PATRICK McDONNELL

Our Little Kat King

Andrews McMeel
Publishing, LLC
Kansas City · Sydney · London

A **MUTTS** TREASURY

Other Books by Patrick McDonnell

Mutts
Cats and Dogs: Mutts II
More Shtuff: Mutts III
Yesh!: Mutts IV
Our Mutts: Five
A Little Look-See: Mutts VI
What Now: Mutts VII
I Want to Be the Kitty: Mutts VIII
Dog-Eared: Mutts IX
Who Let the Cat Out: Mutts X
Everyday Mutts
Animal Friendly
Call of the Wild
Stop and Smell the Roses
Earl & Mooch

Mutts Sundays
Sunday Mornings
Sunday Afternoons
Sunday Evenings

The Best of Mutts

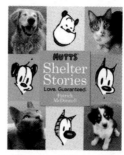

Shelter Stories

Mutts is distributed internationally by King Features Syndicate, Inc. For information, write to King Features Syndicate, Inc., 300 West Fifty-Seventh Street, New York, New York 10019, or visit www.KingFeatures.com.

www.andrewsmcmeel.com

11 12 13 14 15 BAM 10 9 8 7 6 5 4 3 2 1

ISBN: 978-1-4494-0800-8

Library of Congress Control Number: 2011921391

Our Little Kat King is printed on recycled paper.

Mutts can be found on the Internet at
www.muttscomics.com

Cover design by Jeff Schulz.

ATTENTION: SCHOOLS AND BUSINESSES

Andrews McMeel books are available at quantity discounts with bulk purchase for educational, business, or sales promotional use. For information, please e-mail the Andrews McMeel Publishing Special Sales Department: specialsales@amuniversal.com.

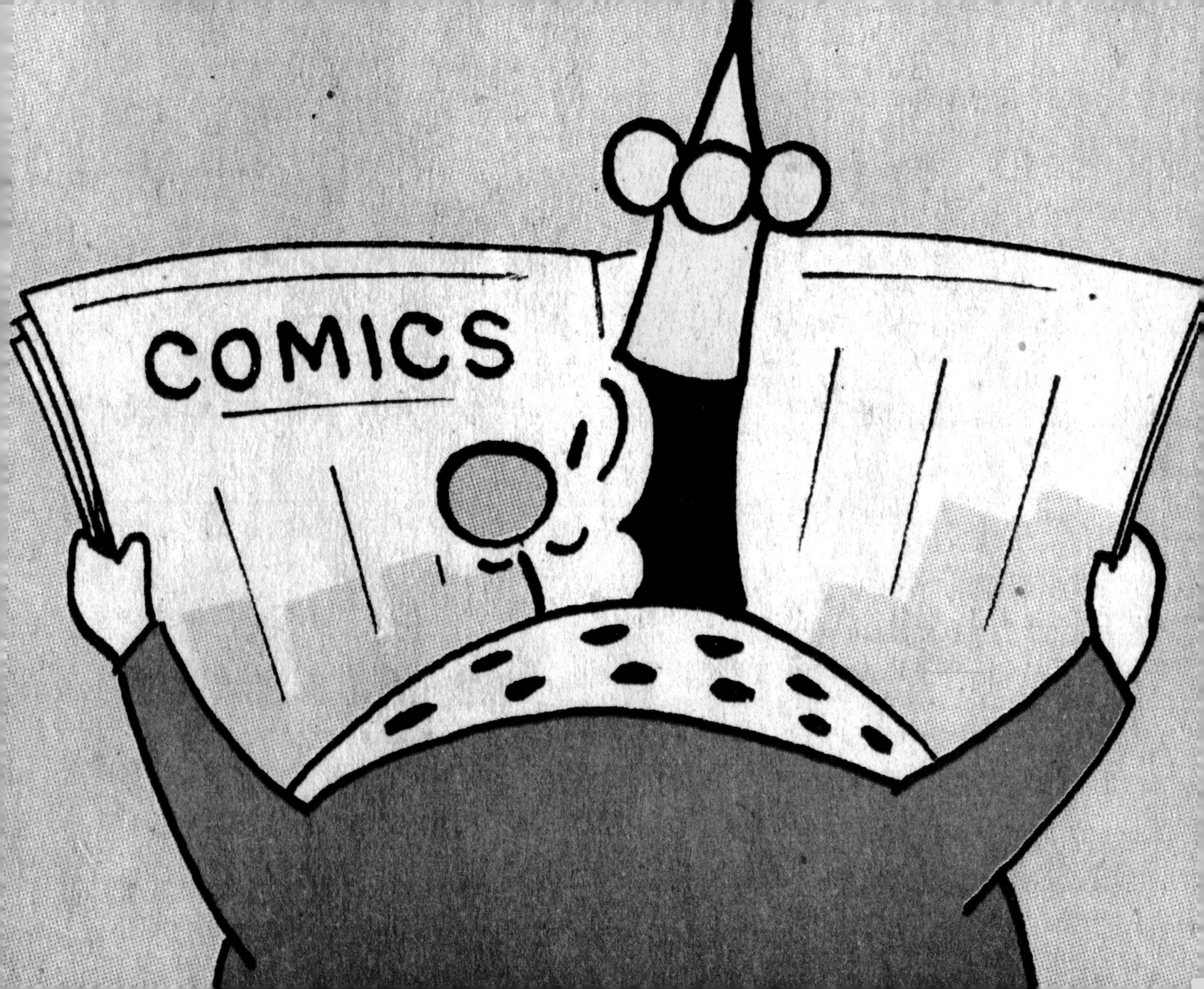
COMICS

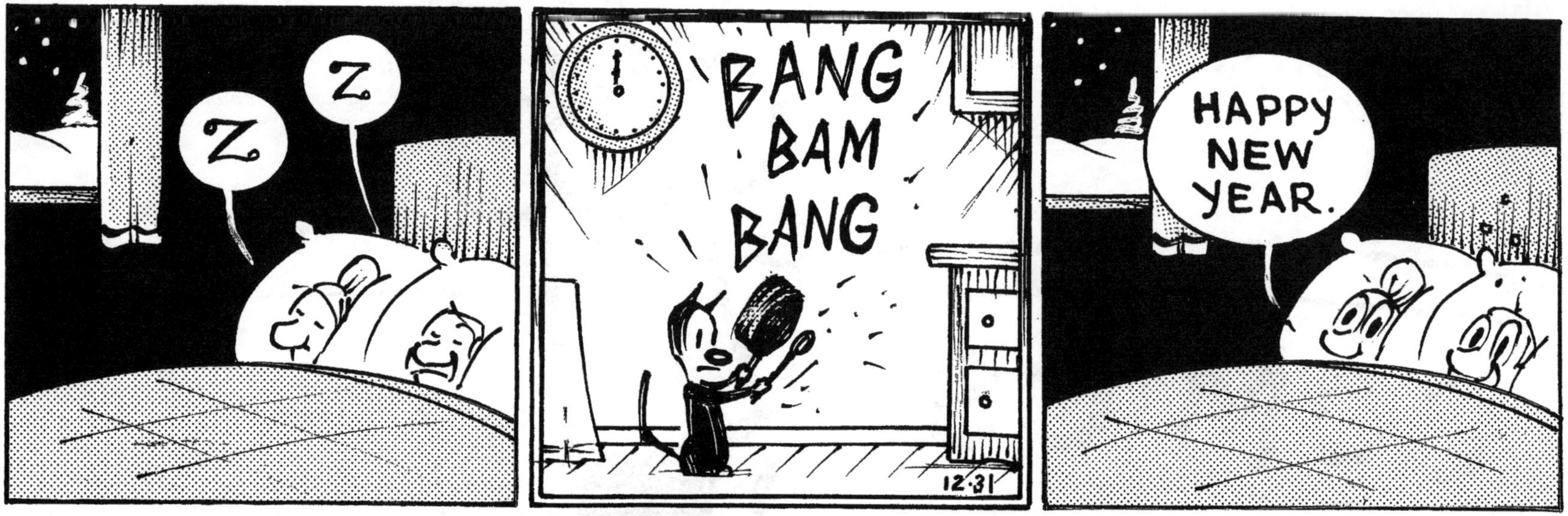
Z
Z
BANG BAM BANG
12·31
HAPPY NEW YEAR.

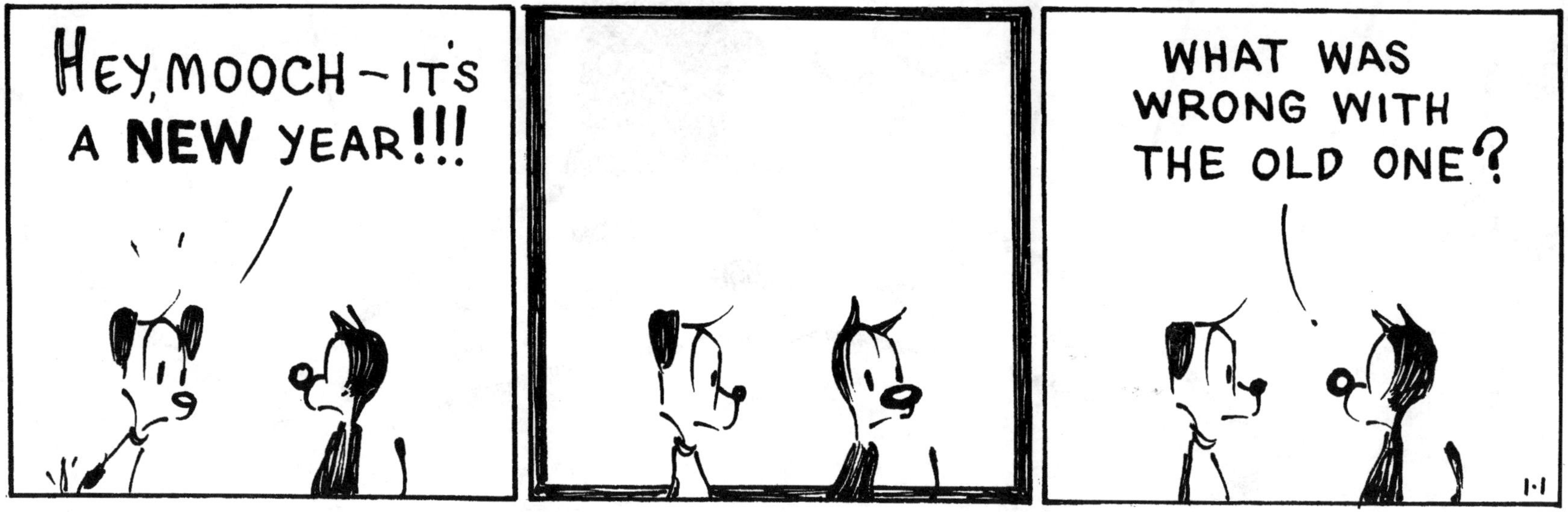
HEY, MOOCH – IT'S A **NEW** YEAR!!!
WHAT WAS WRONG WITH THE OLD ONE?
1·1

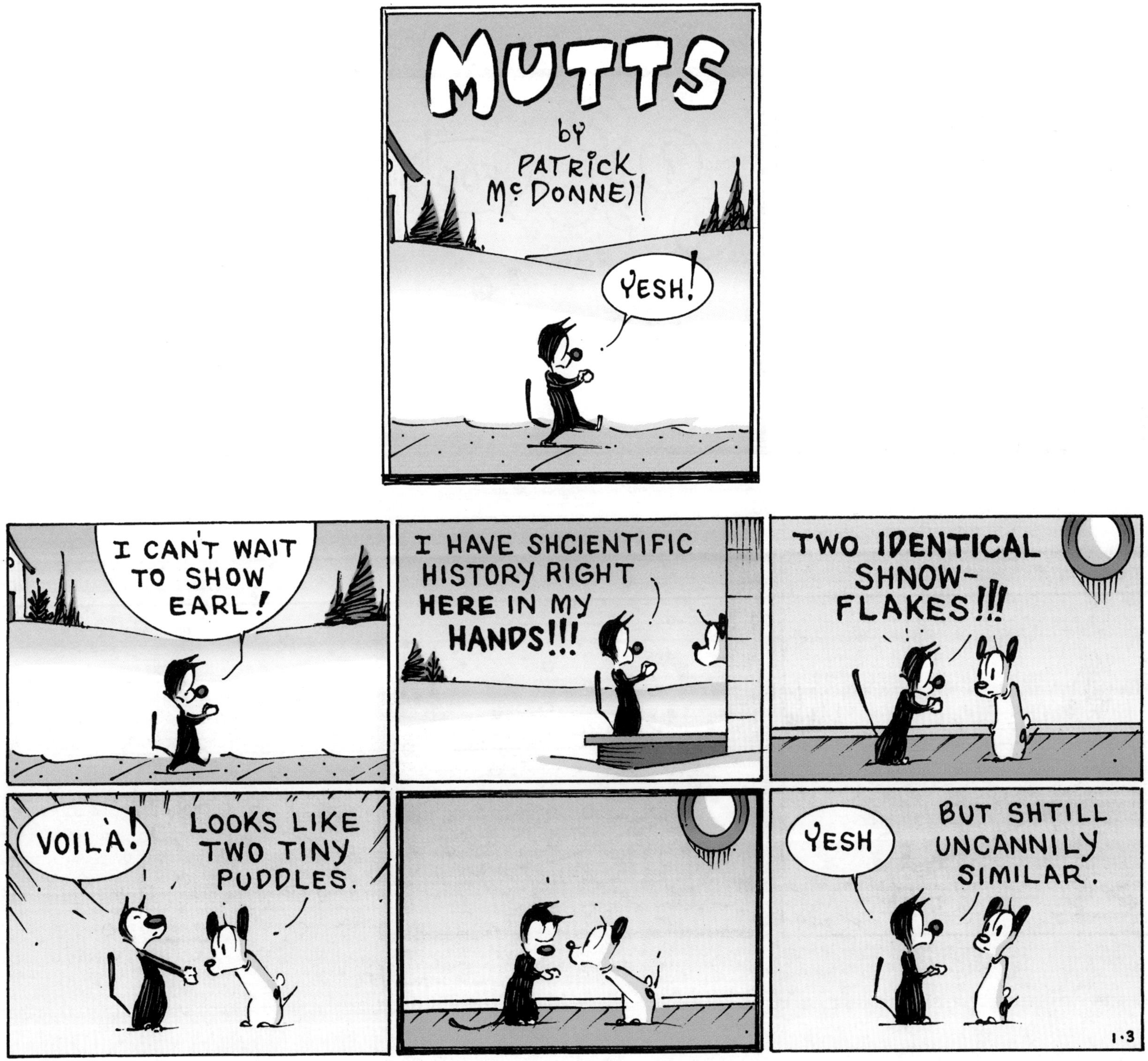
MUTTS
by
PATRICK
McDONNELL
YESH!
I CAN'T WAIT TO SHOW EARL!
I HAVE SHCIENTIFIC HISTORY RIGHT HERE IN MY HANDS!!!
TWO IDENTICAL SHNOW-FLAKES!!!
VOILÀ!
LOOKS LIKE TWO TINY PUDDLES.
YESH
BUT SHTILL UNCANNILY SIMILAR.
1·3

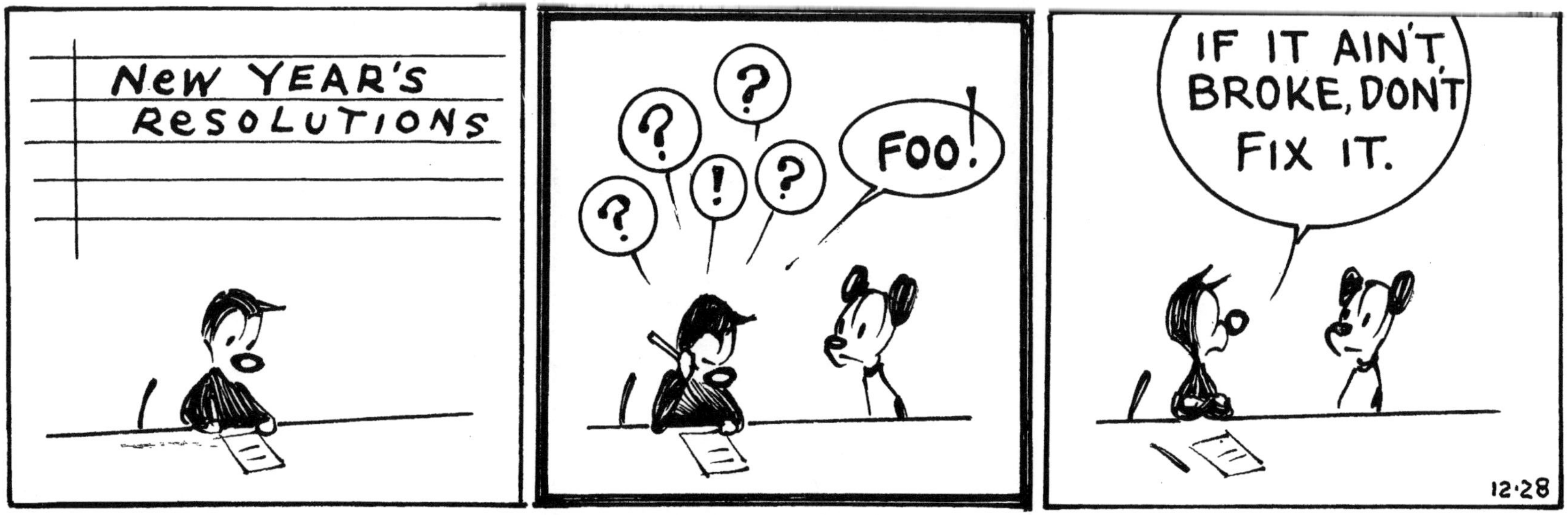
NEW YEAR'S RESOLUTIONS
? ? ! ? ?
FOO!
IF IT AIN'T BROKE, DON'T FIX IT.
12·28

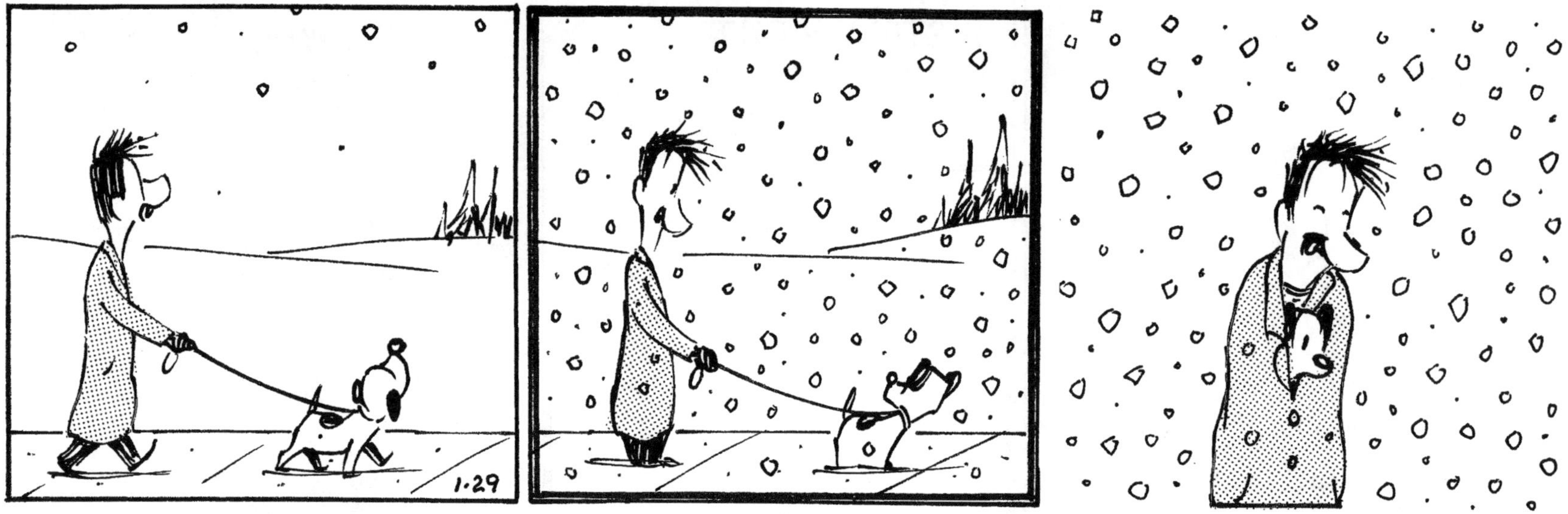
1·29

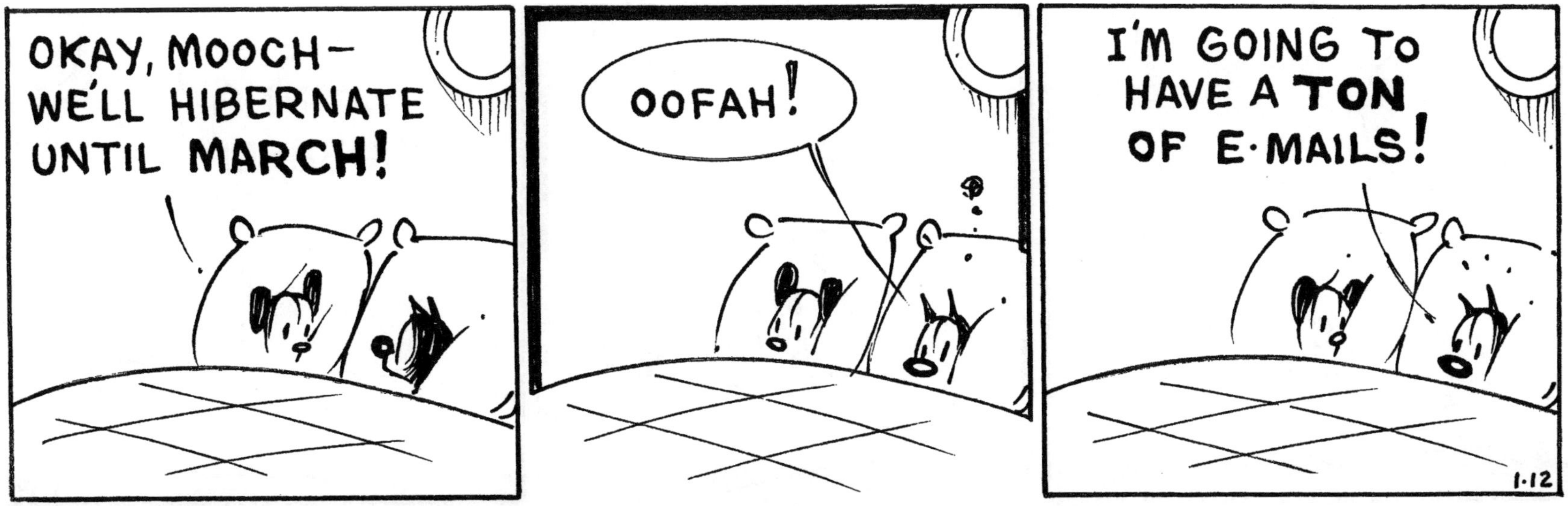
OKAY, MOOCH—
WE'LL HIBERNATE
UNTIL MARCH!
OOFAH!
I'M GOING TO
HAVE A TON
OF E·MAILS!
1·12

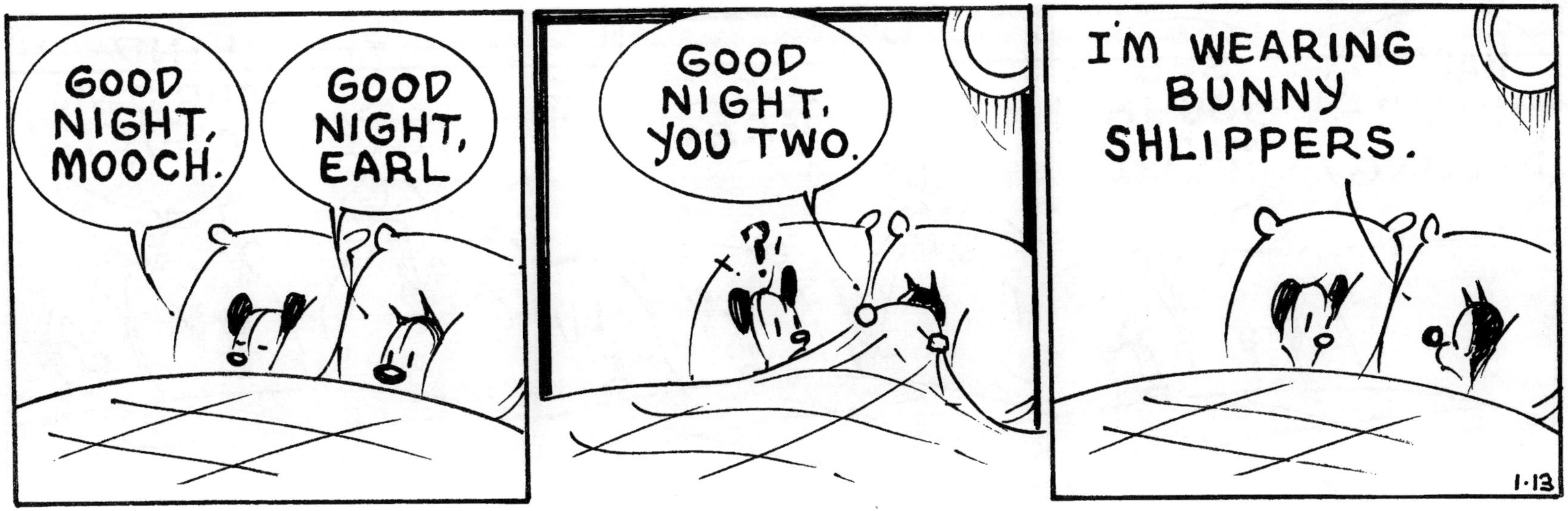
GOOD NIGHT, MOOCH.
GOOD NIGHT, EARL.
GOOD NIGHT, YOU TWO.
I'M WEARING
BUNNY
SHLIPPERS.
1·13

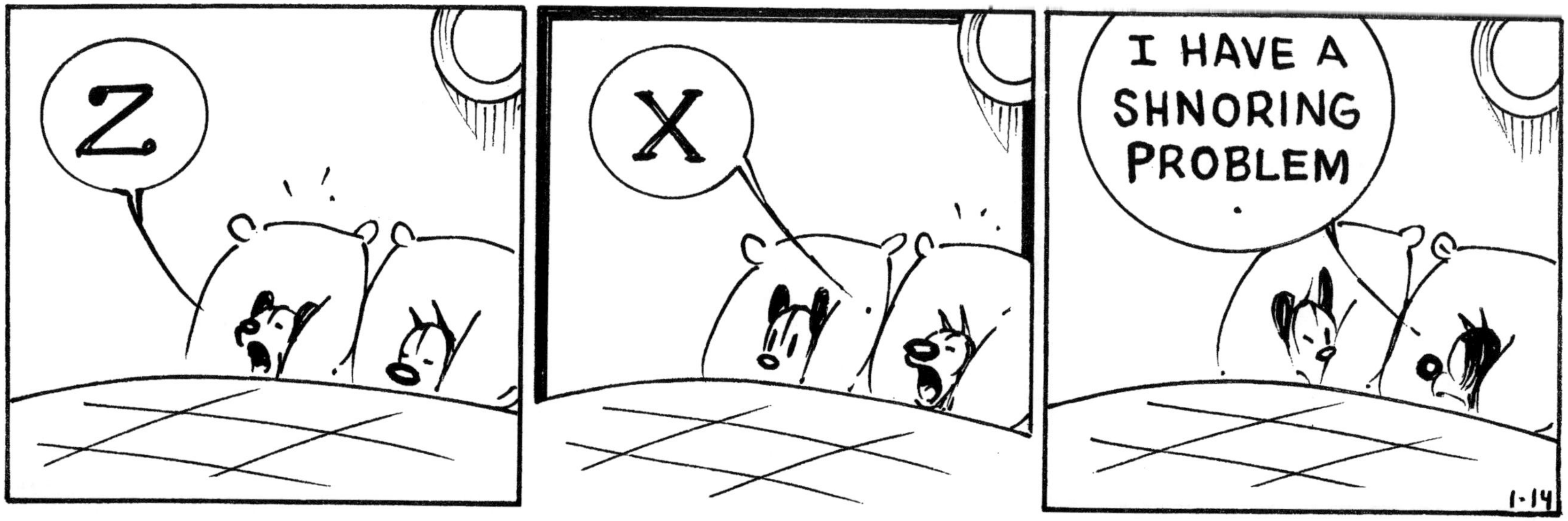
Z
X
I HAVE A SHNORING PROBLEM.
1-14

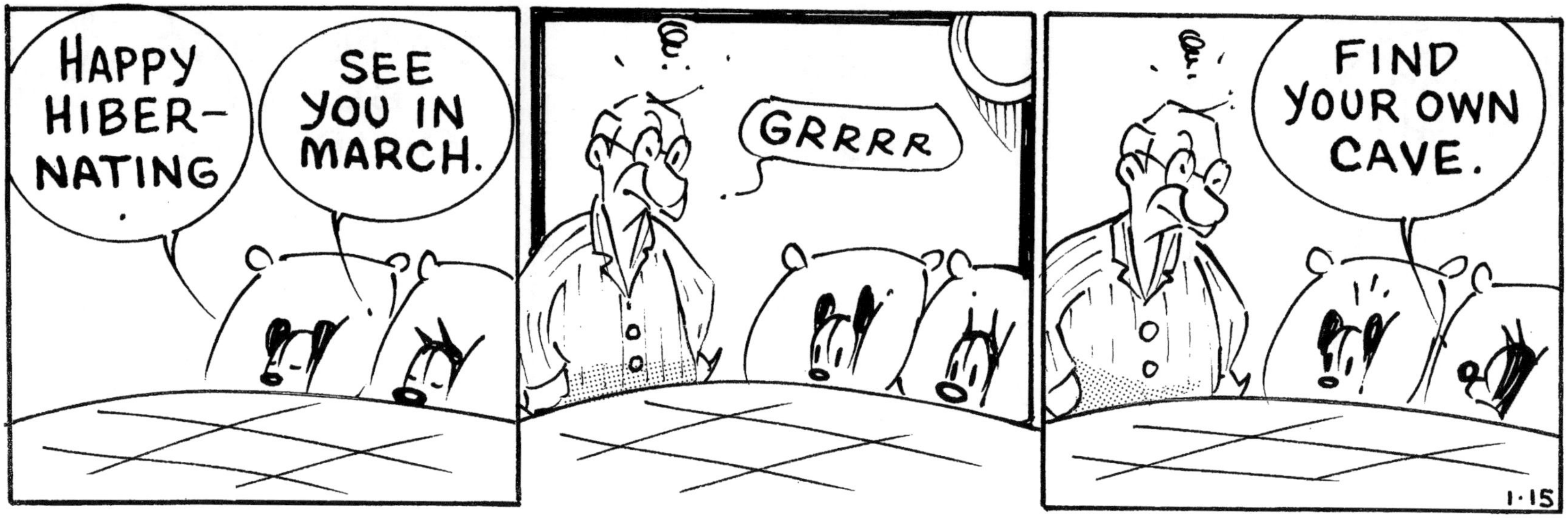
HAPPY HIBER-NATING.
SEE YOU IN MARCH.
GRRRR
FIND YOUR OWN CAVE.
1-15

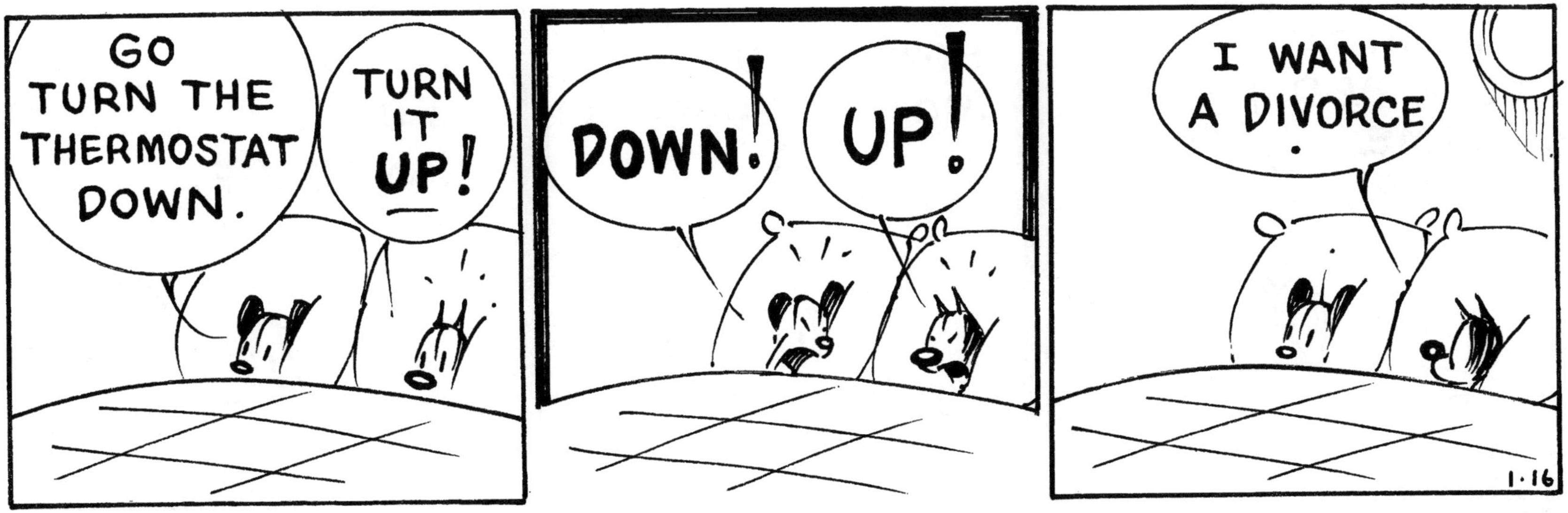
GO TURN THE THERMOSTAT DOWN.
TURN IT UP!
DOWN!
UP!
I WANT A DIVORCE.
1·16

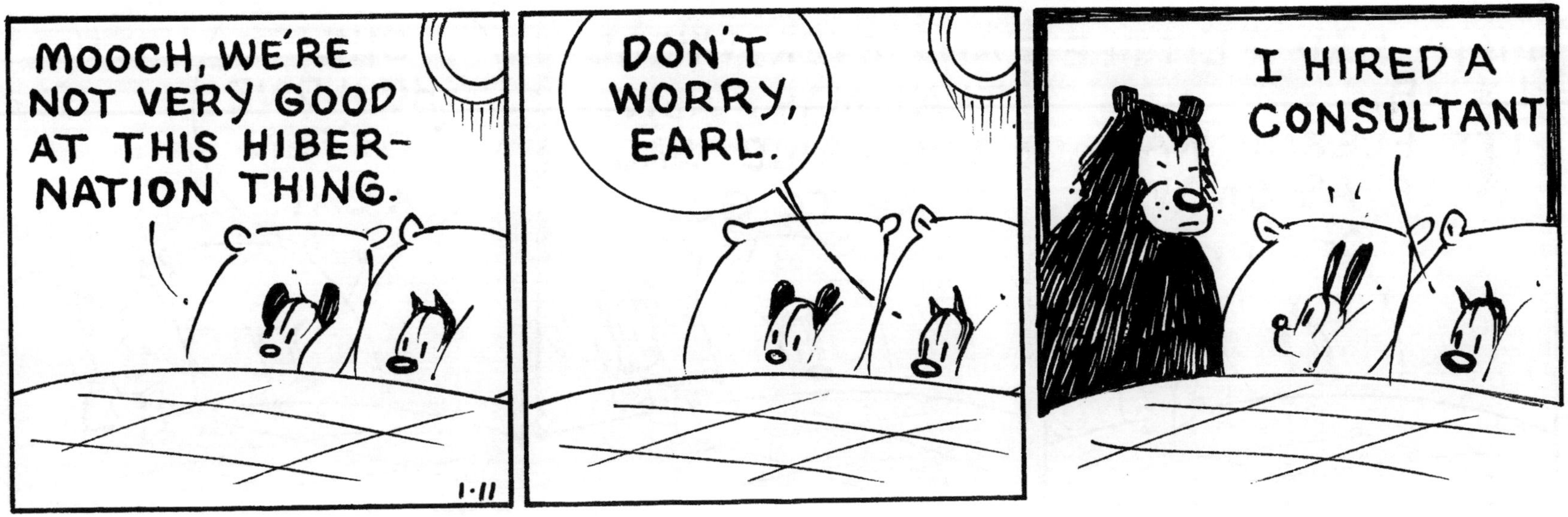
MOOCH, WE'RE NOT VERY GOOD AT THIS HIBER-NATION THING.
1·11
DON'T WORRY, EARL.
I HIRED A CONSULTANT

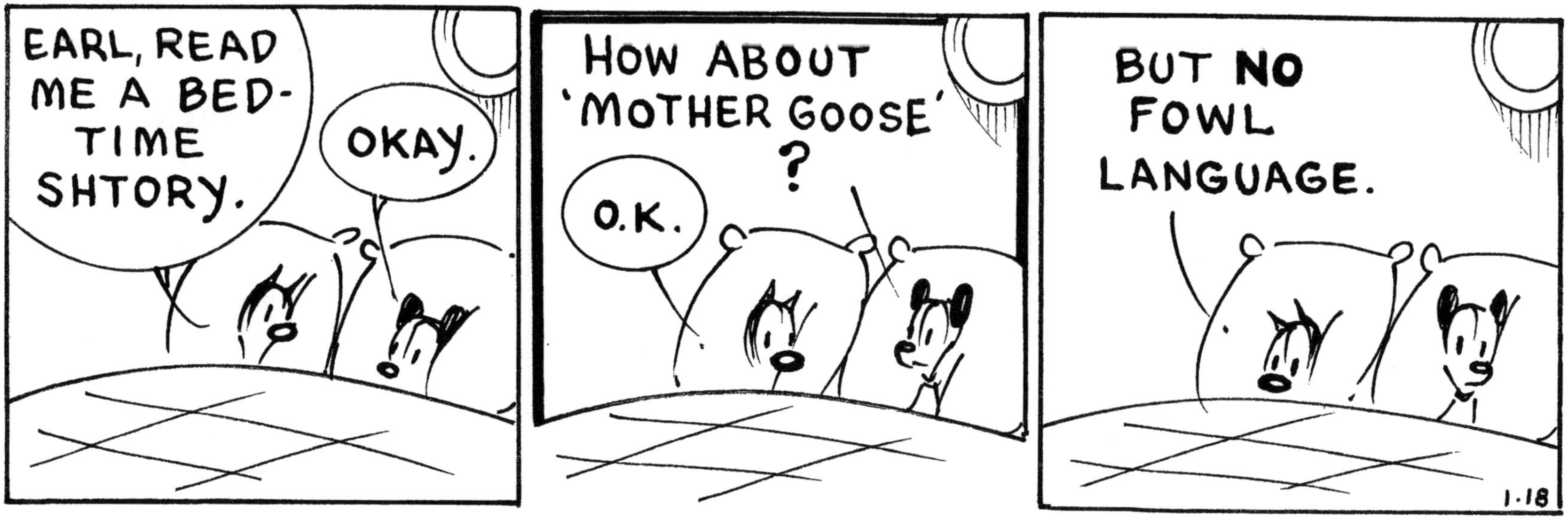
EARL, READ ME A BED-TIME SHTORY.
OKAY.
HOW ABOUT 'MOTHER GOOSE'?
O.K.
BUT **NO** FOWL LANGUAGE.
1·18

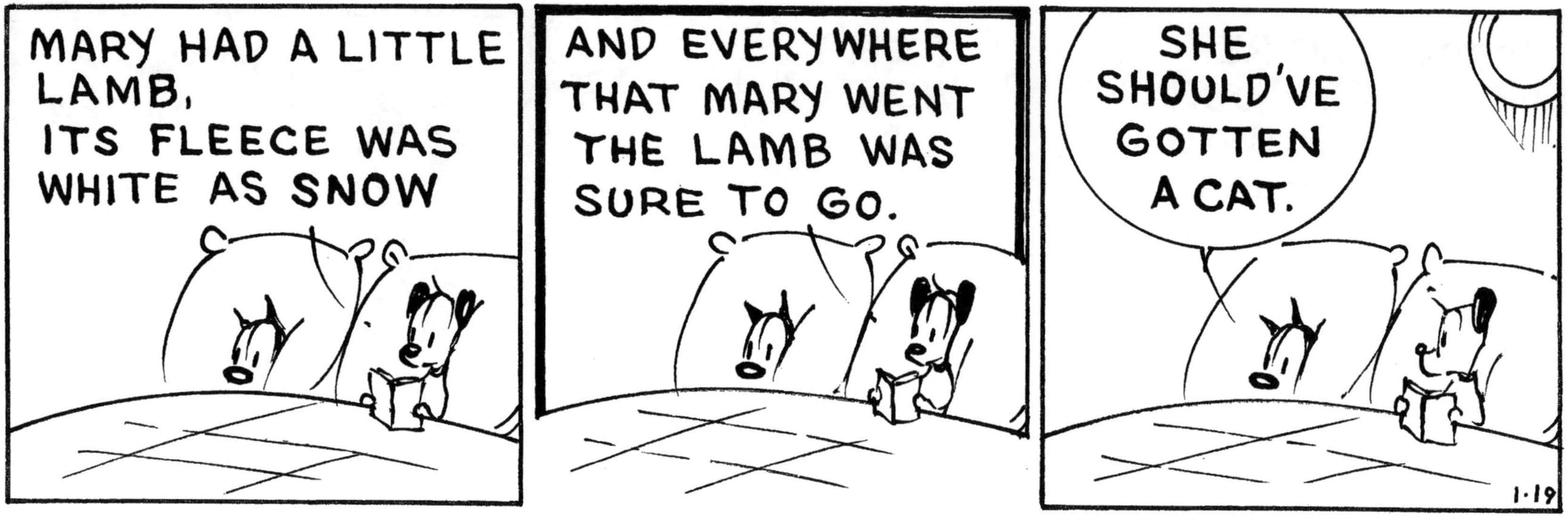
MARY HAD A LITTLE LAMB, ITS FLEECE WAS WHITE AS SNOW
AND EVERYWHERE THAT MARY WENT THE LAMB WAS SURE TO GO.
SHE SHOULD'VE GOTTEN A CAT.
1·19

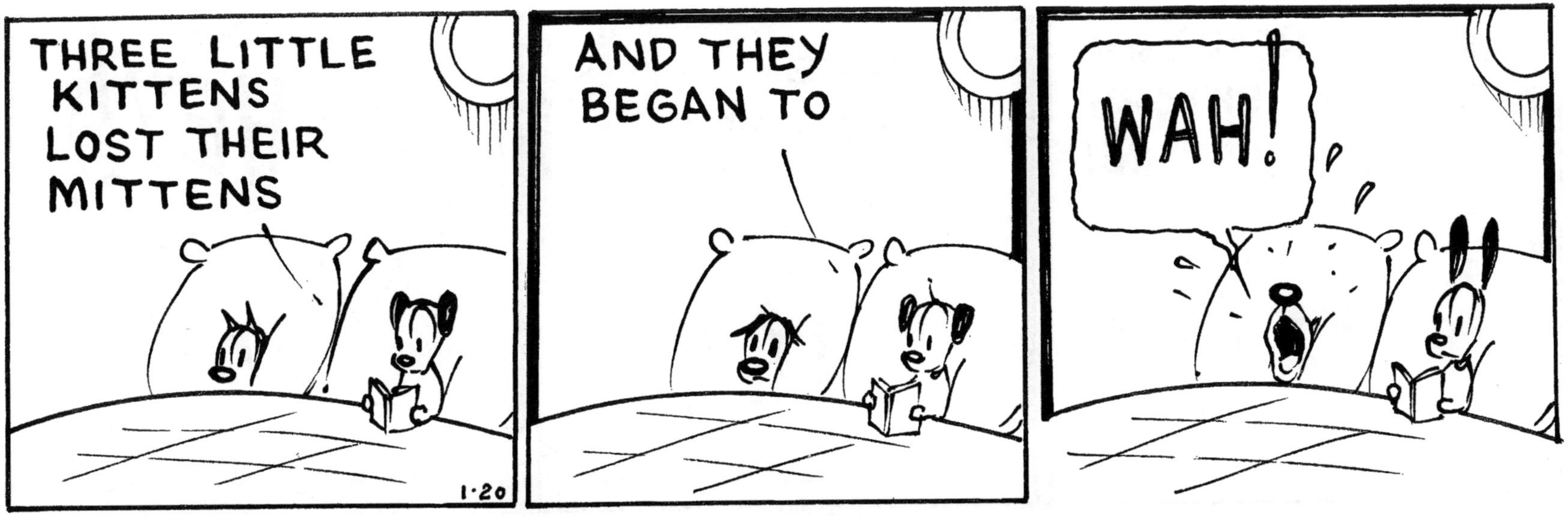
THREE LITTLE KITTENS LOST THEIR MITTENS
1·20
AND THEY BEGAN TO
WAH!

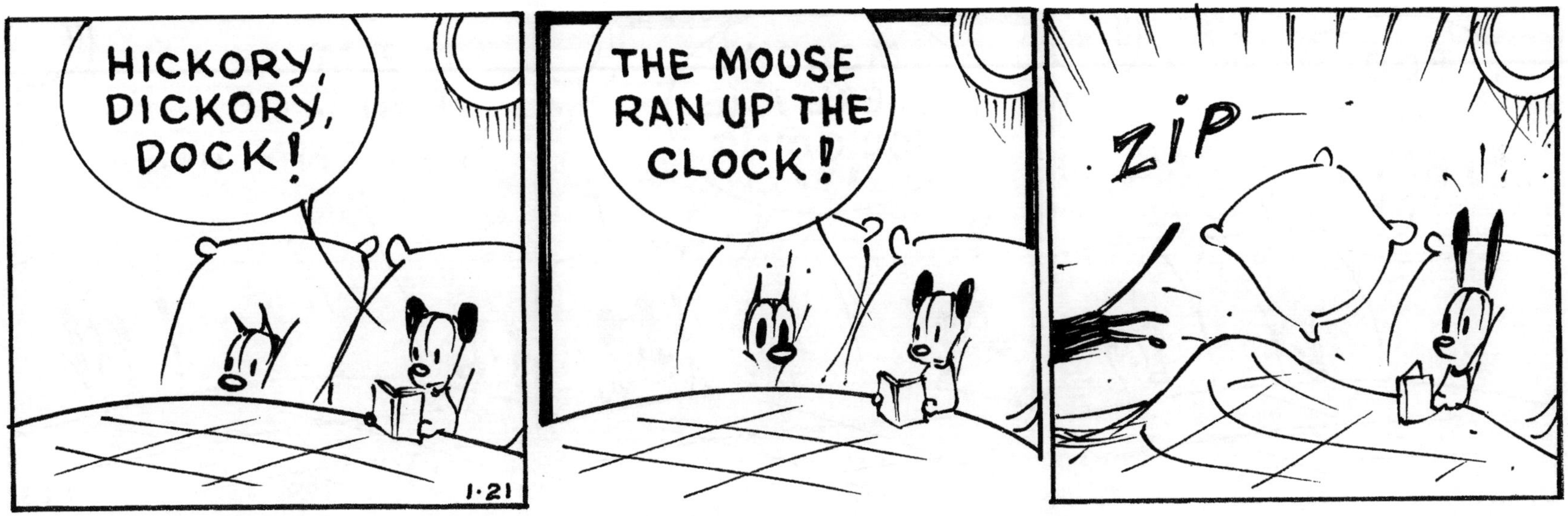
HICKORY, DICKORY, DOCK!
1·21
THE MOUSE RAN UP THE CLOCK!
ZIP

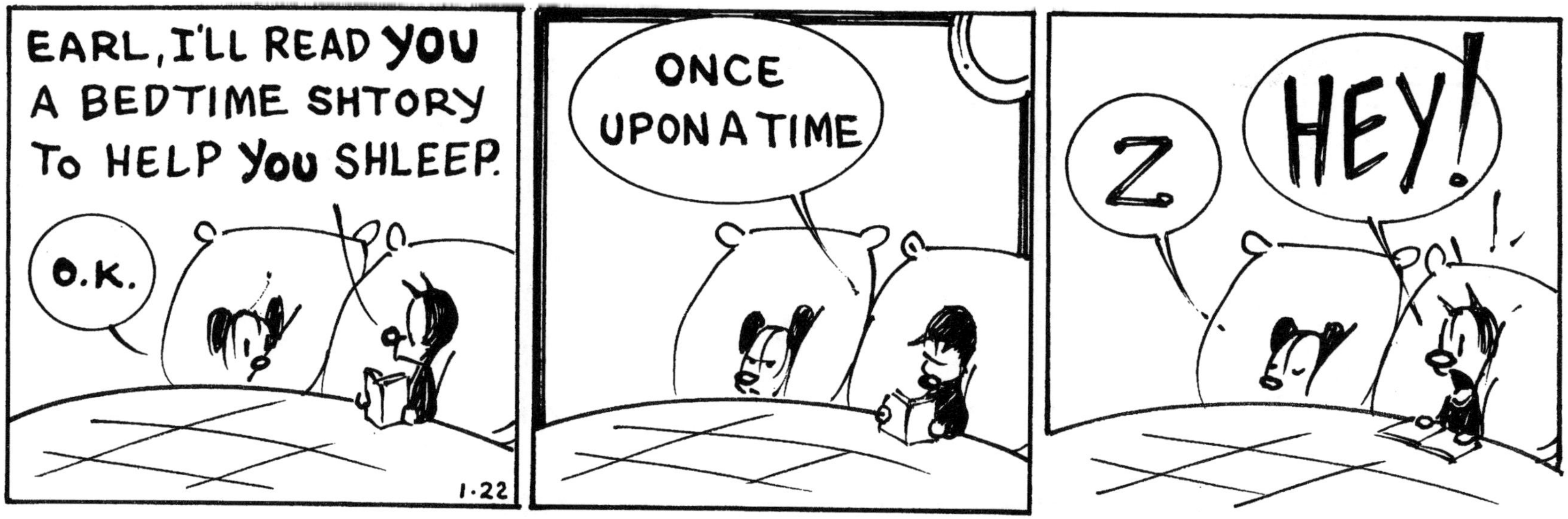
EARL, I'LL READ YOU A BEDTIME SHTORY TO HELP YOU SHLEEP.
O.K.
1.22
ONCE UPON A TIME
Z
HEY!

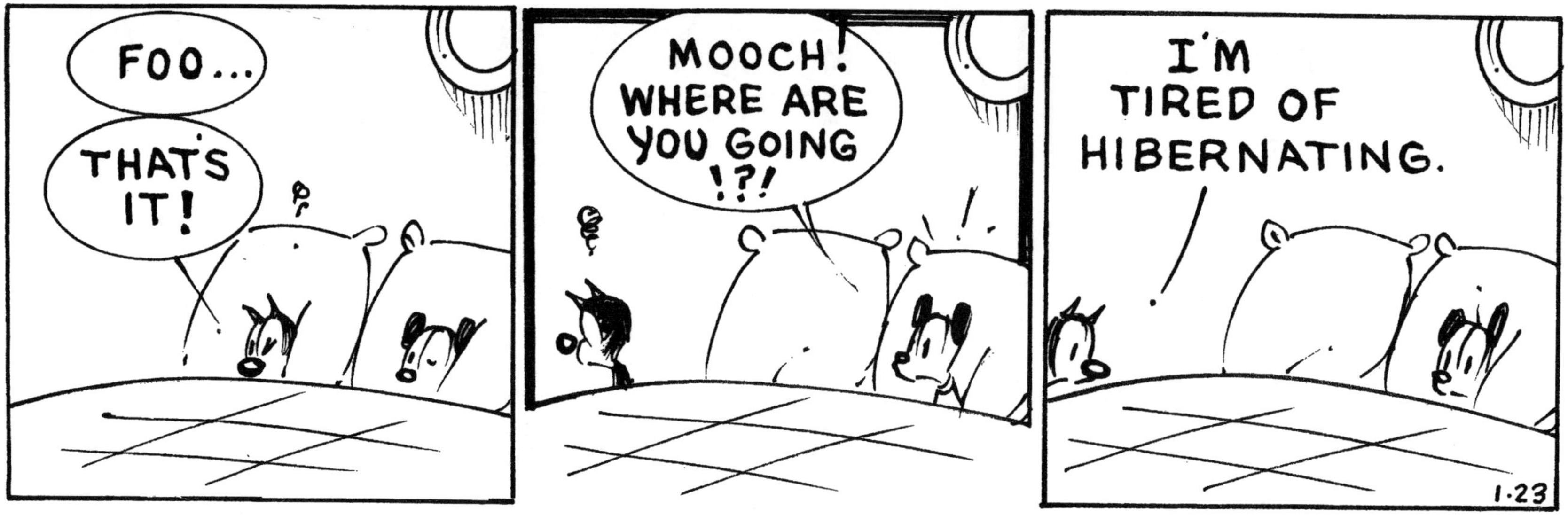
FOO...
THAT'S IT!
MOOCH! WHERE ARE YOU GOING !?!
I'M TIRED OF HIBERNATING.
1.23

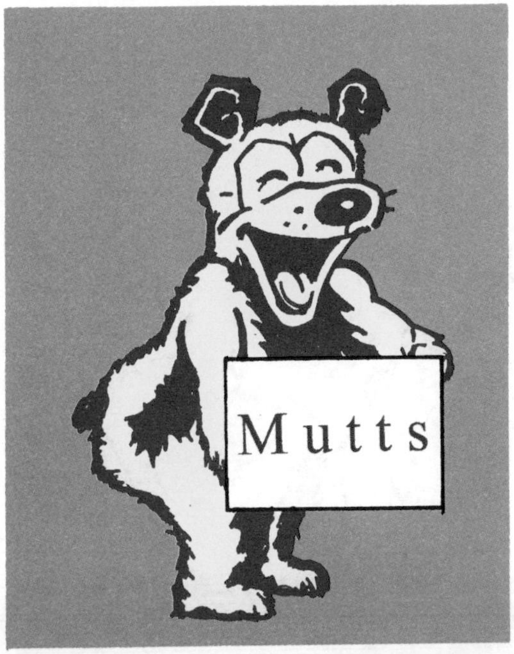
Mutts

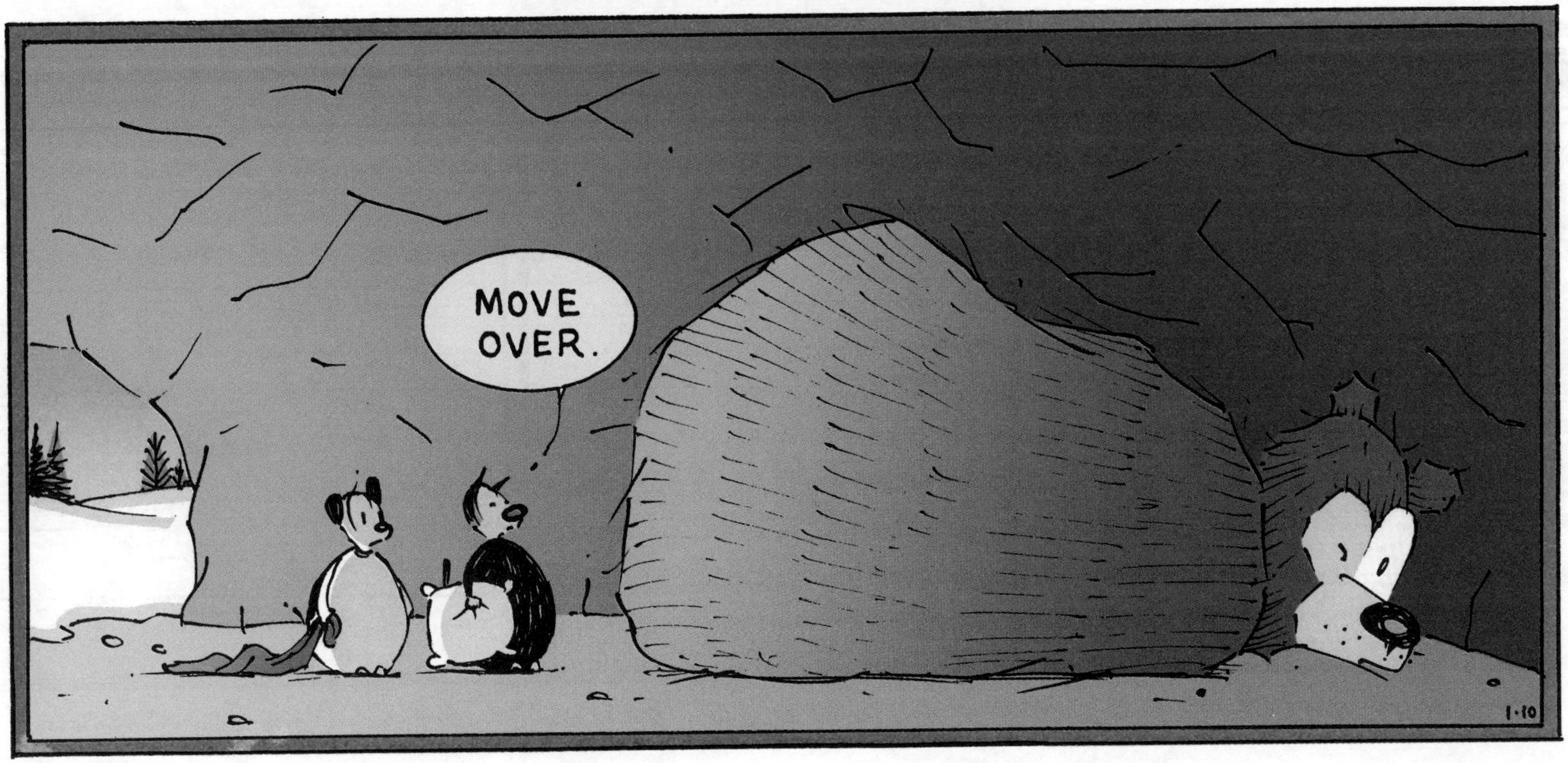
MOVE OVER.
1·10

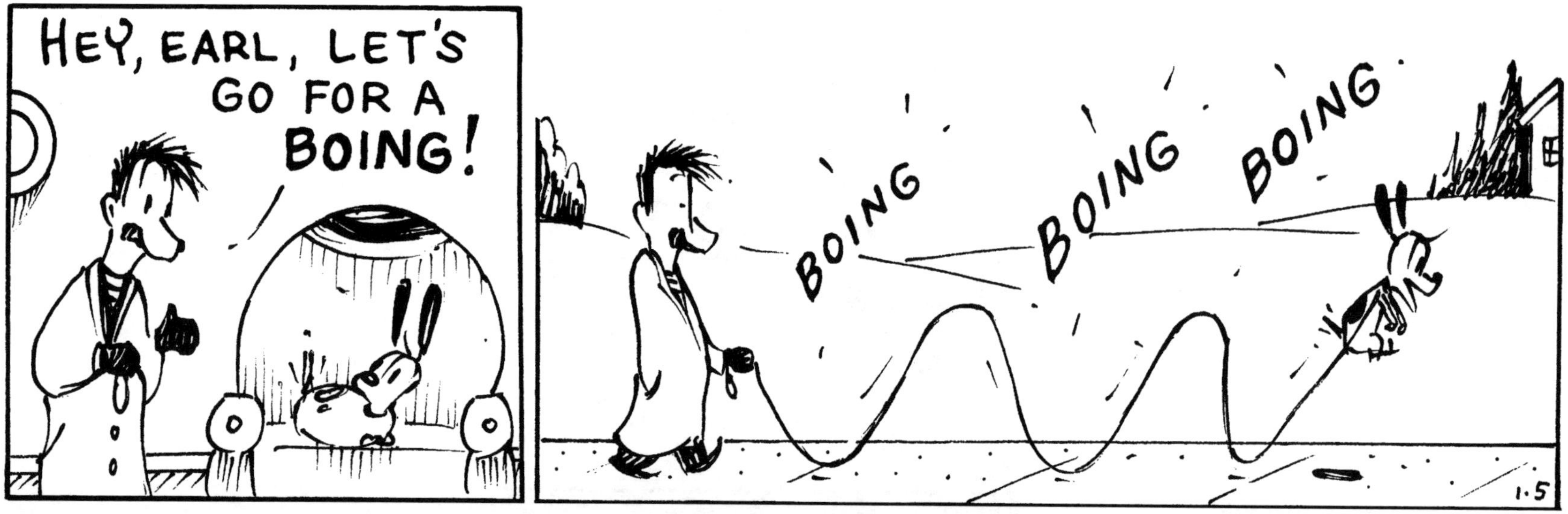
HEY, EARL, LET'S GO FOR A BOING!
BOING
BOING
BOING
1·5

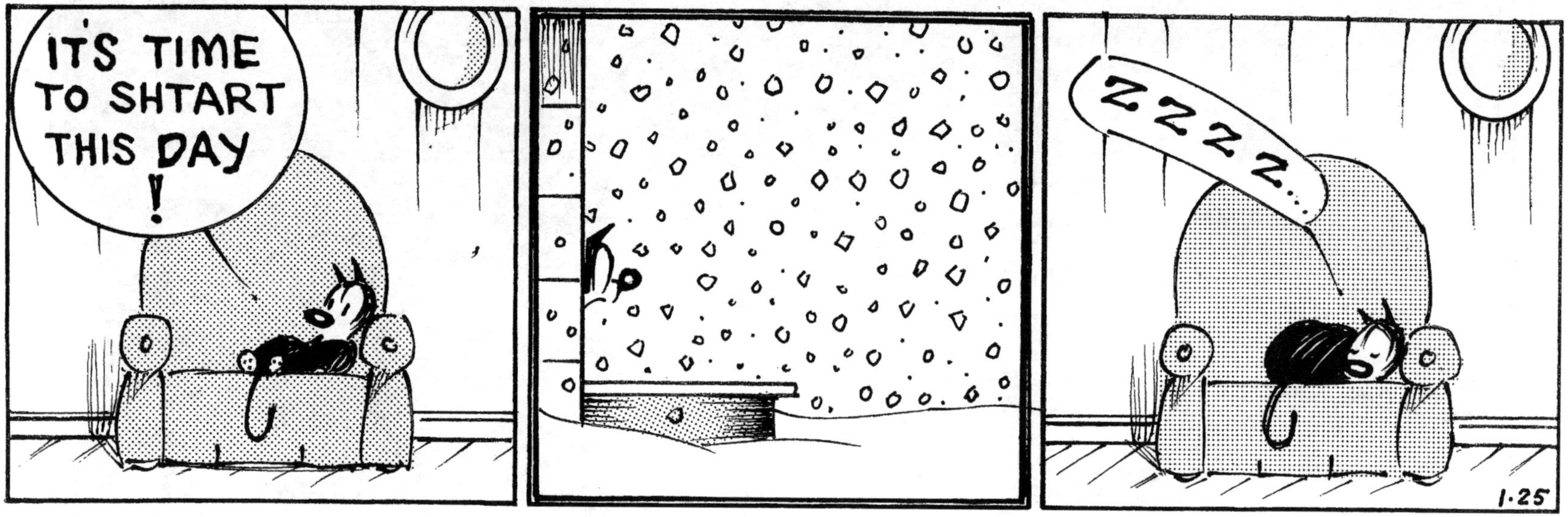
IT'S TIME TO SHTART THIS DAY!
ZZZZZ...
1·25

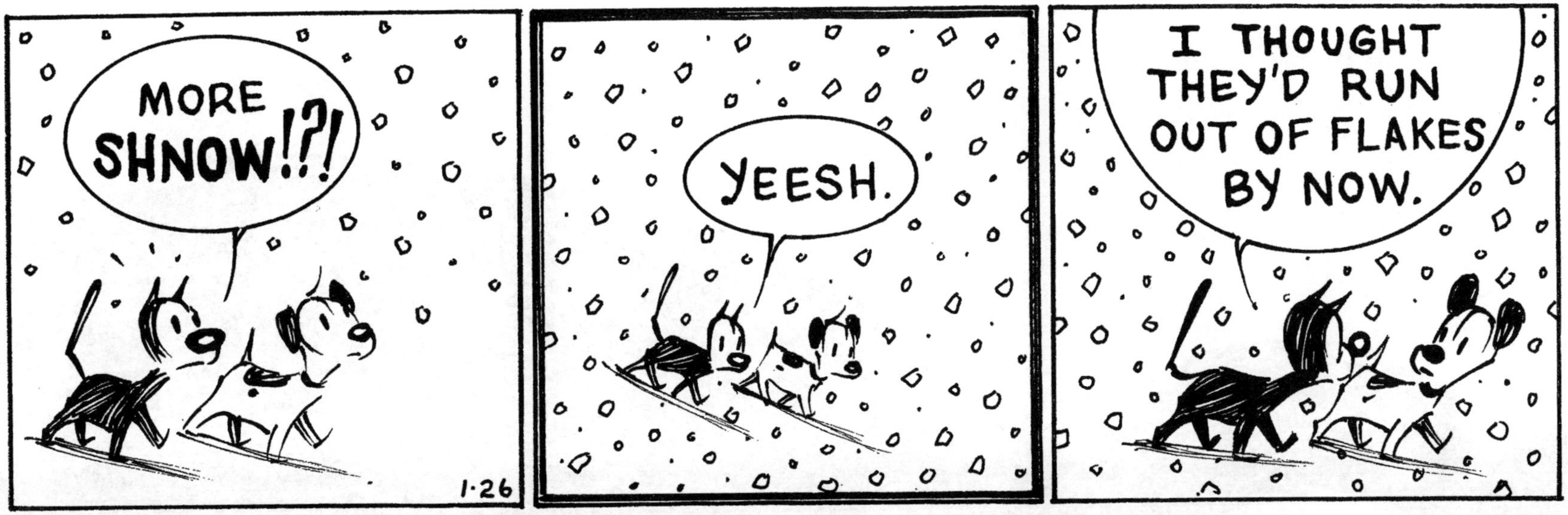
MORE SHNOW!?!
1·26
YEESH.
I THOUGHT THEY'D RUN OUT OF FLAKES BY NOW.

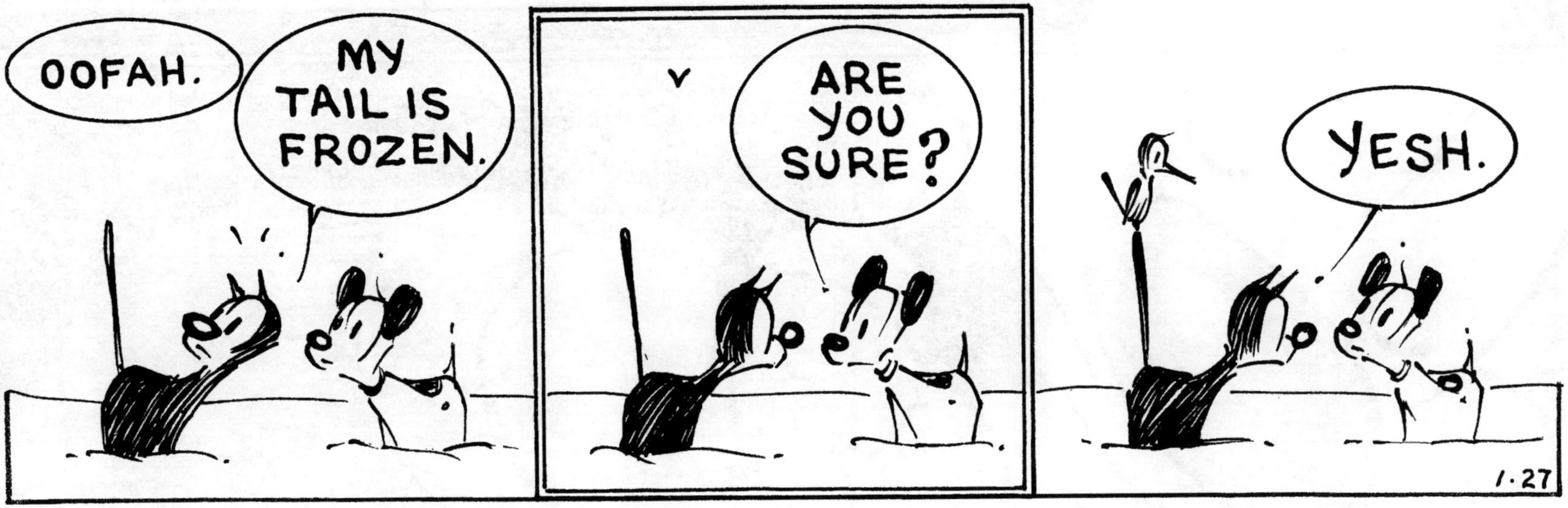
OOFAH.
MY TAIL IS FROZEN.
ARE YOU SURE?
YESH.
1·27

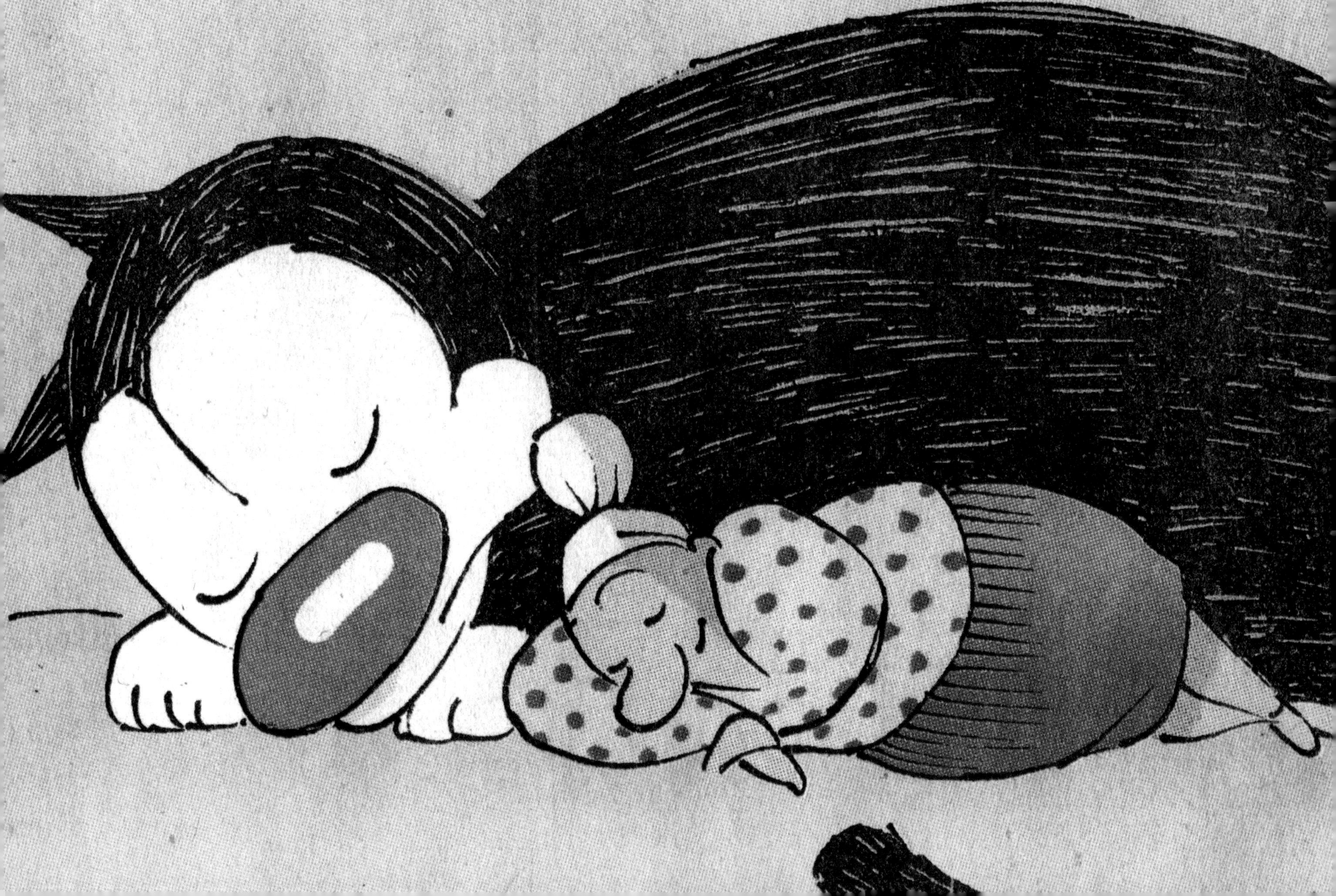

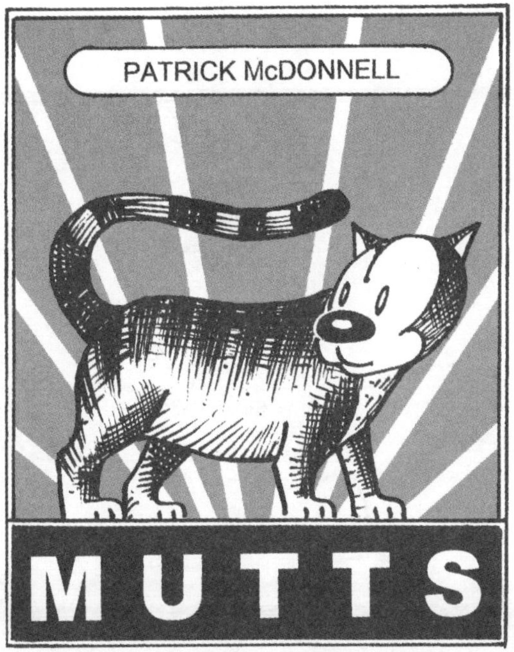
PATRICK McDONNELL
MUTTS

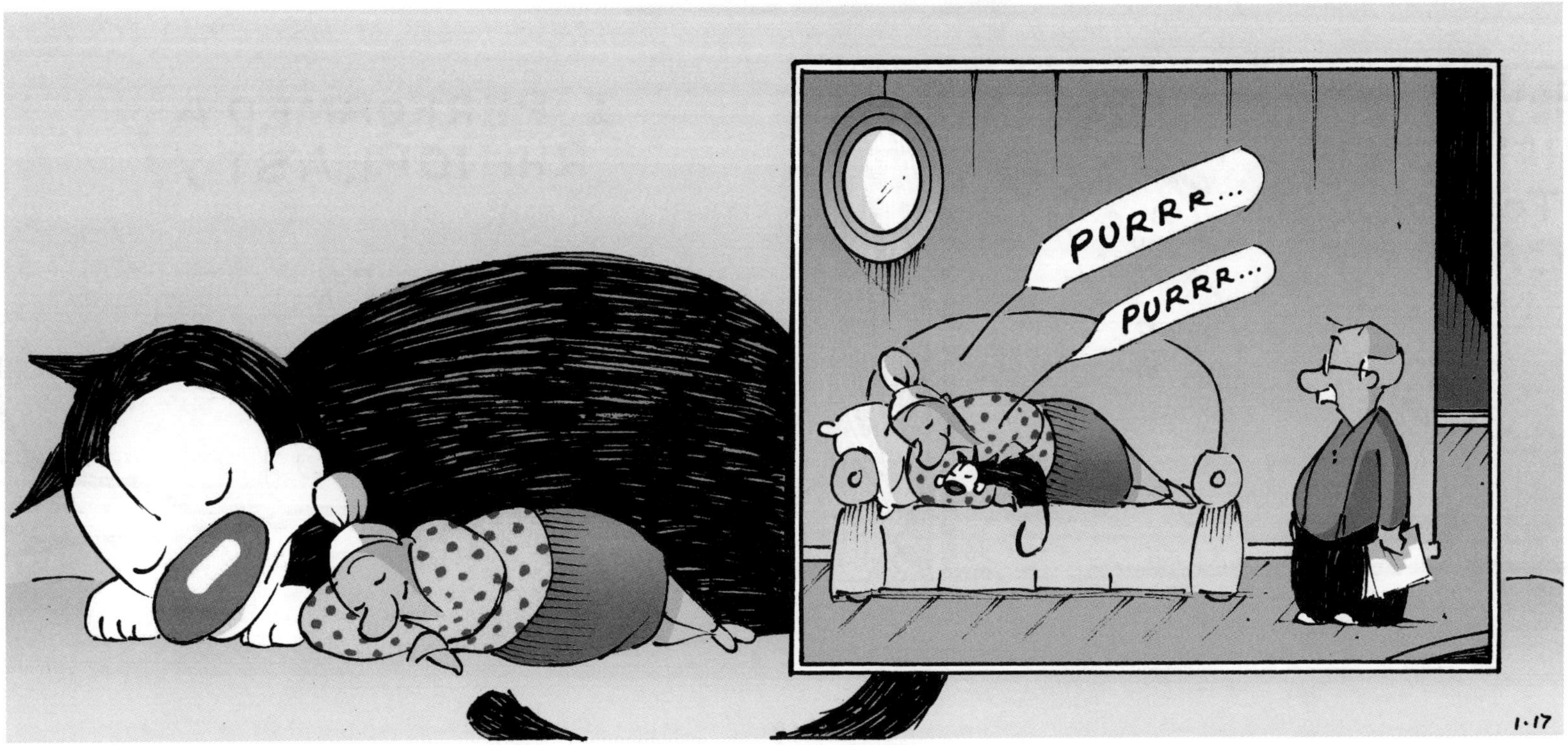
PURRR...
PURRR...
1·17

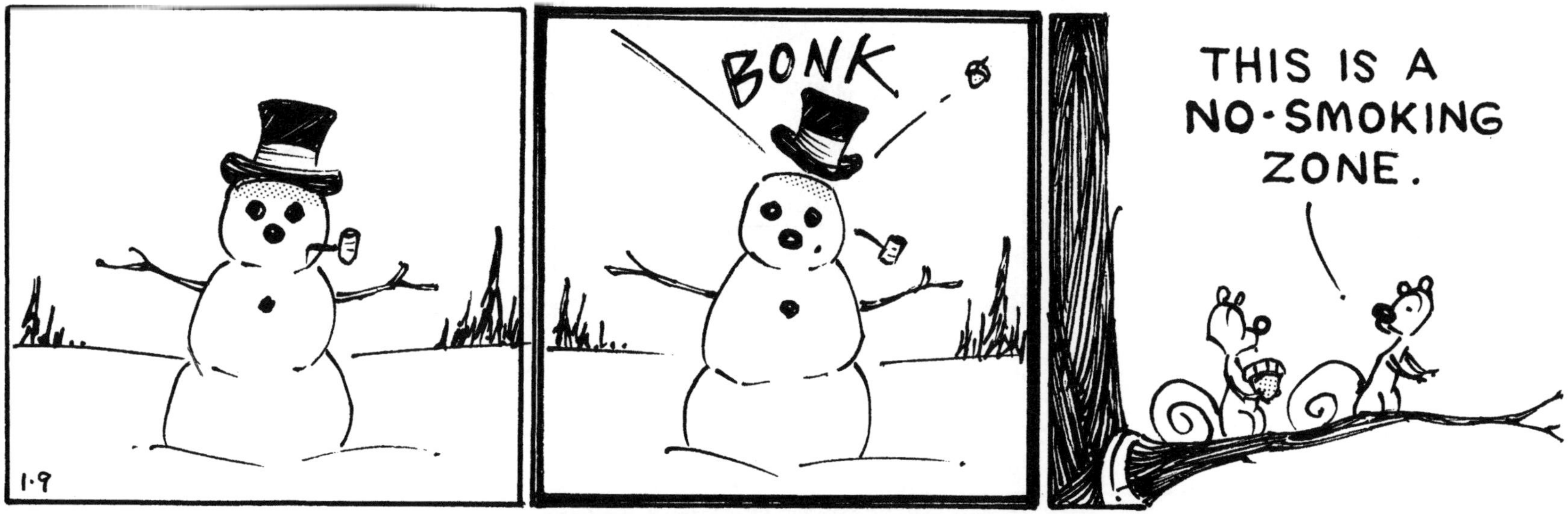
1·9
BONK
THIS IS A NO-SMOKING ZONE.

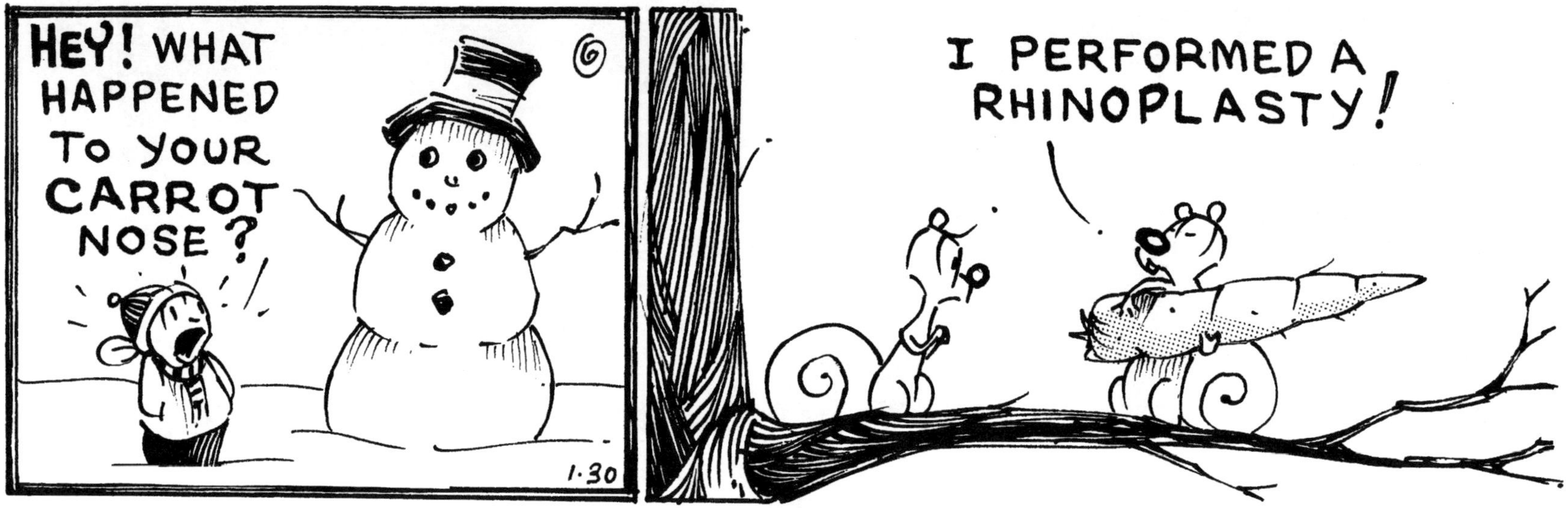
HEY! WHAT HAPPENED TO YOUR CARROT NOSE?
1·30
I PERFORMED A RHINOPLASTY!

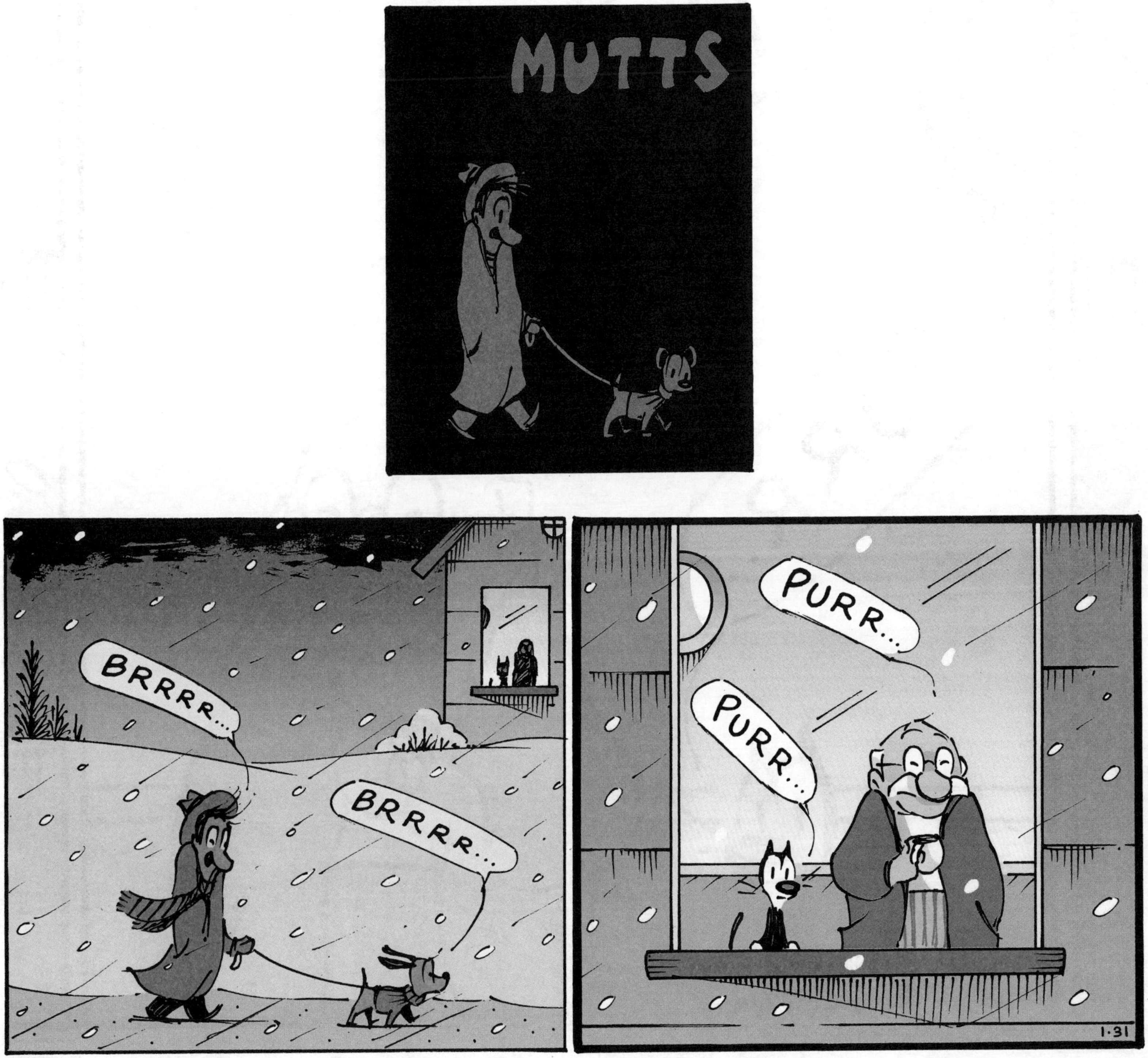
MUTTS
BRRRRR...
BRRRRR...
PURR...
PURR...
1·31

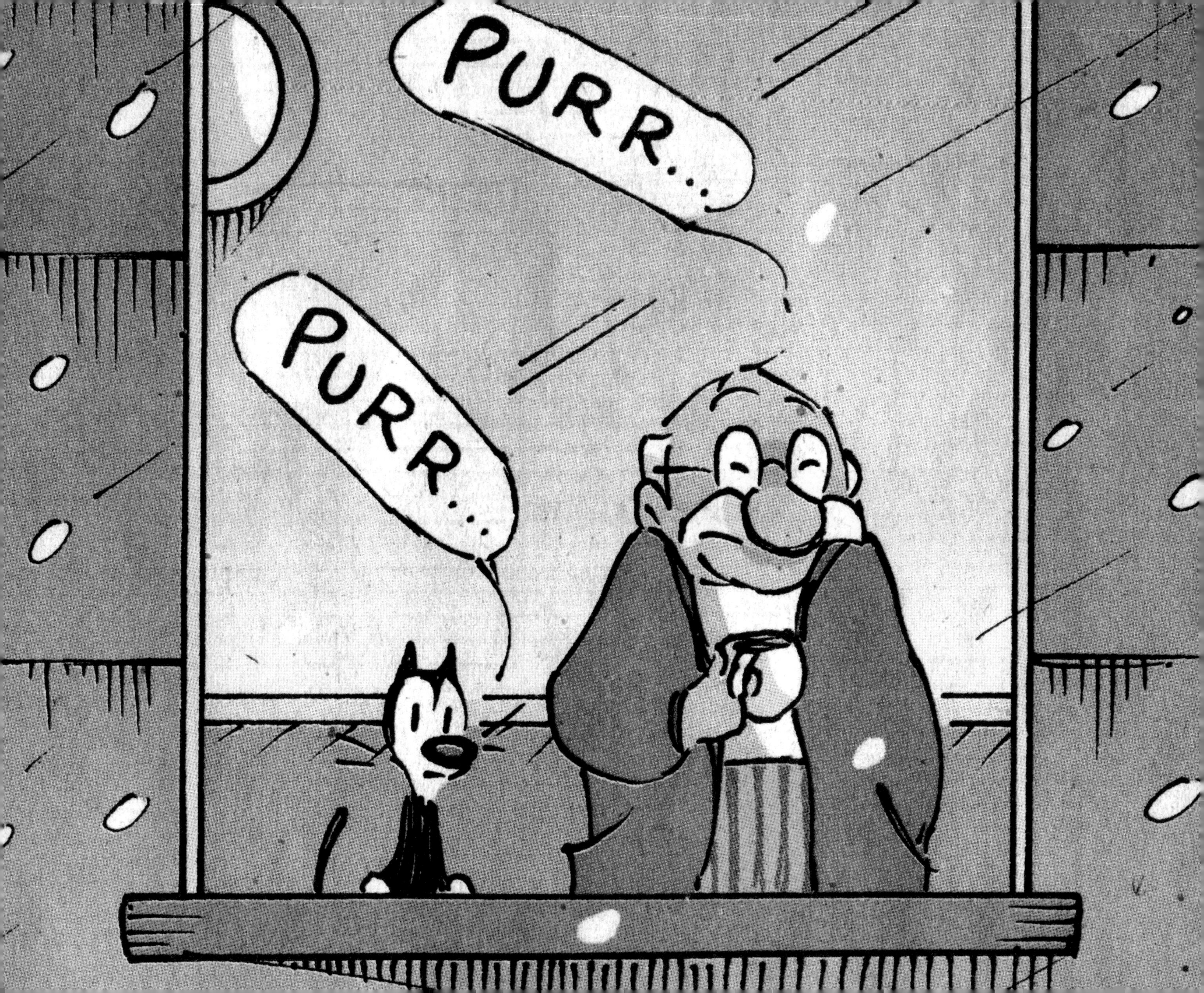
PURR...
PURR...

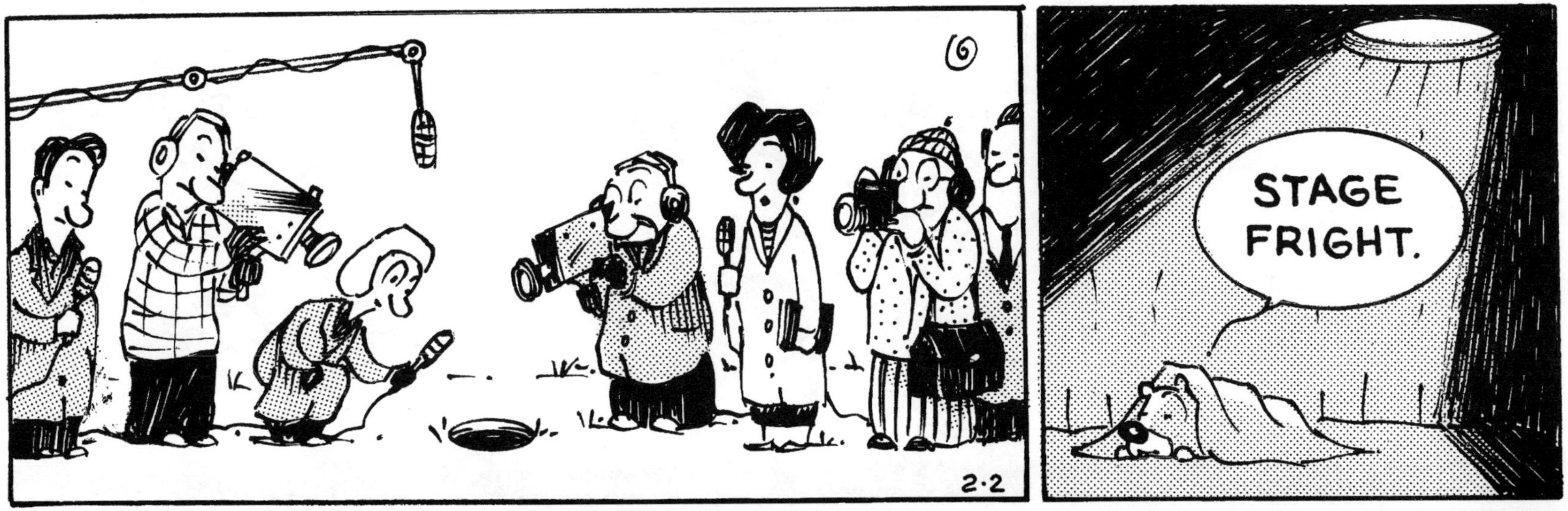
STAGE FRIGHT.
2·2

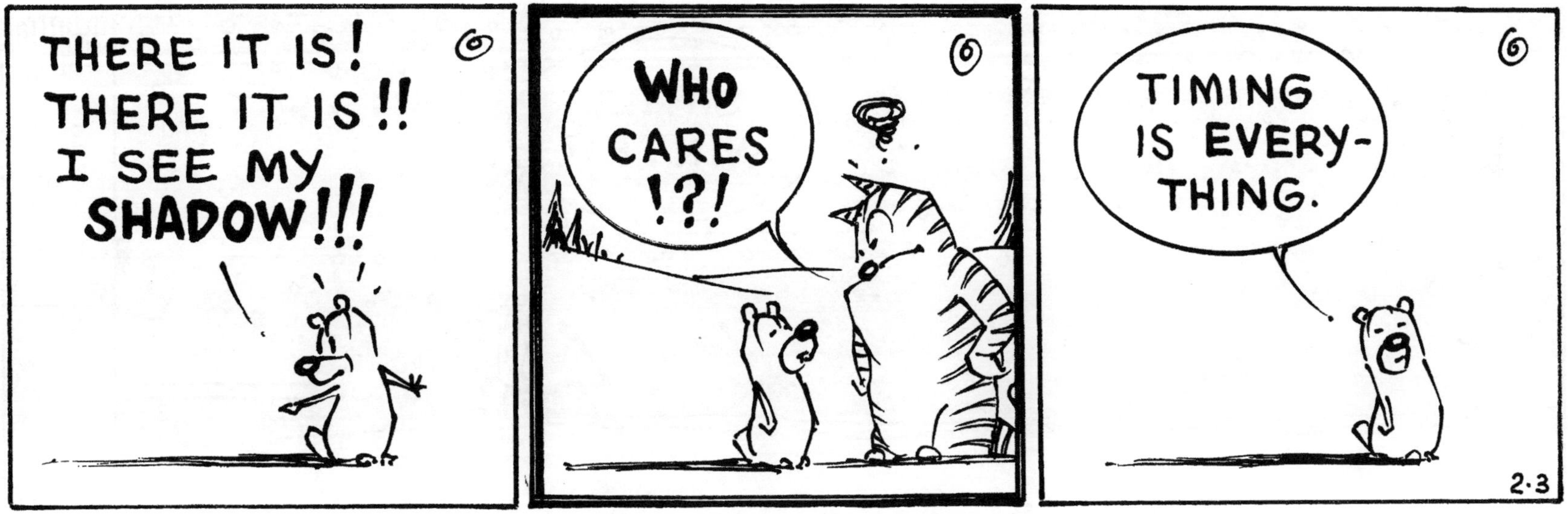
THERE IT IS! THERE IT IS!! I SEE MY SHADOW!!!
WHO CARES !?!
TIMING IS EVERY-THING.
2·3

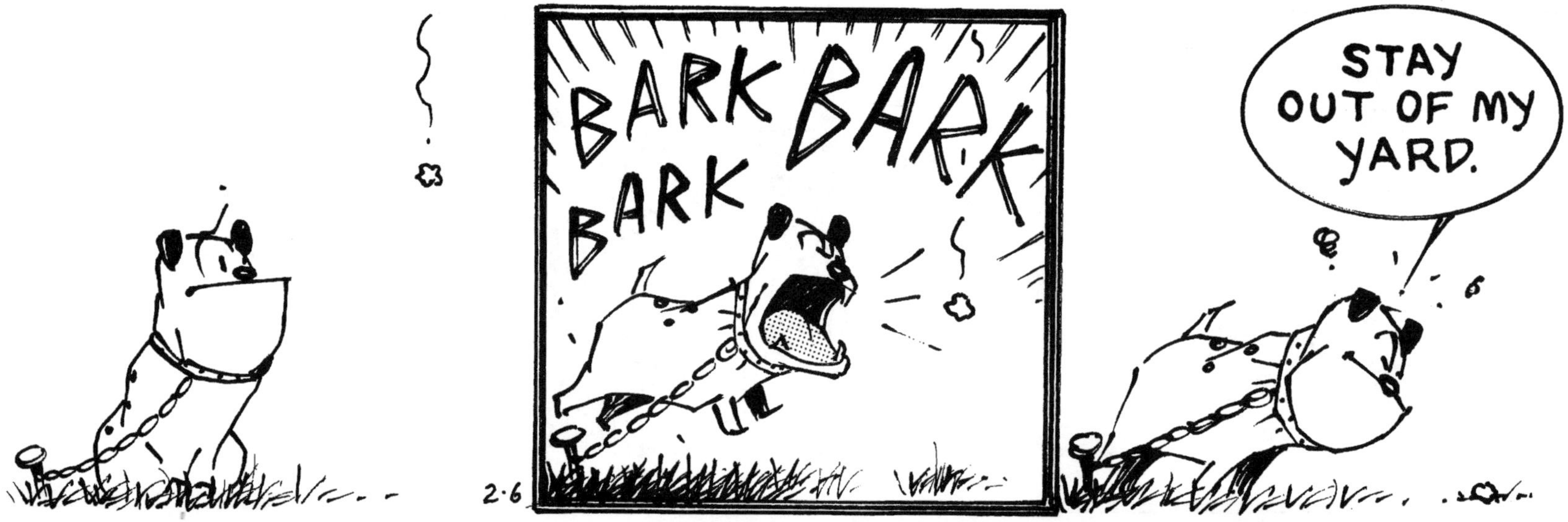
BARK BARK
BARK
STAY OUT OF MY YARD.
2·6

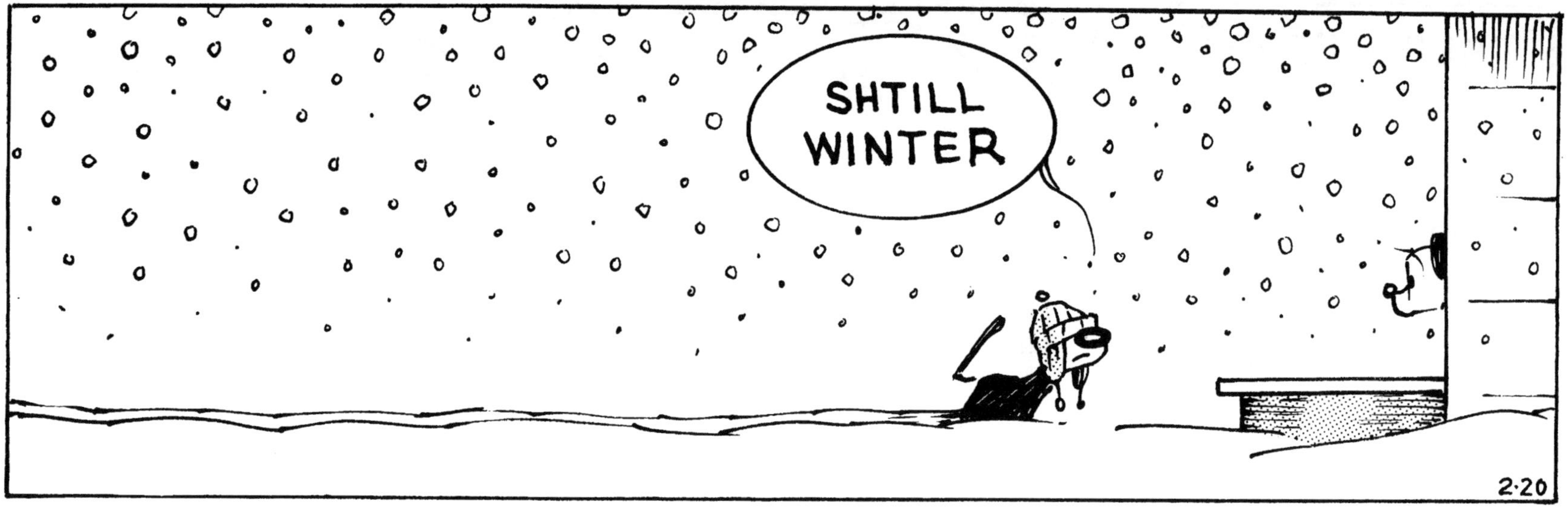
SHTILL WINTER
2·20

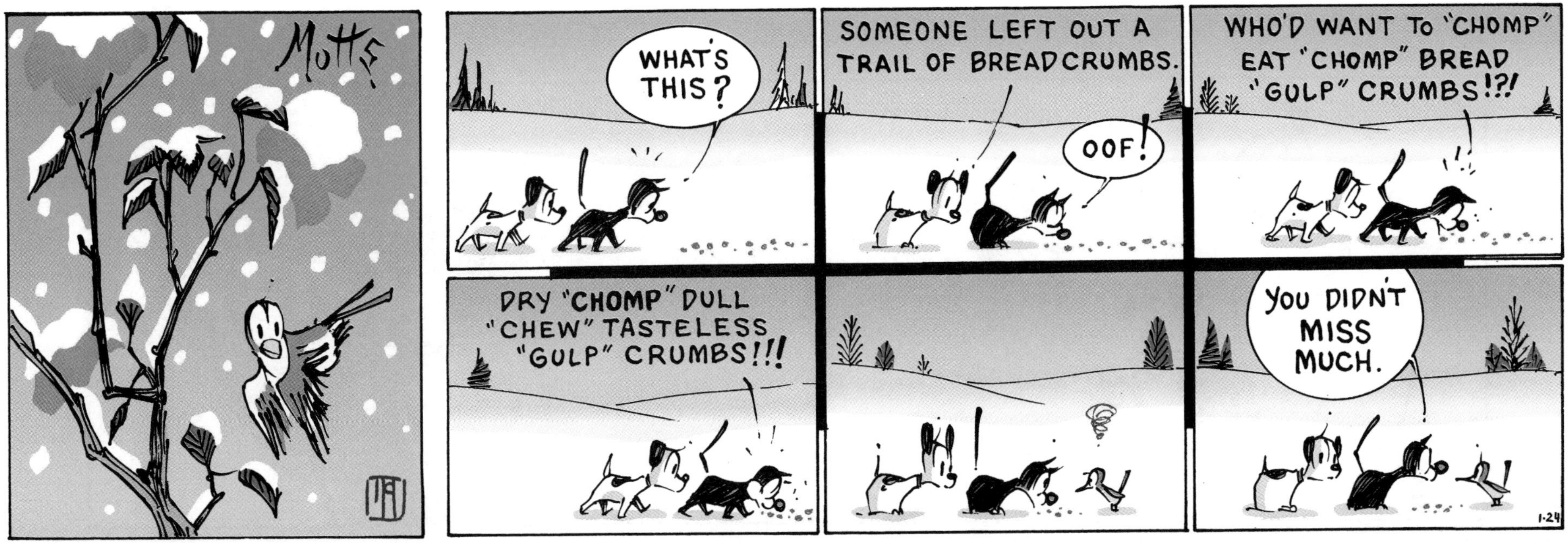

MUTTS
WHAT'S THIS?
SOMEONE LEFT OUT A TRAIL OF BREADCRUMBS.
OOF!
WHO'D WANT TO "CHOMP" EAT "CHOMP" BREAD "GULP" CRUMBS!?!
DRY "CHOMP" DULL "CHEW" TASTELESS "GULP" CRUMBS!!!
YOU DIDN'T MISS MUCH.
1·24

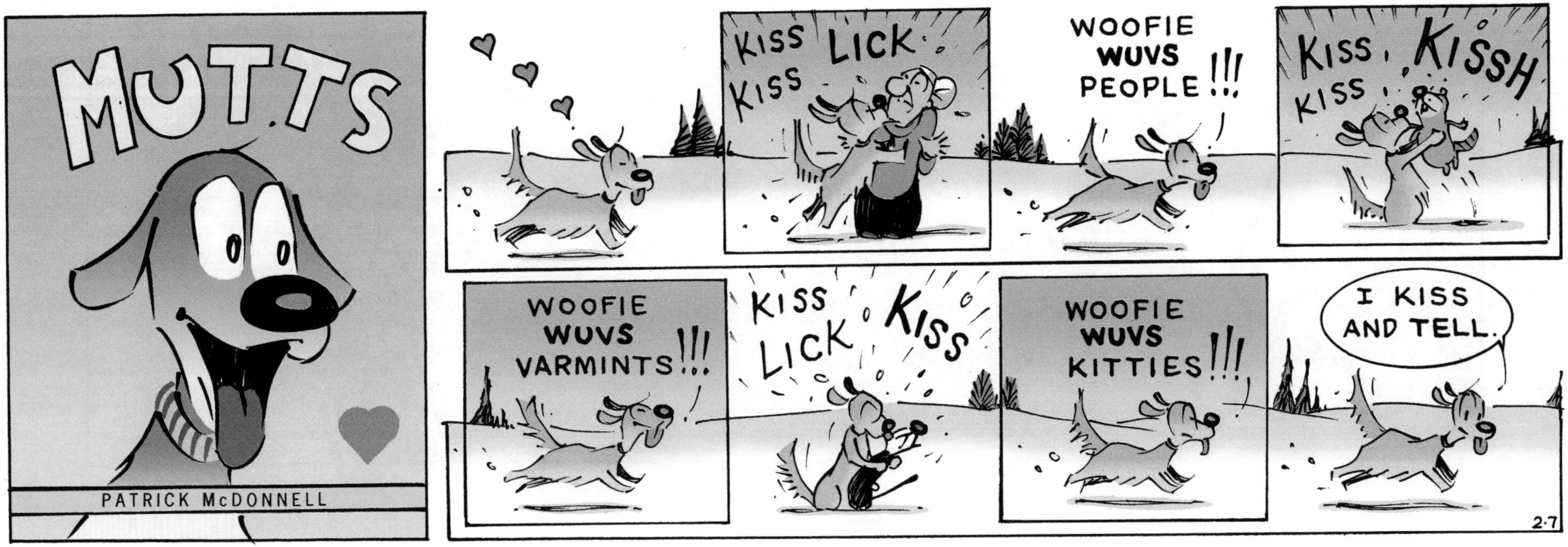

MUTTS
PATRICK McDONNELL
KISS KISS LICK
WOOFIE WUVS PEOPLE!!!
KISS, KISSH KISS
WOOFIE WUVS VARMINTS!!!
KISS LICK KISS
WOOFIE WUVS KITTIES!!!
I KISS AND TELL.
2·7

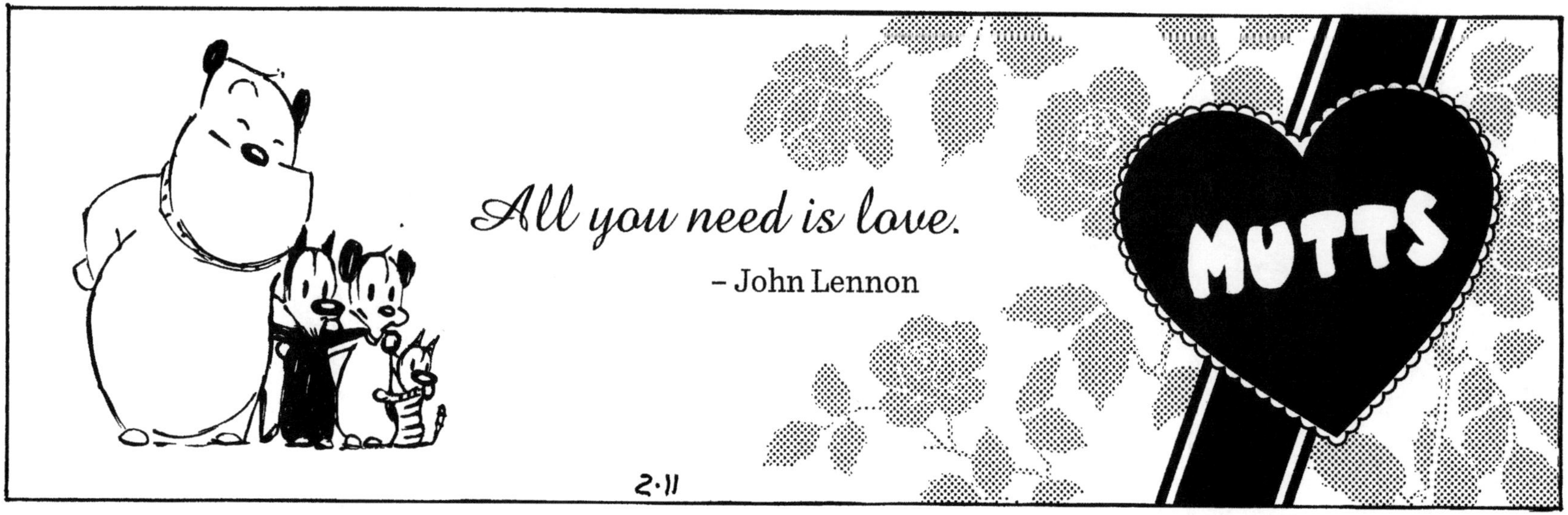
All you need is love.
– John Lennon
MUTTS
2·11

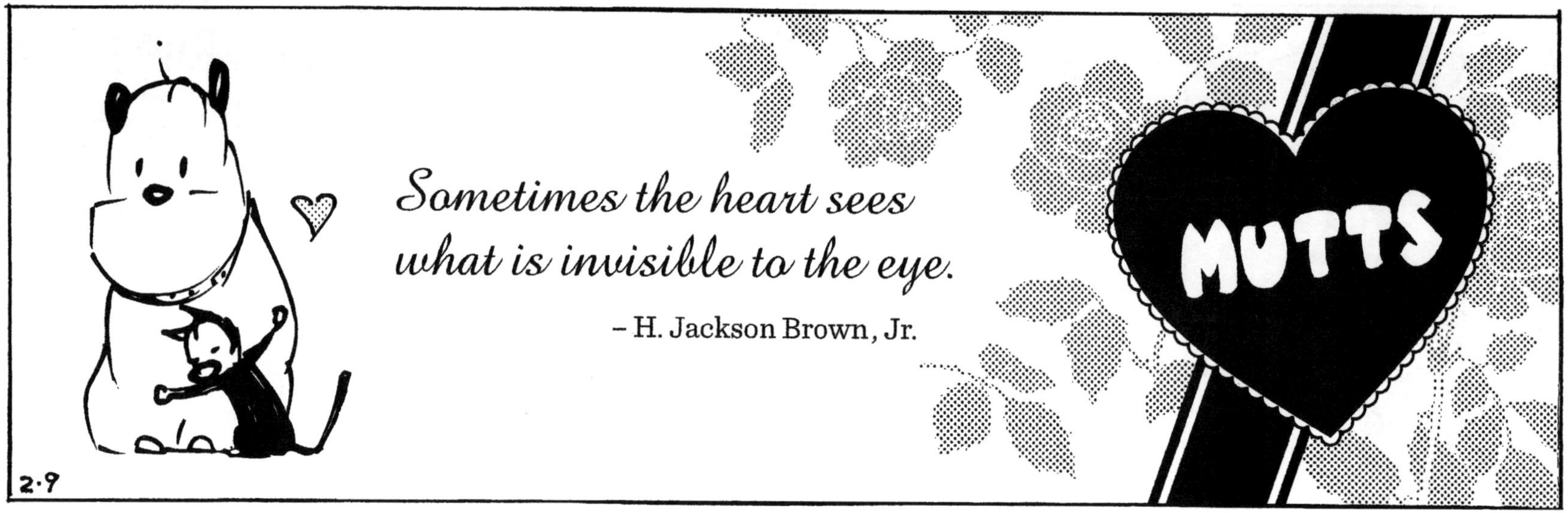
Sometimes the heart sees
what is invisible to the eye.
– H. Jackson Brown, Jr.
MUTTS
2·9

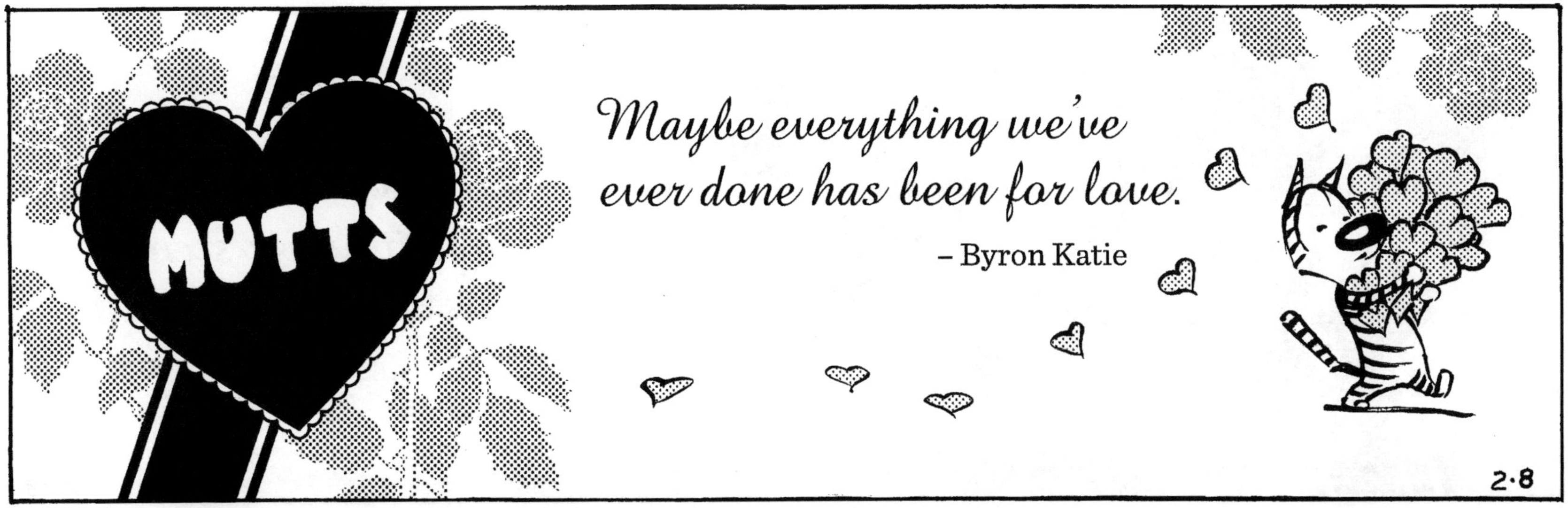
MUTTS
Maybe everything we've ever done has been for love.
– Byron Katie
2·8

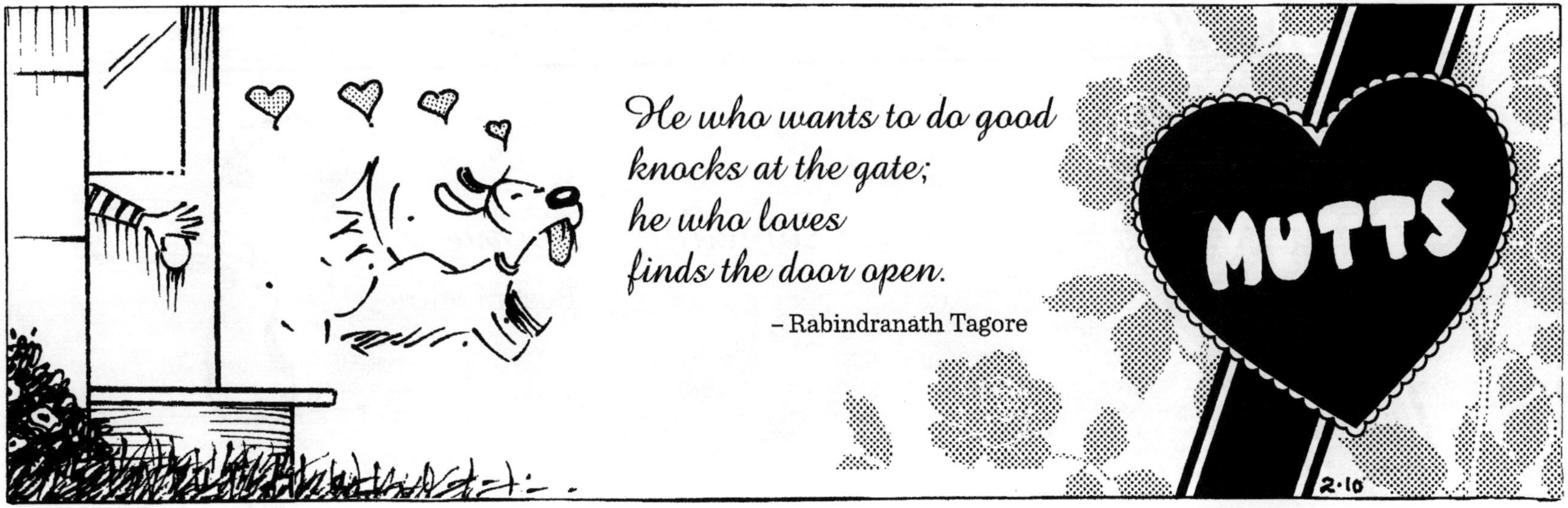
He who wants to do good knocks at the gate; he who loves finds the door open.
– Rabindranath Tagore
MUTTS
2·10

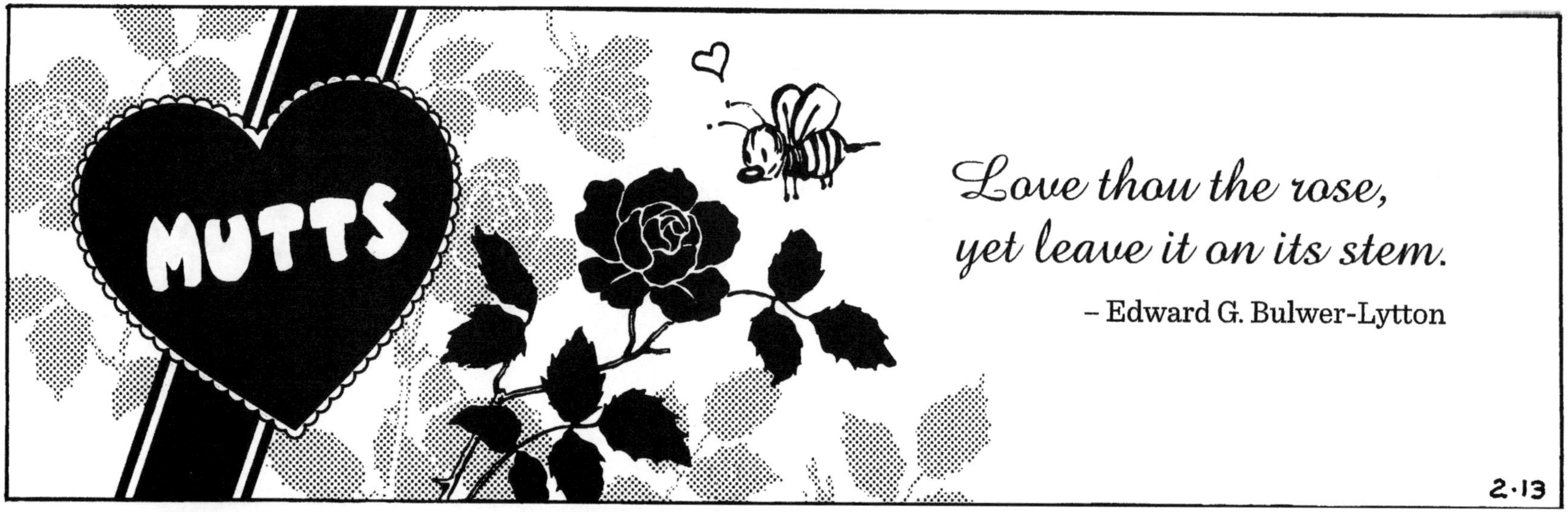
MUTTS
Love thou the rose,
yet leave it on its stem.
– Edward G. Bulwer-Lytton
2·13

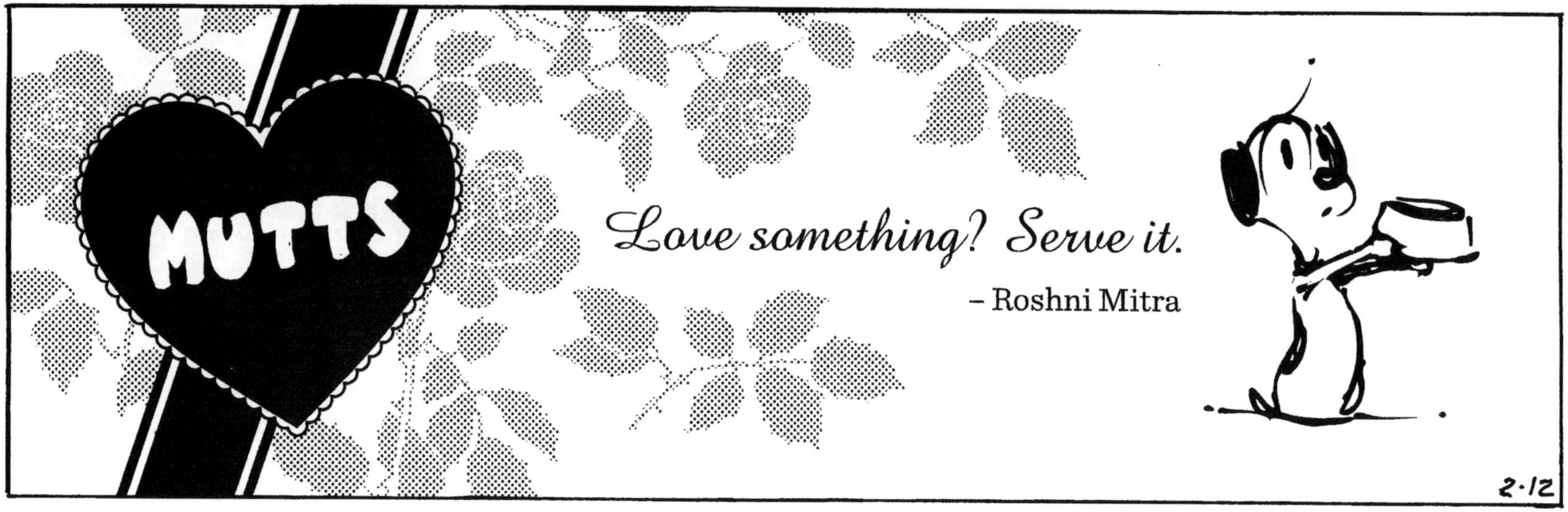
MUTTS
Love something? Serve it.
– Roshni Mitra
2·12

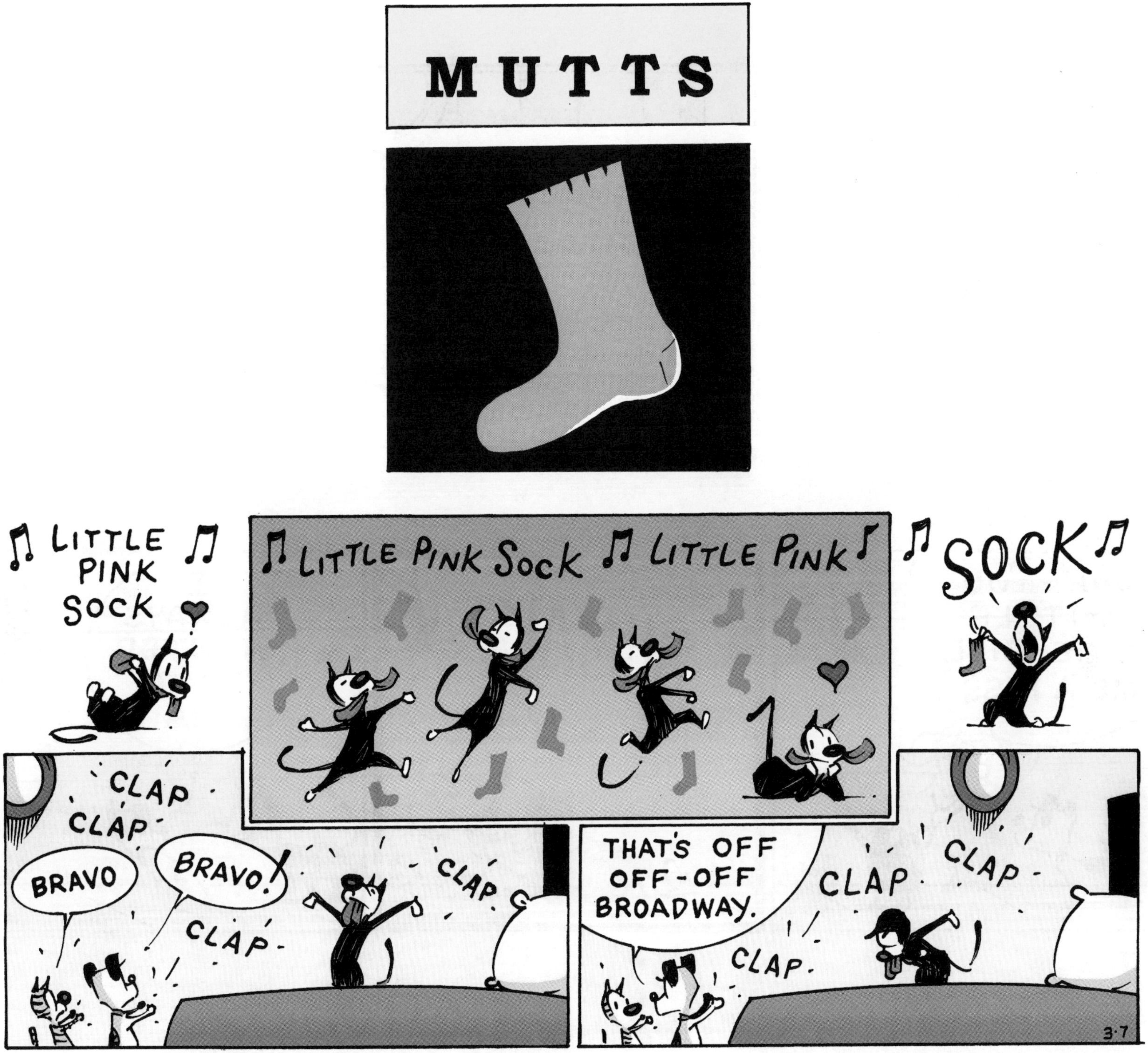
MUTTS
♫ LITTLE PINK SOCK ♫
♫ LITTLE PINK SOCK ♫ LITTLE PINK ♫
♫ SOCK ♫
CLAP
CLAP
BRAVO
BRAVO!
CLAP
CLAP
THAT'S OFF OFF-OFF BROADWAY.
CLAP
CLAP
CLAP
3·7

MOOCH, CAN YOU MOVE?
O.K.
FWIP FWIP FWIP
1·6
I NEEDED A LITTLE "WIGGLE" ROOM.

OOOH-YOU WITTLE CUTIE-GIVE ME A KISS!
SHMAK
I ALWAYS WANTED TO DO THAT.
1·7

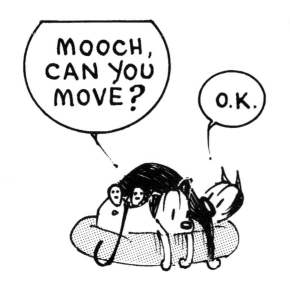

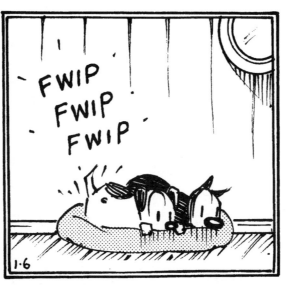

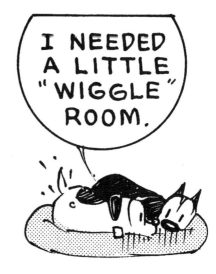

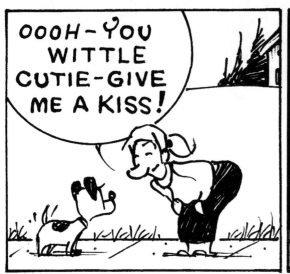

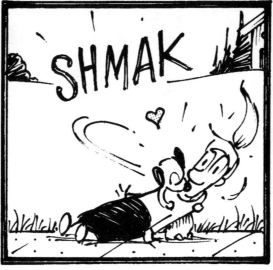

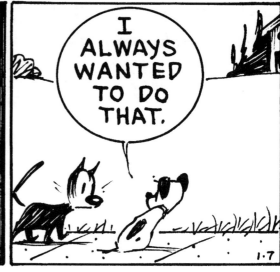

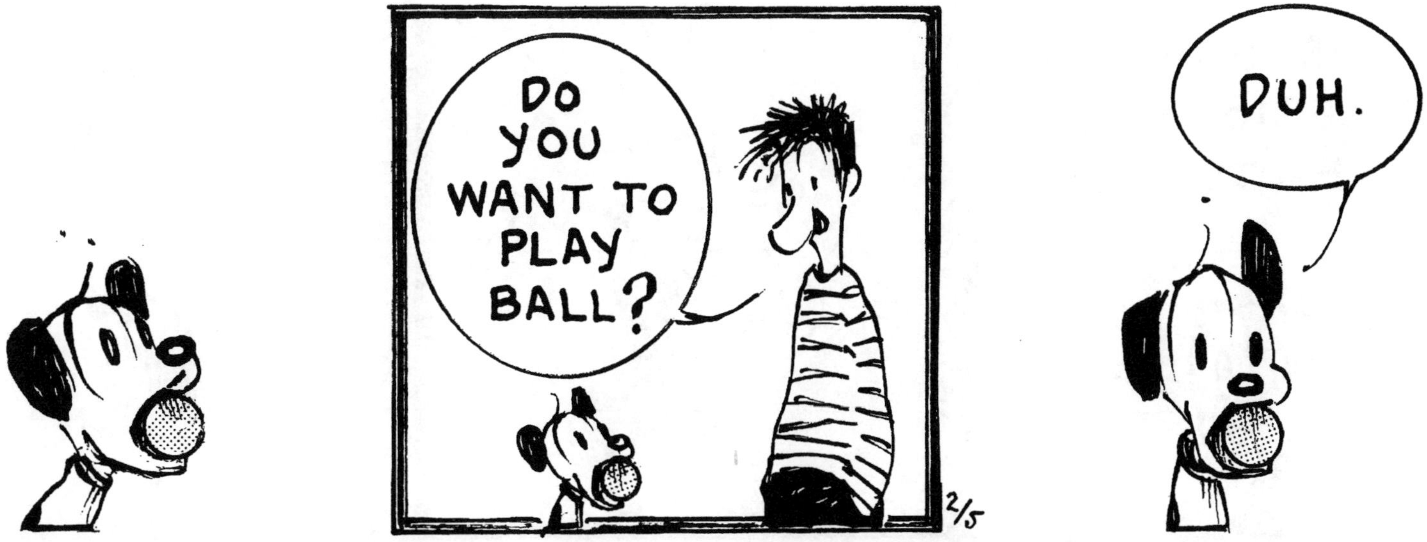
DO YOU WANT TO PLAY BALL?
DUH.
2/5

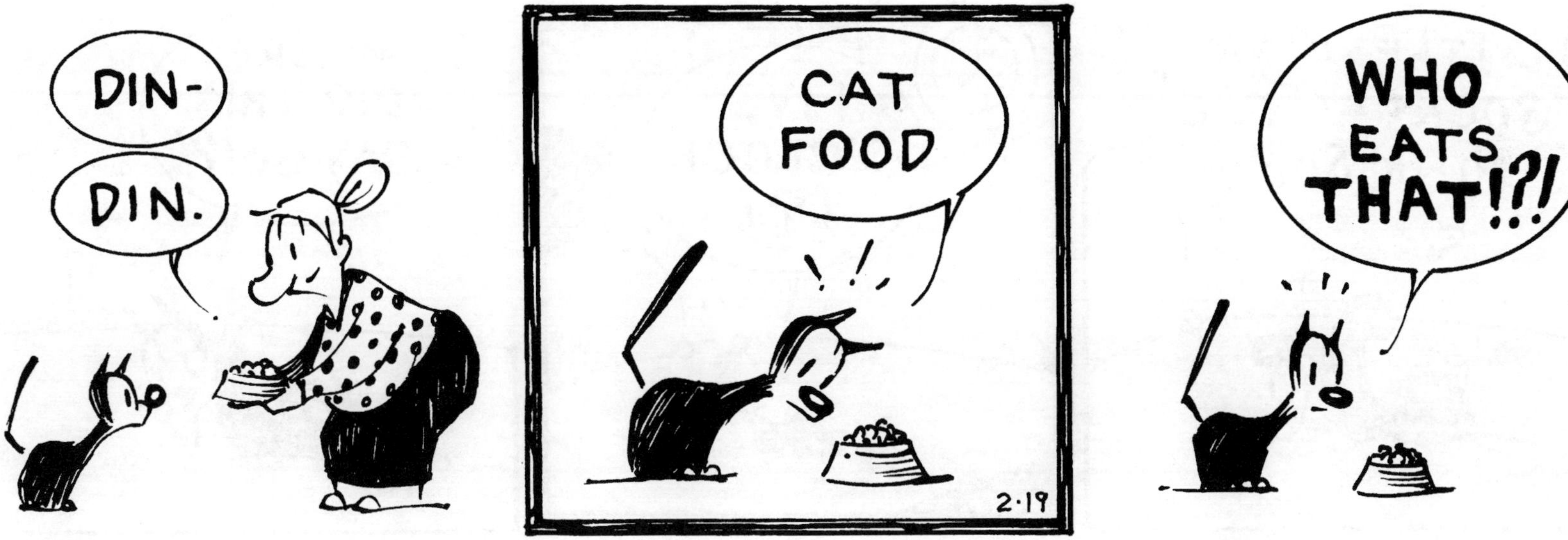
DIN-
DIN.
CAT FOOD
WHO EATS THAT!?!
2·19

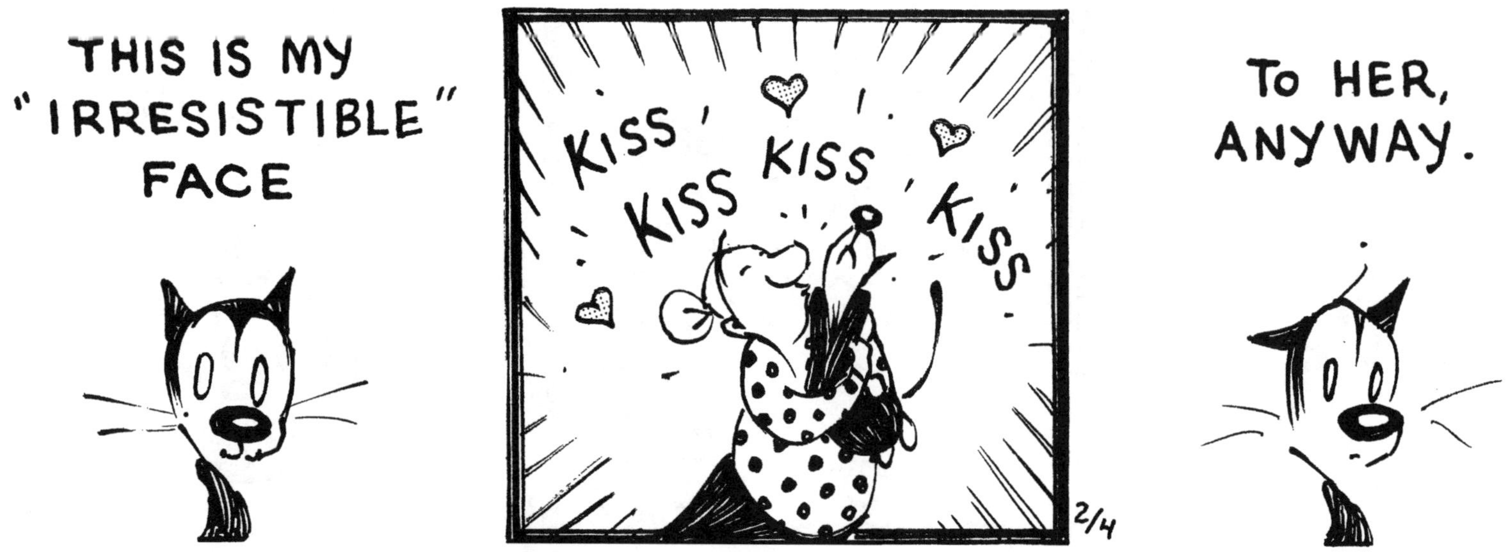
THIS IS MY "IRRESISTIBLE" FACE
KISS KISS KISS KISS
2/4
TO HER, ANYWAY.

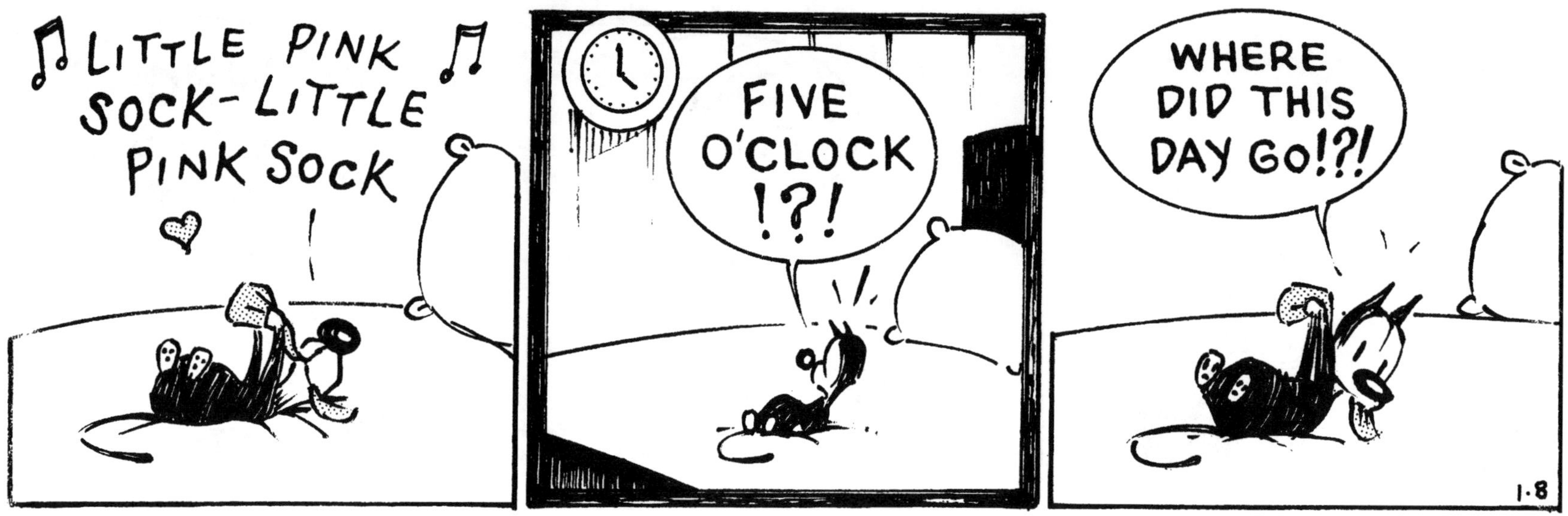
♫ LITTLE PINK SOCK- LITTLE PINK SOCK ♫
FIVE O'CLOCK !?!
WHERE DID THIS DAY GO!?!
1·8

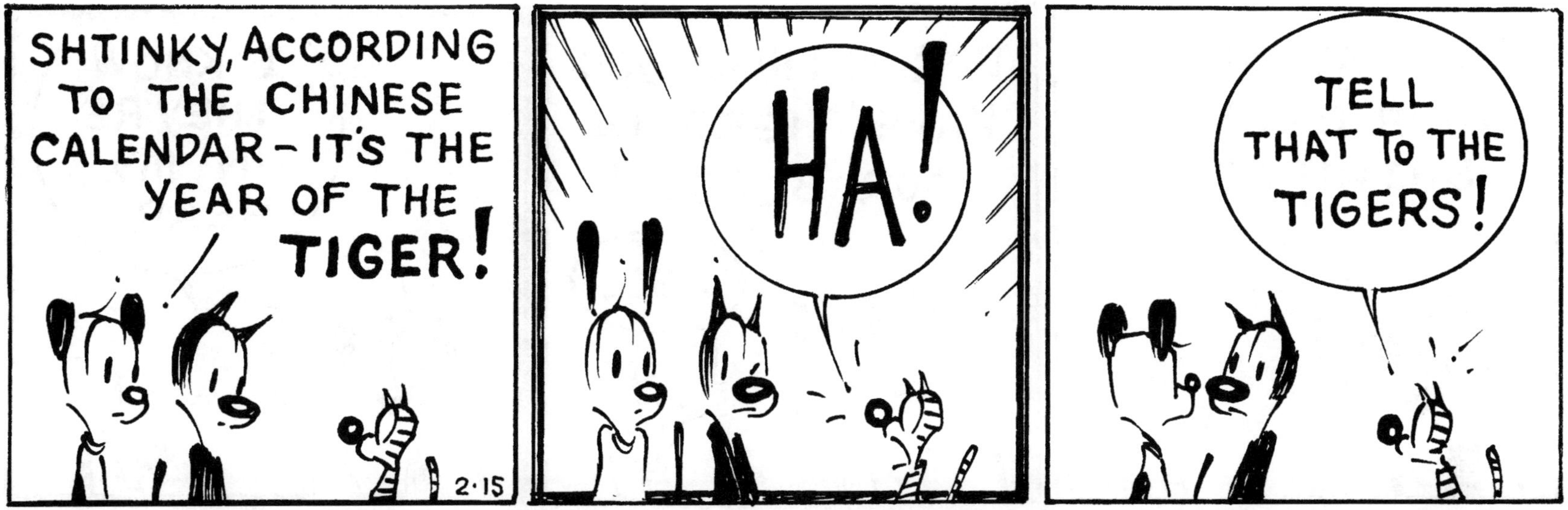
SHTINKY, ACCORDING TO THE CHINESE CALENDAR - IT'S THE YEAR OF THE TIGER!
2·15
HA!
TELL THAT TO THE TIGERS!

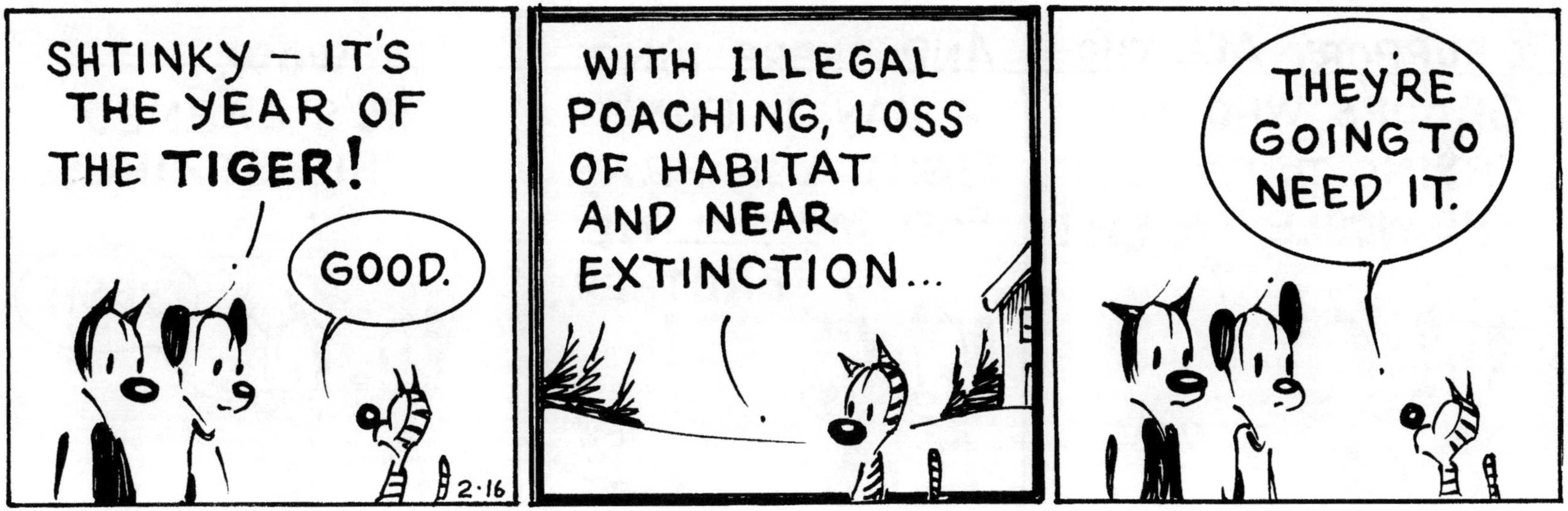
SHTINKY - IT'S THE YEAR OF THE TIGER!
GOOD.
2·16
WITH ILLEGAL POACHING, LOSS OF HABITAT AND NEAR EXTINCTION...
THEY'RE GOING TO NEED IT.

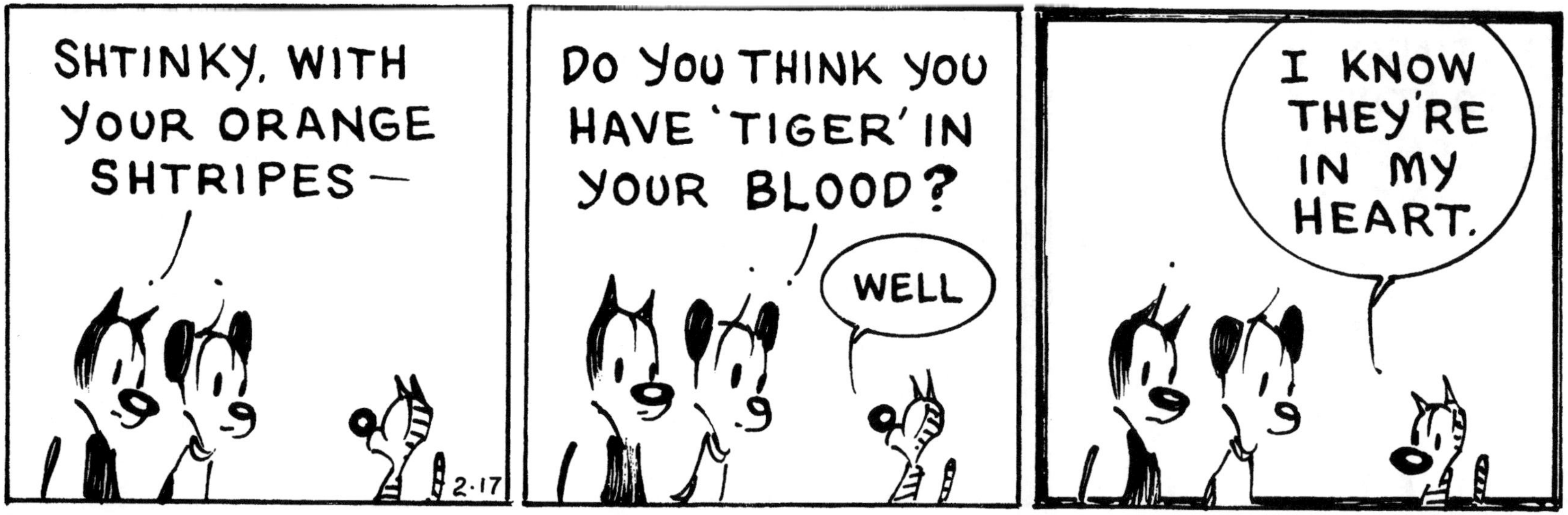
SHTINKY, WITH YOUR ORANGE SHTRIPES—
2.17
DO YOU THINK YOU HAVE 'TIGER' IN YOUR BLOOD?
WELL
I KNOW THEY'RE IN MY HEART.

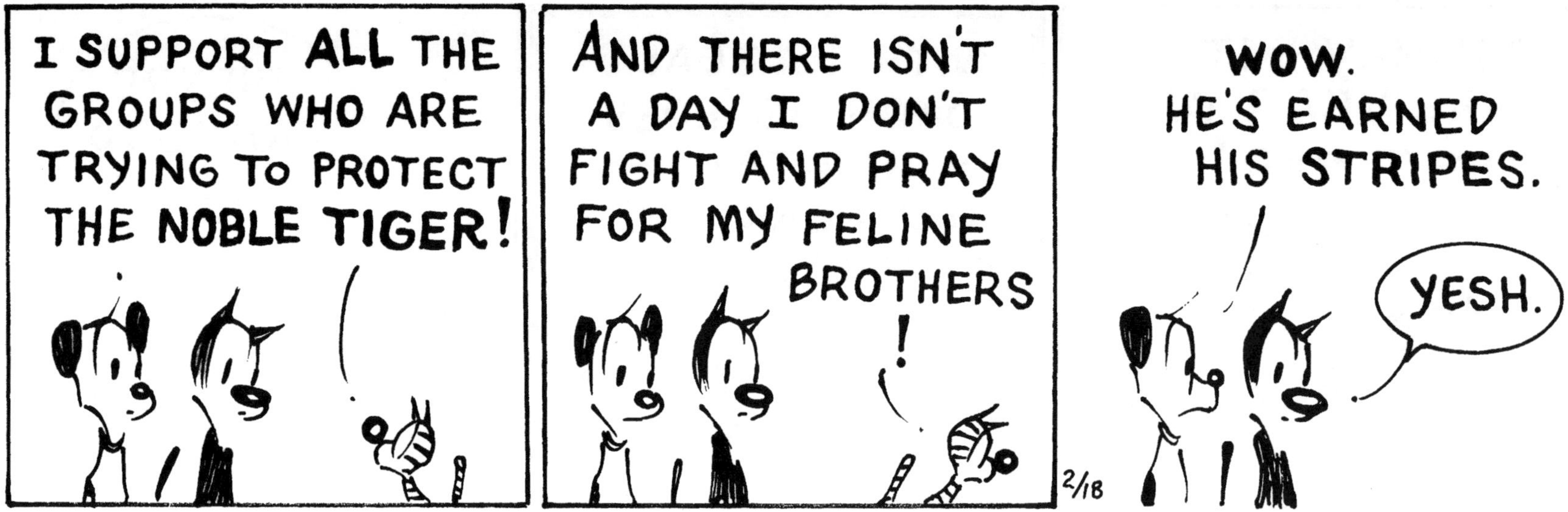
I SUPPORT **ALL** THE GROUPS WHO ARE TRYING TO PROTECT THE **NOBLE TIGER**!
AND THERE ISN'T A DAY I DON'T FIGHT AND PRAY FOR MY FELINE BROTHERS
!
2/18
WOW. HE'S EARNED HIS **STRIPES**.
YESH.

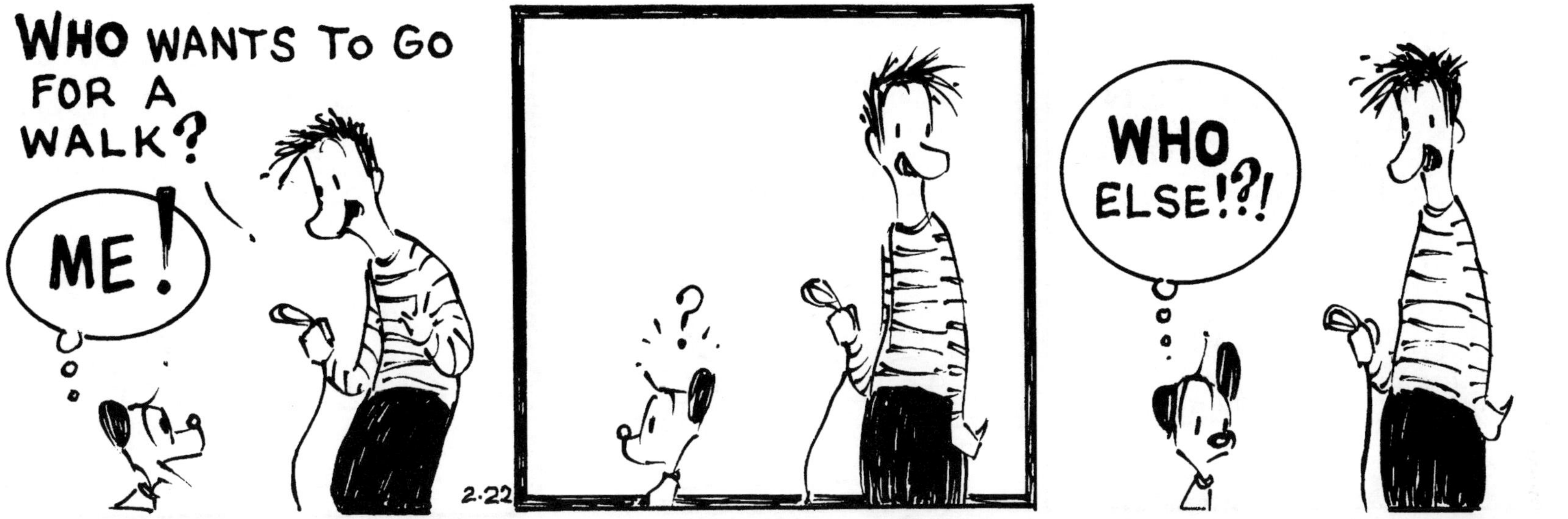
WHO WANTS TO GO FOR A WALK?
ME!
2·22
WHO ELSE!?!

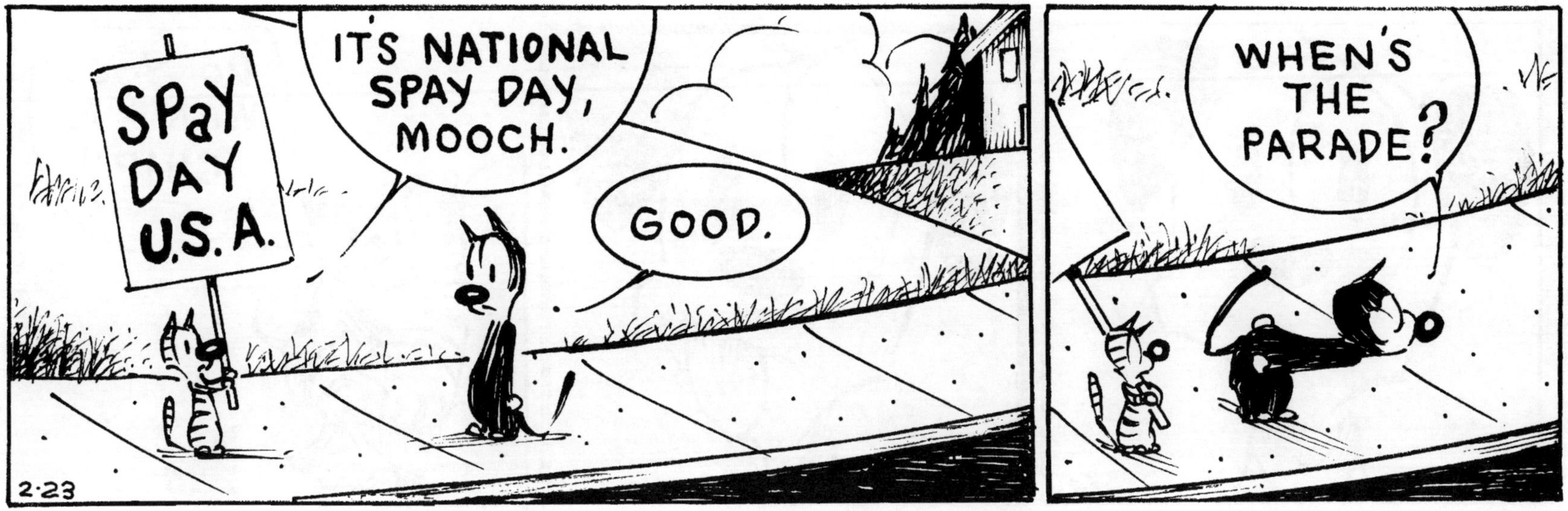
SPaY DAY U.S.A.
IT'S NATIONAL SPAY DAY, MOOCH.
GOOD.
2·23
WHEN'S THE PARADE?

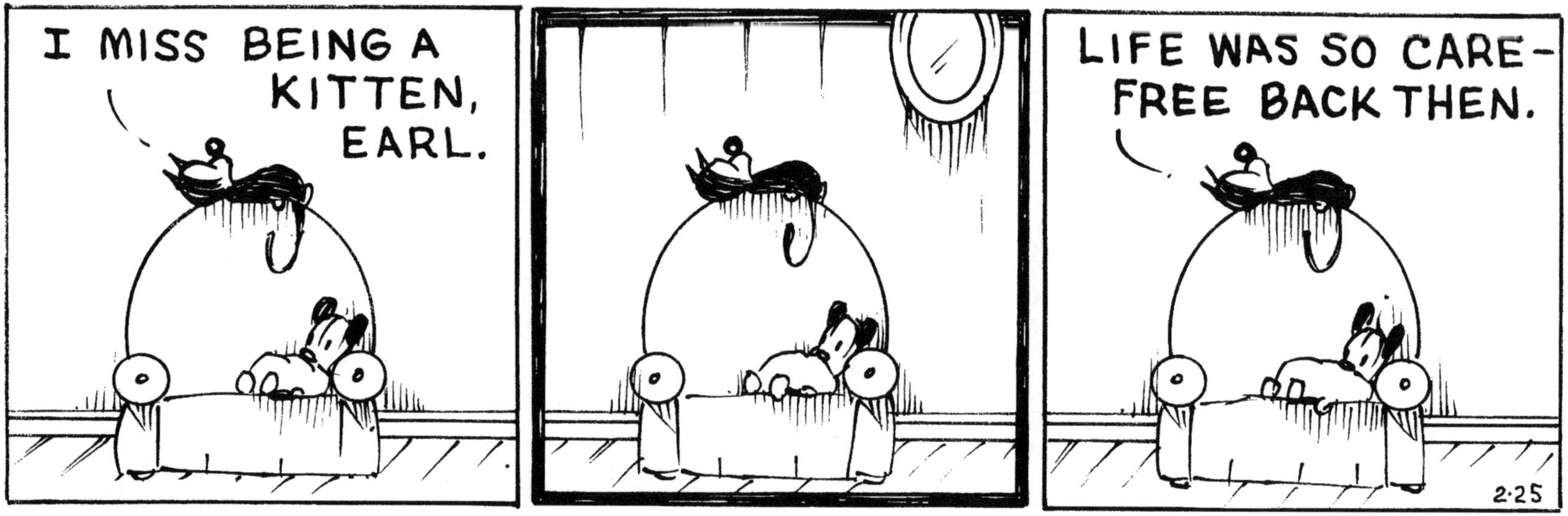
I MISS BEING A KITTEN, EARL.
LIFE WAS SO CARE-FREE BACK THEN.
2·25

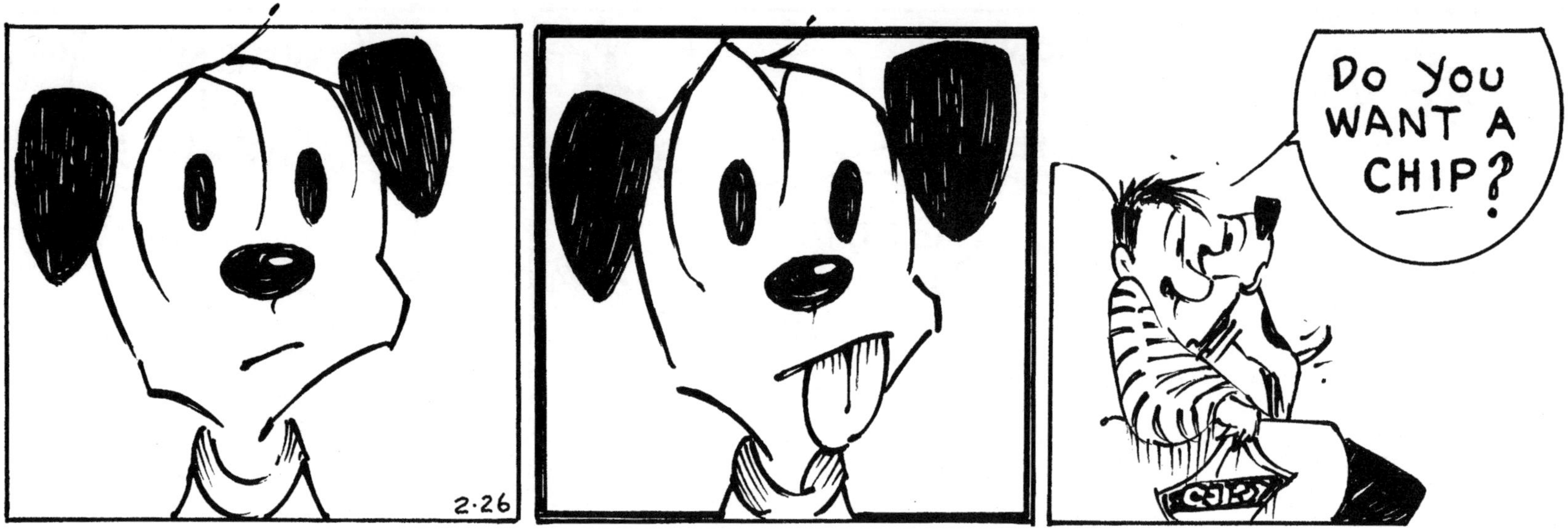
2·26
DO YOU WANT A CHIP?

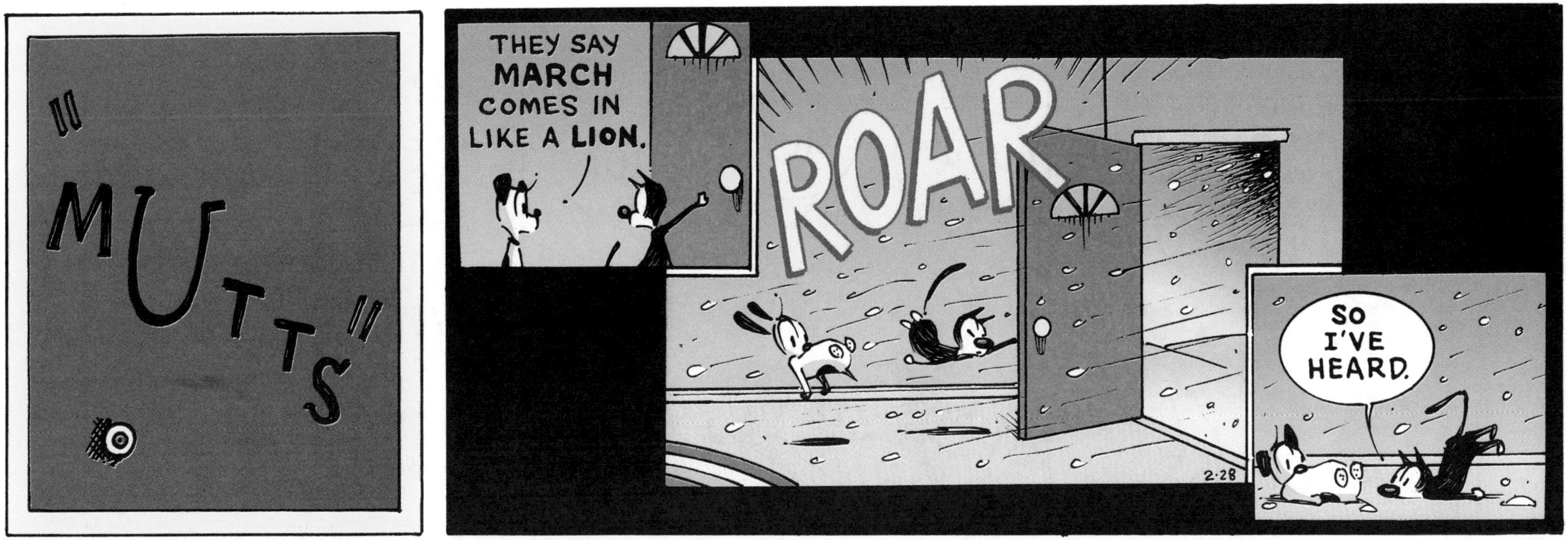
"MUTTS"
THEY SAY MARCH COMES IN LIKE A LION.
ROAR
SO I'VE HEARD.
2·28

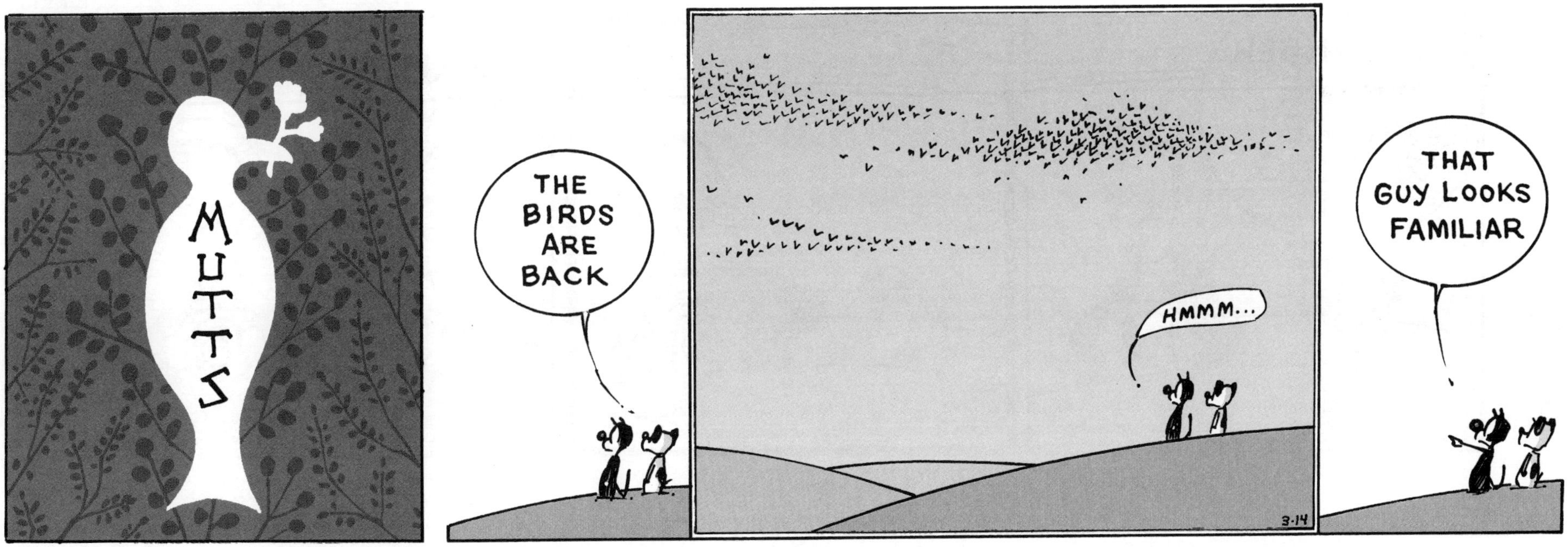
MUTTS
THE BIRDS ARE BACK
HMMM...
THAT GUY LOOKS FAMILIAR
3·14

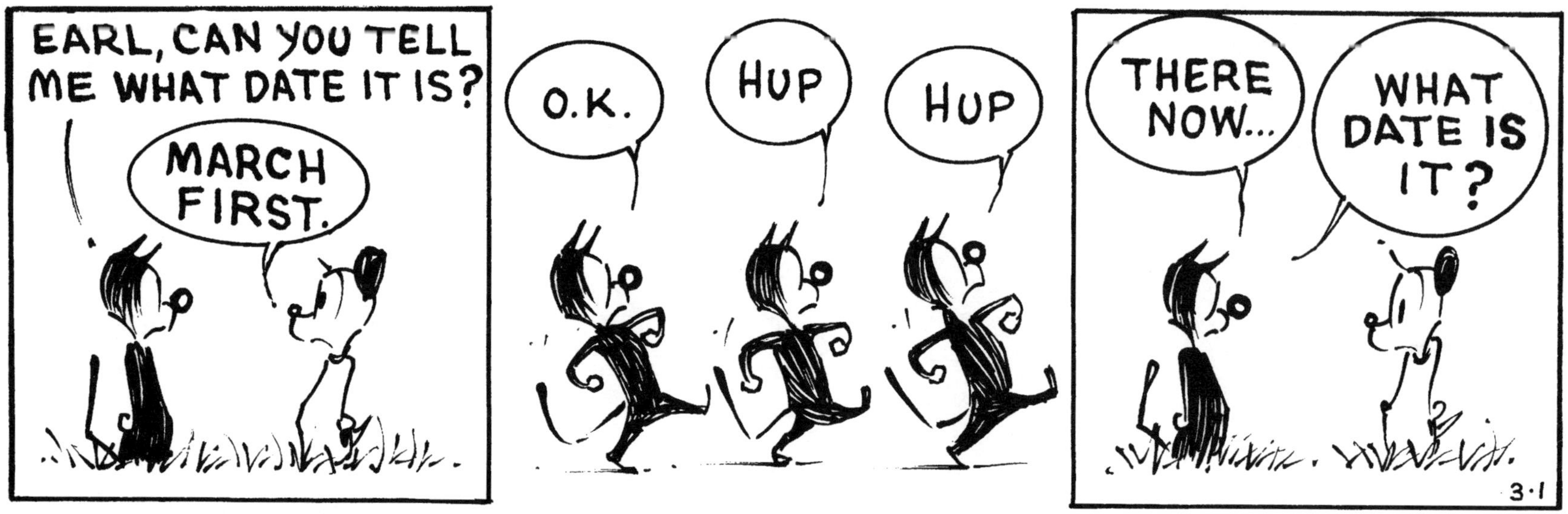
EARL, CAN YOU TELL ME WHAT DATE IT IS?
MARCH FIRST.
O.K.
HUP
HUP
THERE NOW...
WHAT DATE IS IT?
3·1

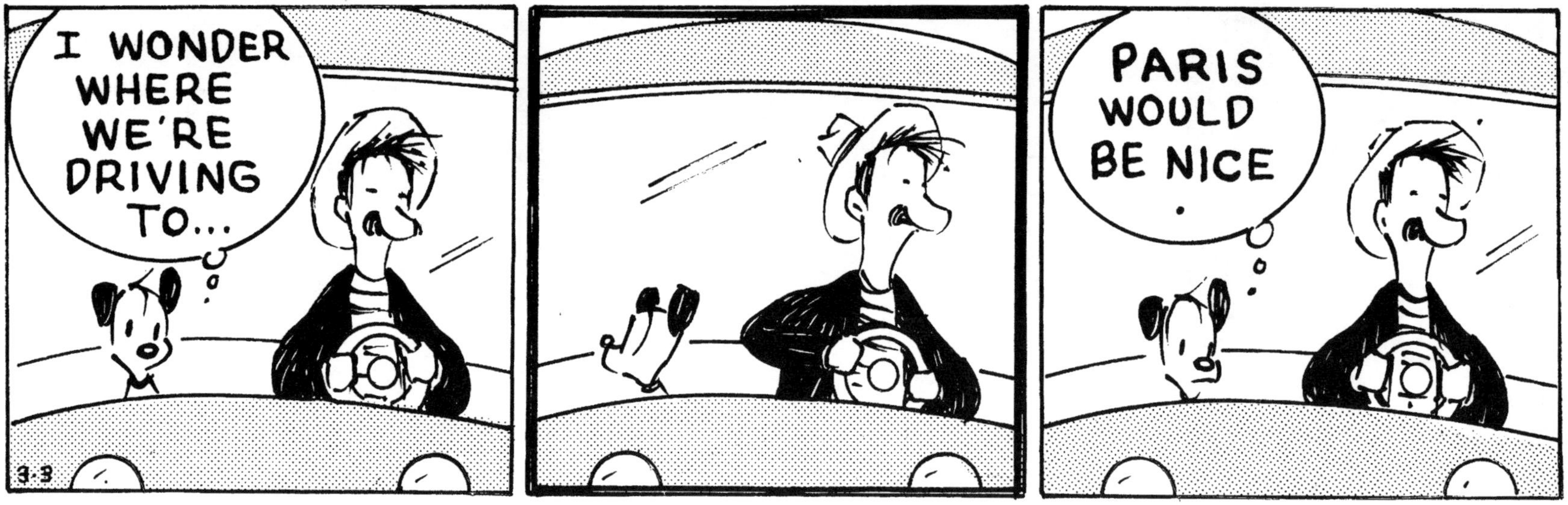
I WONDER WHERE WE'RE DRIVING TO...
3·3
PARIS WOULD BE NICE.

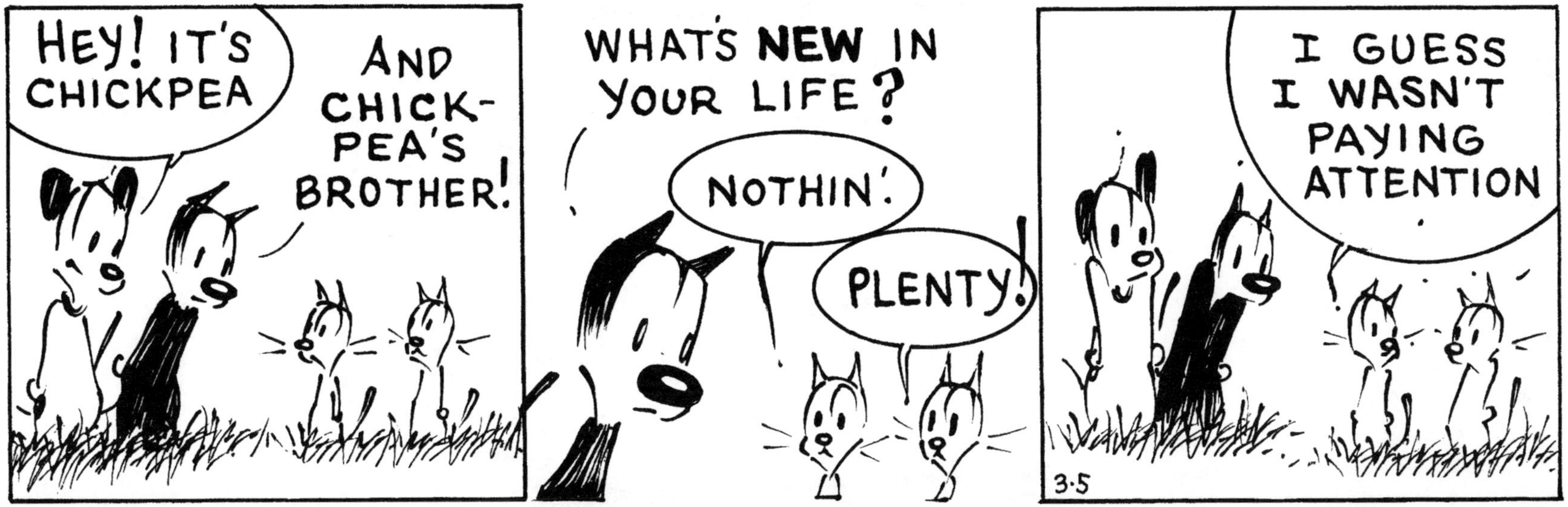
HEY! IT'S CHICKPEA
AND CHICK-PEA'S BROTHER!
WHAT'S NEW IN YOUR LIFE?
NOTHIN'.
PLENTY!
I GUESS I WASN'T PAYING ATTENTION.
3·5

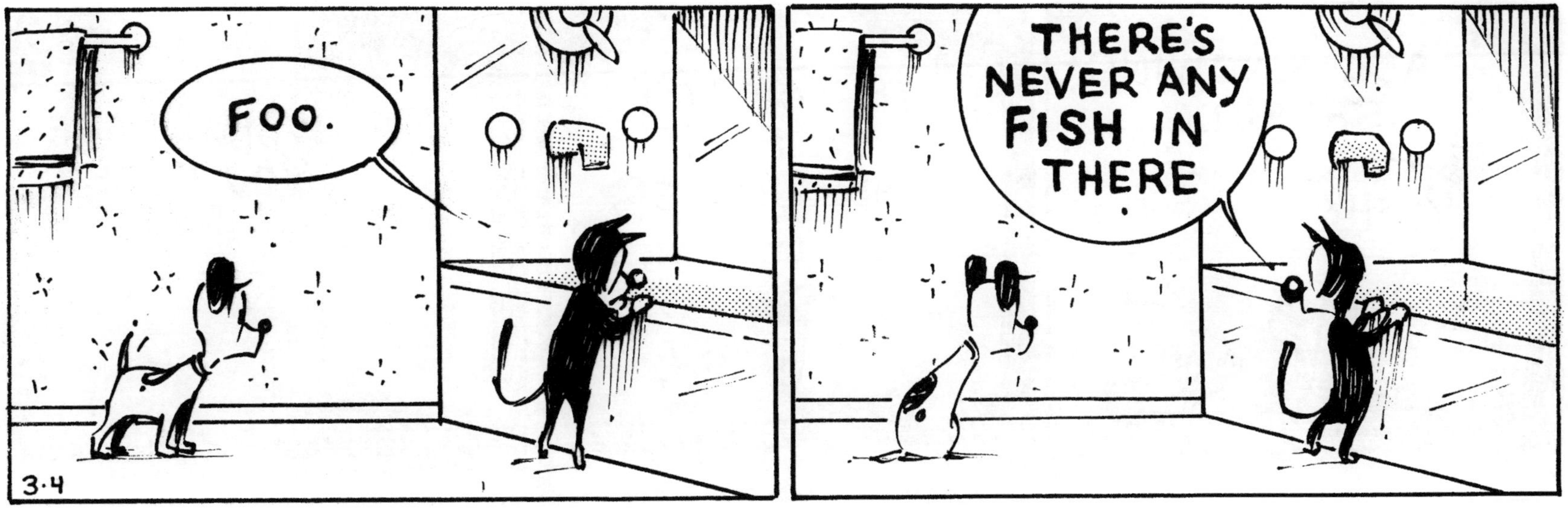
FOO.
THERE'S NEVER ANY FISH IN THERE.
3·4

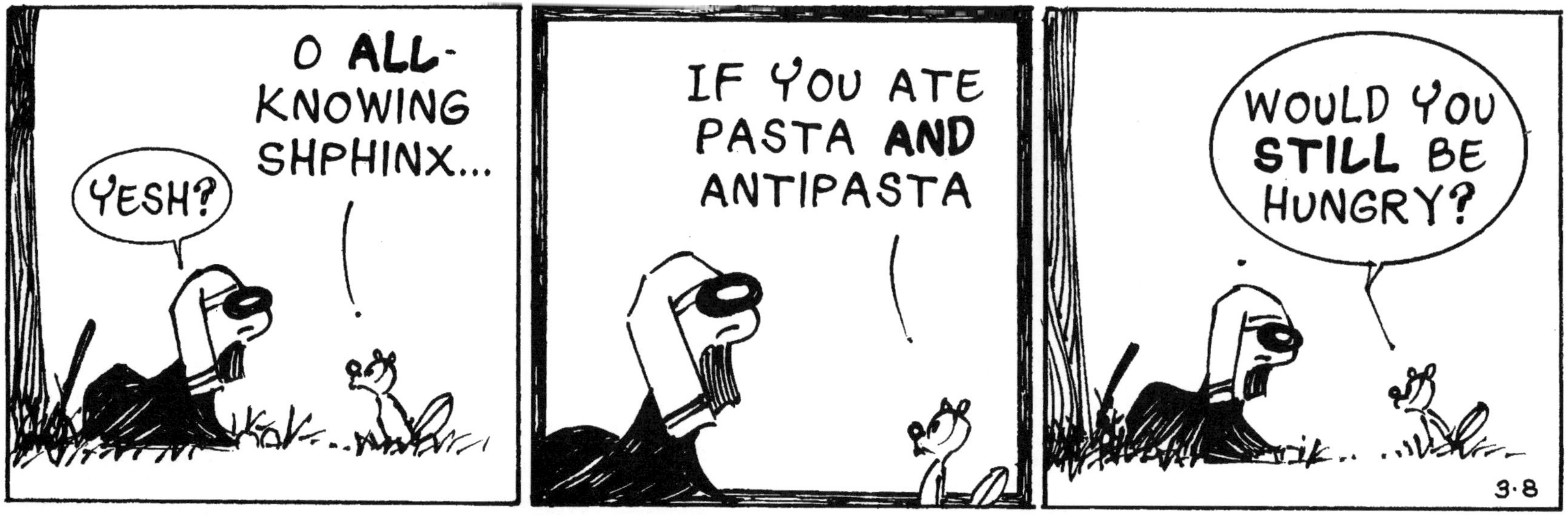
O ALL-KNOWING SHPHINX...
YESH?
IF YOU ATE PASTA AND ANTIPASTA
WOULD YOU STILL BE HUNGRY?
3·8

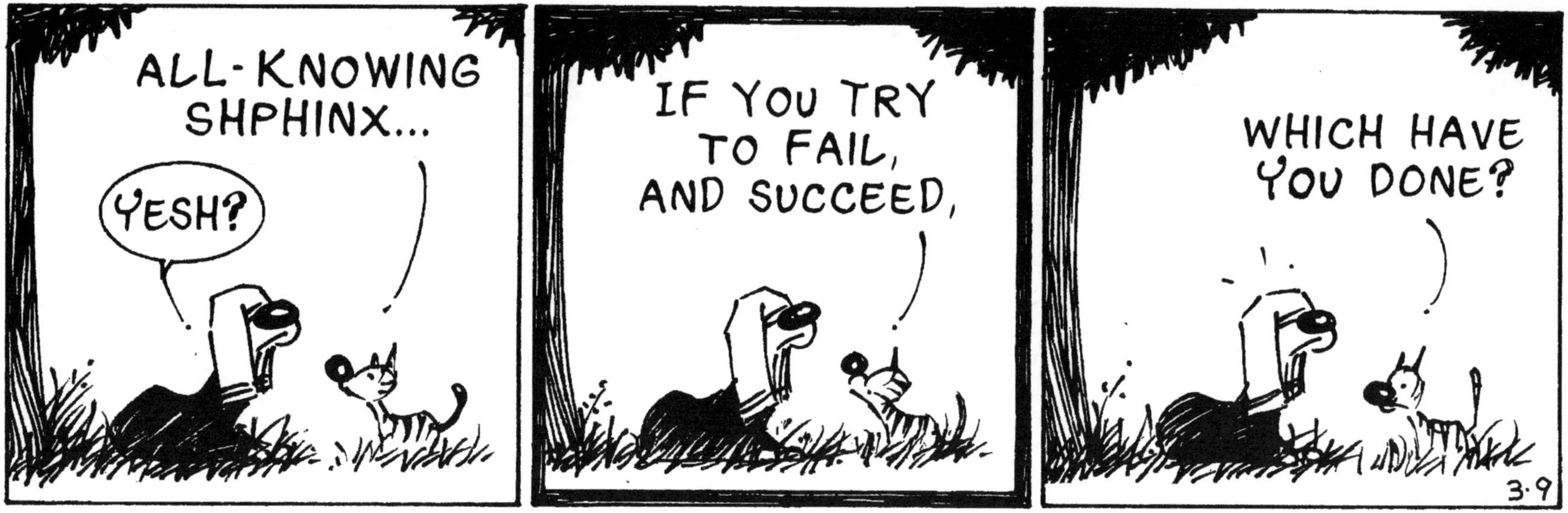
ALL-KNOWING SHPHINX...
YESH?
IF YOU TRY TO FAIL, AND SUCCEED,
WHICH HAVE YOU DONE?
3·9

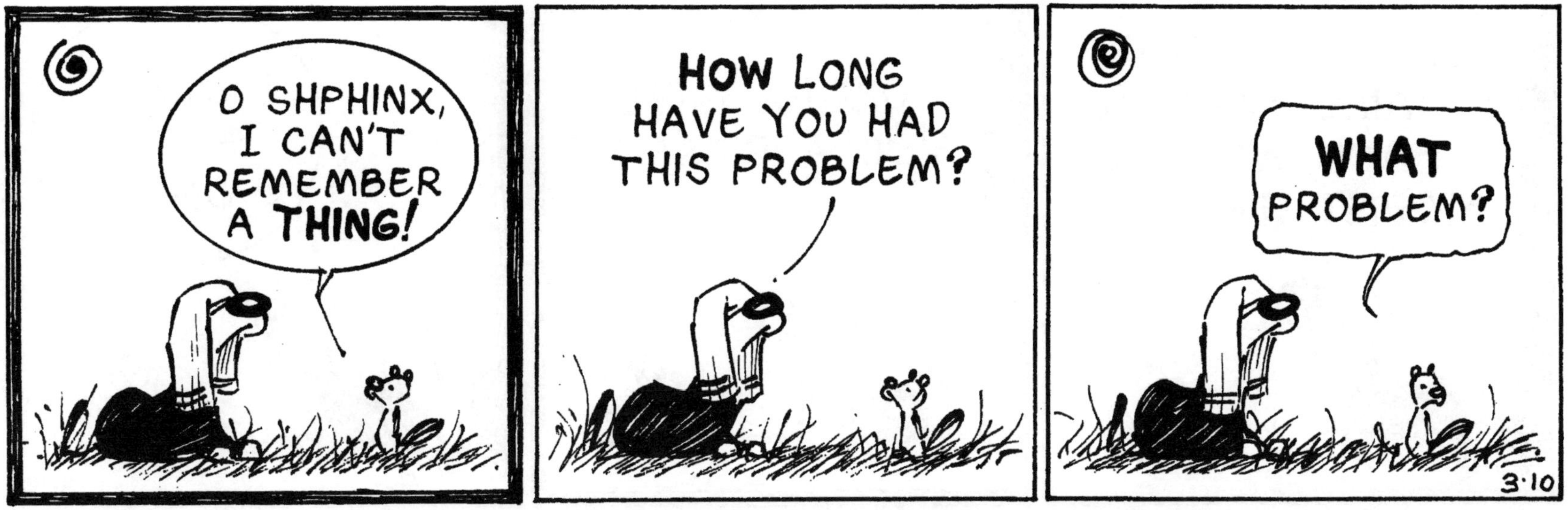
O SHPHINX, I CAN'T REMEMBER A **THING**!
HOW LONG HAVE YOU HAD THIS PROBLEM?
WHAT PROBLEM?
3·10

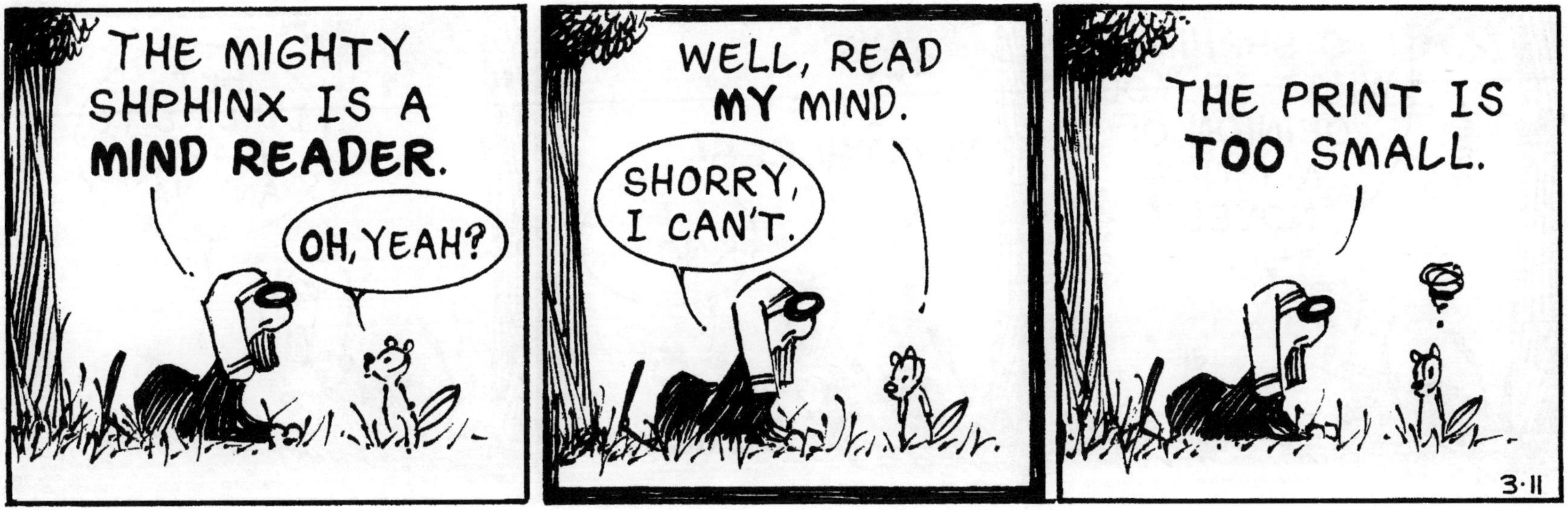
THE MIGHTY SHPHINX IS A **MIND READER**.
OH, YEAH?
WELL, READ **MY** MIND.
SHORRY, I CAN'T.
THE PRINT IS **TOO** SMALL.
3·11

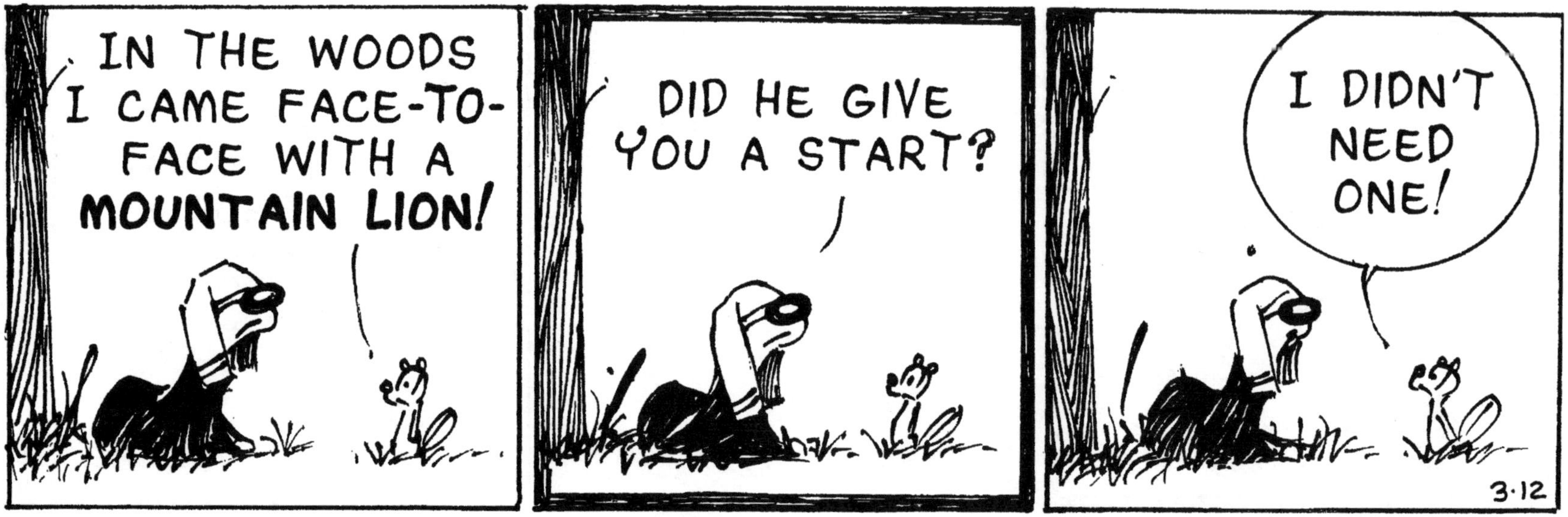
IN THE WOODS I CAME FACE-TO-FACE WITH A **MOUNTAIN LION!**
DID HE GIVE YOU A START?
I DIDN'T NEED ONE!
3·12

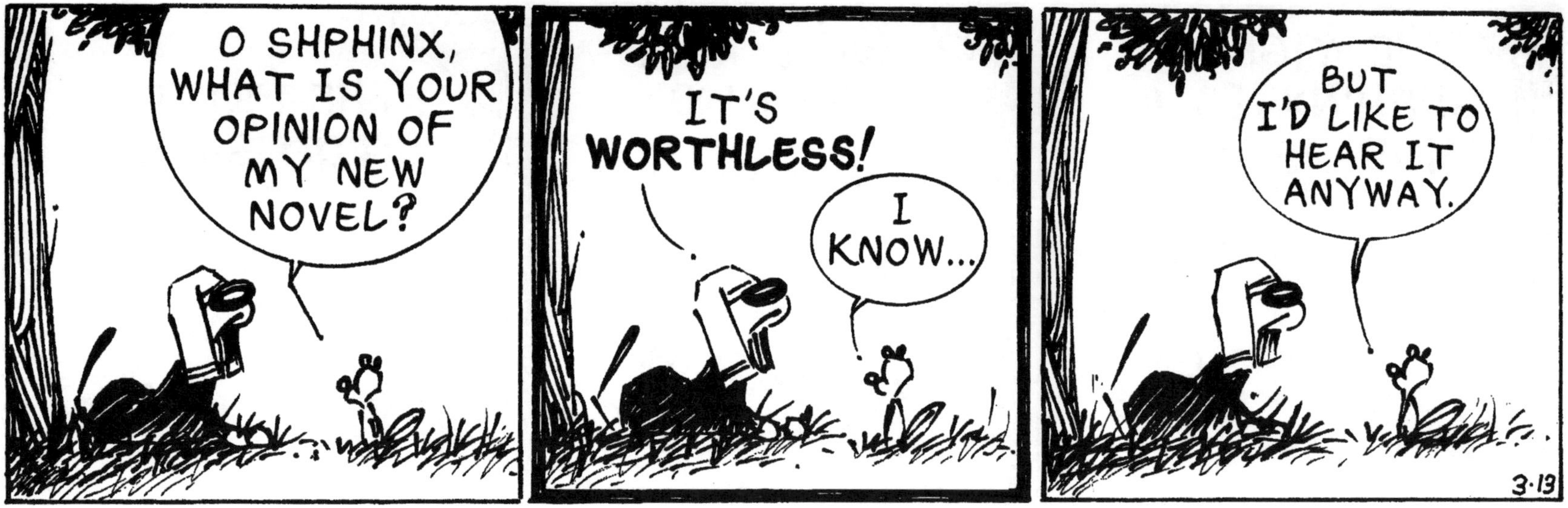
O SHPHINX, WHAT IS YOUR OPINION OF MY NEW NOVEL?
IT'S **WORTHLESS!**
I KNOW...
BUT I'D LIKE TO HEAR IT ANYWAY.
3·13

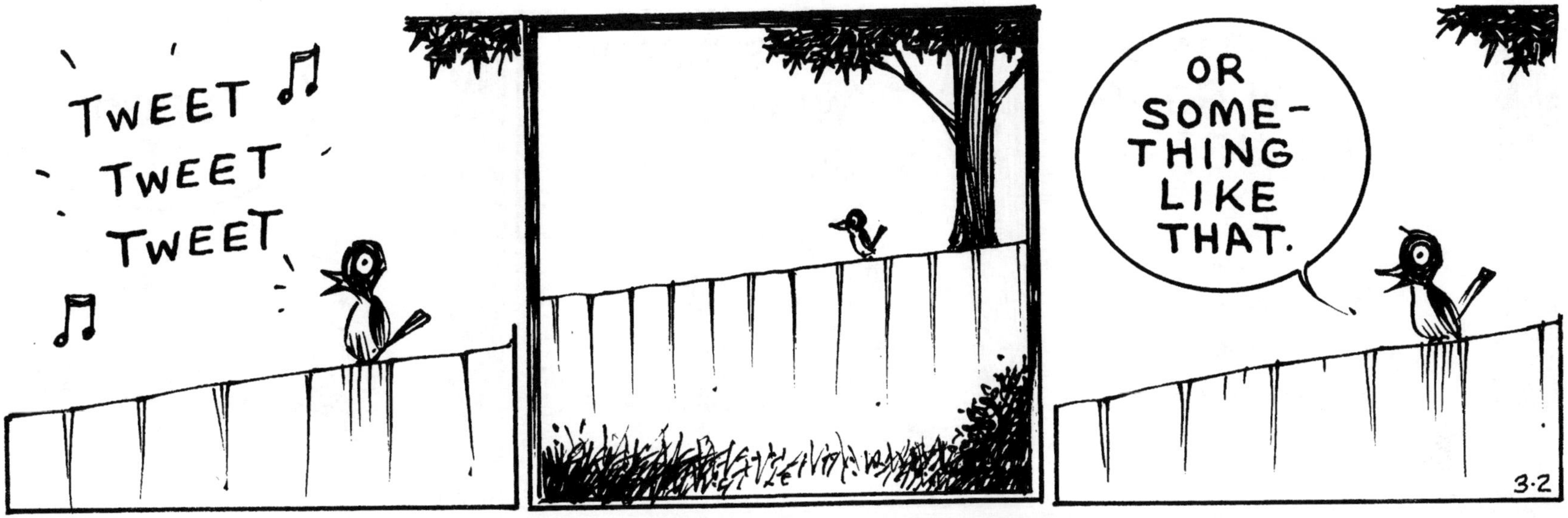
TWEET
TWEET
TWEET
OR SOMETHING LIKE THAT.
3·2

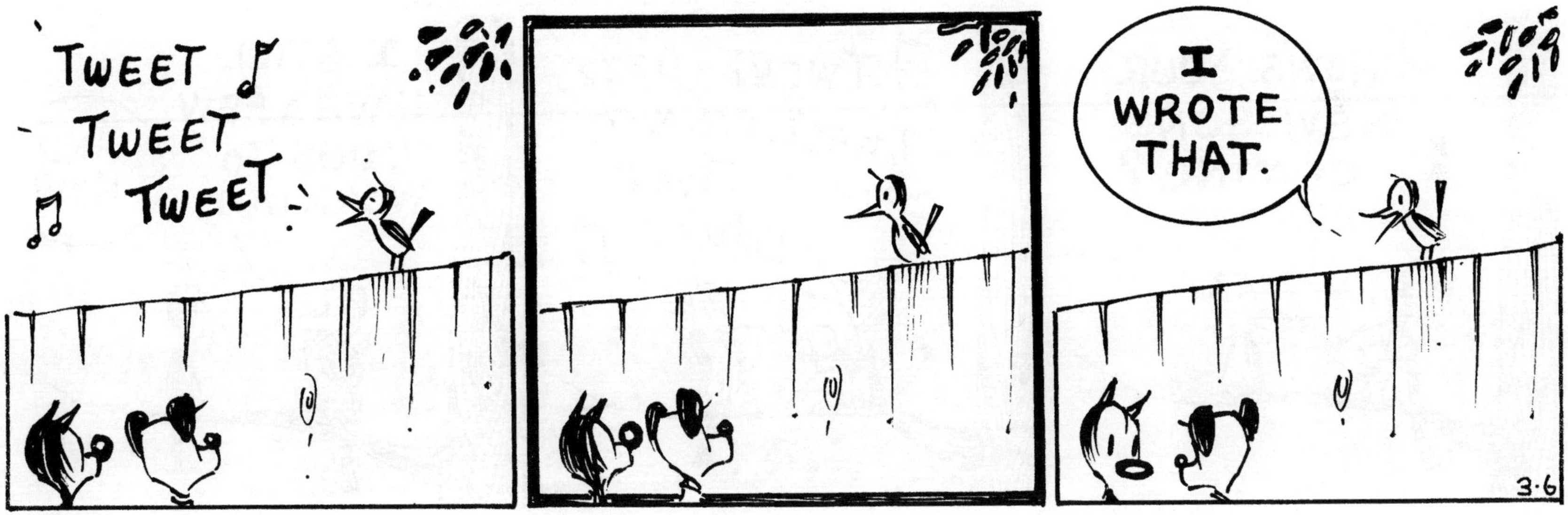
TWEET
TWEET
TWEET
I WROTE THAT.
3·6

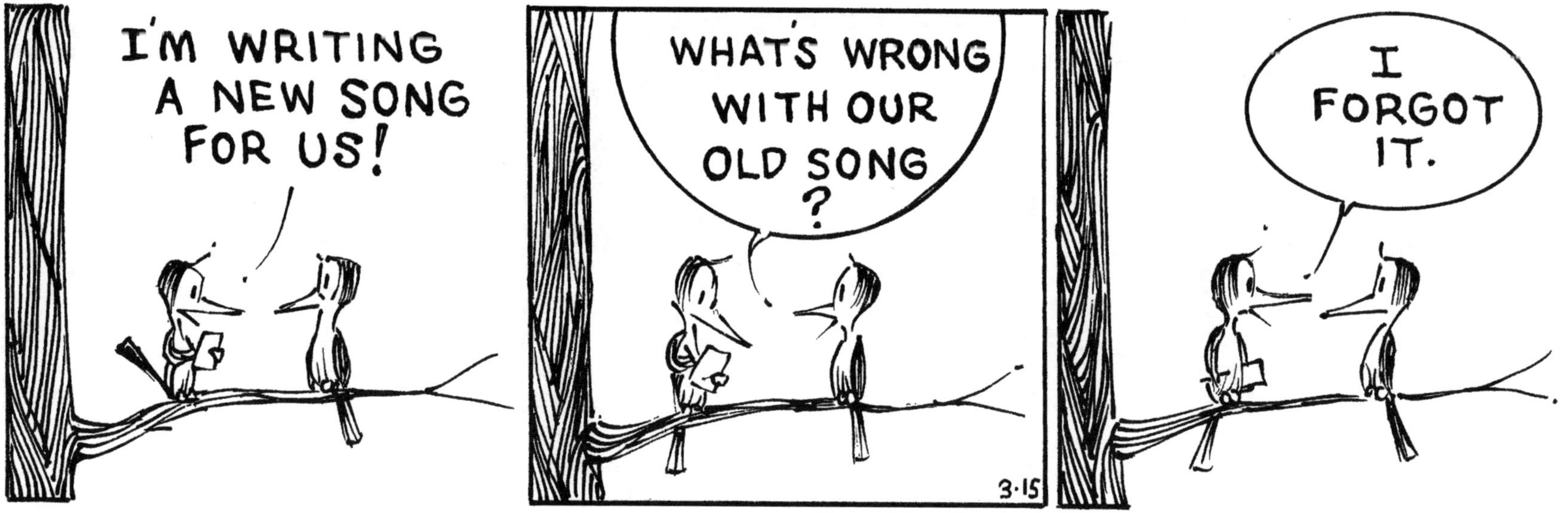
I'M WRITING A NEW SONG FOR US!
WHAT'S WRONG WITH OUR OLD SONG?
I FORGOT IT.
3·15

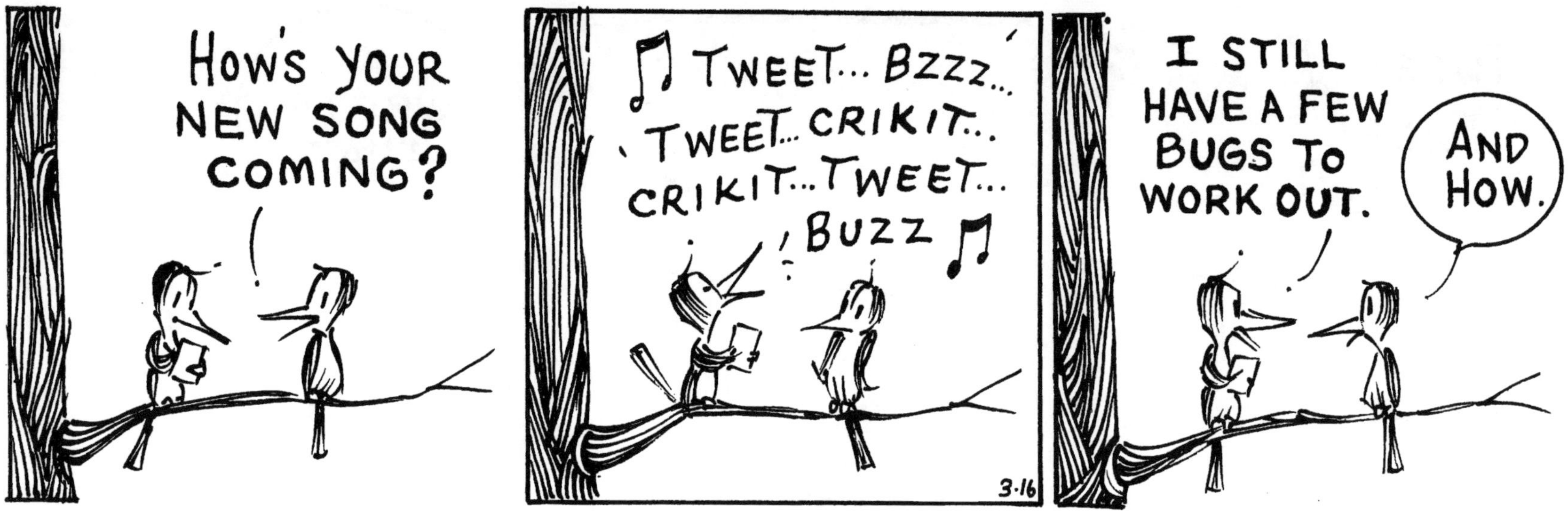
HOW'S YOUR NEW SONG COMING?
TWEET... BZZZ... TWEET... CRIKIT... CRIKIT... TWEET... BUZZ
I STILL HAVE A FEW BUGS TO WORK OUT.
AND HOW.
3·16

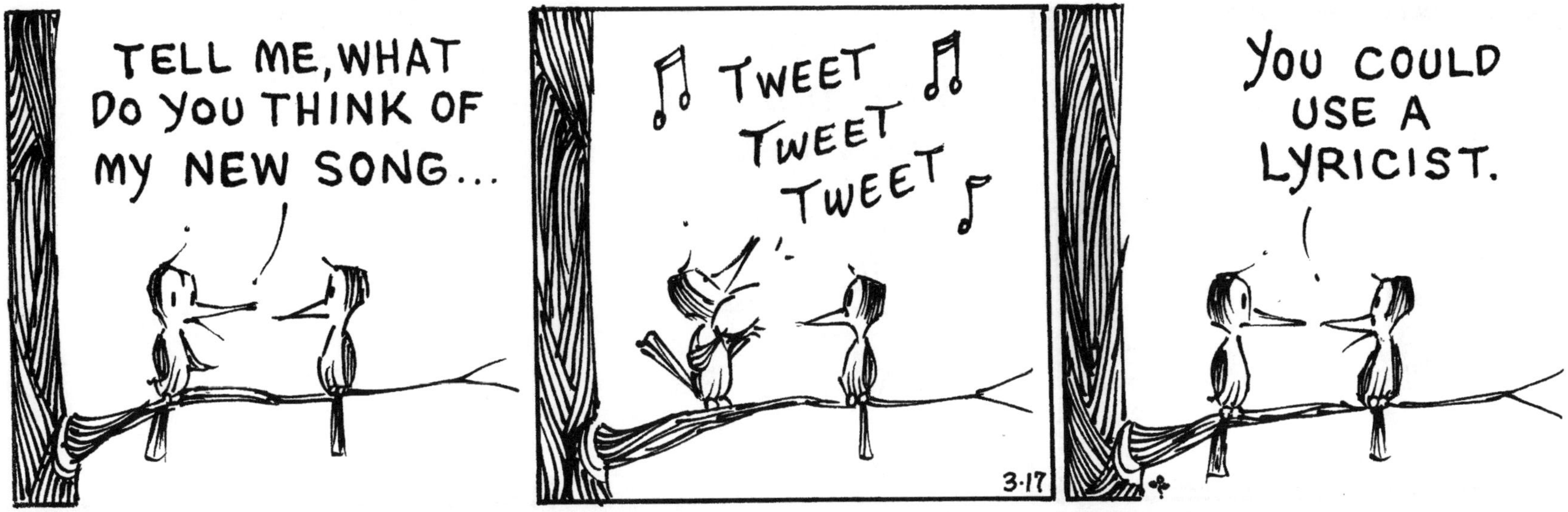
TELL ME, WHAT DO YOU THINK OF MY NEW SONG...
TWEET TWEET TWEET
3·17
YOU COULD USE A LYRICIST.

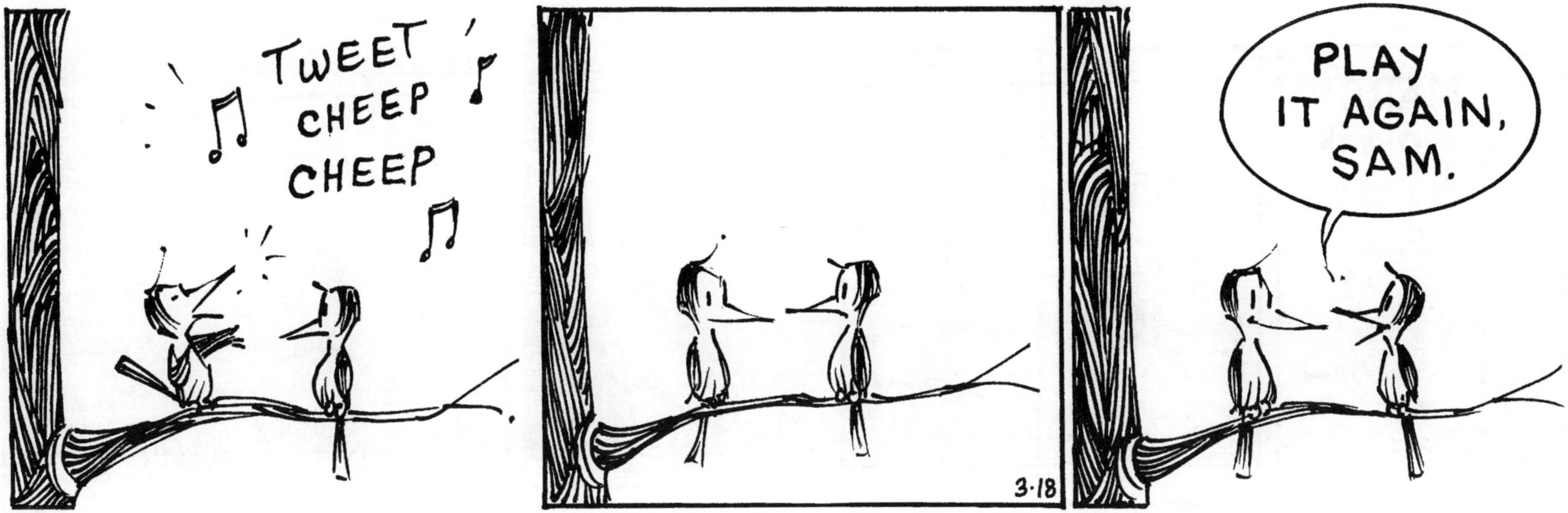
TWEET CHEEP CHEEP
3·18
PLAY IT AGAIN, SAM.

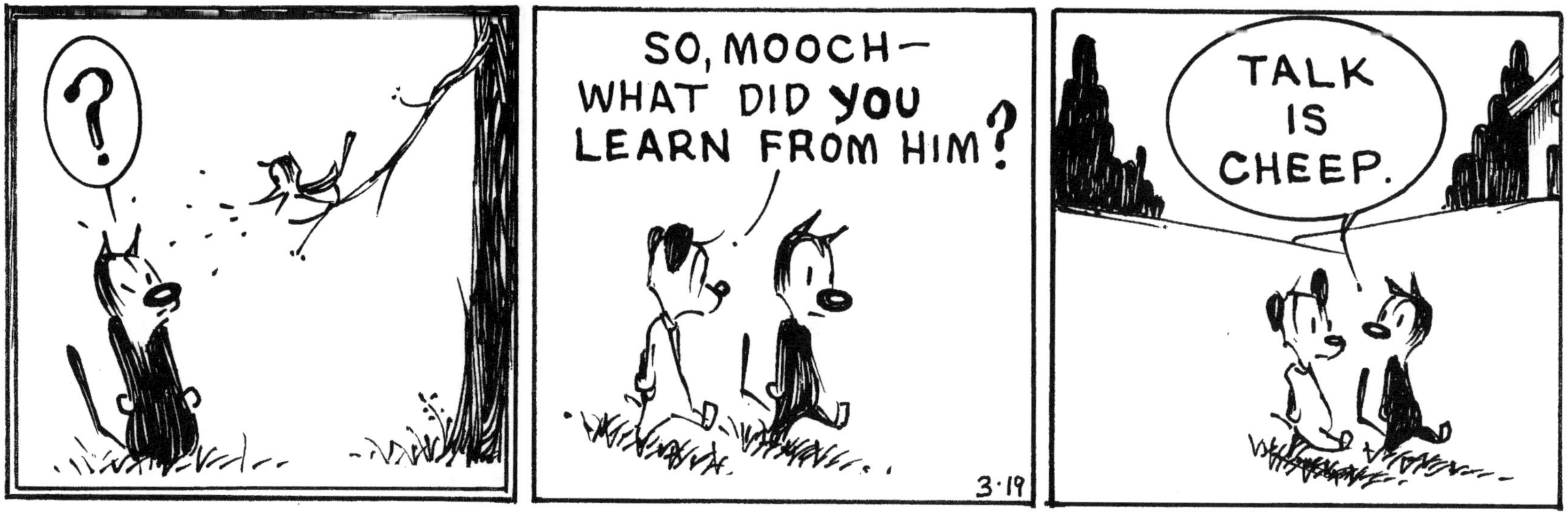
?
SO, MOOCH— WHAT DID YOU LEARN FROM HIM?
3·19
TALK IS CHEEP.

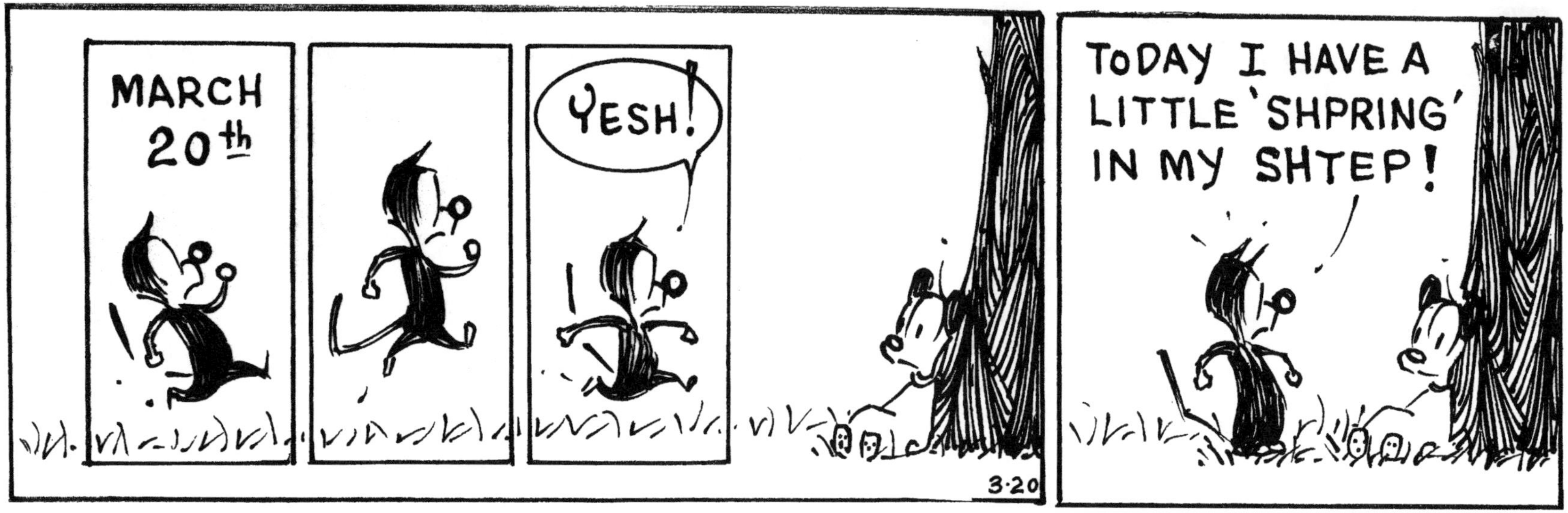
MARCH 20th
YESH!
3·20
TODAY I HAVE A LITTLE 'SHPRING' IN MY SHTEP!

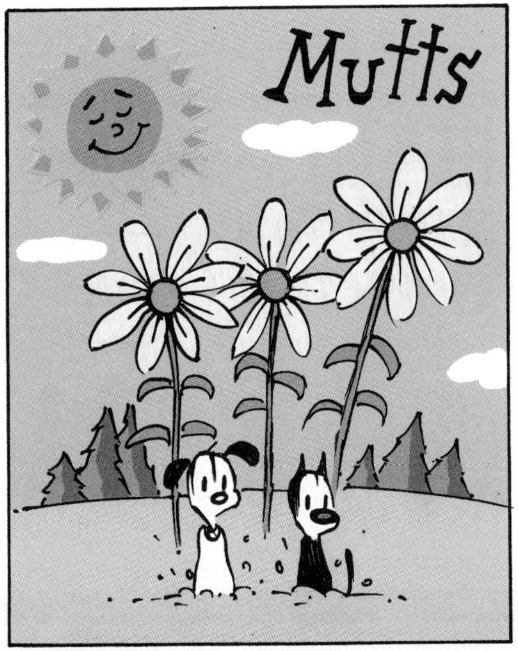
Mutts

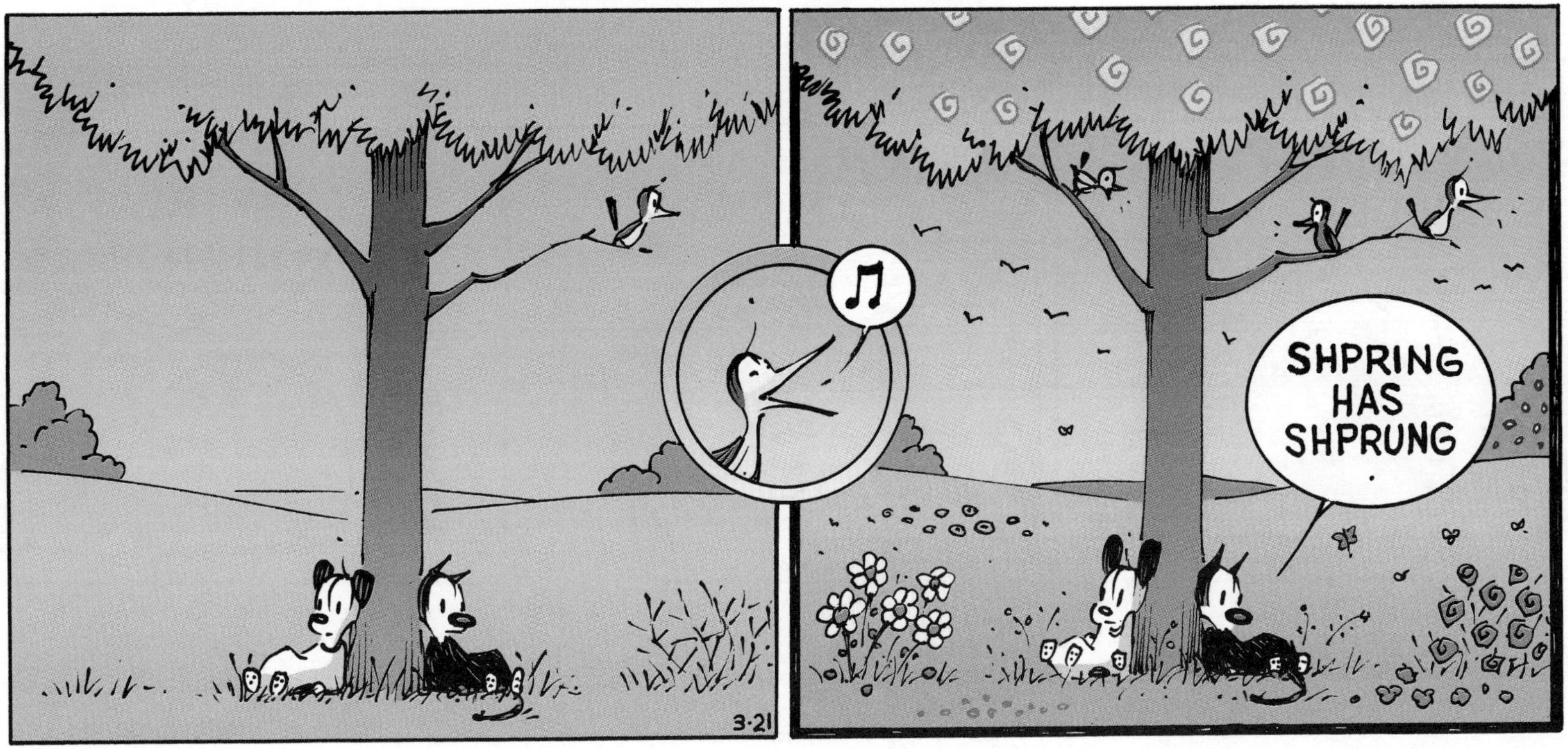
♫
3·21
SHPRING HAS SHPRUNG

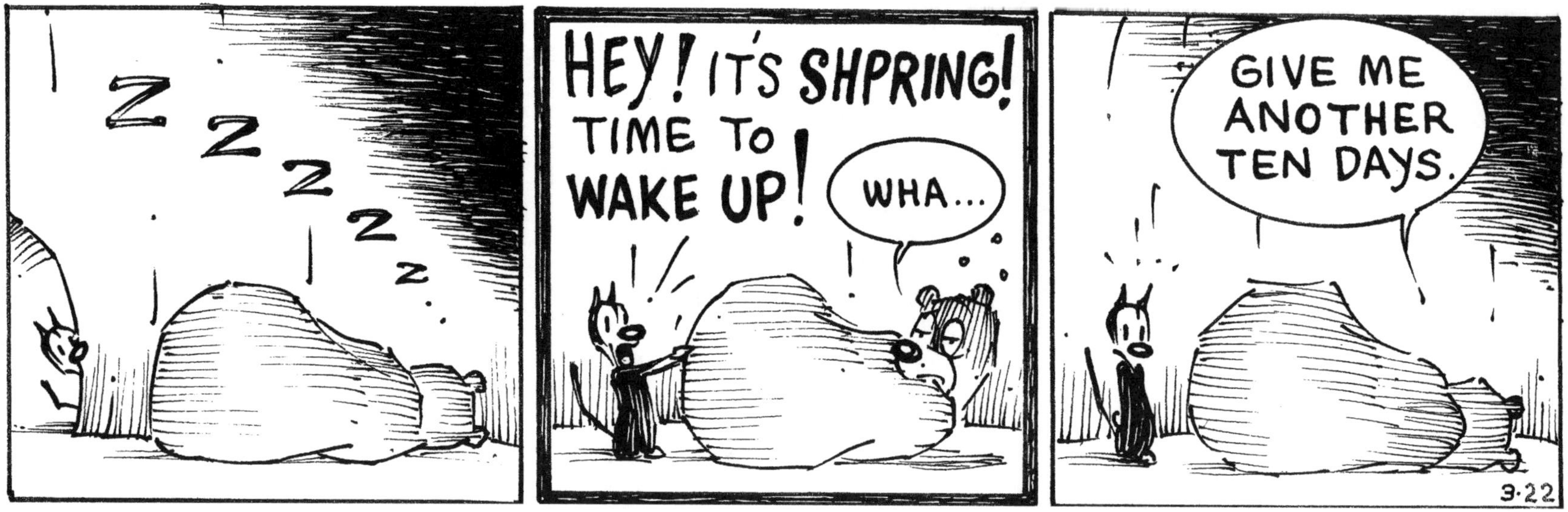
Z Z Z Z Z
HEY! IT'S SHPRING! TIME TO WAKE UP!
WHA...
GIVE ME ANOTHER TEN DAYS.
3·22

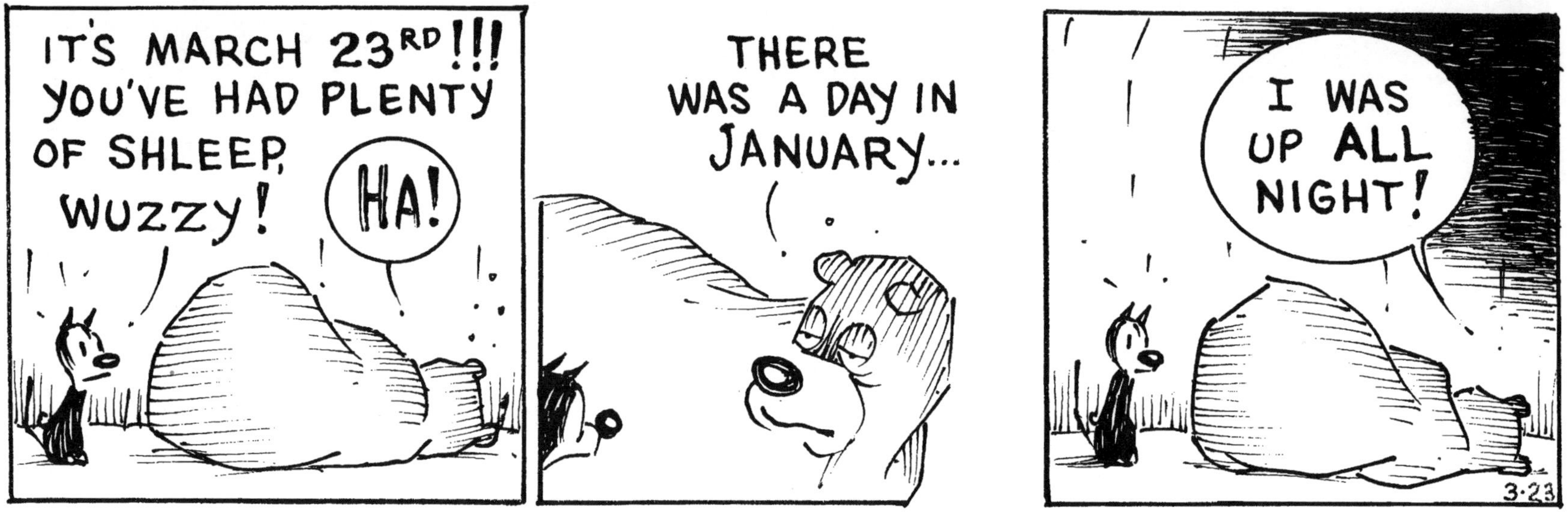
IT'S MARCH 23RD!!! YOU'VE HAD PLENTY OF SHLEEP, WUZZY!
HA!
THERE WAS A DAY IN JANUARY...
I WAS UP ALL NIGHT!
3·23

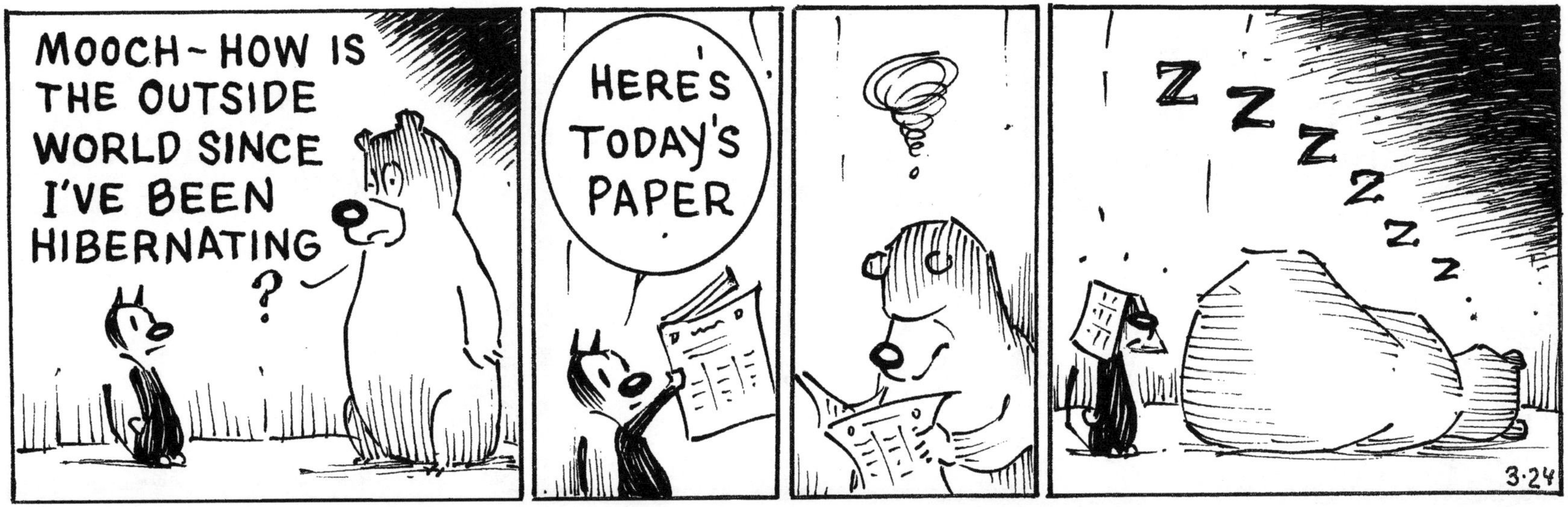
MOOCH ~ HOW IS THE OUTSIDE WORLD SINCE I'VE BEEN HIBERNATING?
HERE'S TODAY'S PAPER
ZZZZZZ
3·24

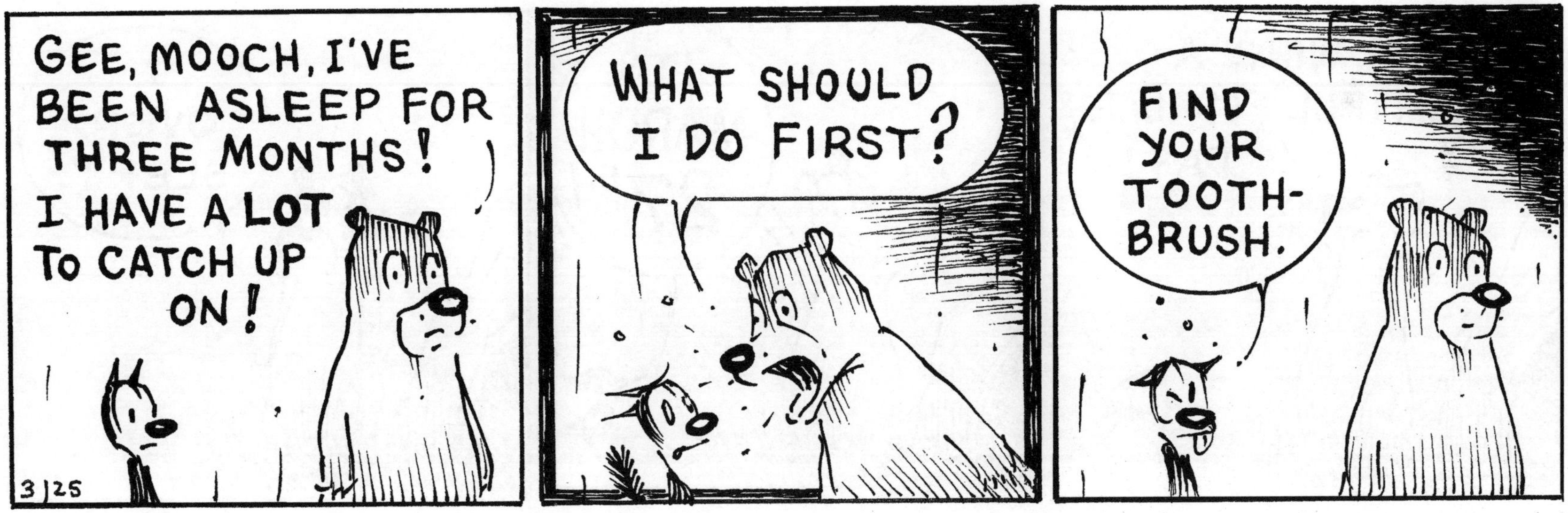
GEE, MOOCH, I'VE BEEN ASLEEP FOR THREE MONTHS! I HAVE A **LOT** TO CATCH UP ON!
3/25
WHAT SHOULD I DO FIRST?
FIND YOUR TOOTH-BRUSH.

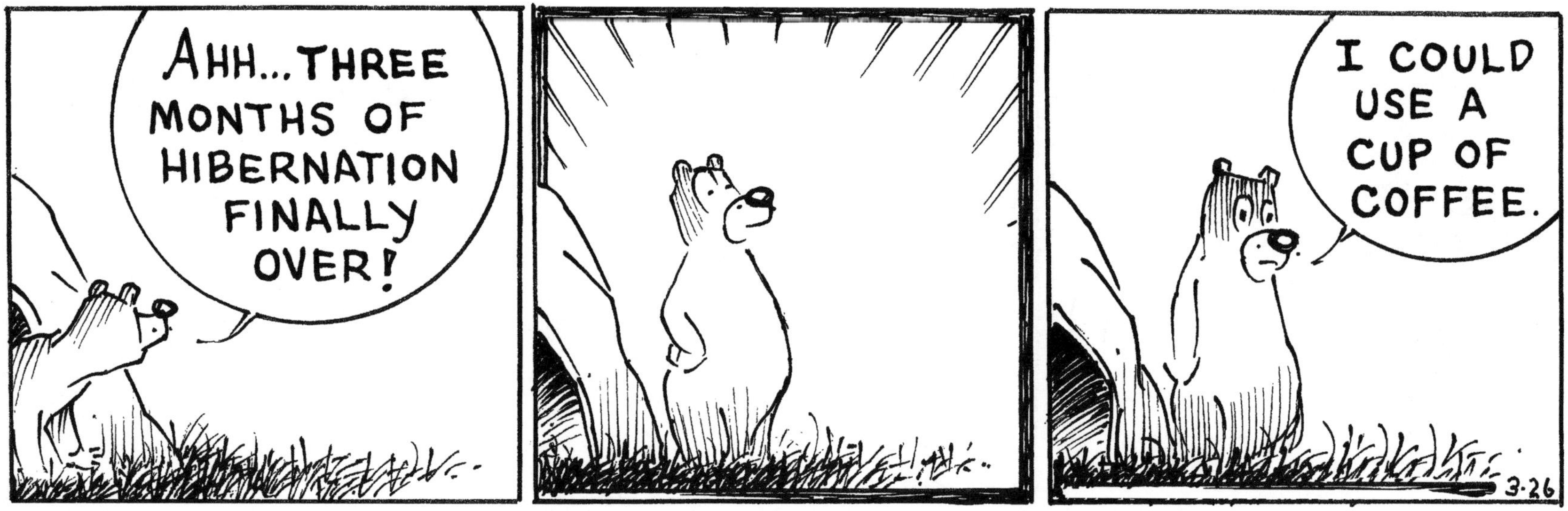
AHH... THREE MONTHS OF HIBERNATION FINALLY OVER!
I COULD USE A CUP OF COFFEE.
3·26

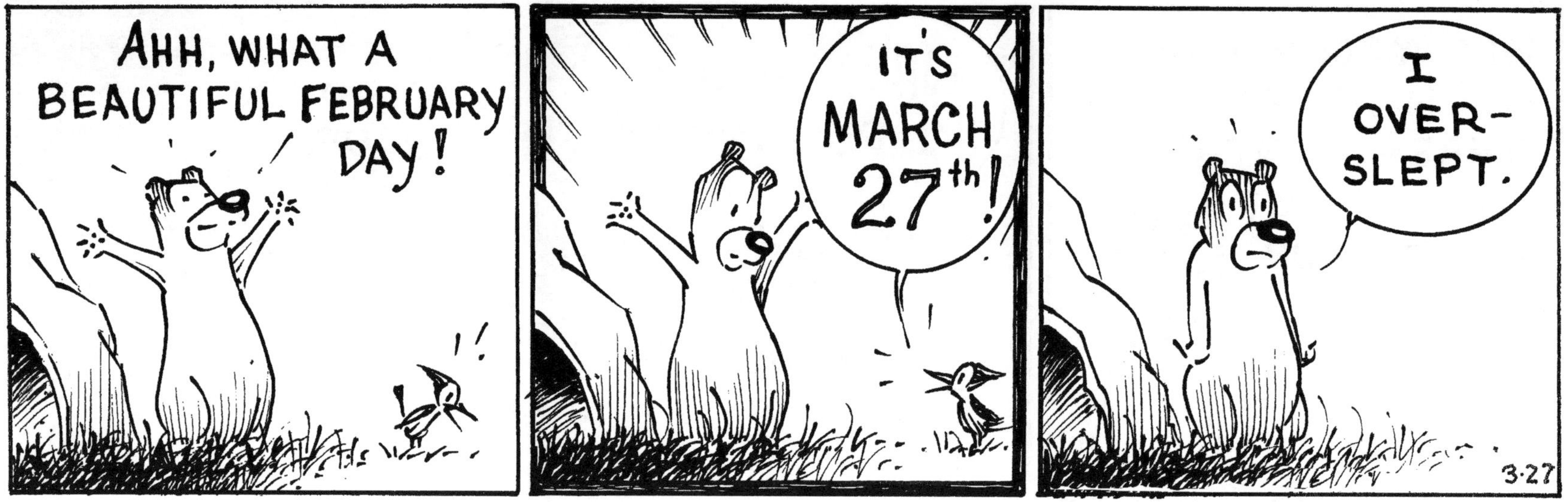
AHH, WHAT A BEAUTIFUL FEBRUARY DAY!
IT'S MARCH 27th!
I OVER-SLEPT.
3·27

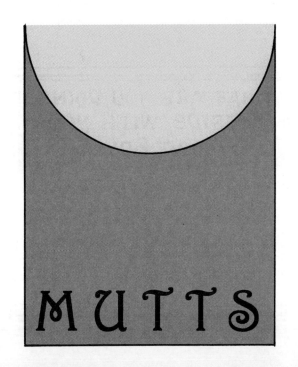

MUTTS

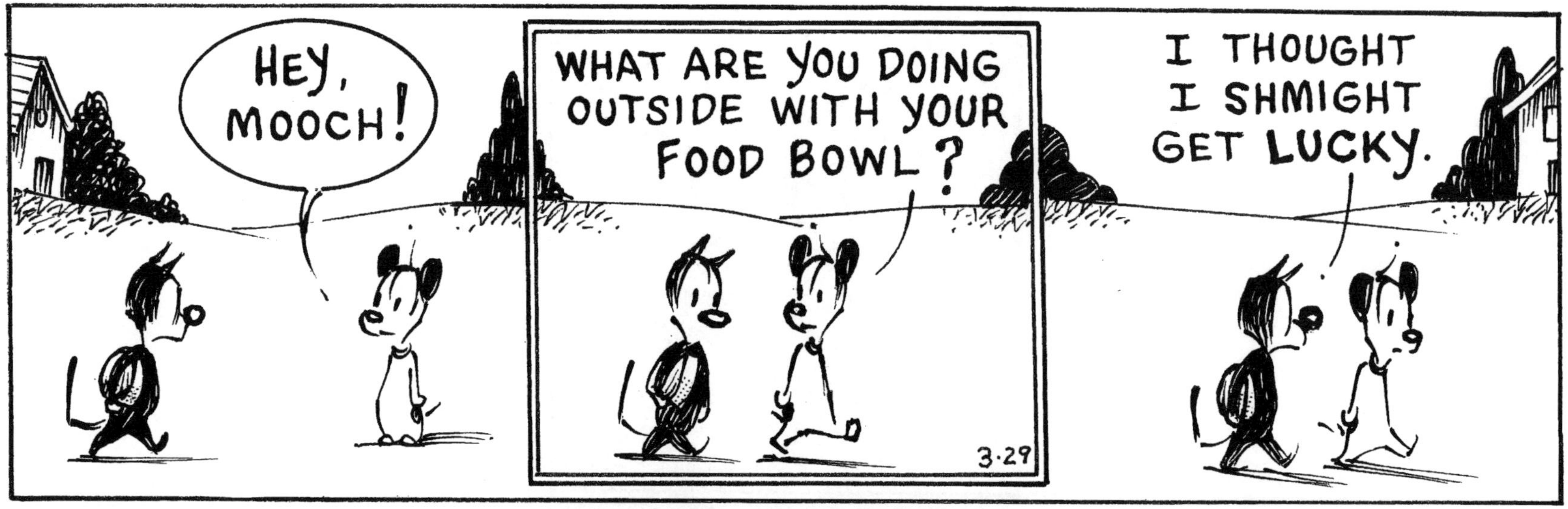
HEY, MOOCH!
WHAT ARE YOU DOING OUTSIDE WITH YOUR FOOD BOWL?
3·29
I THOUGHT I SHMIGHT GET LUCKY.

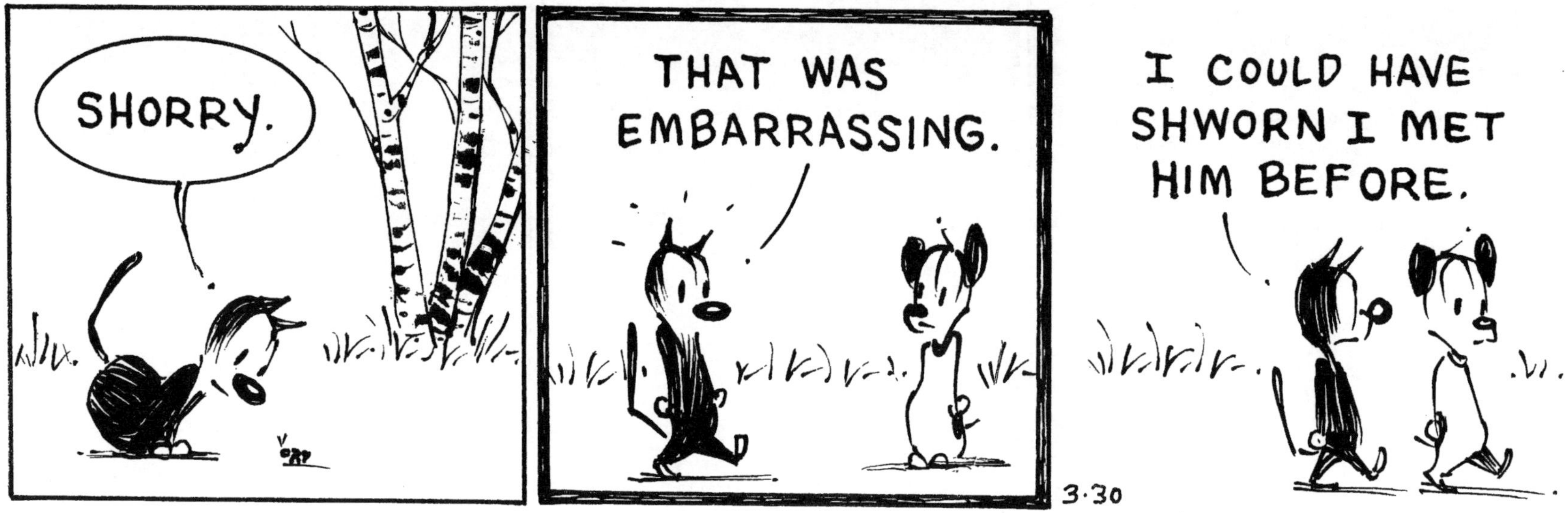
SHORRY.
THAT WAS EMBARRASSING.
3·30
I COULD HAVE SHWORN I MET HIM BEFORE.

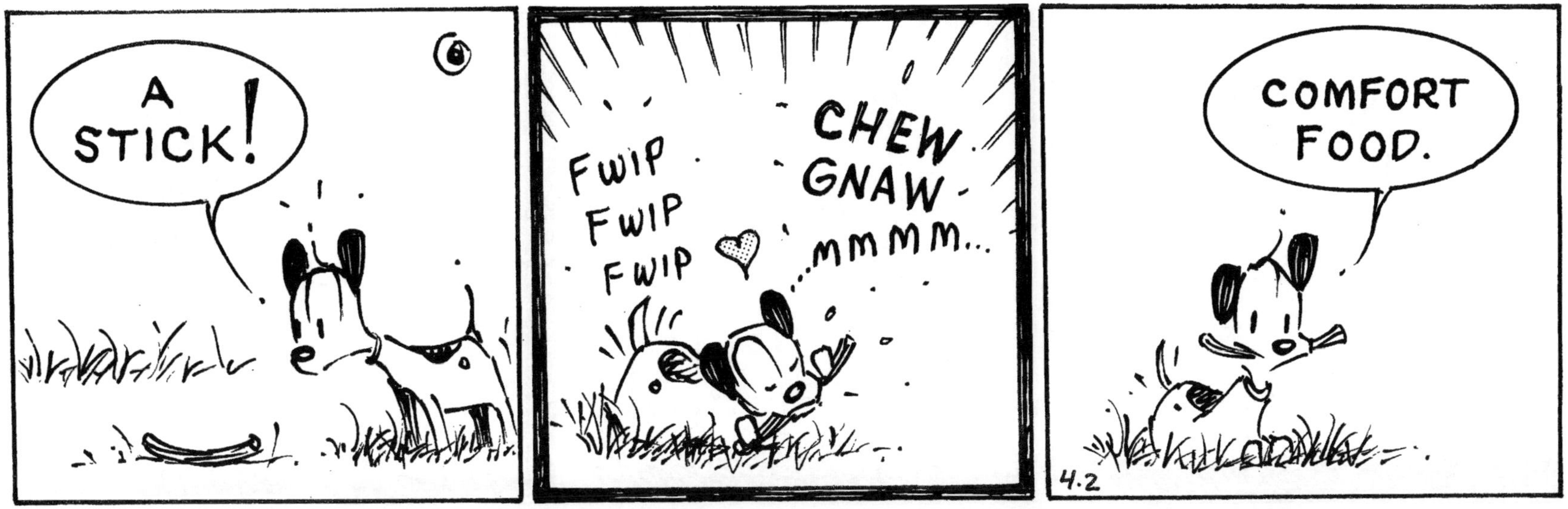
A STICK!
FWIP FWIP FWIP
CHEW GNAW MMMM...
COMFORT FOOD.
4.2

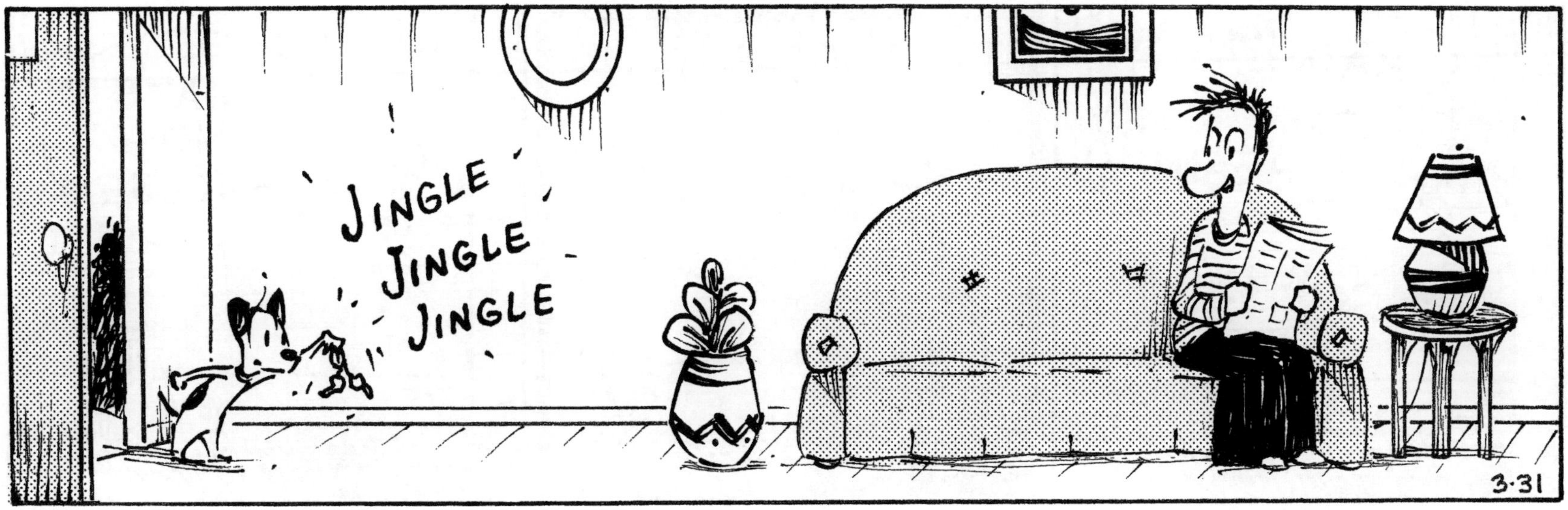
JINGLE JINGLE JINGLE
3.31

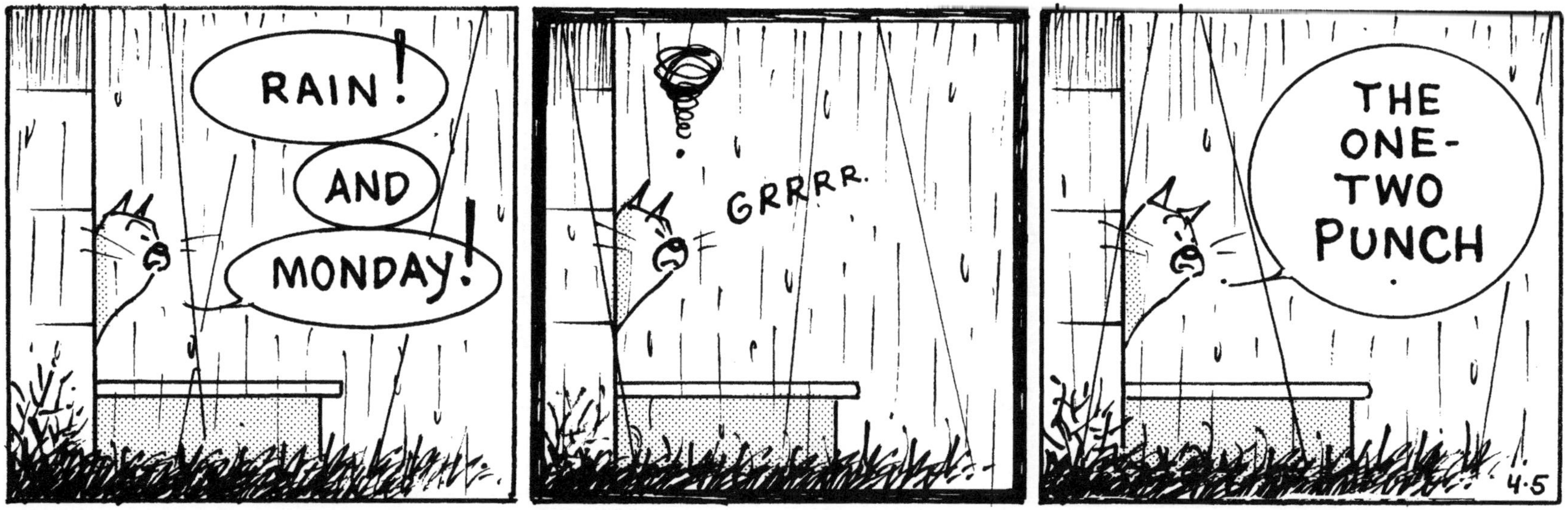
RAIN!
AND
MONDAY!
GRRRR.
THE ONE-TWO PUNCH.
4·5

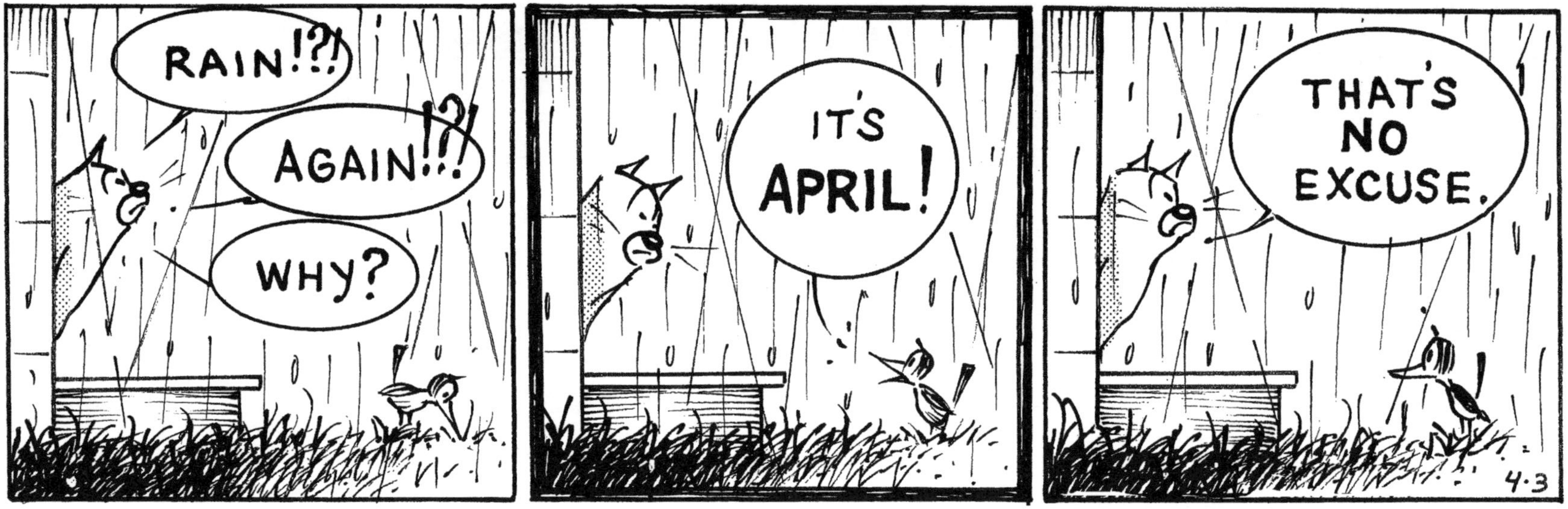
RAIN!?!
AGAIN!?!
WHY?
IT'S APRIL!
THAT'S NO EXCUSE.
4·3

MUTTS
WOW
WHAT A SPECIAL LITTLE UMBRELLA !!!
OH,
YES
AND IT SMELLS LIKE PINA COLADA!
3·28

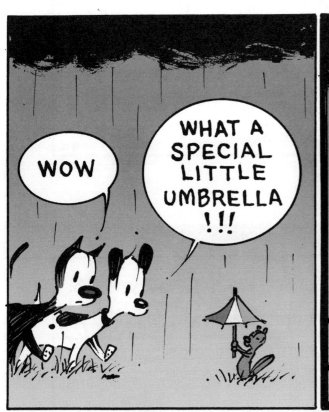

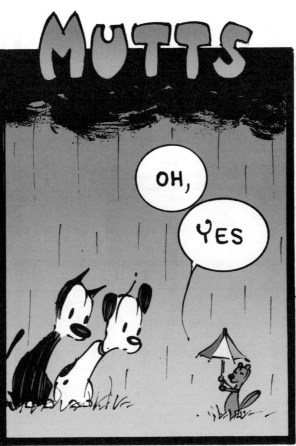

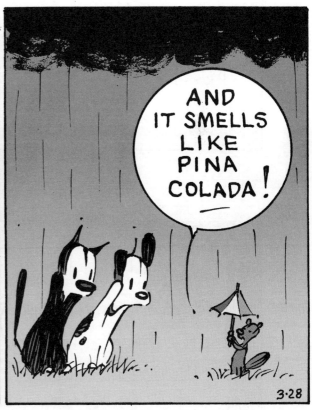

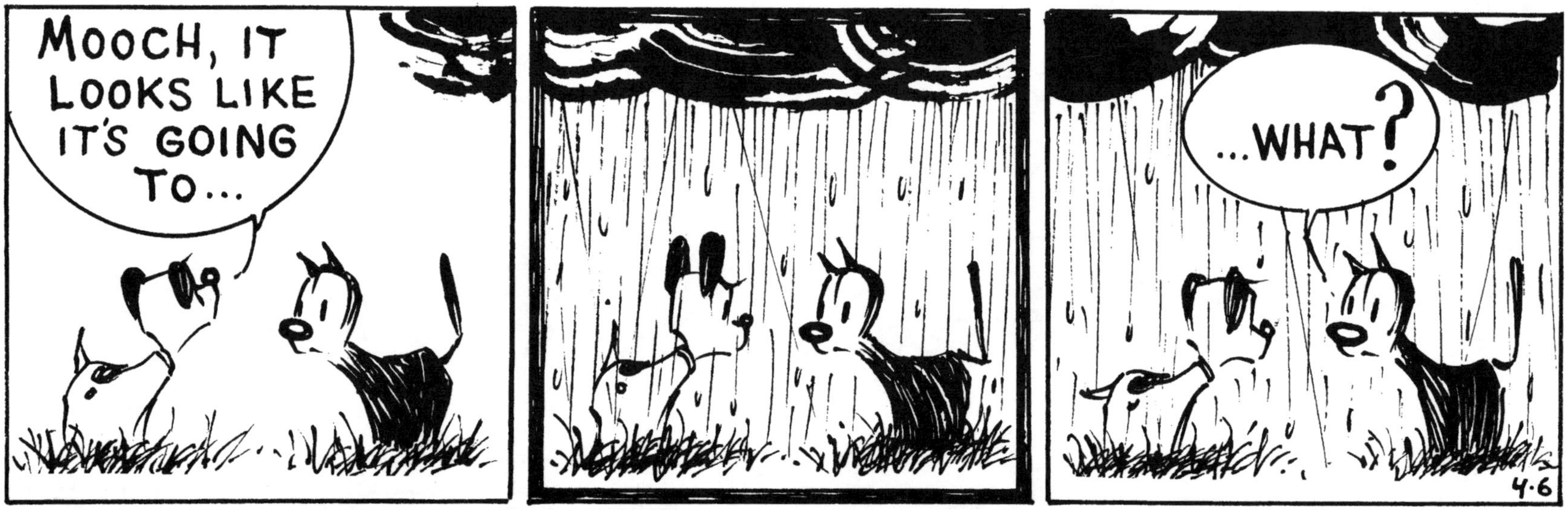
MOOCH, IT LOOKS LIKE IT'S GOING TO...
...WHAT?
4·6

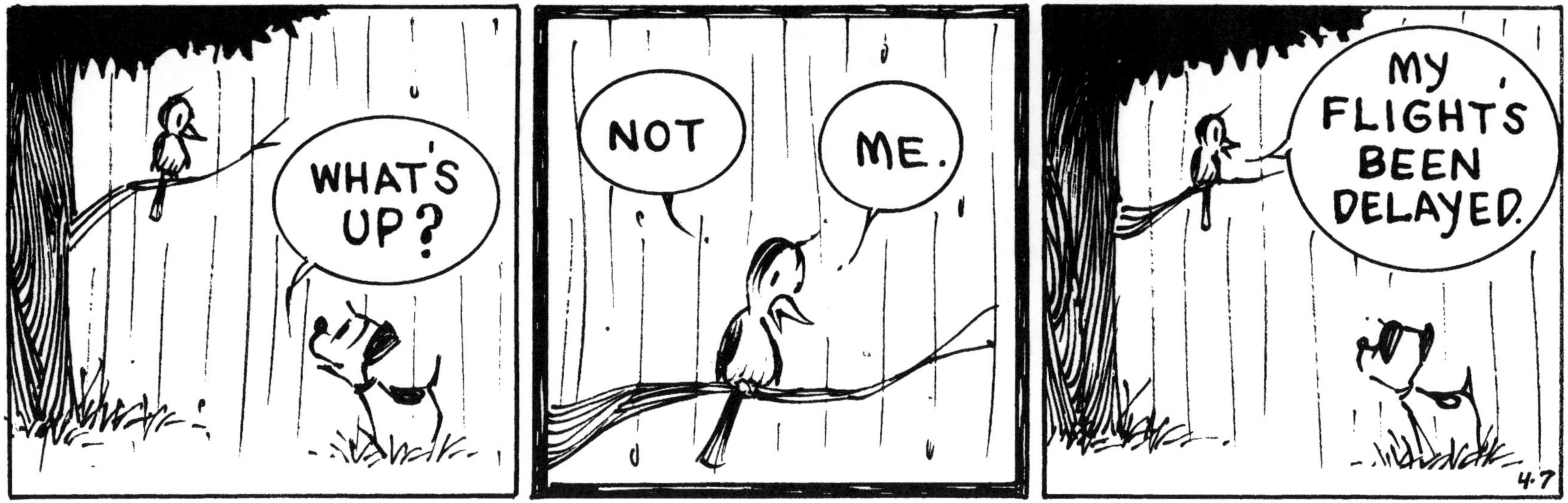
WHAT'S UP?
NOT
ME.
MY FLIGHT'S BEEN DELAYED.
4·7

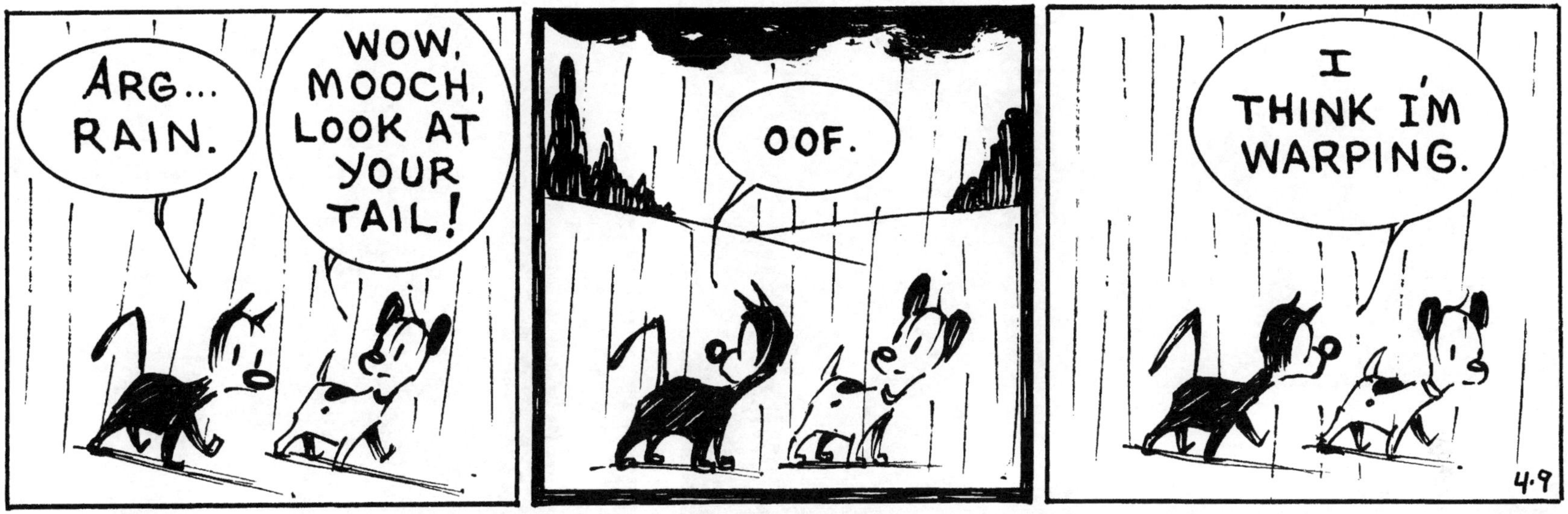
ARG... RAIN.
WOW, MOOCH, LOOK AT YOUR TAIL!
OOF.
I THINK I'M WARPING.
4·9

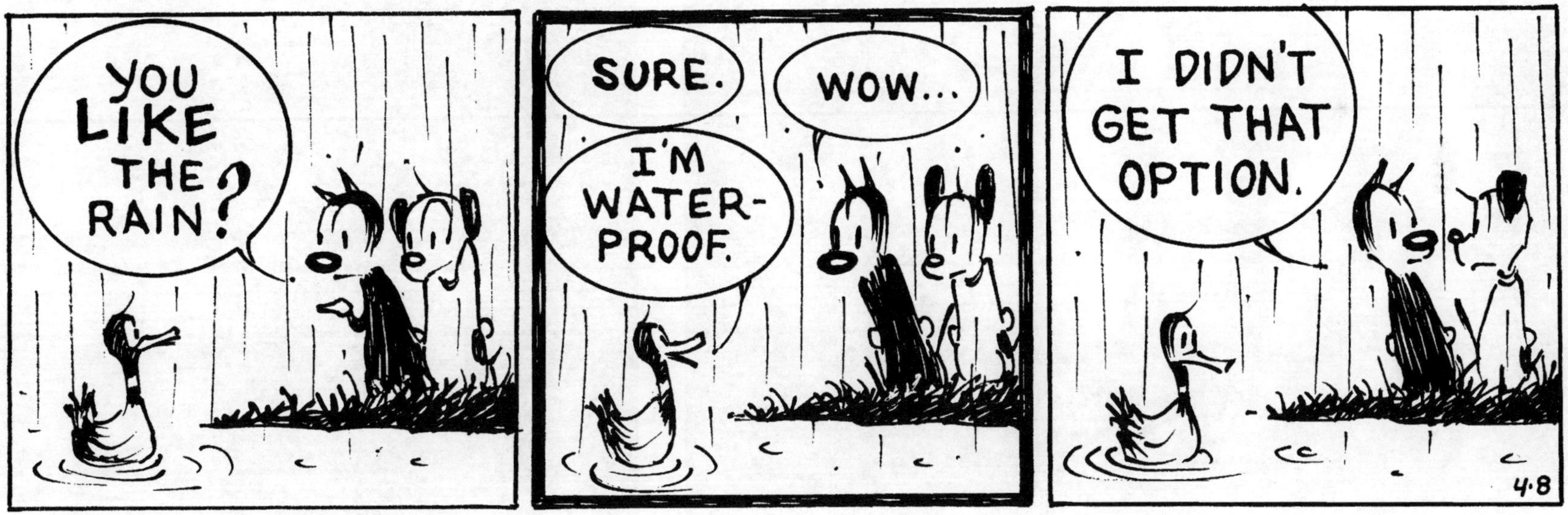
YOU LIKE THE RAIN?
SURE.
I'M WATER-PROOF.
WOW...
I DIDN'T GET THAT OPTION.
4·8

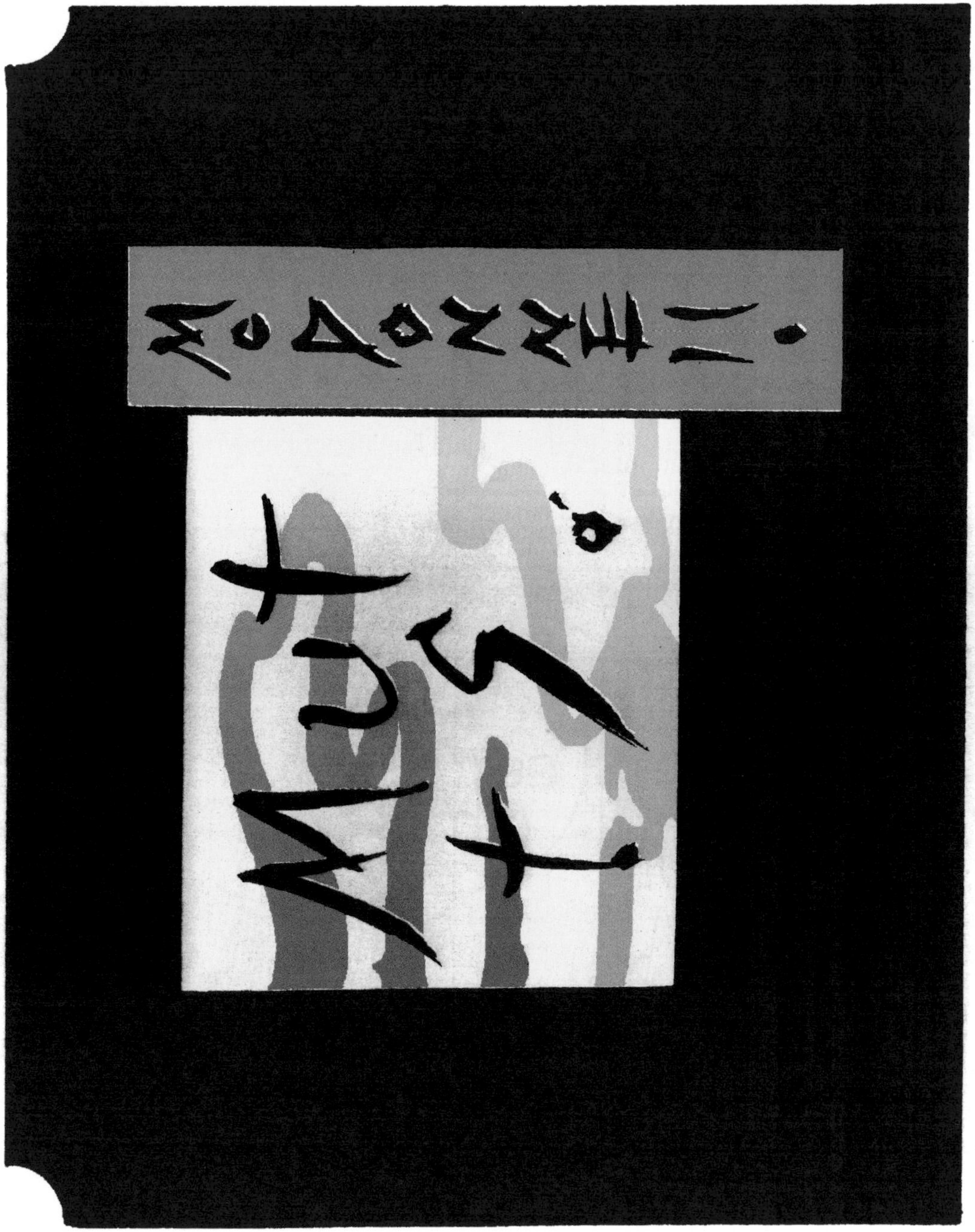

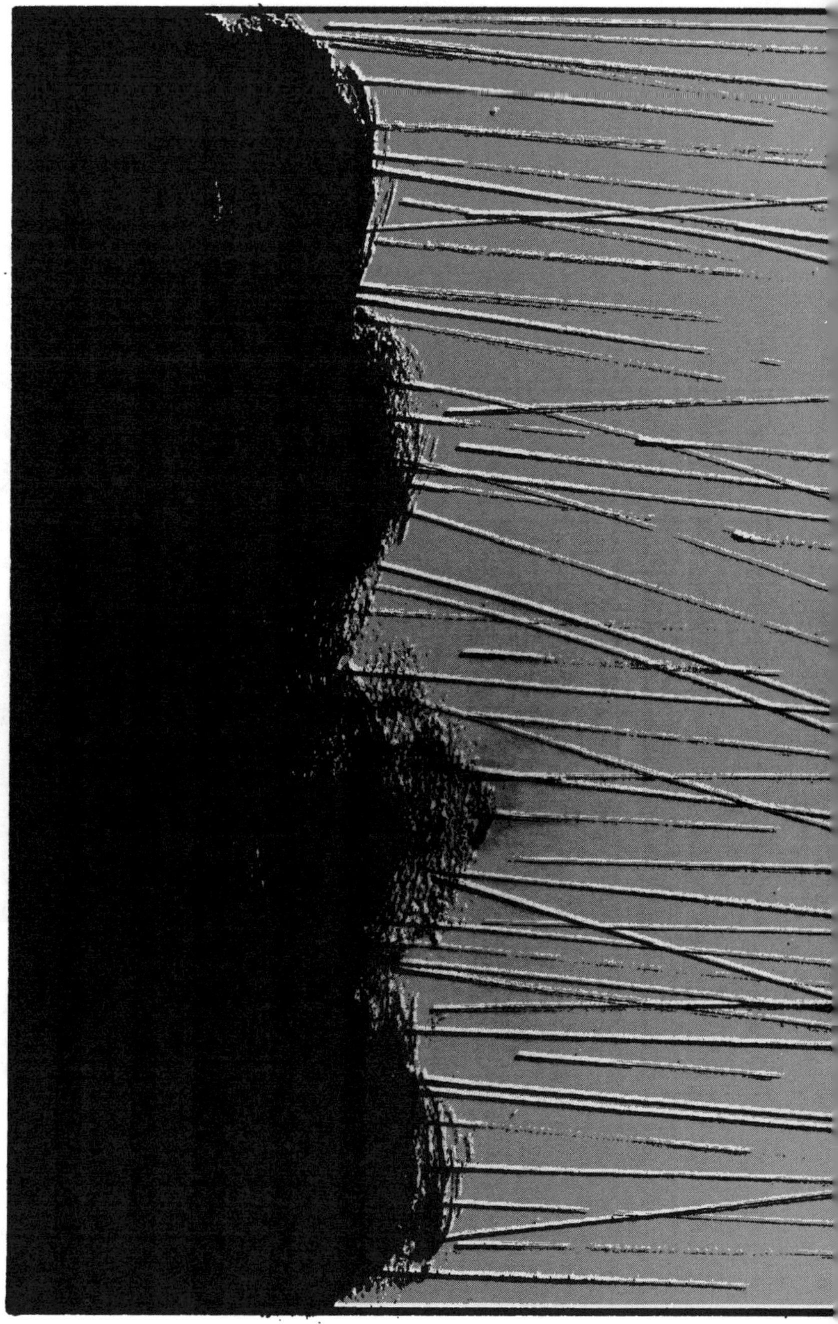

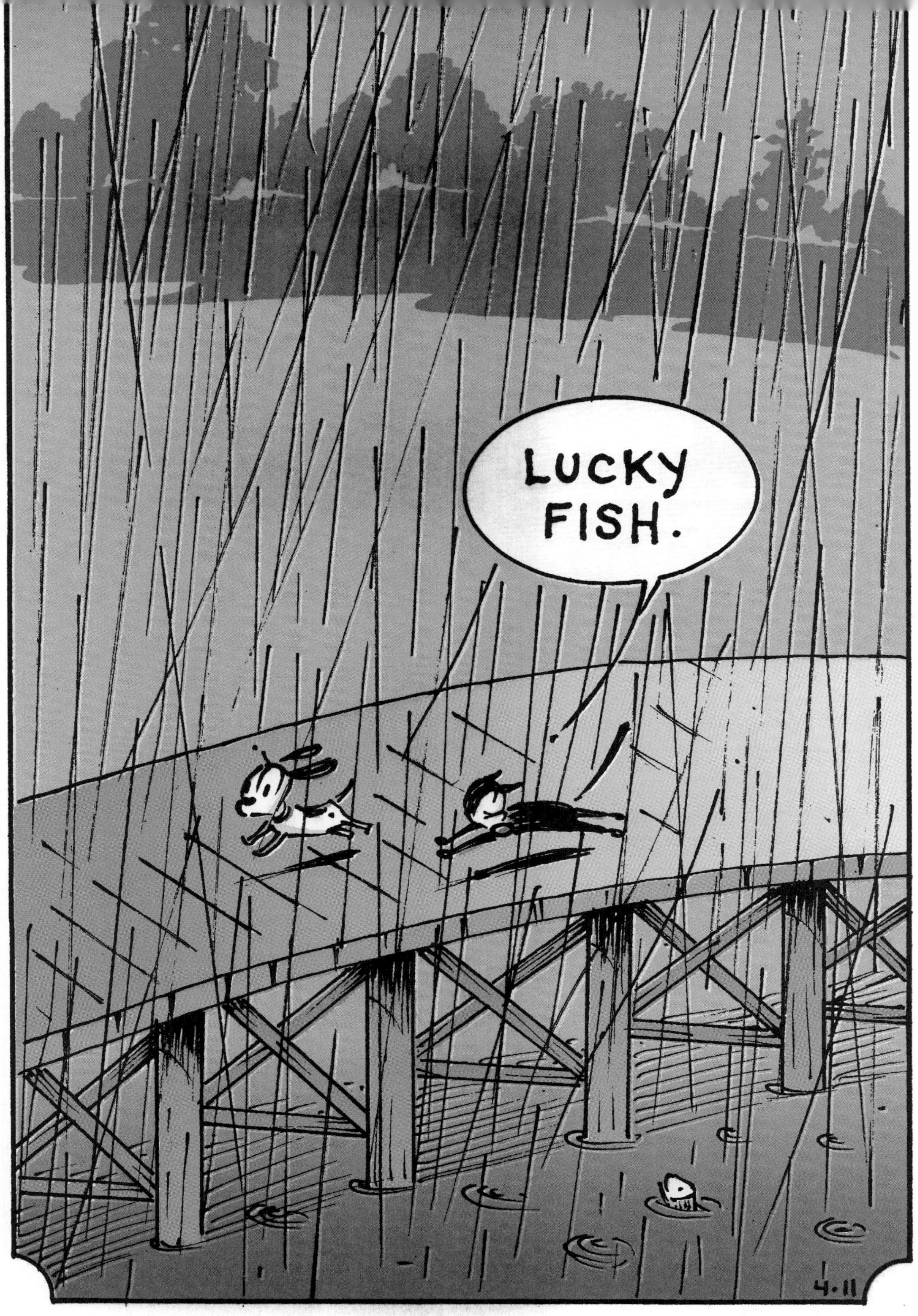

LUCKY FISH.
4.11

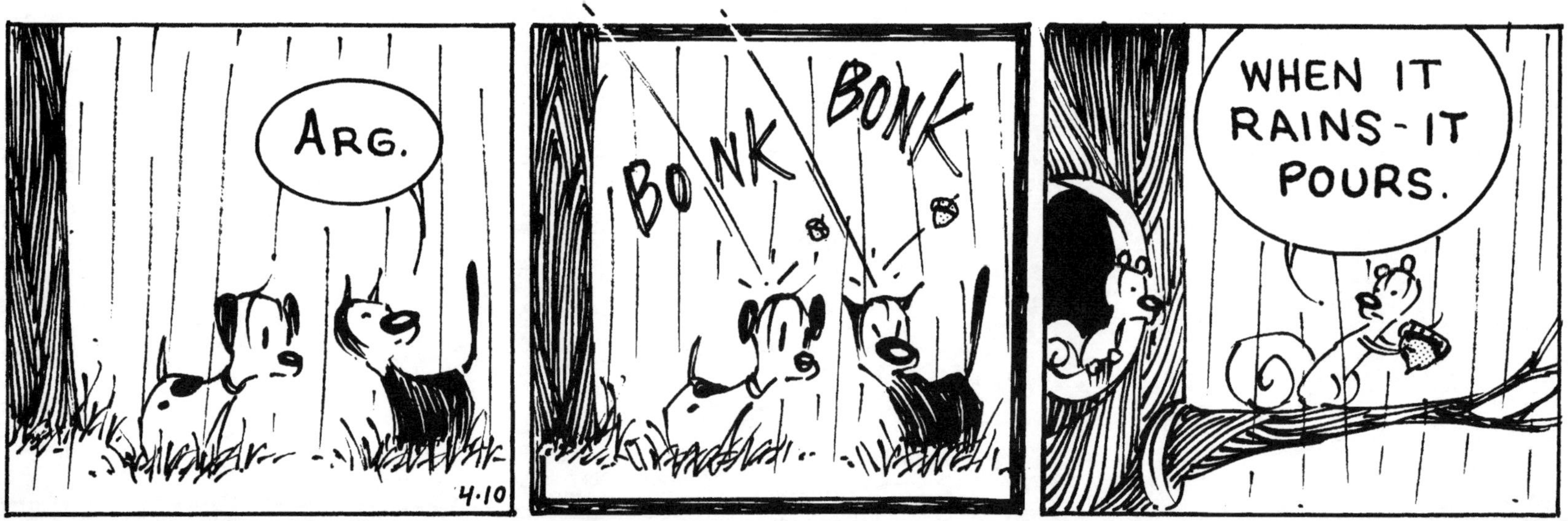
ARG.
BONK
BONK
WHEN IT RAINS - IT POURS.
4·10

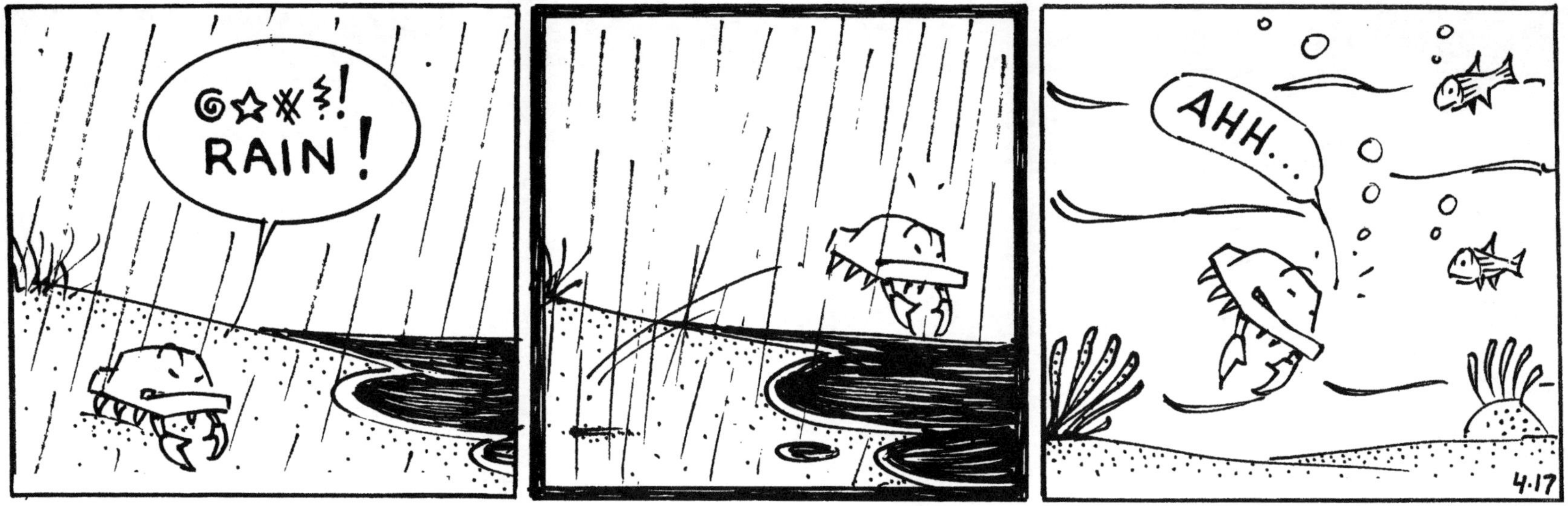
RAIN!
AHH...
4·17

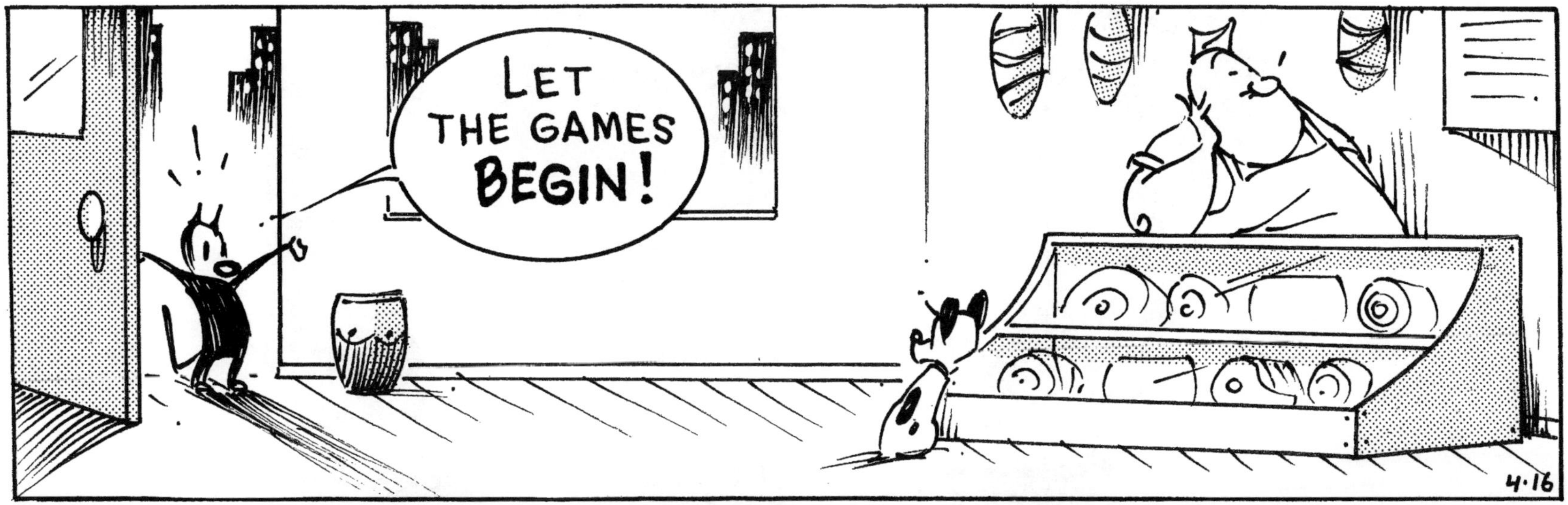
LET THE GAMES BEGIN!
4·16

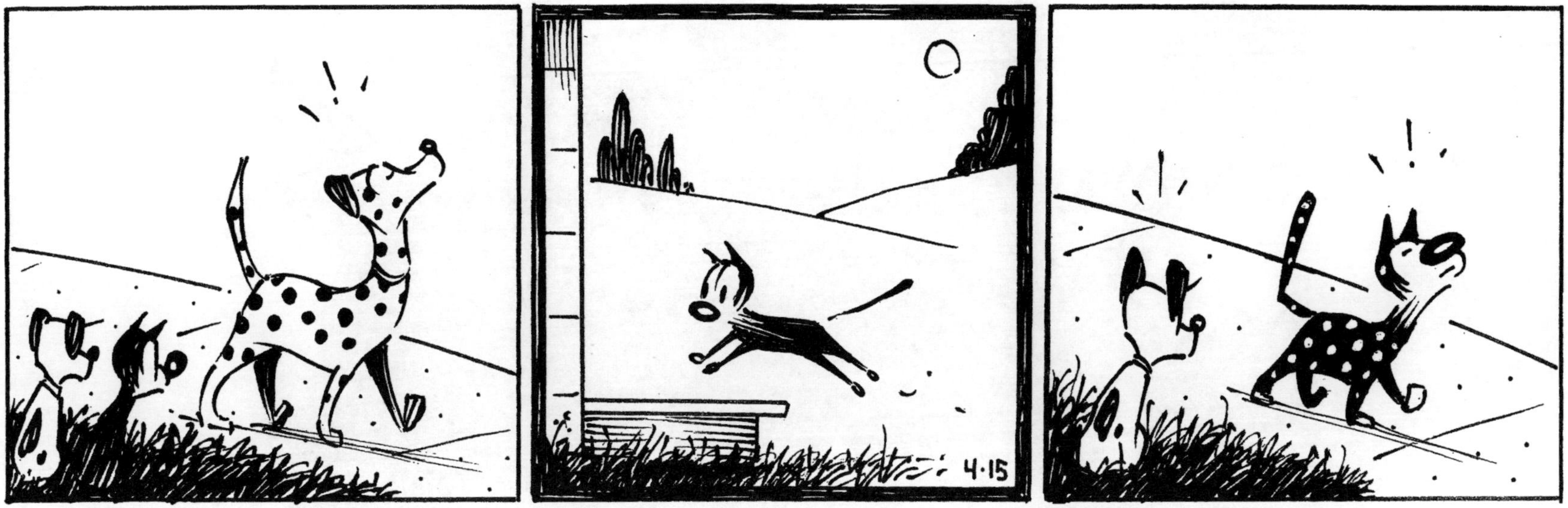
4·15

MUTTS

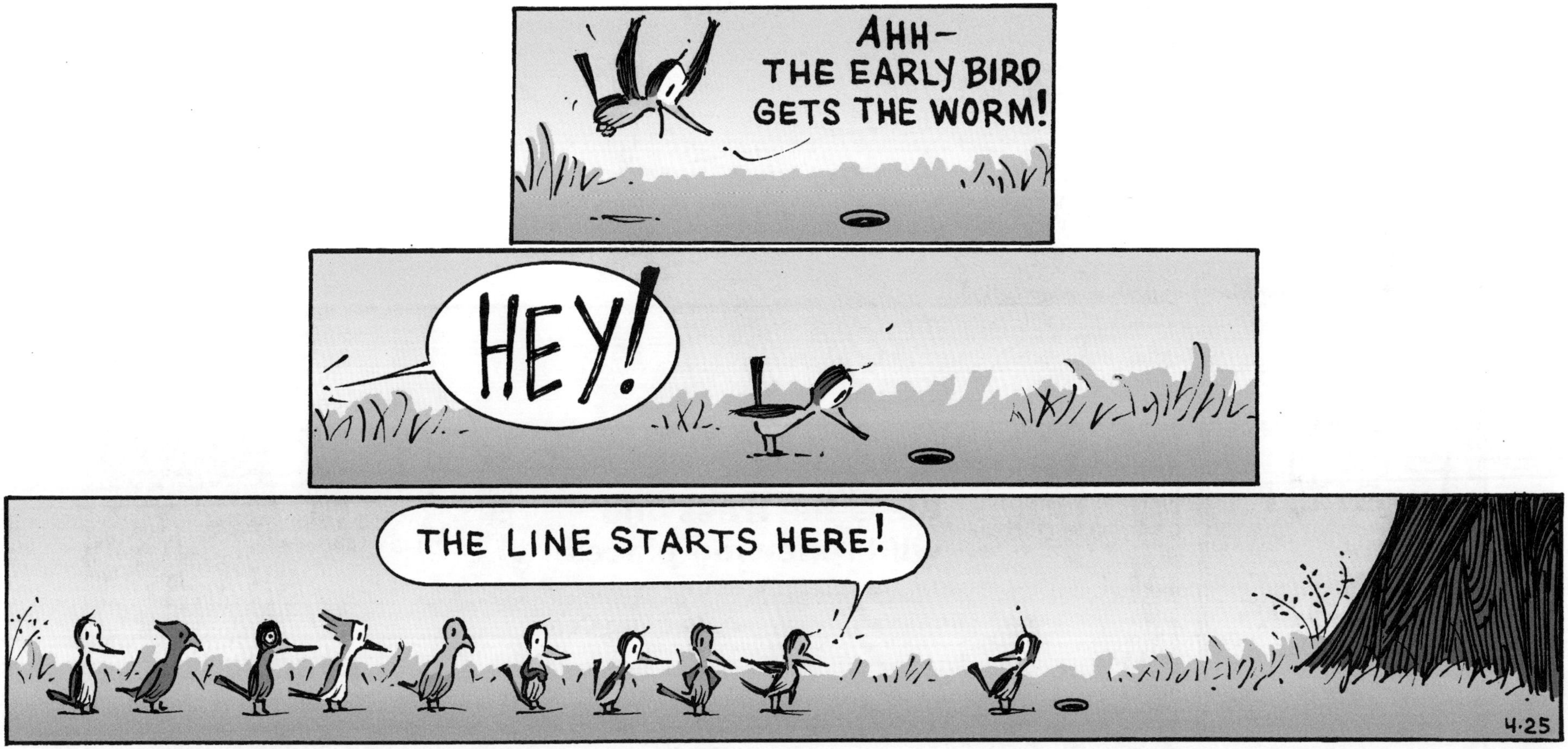
AHH- THE EARLY BIRD GETS THE WORM!
HEY!
THE LINE STARTS HERE!
4·25

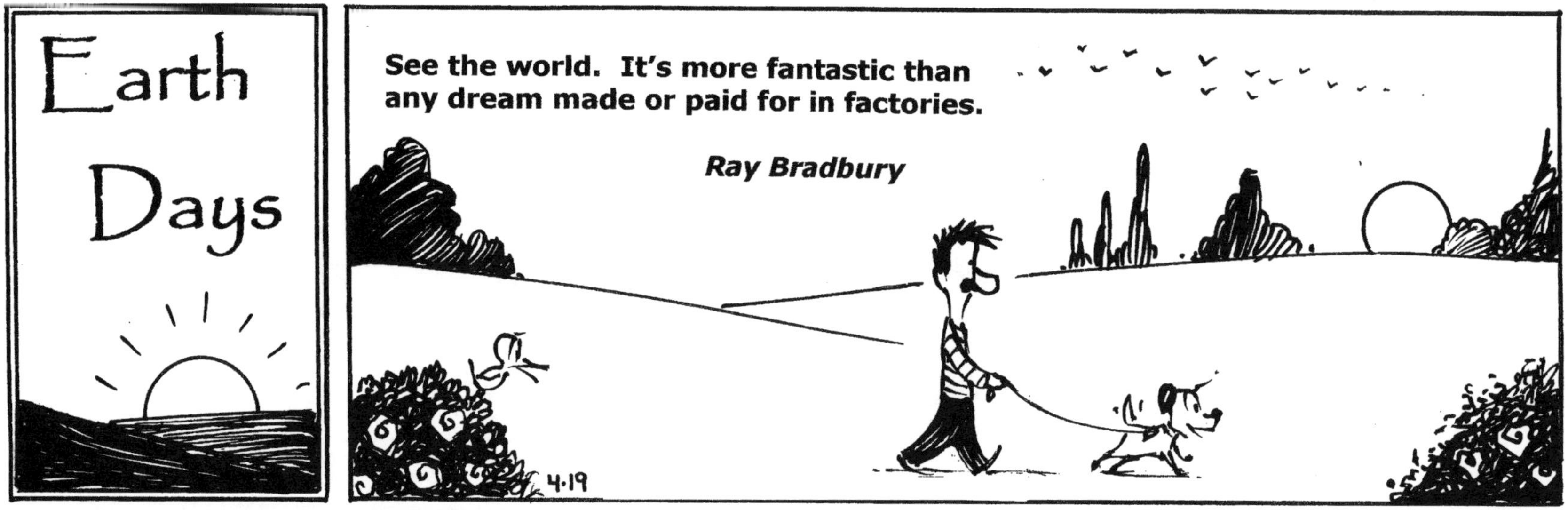
Earth Days
See the world. It's more fantastic than any dream made or paid for in factories.
Ray Bradbury
4·19

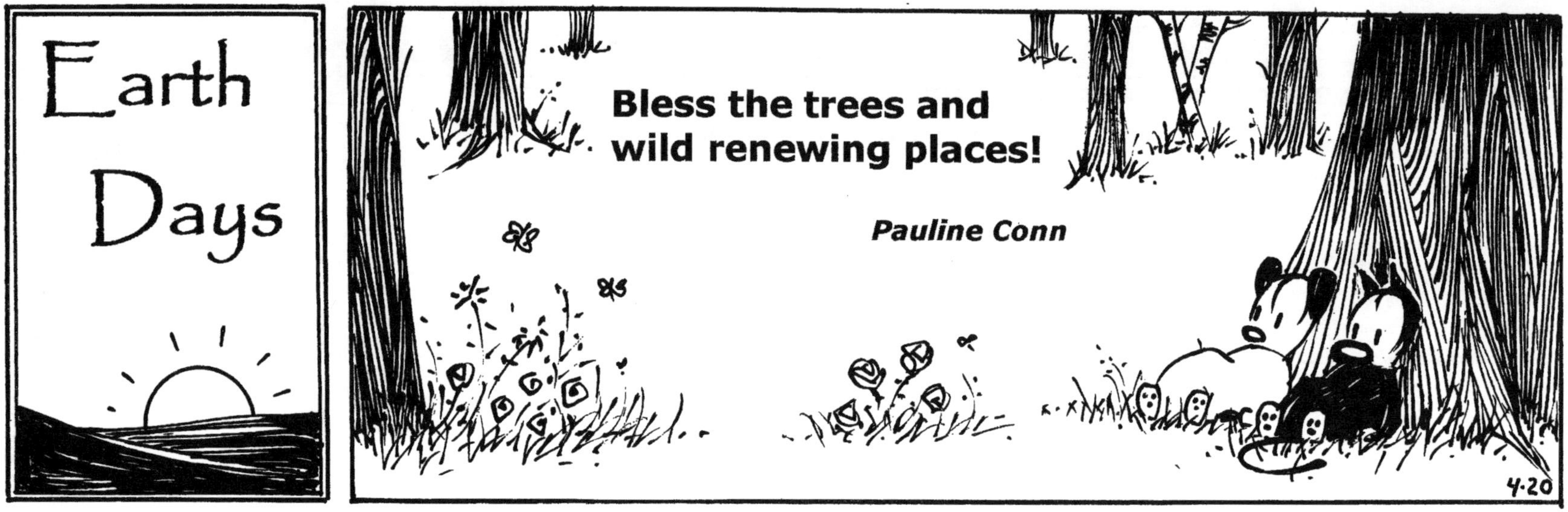
Earth Days
Bless the trees and wild renewing places!
Pauline Conn
4·20

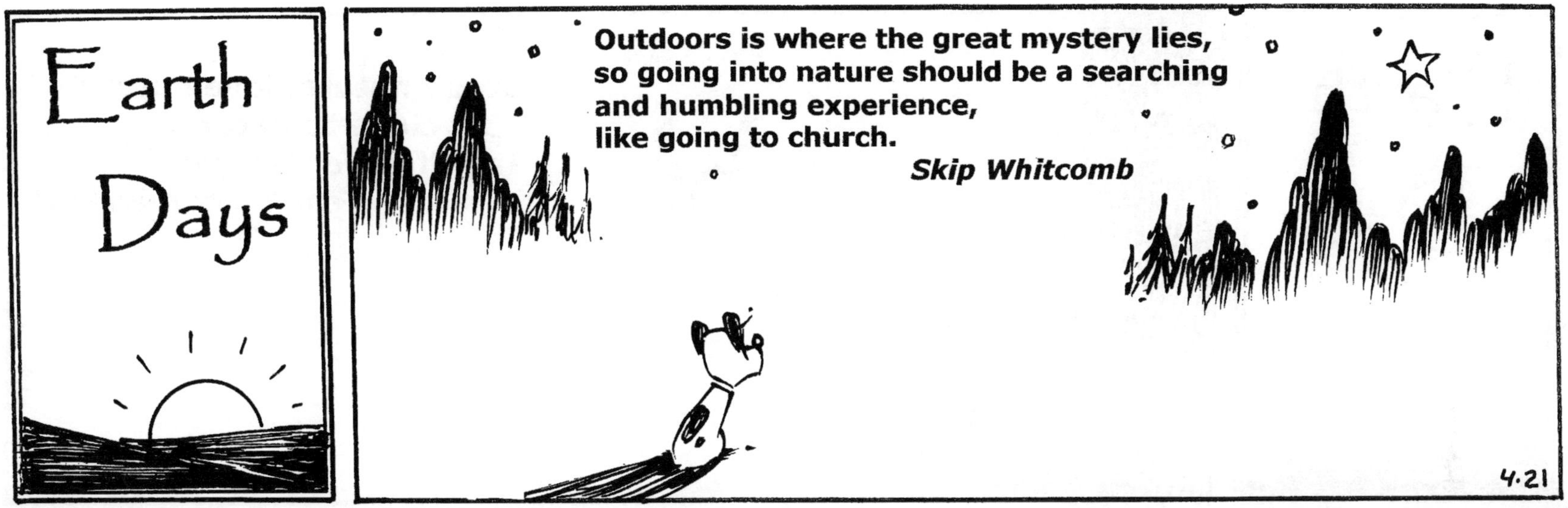
Earth Days
Outdoors is where the great mystery lies,
so going into nature should be a searching
and humbling experience,
like going to church.
Skip Whitcomb
4.21

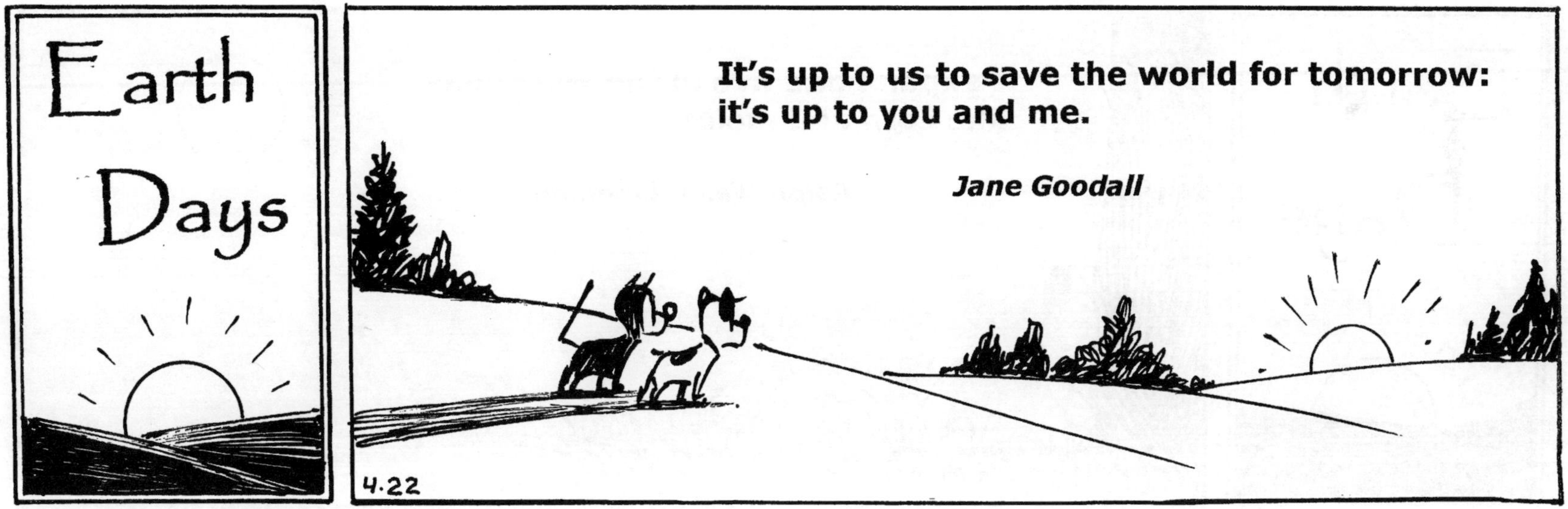
Earth Days
It's up to us to save the world for tomorrow:
it's up to you and me.
Jane Goodall
4.22

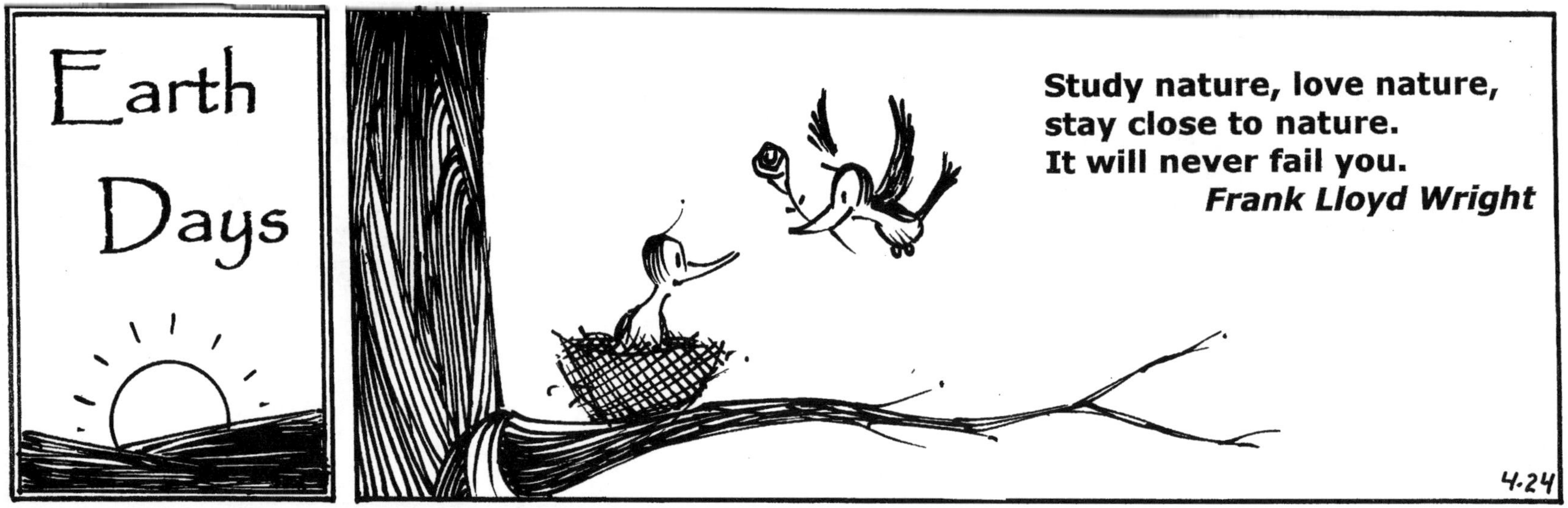
Earth Days
Study nature, love nature,
stay close to nature.
It will never fail you.
Frank Lloyd Wright
4·24

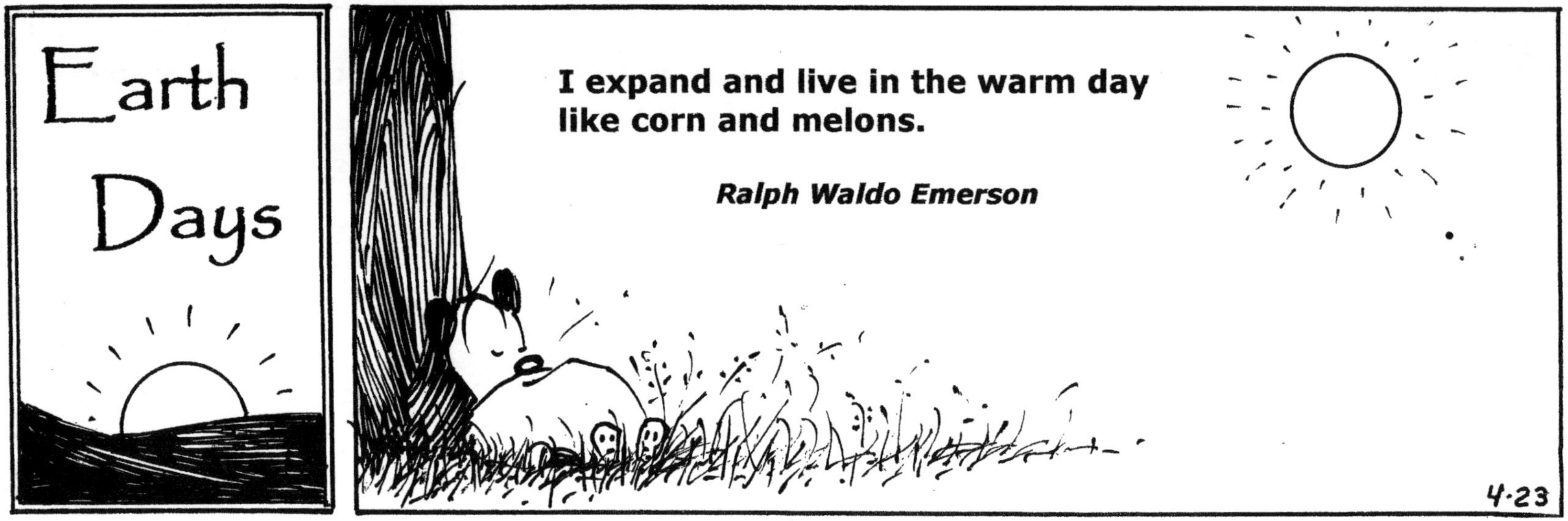
Earth Days
I expand and live in the warm day
like corn and melons.
Ralph Waldo Emerson
4·23

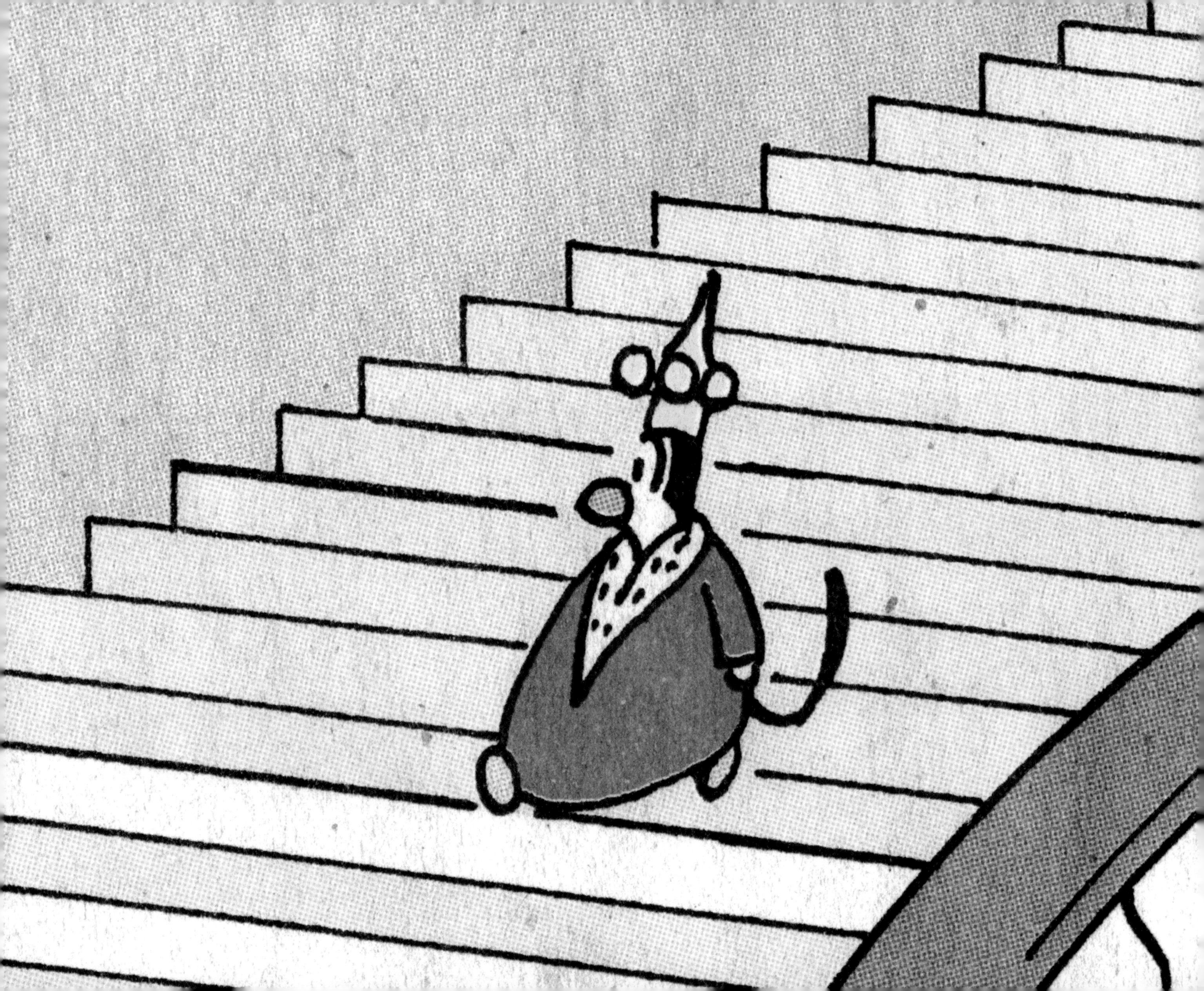

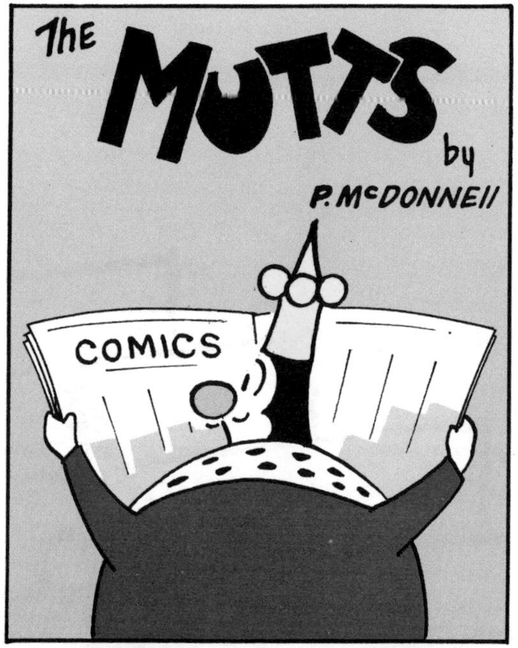
The MUTTS by P. McDONNELL
COMICS

The Little Kat King

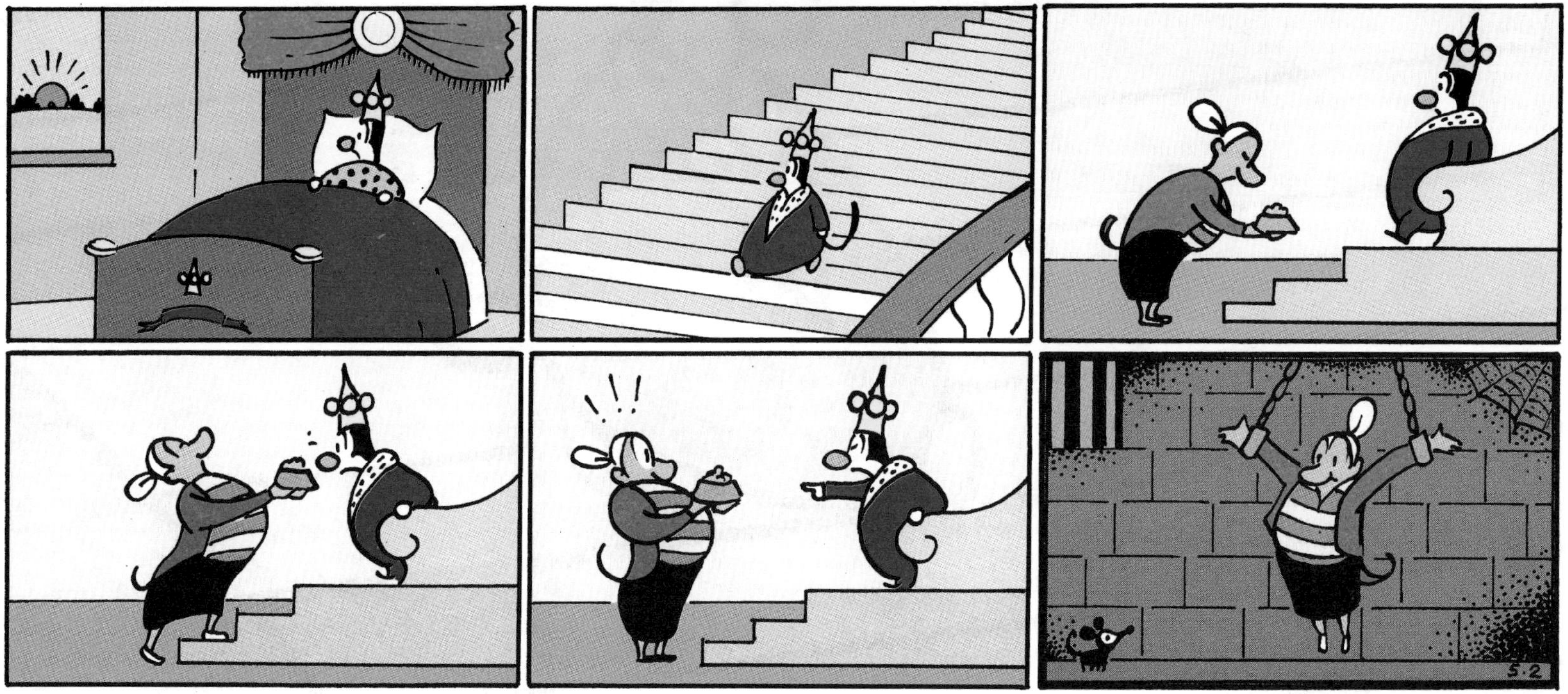
5·2

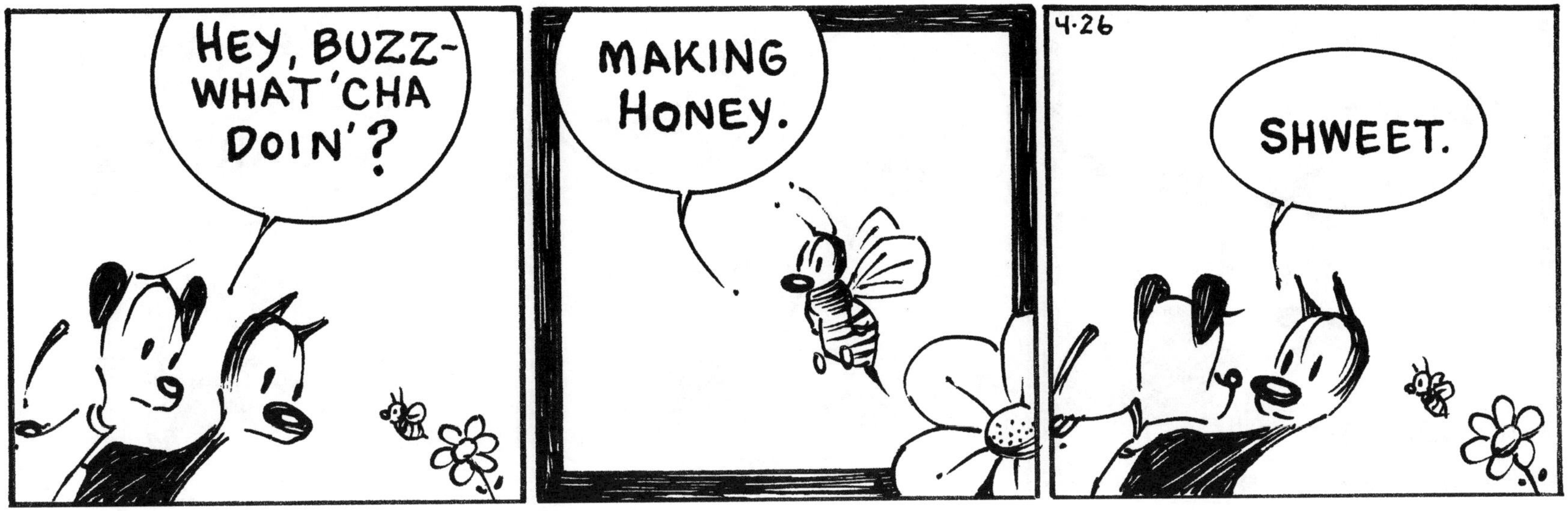
HEY, BUZZ-
WHAT'CHA
DOIN'?
MAKING
HONEY.
4·26
SHWEET.

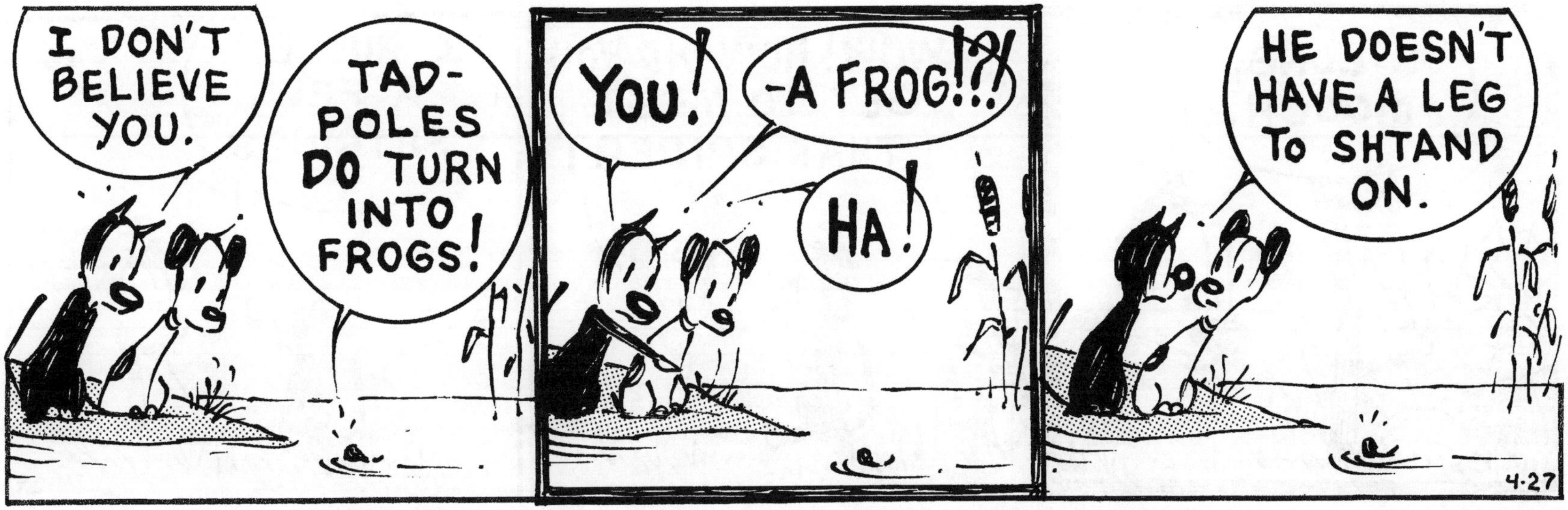
I DON'T
BELIEVE
YOU.
TAD-
POLES
DO TURN
INTO
FROGS!
YOU!
-A FROG!?!
HA!
HE DOESN'T
HAVE A LEG
TO SHTAND
ON.
4·27

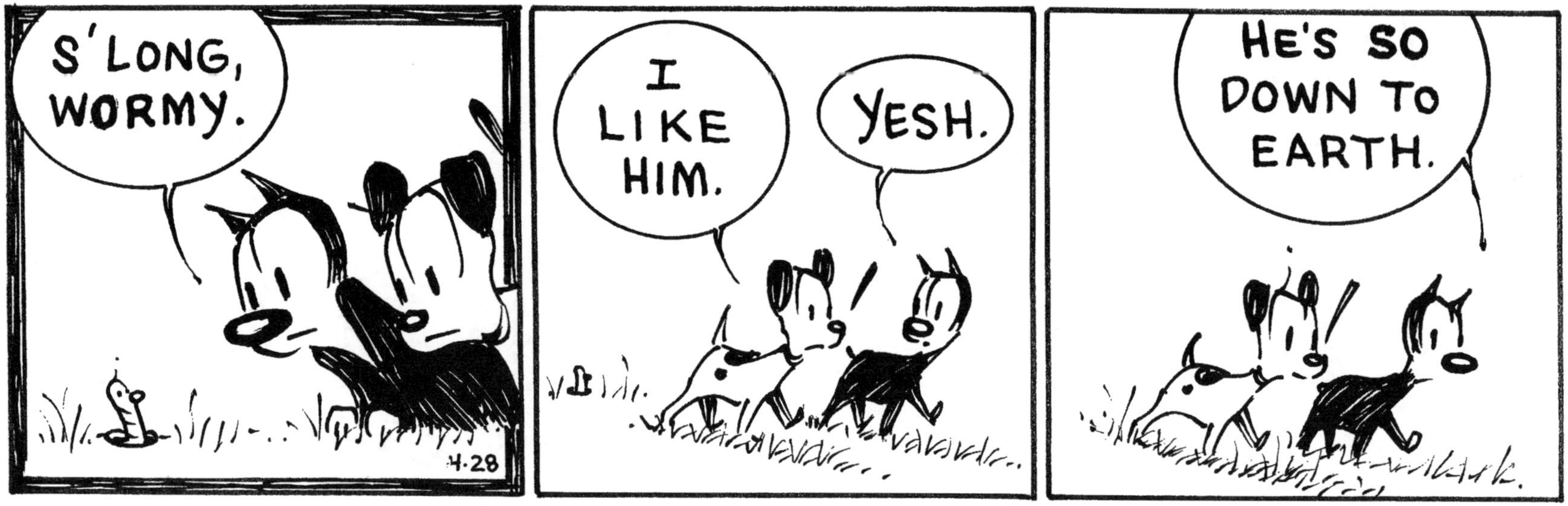
S'LONG, WORMY.
4·28
I LIKE HIM.
YESH.
HE'S SO DOWN TO EARTH.

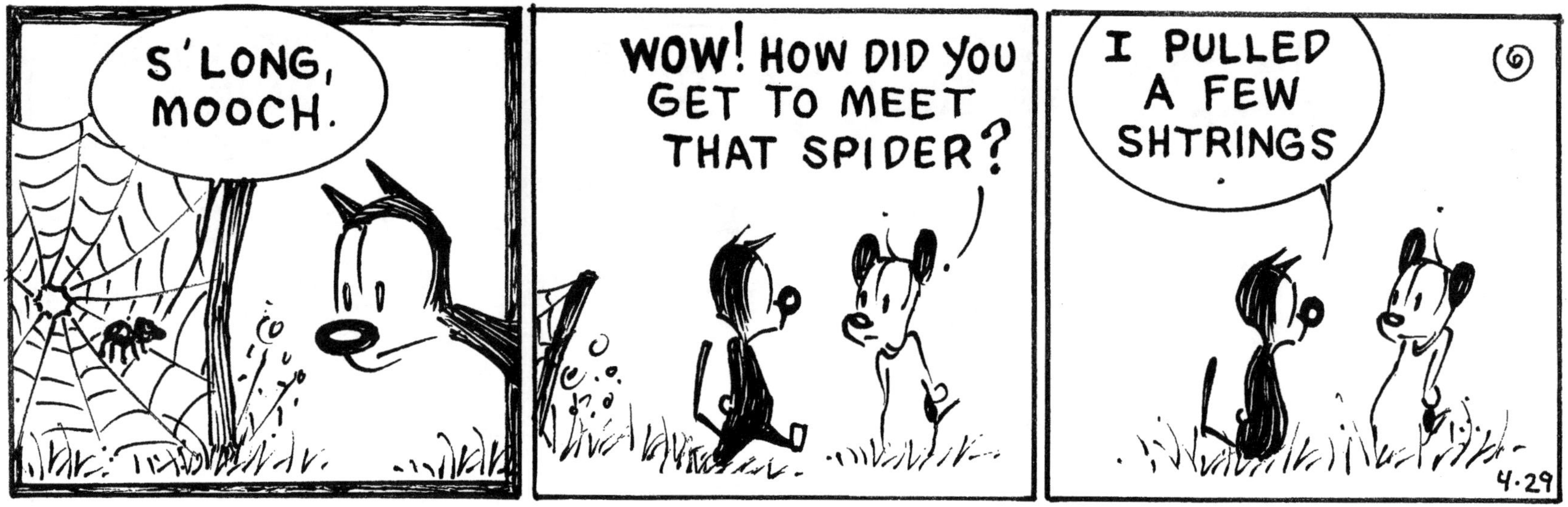
S'LONG, MOOCH.
WOW! HOW DID YOU GET TO MEET THAT SPIDER?
I PULLED A FEW SHTRINGS
4·29

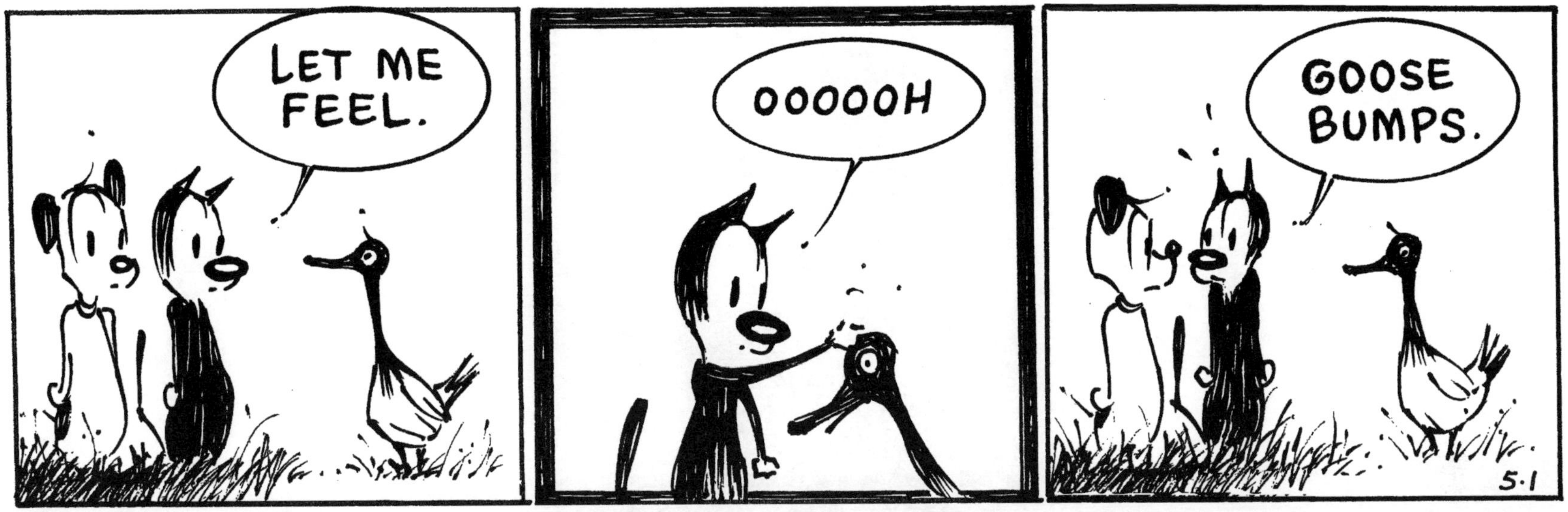
LET ME FEEL.
OOOOOH
GOOSE BUMPS.
5·1

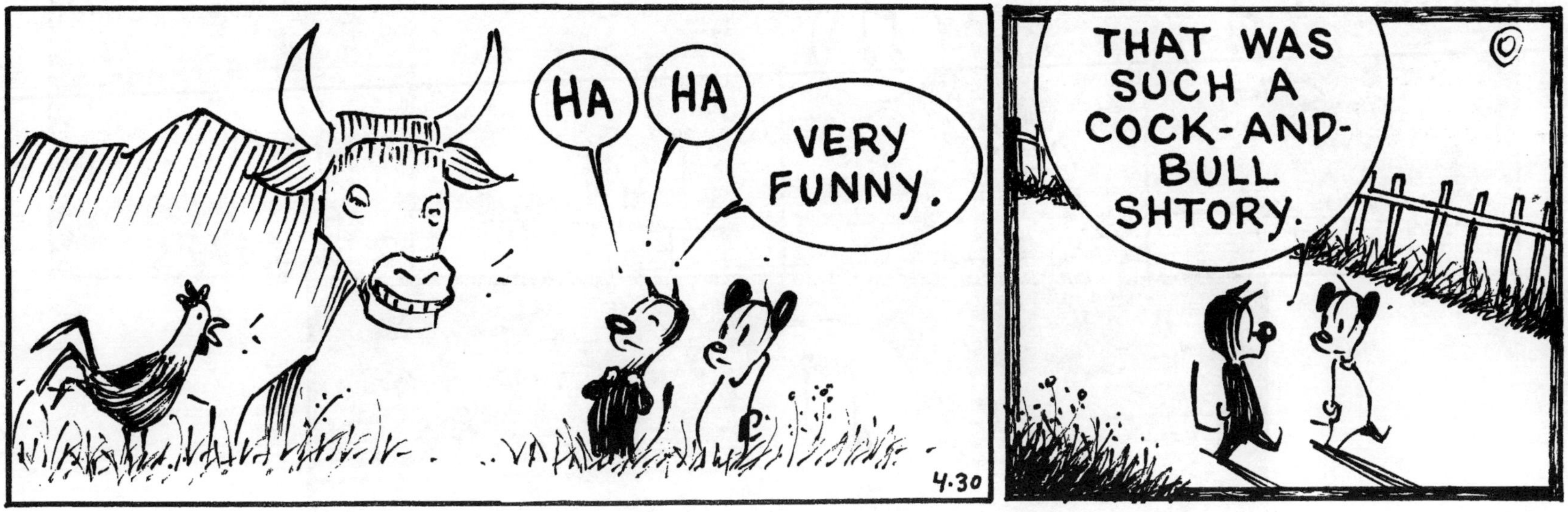
HA
HA
VERY FUNNY.
4·30
THAT WAS SUCH A COCK-AND-BULL SHTORY.
©

MUTTS

5·16

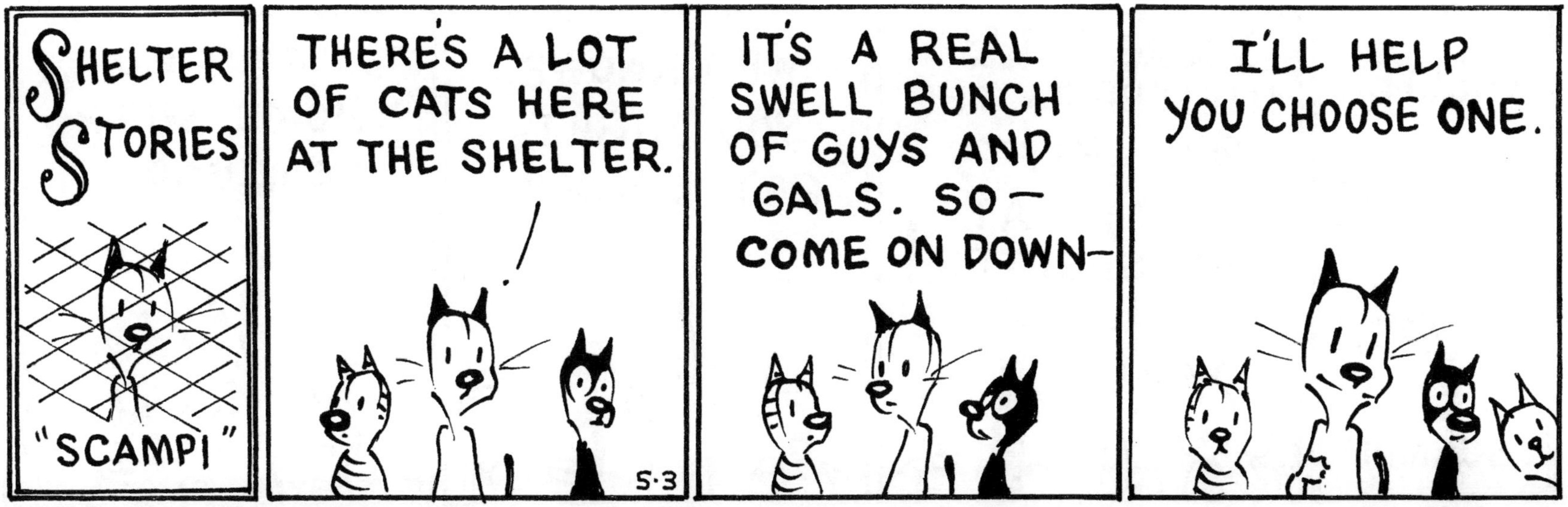
SHELTER STORIES
"SCAMPI"
THERE'S A LOT OF CATS HERE AT THE SHELTER.
5·3
IT'S A REAL SWELL BUNCH OF GUYS AND GALS. SO— COME ON DOWN—
I'LL HELP YOU CHOOSE ONE.

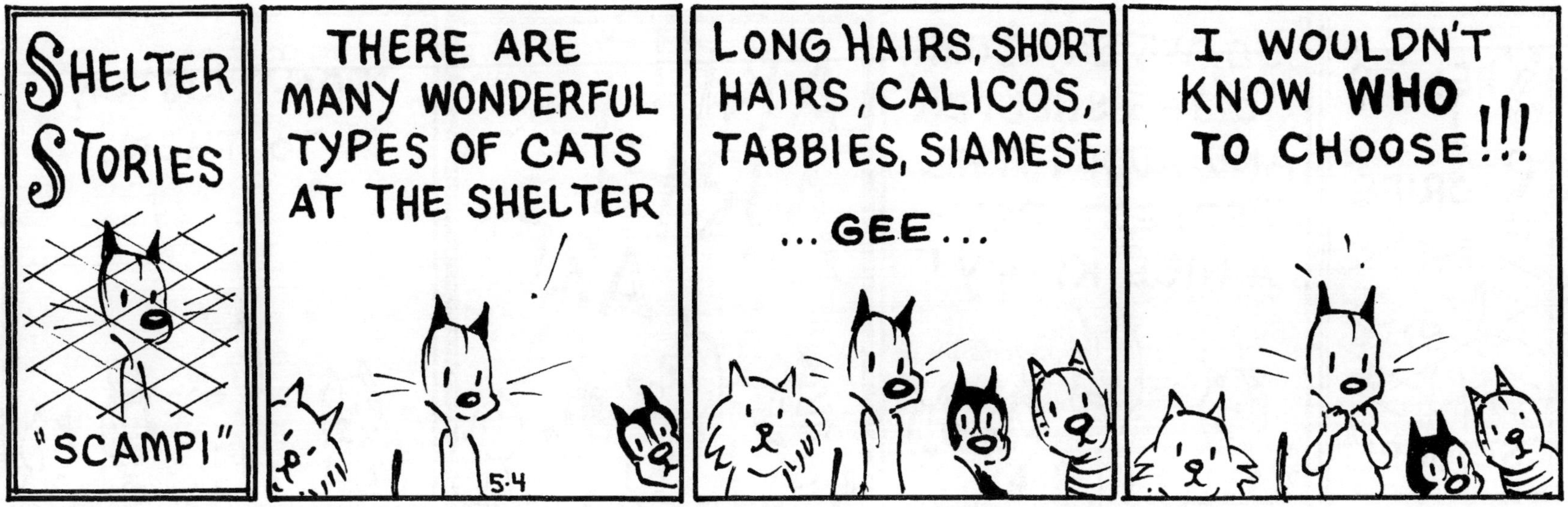
SHELTER STORIES
"SCAMPI"
THERE ARE MANY WONDERFUL TYPES OF CATS AT THE SHELTER
5·4
LONG HAIRS, SHORT HAIRS, CALICOS, TABBIES, SIAMESE
... GEE ...
I WOULDN'T KNOW WHO TO CHOOSE!!!

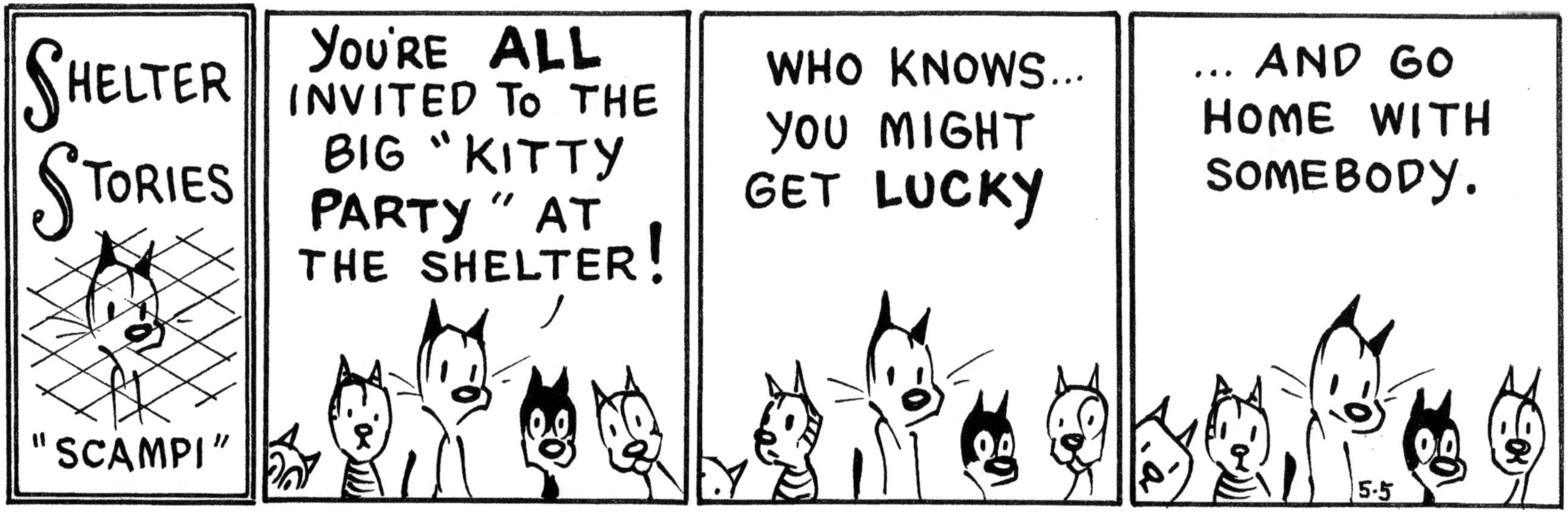
SHELTER STORIES
"SCAMPI"
YOU'RE **ALL** INVITED TO THE BIG "KITTY **PARTY**" AT THE SHELTER!
WHO KNOWS... YOU MIGHT GET **LUCKY**
... AND GO HOME WITH SOMEBODY.
5·5

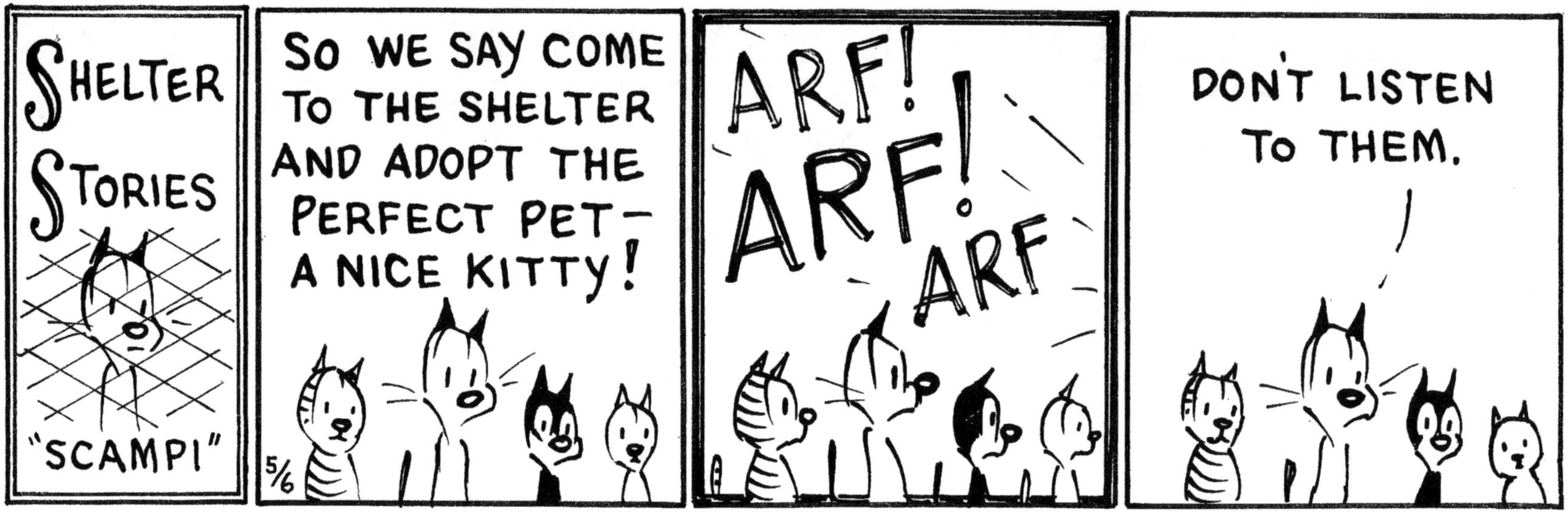
SHELTER STORIES
"SCAMPI"
SO WE SAY COME TO THE SHELTER AND ADOPT THE PERFECT PET— A NICE KITTY!
5/6
ARF! ARF! ARF
DON'T LISTEN TO THEM.

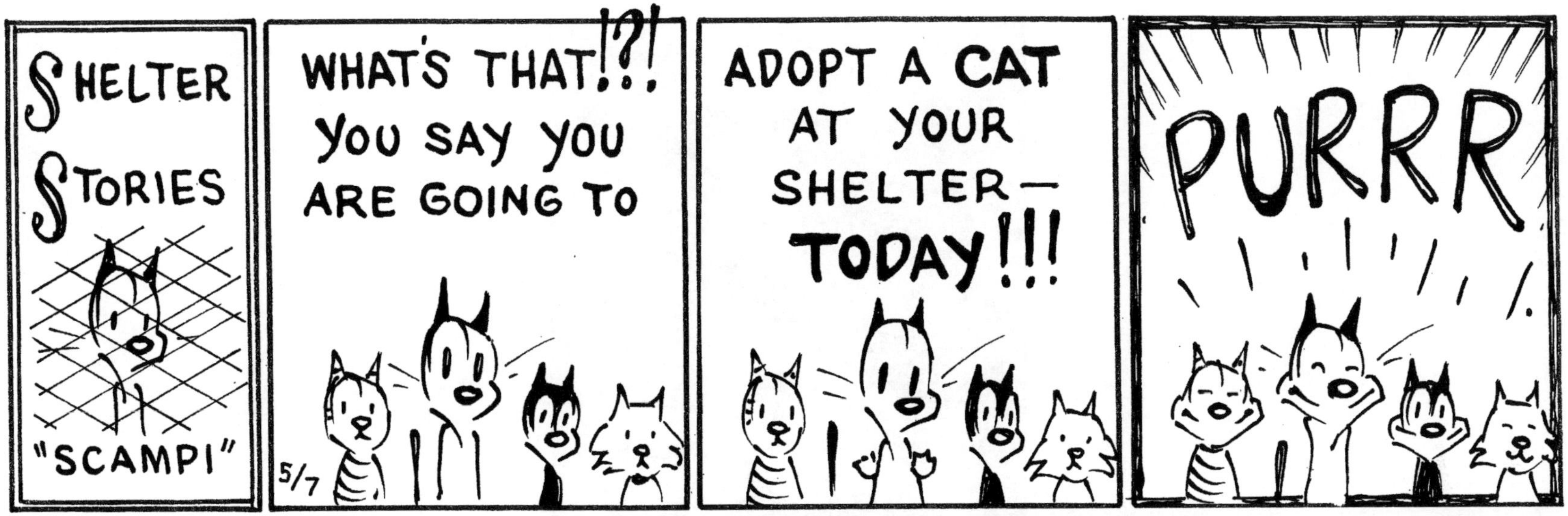
SHELTER STORIES
"SCAMPI"
5/7
WHAT'S THAT!?! YOU SAY YOU ARE GOING TO
ADOPT A CAT AT YOUR SHELTER— TODAY!!!
PURRR

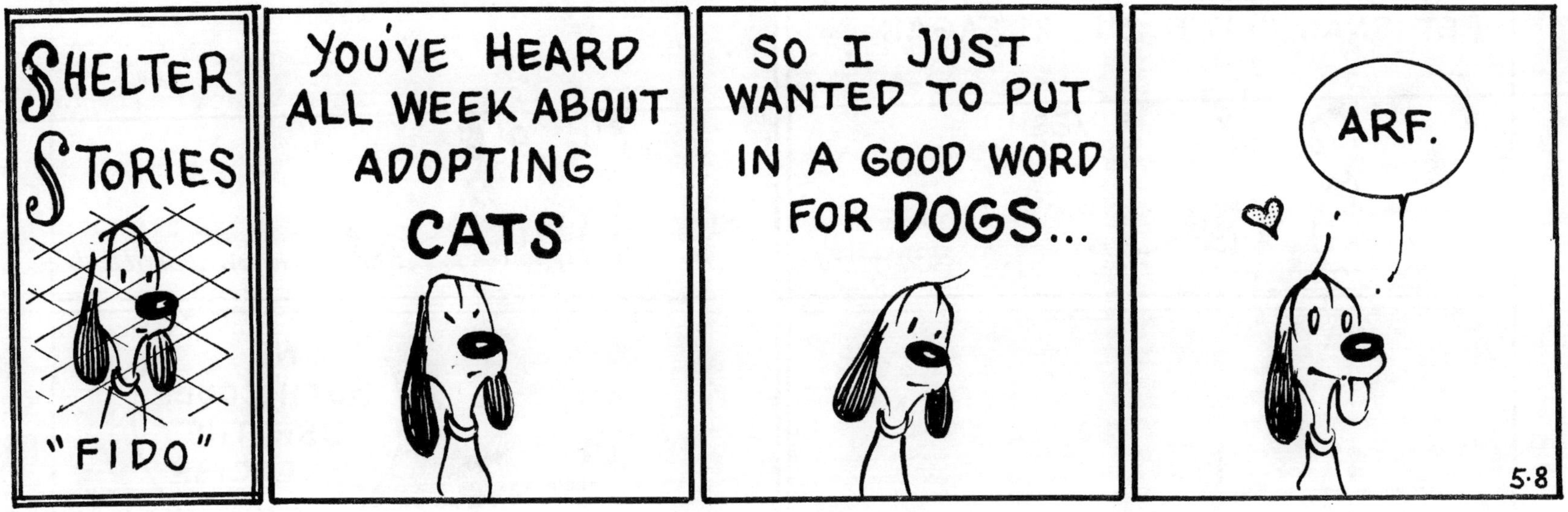
SHELTER STORIES
"FIDO"
YOU'VE HEARD ALL WEEK ABOUT ADOPTING CATS
SO I JUST WANTED TO PUT IN A GOOD WORD FOR DOGS...
ARF.
5·8

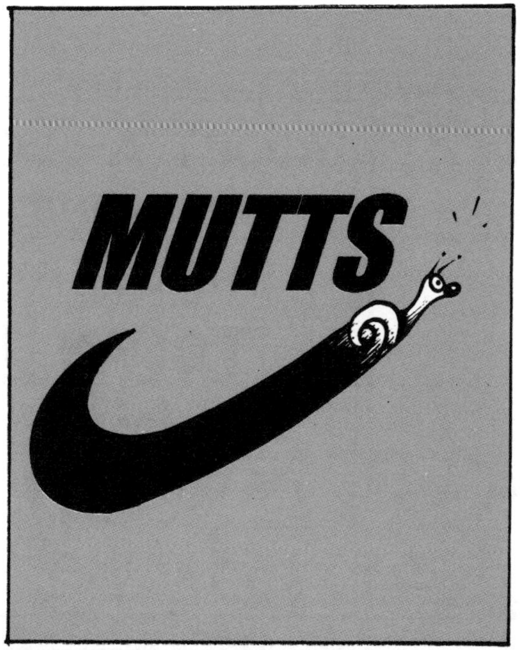
MUTTS

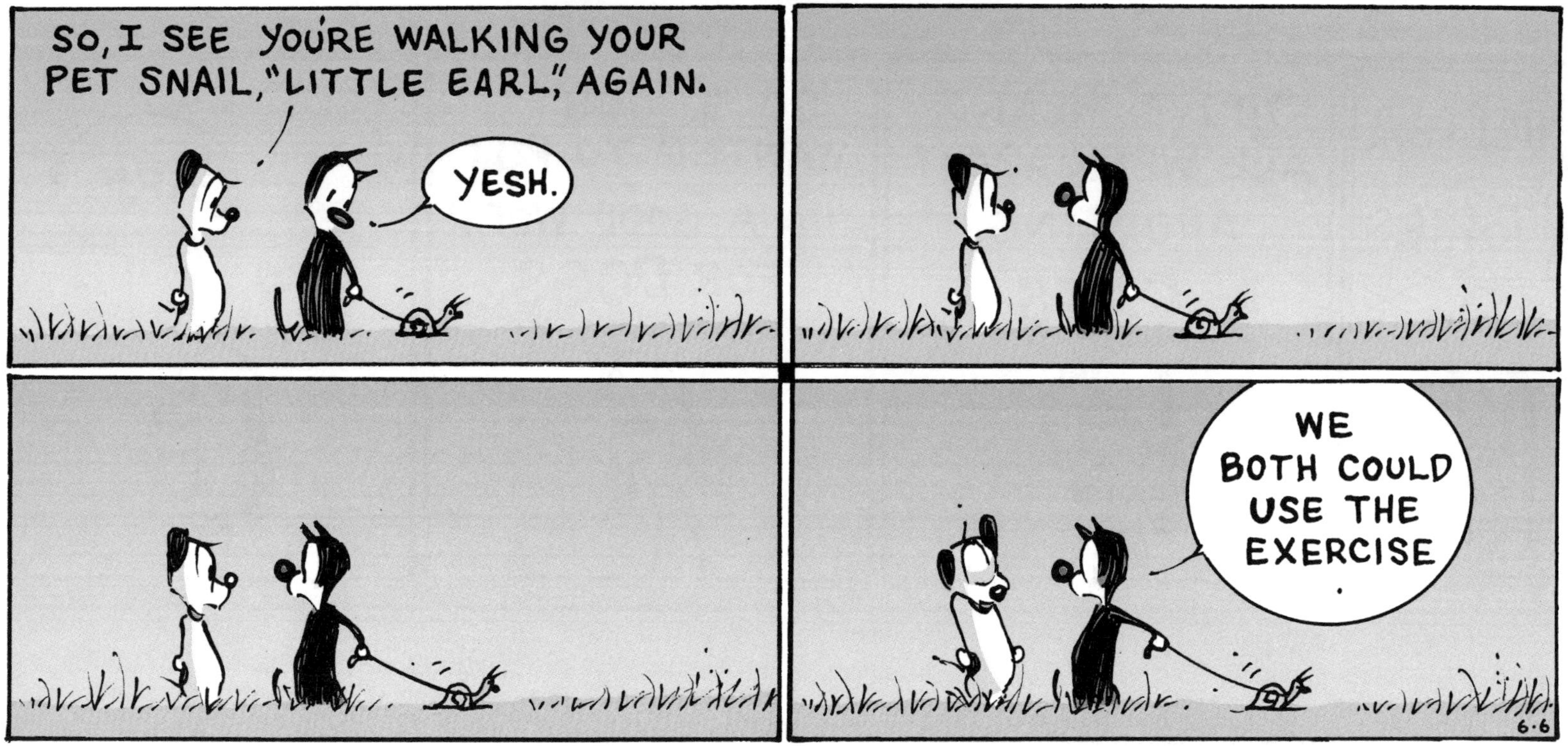
SO, I SEE YOU'RE WALKING YOUR PET SNAIL, "LITTLE EARL," AGAIN.
YESH.
WE BOTH COULD USE THE EXERCISE.
6·6

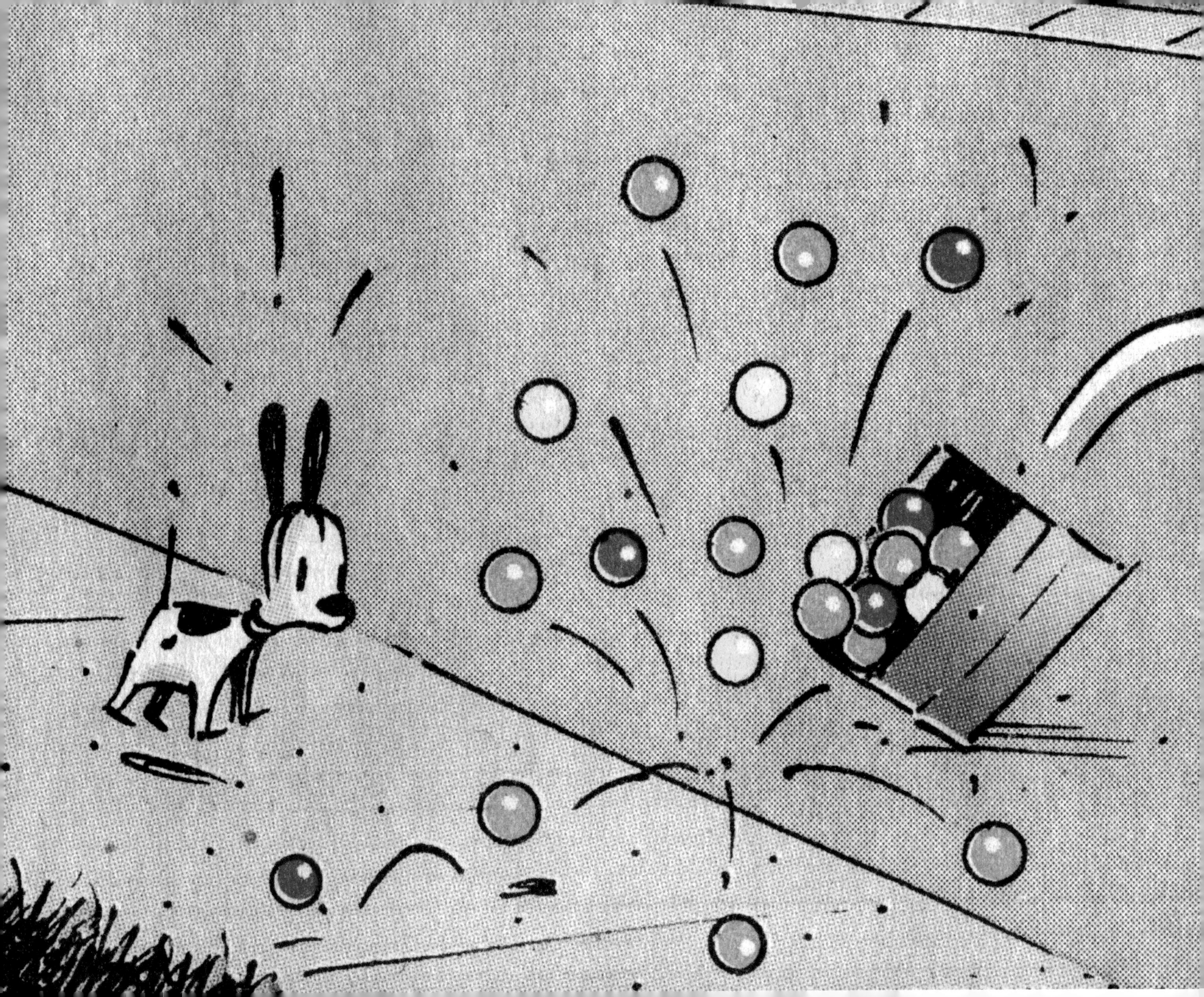

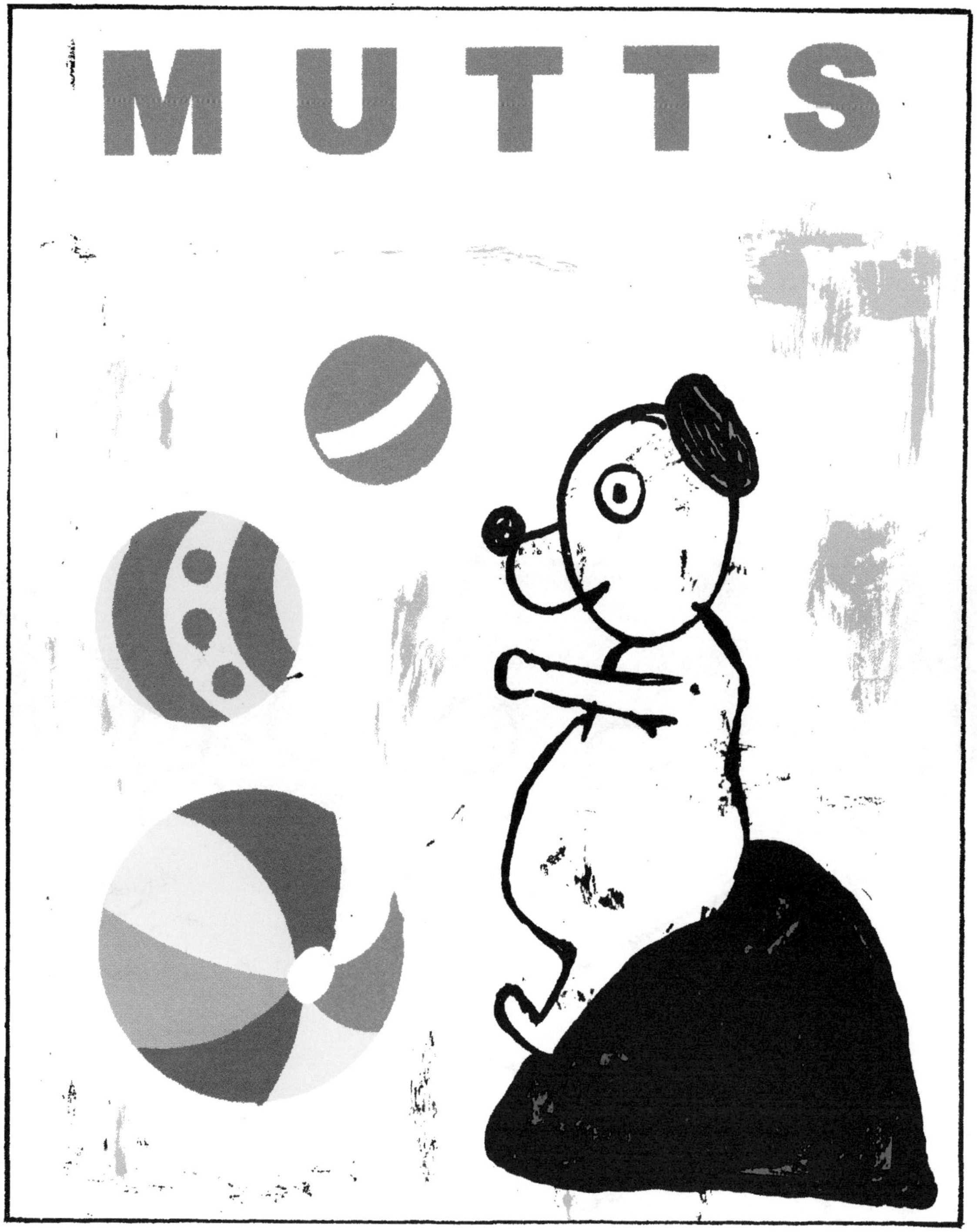
MUTTS

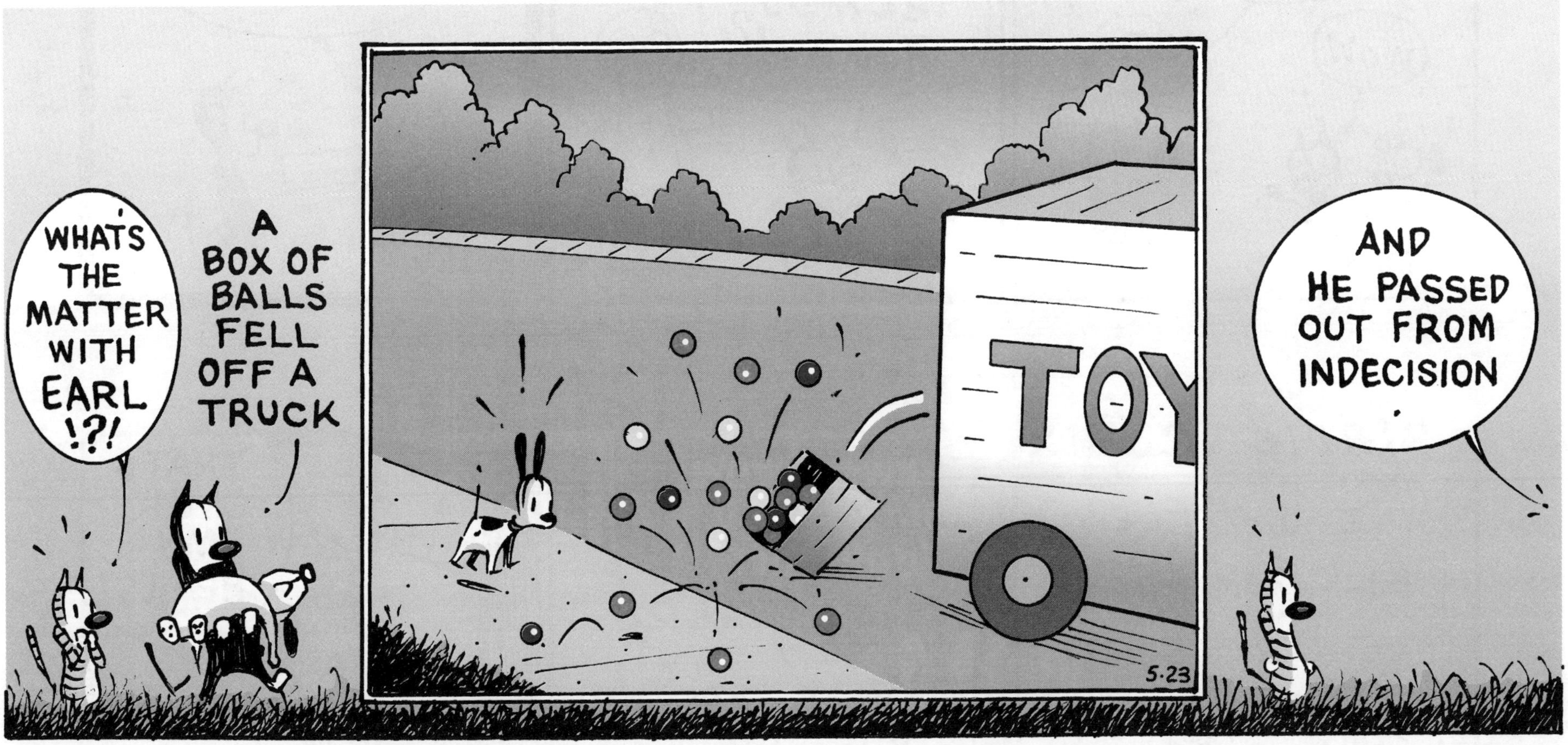
WHAT'S THE MATTER WITH EARL !?!
A BOX OF BALLS FELL OFF A TRUCK
TOY
5·23
AND HE PASSED OUT FROM INDECISION

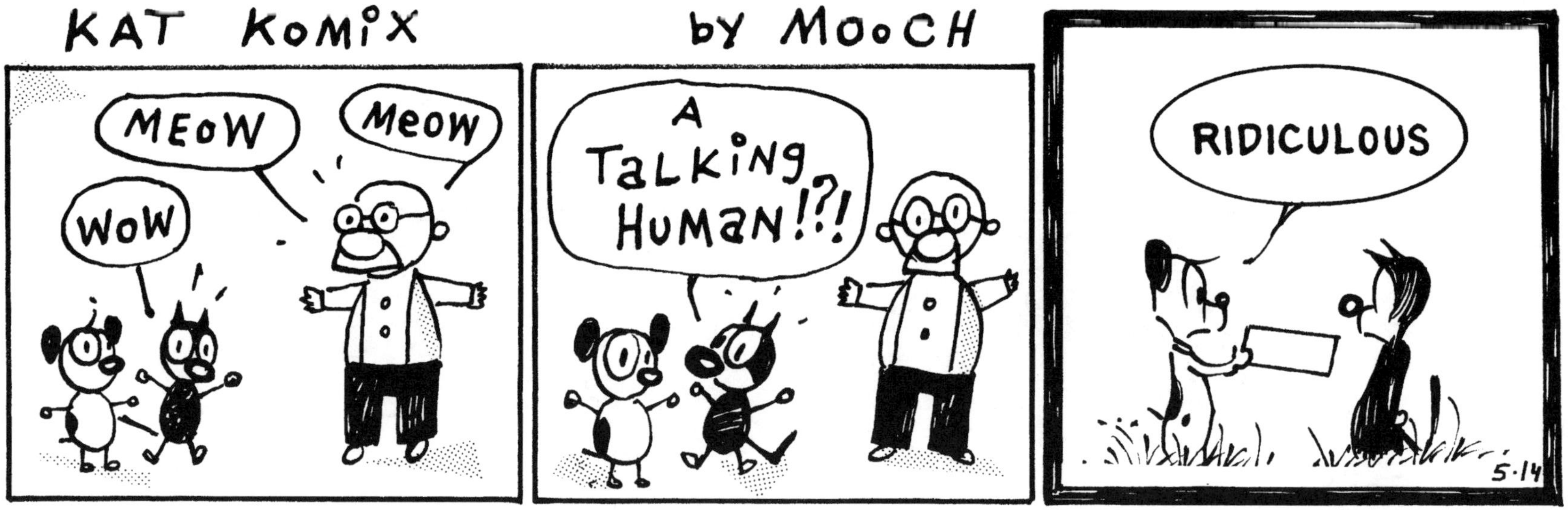
KAT KOMIX
by MOOCH
MEOW
Meow
WOW
A TaLKing HuMaN!?!
RIDICULOUS
5·14

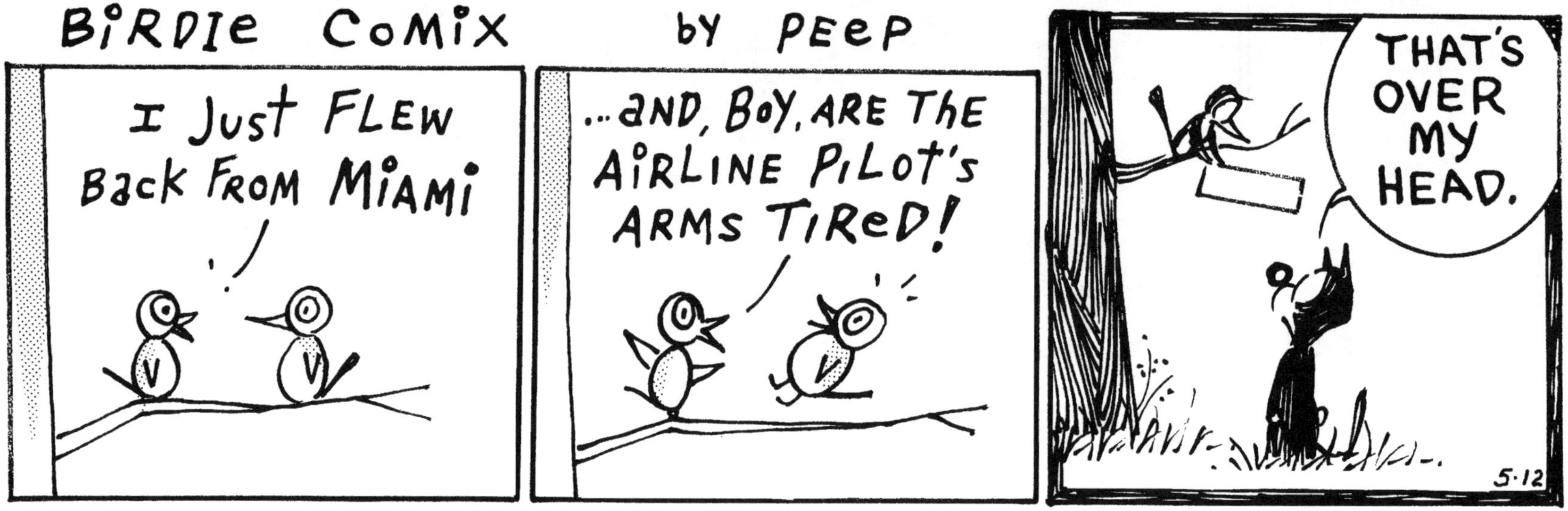
BiRDIE CoMiX
by PEEP
I Just FLEW Back FROM MiAMi
...aND, Boy, ARE ThE AiRLINE PiLot's ARMS TiReD!
THAT'S OVER MY HEAD.
5·12

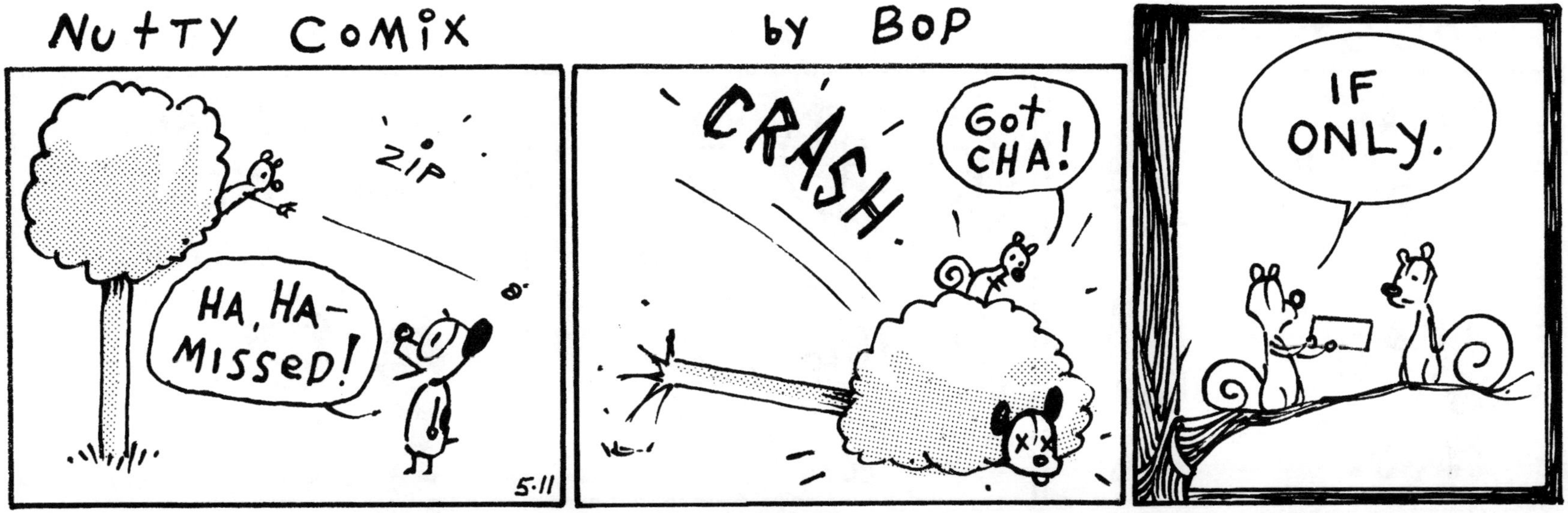
NUTTY COMIX
by BOP
ZIP
HA, HA- MISSED!
5·11
CRASH.
Got CHA!
IF ONLY.

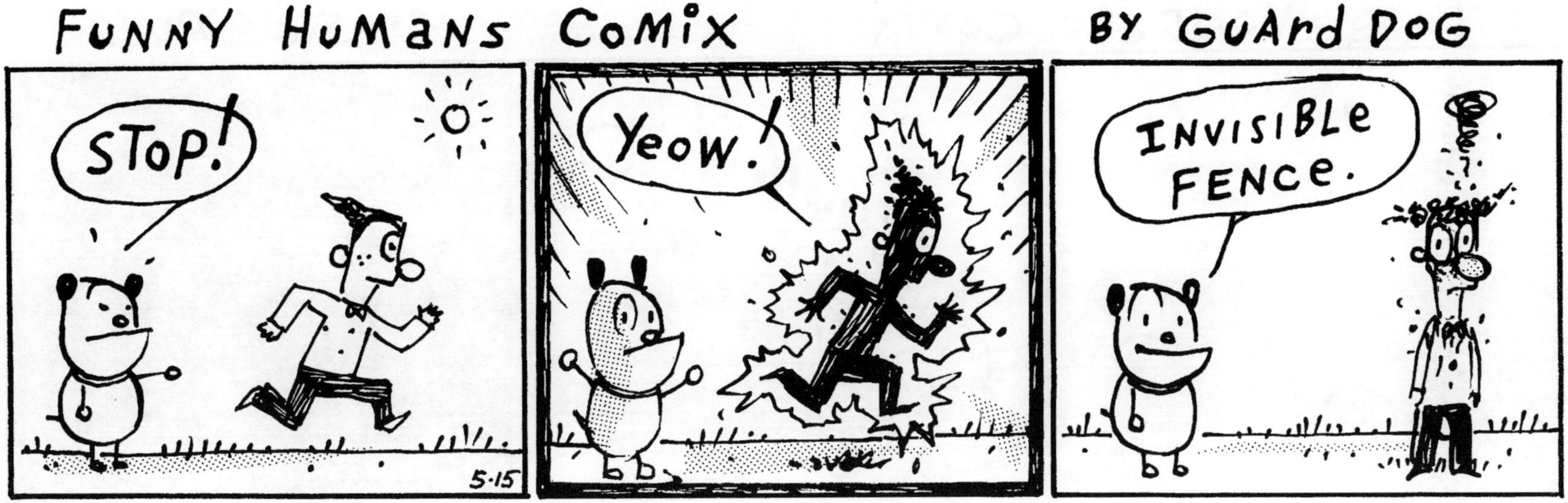
FUNNY HUMANS COMIX
BY GUARD DOG
STOP!
5·15
Yeow.!
INVISIBLE FENCE.

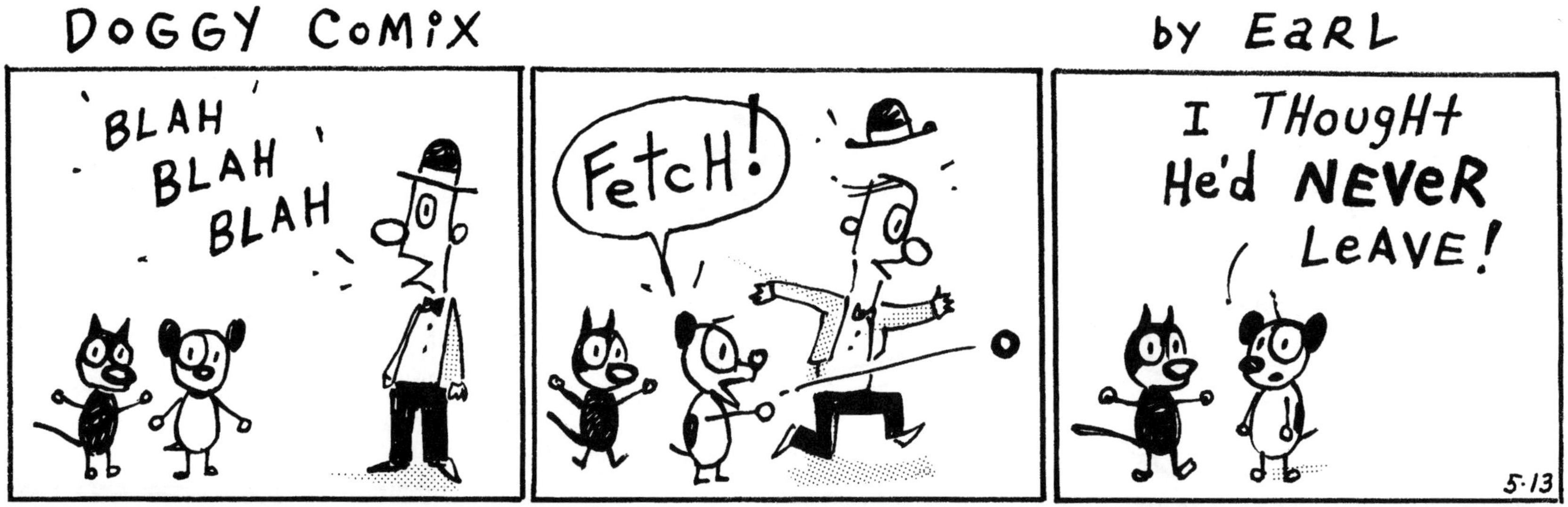
DOGGY COMIX
by EARL
BLAH BLAH BLAH
FETCH!
I THOUGHT HE'D NEVER LEAVE!
5·13

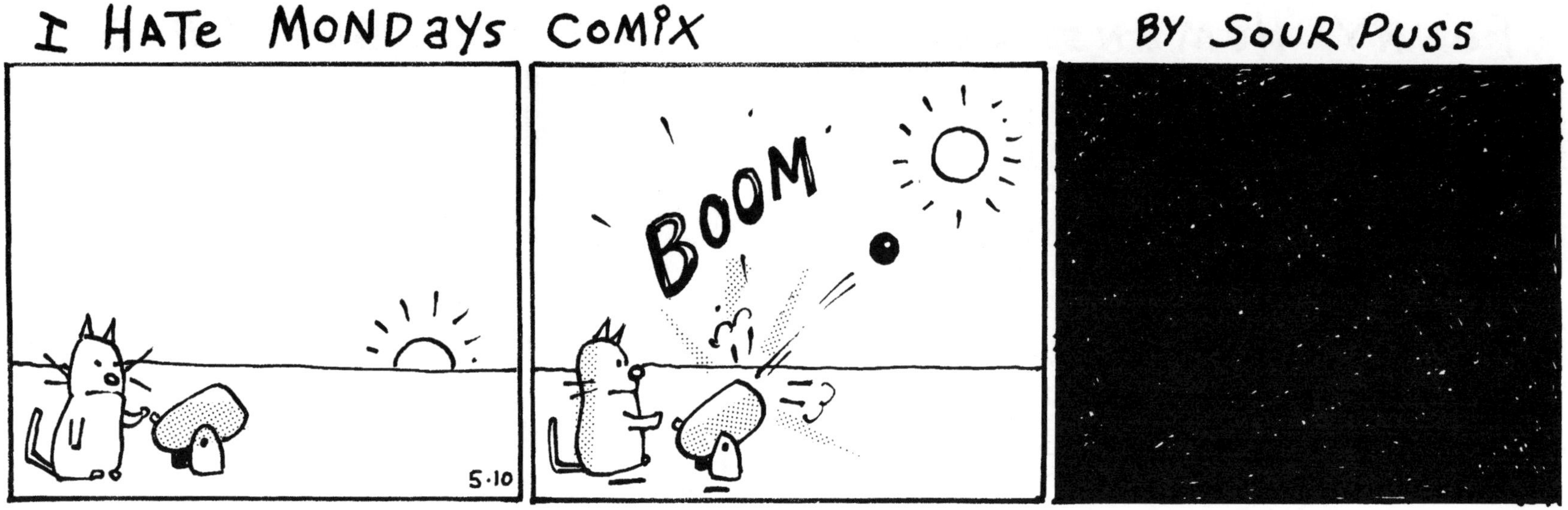
I HATE MONDAYS COMIX
BY SOUR PUSS
5·10
BOOM

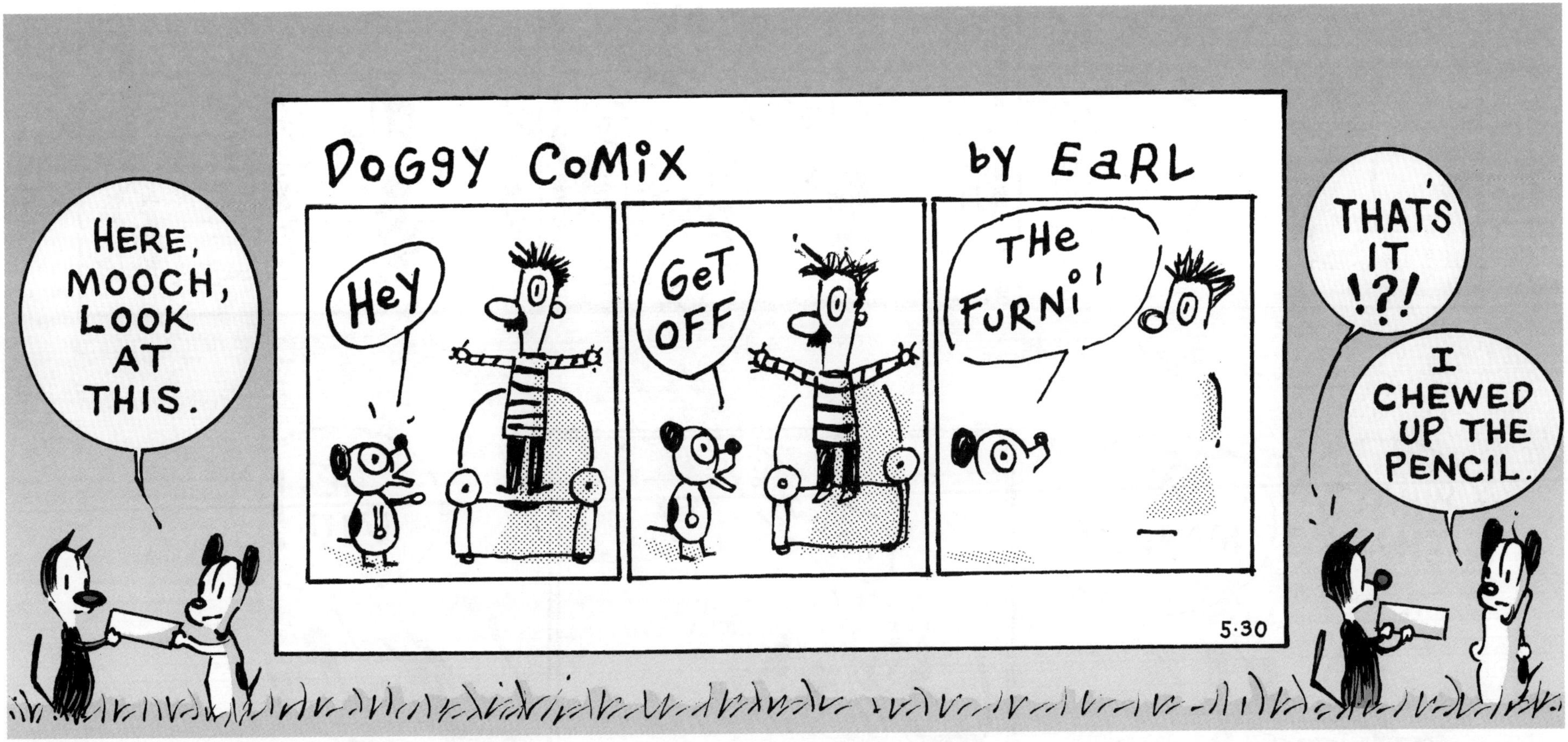
HERE, MOOCH, LOOK AT THIS.
DoGGY CoMiX
by EaRL
Hey
GeT OFF
THe FuRNi
5·30
THAT'S IT !?!
I CHEWED UP THE PENCIL.

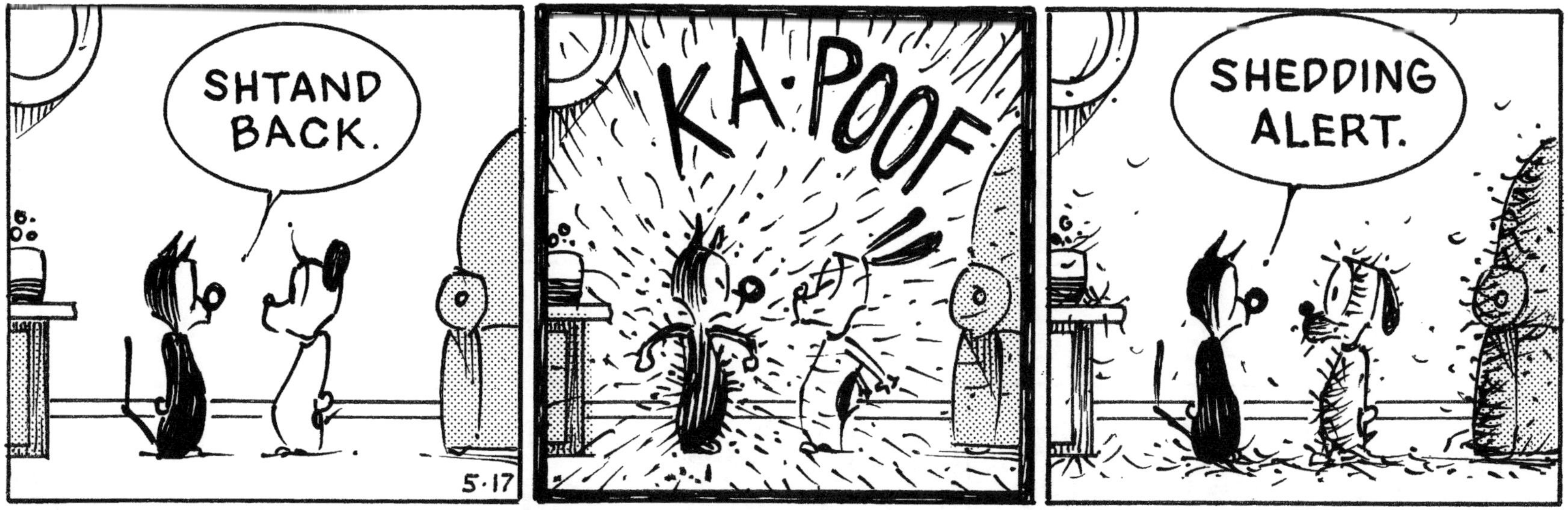
SHTAND BACK.
KA-POOF
SHEDDING ALERT.
5·17

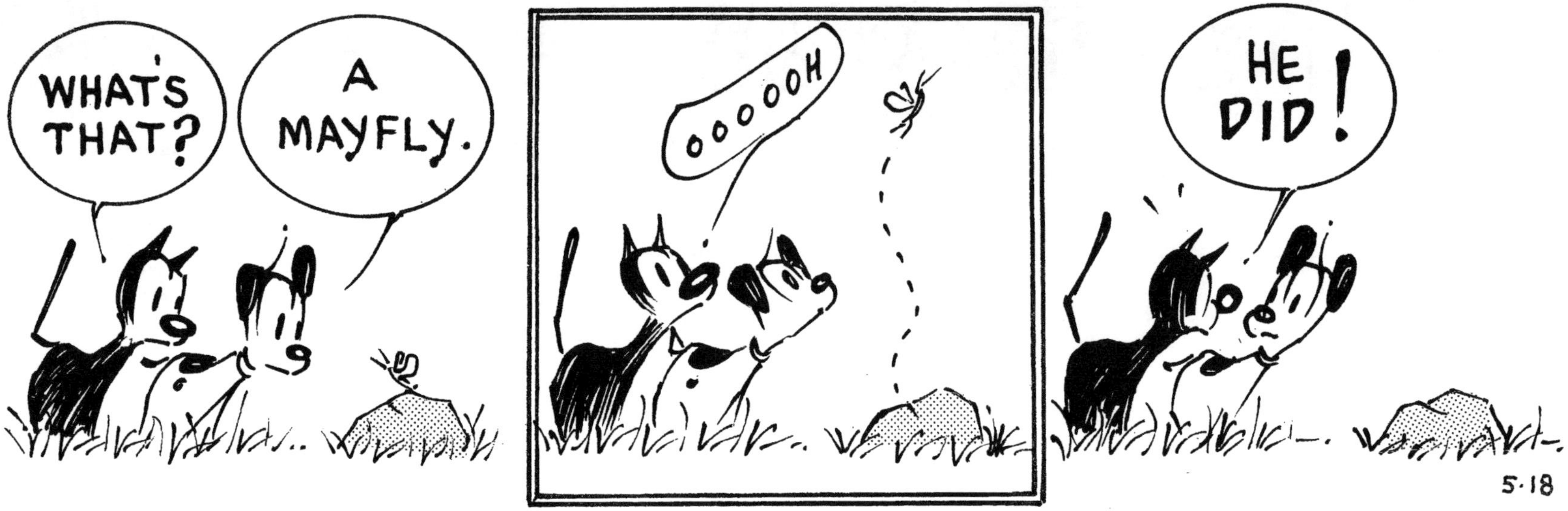
WHAT'S THAT?
A MAYFLY.
OOOOOH
HE DID!
5·18

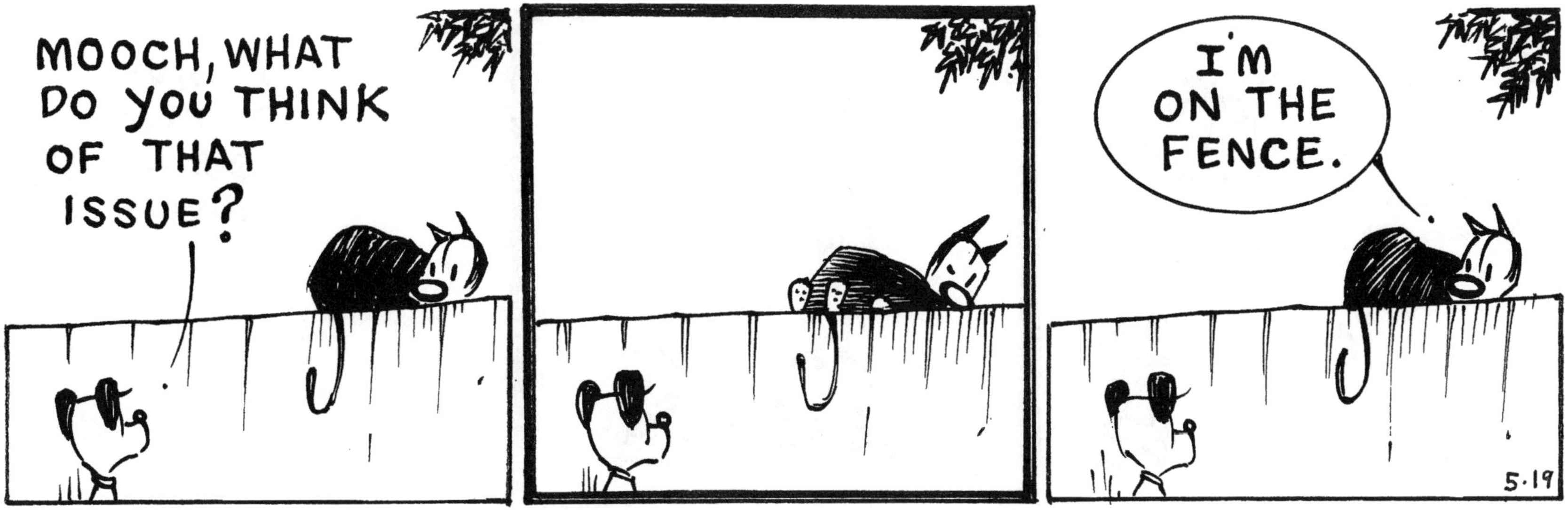
MOOCH, WHAT DO YOU THINK OF THAT ISSUE?
I'M ON THE FENCE.
5·19

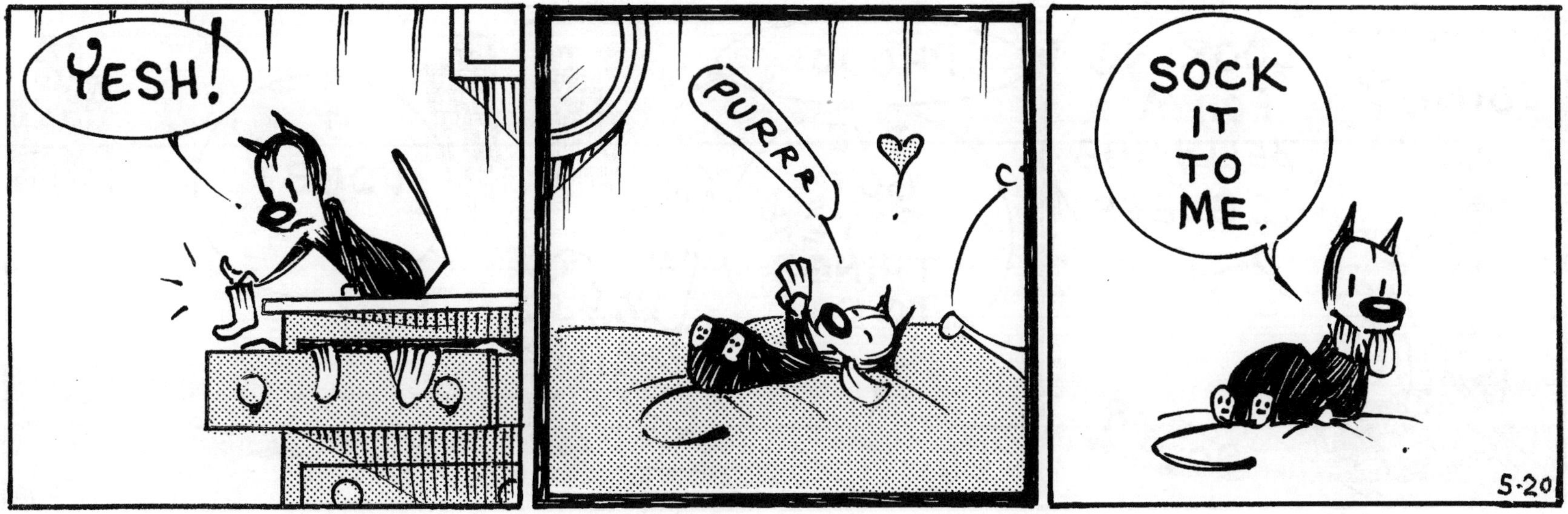
YESH!
PURRR
SOCK IT TO ME.
5·20

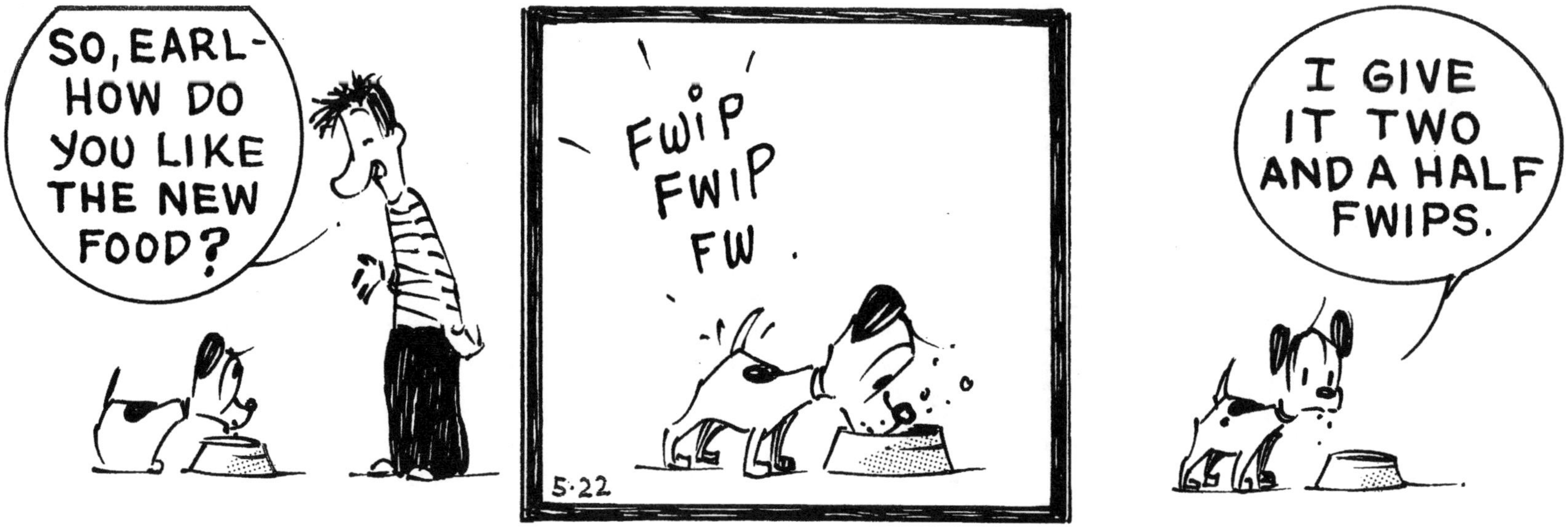
SO, EARL- HOW DO YOU LIKE THE NEW FOOD?
FWIP FWIP FW
5·22
I GIVE IT TWO AND A HALF FWIPS.

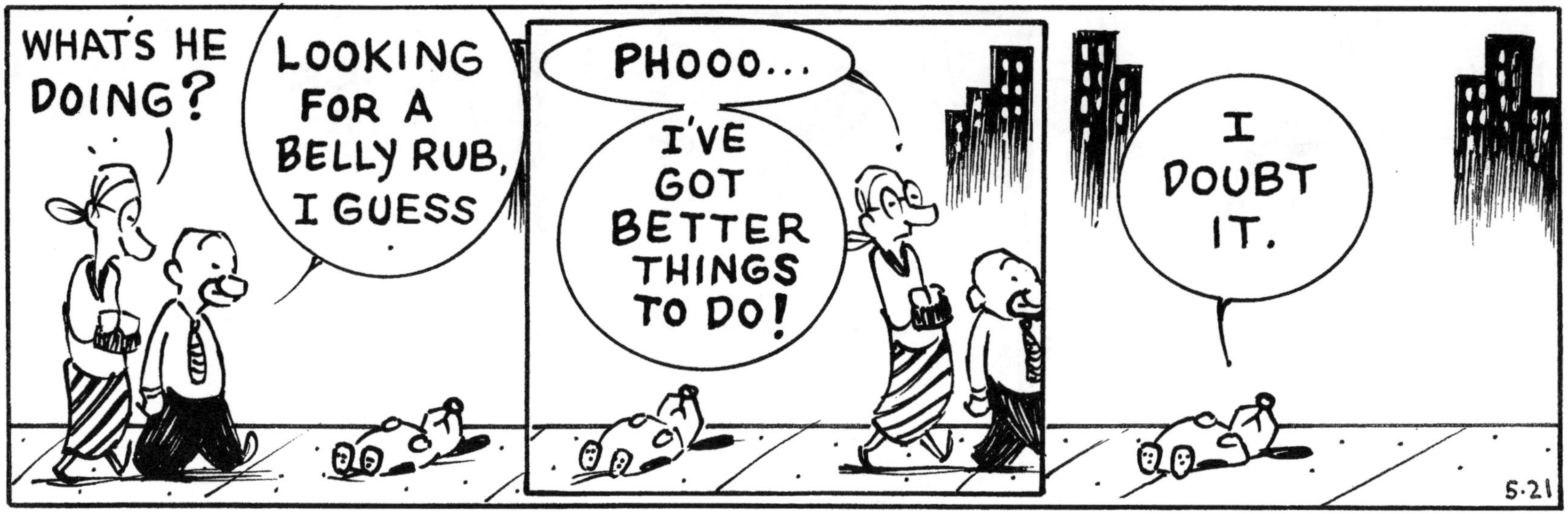
WHAT'S HE DOING?
LOOKING FOR A BELLY RUB, I GUESS
PHOOO...
I'VE GOT BETTER THINGS TO DO!
I DOUBT IT.
5·21

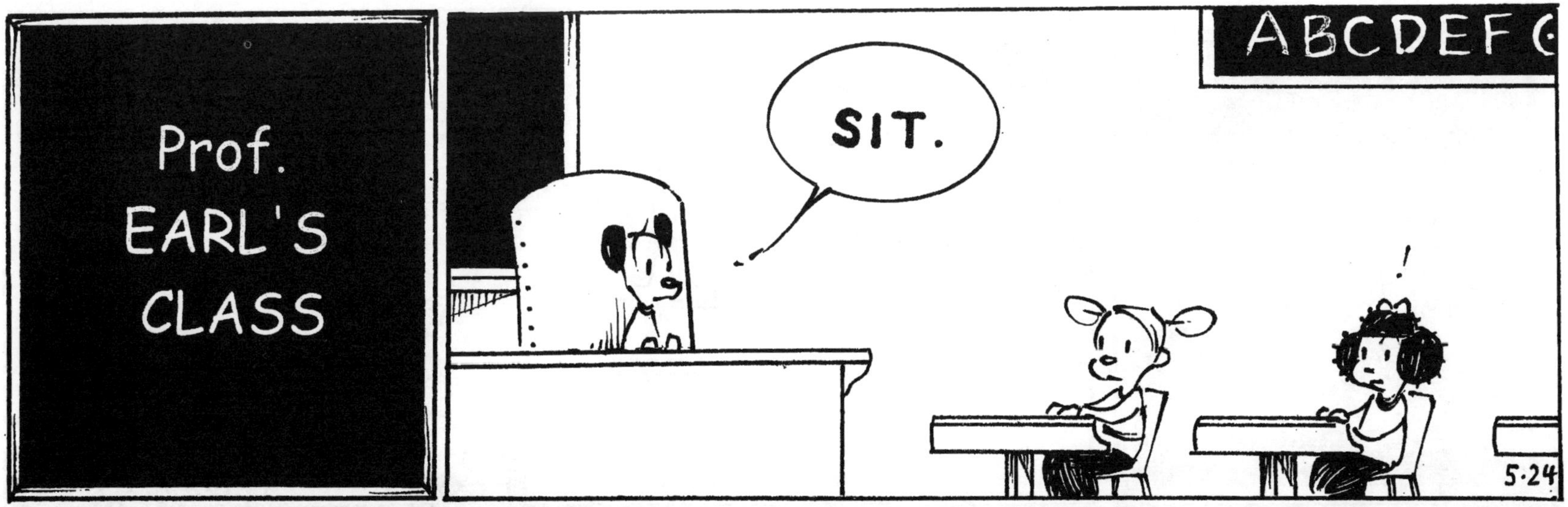
Prof.
EARL'S
CLASS
ABCDEFG
SIT.
!
5·24

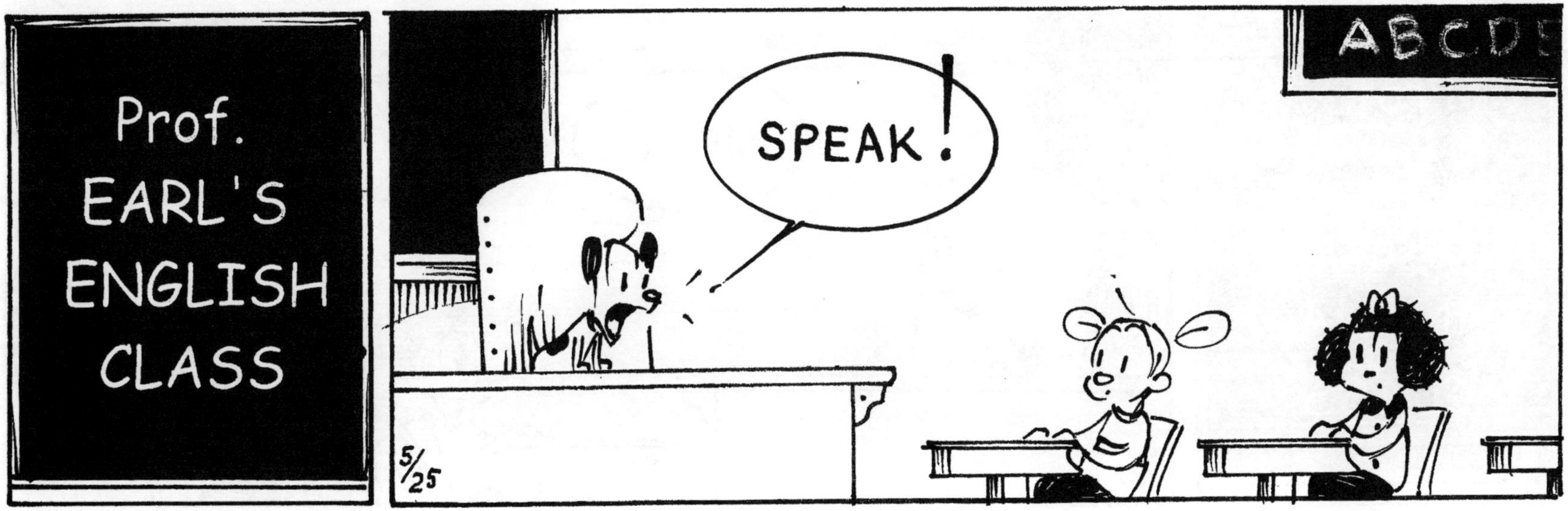
Prof.
EARL'S
ENGLISH
CLASS
ABCDE
SPEAK!
5/25

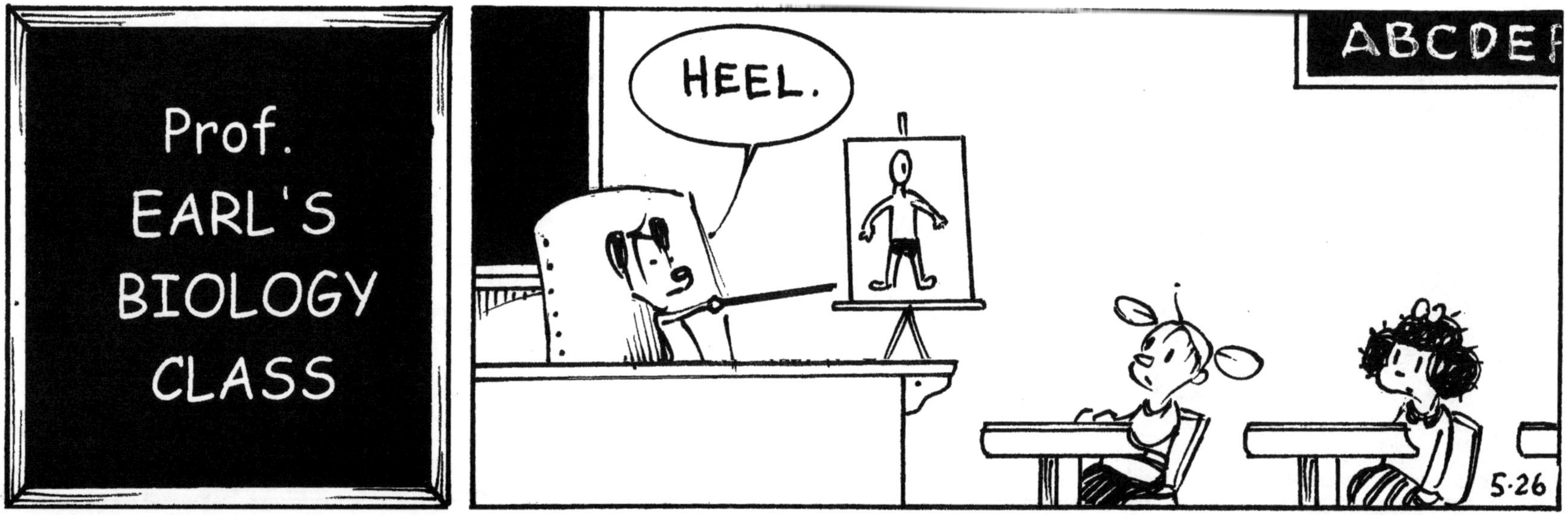
Prof.
EARL'S
BIOLOGY
CLASS
ABCDE
HEEL.
5·26

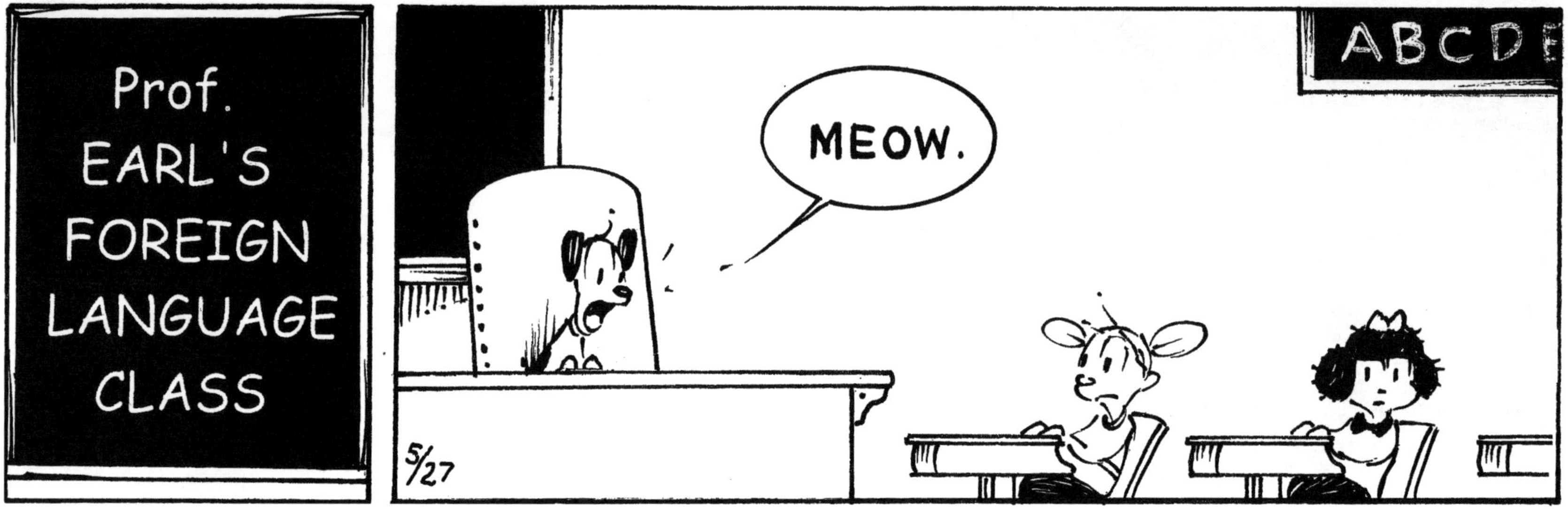
Prof.
EARL'S
FOREIGN
LANGUAGE
CLASS
ABCDE
MEOW.
5/27

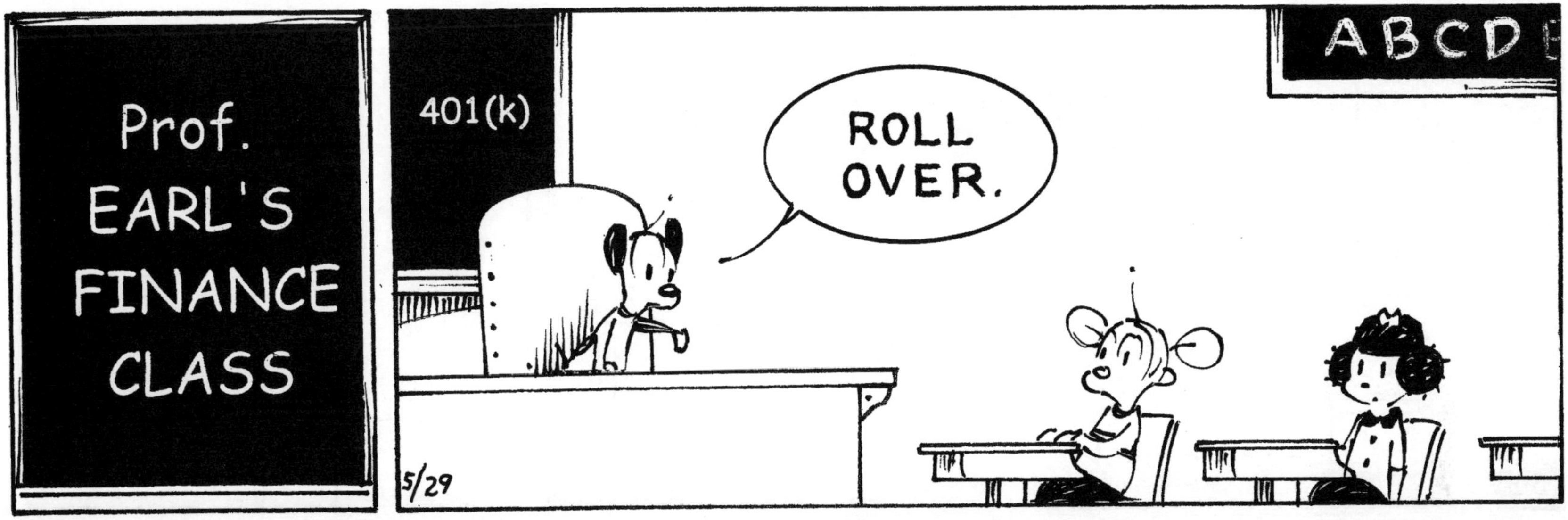
Prof.
EARL'S
FINANCE
CLASS
401(k)
ABCDE
ROLL OVER.
5/29

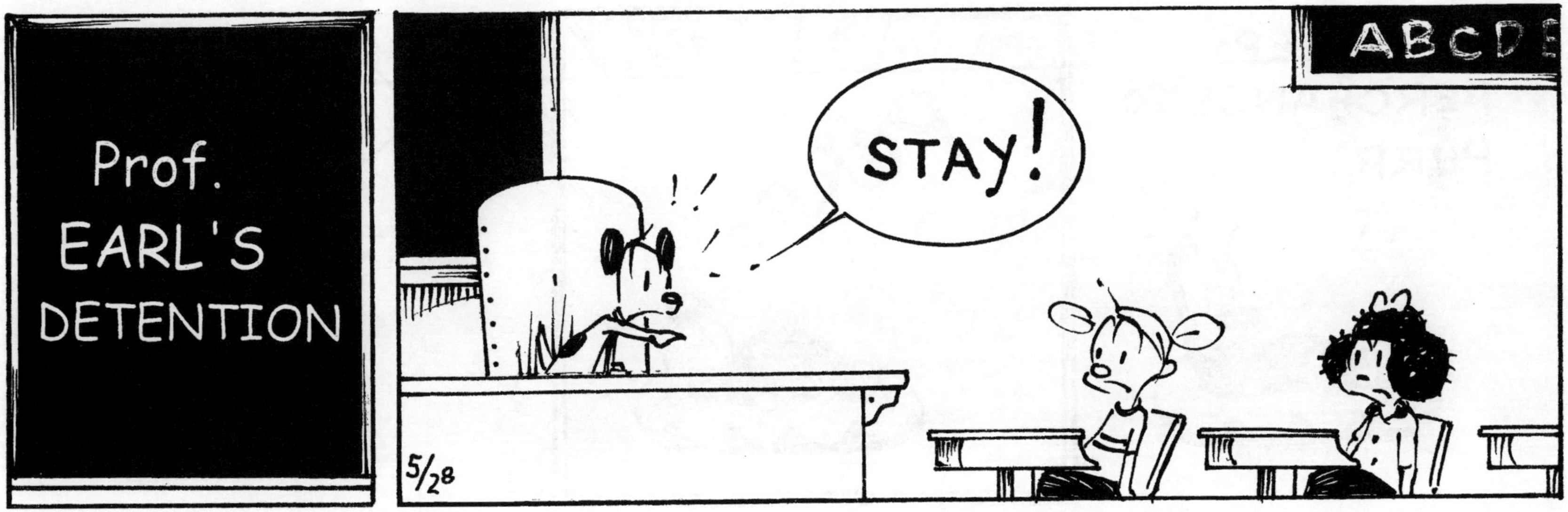
Prof.
EARL'S
DETENTION
ABCDE
STAY!
5/28

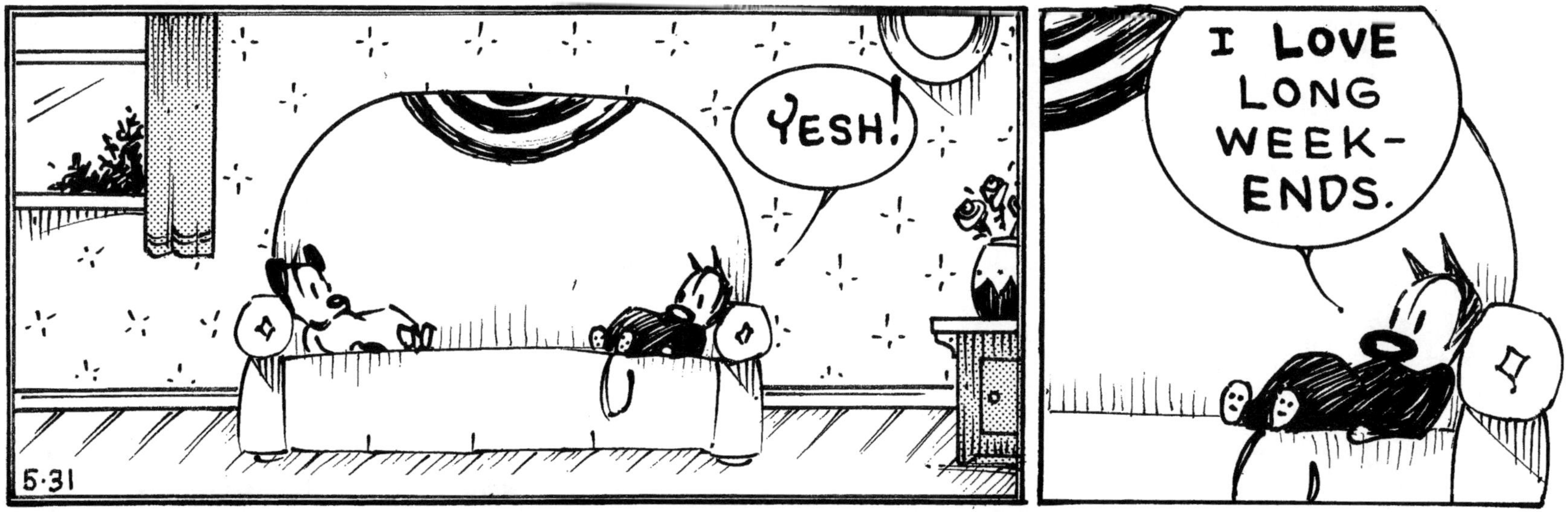
5·31
YESH!
I LOVE LONG WEEK-ENDS.

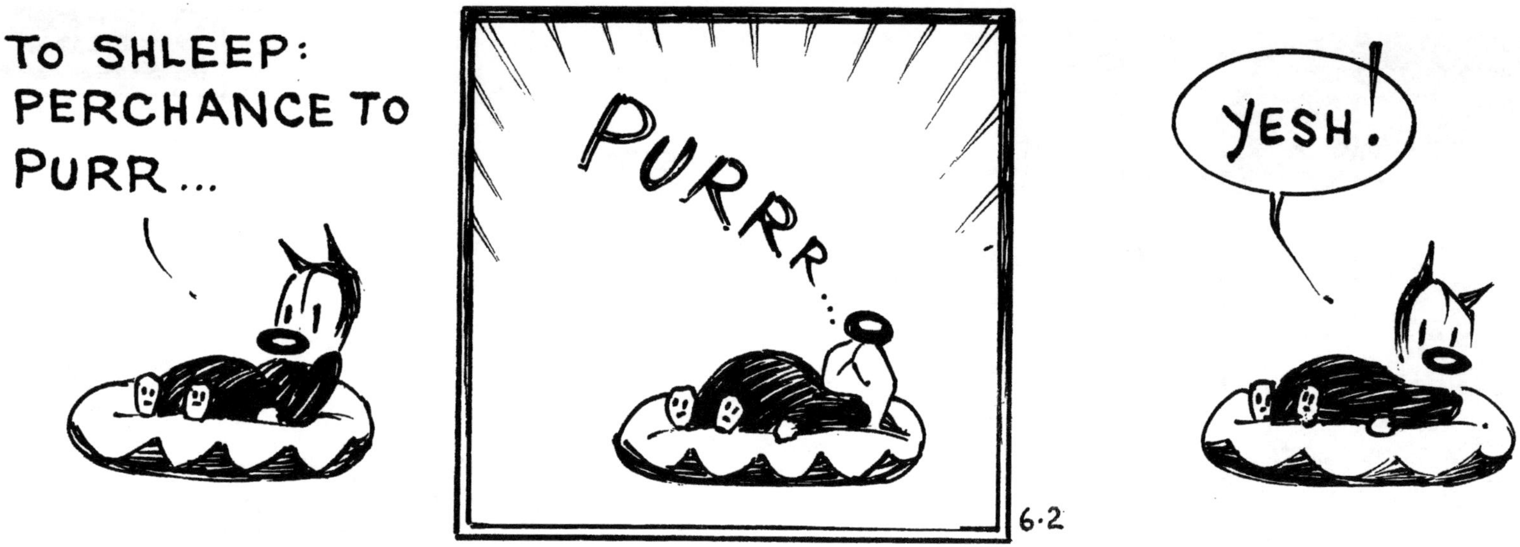
TO SHLEEP: PERCHANCE TO PURR...
PURRR...
6·2
YESH!

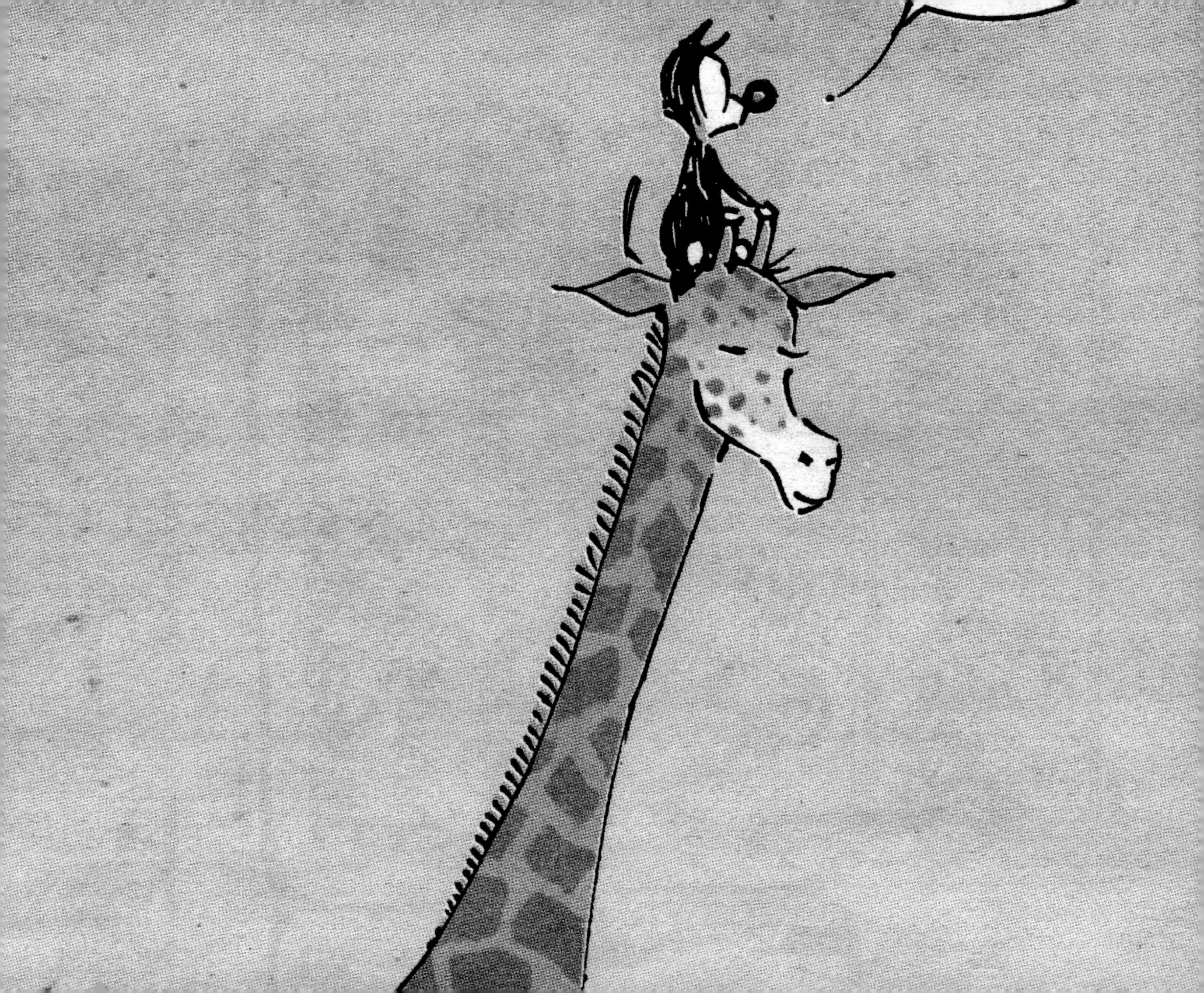

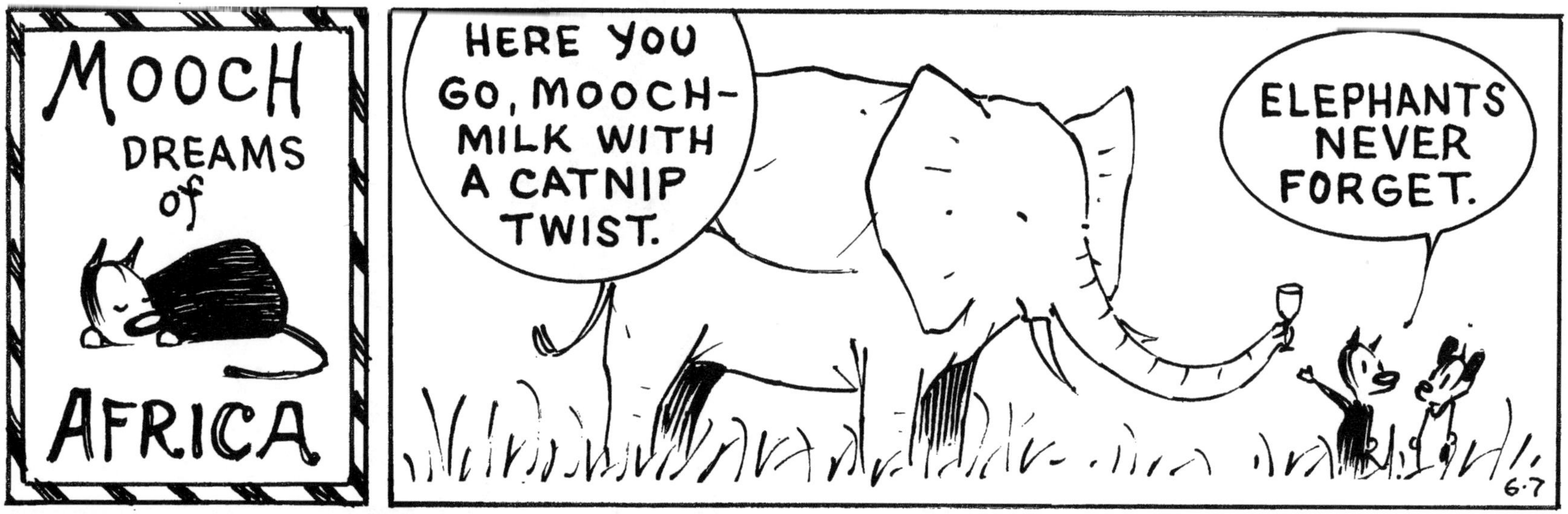
MOOCH DREAMS of AFRICA
HERE YOU GO, MOOCH-MILK WITH A CATNIP TWIST.
ELEPHANTS NEVER FORGET.
6·7

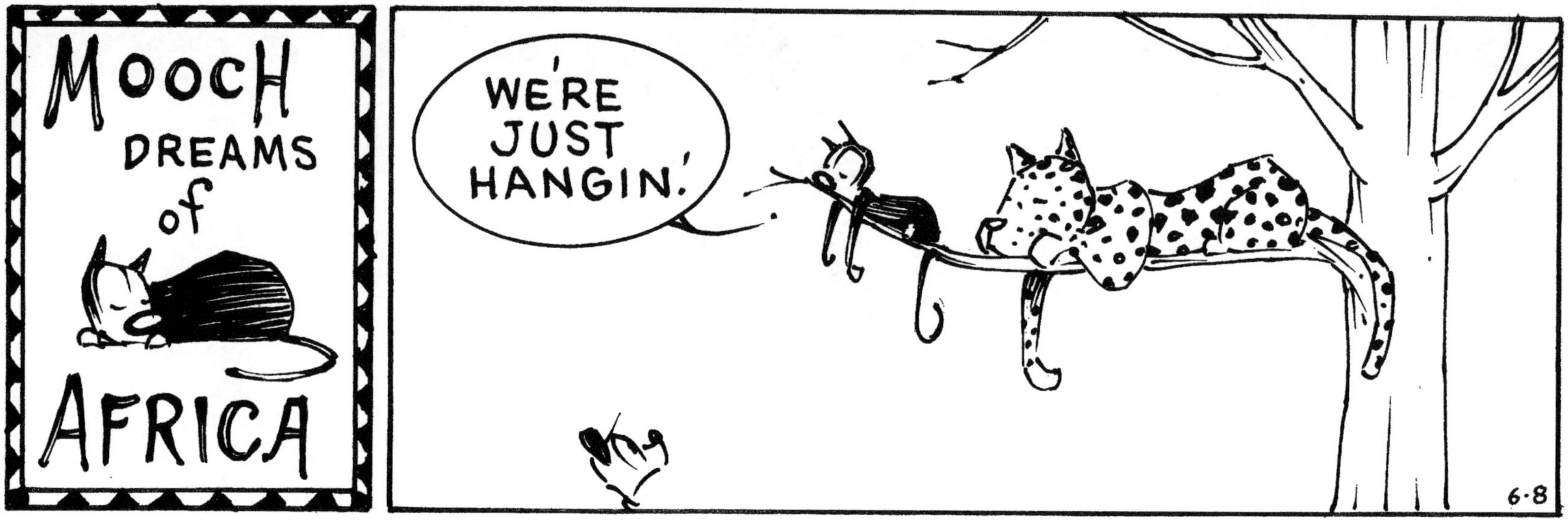
MOOCH DREAMS of AFRICA
WE'RE JUST HANGIN'.
6·8

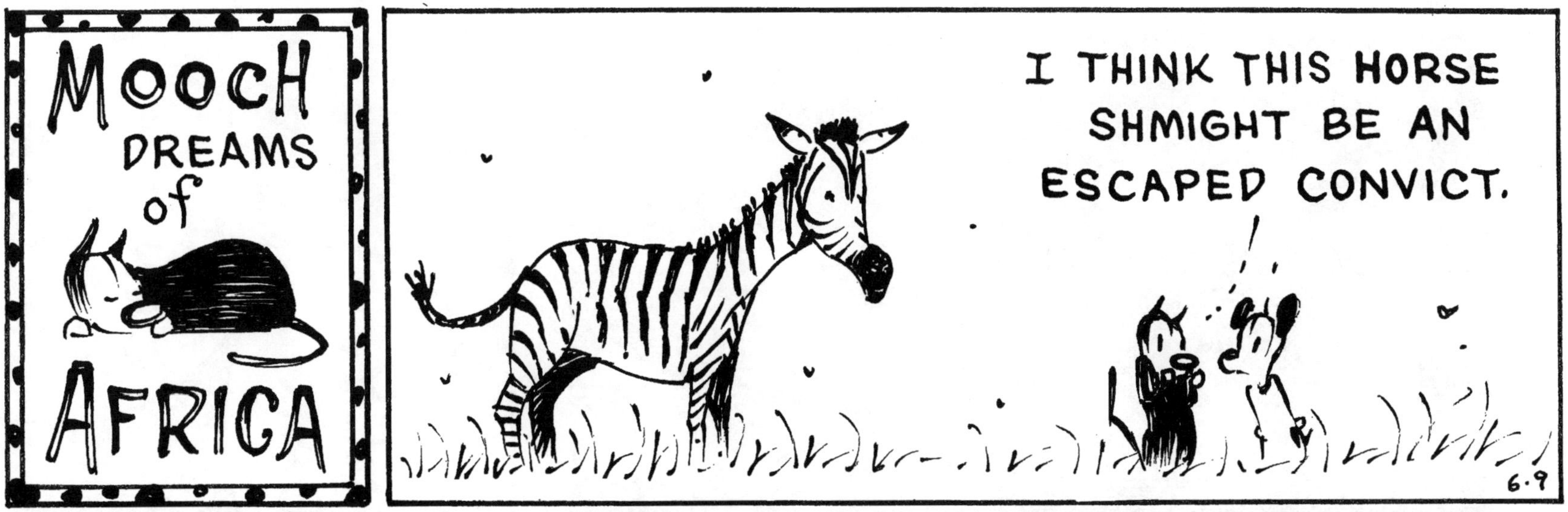
MOOCH DREAMS of AFRICA
I THINK THIS HORSE SHMIGHT BE AN ESCAPED CONVICT.
6·9

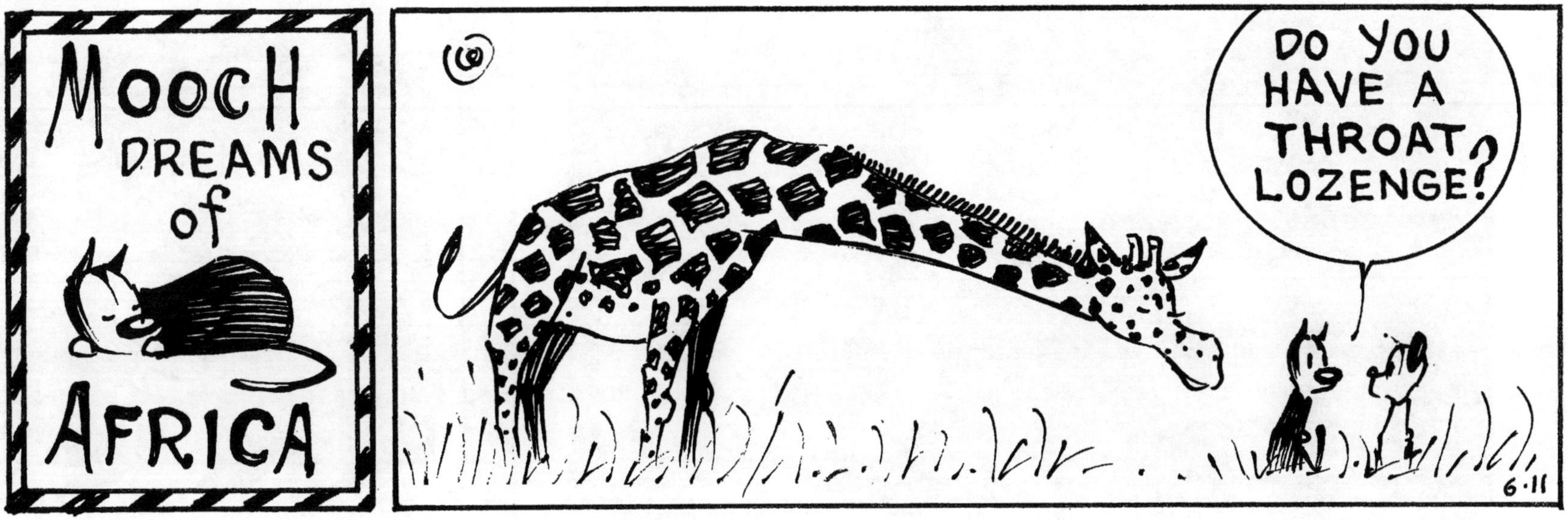
MOOCH DREAMS of AFRICA
DO YOU HAVE A THROAT LOZENGE?
6·11

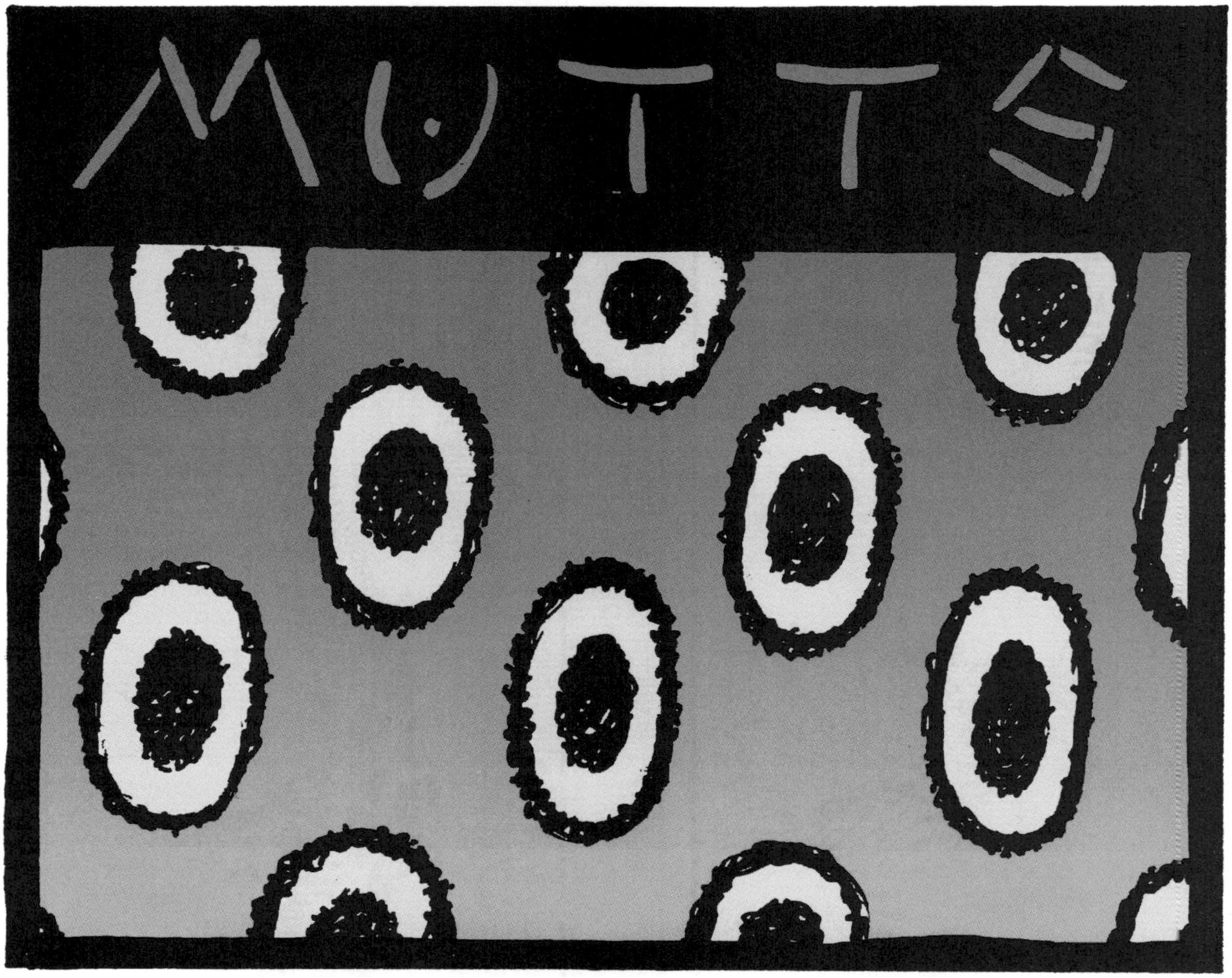
MUTTS

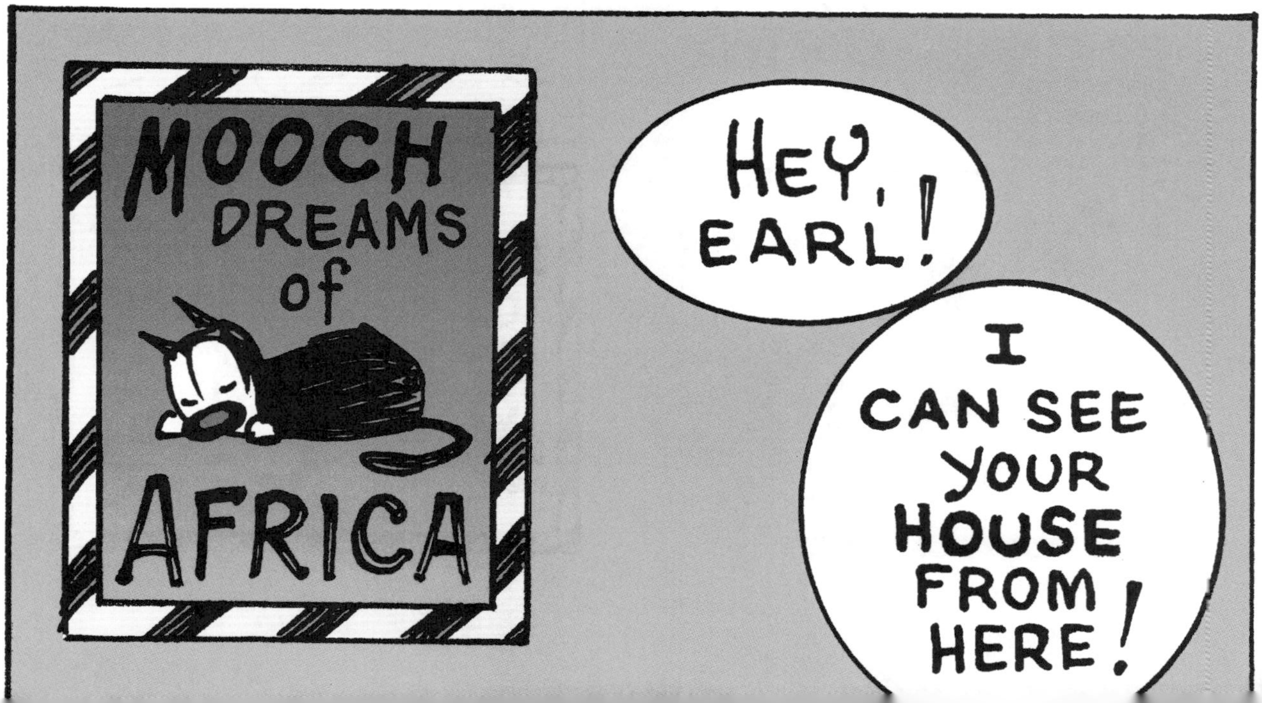
MOOCH DREAMS of AFRICA
HEY, EARL!
I CAN SEE YOUR HOUSE FROM HERE!

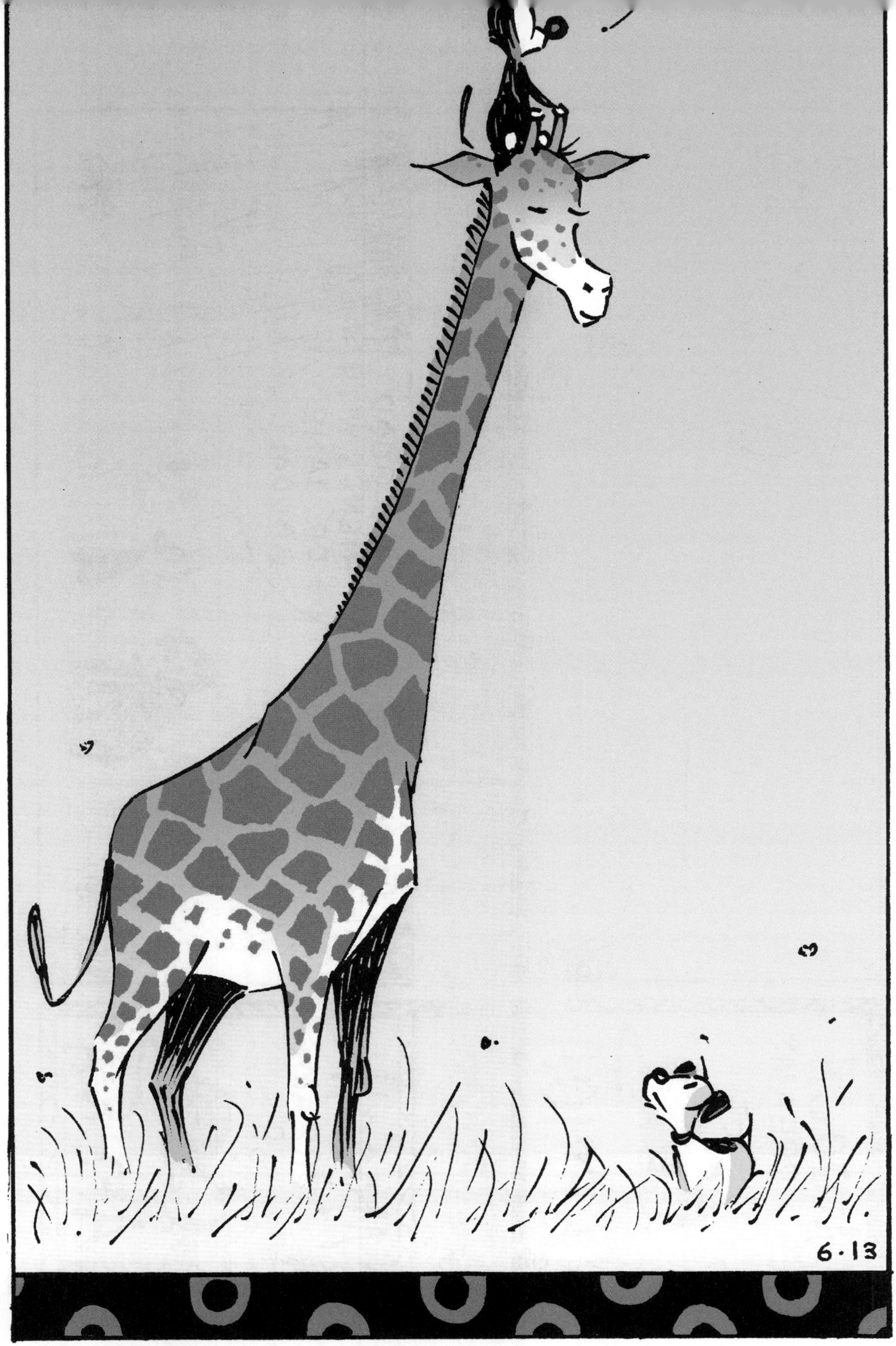
6-13

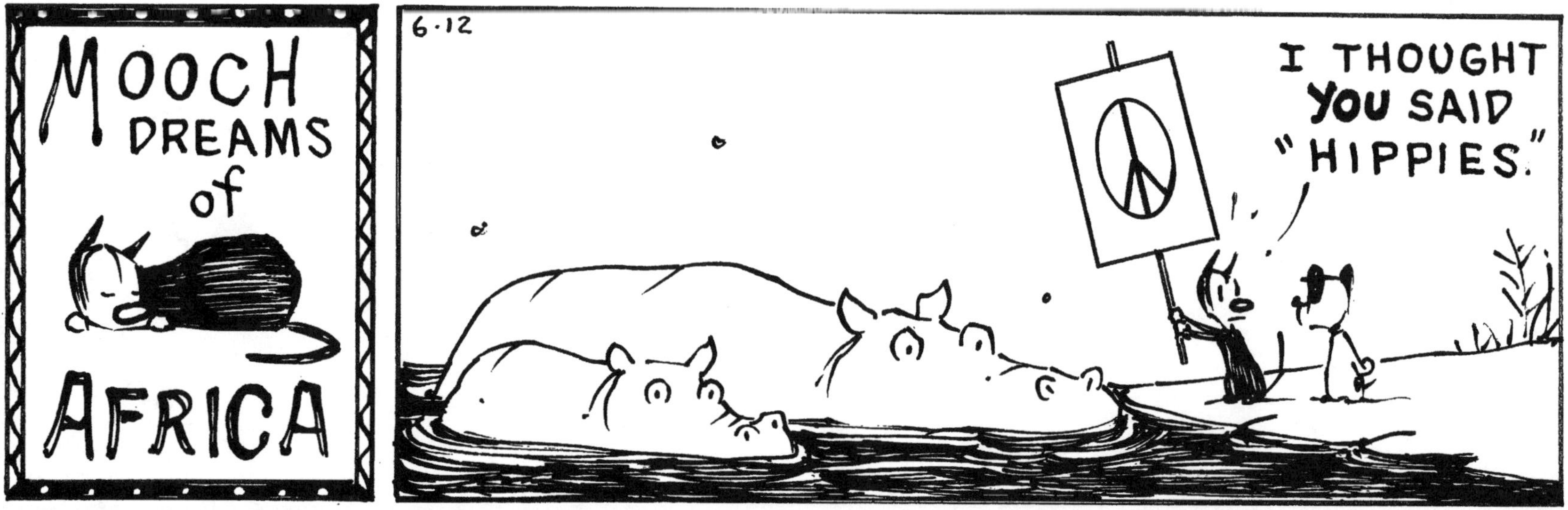
MOOCH DREAMS of AFRICA
6·12
I THOUGHT YOU SAID "HIPPIES."

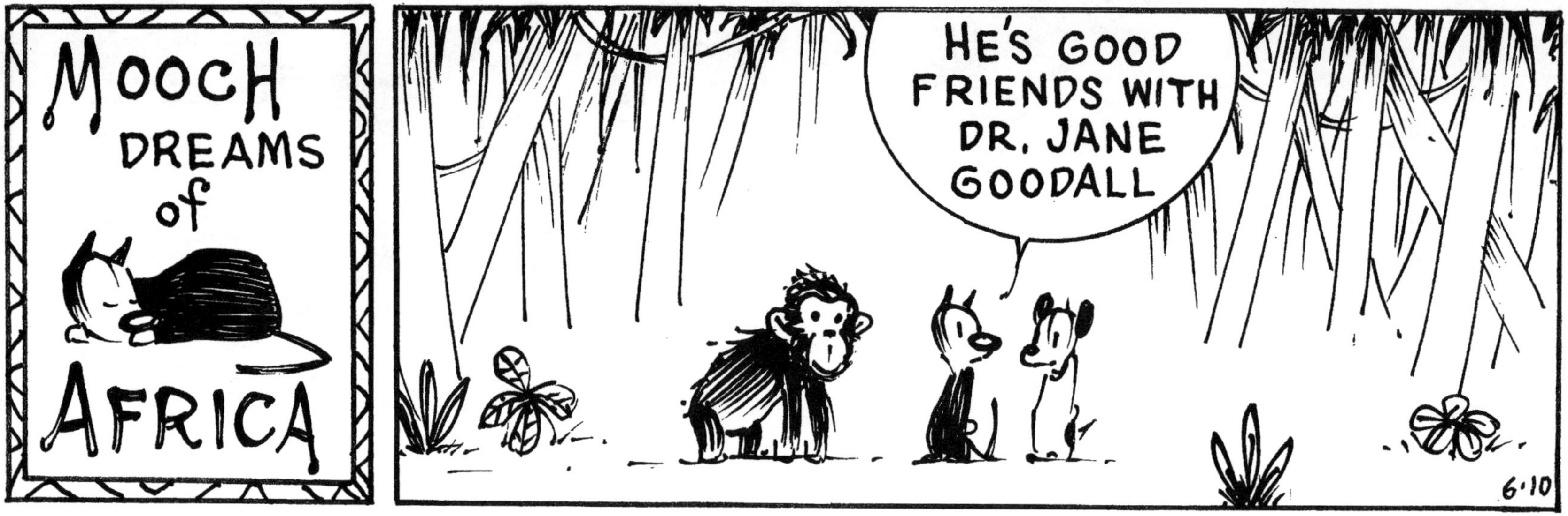
MOOCH DREAMS of AFRICA
HE'S GOOD FRIENDS WITH DR. JANE GOODALL
6·10

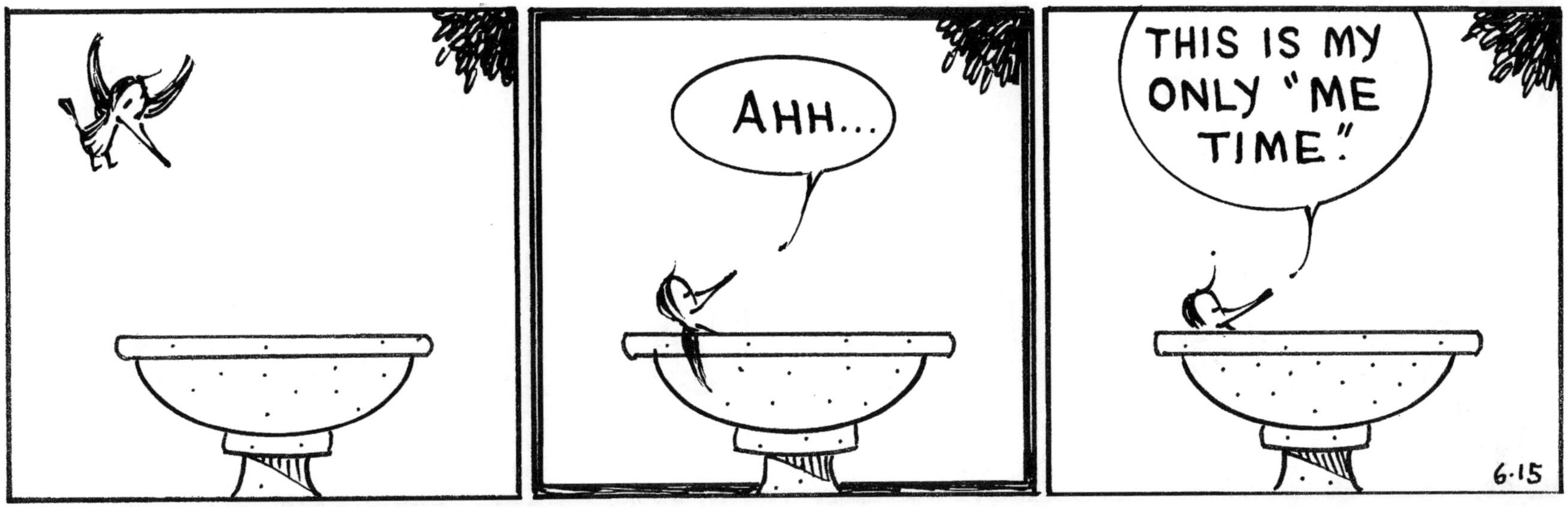
AHH...
THIS IS MY ONLY "ME TIME."
6·15

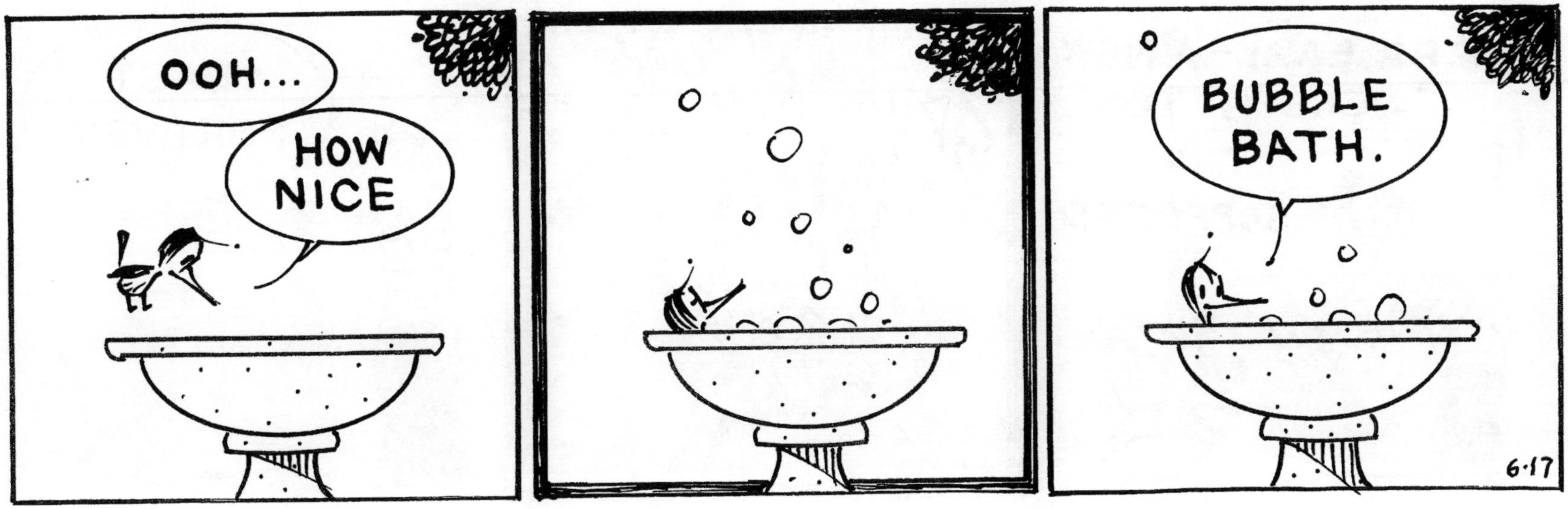
OOH...
HOW NICE
BUBBLE BATH.
6·17

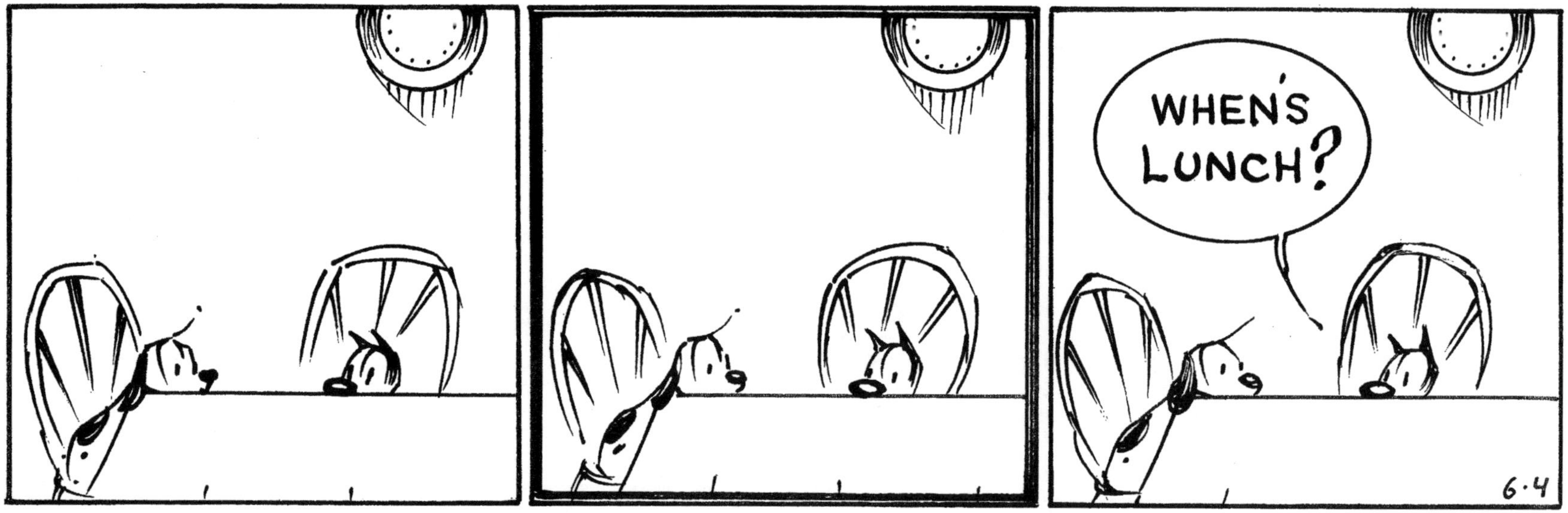
WHEN'S LUNCH?
6·4

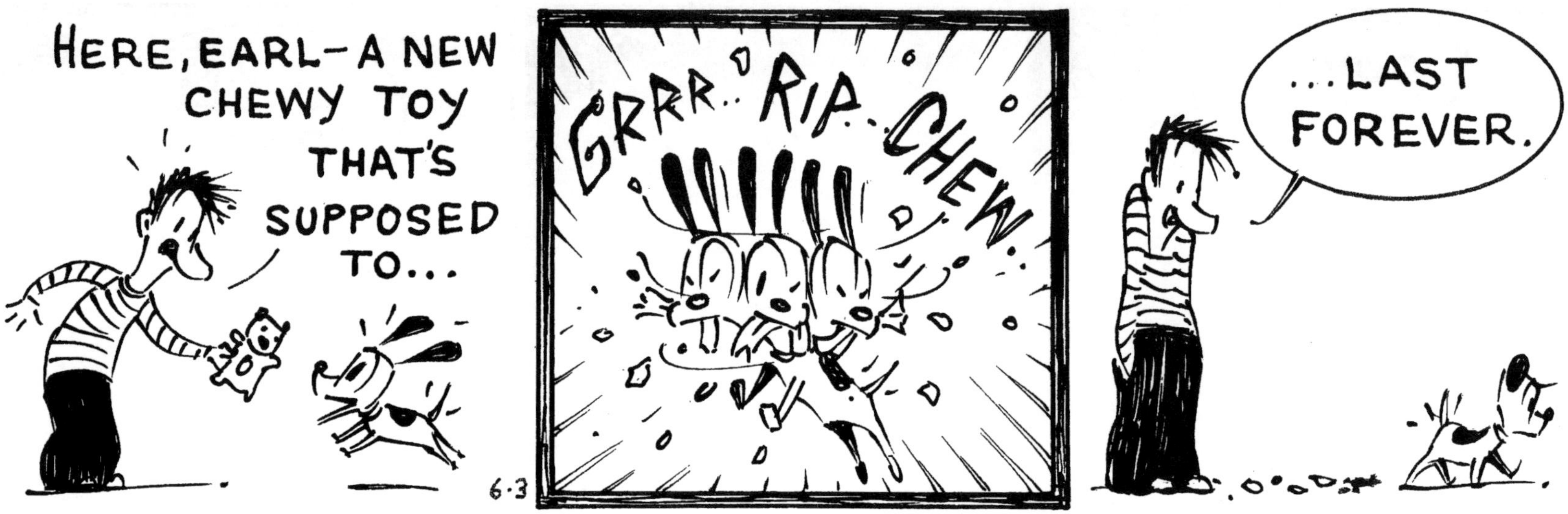
HERE, EARL—A NEW CHEWY TOY THAT'S SUPPOSED TO...
6·3
GRRR.. RIP.. CHEW..
...LAST FOREVER.

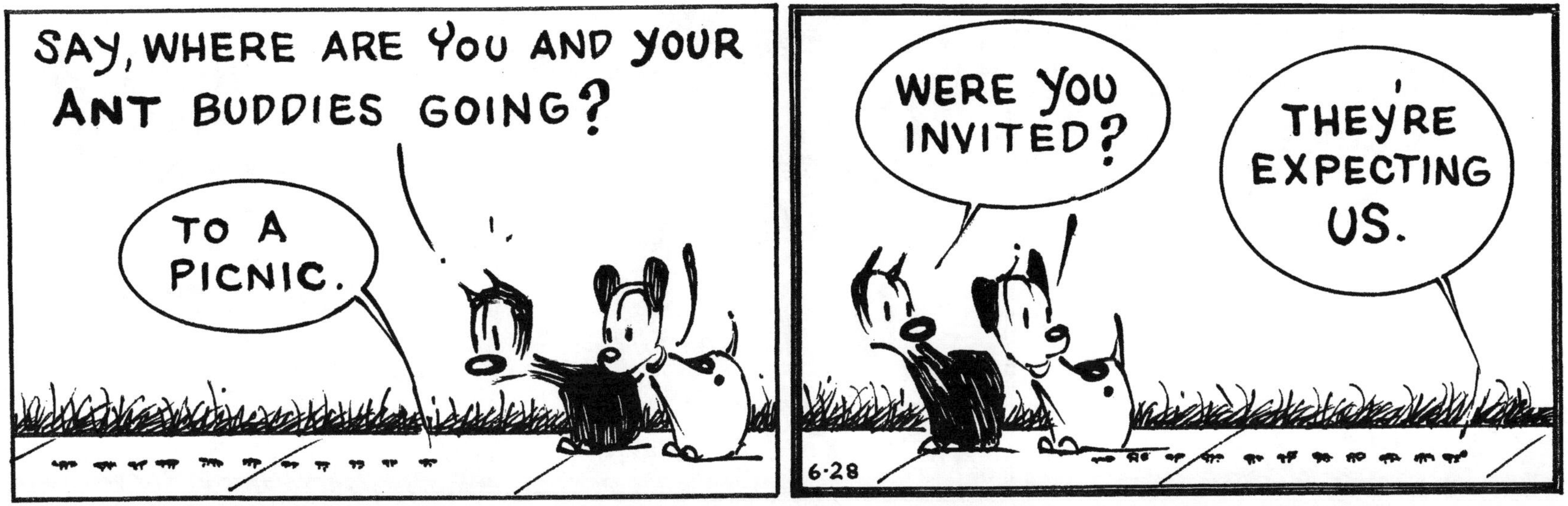
SAY, WHERE ARE YOU AND YOUR ANT BUDDIES GOING?
TO A PICNIC.
WERE YOU INVITED?
THEY'RE EXPECTING US.
6·28

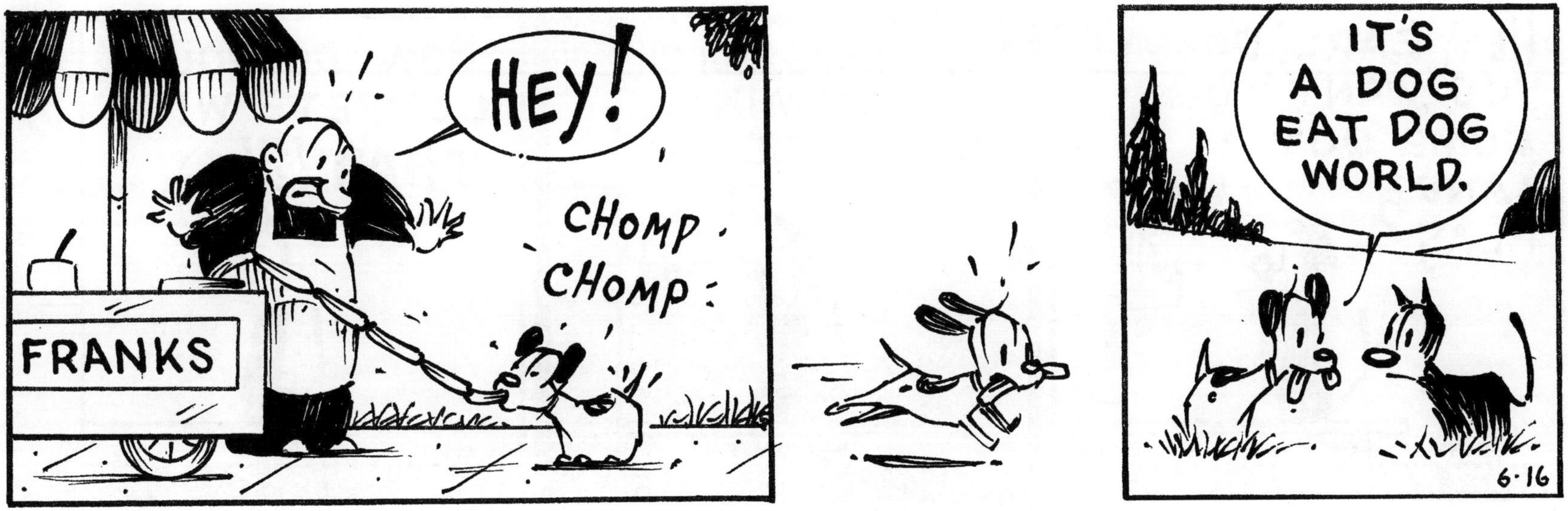
FRANKS
HEY!
CHOMP CHOMP
IT'S A DOG EAT DOG WORLD.
6·16

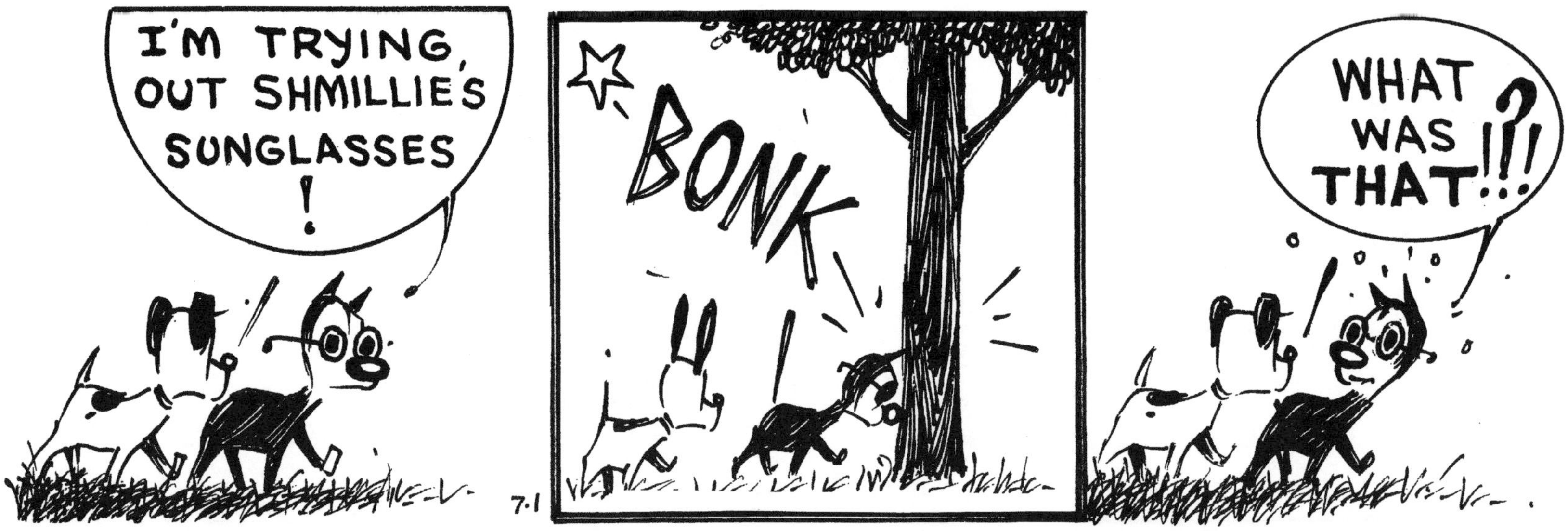
I'M TRYING, OUT SHMILLIE'S SUNGLASSES!
7·1
BONK
WHAT WAS THAT?!!!

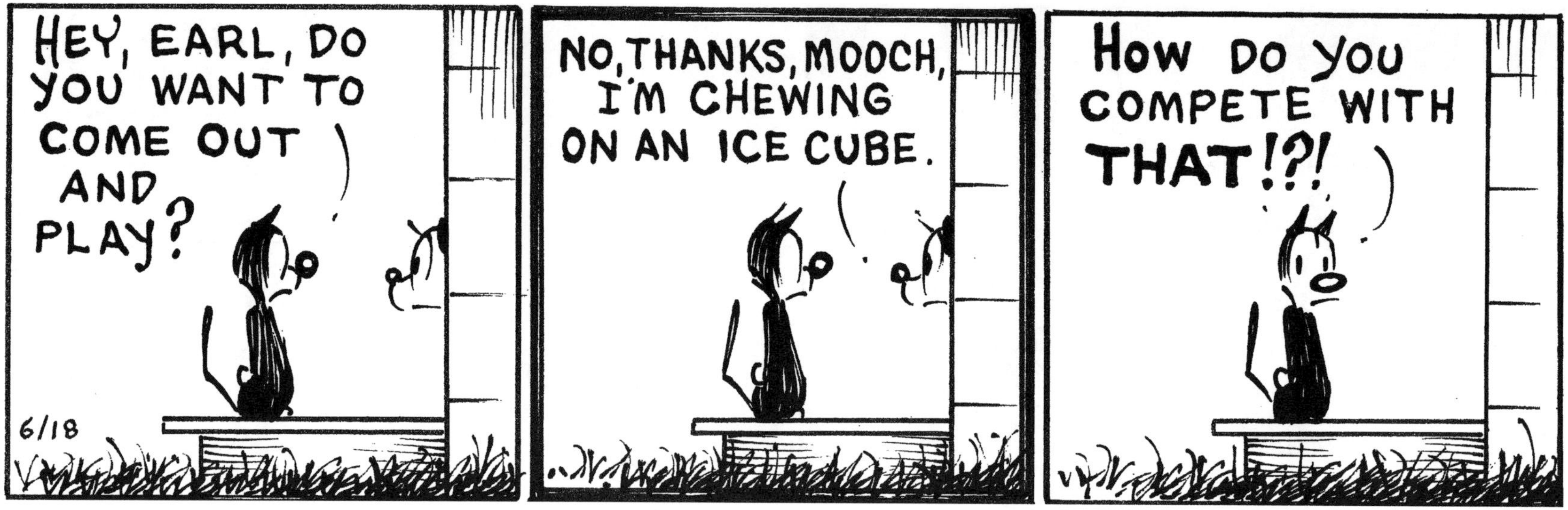
HEY, EARL, DO YOU WANT TO COME OUT AND PLAY?
6/18
NO, THANKS, MOOCH, I'M CHEWING ON AN ICE CUBE.
HOW DO YOU COMPETE WITH THAT!?!

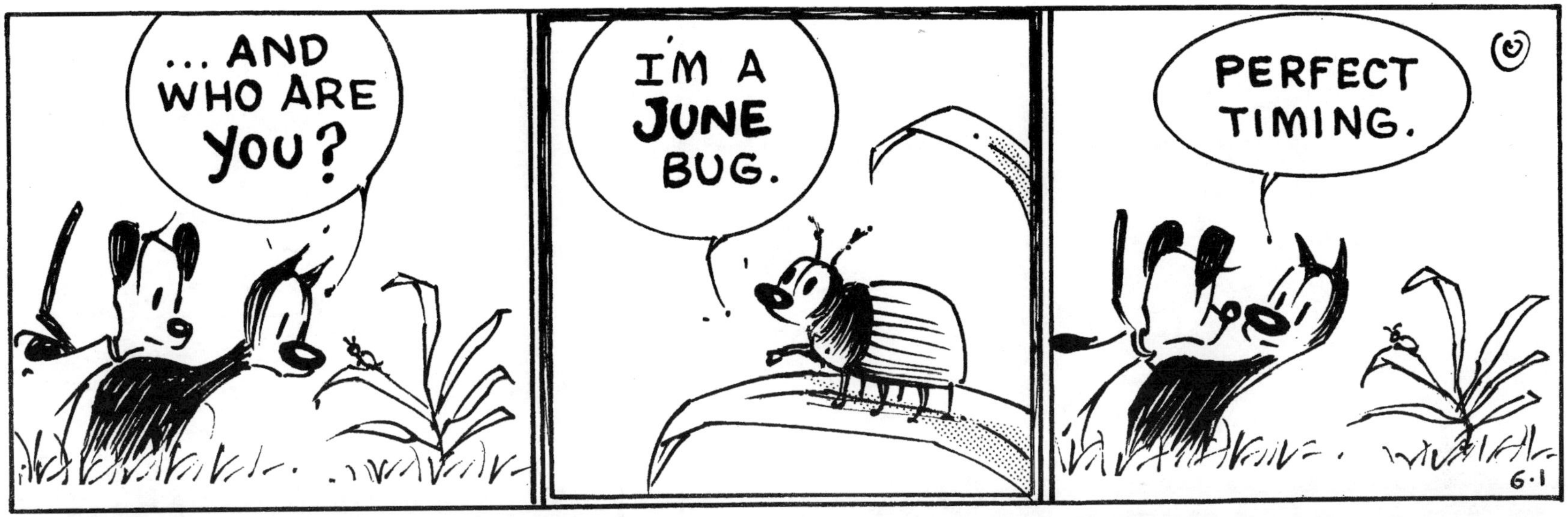
... AND WHO ARE YOU?
I'M A JUNE BUG.
PERFECT TIMING.
6·1

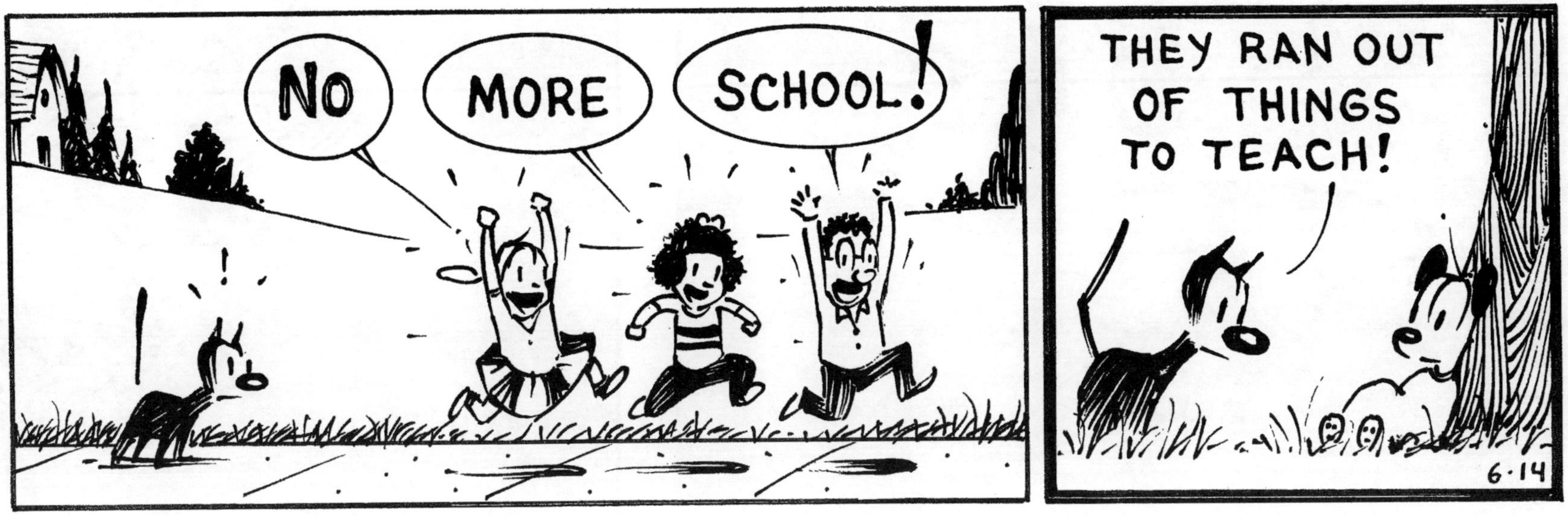
NO
MORE
SCHOOL!
THEY RAN OUT OF THINGS TO TEACH!
6·14

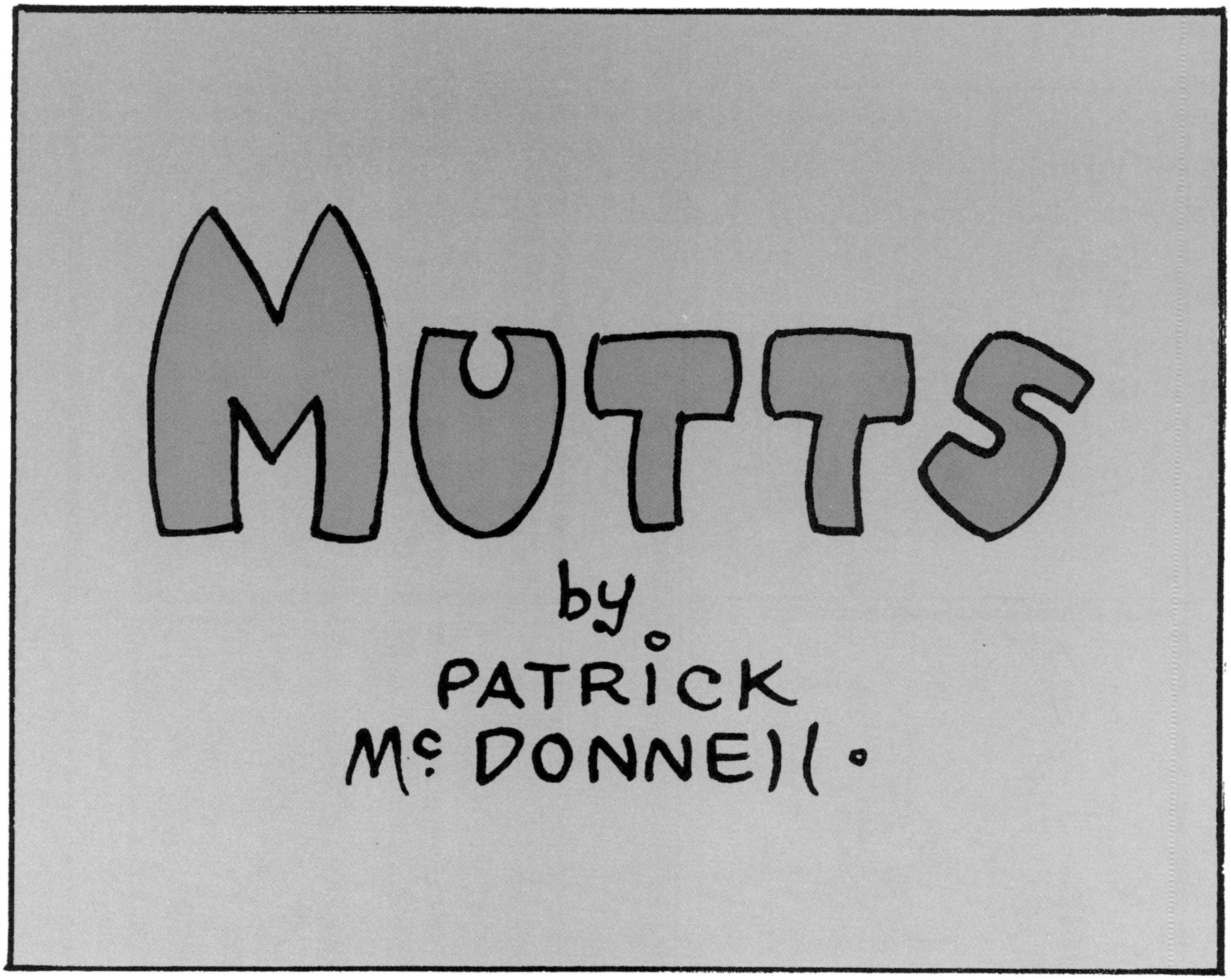
MUTTS
by
PATRICK
McDONNELL

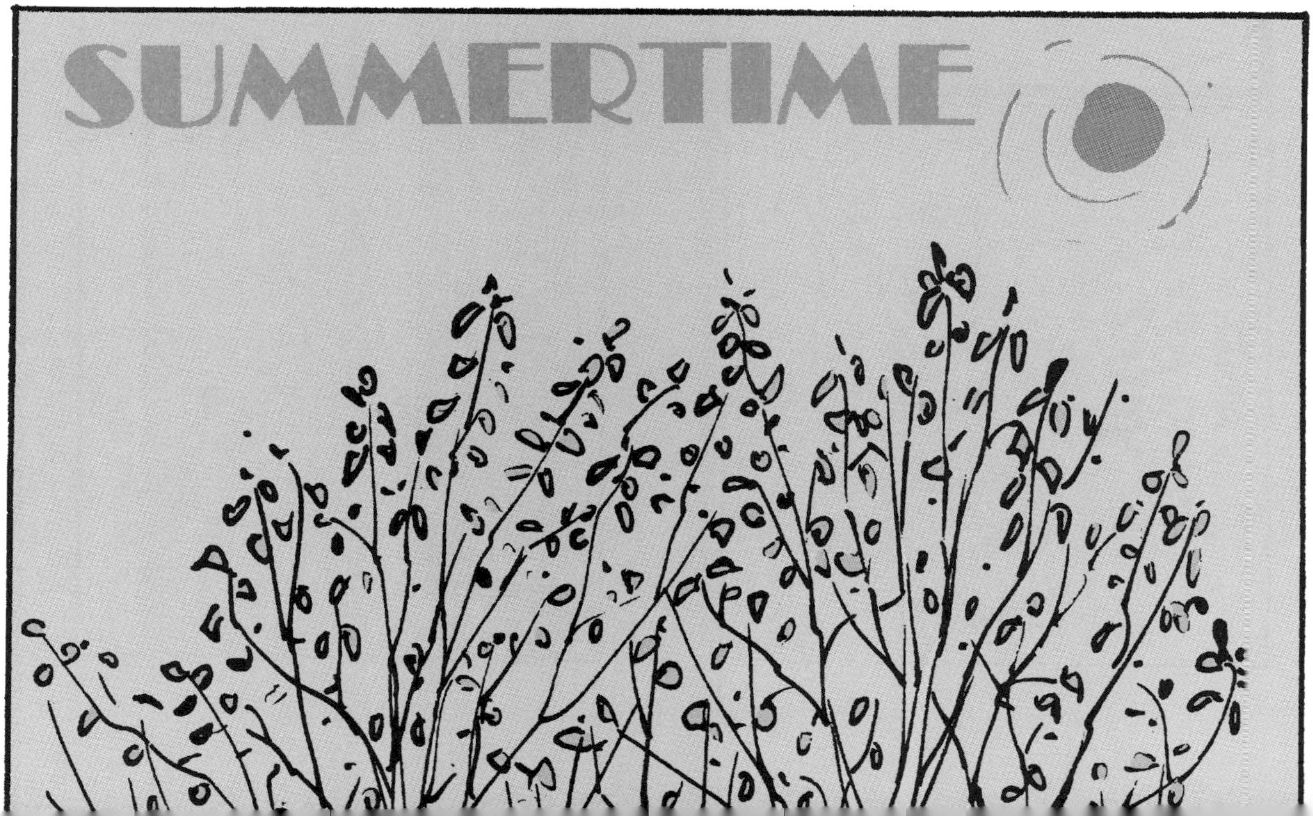
SUMMERTIME

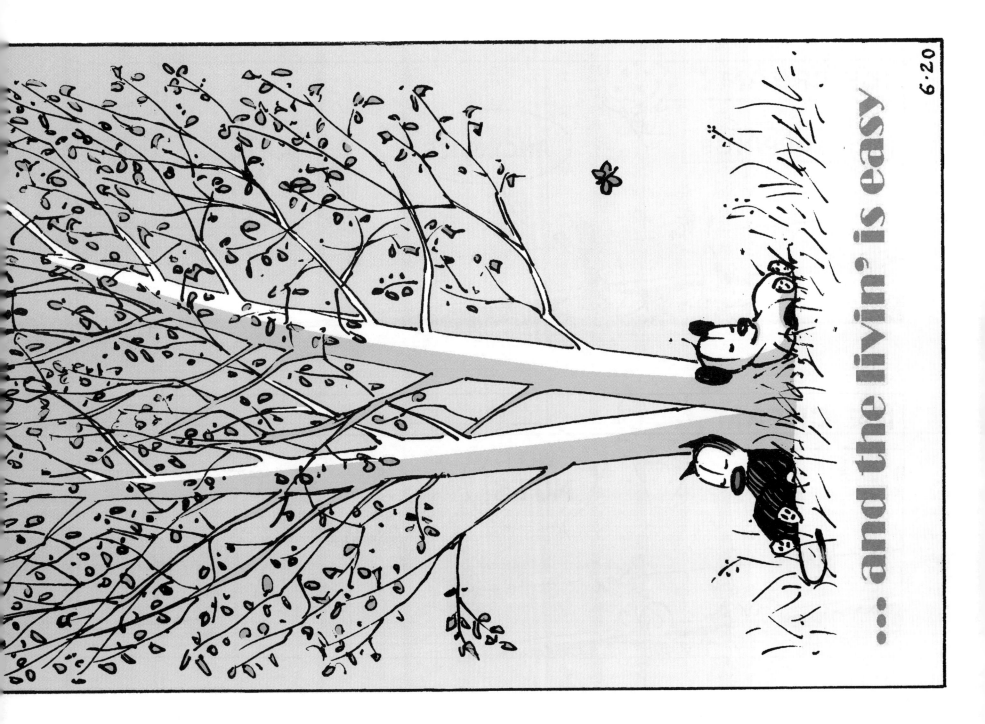

... and the livin' is easy

6.20

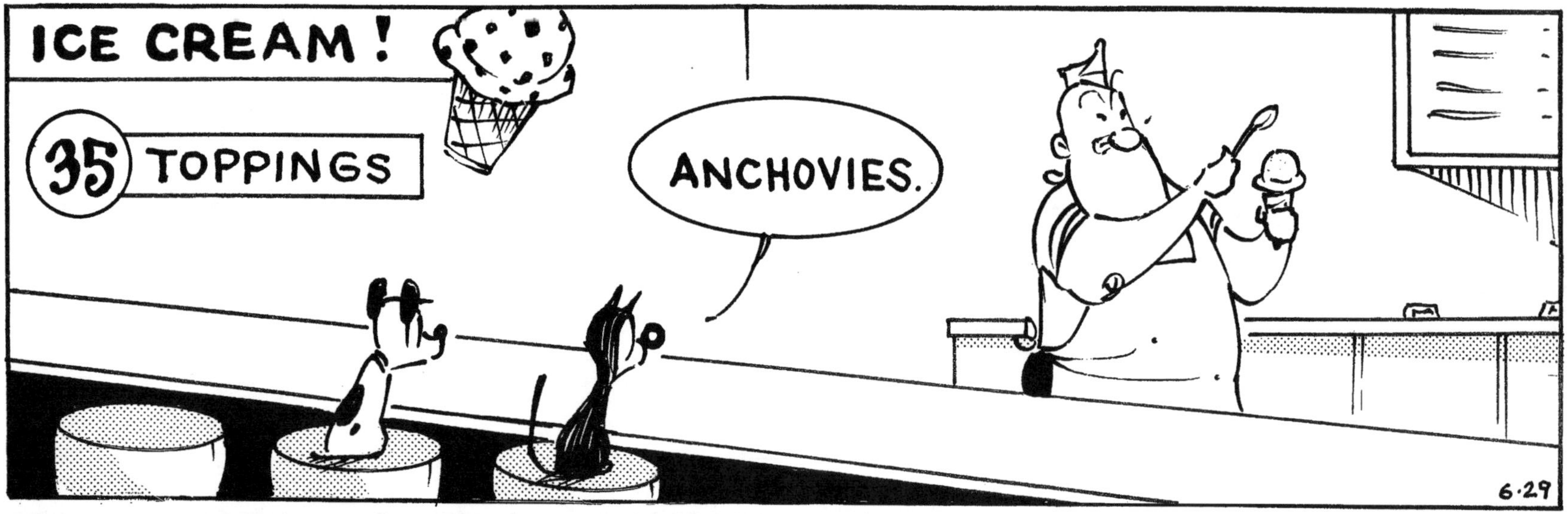
ICE CREAM!
35 TOPPINGS
ANCHOVIES.
6·29

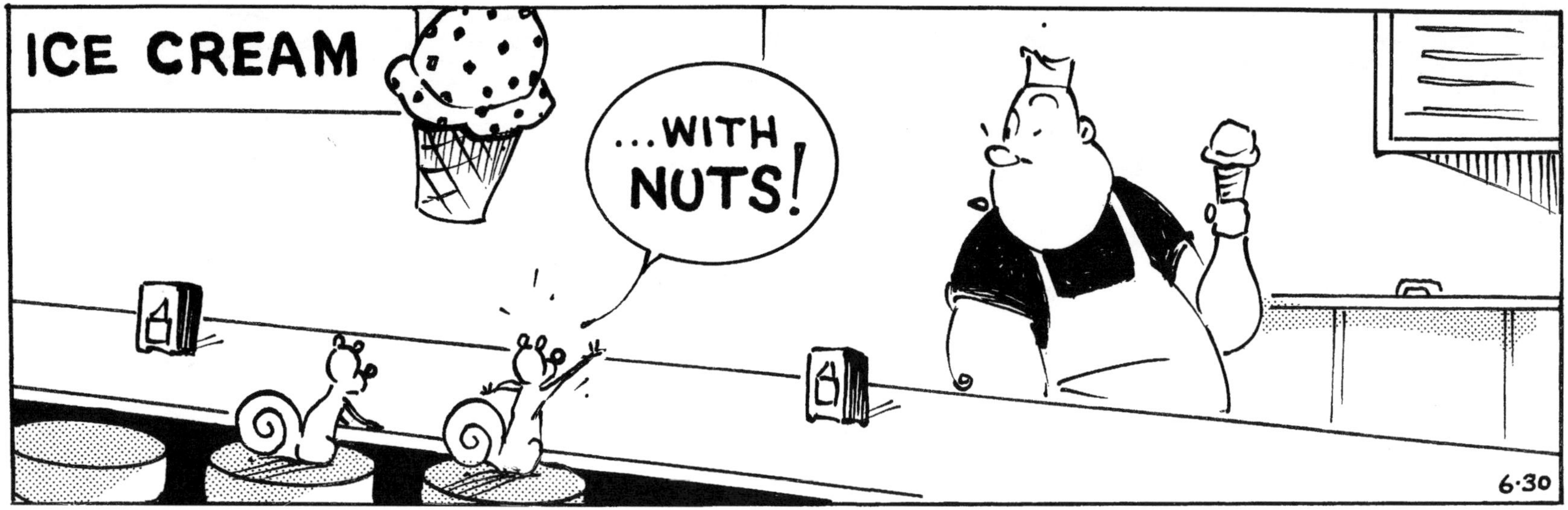
ICE CREAM
...WITH NUTS!
6·30

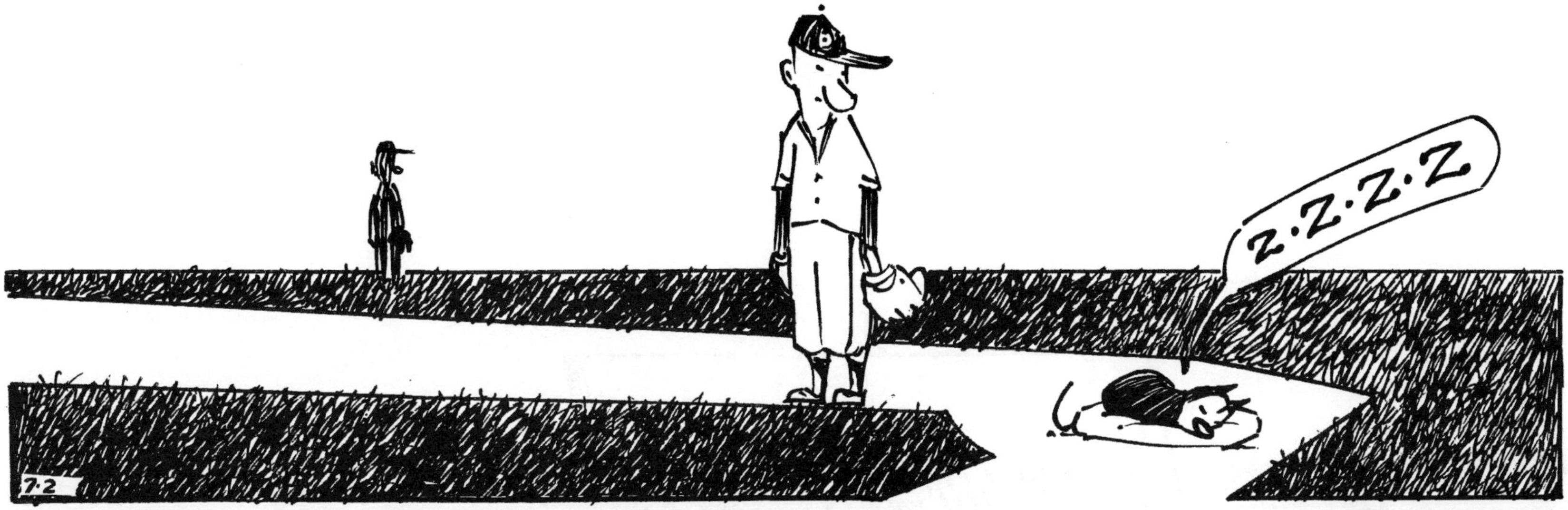

Z·Z·Z·Z·Z
7·2

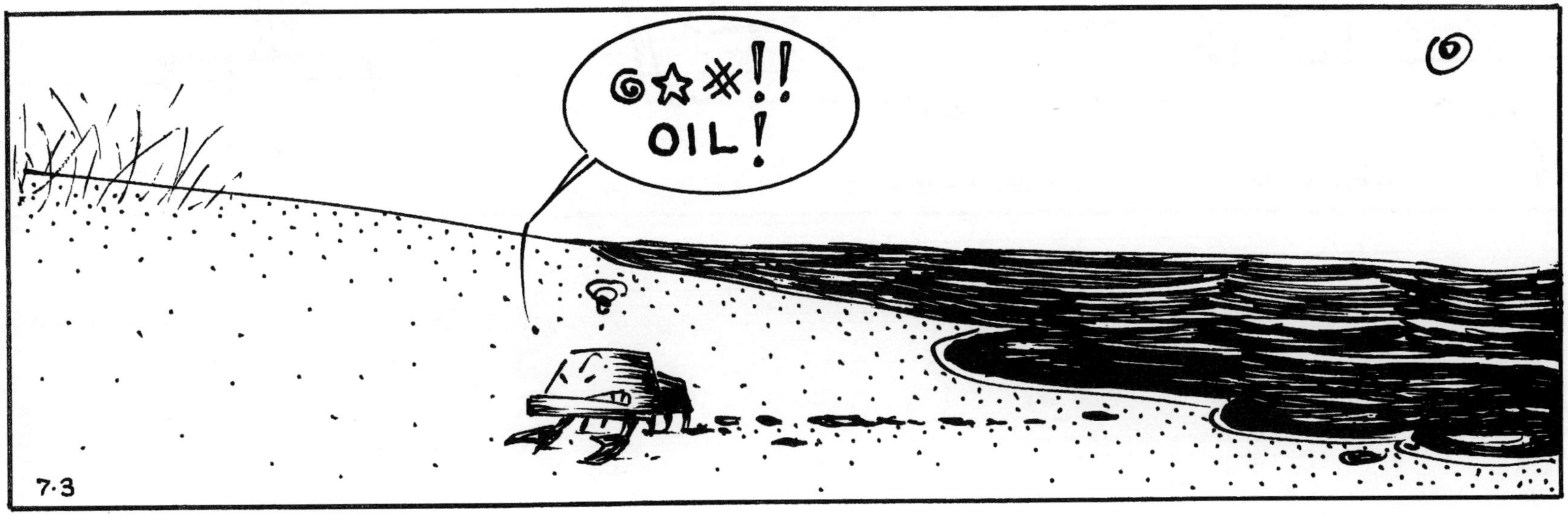

@☆※!! OIL!
7·3

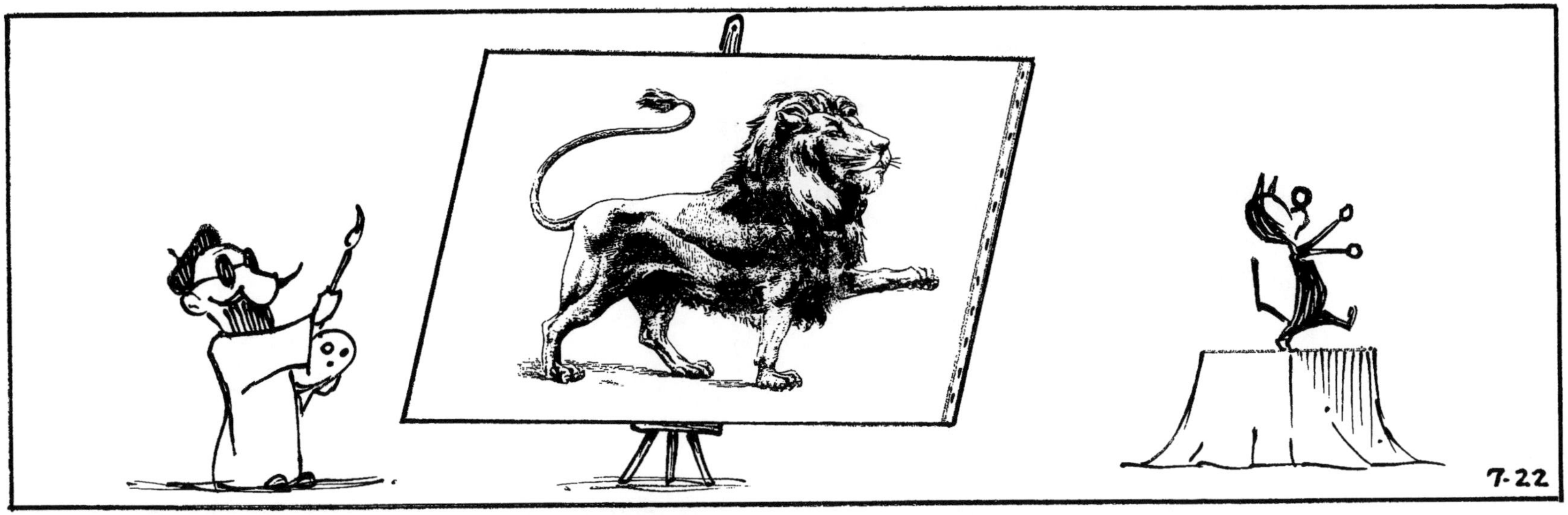
7-22

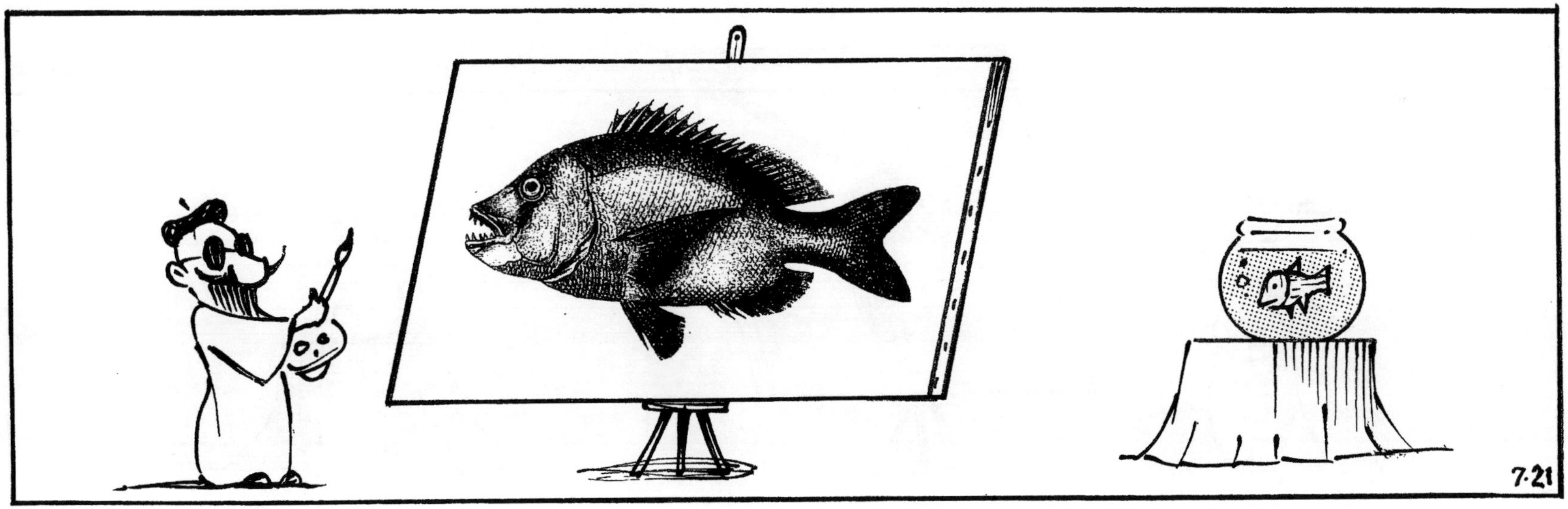
7-21

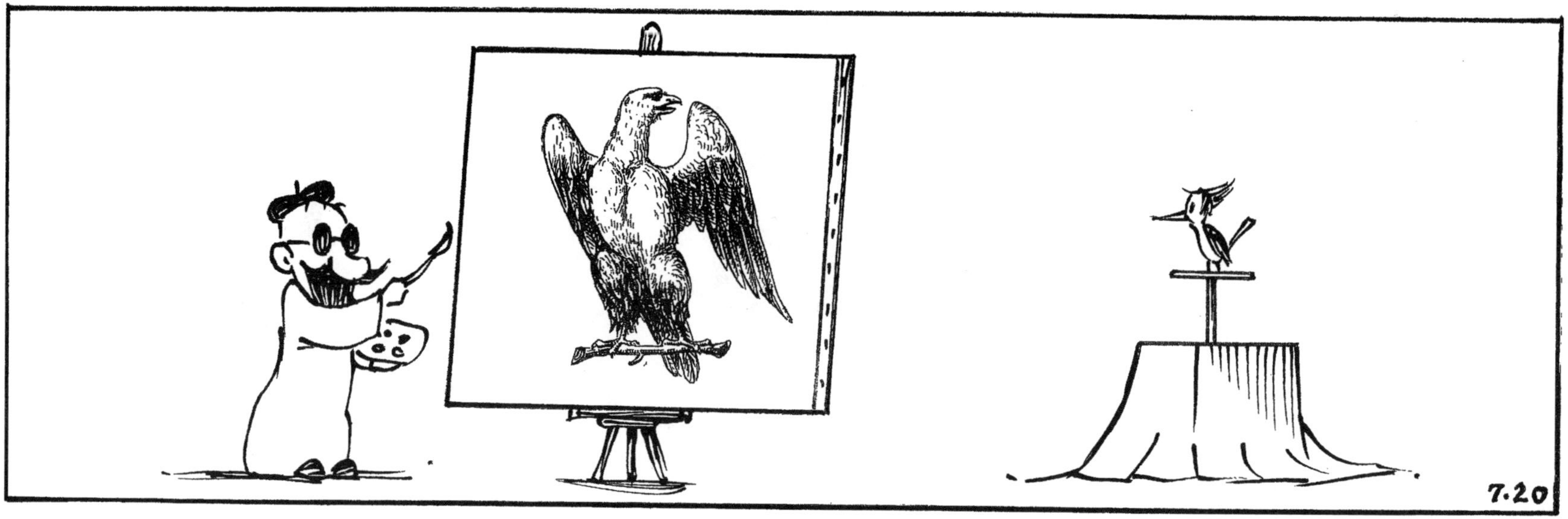
7.20

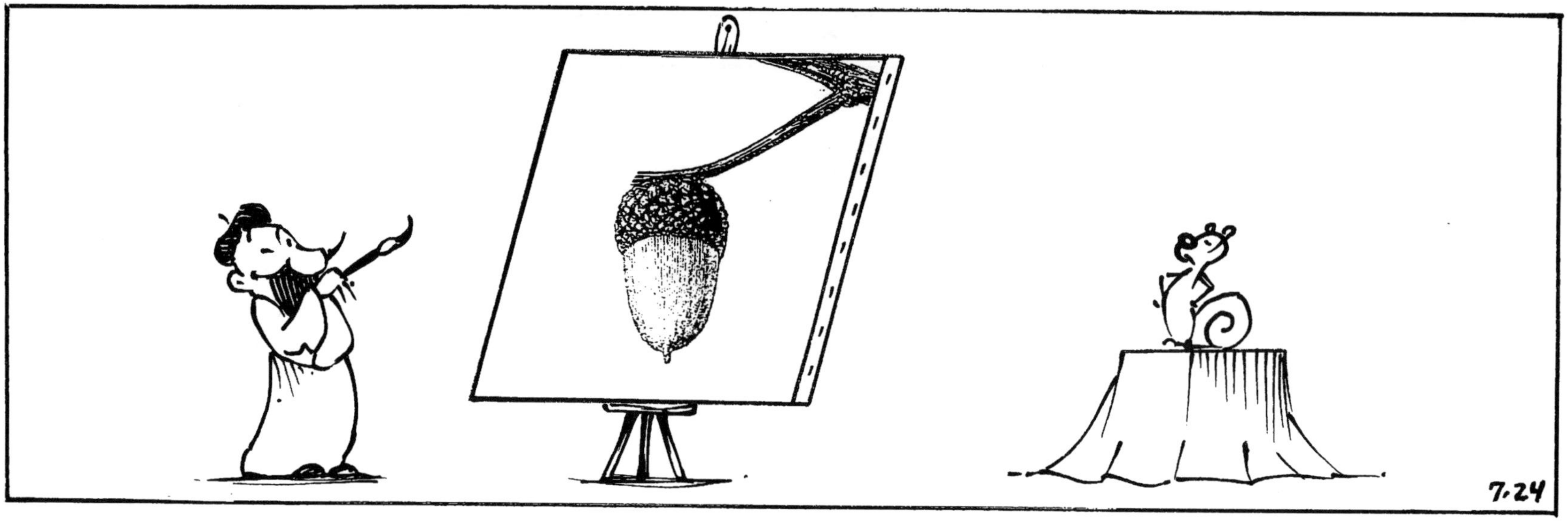
7.24

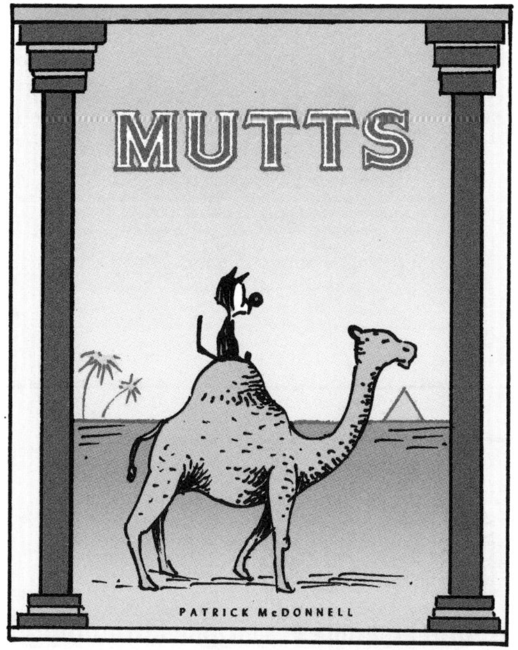
MUTTS
PATRICK McDONNELL

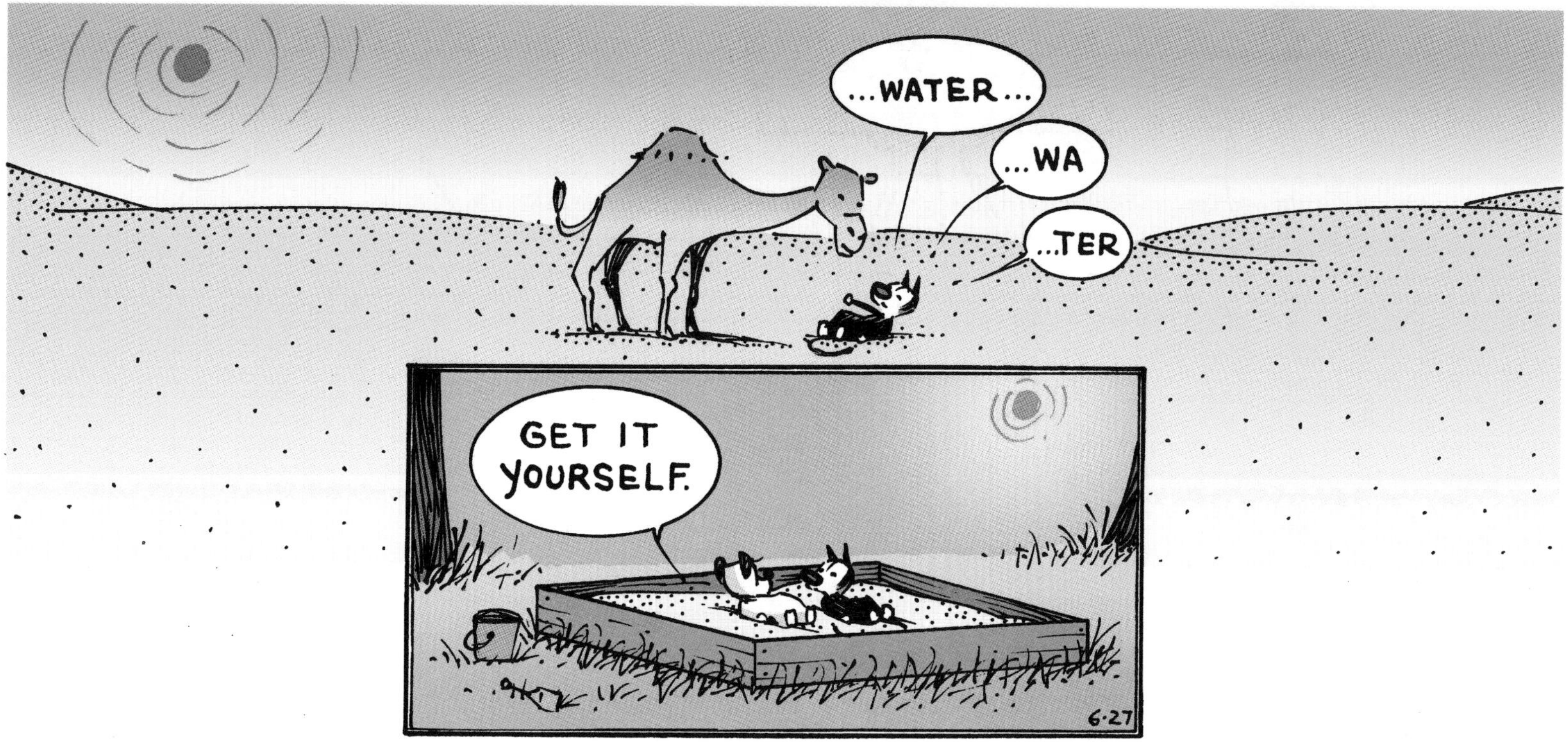
...WATER...
...WA
...TER
GET IT YOURSELF.
6-27

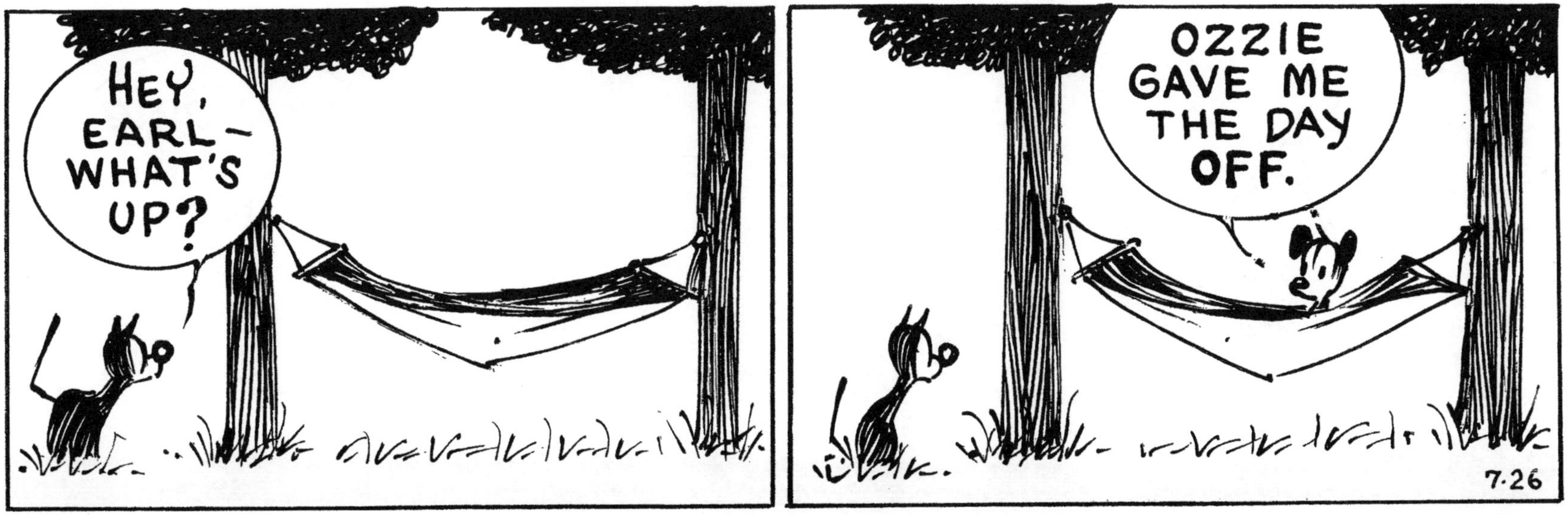
HEY, EARL– WHAT'S UP?
OZZIE GAVE ME THE DAY OFF.
7·26

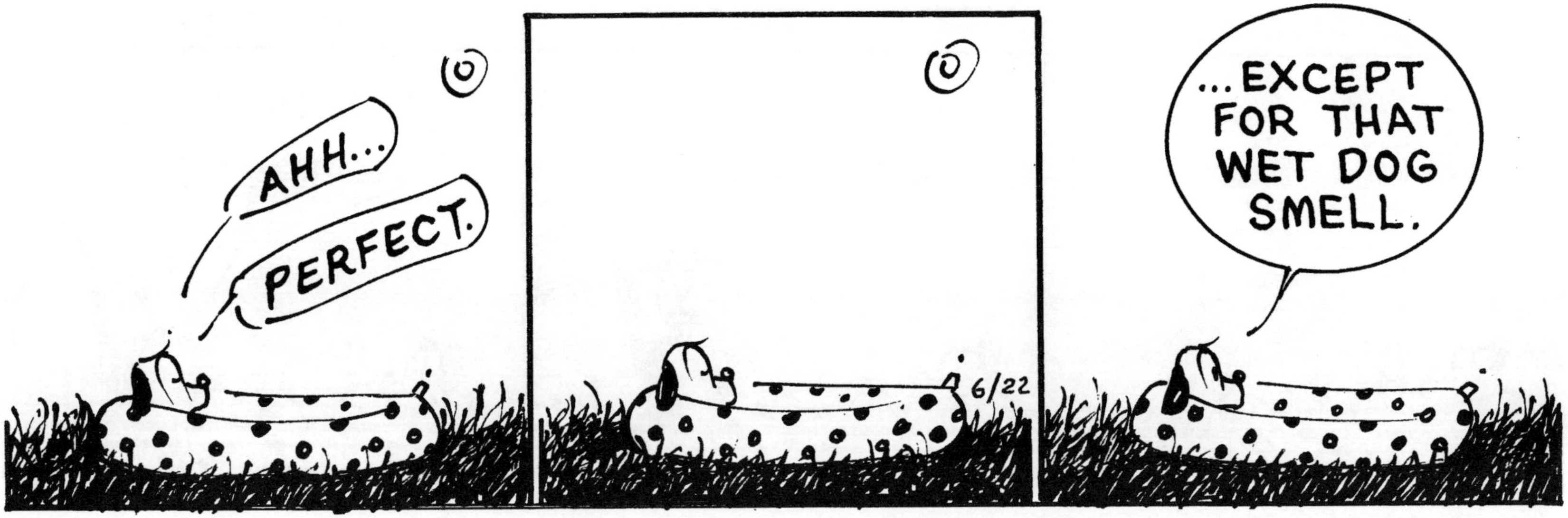
AHH...
PERFECT.
6/22
...EXCEPT FOR THAT WET DOG SMELL.

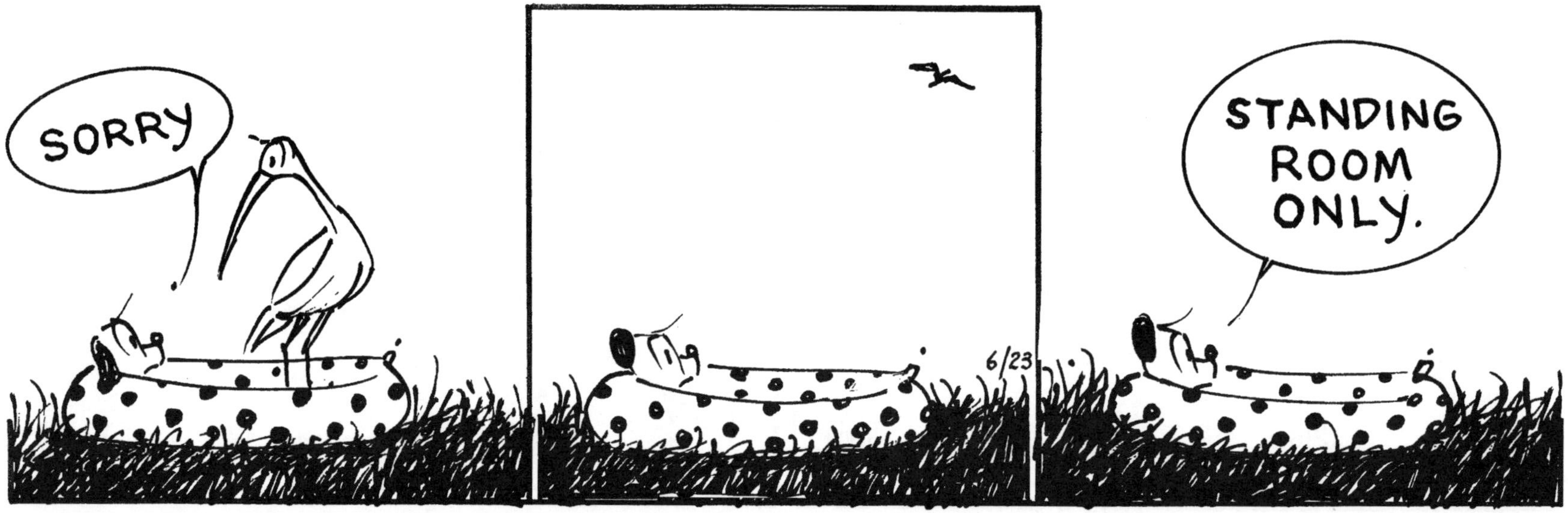
SORRY
6/23
STANDING ROOM ONLY.

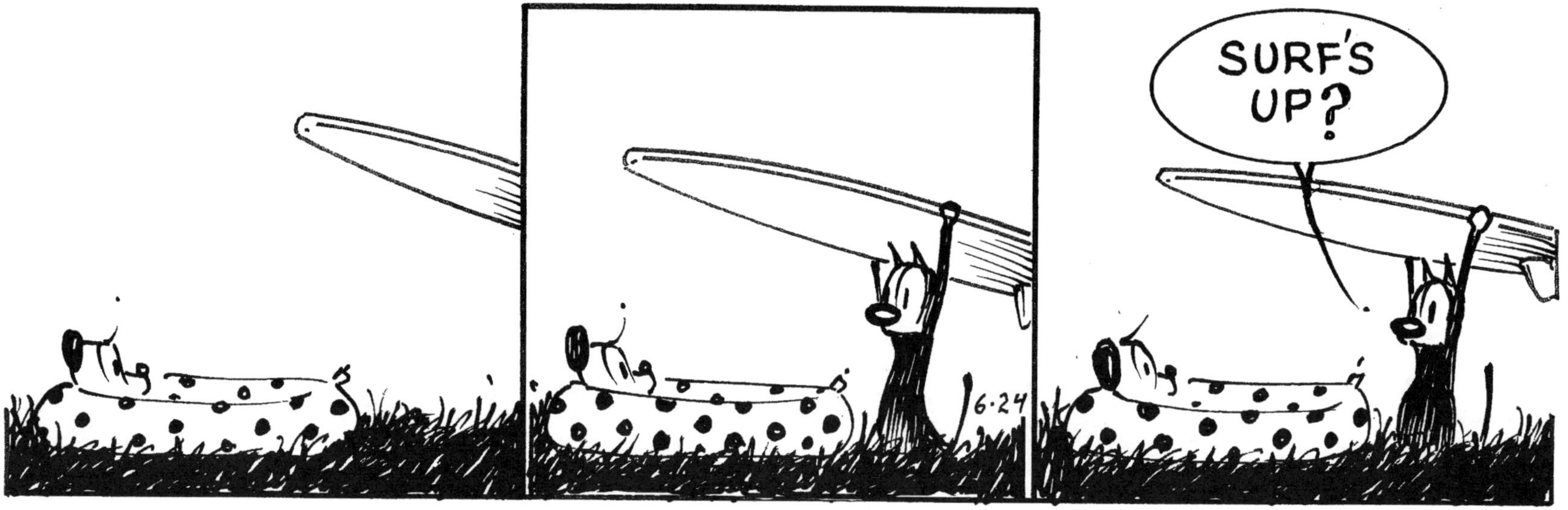
6·24
SURF'S UP?

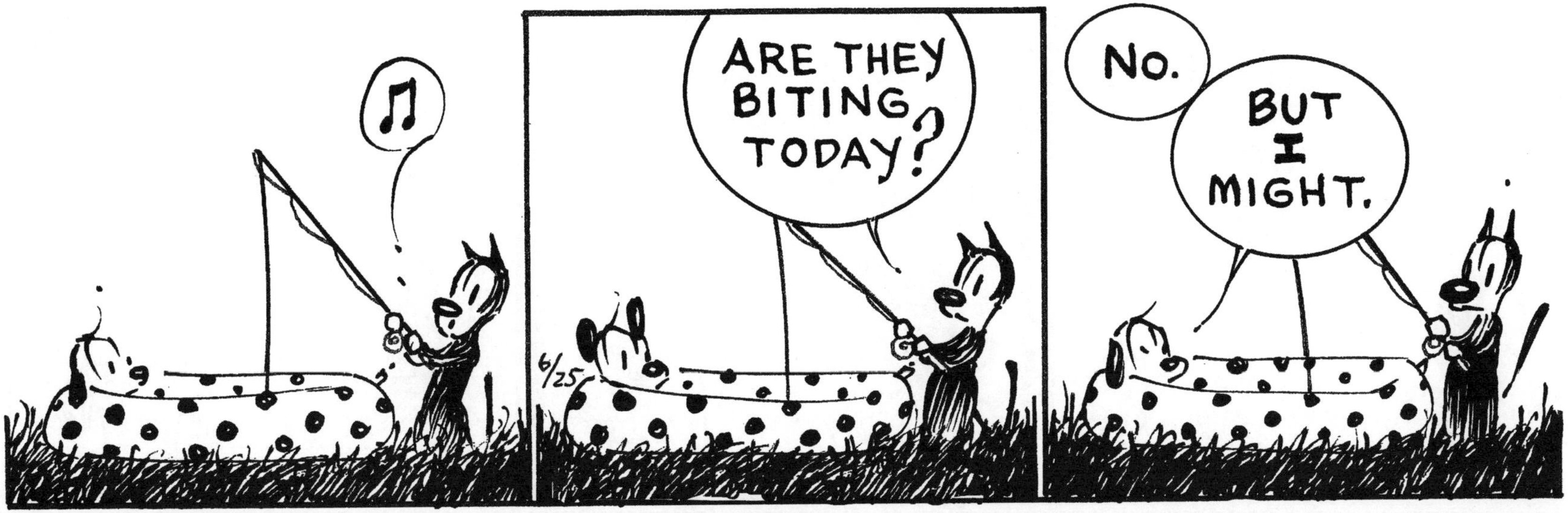
ARE THEY BITING TODAY?
6/25
NO.
BUT I MIGHT.

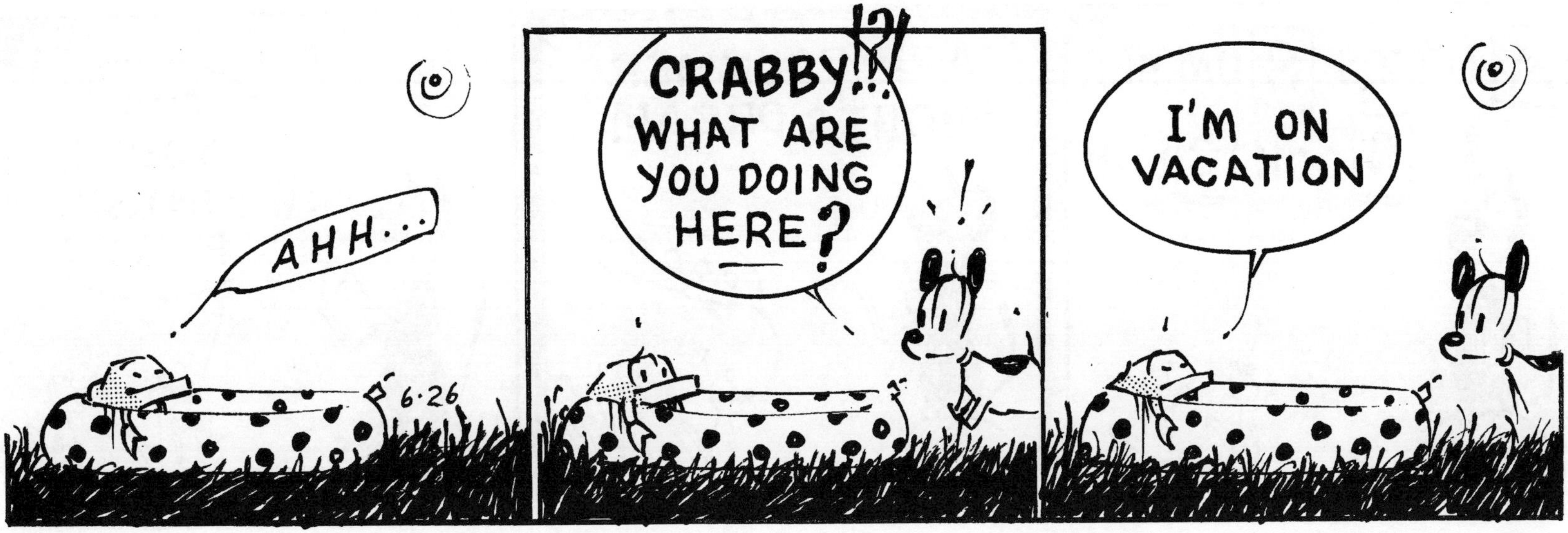
AHH...
6·26
CRABBY!!
WHAT ARE YOU DOING HERE?
I'M ON VACATION

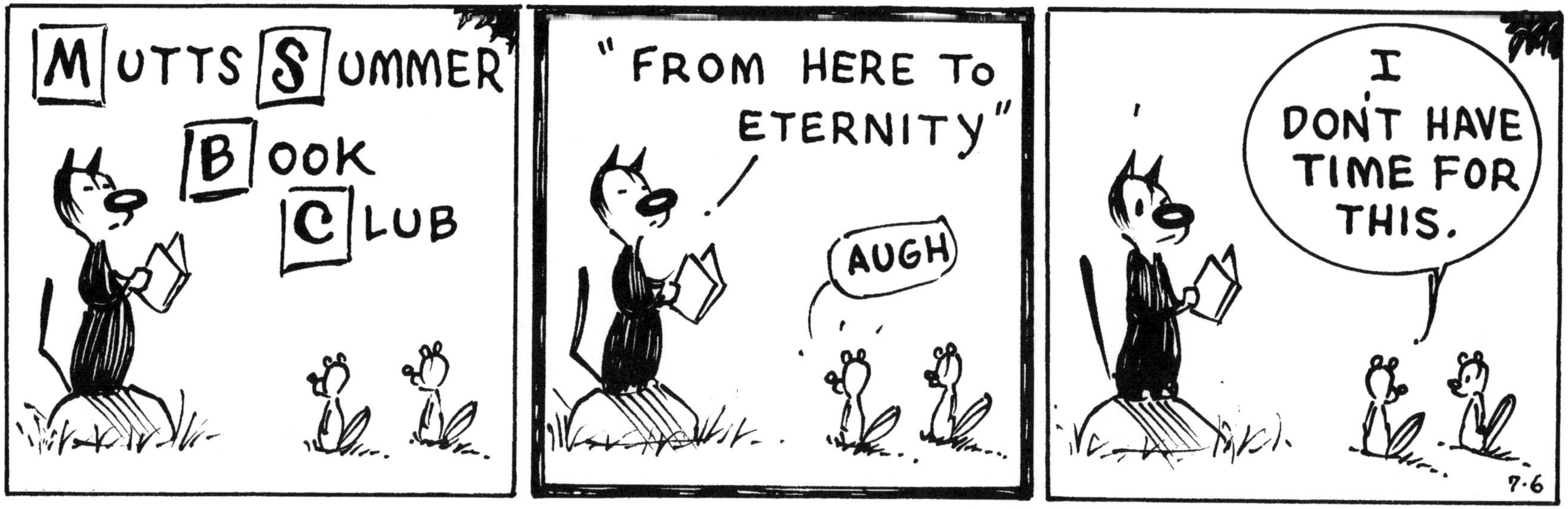
MUTTS SUMMER BOOK CLUB
"FROM HERE TO ETERNITY"
AUGH
I DON'T HAVE TIME FOR THIS.
7·6

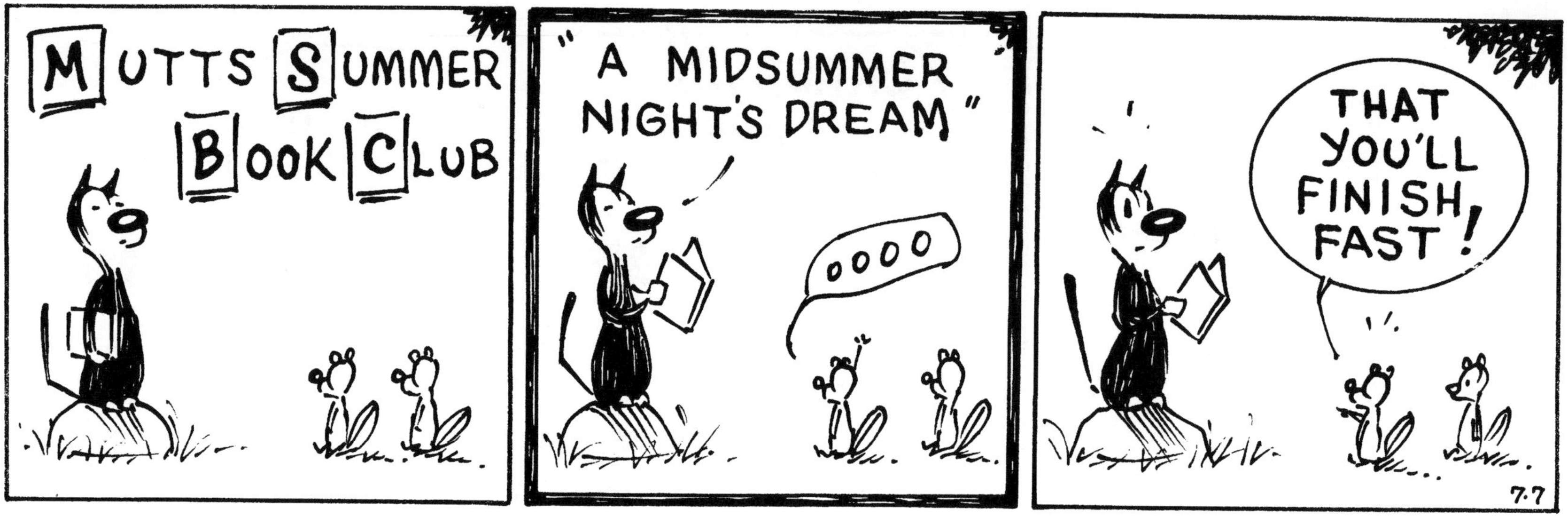
MUTTS SUMMER BOOK CLUB
"A MIDSUMMER NIGHT'S DREAM"
OOOO
THAT YOU'LL FINISH, FAST!
7·7

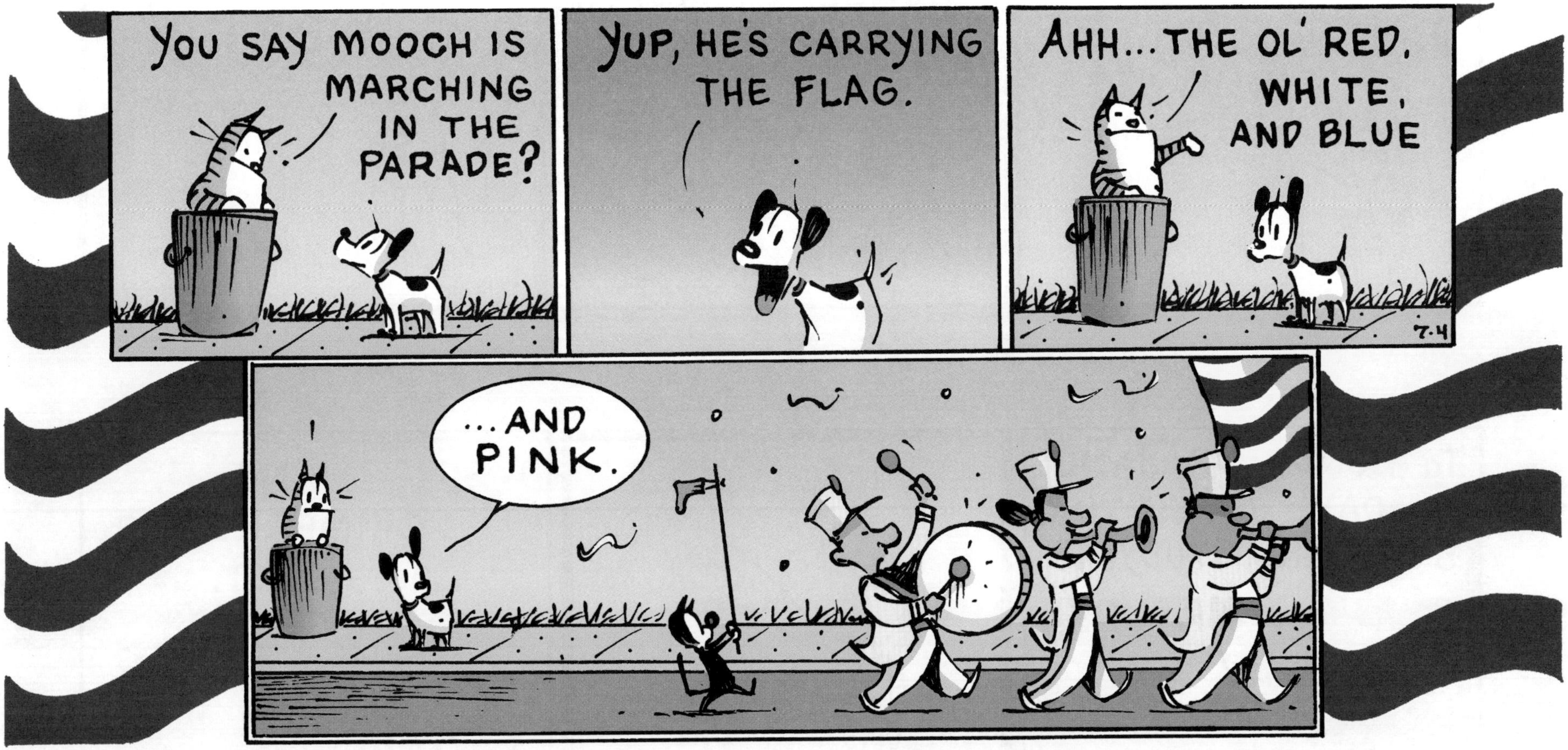
YOU SAY MOOCH IS MARCHING IN THE PARADE?
YUP, HE'S CARRYING THE FLAG.
AHH... THE OL' RED, WHITE, AND BLUE
7-4
...AND PINK.

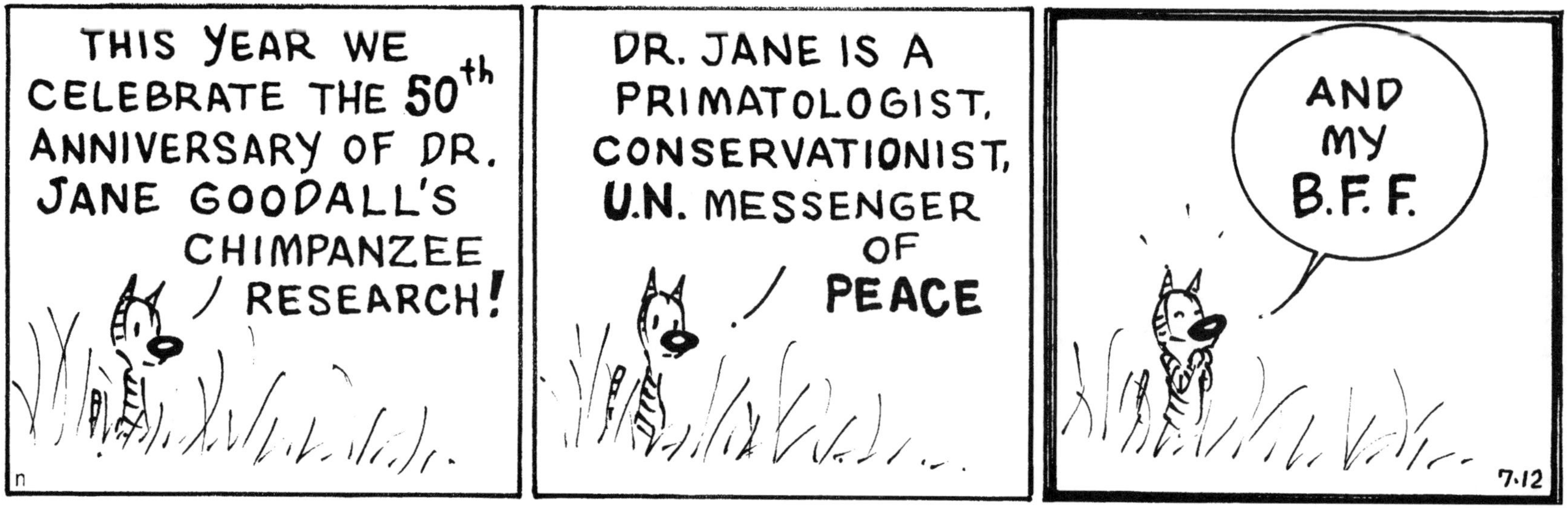
THIS YEAR WE CELEBRATE THE 50th ANNIVERSARY OF DR. JANE GOODALL'S CHIMPANZEE RESEARCH!
DR. JANE IS A PRIMATOLOGIST, CONSERVATIONIST, U.N. MESSENGER OF PEACE
AND MY B.F.F.
7·12

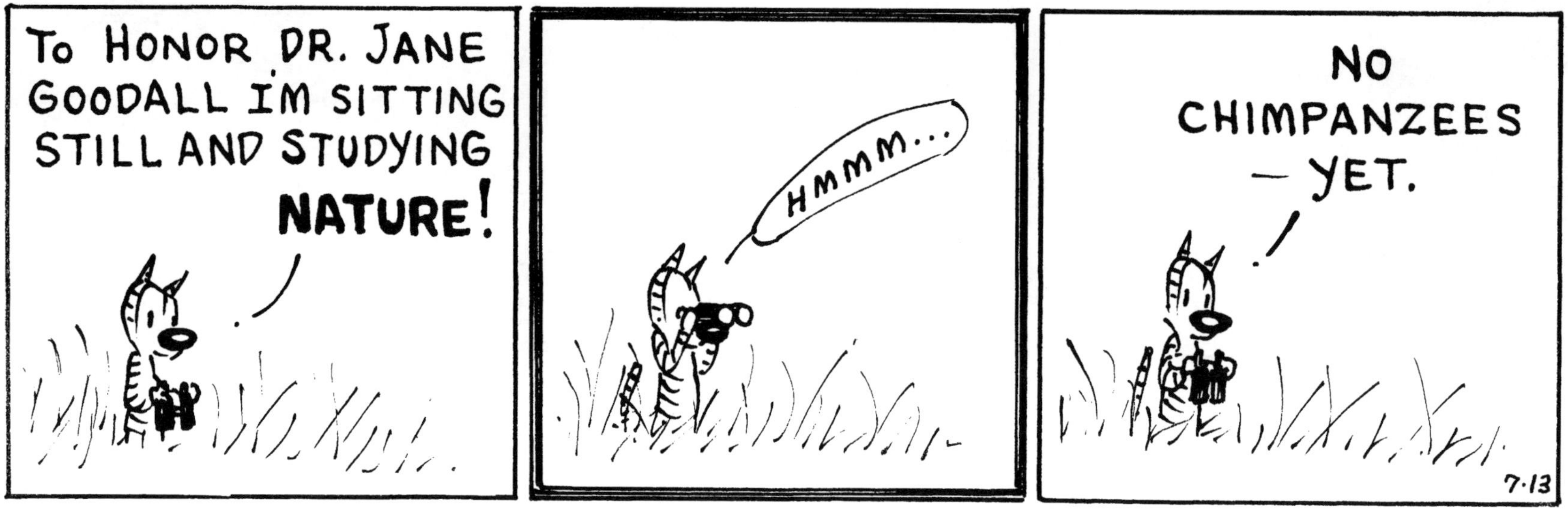
To HONOR DR. JANE GOODALL I'M SITTING STILL AND STUDYING NATURE!
HMMM...
NO CHIMPANZEES — YET.
7·13

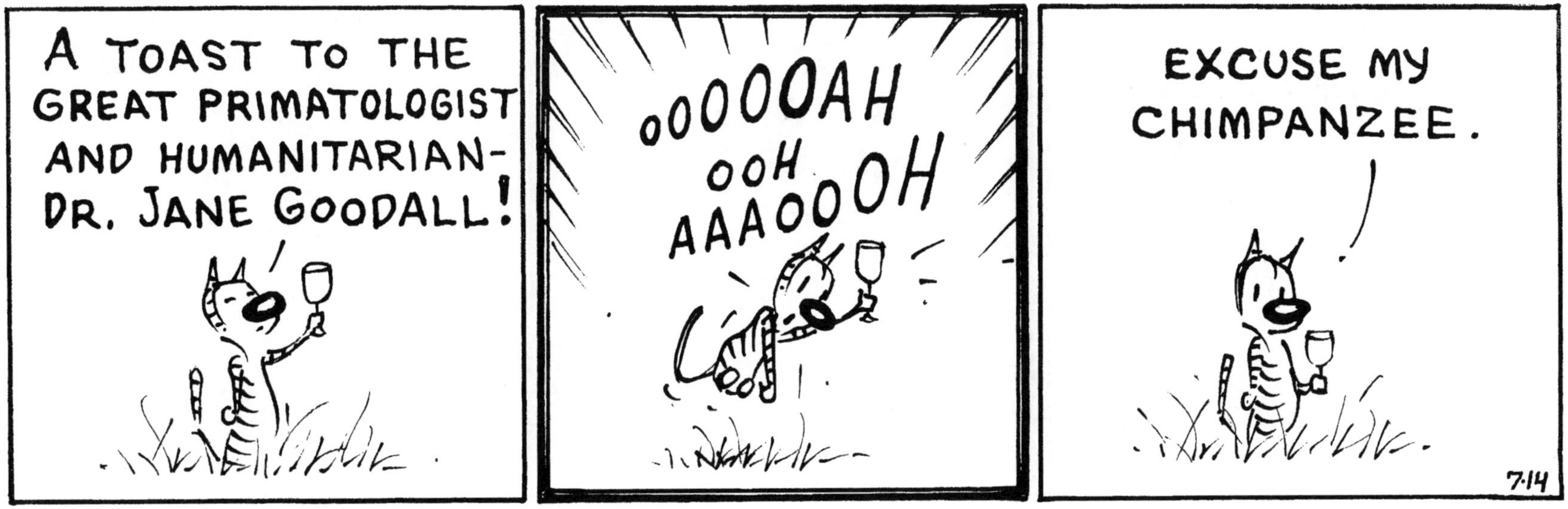
A TOAST TO THE GREAT PRIMATOLOGIST AND HUMANITARIAN- DR. JANE GOODALL!
oOOOOAH
OOH
AAAOOOOH
EXCUSE MY CHIMPANZEE.
7·14

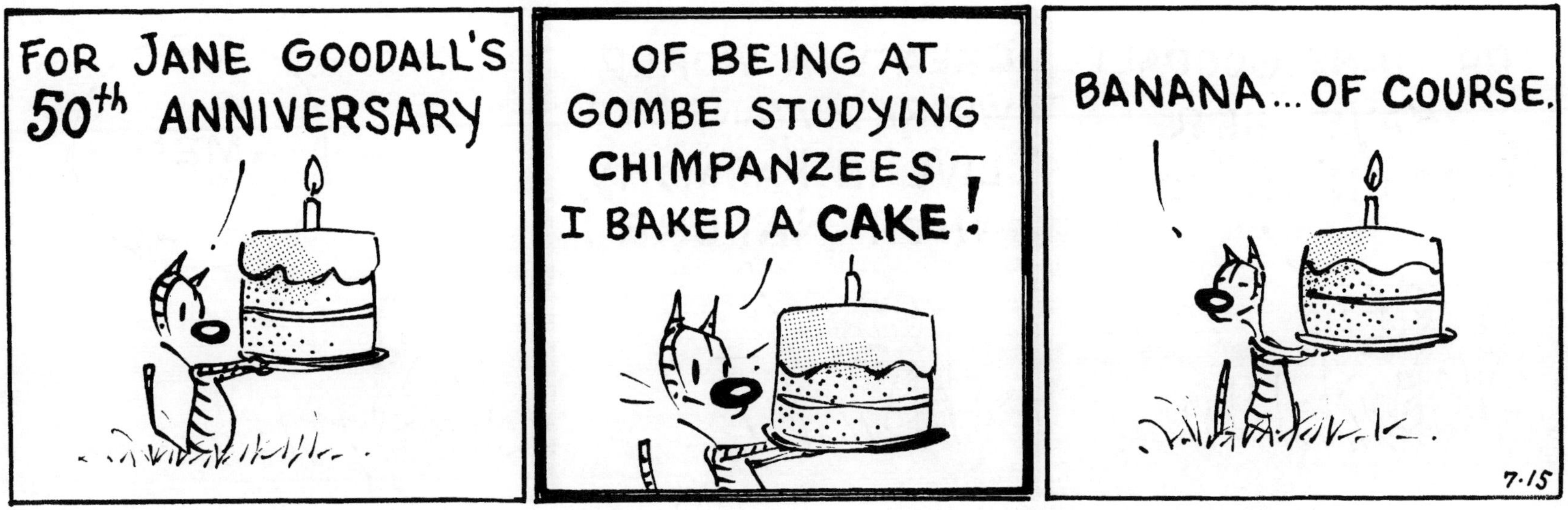
FOR JANE GOODALL'S 50th ANNIVERSARY
OF BEING AT GOMBE STUDYING CHIMPANZEES— I BAKED A CAKE!
BANANA... OF COURSE.
7·15

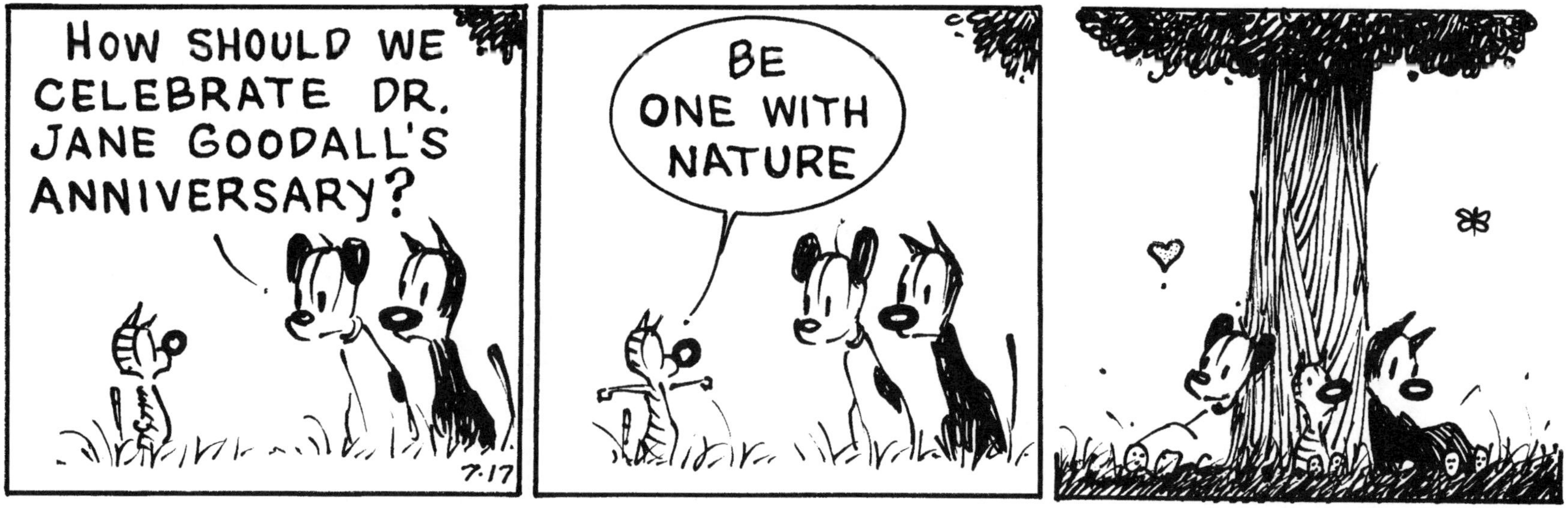
HOW SHOULD WE CELEBRATE DR. JANE GOODALL'S ANNIVERSARY?
BE ONE WITH NATURE
7·17

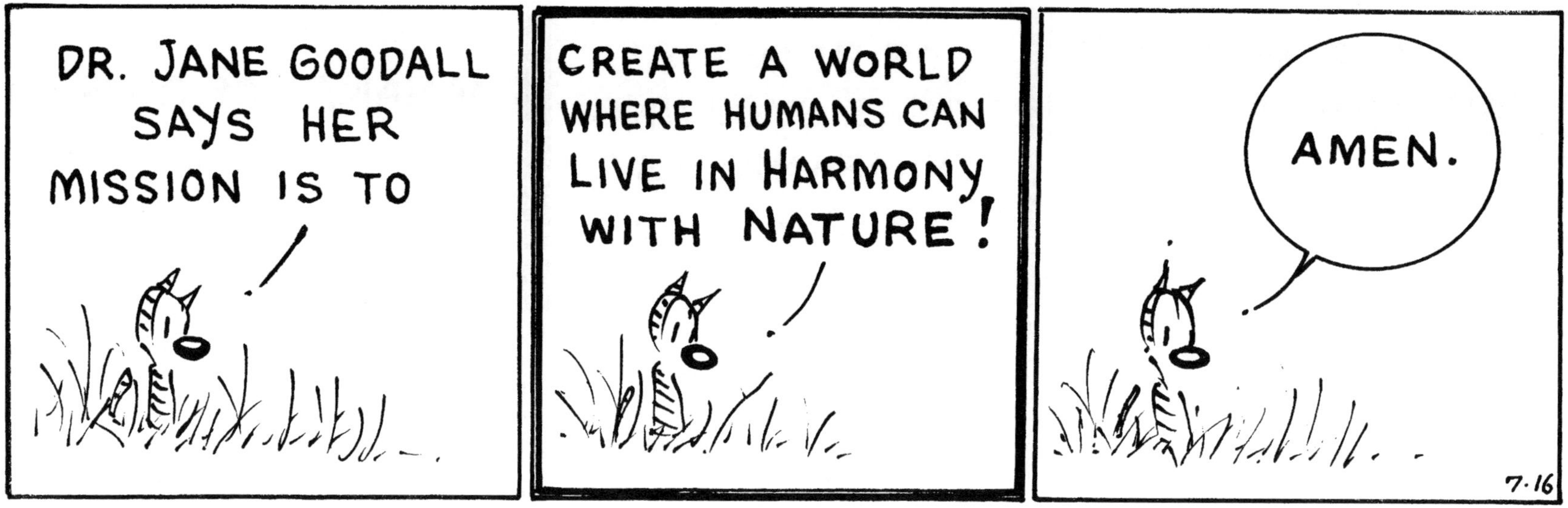
DR. JANE GOODALL SAYS HER MISSION IS TO
CREATE A WORLD WHERE HUMANS CAN LIVE IN HARMONY WITH NATURE!
AMEN.
7·16

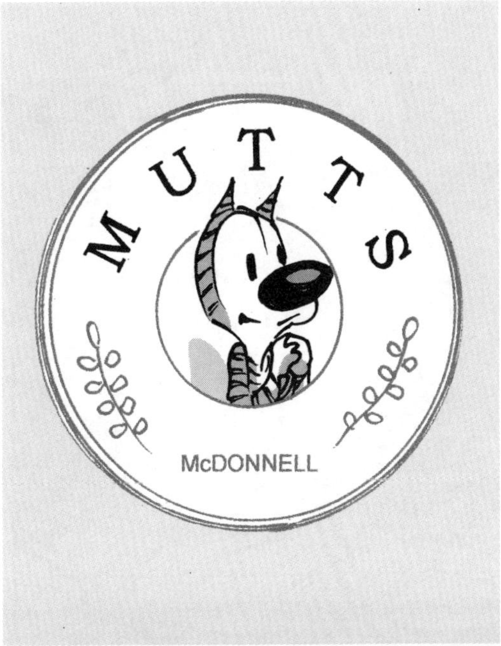
MUTTS
McDONNELL

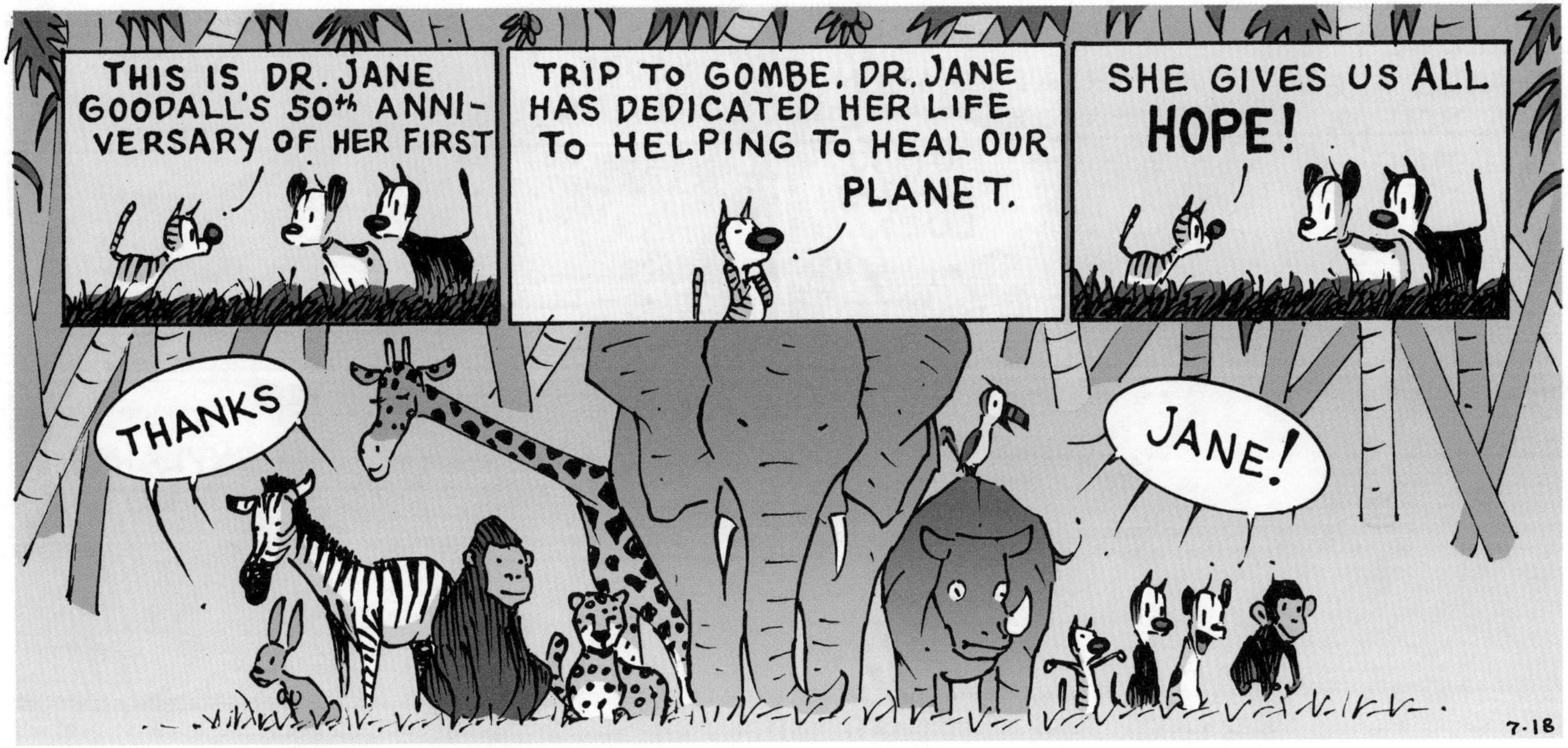
THIS IS DR. JANE GOODALL'S 50th ANNIVERSARY OF HER FIRST
TRIP TO GOMBE. DR. JANE HAS DEDICATED HER LIFE TO HELPING TO HEAL OUR PLANET.
SHE GIVES US ALL HOPE!
THANKS
JANE!
7·18

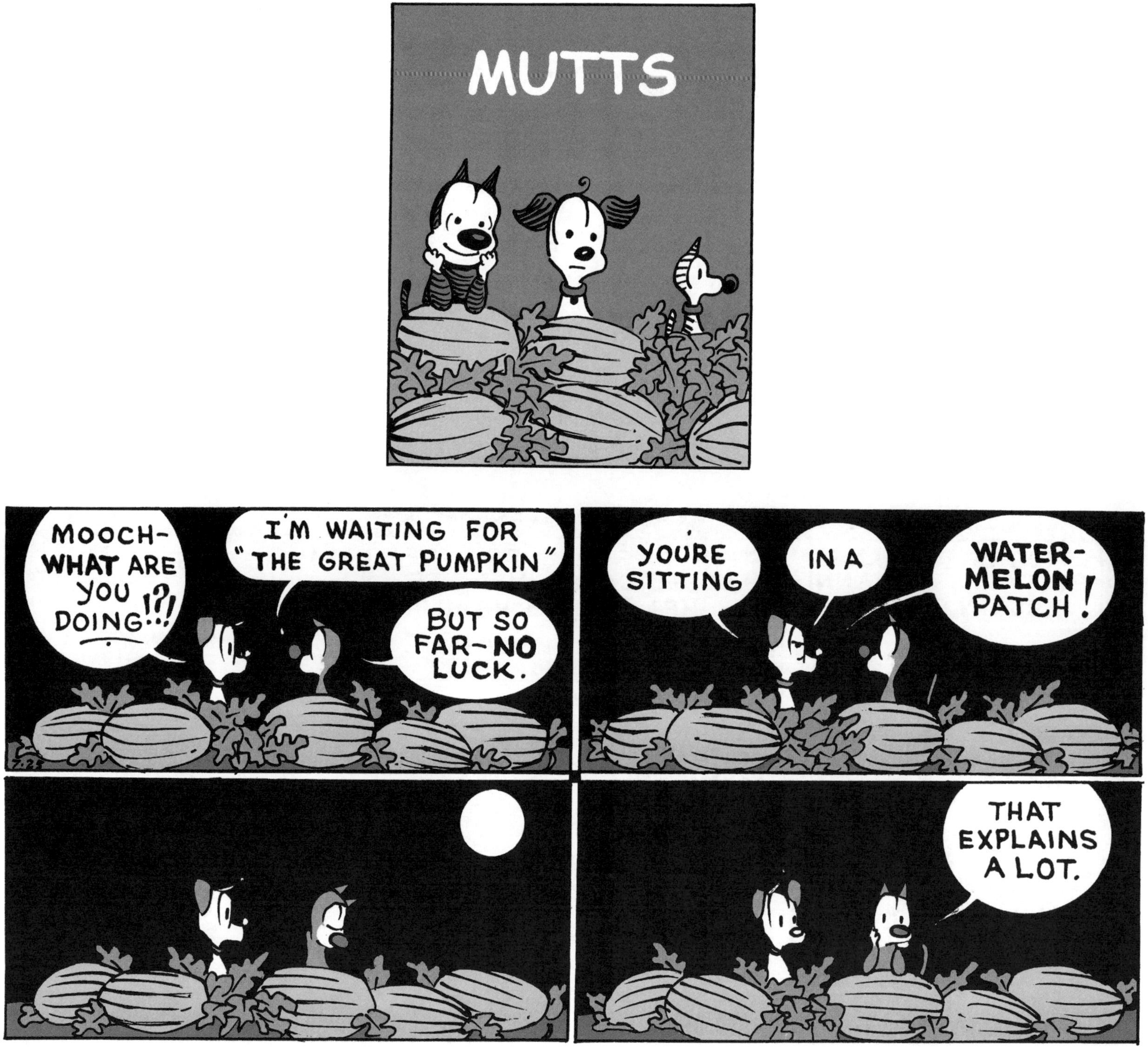
MUTTS
MOOCH- WHAT ARE YOU DOING!?!
I'M WAITING FOR "THE GREAT PUMPKIN"
BUT SO FAR-NO LUCK.
YOU'RE SITTING
IN A
WATER-MELON PATCH!
THAT EXPLAINS A LOT.

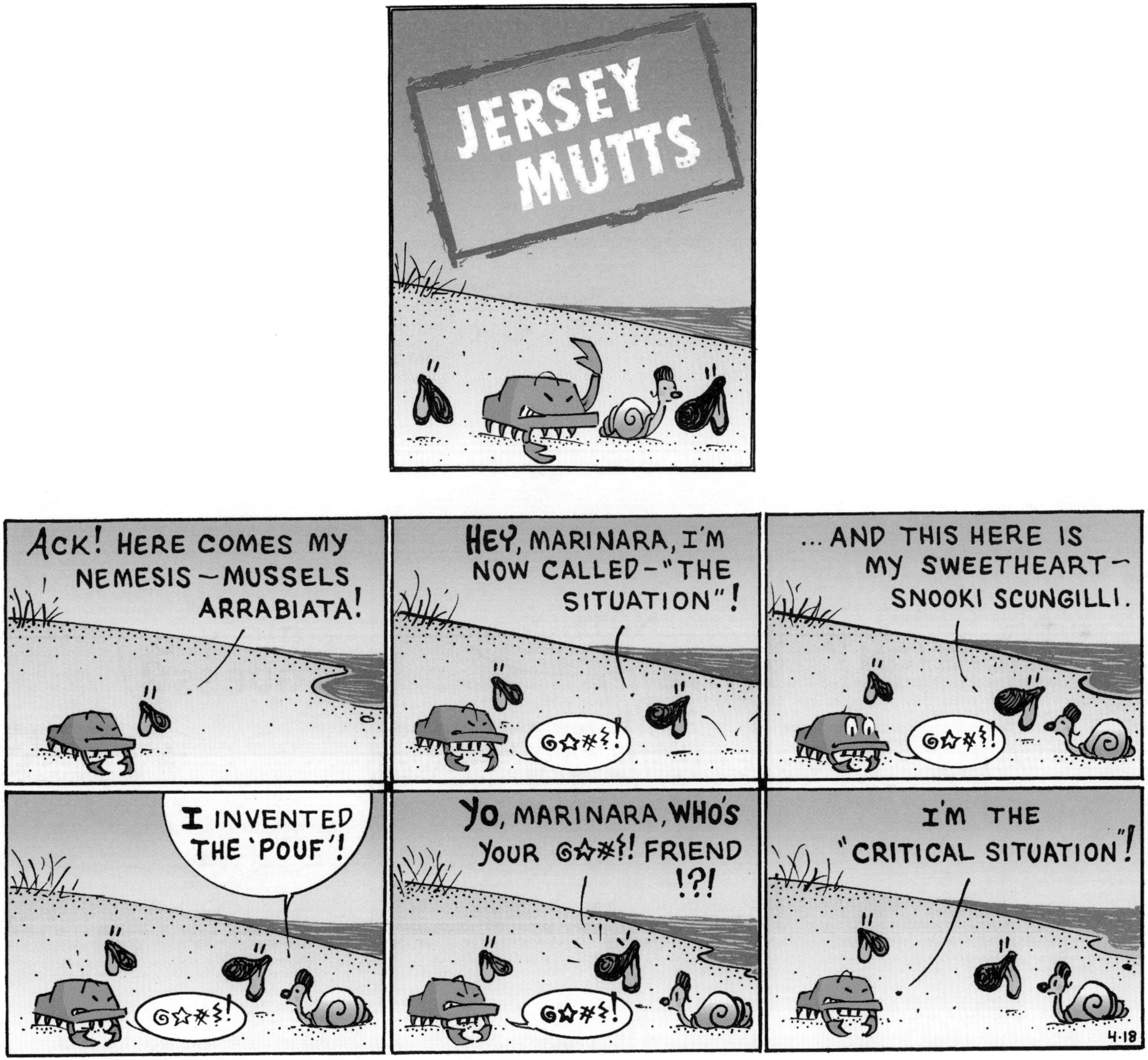
JERSEY MUTTS
ACK! HERE COMES MY NEMESIS—MUSSELS ARRABIATA!
HEY, MARINARA, I'M NOW CALLED—"THE SITUATION"!
@☆#$!
...AND THIS HERE IS MY SWEETHEART—SNOOKI SCUNGILLI.
@☆#$!
I INVENTED THE 'POUF'!
@☆#$!
YO, MARINARA, WHO'S YOUR @☆#$! FRIEND !?!
@☆#$!
I'M THE "CRITICAL SITUATION"!
4·18

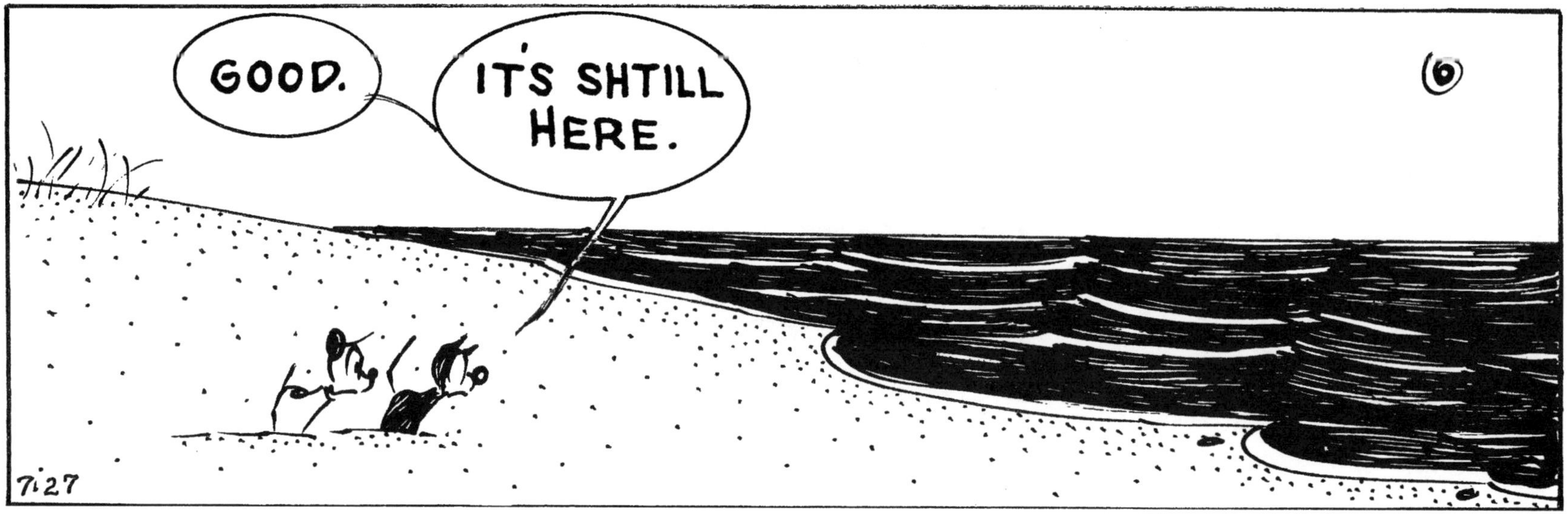
GOOD.
IT'S SHTILL HERE.
7.27

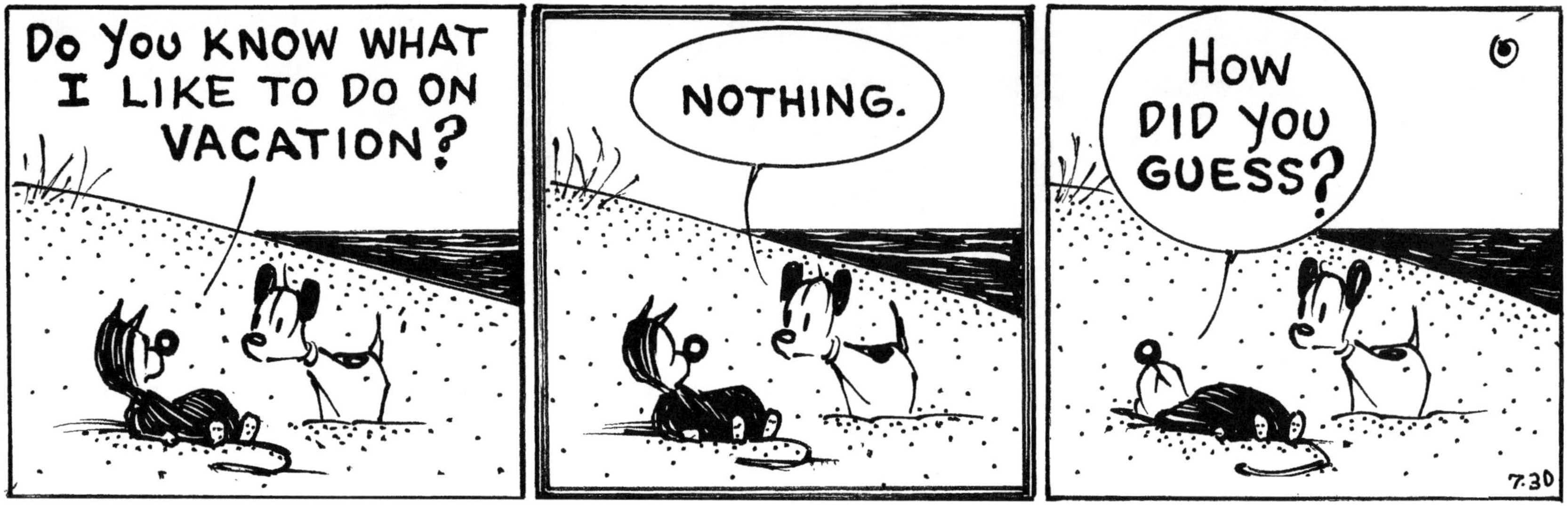
DO YOU KNOW WHAT I LIKE TO DO ON VACATION?
NOTHING.
HOW DID YOU GUESS?
7.30

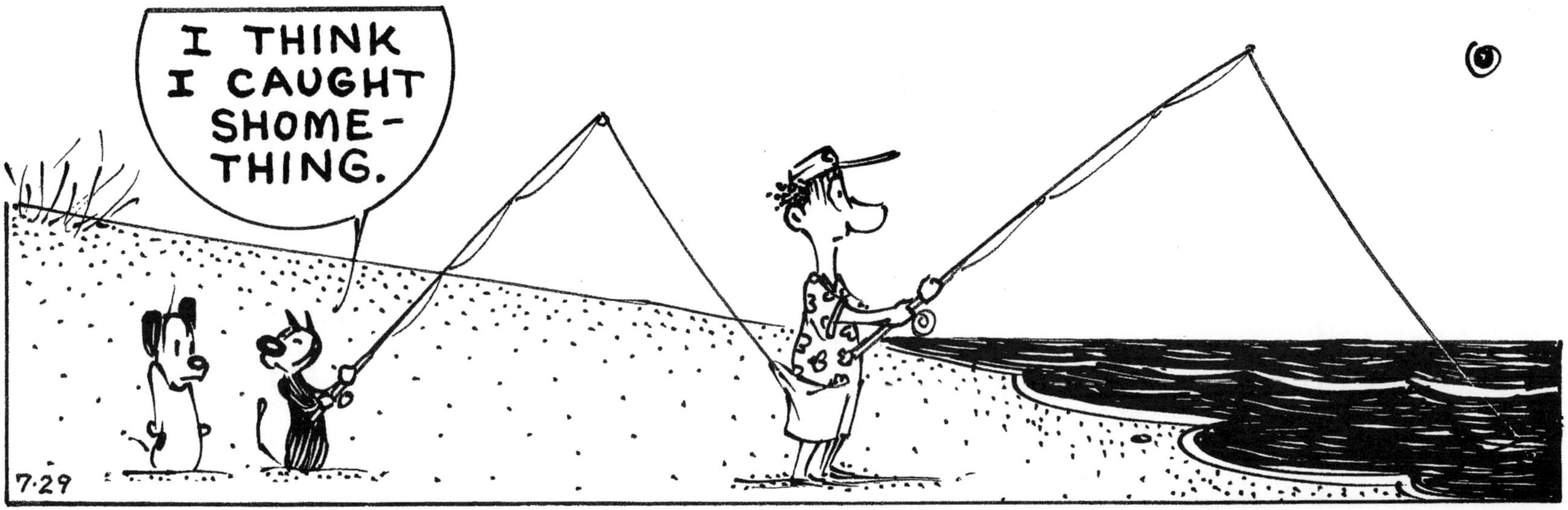
I THINK I CAUGHT SHOME-THING.
7·29

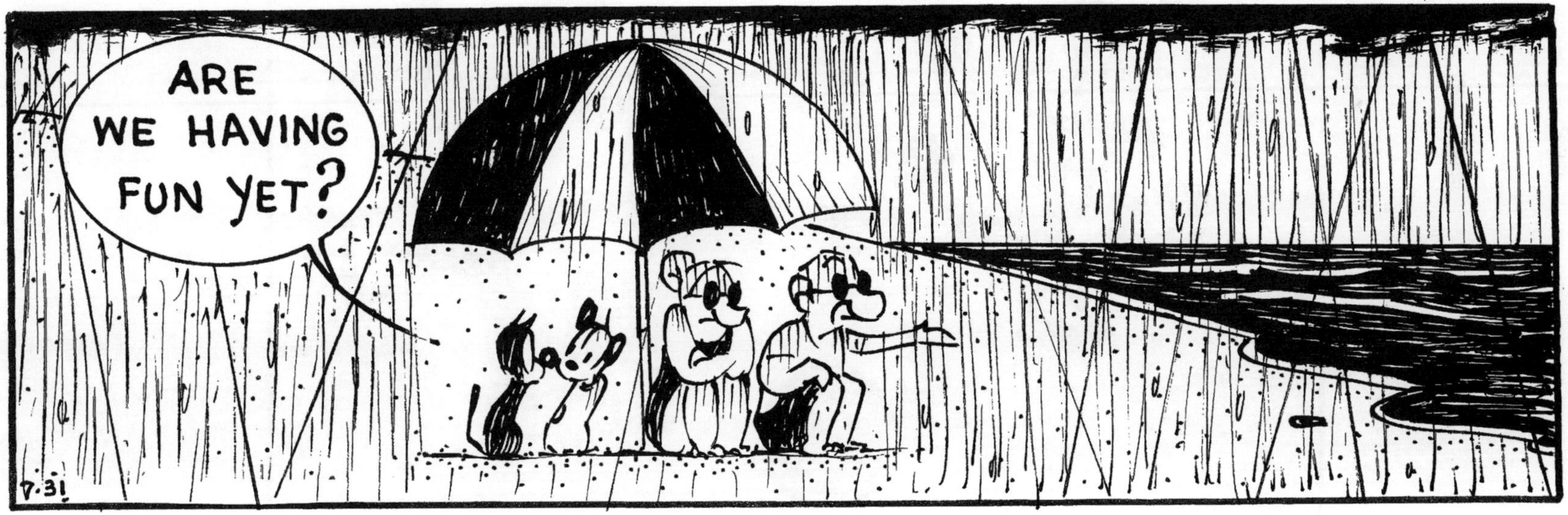
ARE WE HAVING FUN YET?
7·31

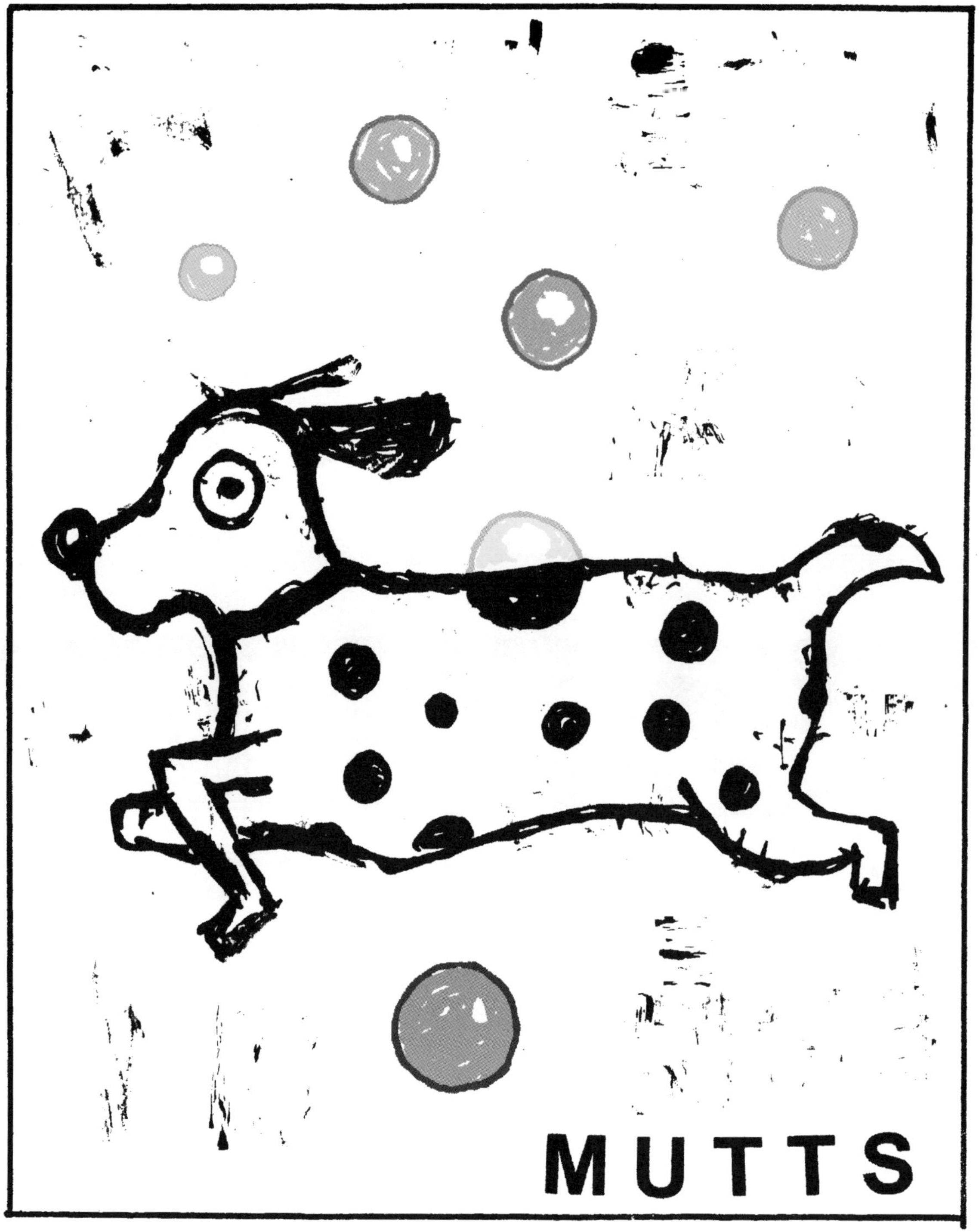
MUTTS

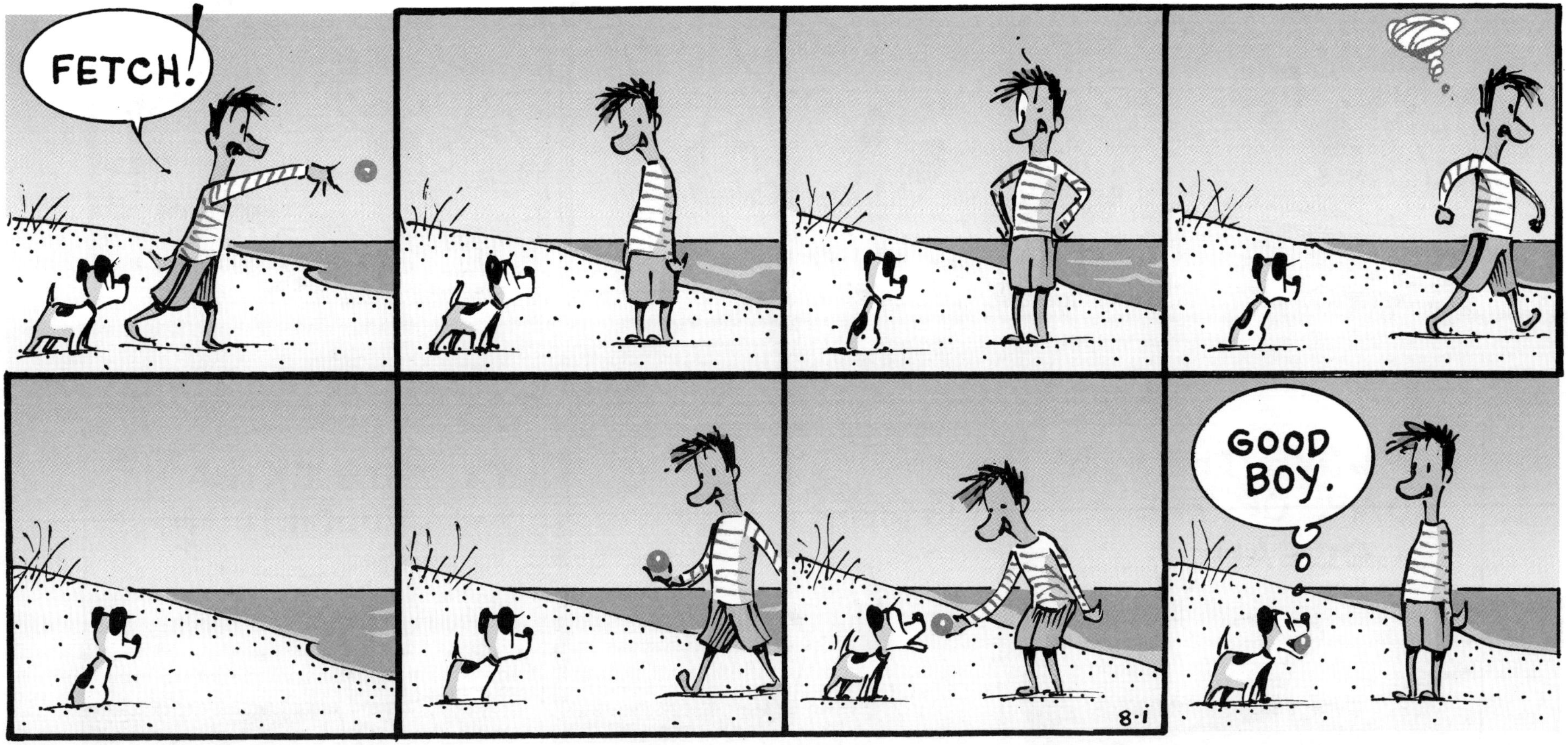
FETCH!
GOOD BOY.
8·1

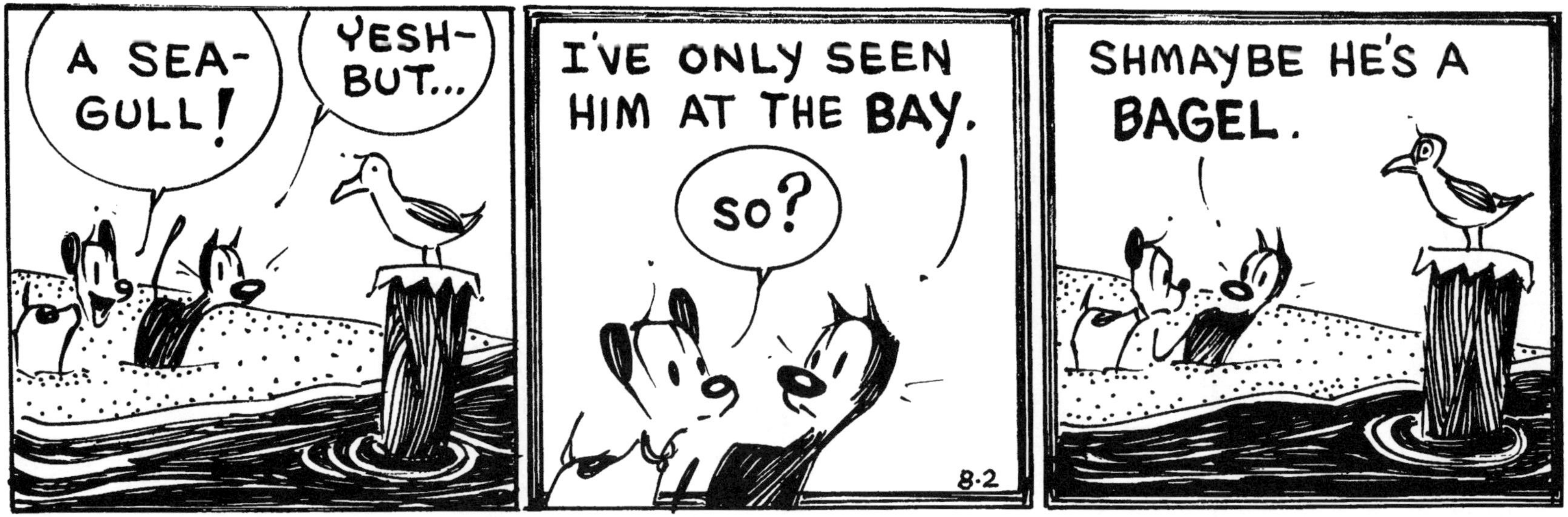
A SEA-GULL!
YESH-BUT...
I'VE ONLY SEEN HIM AT THE BAY.
SO?
8·2
SHMAYBE HE'S A BAGEL.

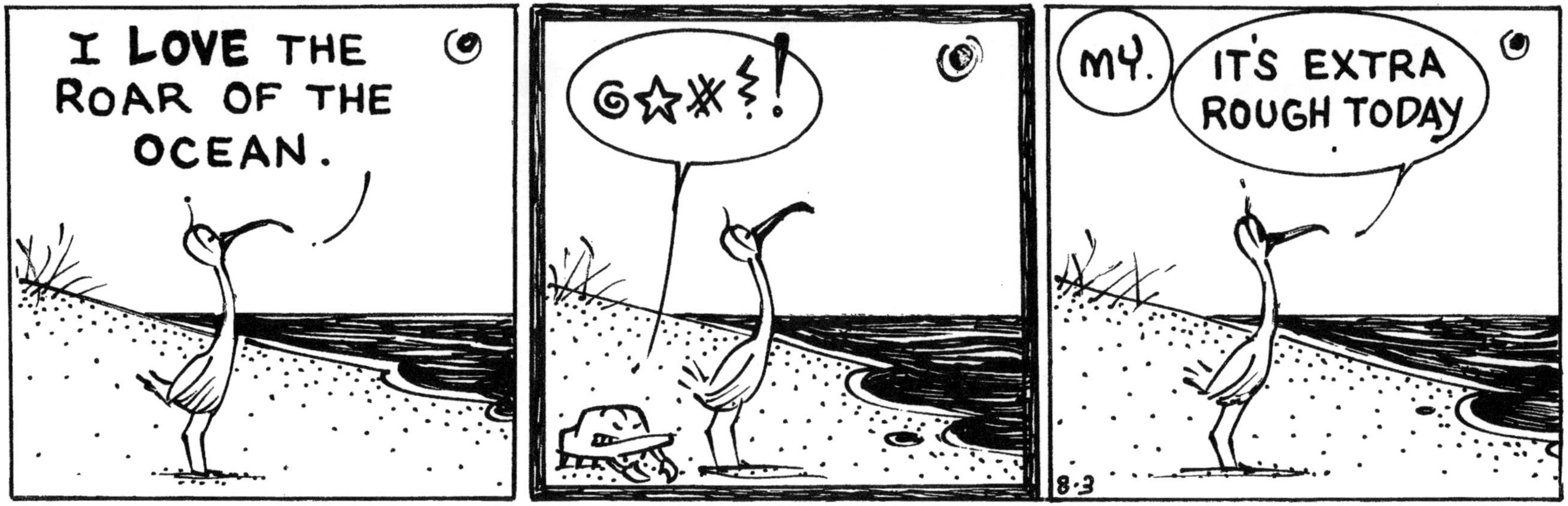
I LOVE THE ROAR OF THE OCEAN.
MY.
IT'S EXTRA ROUGH TODAY
8·3

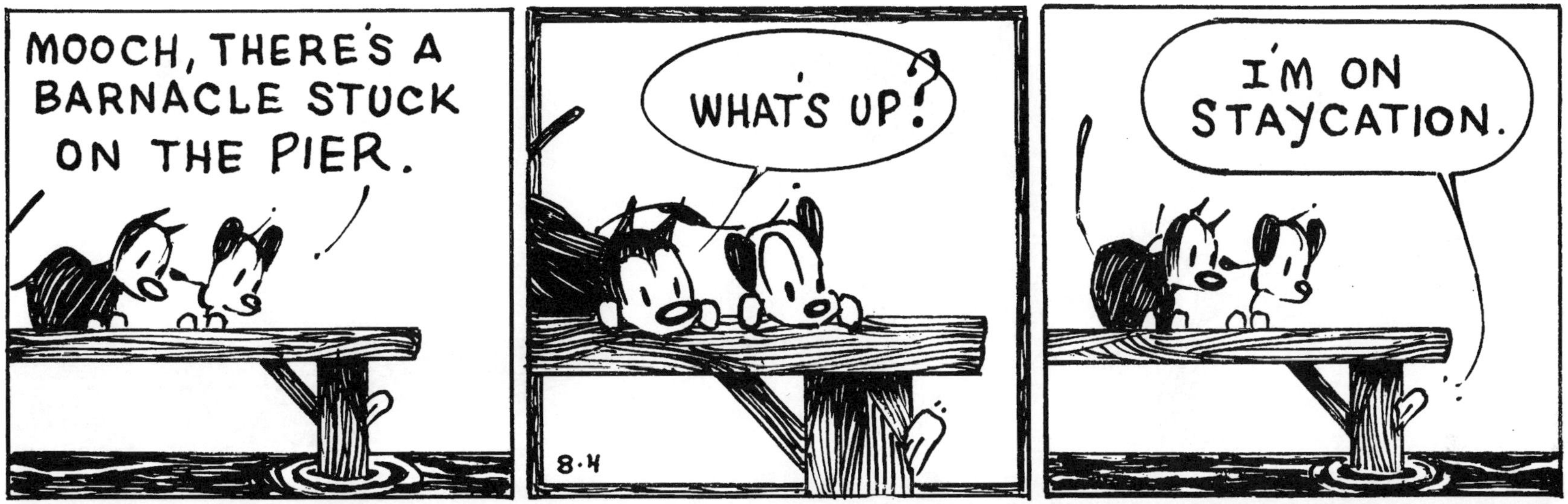
MOOCH, THERE'S A BARNACLE STUCK ON THE PIER.
WHAT'S UP?
I'M ON STAYCATION.
8·4

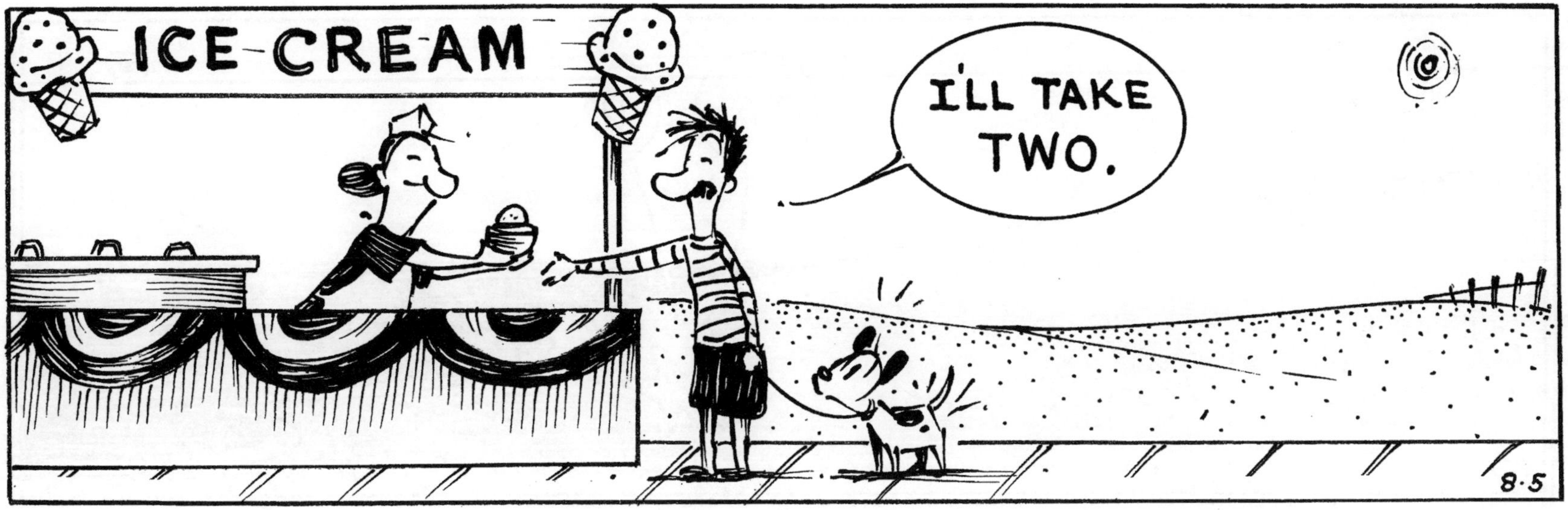
ICE CREAM
I'LL TAKE TWO.
8·5

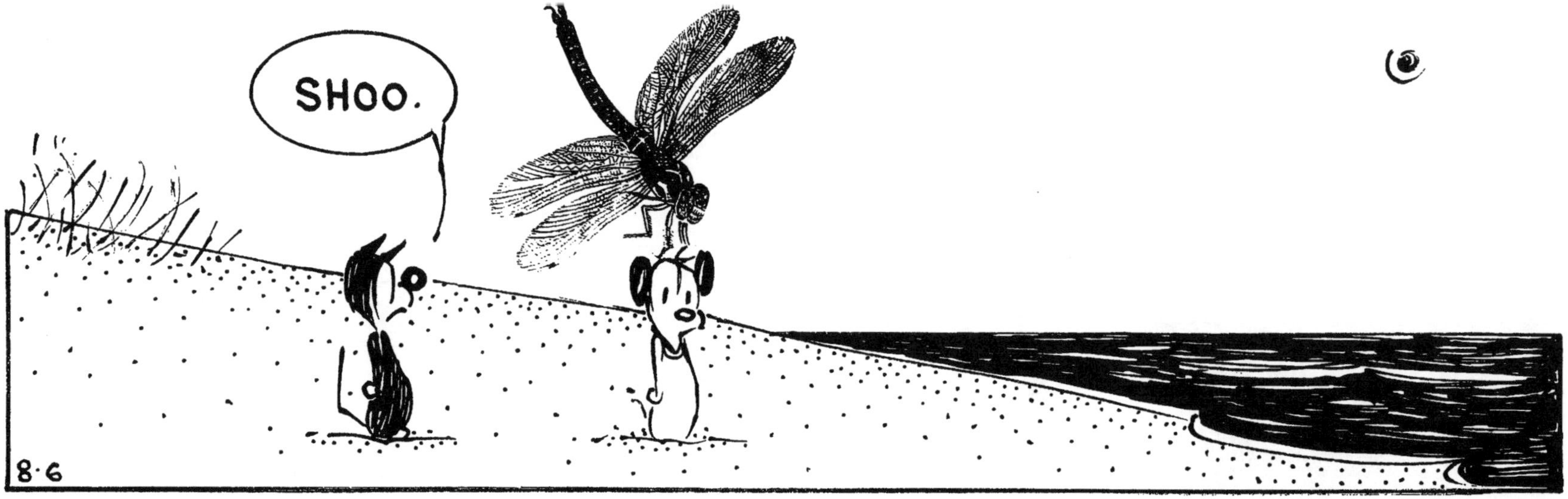
SHOO.
8·6

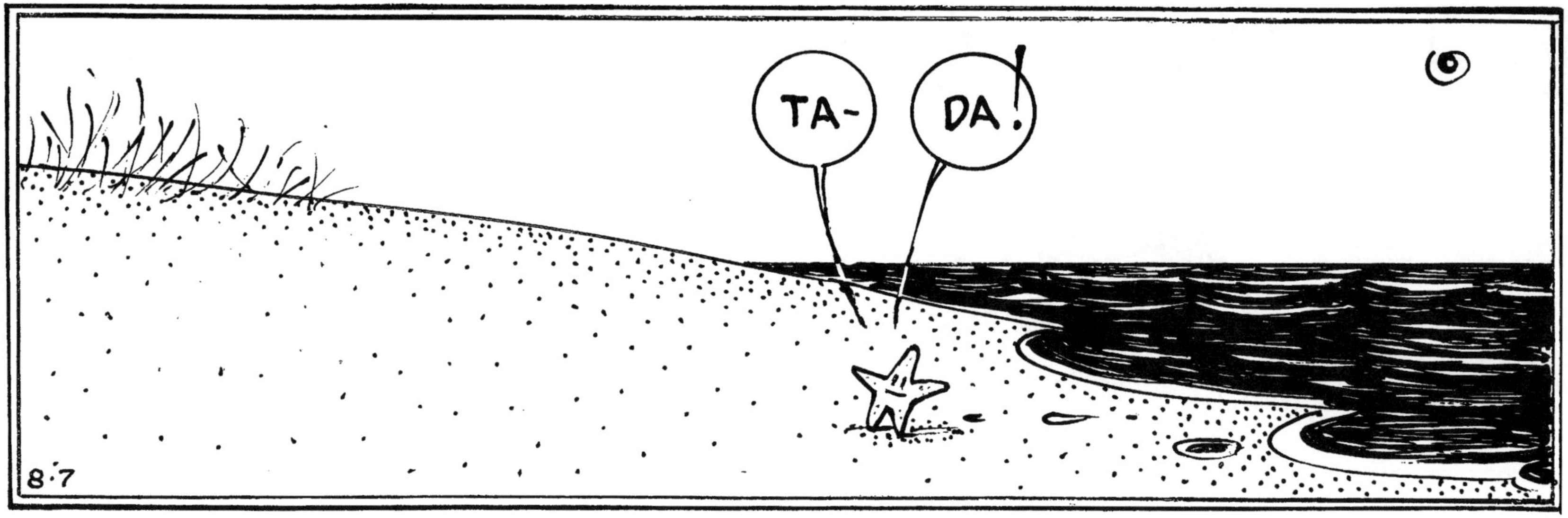
TA-
DA!
8·7

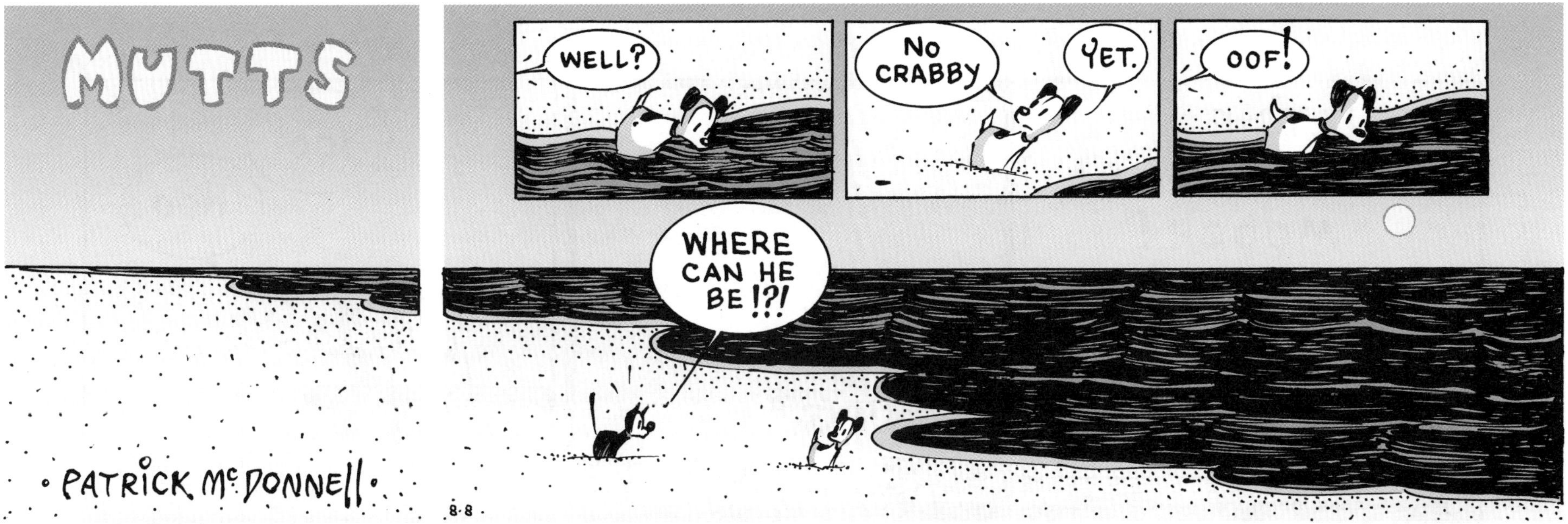
MUTTS
• PATRICK McDONNELL •
WELL?
NO CRABBY
YET.
OOF!
WHERE CAN HE BE!?!
8·8

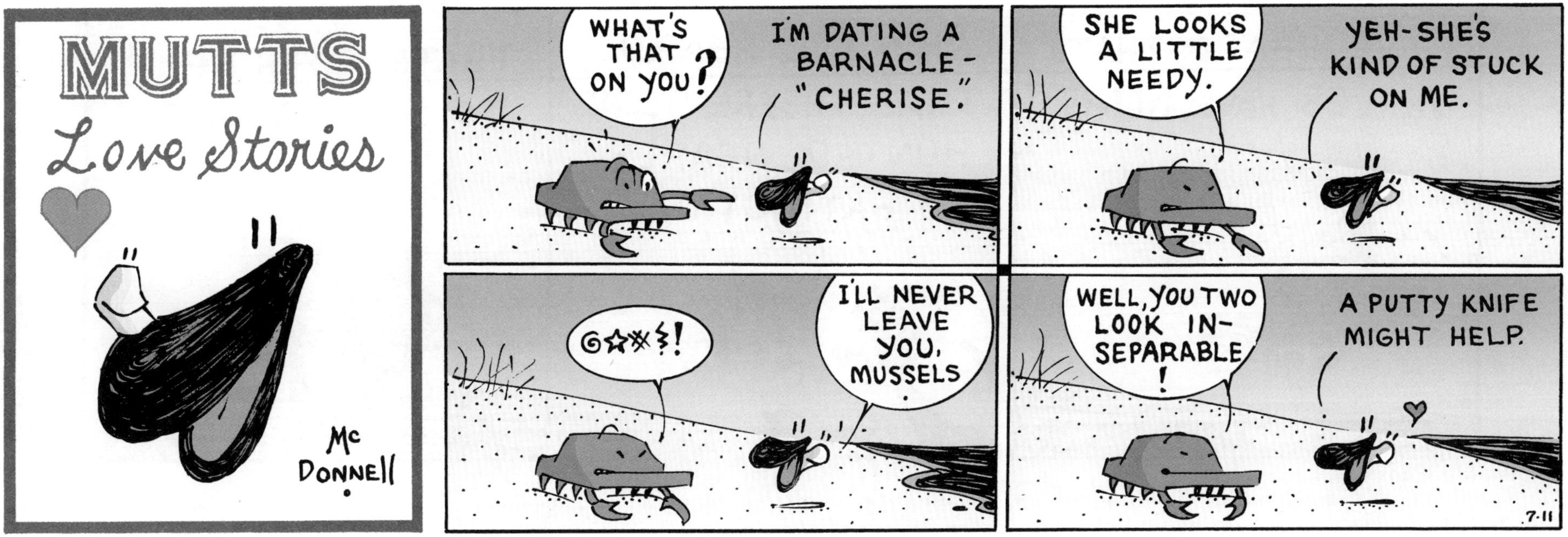
MUTTS
Love Stories
McDONNELL
WHAT'S THAT ON YOU?
I'M DATING A BARNACLE - "CHERISE."
SHE LOOKS A LITTLE NEEDY.
YEH-SHE'S KIND OF STUCK ON ME.
I'LL NEVER LEAVE YOU, MUSSELS.
WELL, YOU TWO LOOK IN-SEPARABLE!
A PUTTY KNIFE MIGHT HELP.
7·11

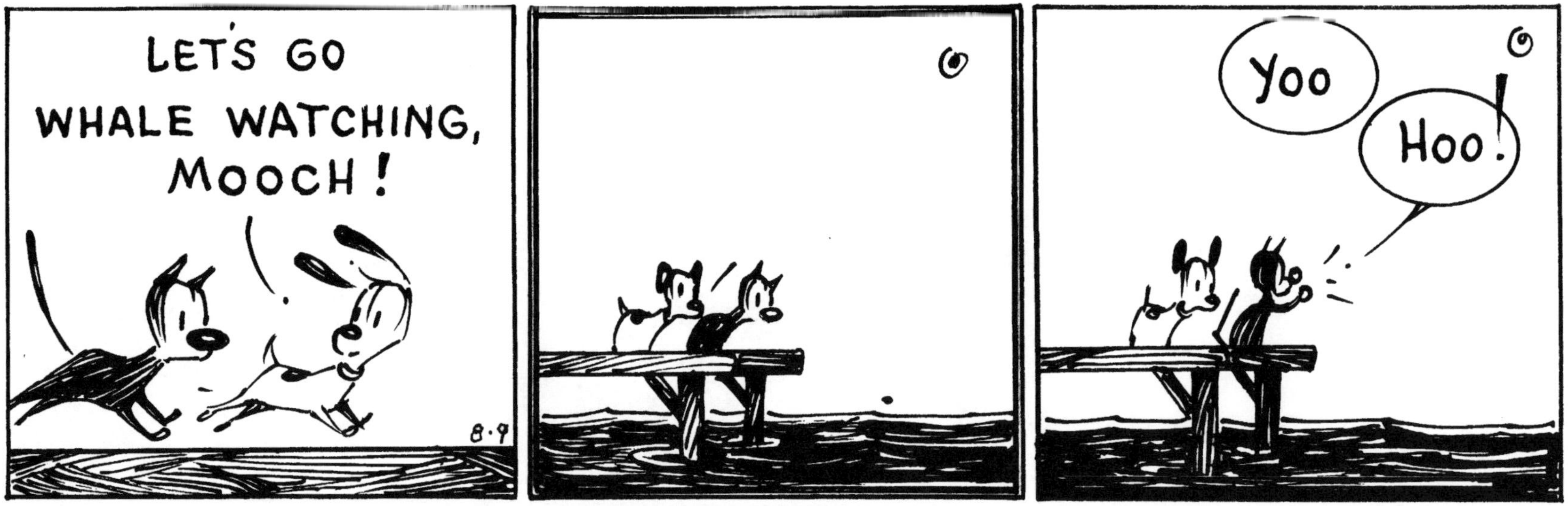
LET'S GO WHALE WATCHING, MOOCH!
8·9
Yoo
Hoo!

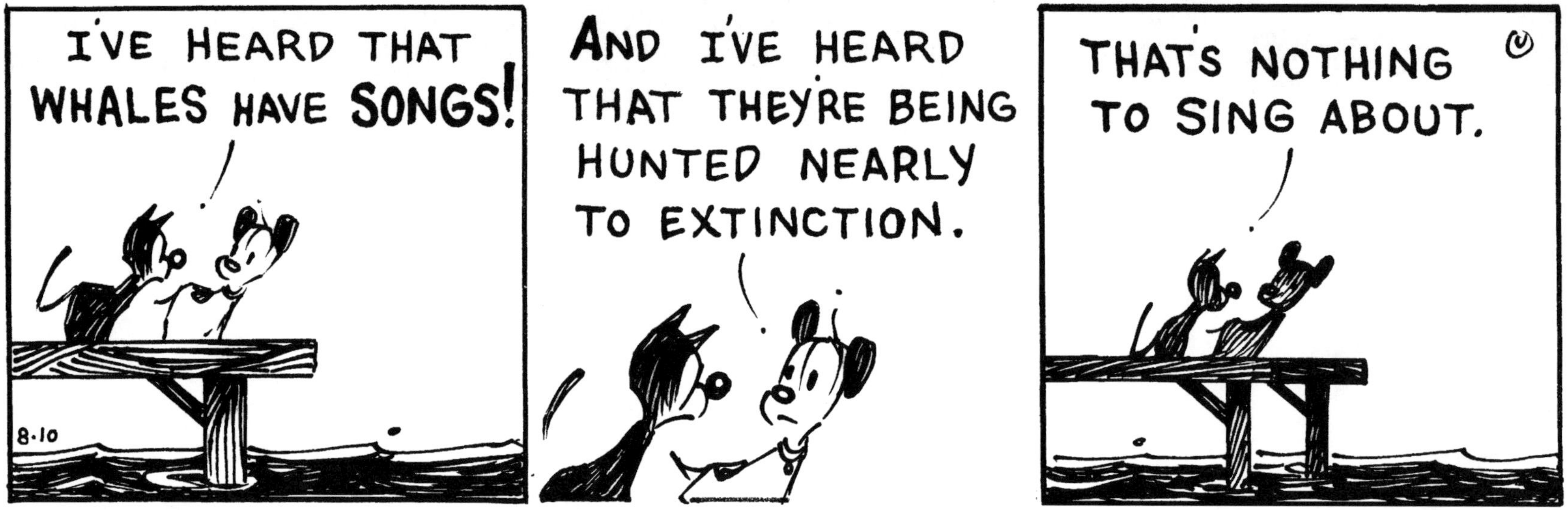
I'VE HEARD THAT WHALES HAVE SONGS!
8·10
AND I'VE HEARD THAT THEY'RE BEING HUNTED NEARLY TO EXTINCTION.
THAT'S NOTHING TO SING ABOUT.

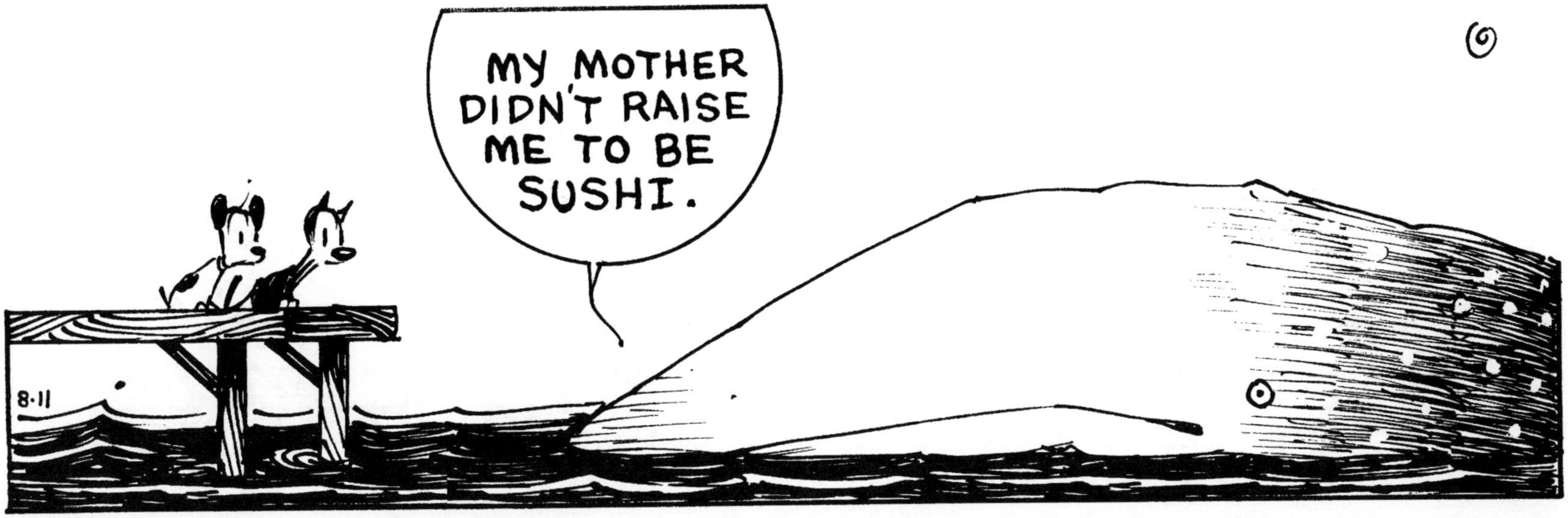
8·11
MY MOTHER DIDN'T RAISE ME TO BE SUSHI.

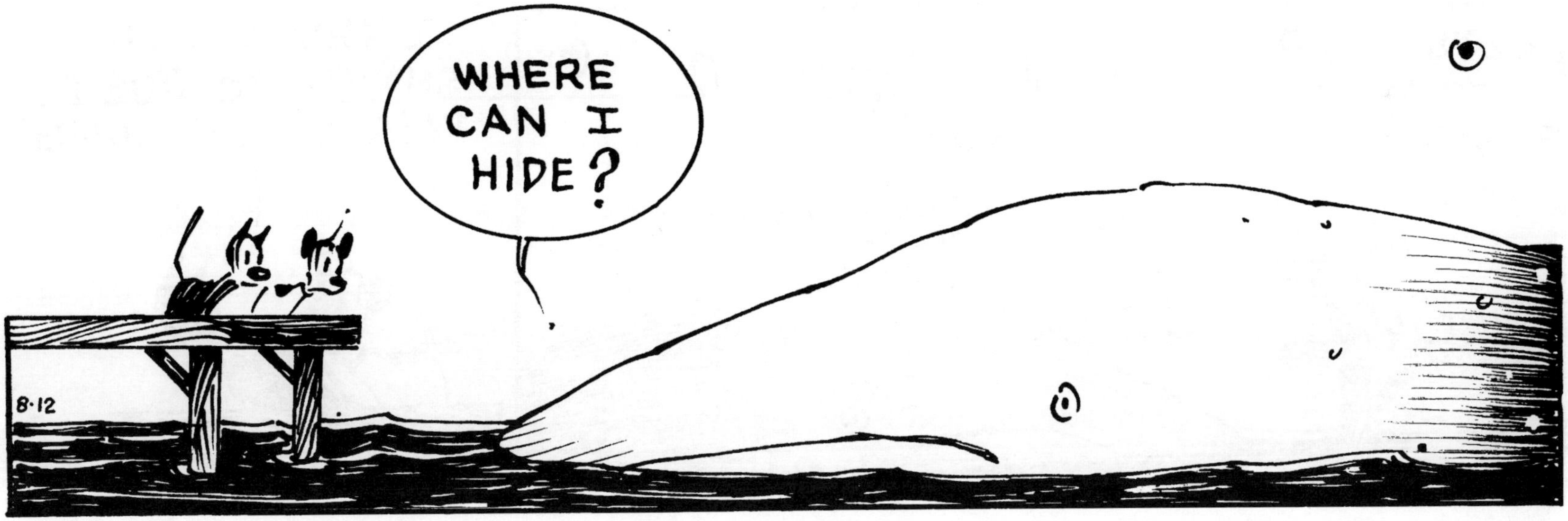
8·12
WHERE CAN I HIDE?

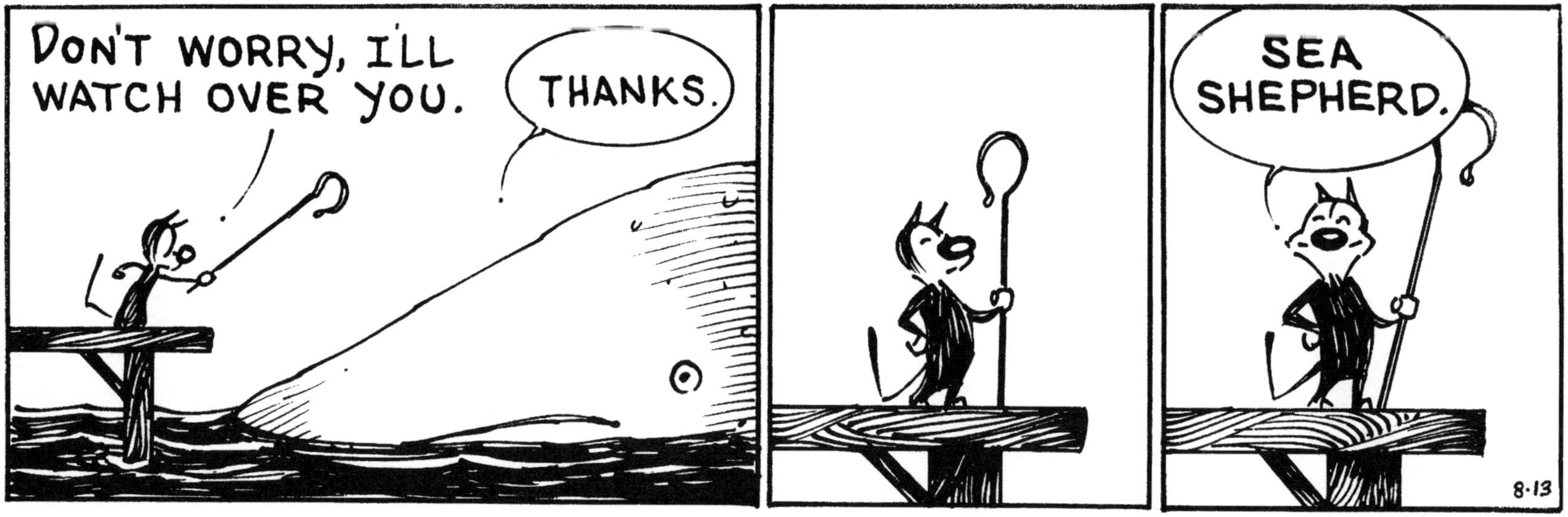
DON'T WORRY, I'LL WATCH OVER YOU.
THANKS.
SEA SHEPHERD.
8·13

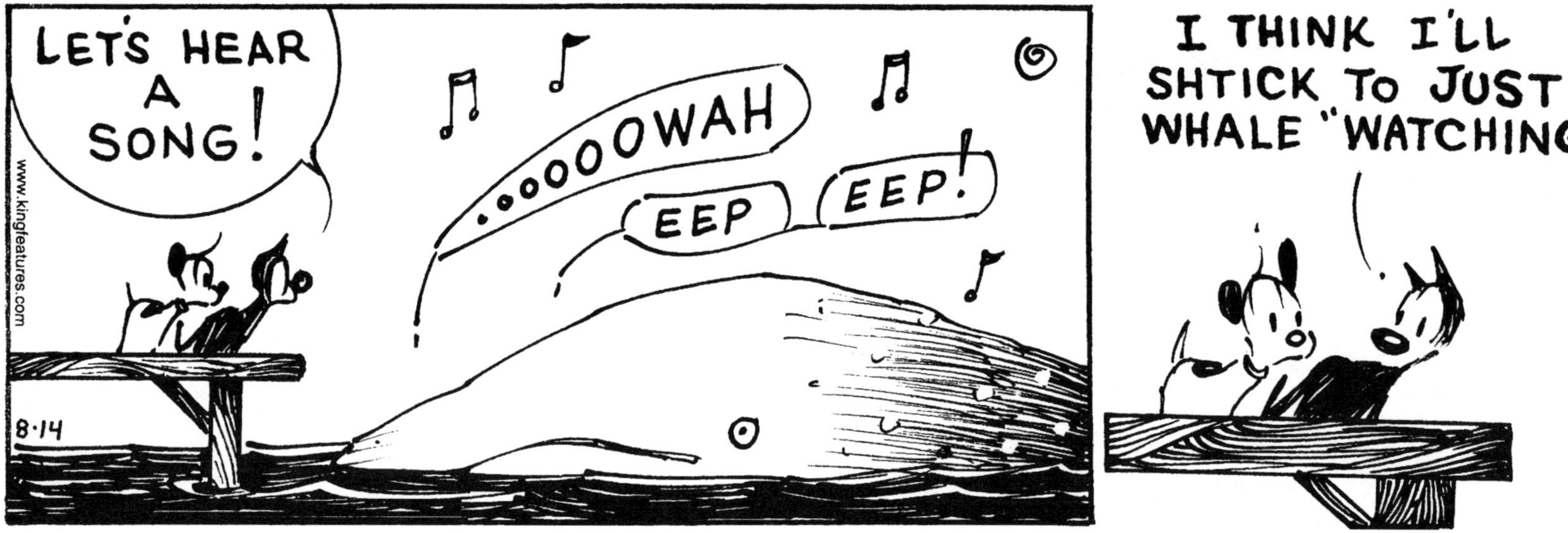
LET'S HEAR A SONG!
.oooOOWAH
EEP
EEP!
www.kingfeatures.com
8·14
I THINK I'LL SHTICK TO JUST WHALE "WATCHING"

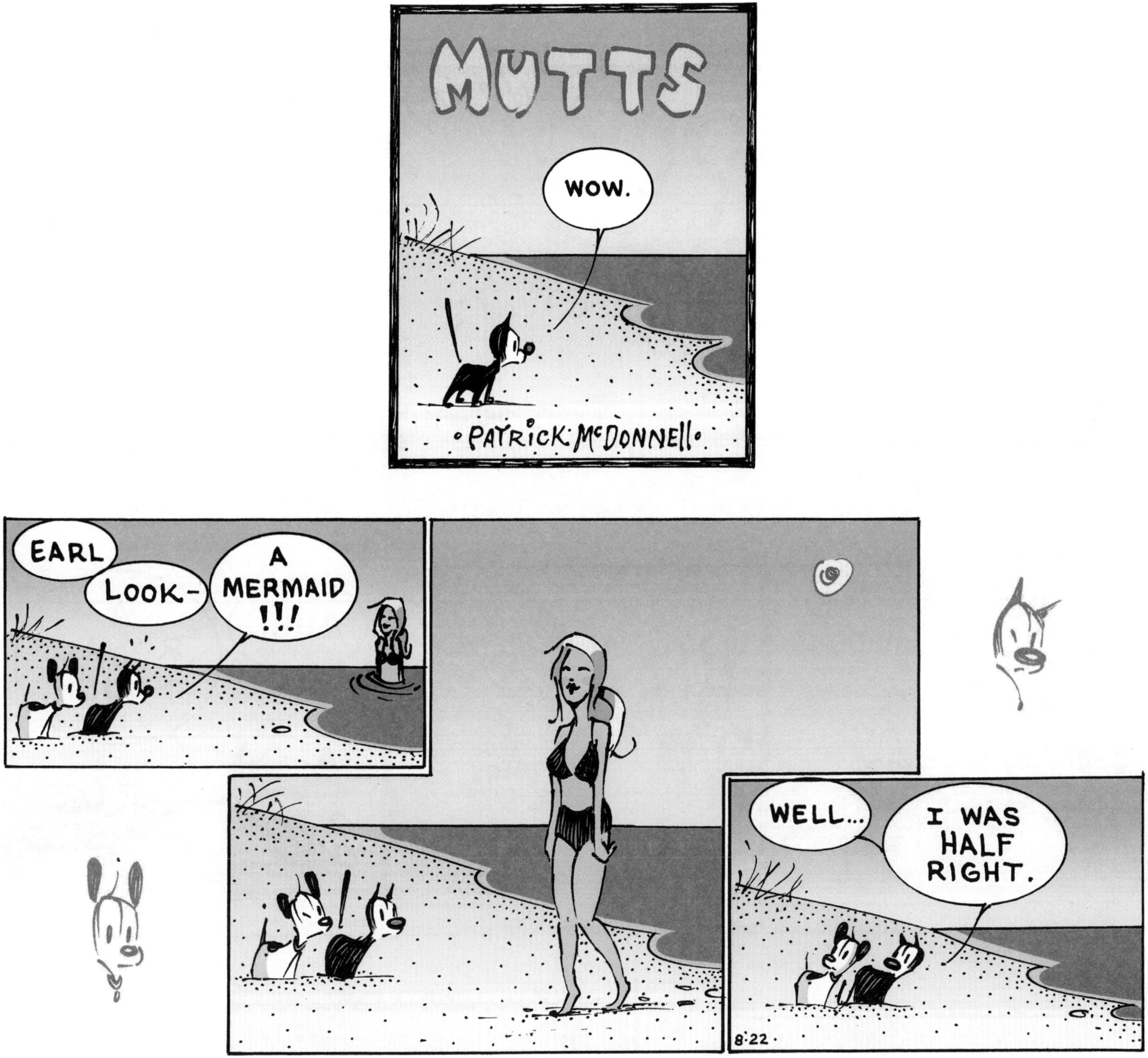
MUTTS
WOW.
PATRICK McDONNELL
EARL
LOOK-
A MERMAID !!!
WELL...
I WAS HALF RIGHT.
8·22

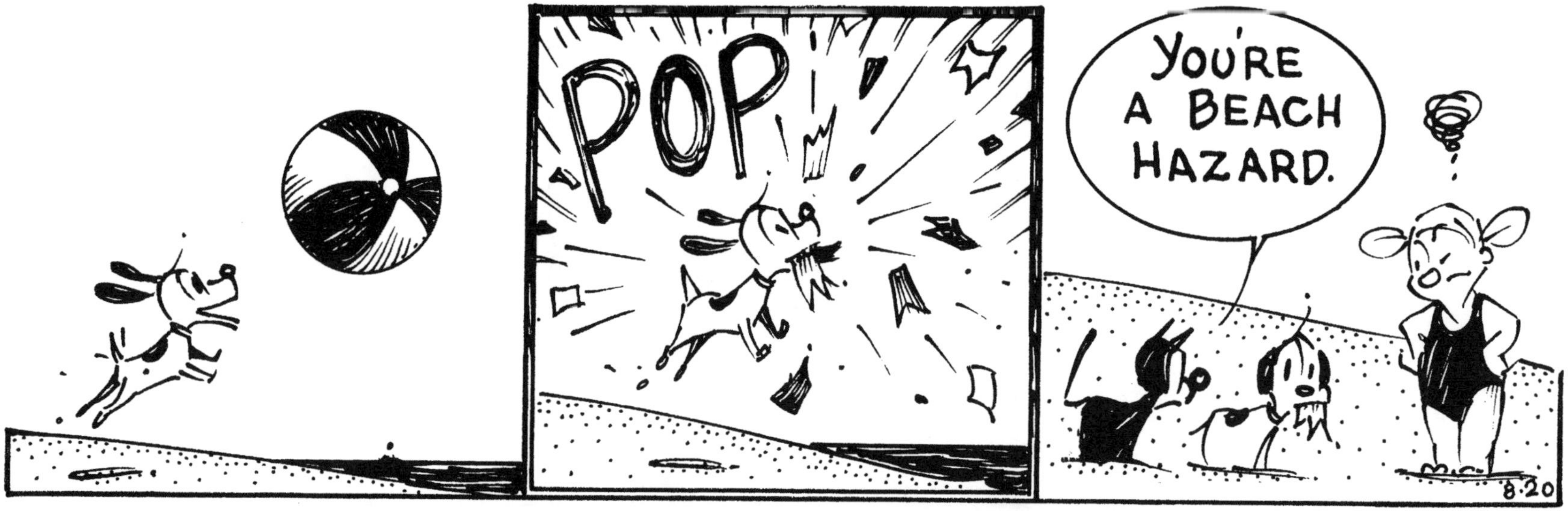
POP
YOU'RE A BEACH HAZARD.
8·20

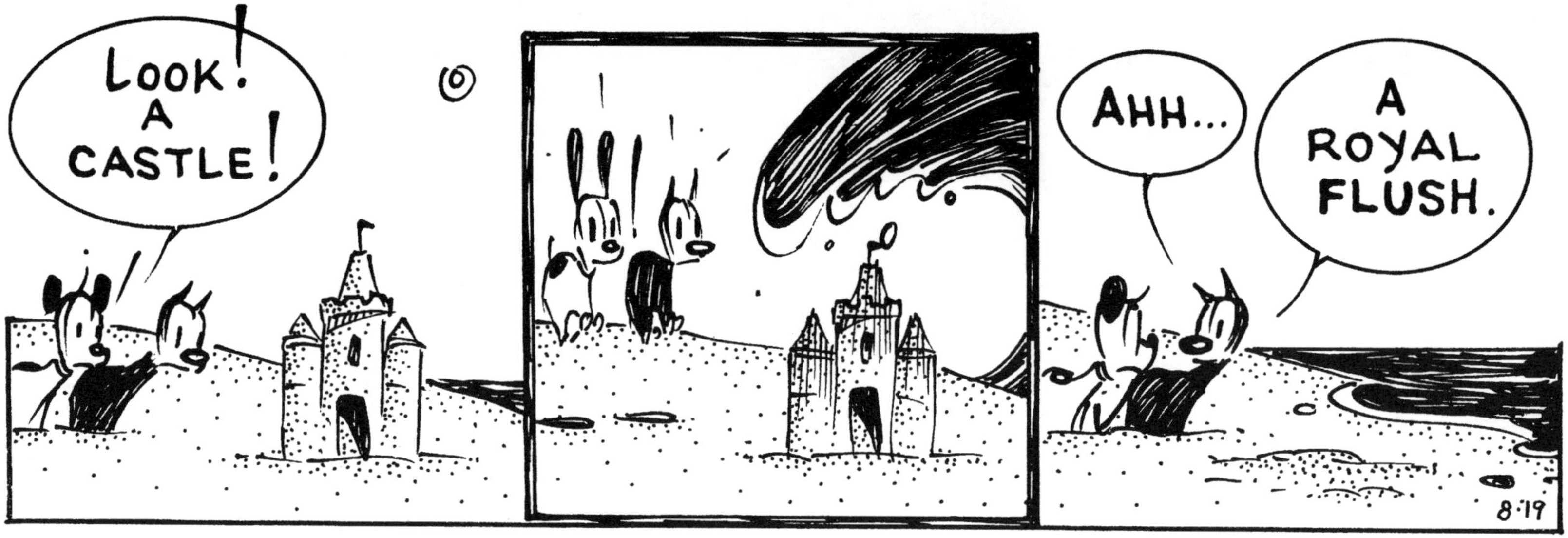
LOOK! A CASTLE!
AHH...
A ROYAL FLUSH.
8·19

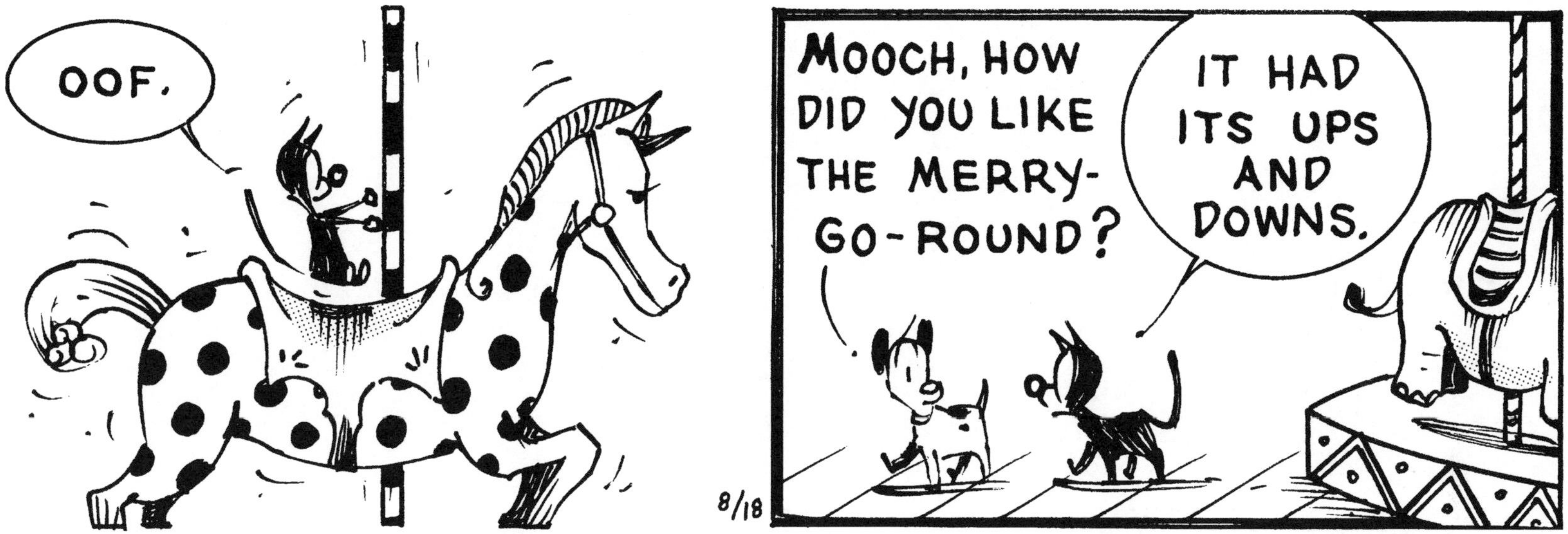
OOF.
8/18
MOOCH, HOW DID YOU LIKE THE MERRY-GO-ROUND?
IT HAD ITS UPS AND DOWNS.

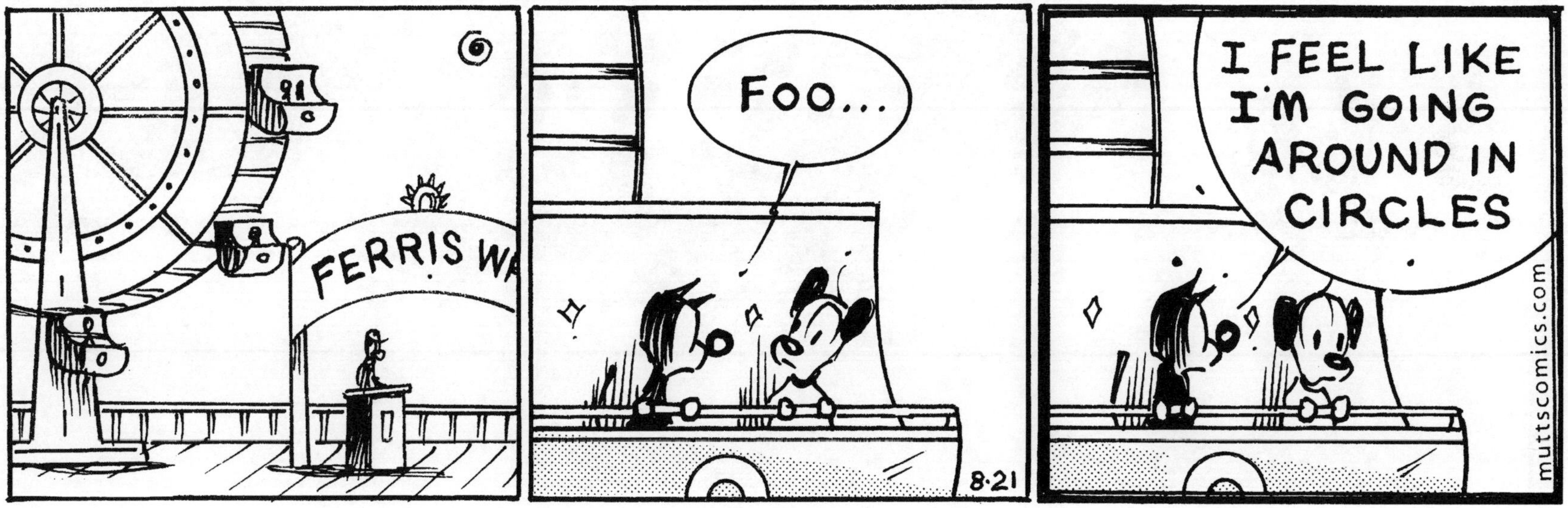
FERRIS WH
FOO...
8·21
I FEEL LIKE I'M GOING AROUND IN CIRCLES
muttscomics.com

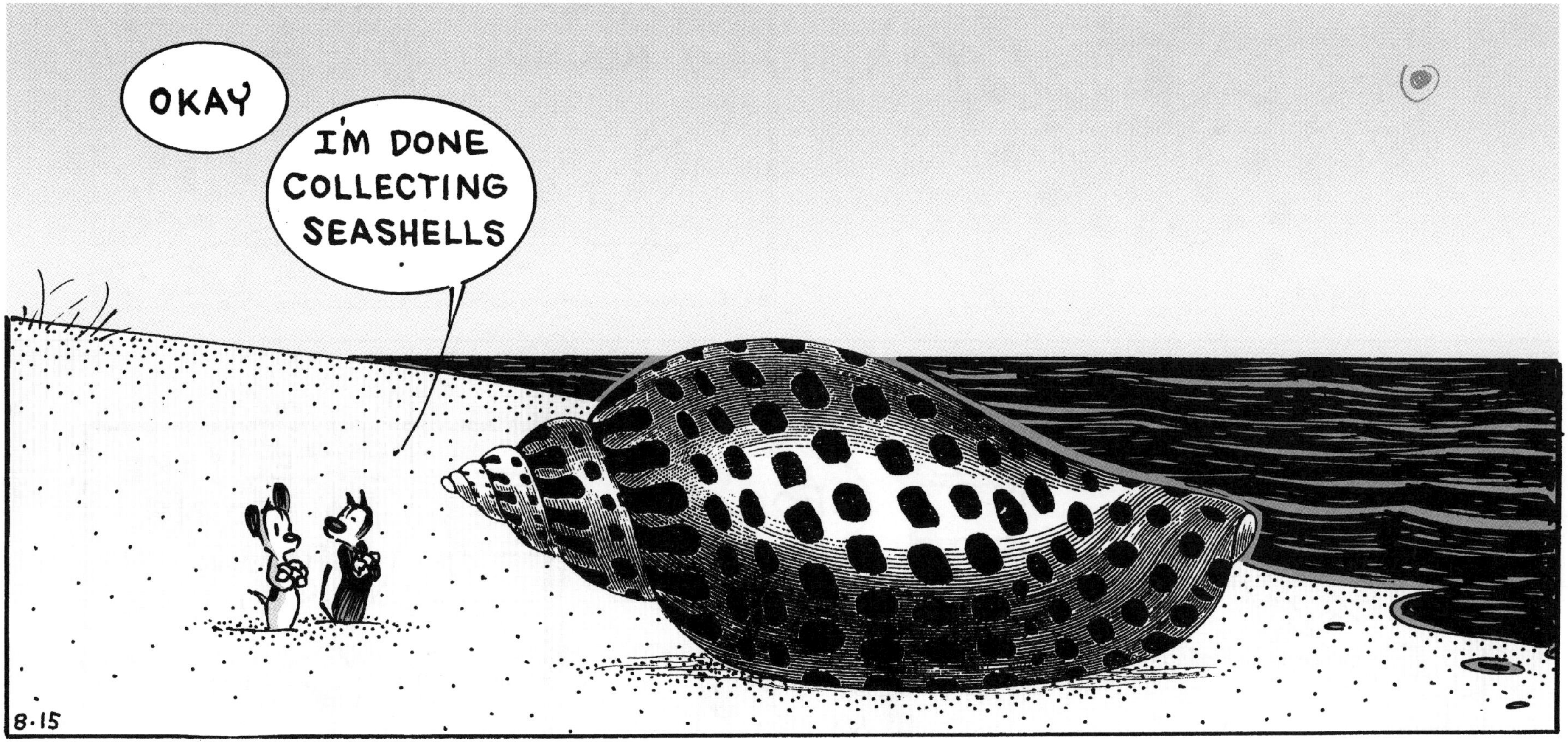
OKAY
I'M DONE COLLECTING SEASHELLS
8·15

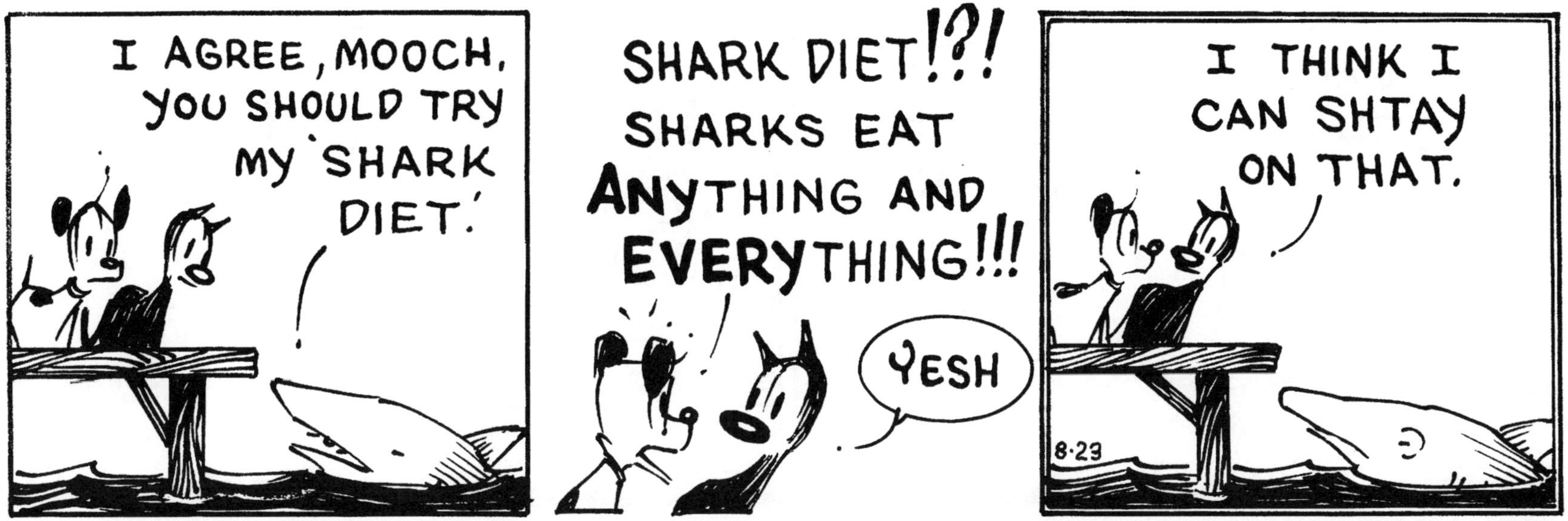
I AGREE, MOOCH, YOU SHOULD TRY MY 'SHARK DIET.'
SHARK DIET!?! SHARKS EAT ANYTHING AND EVERYTHING!!!
YESH
I THINK I CAN SHTAY ON THAT.
8·23

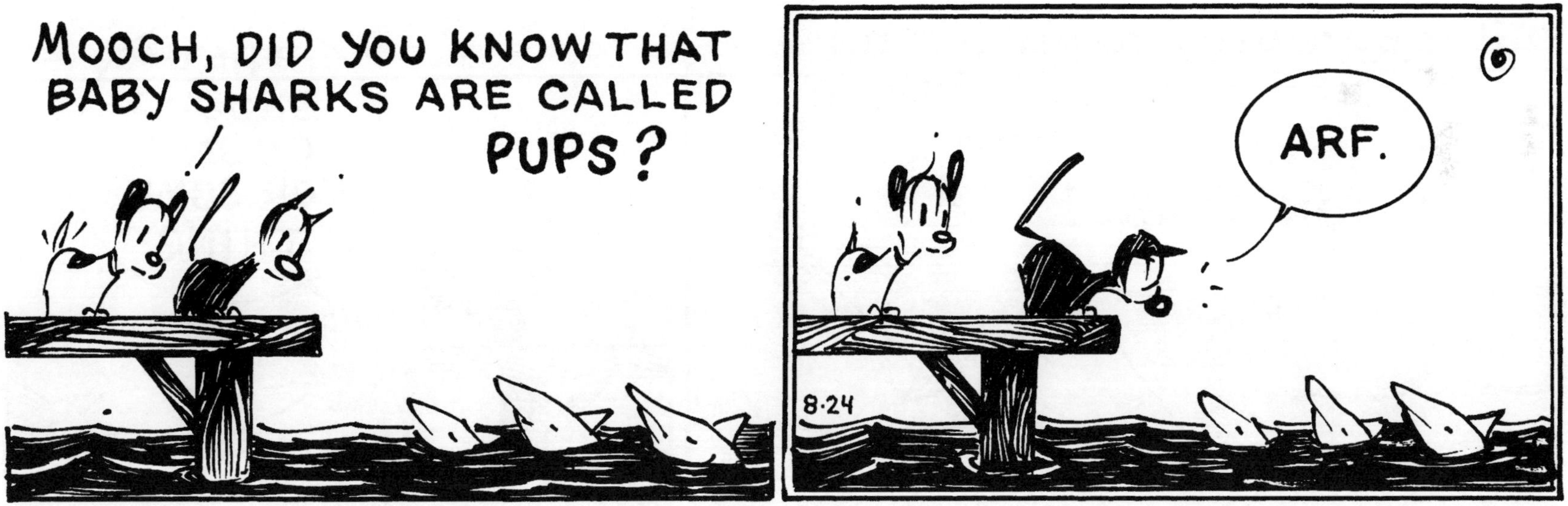
MOOCH, DID YOU KNOW THAT BABY SHARKS ARE CALLED PUPS?
ARF.
8·24

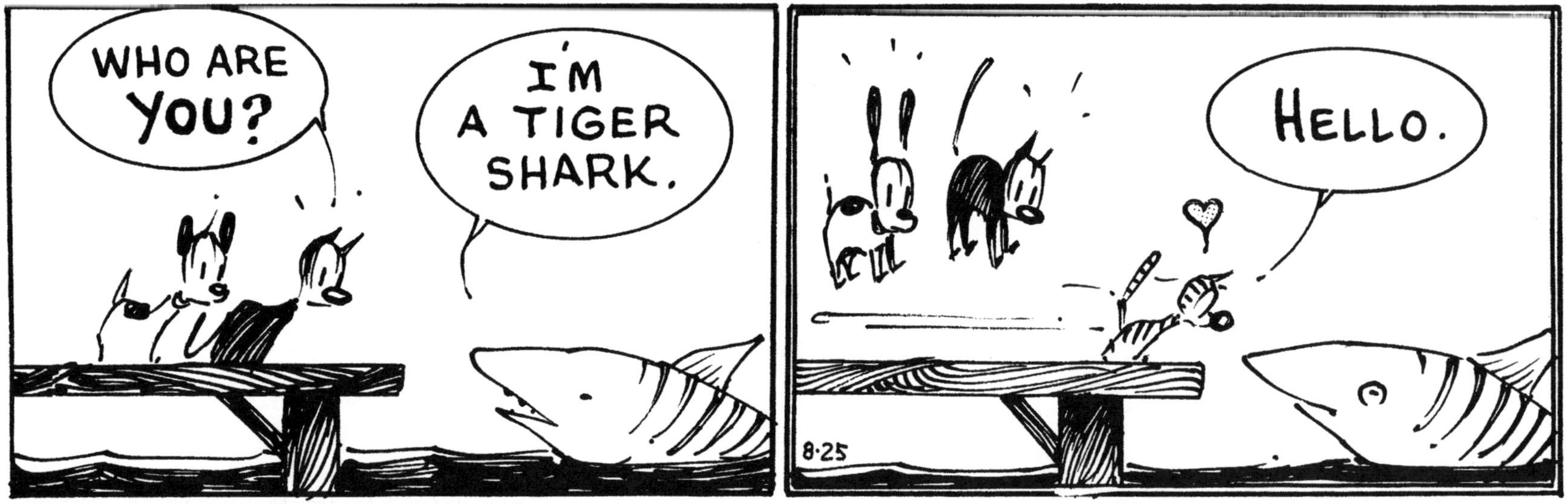
WHO ARE YOU?
I'M A TIGER SHARK.
HELLO.
8·25

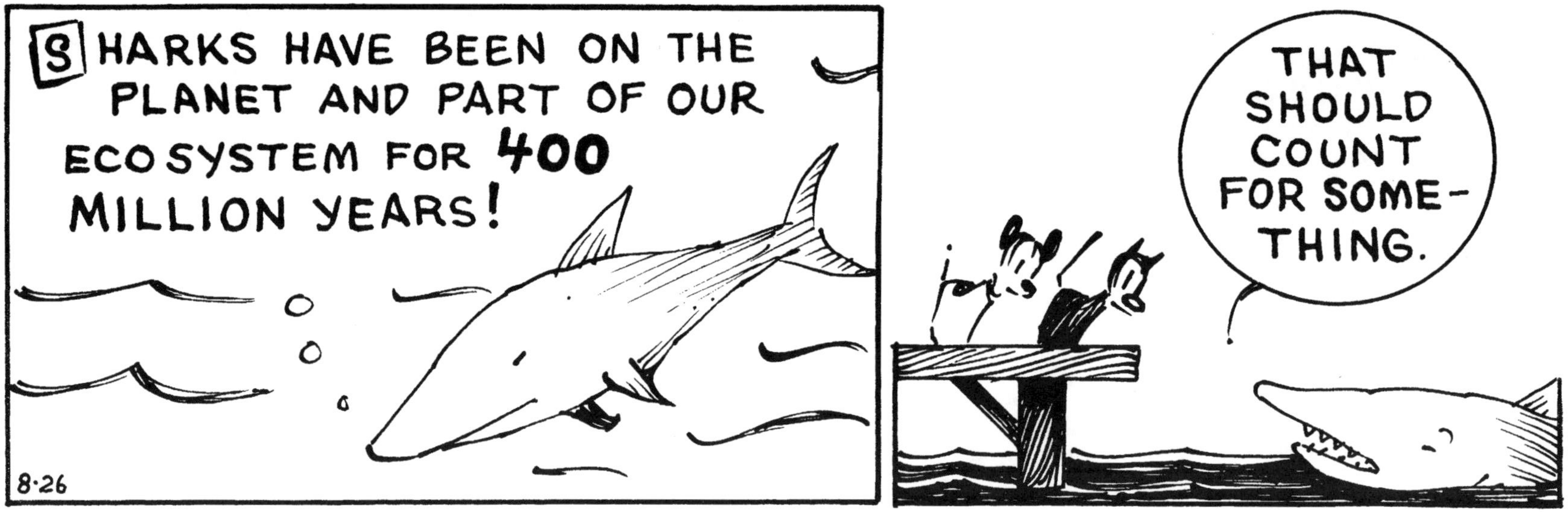
SHARKS HAVE BEEN ON THE PLANET AND PART OF OUR ECOSYSTEM FOR 400 MILLION YEARS!
8·26
THAT SHOULD COUNT FOR SOME-THING.

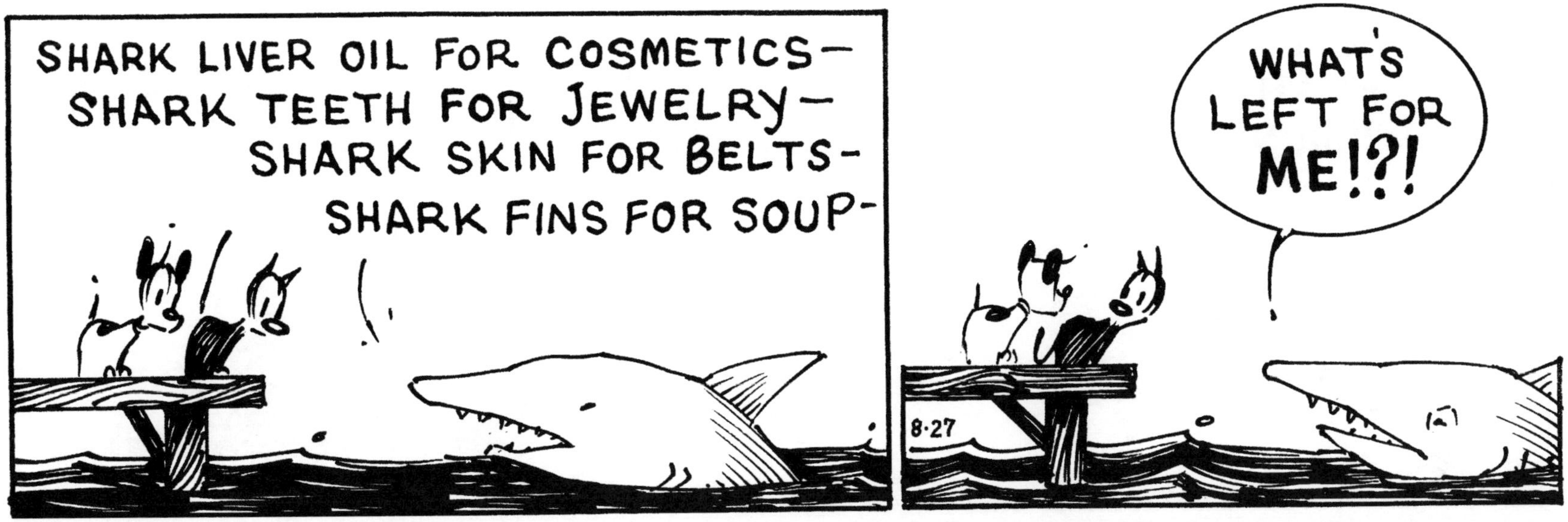
SHARK LIVER OIL FOR COSMETICS—
SHARK TEETH FOR JEWELRY—
SHARK SKIN FOR BELTS-
SHARK FINS FOR SOUP-
WHAT'S LEFT FOR ME!?!
8·27

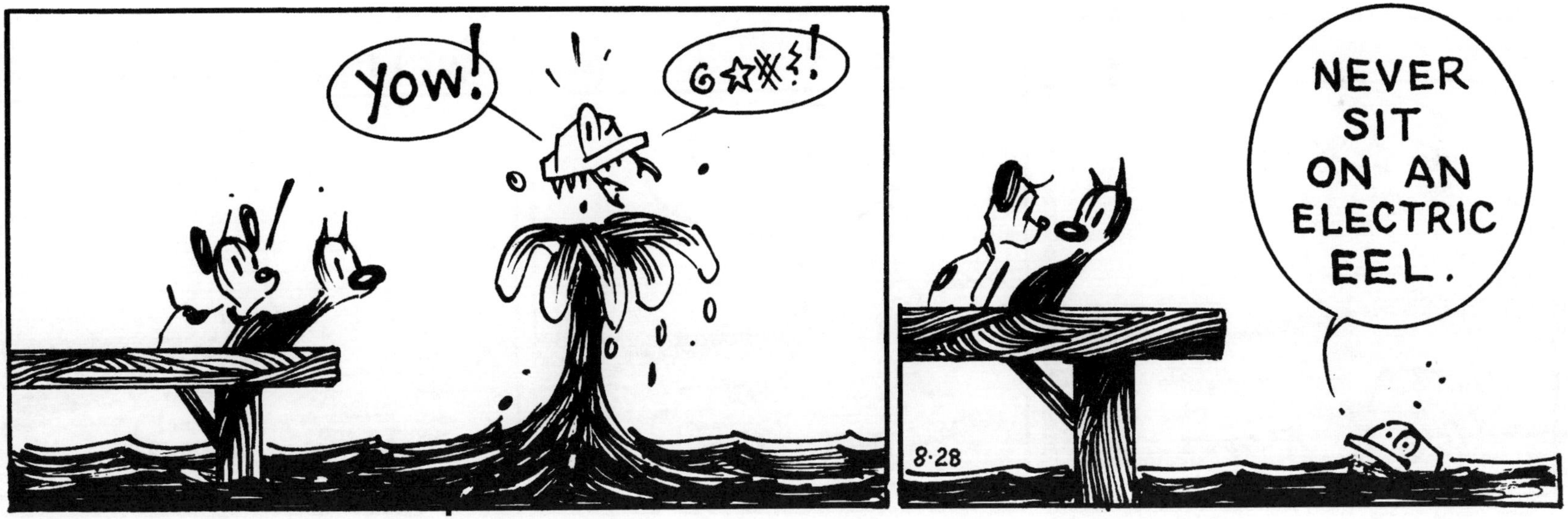
YOW!
NEVER SIT ON AN ELECTRIC EEL.
8·28

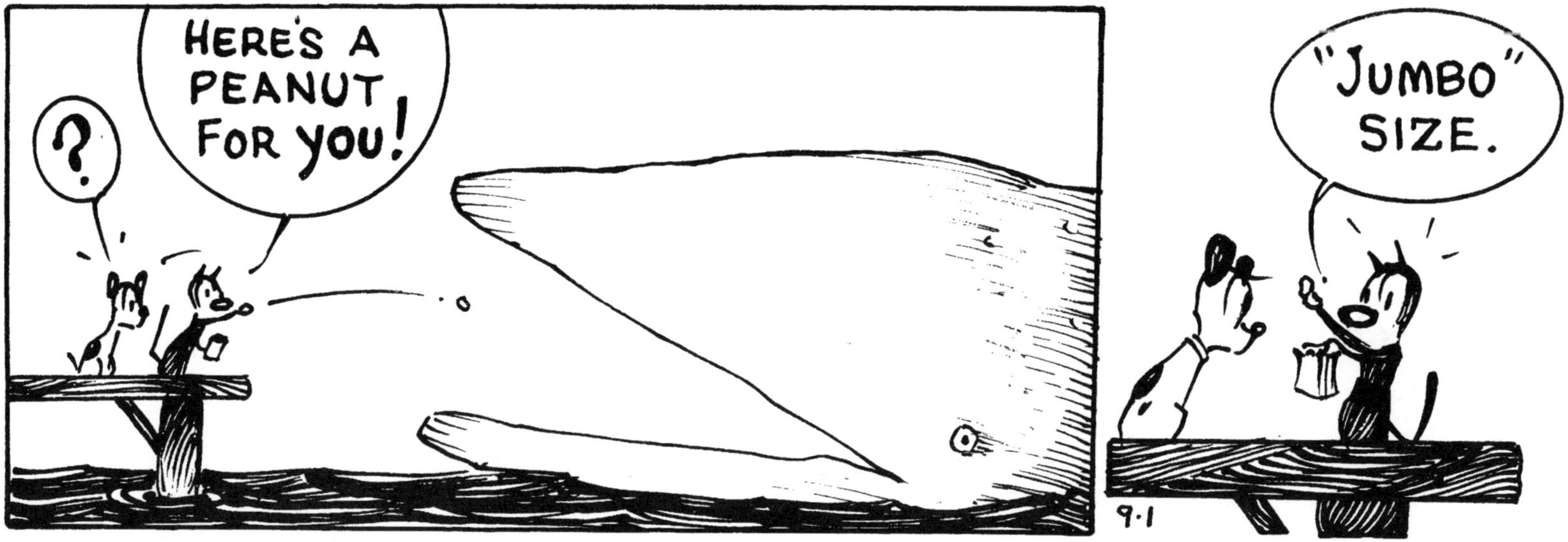
?
HERE'S A PEANUT FOR YOU!
"JUMBO" SIZE.
9·1

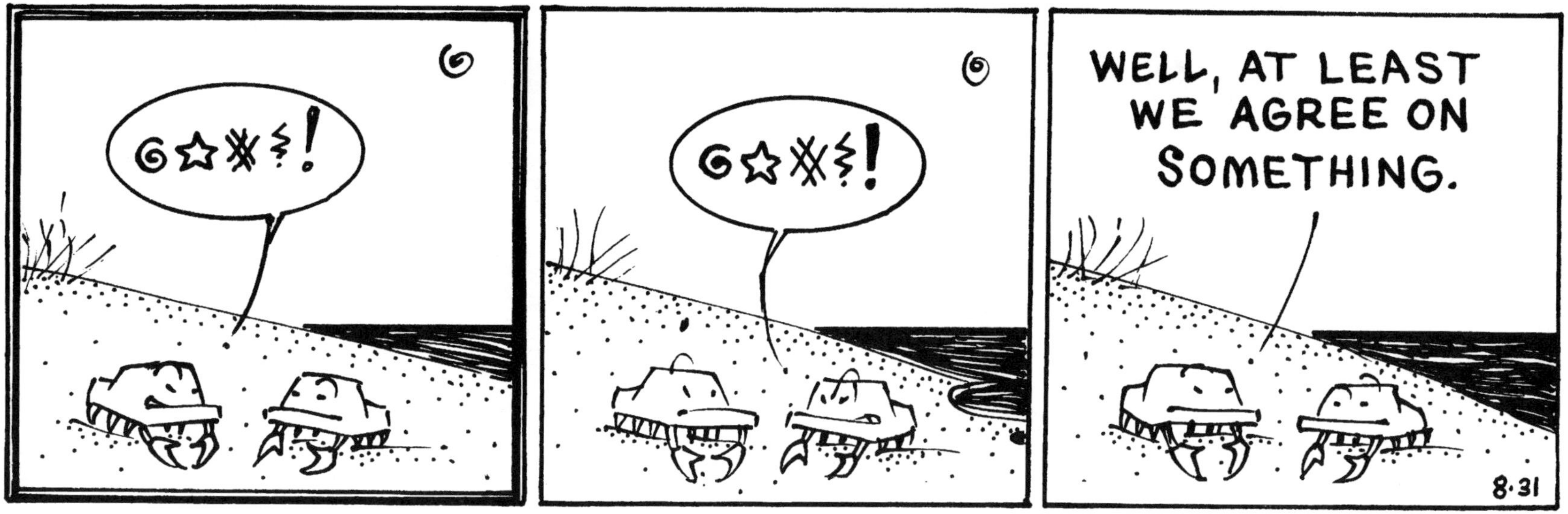
WELL, AT LEAST WE AGREE ON SOMETHING.
8·31

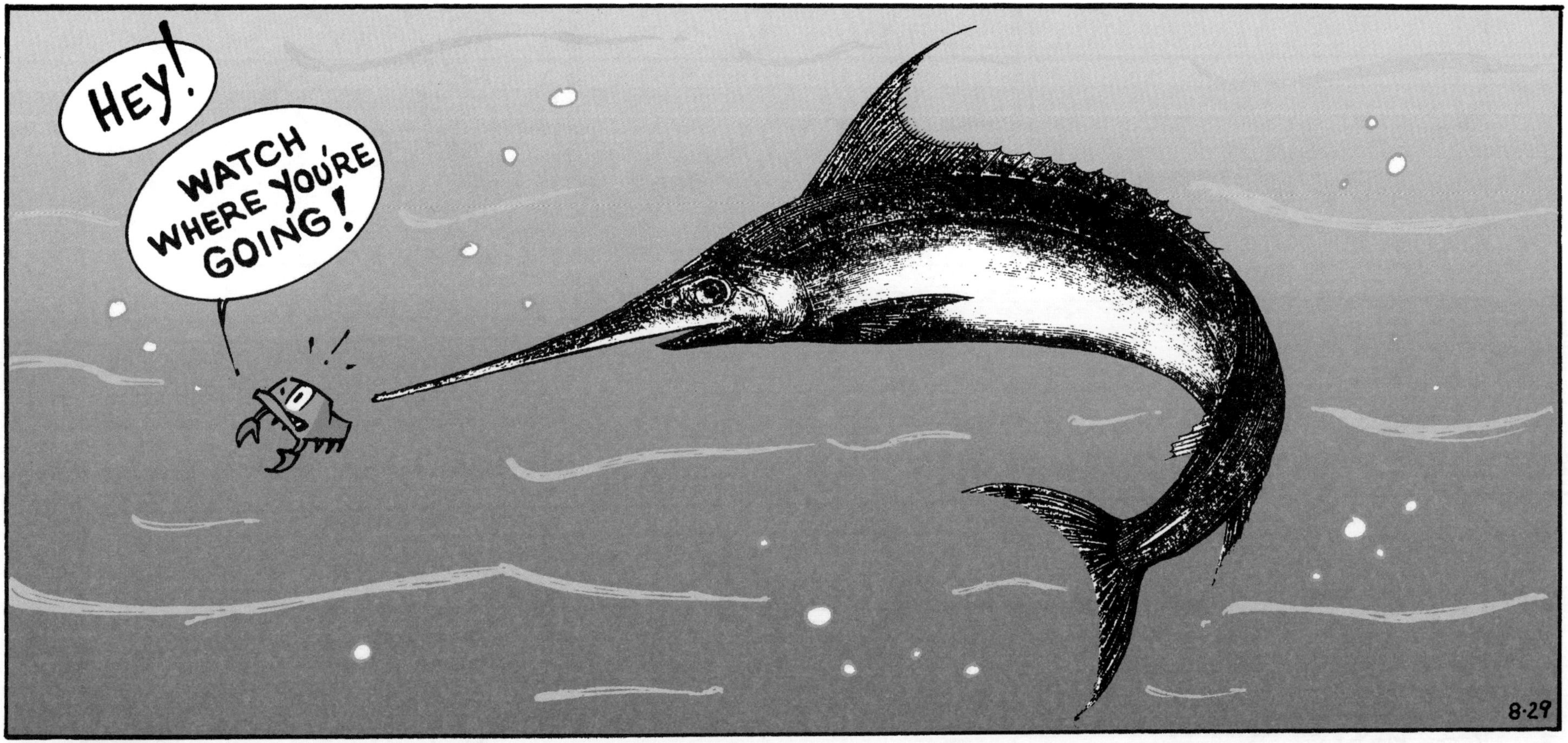
HEY!
WATCH WHERE YOU'RE GOING!
8·29

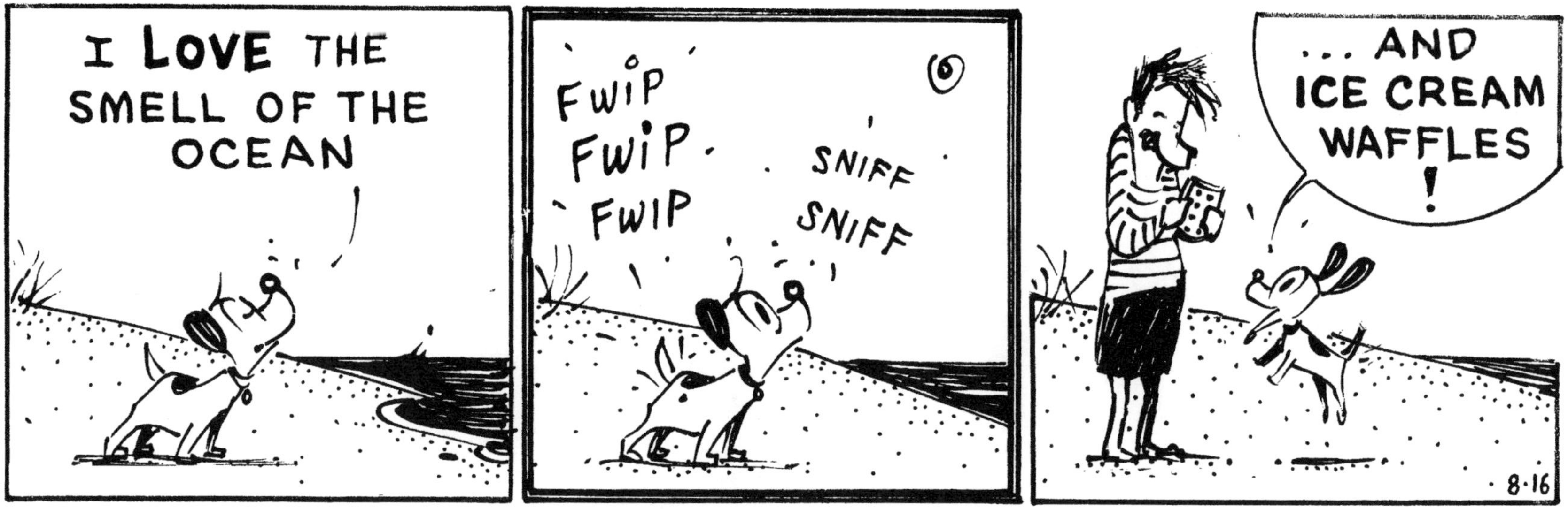
I LOVE THE SMELL OF THE OCEAN
FWIP FWIP FWIP
SNIFF SNIFF
...AND ICE CREAM WAFFLES!
8·16

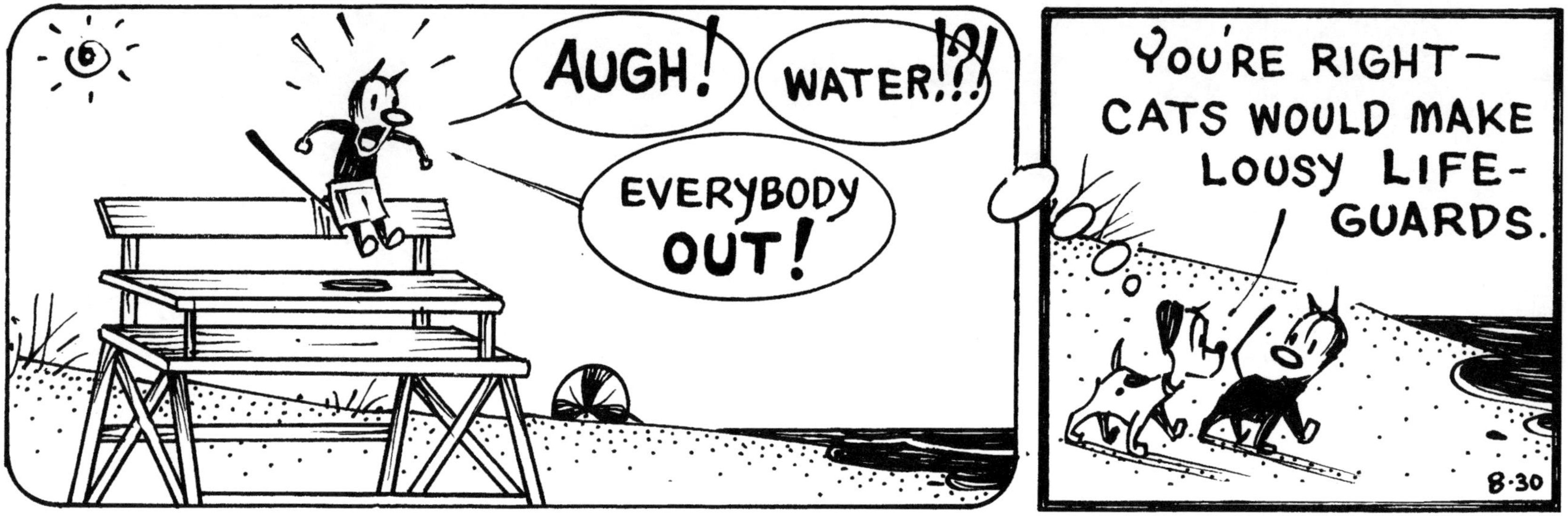
AUGH!
WATER!?!
EVERYBODY OUT!
YOU'RE RIGHT— CATS WOULD MAKE LOUSY LIFE-GUARDS.
8·30

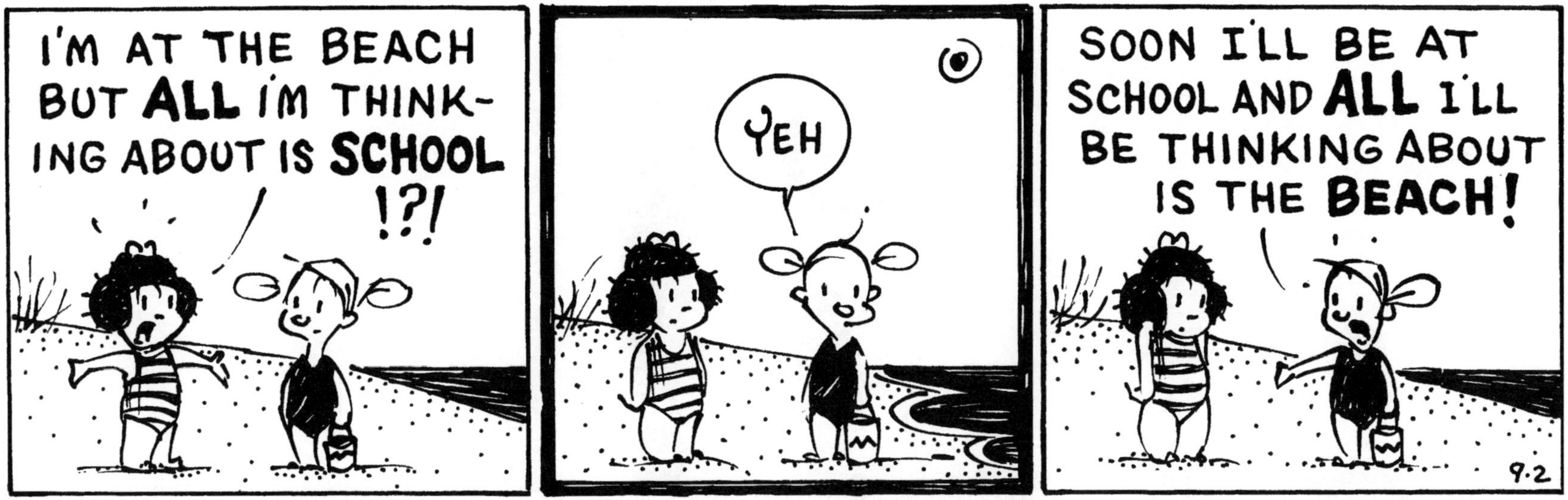
I'M AT THE BEACH BUT ALL I'M THINKING ABOUT IS SCHOOL !?!
YEH
SOON I'LL BE AT SCHOOL AND ALL I'LL BE THINKING ABOUT IS THE BEACH!
9·2

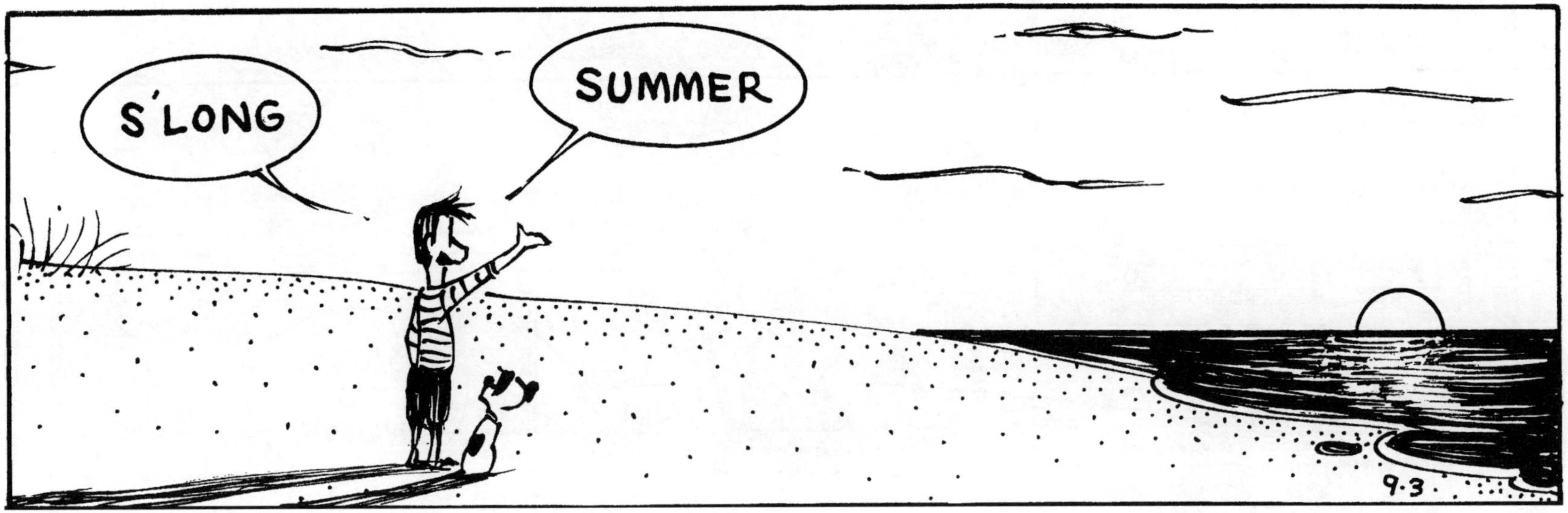
S'LONG
SUMMER
9·3

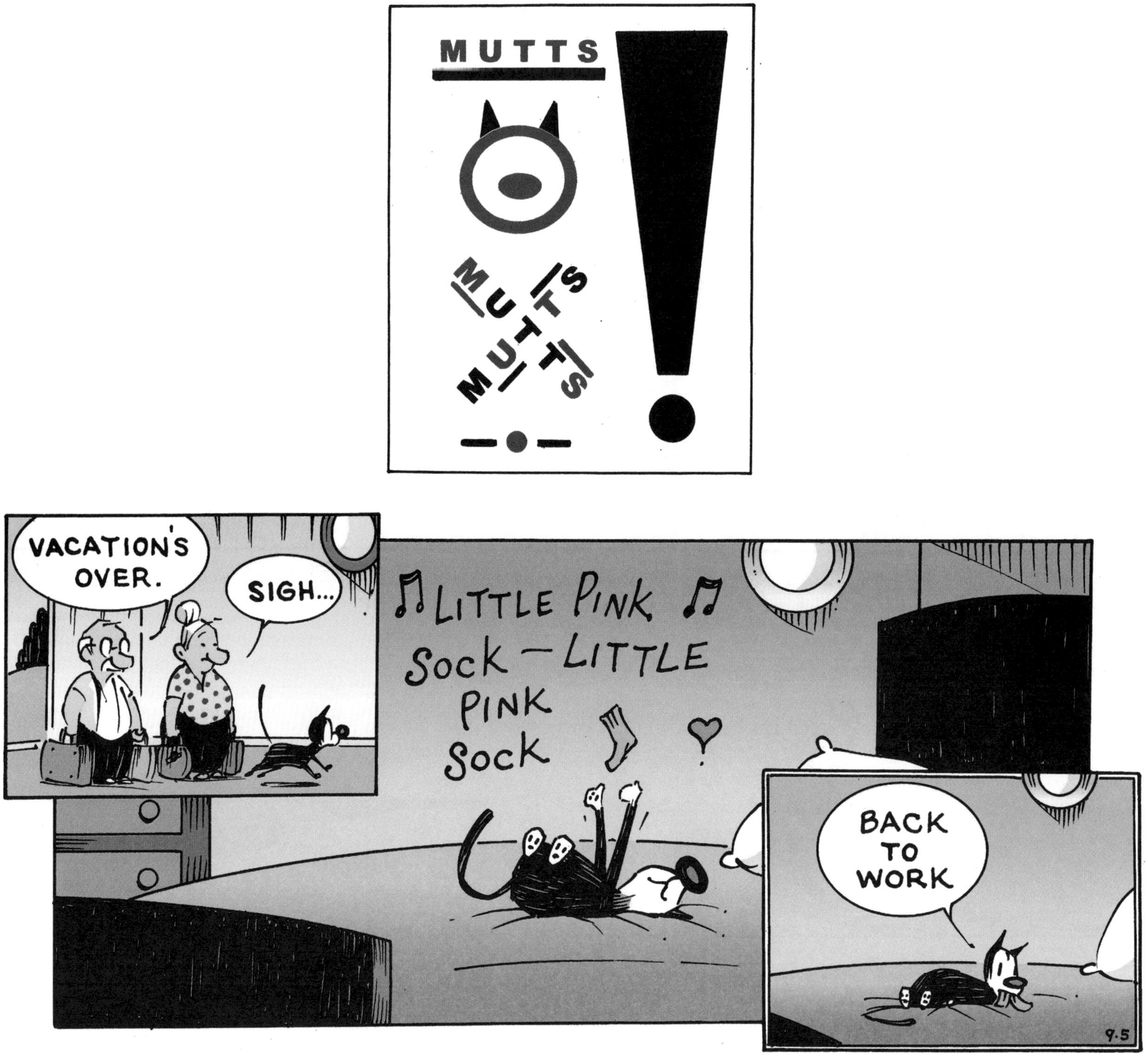
MUTTS
MUTTS
MUTTS
VACATION'S OVER.
SIGH...
LITTLE PINK SOCK — LITTLE PINK SOCK
BACK TO WORK
9.5

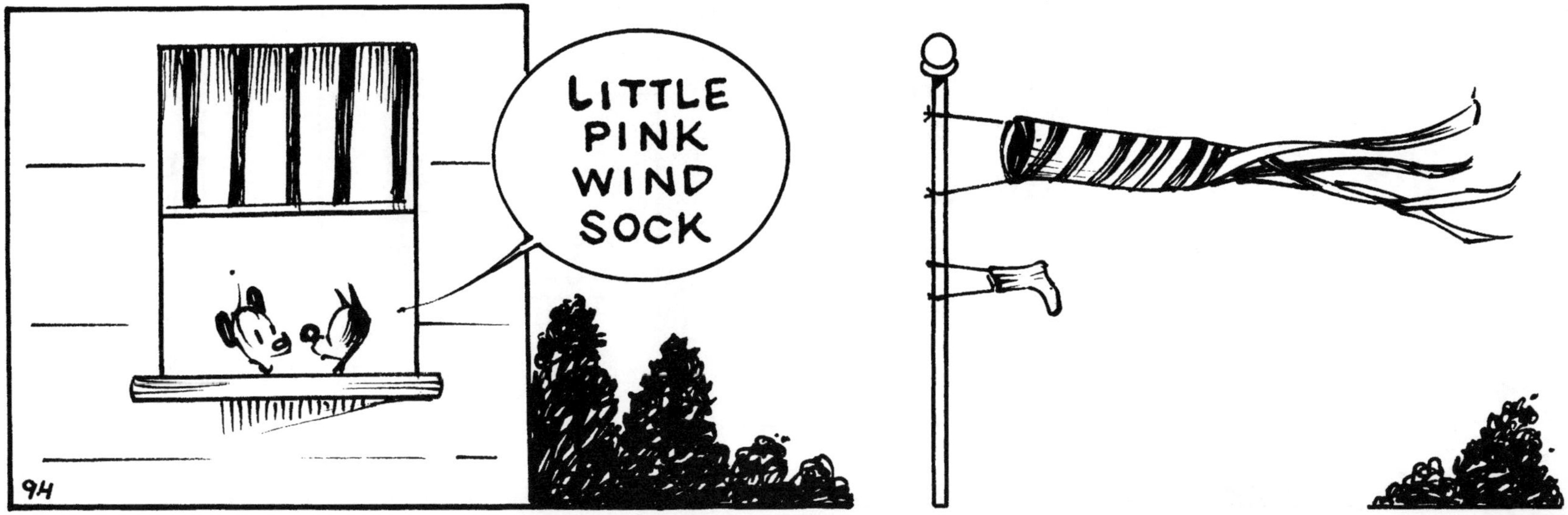
LITTLE PINK WIND SOCK
94

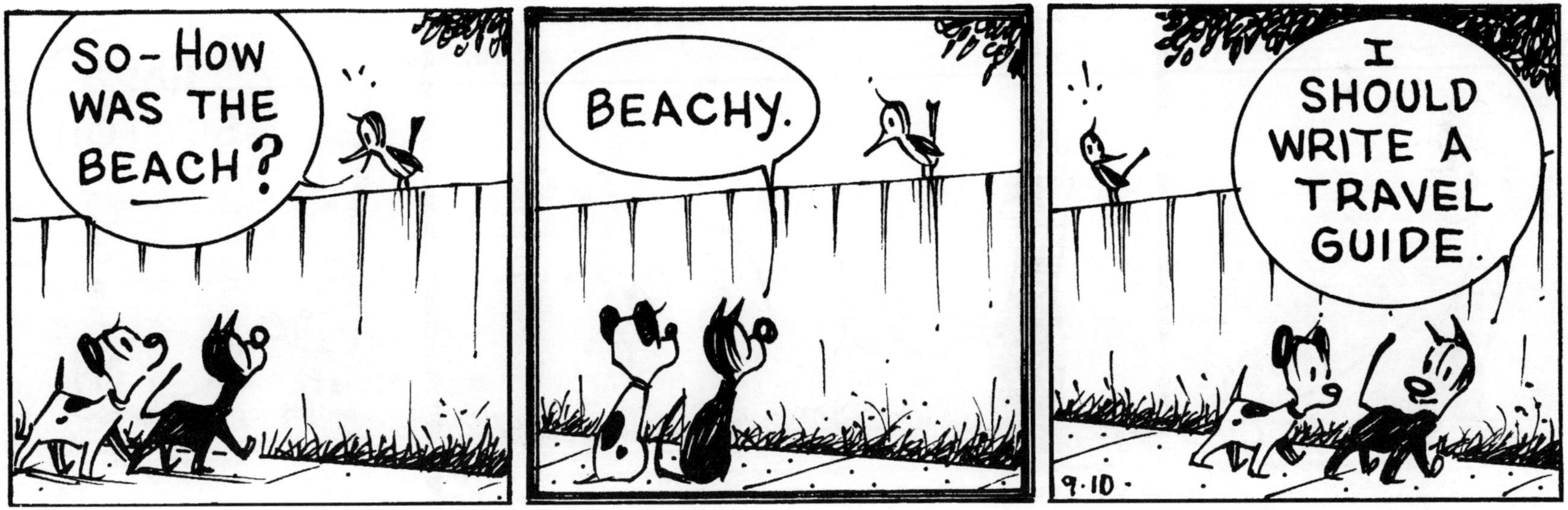
SO-HOW WAS THE BEACH?
BEACHY.
I SHOULD WRITE A TRAVEL GUIDE.
9.10

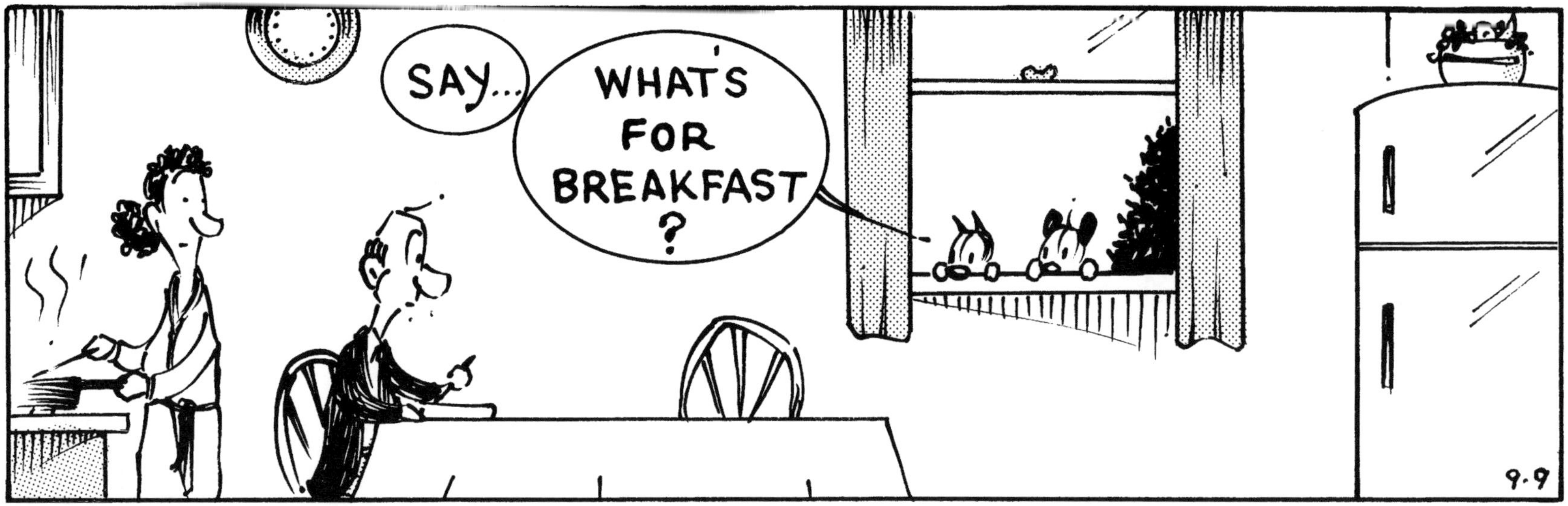
SAY...
WHAT'S FOR BREAKFAST?
9·9

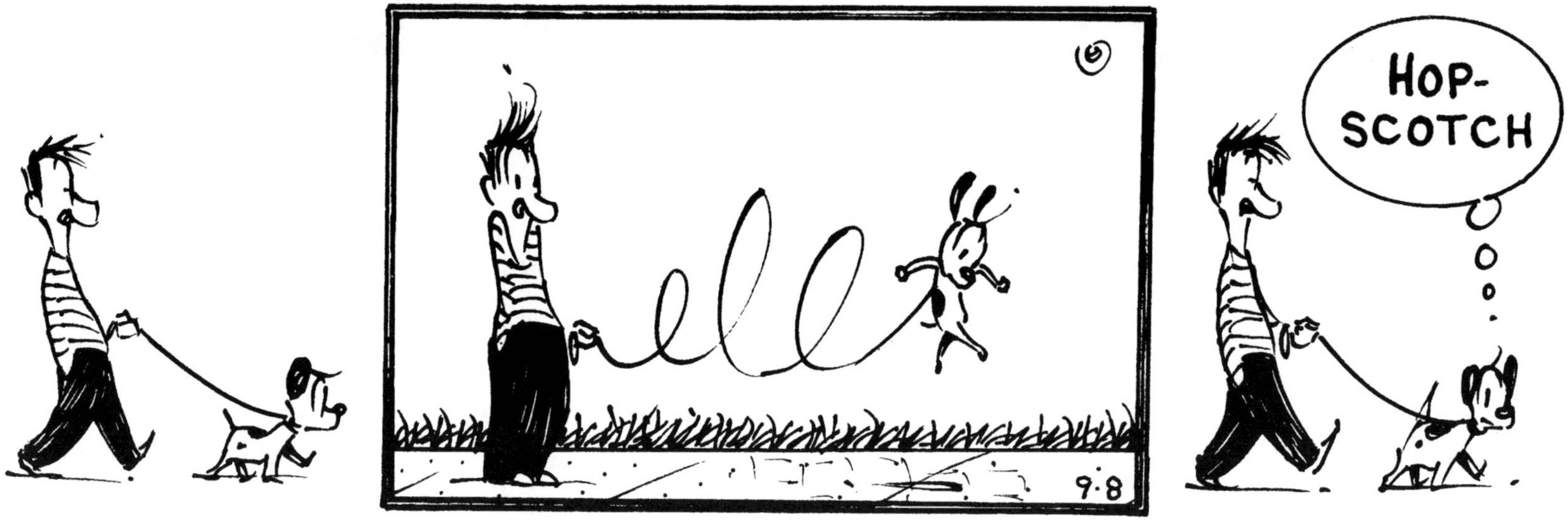
9·8
HOP-SCOTCH

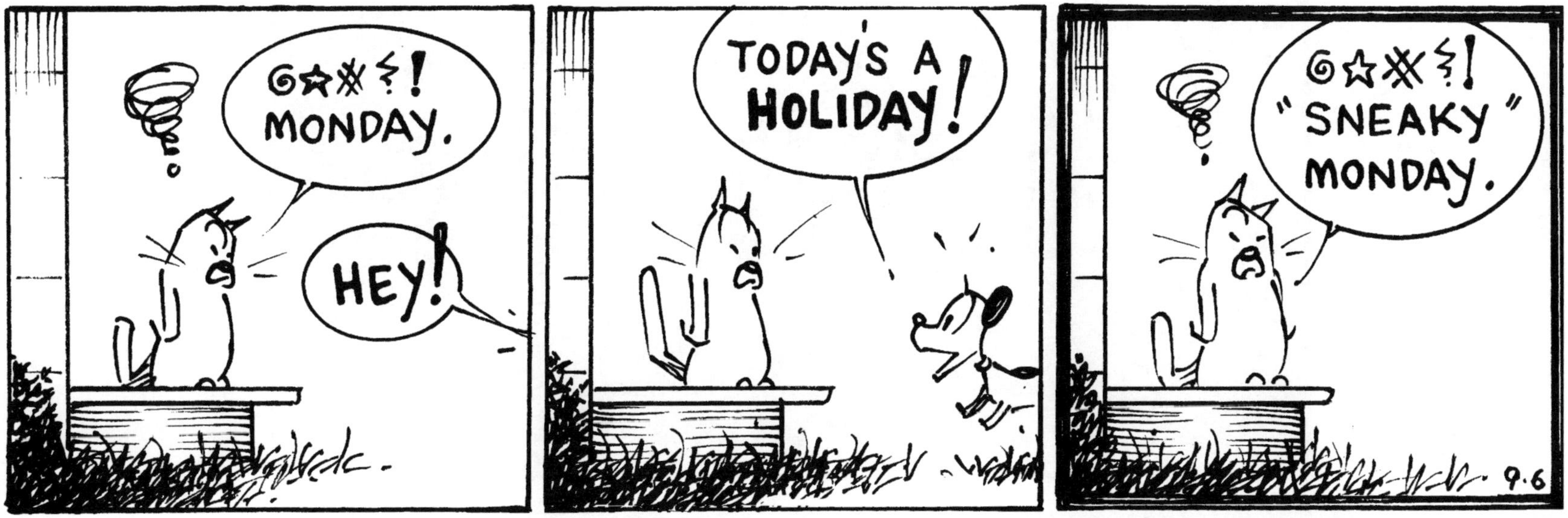
G☆※?! MONDAY.
HEY!
TODAY'S A HOLIDAY!
G☆※?! "SNEAKY" MONDAY.
9·6

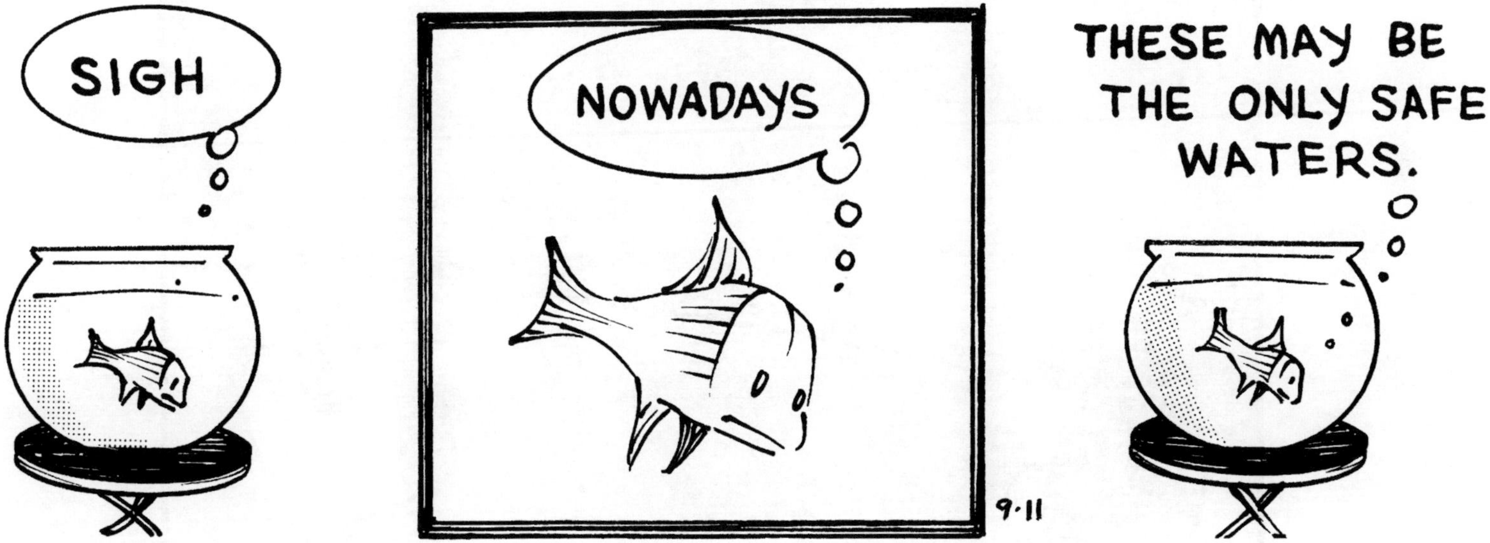
SIGH
NOWADAYS
THESE MAY BE THE ONLY SAFE WATERS.
9·11

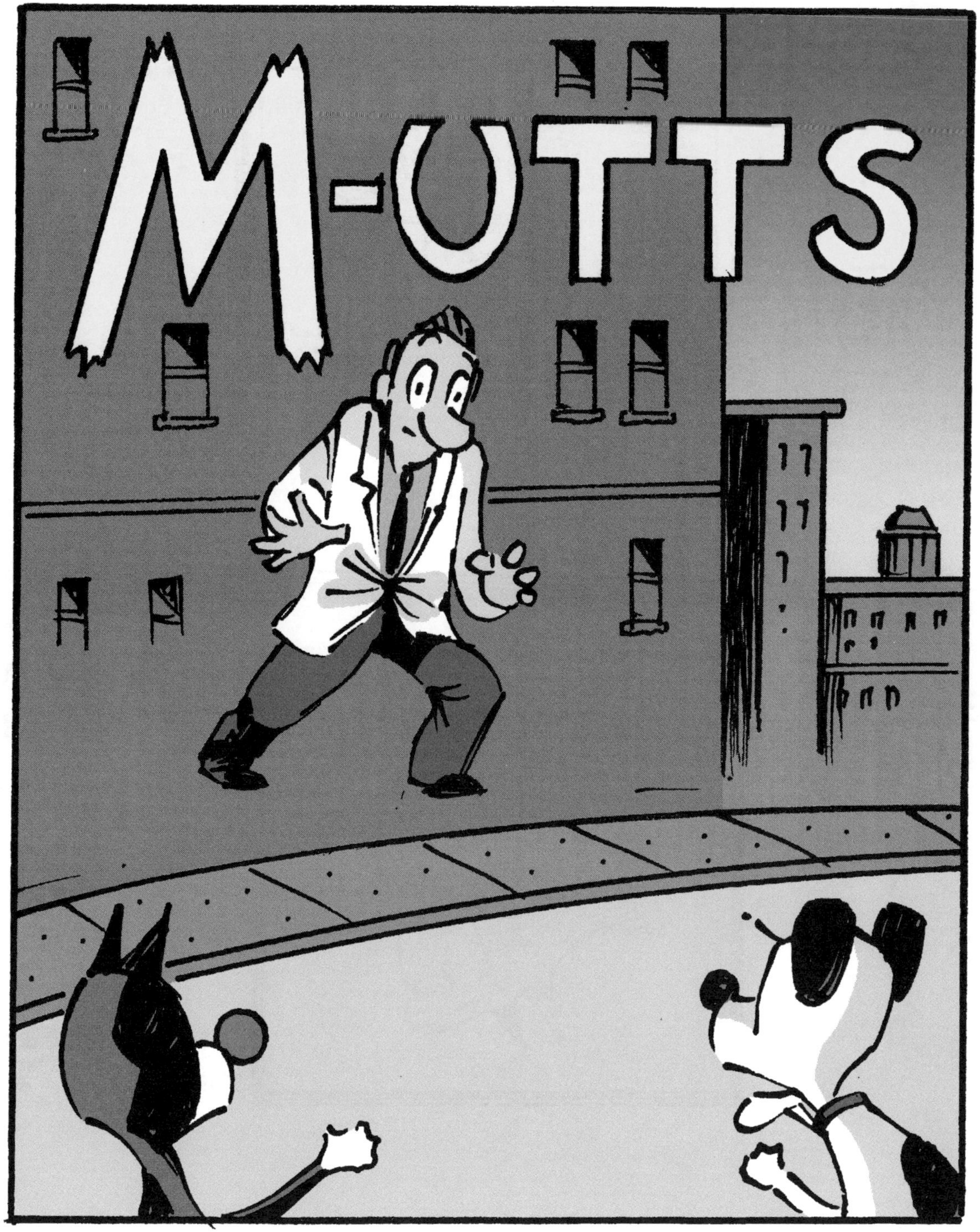
M-UTTS

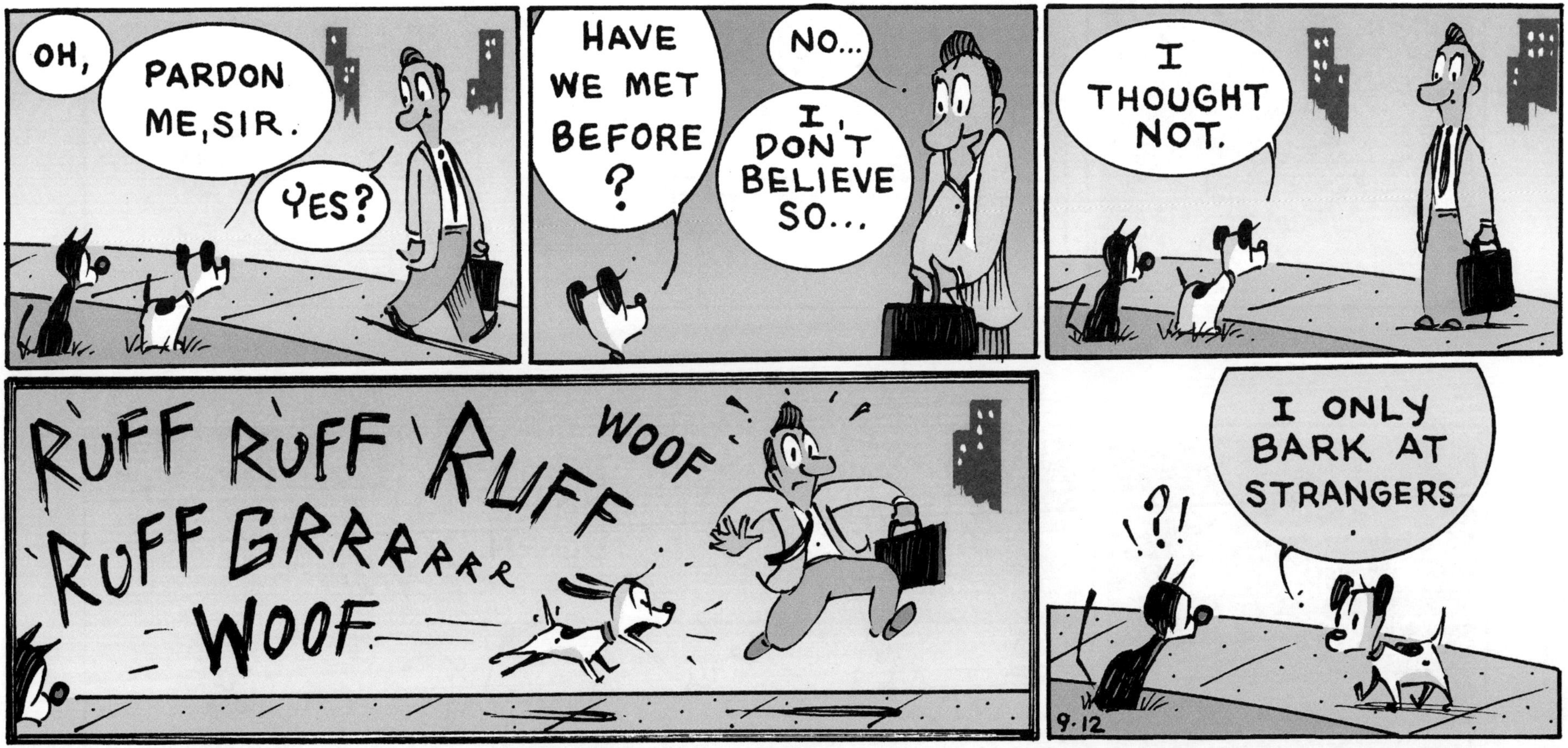
OH,
PARDON ME, SIR.
YES?
HAVE WE MET BEFORE?
NO...
I DON'T BELIEVE SO...
I THOUGHT NOT.
RUFF RUFF RUFF
WOOF
RUFF GRRRRRRR
WOOF
!?!
I ONLY BARK AT STRANGERS.
9.12

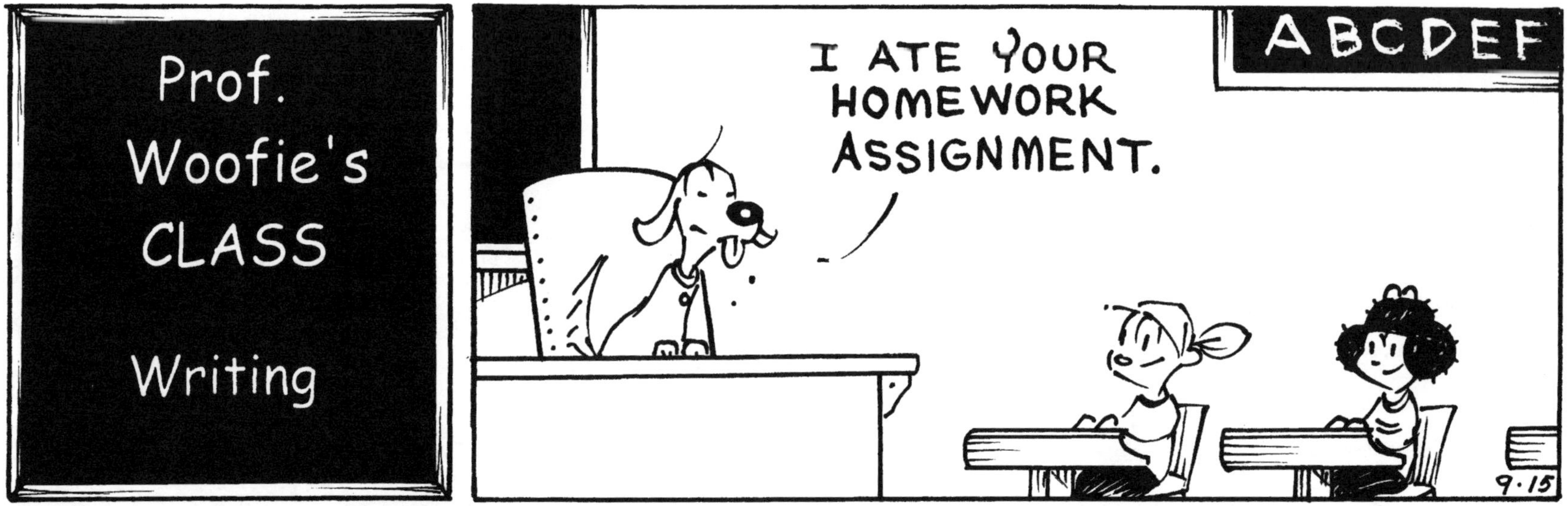
Prof.
Woofie's
CLASS
Writing
ABCDEF
I ATE YOUR HOMEWORK ASSIGNMENT.
9·15

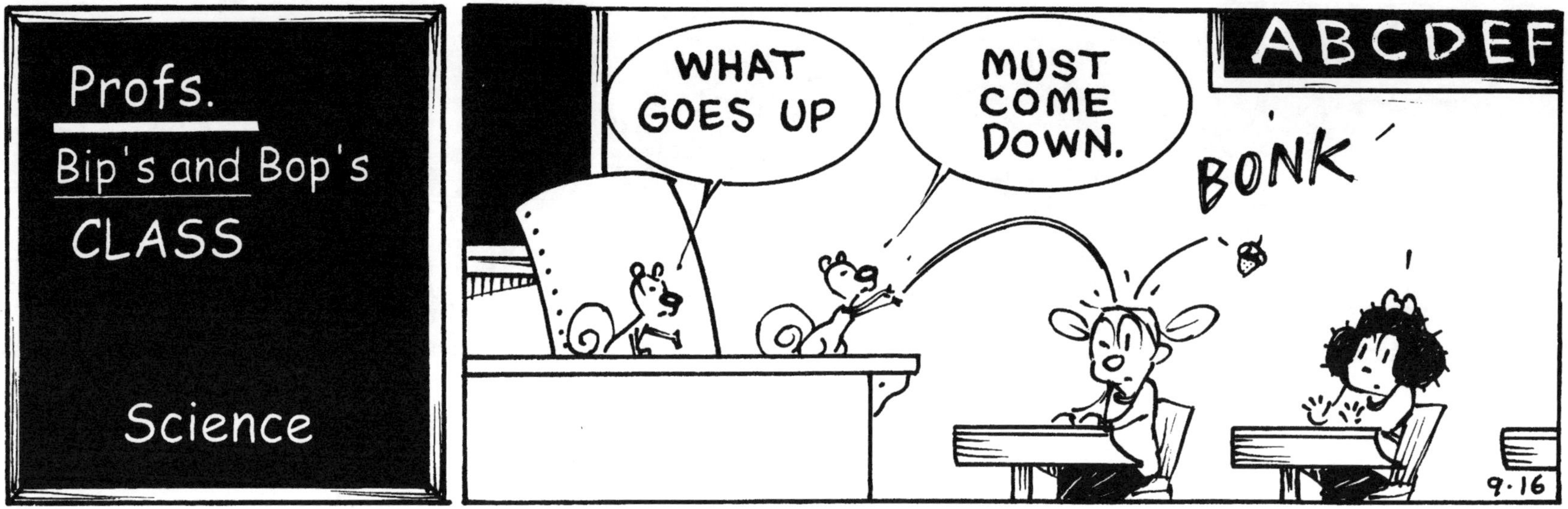
Profs.
Bip's and Bop's
CLASS
Science
ABCDEF
WHAT GOES UP
MUST COME DOWN.
BONK
9·16

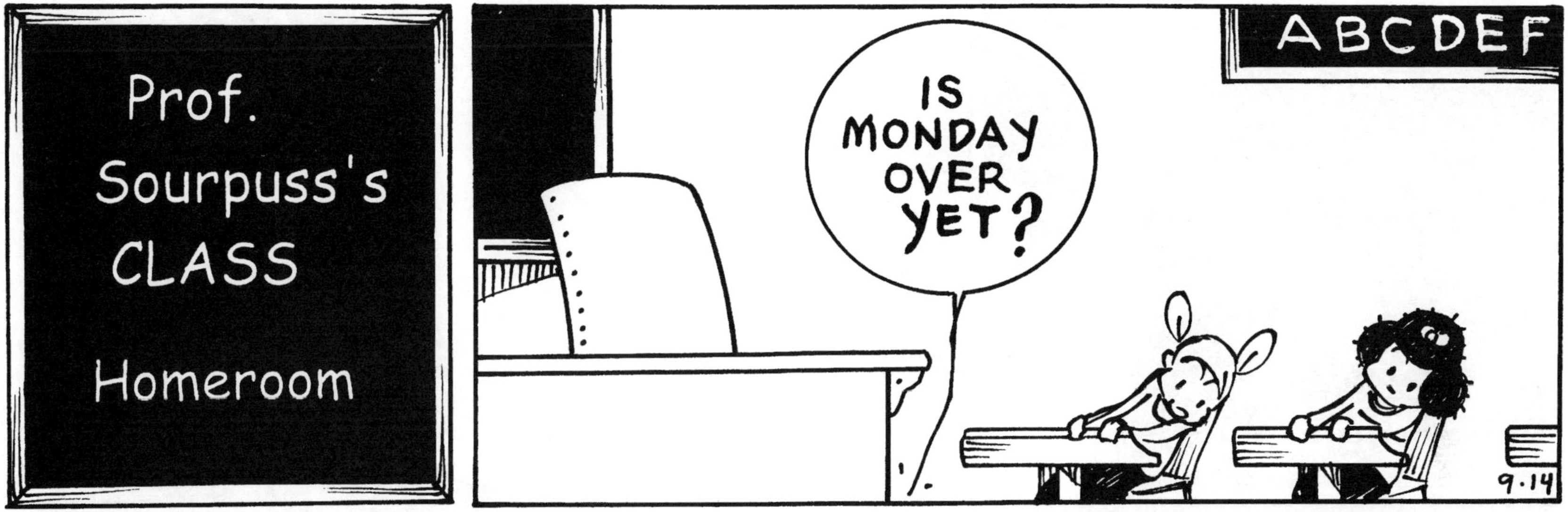
Prof.
Sourpuss's
CLASS
Homeroom
ABCDEF
IS MONDAY OVER YET?
9·14

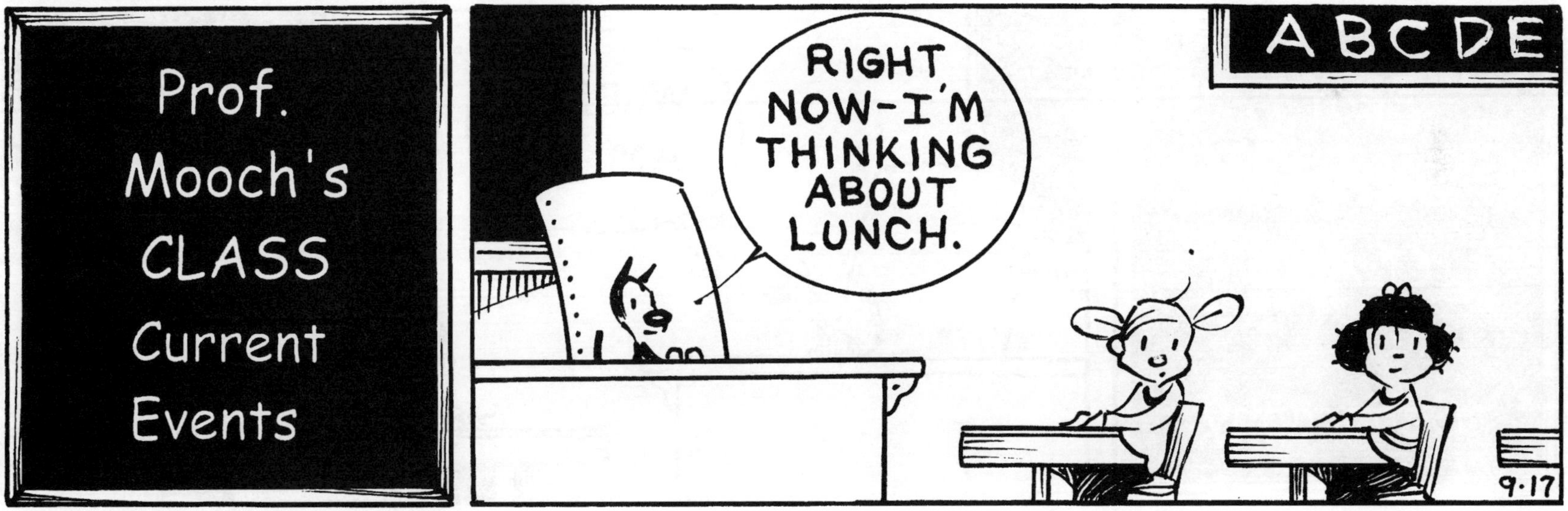
Prof.
Mooch's
CLASS
Current
Events
ABCDE
RIGHT NOW–I'M THINKING ABOUT LUNCH.
9·17

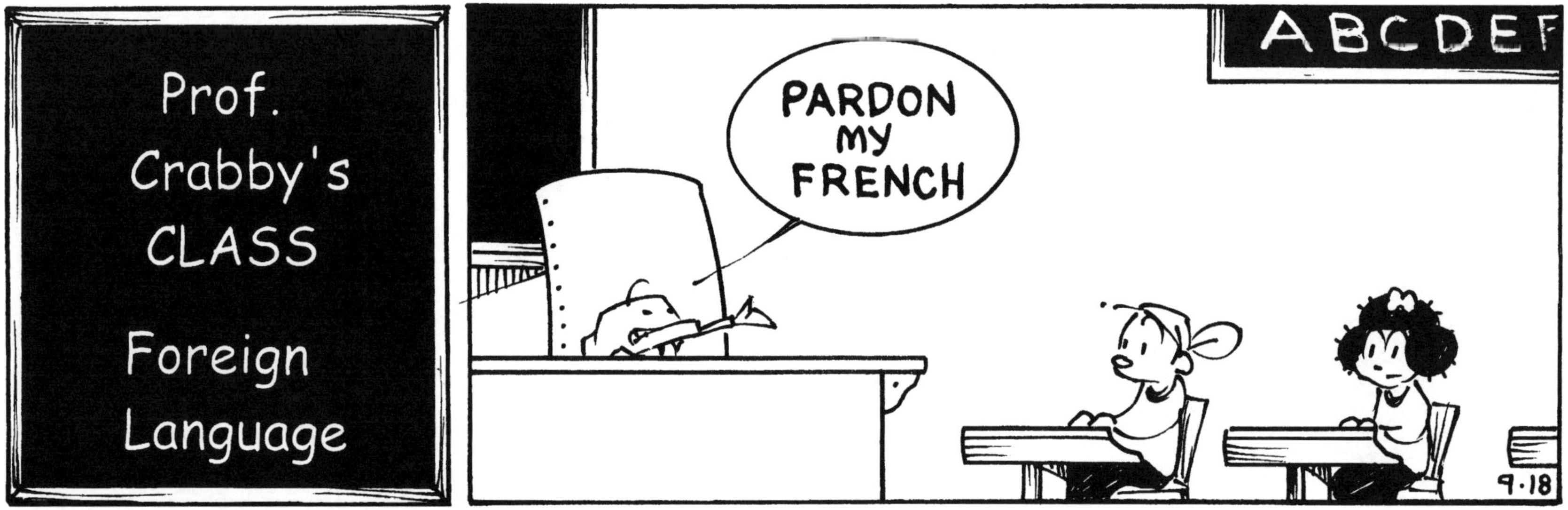
Prof.
Crabby's
CLASS
Foreign
Language
ABCDEF
PARDON MY FRENCH
9·18

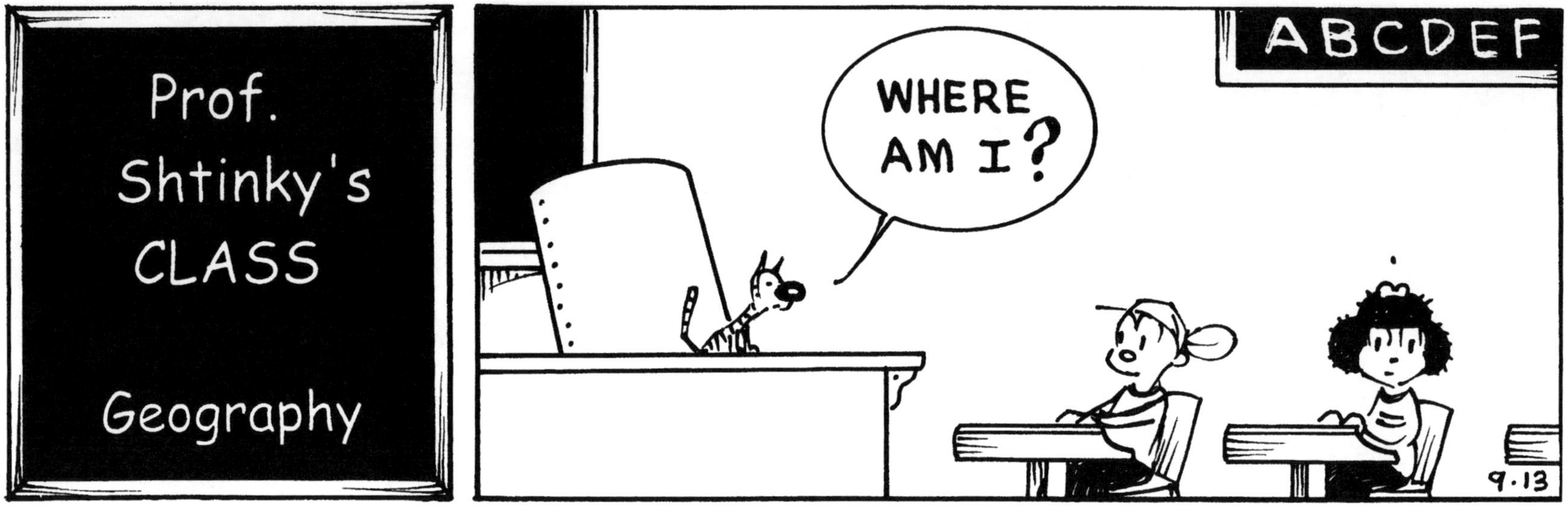
Prof.
Shtinky's
CLASS
Geography
ABCDEF
WHERE AM I?
9·13

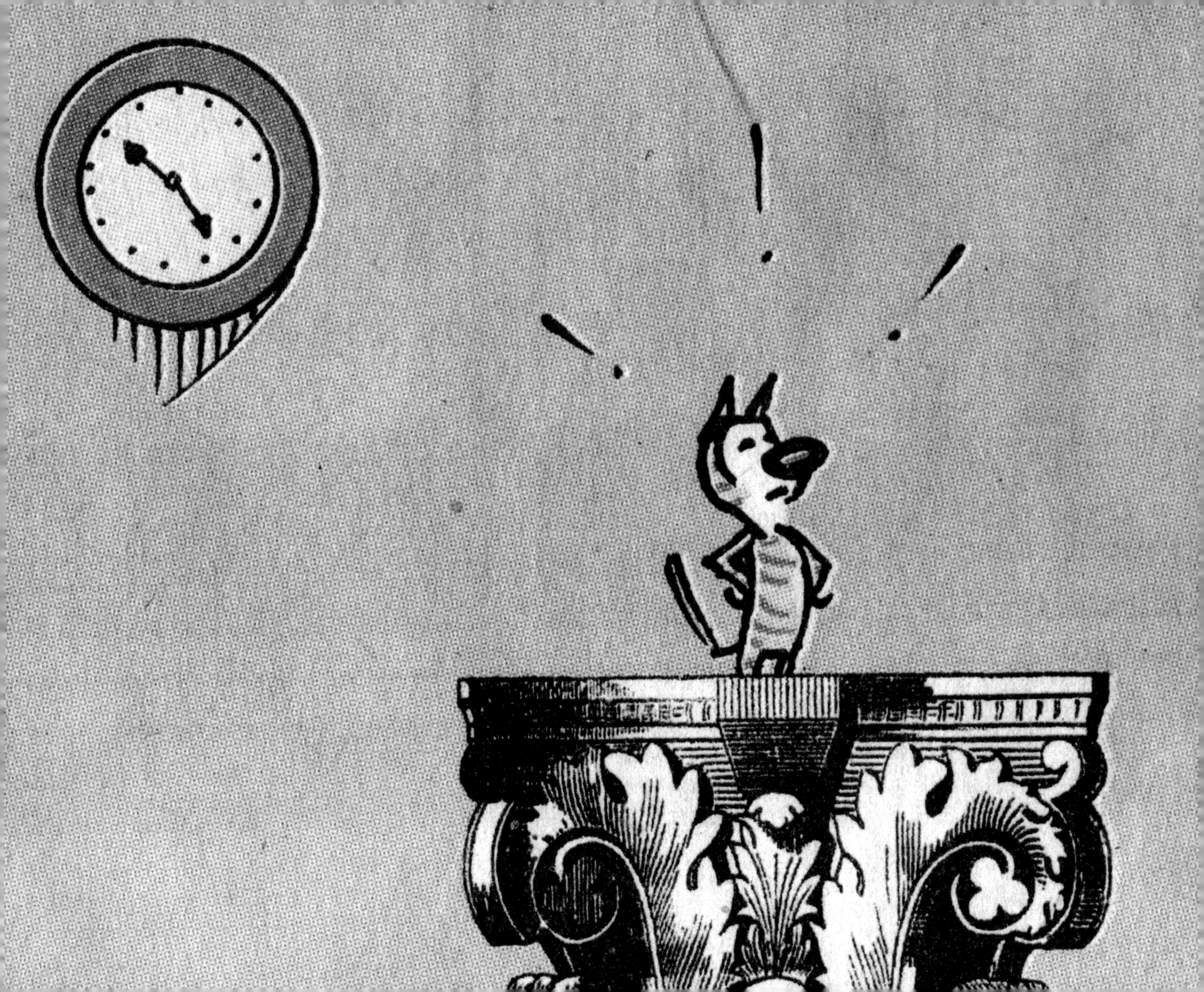

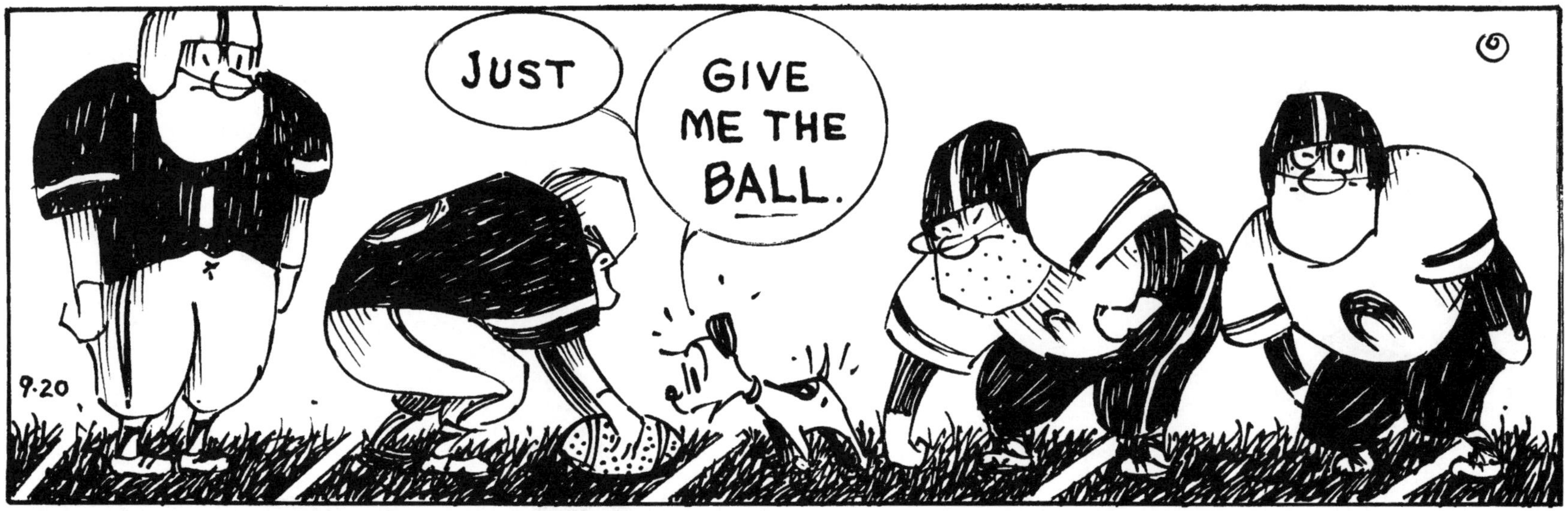
JUST
GIVE ME THE BALL.
9.20

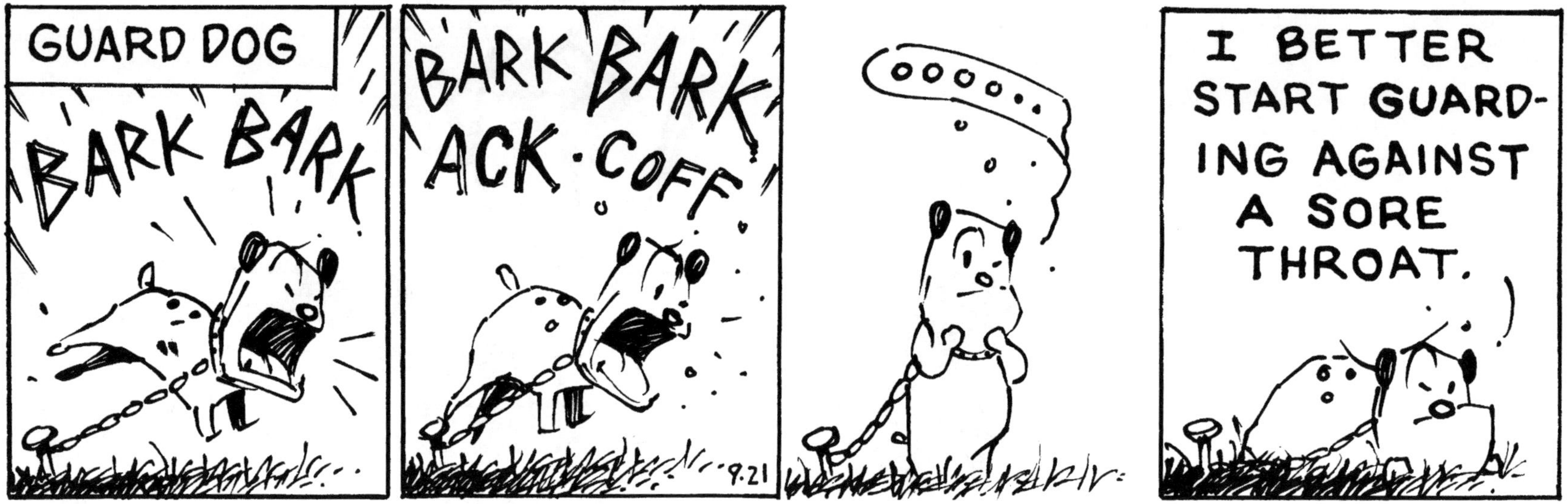
GUARD DOG
BARK BARK
BARK BARK
ACK·COFF
9.21
OOOO..
I BETTER START GUARDING AGAINST A SORE THROAT.

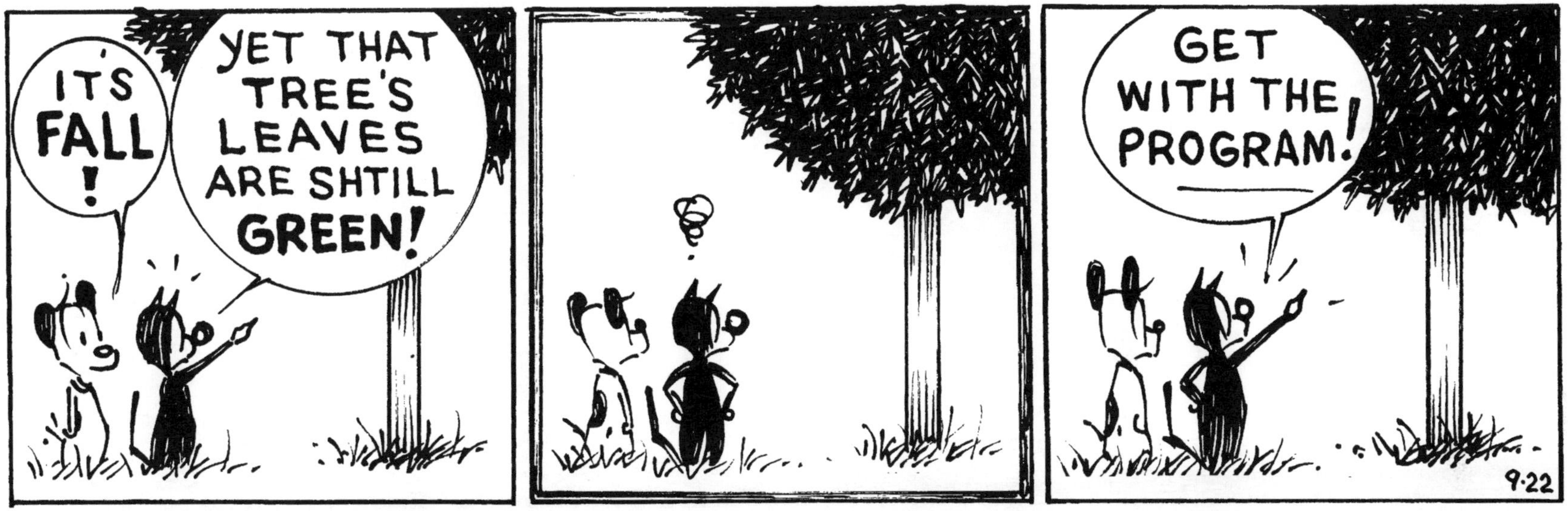
IT'S FALL!
YET THAT TREE'S LEAVES ARE SHTILL GREEN!
GET WITH THE PROGRAM!
9·22

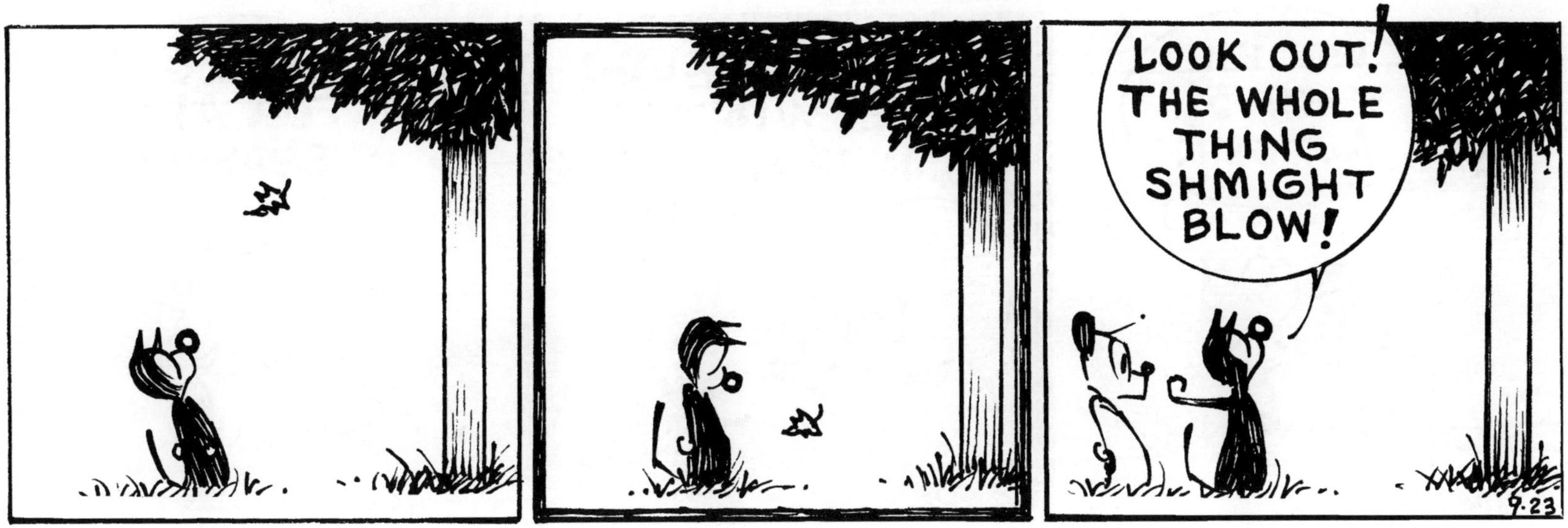
LOOK OUT! THE WHOLE THING SHMIGHT BLOW!
9·23

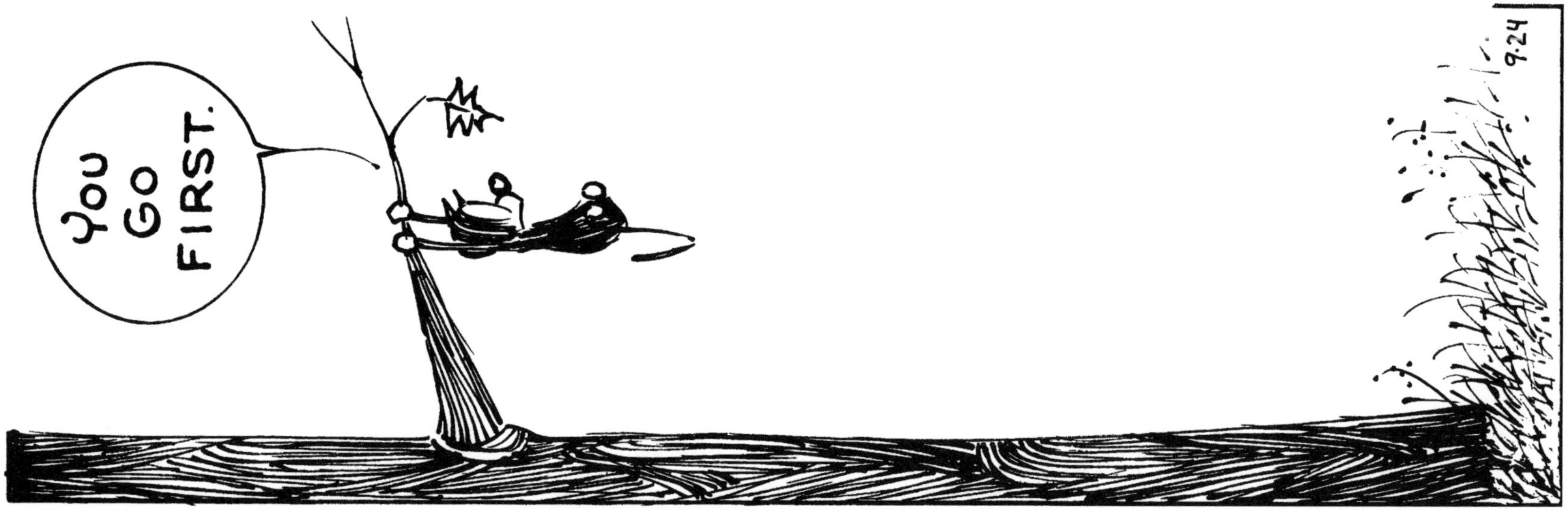
YOU GO FIRST.
9·24

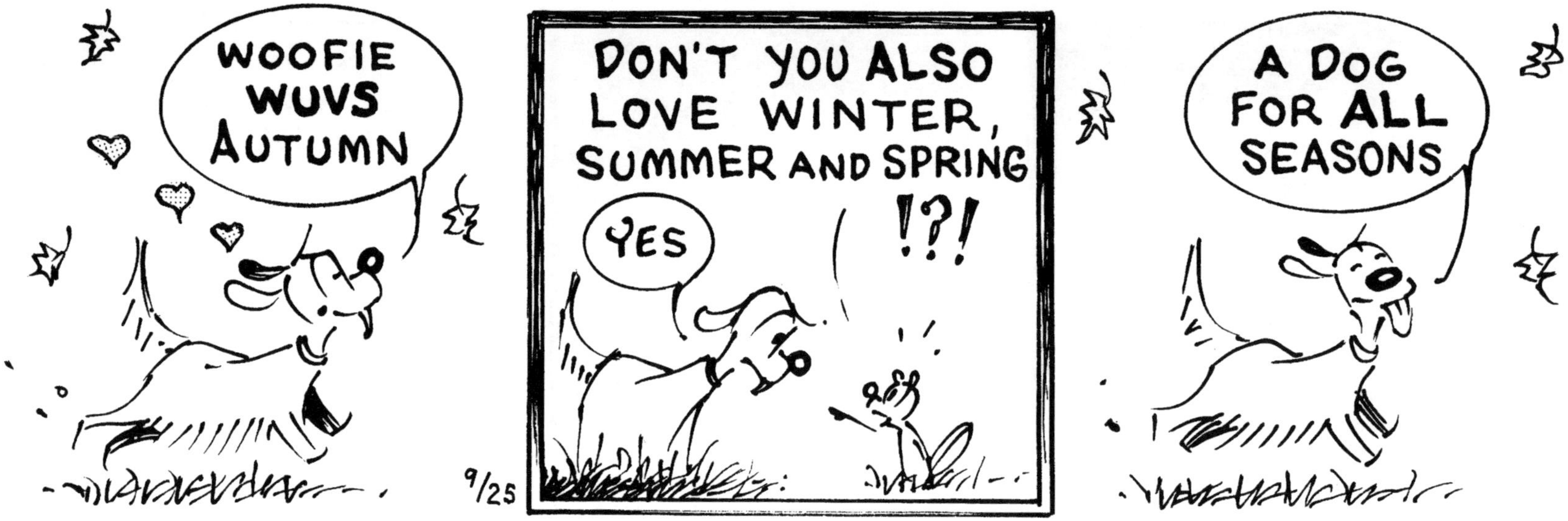
WOOFIE WUVS AUTUMN
9/25
DON'T YOU ALSO LOVE WINTER, SUMMER AND SPRING
YES
!?!
A DOG FOR ALL SEASONS

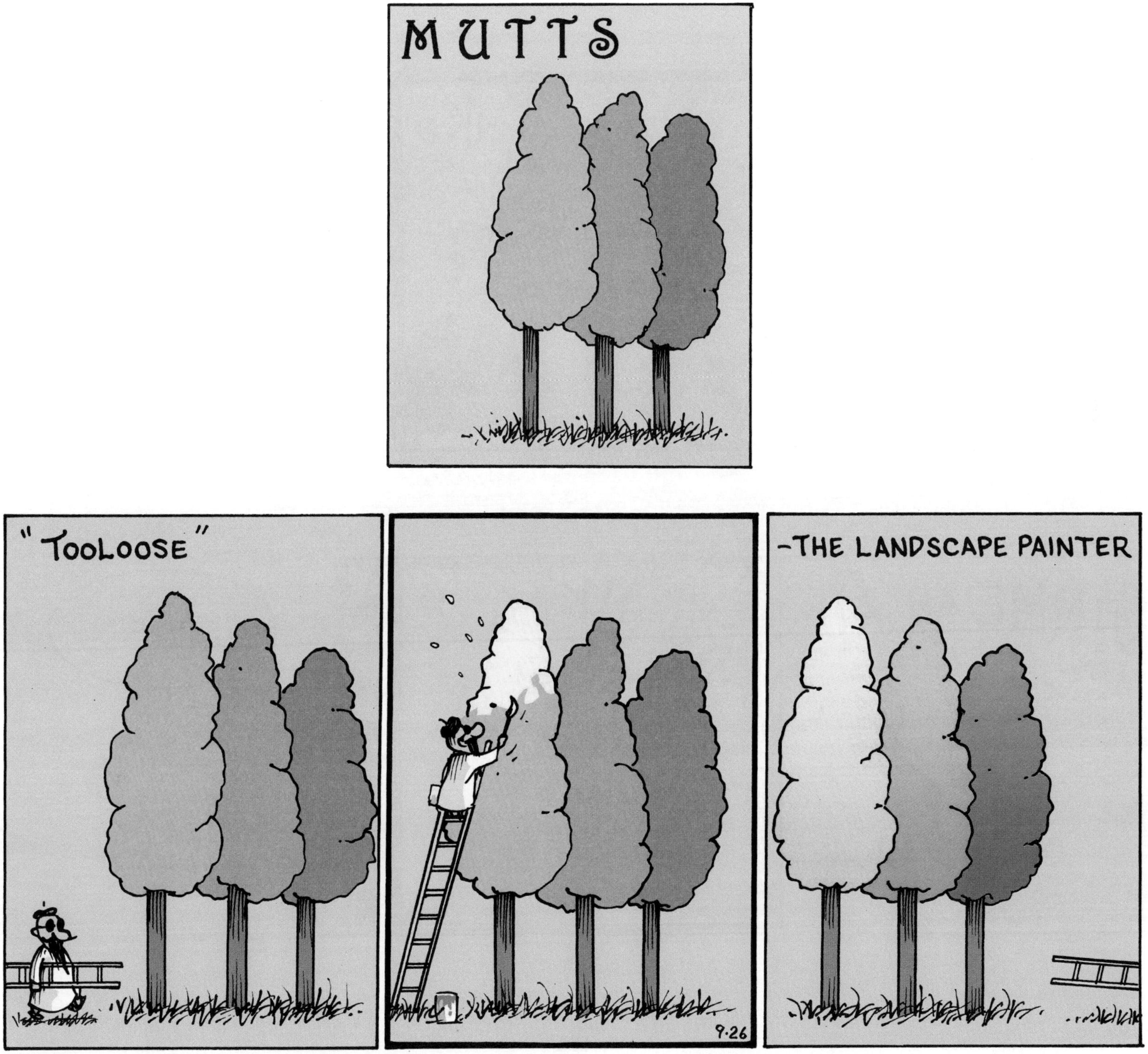
MUTTS
"TOOLOOSE"
-THE LANDSCAPE PAINTER
9·26

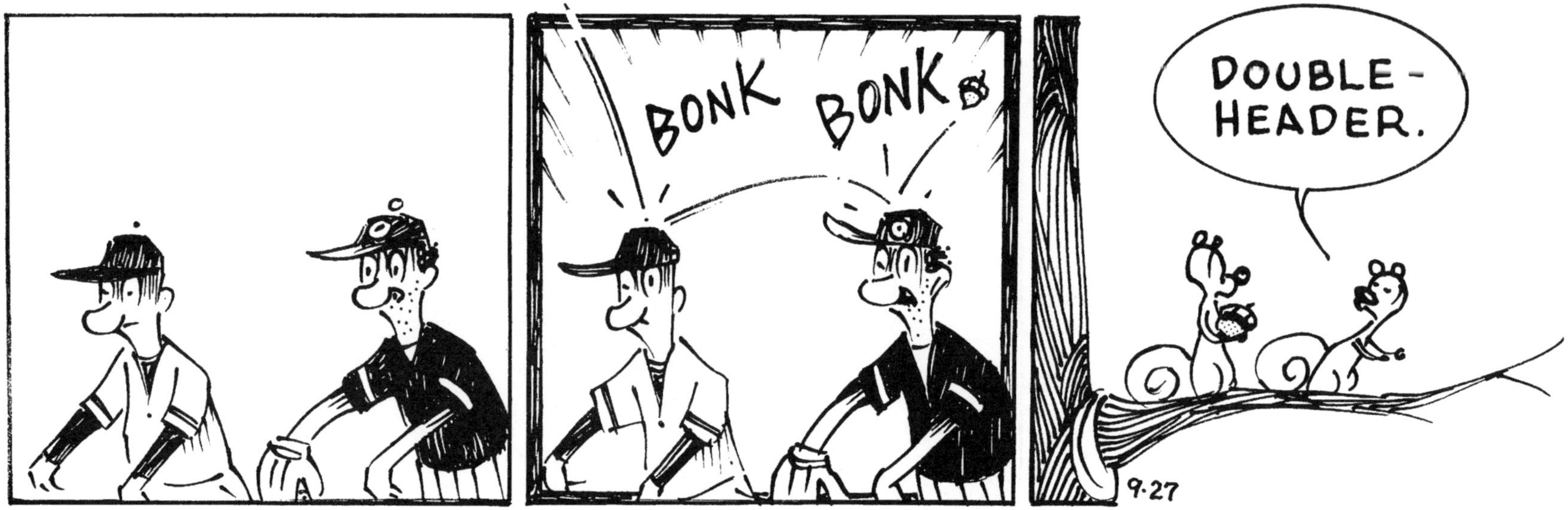
BONK BONK
DOUBLE-HEADER.
9·27

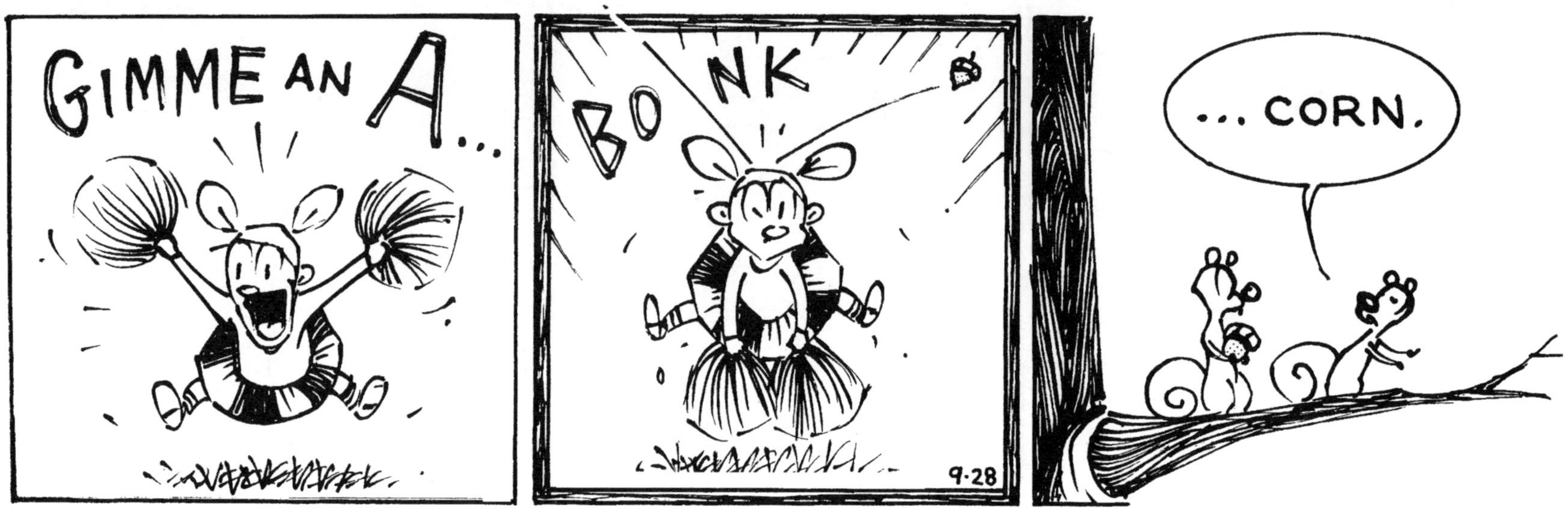
GIMME AN A...
BONK
9·28
...CORN.

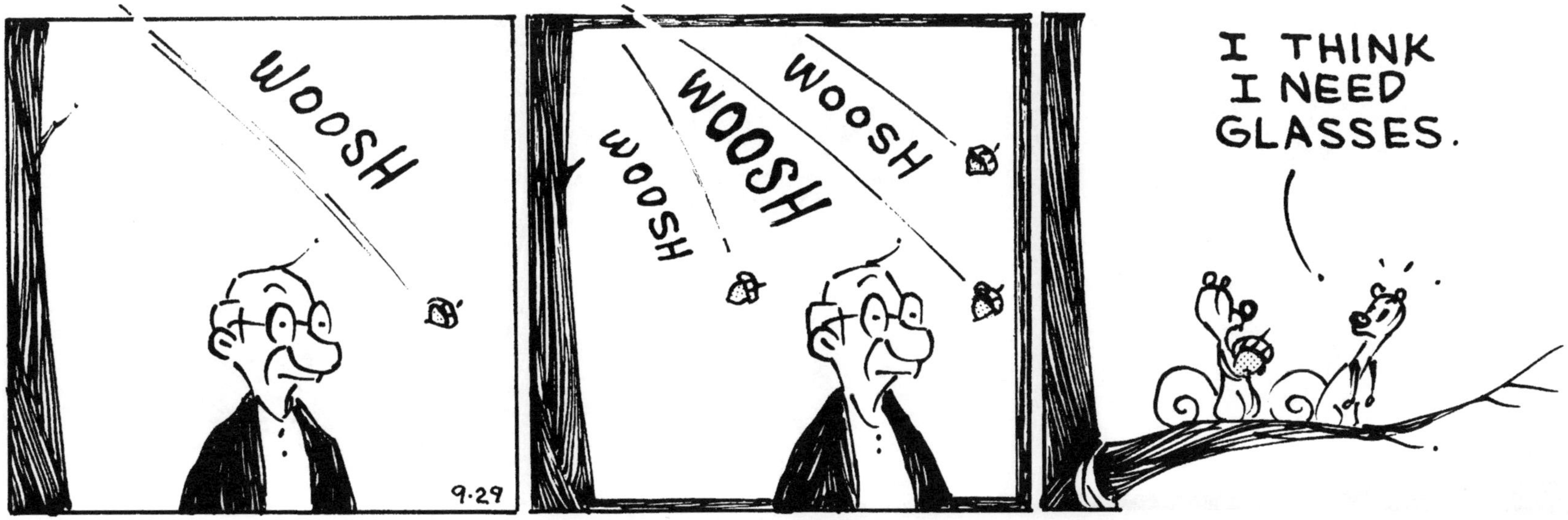
WOOSH
9·29
WOOSH
WOOSH
WOOSH
I THINK I NEED GLASSES.

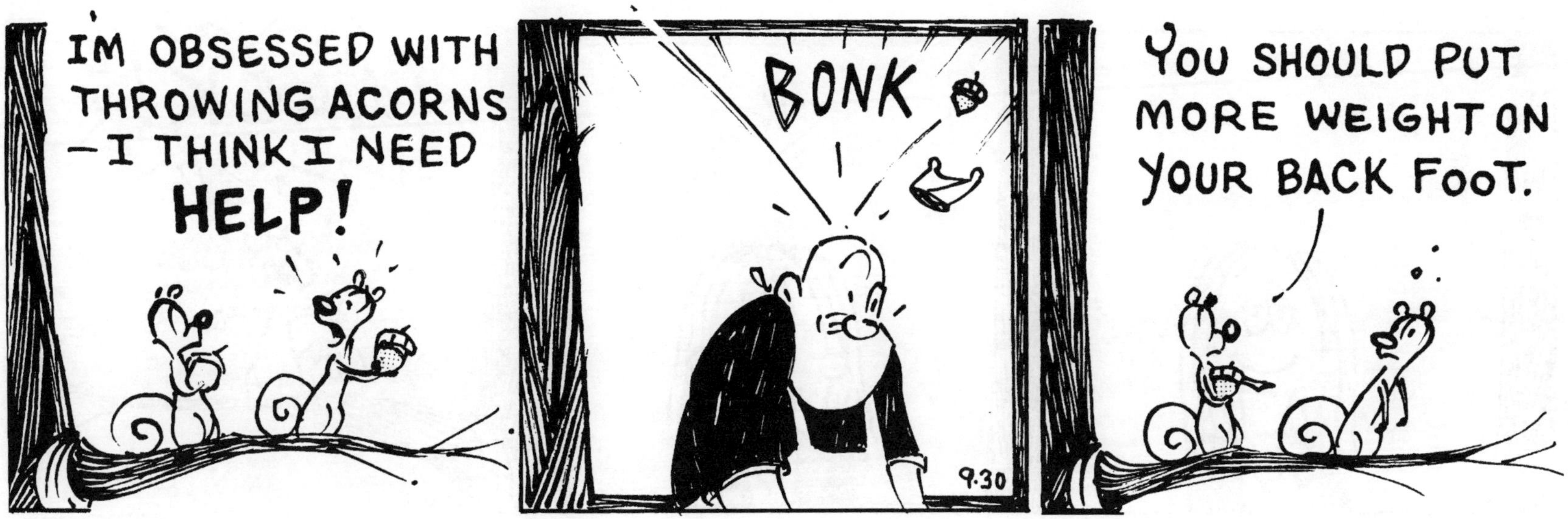
I'M OBSESSED WITH THROWING ACORNS —I THINK I NEED HELP!
BONK
9·30
YOU SHOULD PUT MORE WEIGHT ON YOUR BACK FOOT.

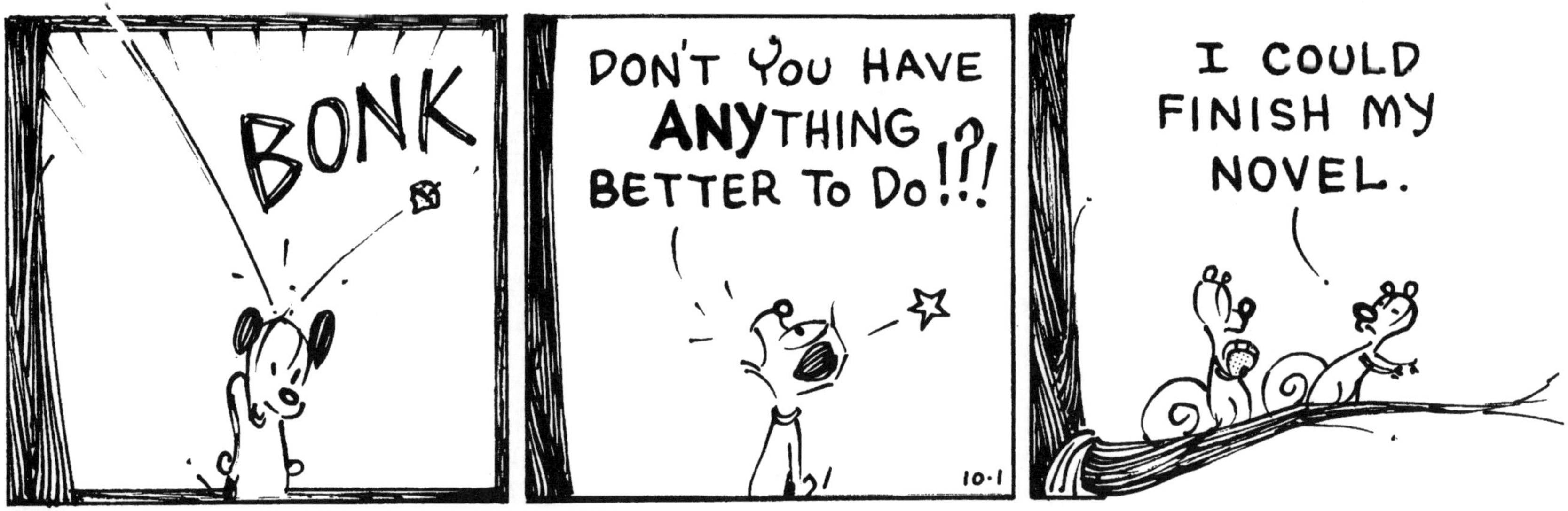
BONK
DON'T YOU HAVE ANYTHING BETTER TO DO!?!
I COULD FINISH MY NOVEL.
10·1

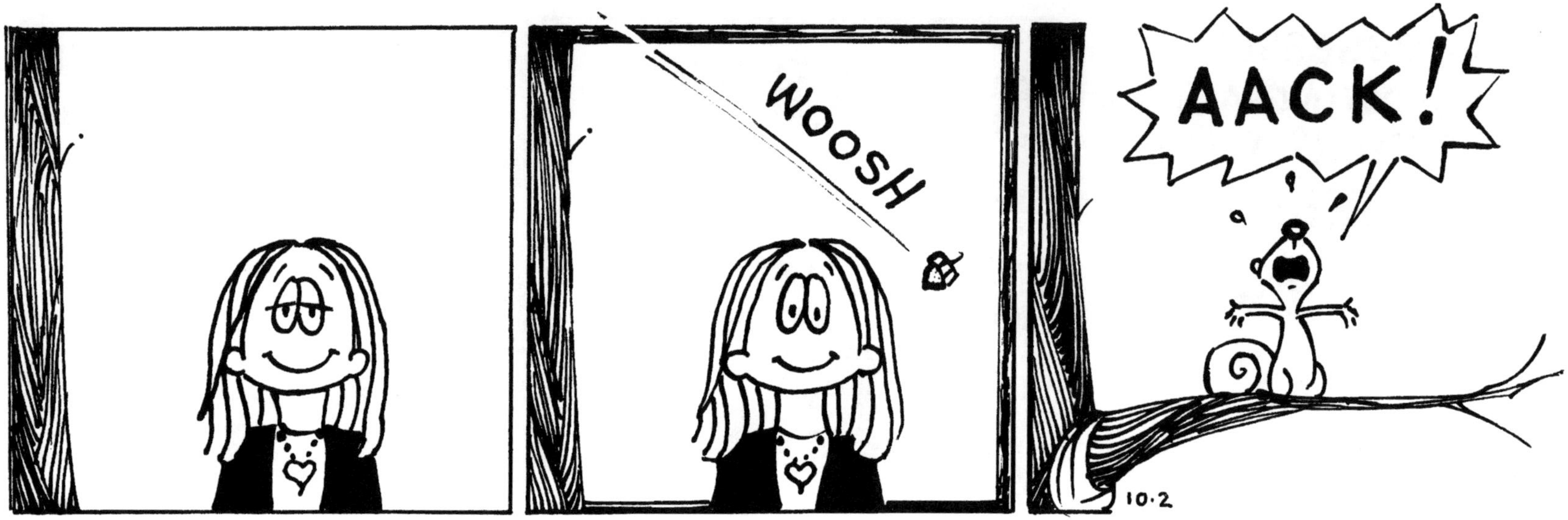
WOOSH
AACK!
10·2

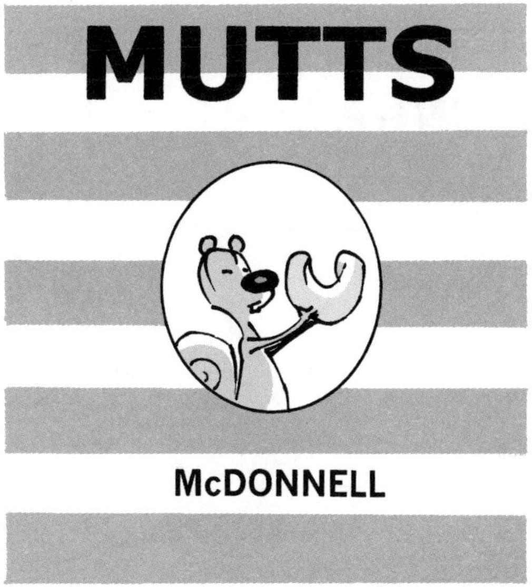
MUTTS
McDONNELL

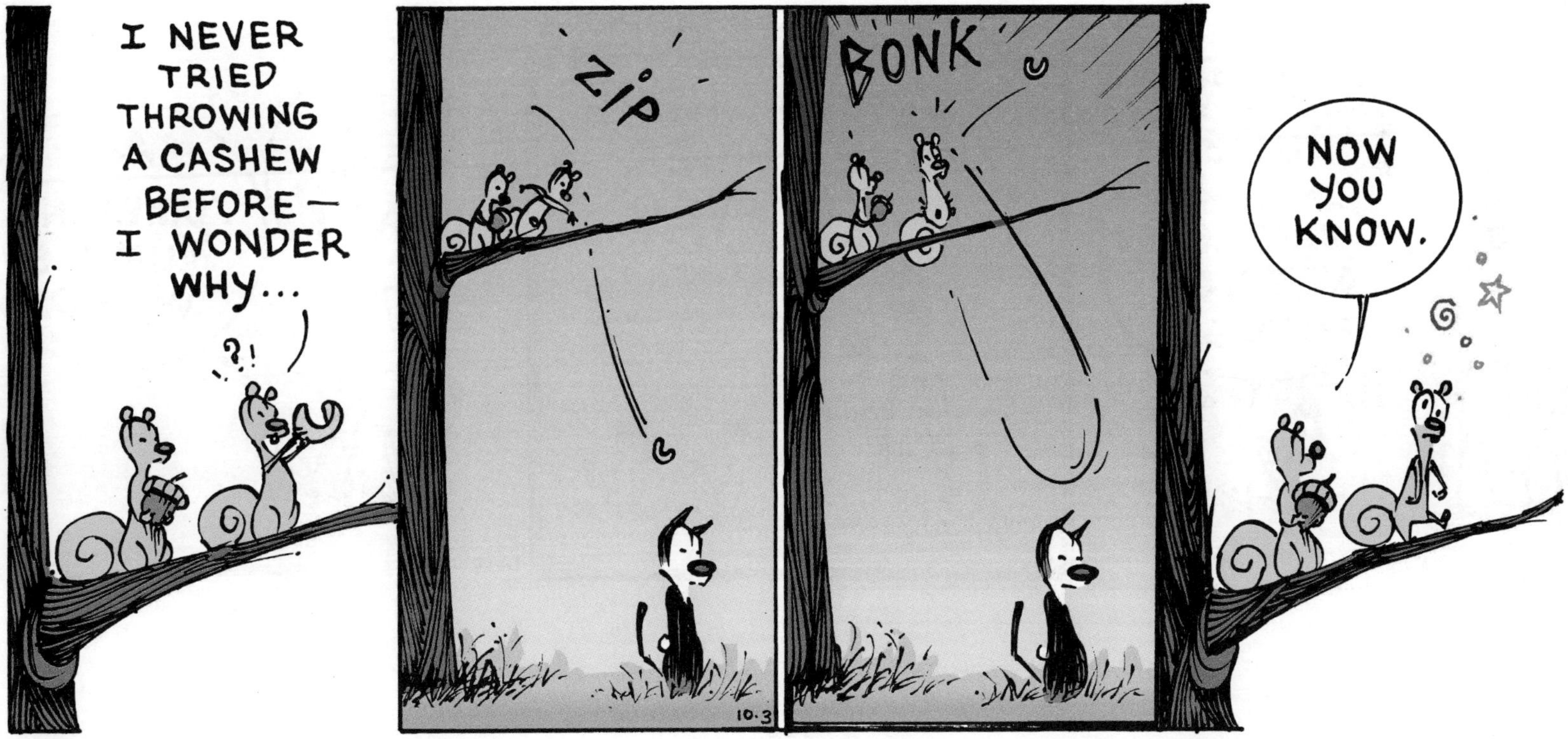
I NEVER TRIED THROWING A CASHEW BEFORE— I WONDER WHY...
?!
ZIP
BONK
NOW YOU KNOW.
10.3

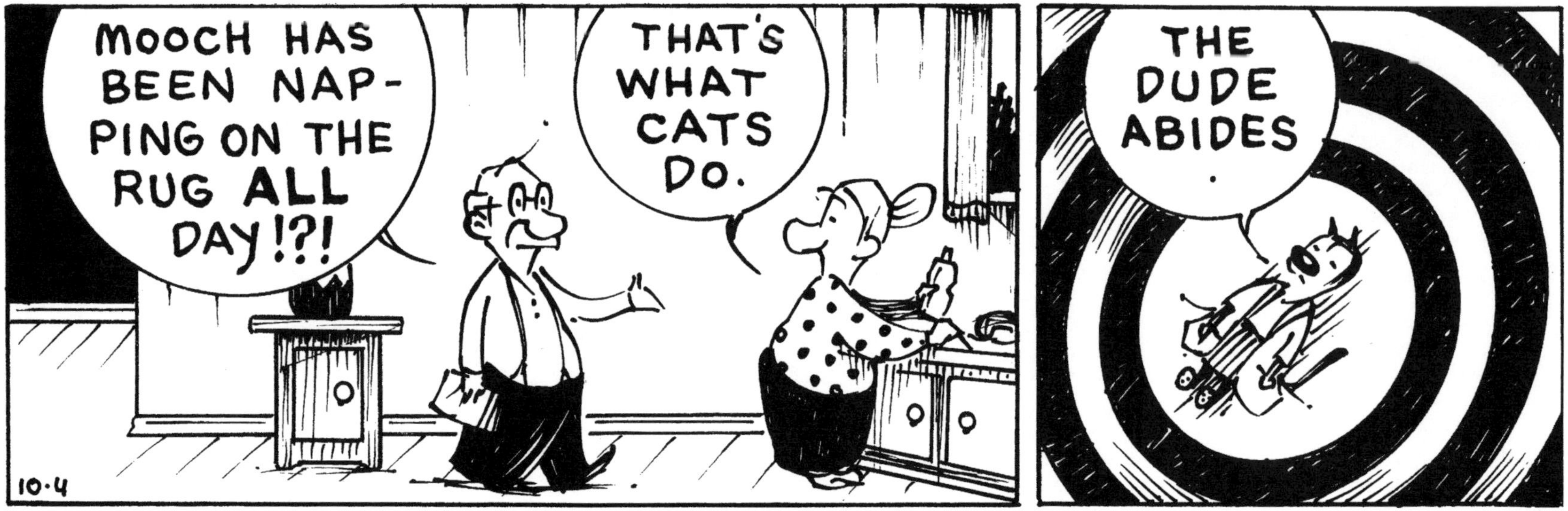
MOOCH HAS BEEN NAPPING ON THE RUG ALL DAY!?!
THAT'S WHAT CATS DO.
THE DUDE ABIDES
10·4

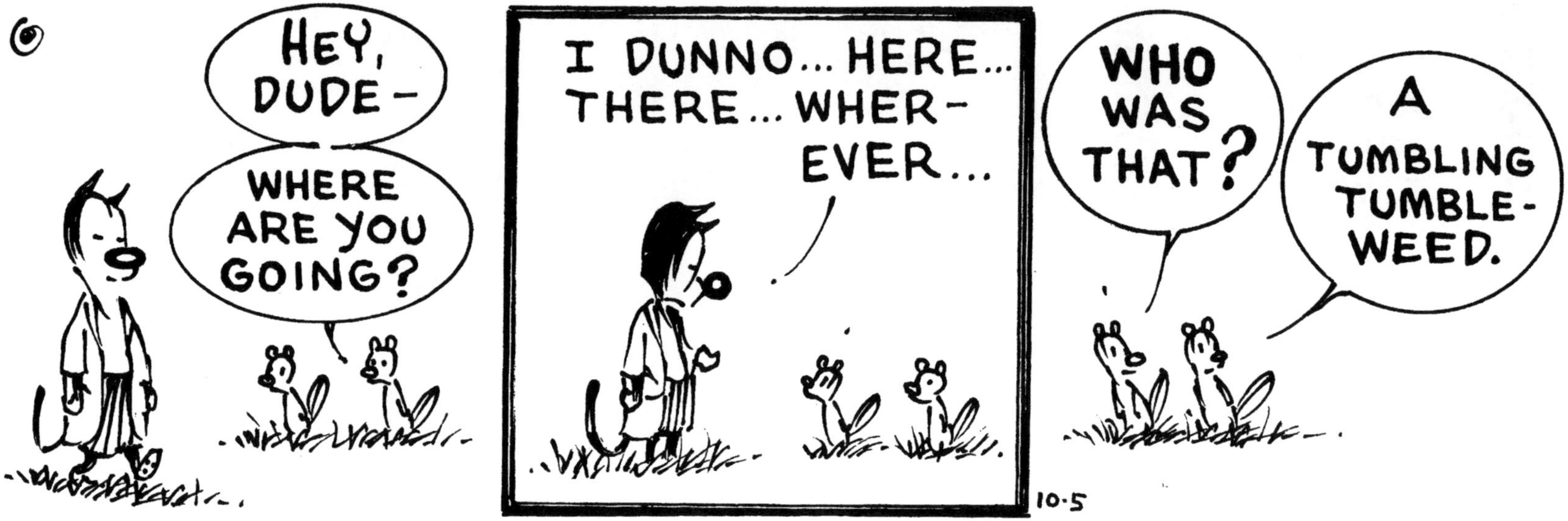
HEY, DUDE-
WHERE ARE YOU GOING?
I DUNNO... HERE... THERE... WHER-EVER...
WHO WAS THAT?
A TUMBLING TUMBLE-WEED.
10·5

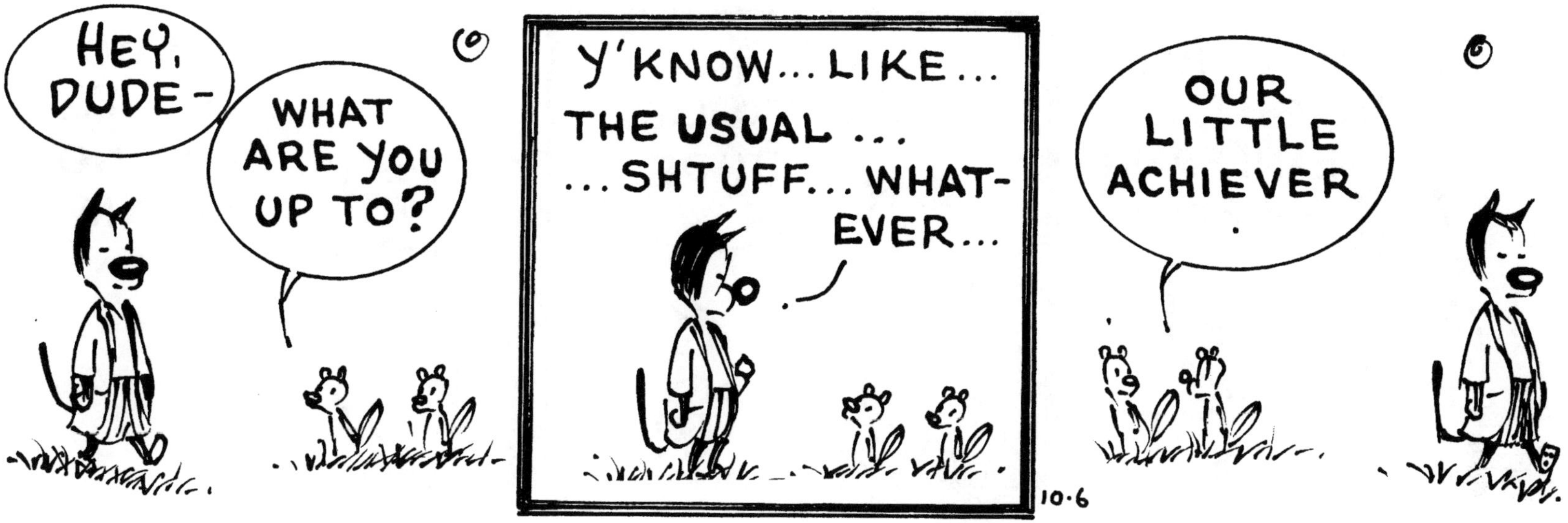
HEY, DUDE-
WHAT ARE YOU UP TO?
Y'KNOW... LIKE... THE USUAL... ...SHTUFF... WHAT-EVER...
OUR LITTLE ACHIEVER.
10·6

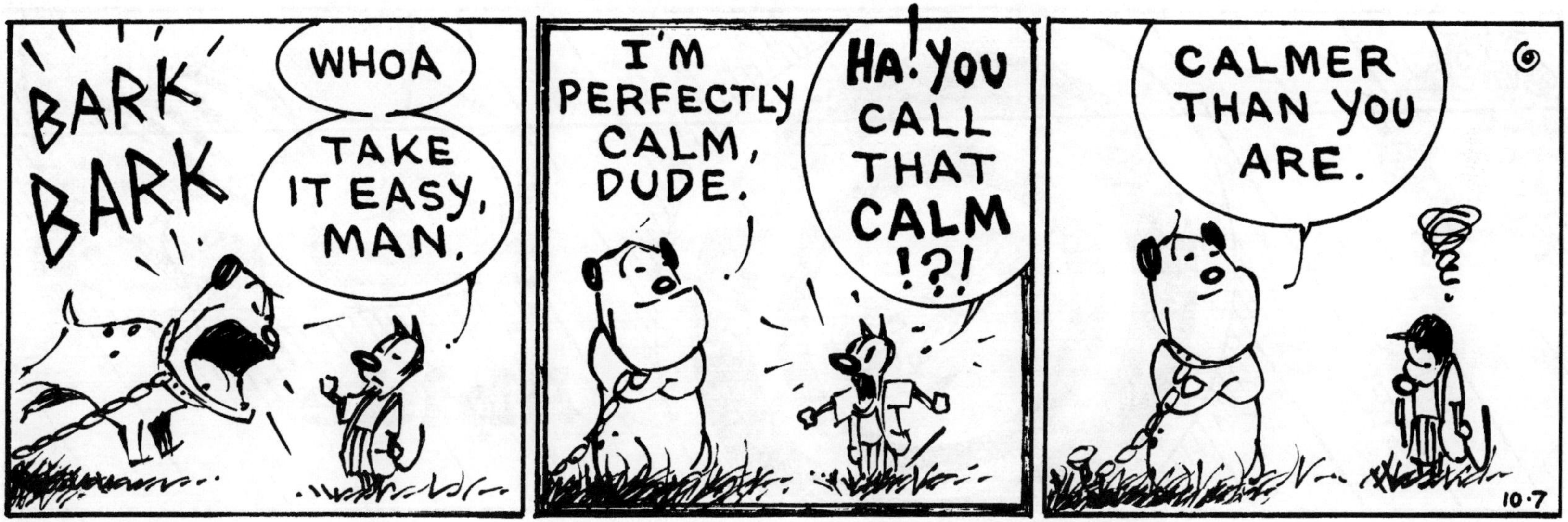
BARK BARK
WHOA
TAKE IT EASY, MAN.
I'M PERFECTLY CALM, DUDE.
HA! YOU CALL THAT CALM !?!
CALMER THAN YOU ARE.
10·7

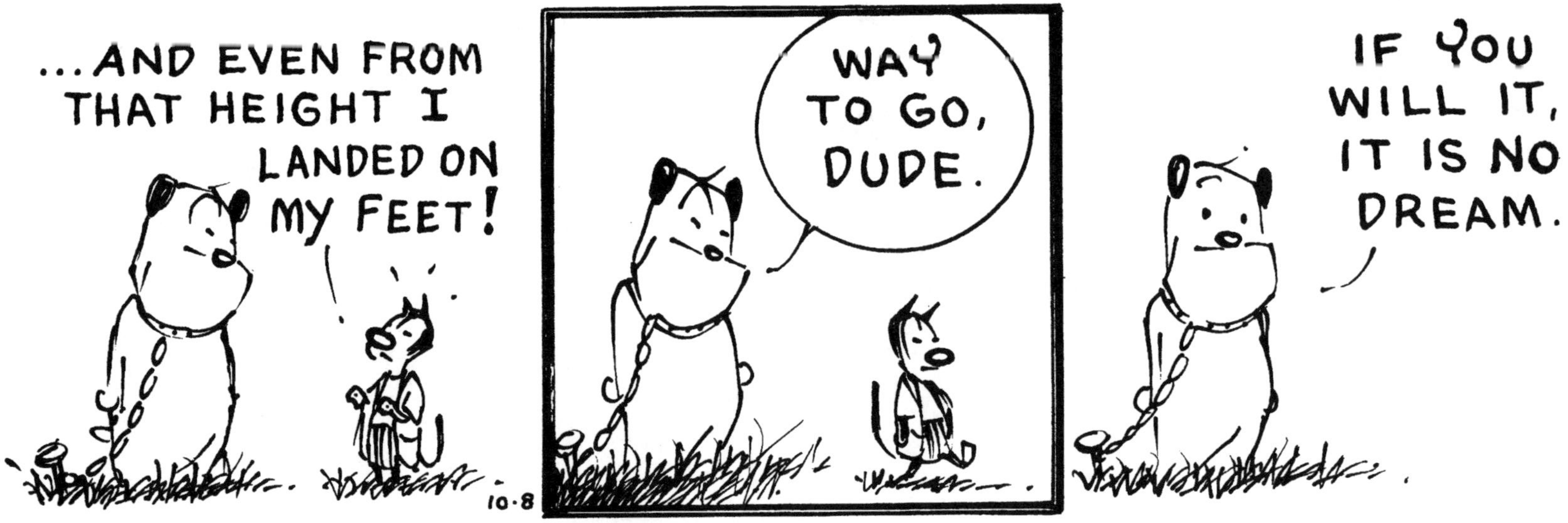
...AND EVEN FROM THAT HEIGHT I LANDED ON MY FEET!
10·8
WAY TO GO, DUDE.
IF YOU WILL IT, IT IS NO DREAM.

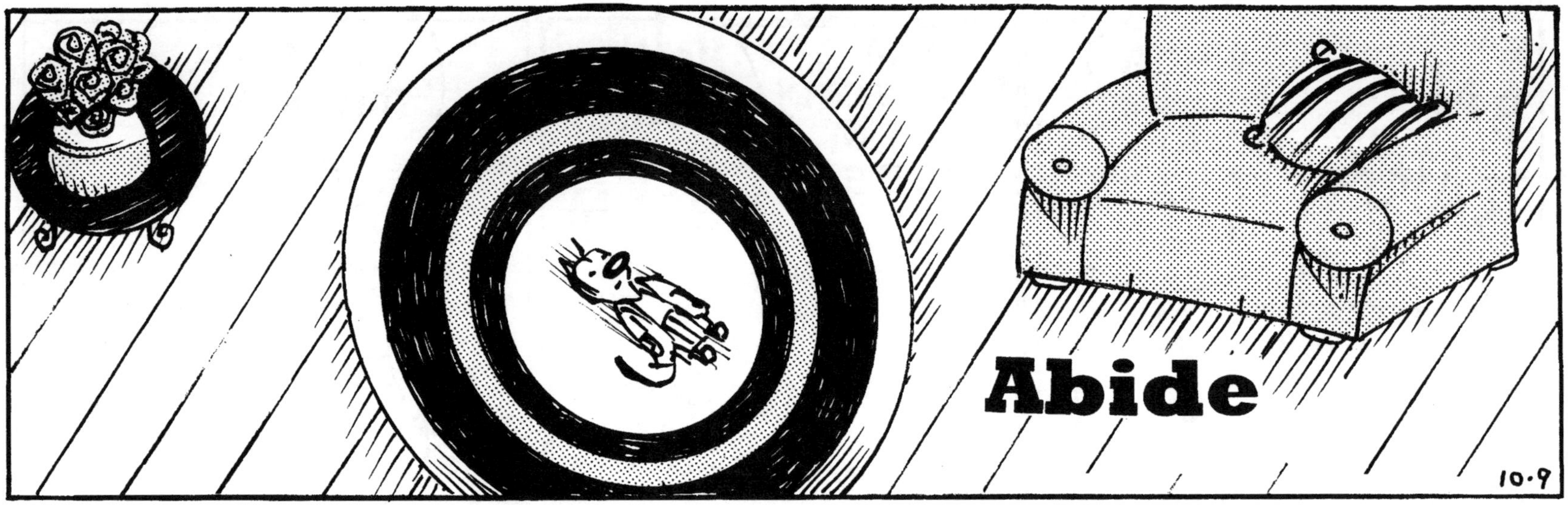
Abide
10·9

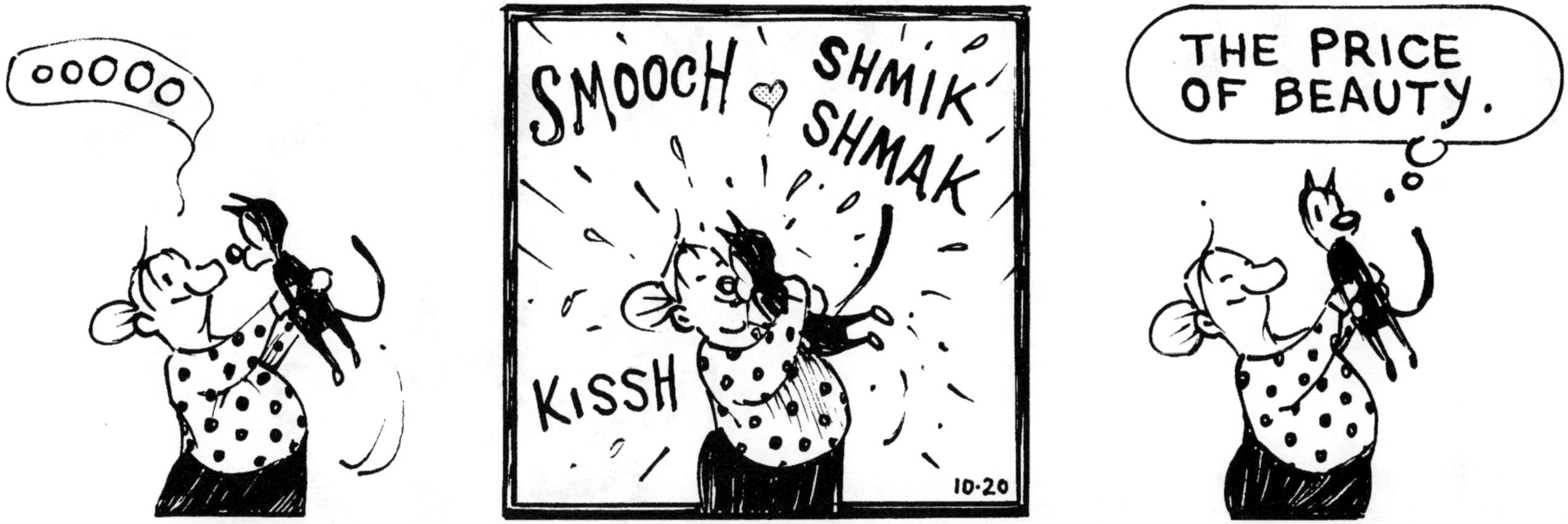
OOOOO
SMOOCH
SHMIK SHMAK
KISSH
10·20
THE PRICE OF BEAUTY.

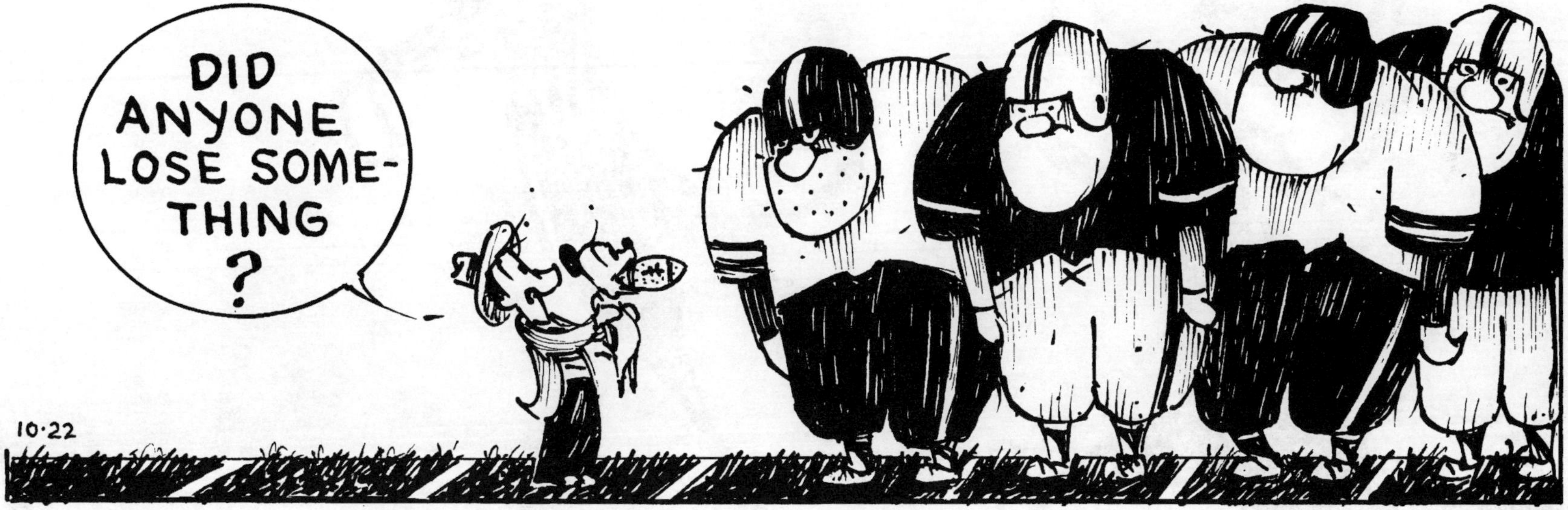
DID ANYONE LOSE SOME-THING ?
10·22

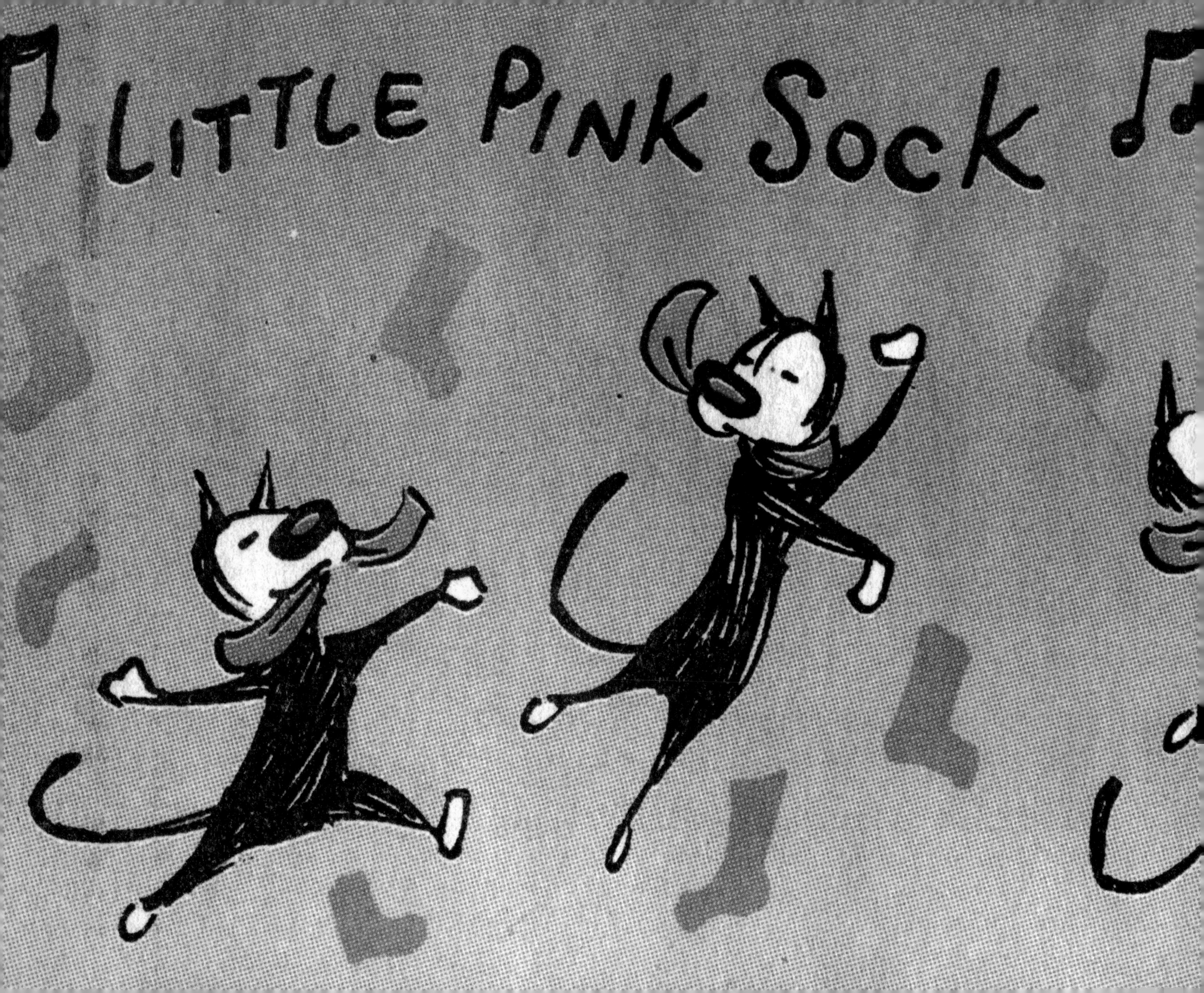
LITTLE PINK SOCK

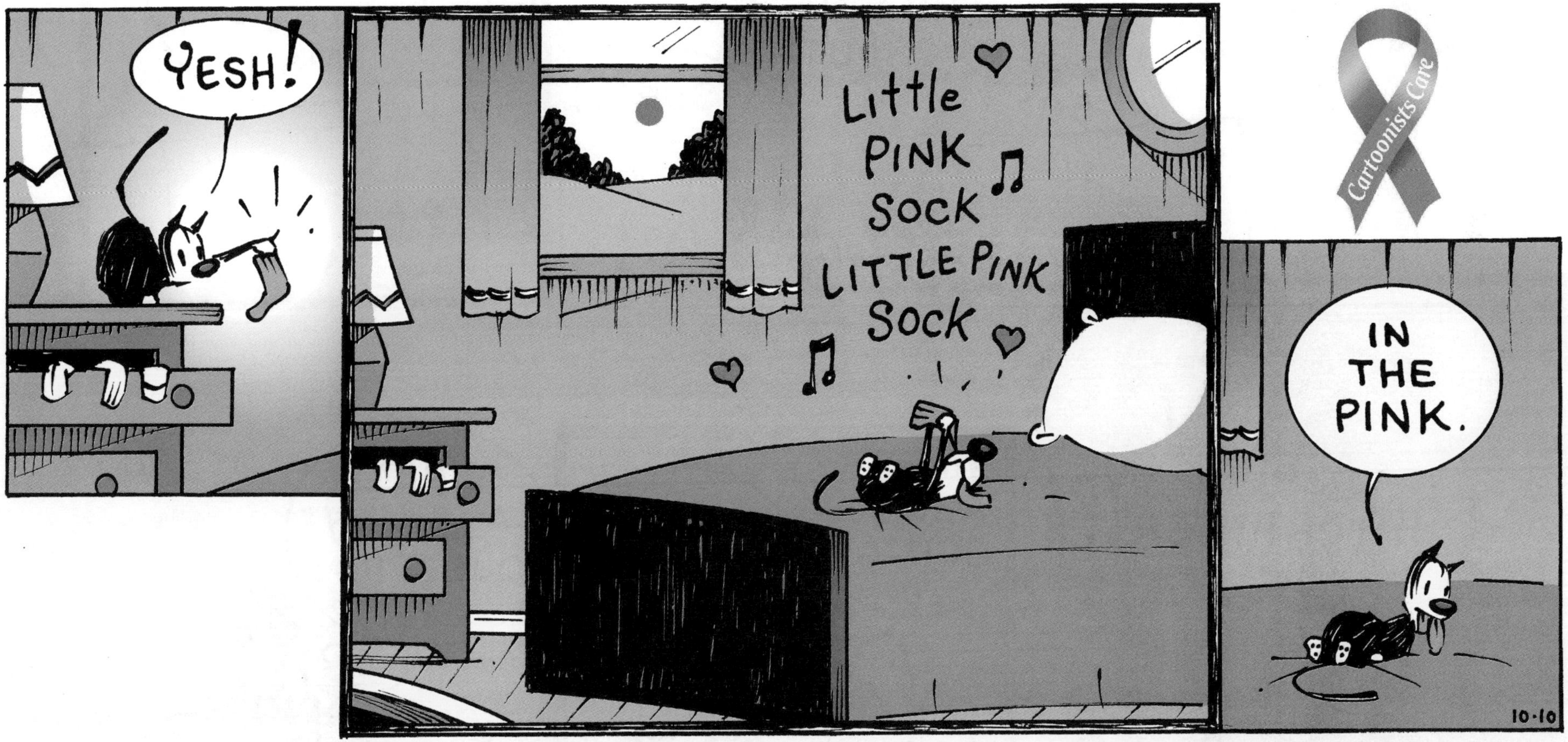
YESH!
Little PINK Sock LITTLE PINK Sock
Cartoonists Care
IN THE PINK.
10-10

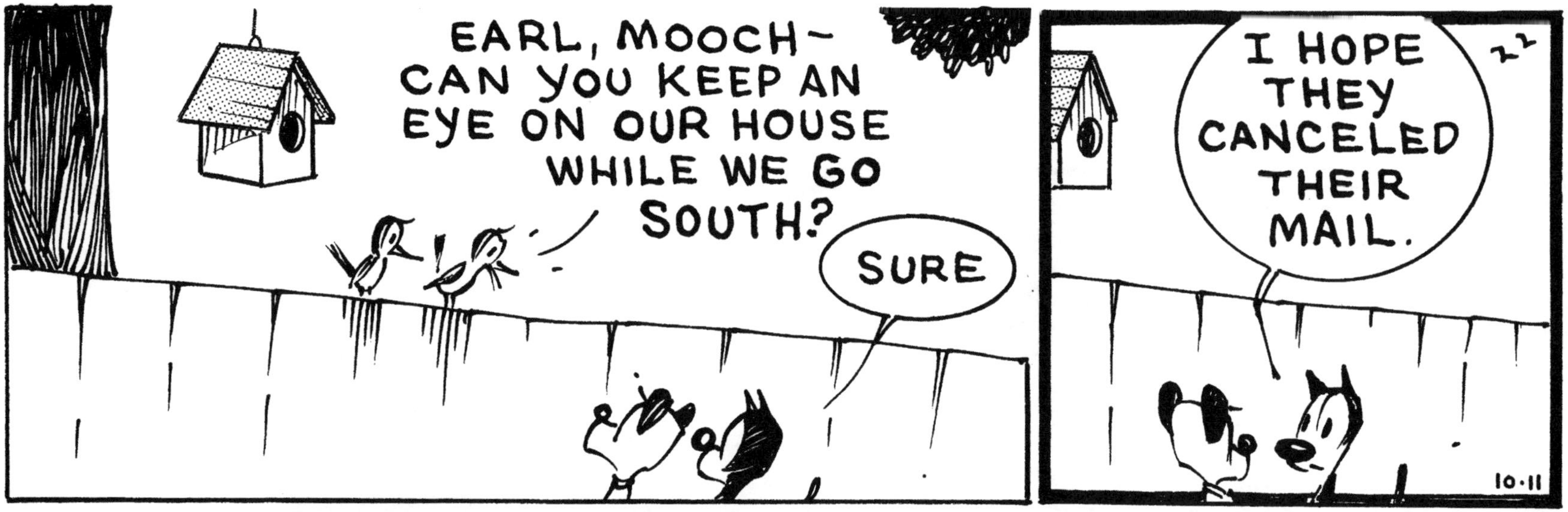
EARL, MOOCH-
CAN YOU KEEP AN EYE ON OUR HOUSE WHILE WE GO SOUTH?
SURE
I HOPE THEY CANCELED THEIR MAIL.
10·11

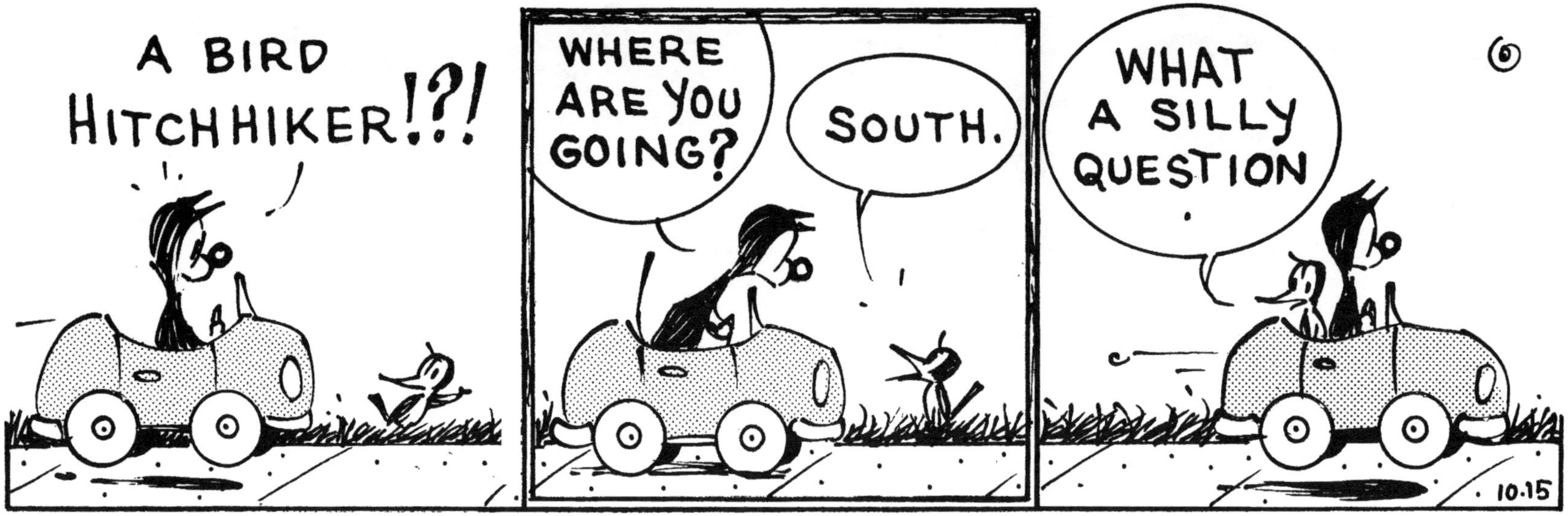
A BIRD HITCHHIKER!?!
WHERE ARE YOU GOING?
SOUTH.
WHAT A SILLY QUESTION
10·15

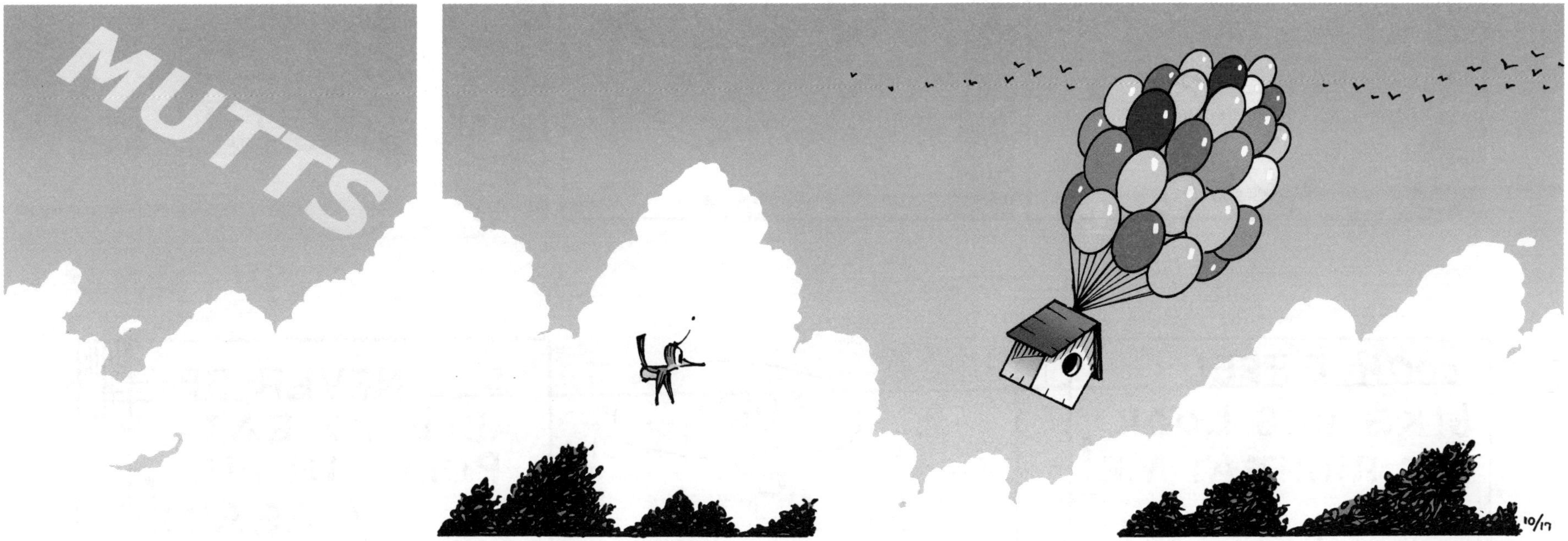
MUTTS
10/17

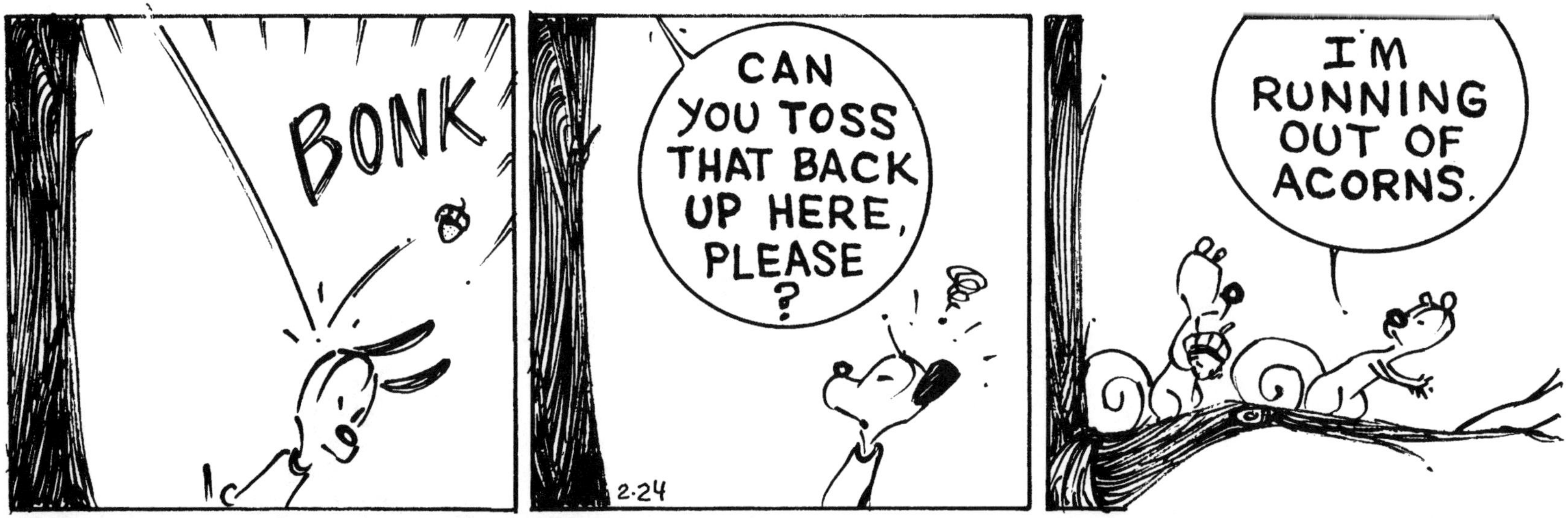
BONK
CAN YOU TOSS THAT BACK UP HERE, PLEASE?
2·24
I'M RUNNING OUT OF ACORNS.

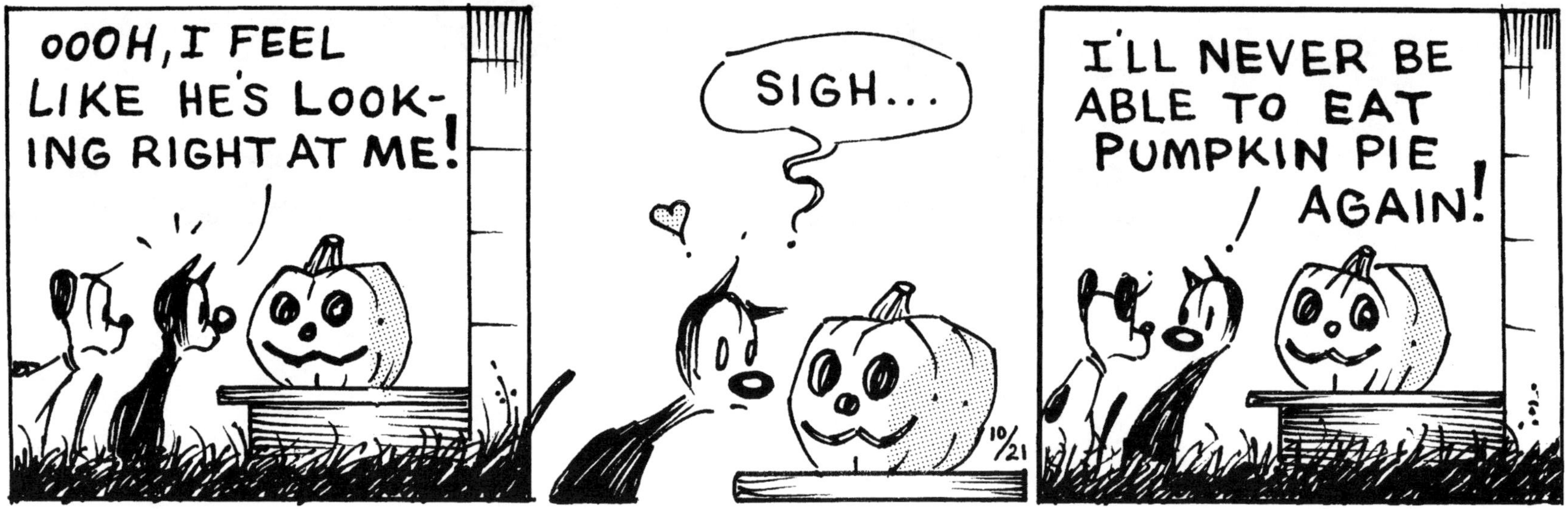
OOOH, I FEEL LIKE HE'S LOOKING RIGHT AT ME!
SIGH...
10/21
I'LL NEVER BE ABLE TO EAT PUMPKIN PIE AGAIN!

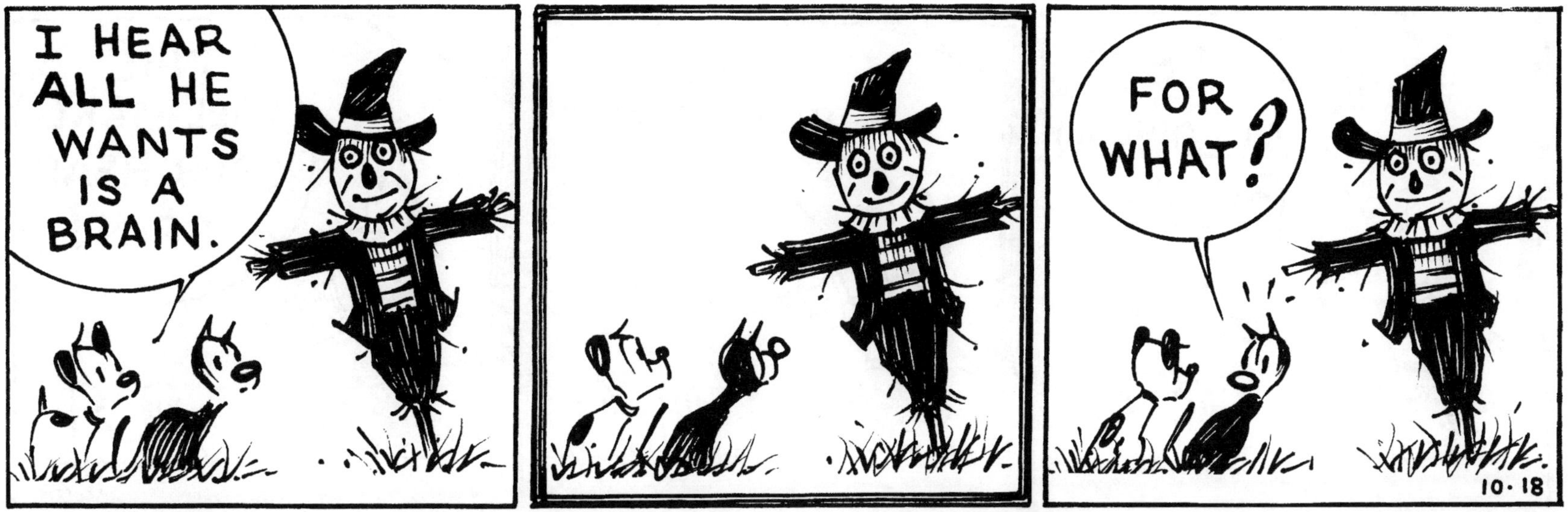
I HEAR ALL HE WANTS IS A BRAIN.
FOR WHAT?
10·18

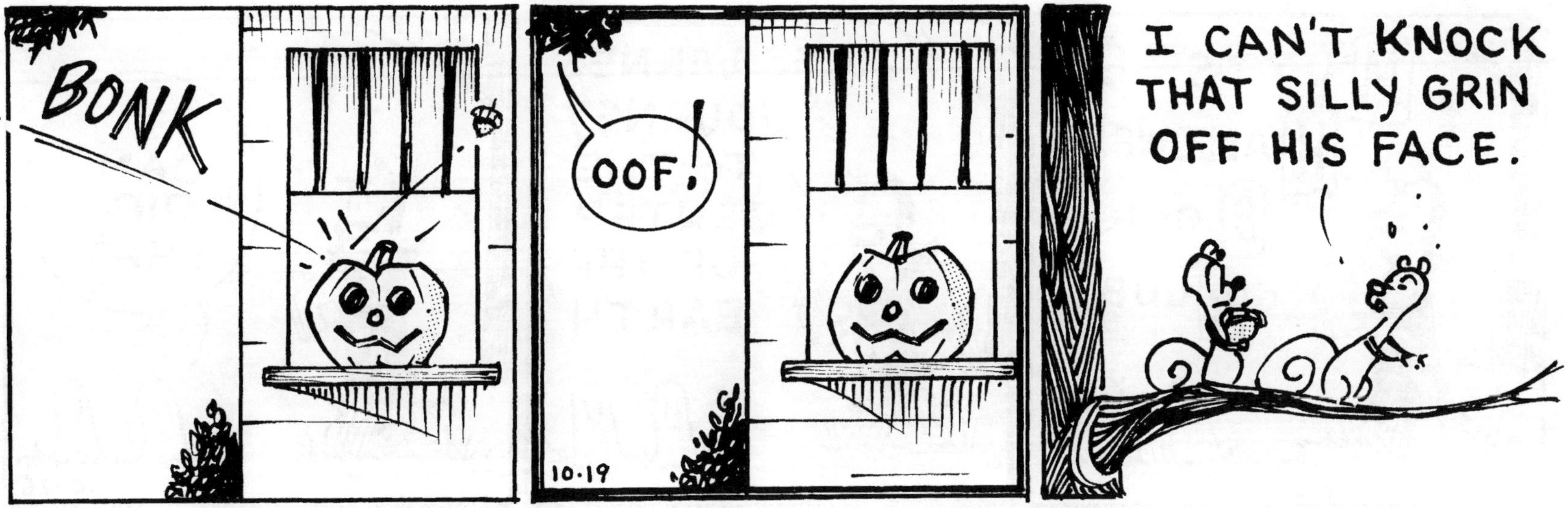
BONK
OOF!
10·19
I CAN'T KNOCK THAT SILLY GRIN OFF HIS FACE.

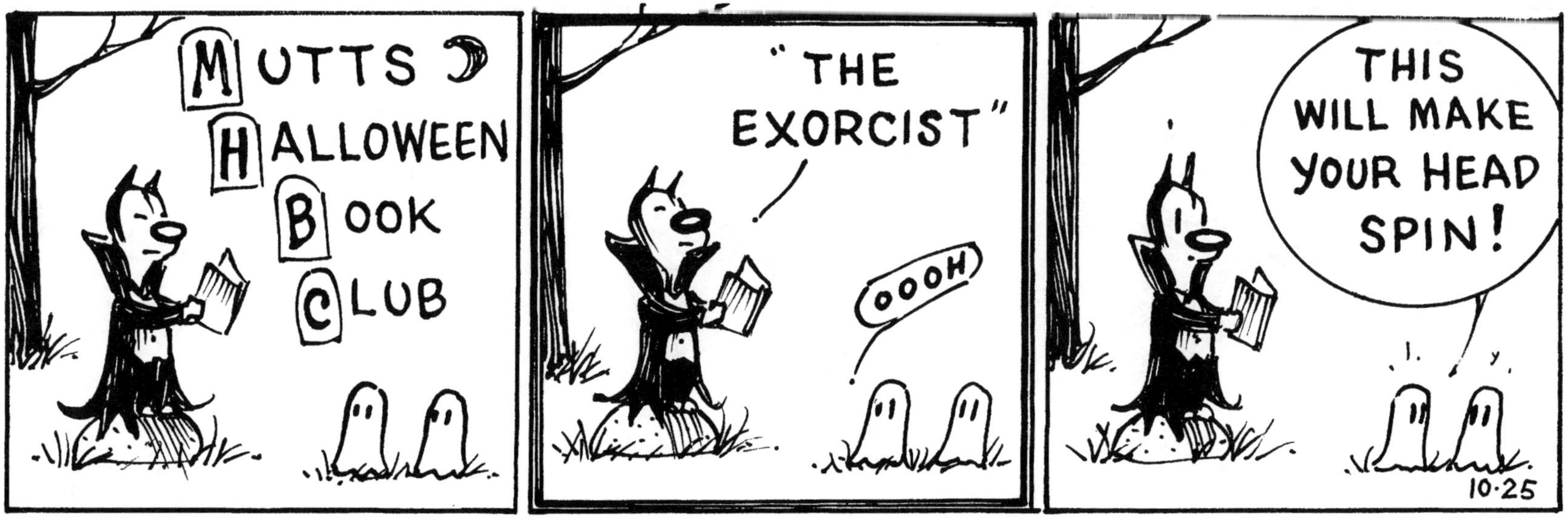
MUTTS HALLOWEEN BOOK CLUB
"THE EXORCIST"
OOOH
THIS WILL MAKE YOUR HEAD SPIN!
10·25

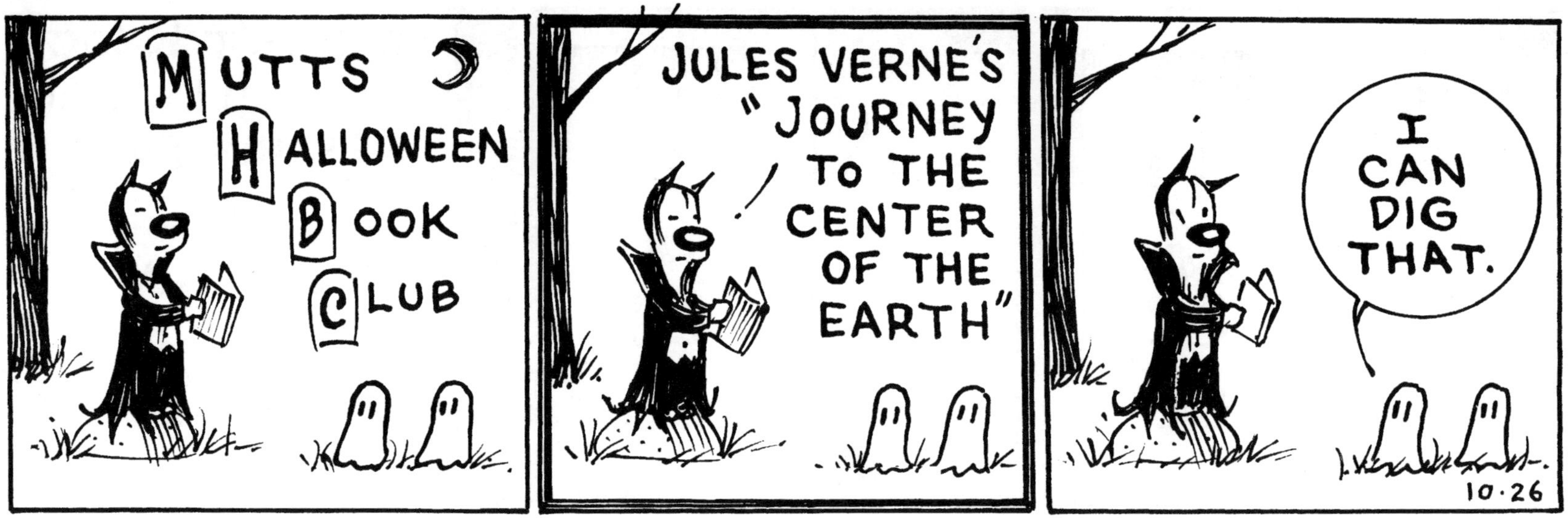
MUTTS HALLOWEEN BOOK CLUB
JULES VERNE'S "JOURNEY TO THE CENTER OF THE EARTH"
I CAN DIG THAT.
10·26

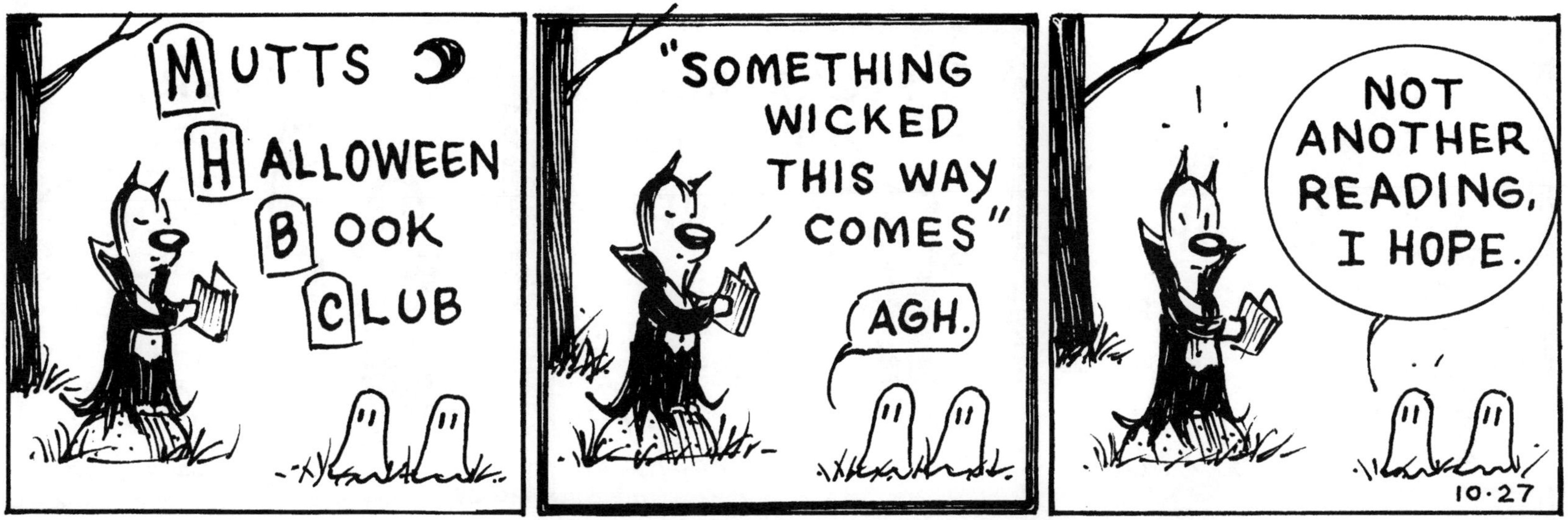
MUTTS
HALLOWEEN
BOOK
CLUB
"SOMETHING WICKED THIS WAY COMES"
AGH.
NOT ANOTHER READING, I HOPE.
10·27

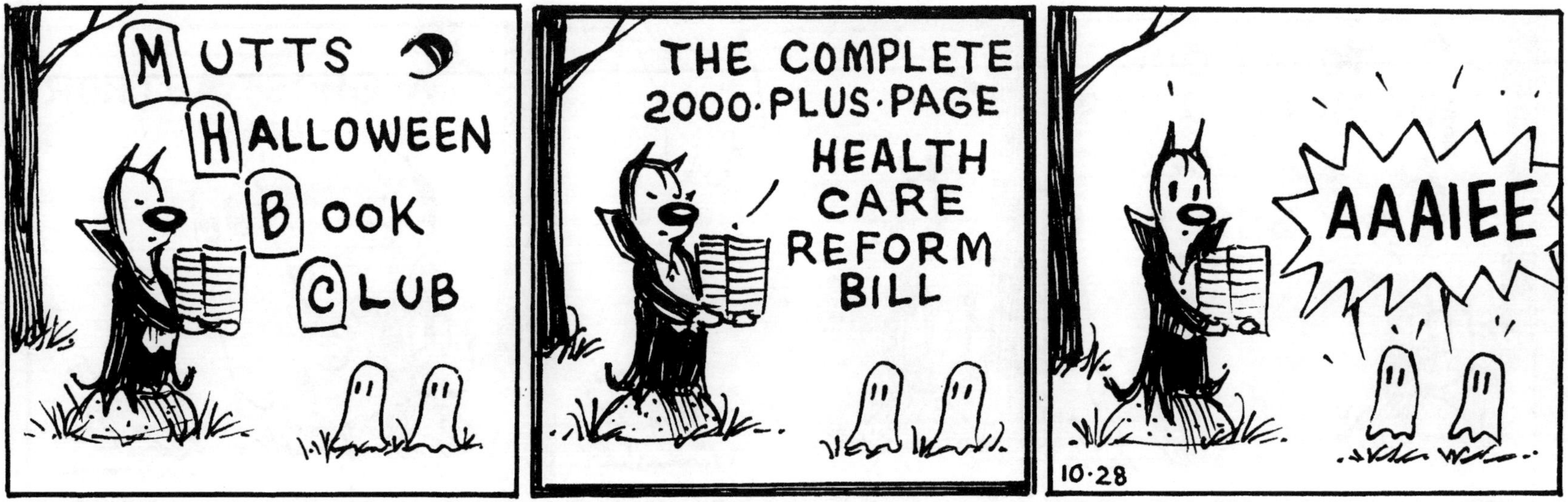
MUTTS
HALLOWEEN
BOOK
CLUB
THE COMPLETE 2000·PLUS·PAGE HEALTH CARE REFORM BILL
AAAIEE
10·28

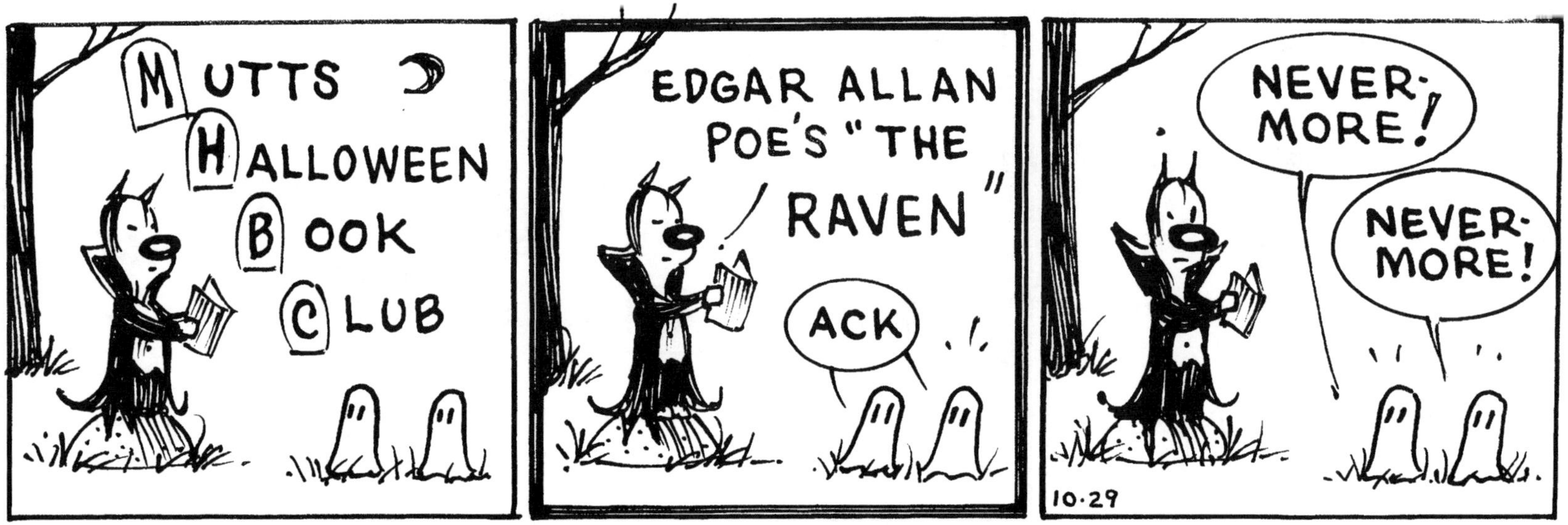
MUTTS
HALLOWEEN
BOOK
CLUB
EDGAR ALLAN POE'S "THE RAVEN"
ACK
NEVER-MORE!
NEVER-MORE!
10·29

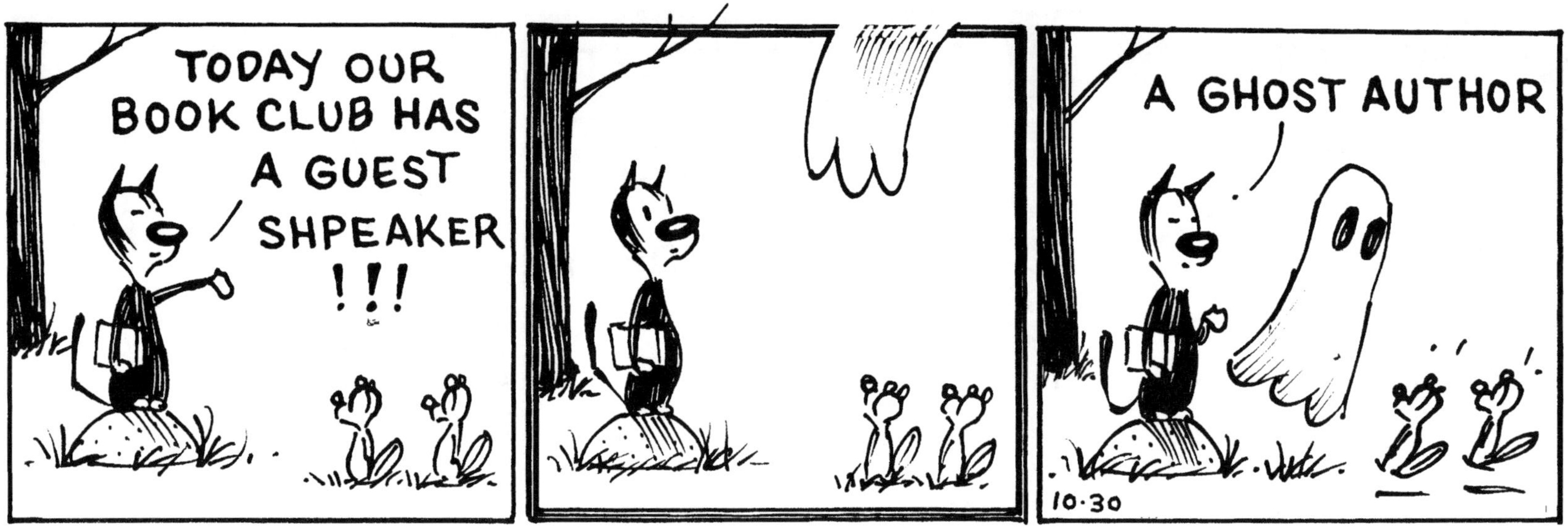
TODAY OUR BOOK CLUB HAS A GUEST SHPEAKER
!!!
A GHOST AUTHOR
10·30

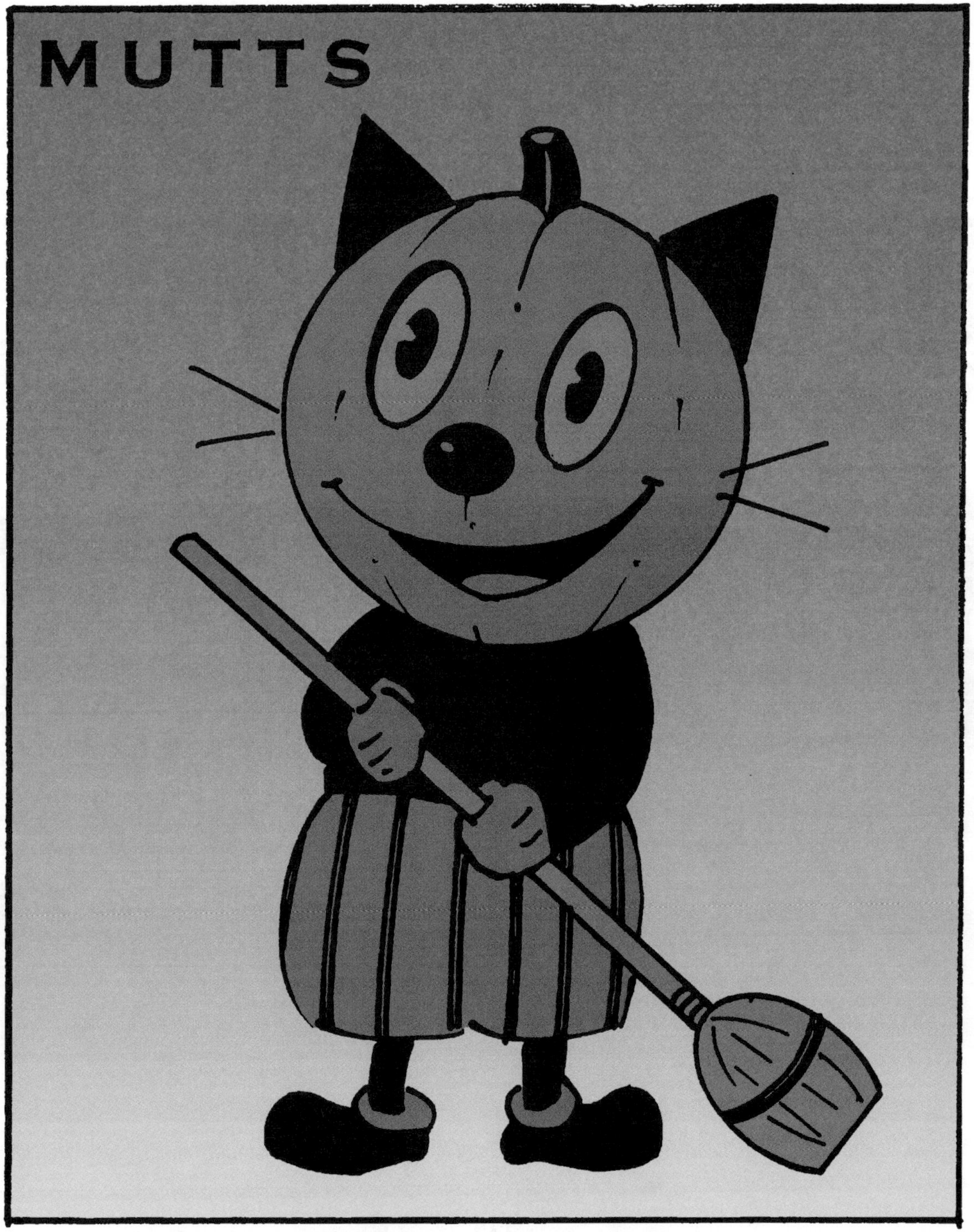
MUTTS

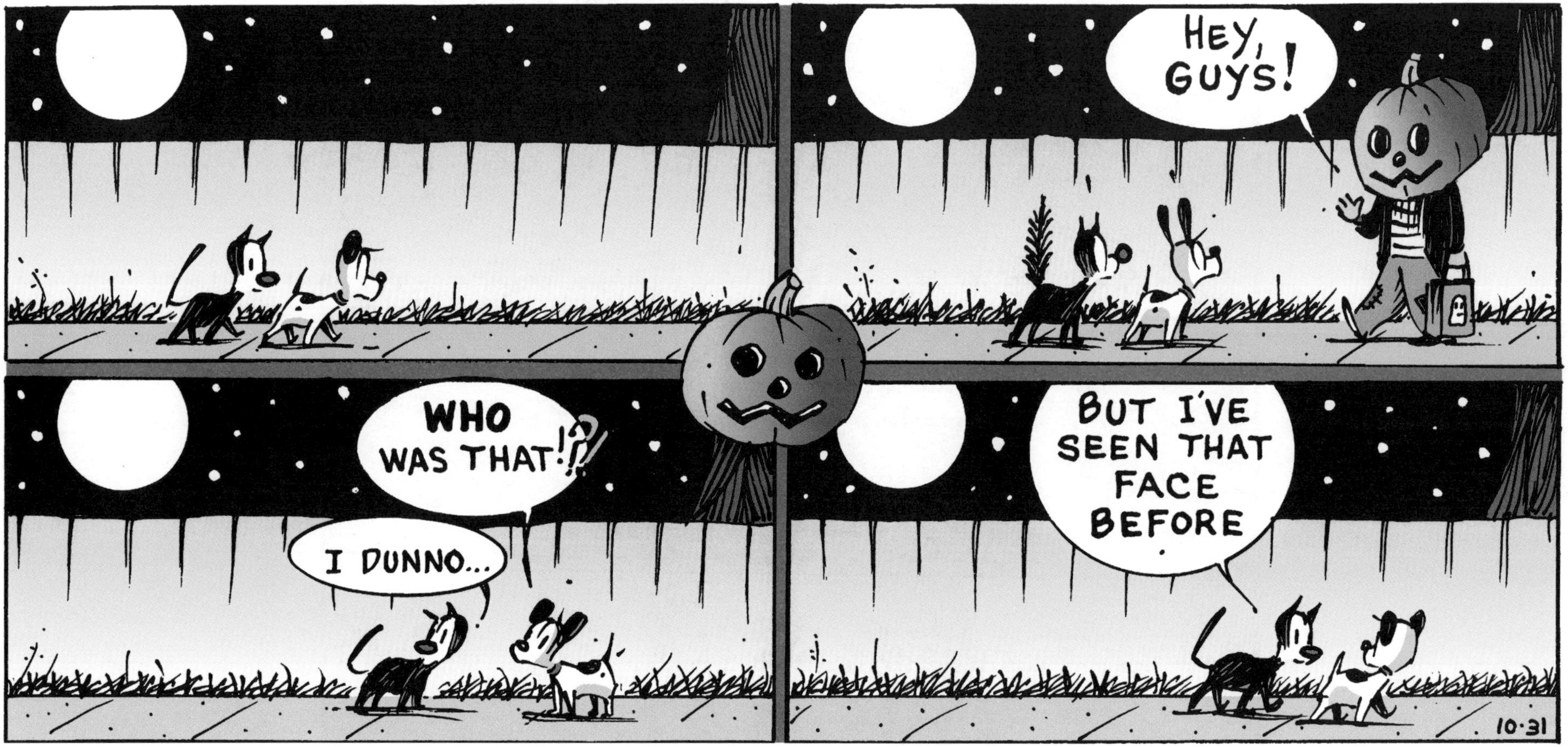
HEY, GUYS!
WHO WAS THAT!?
I DUNNO...
BUT I'VE SEEN THAT FACE BEFORE
10·31

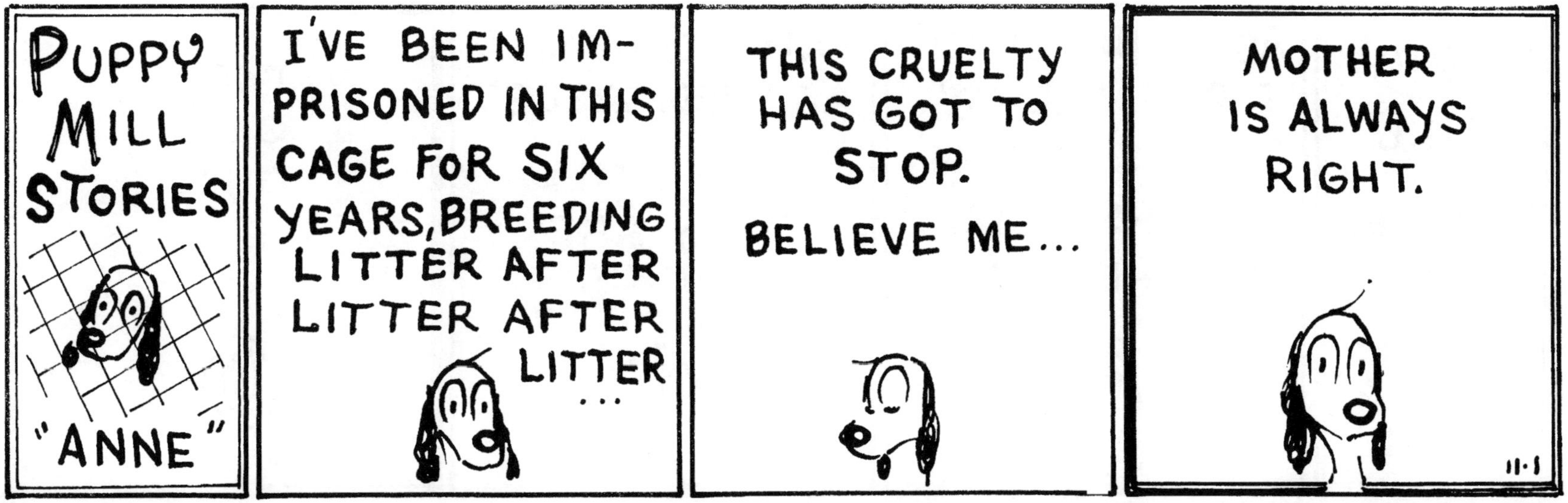
PUPPY MILL STORIES
"ANNE"
I'VE BEEN IMPRISONED IN THIS CAGE FOR SIX YEARS, BREEDING LITTER AFTER LITTER AFTER LITTER...
THIS CRUELTY HAS GOT TO STOP.
BELIEVE ME...
MOTHER IS ALWAYS RIGHT.
11·1

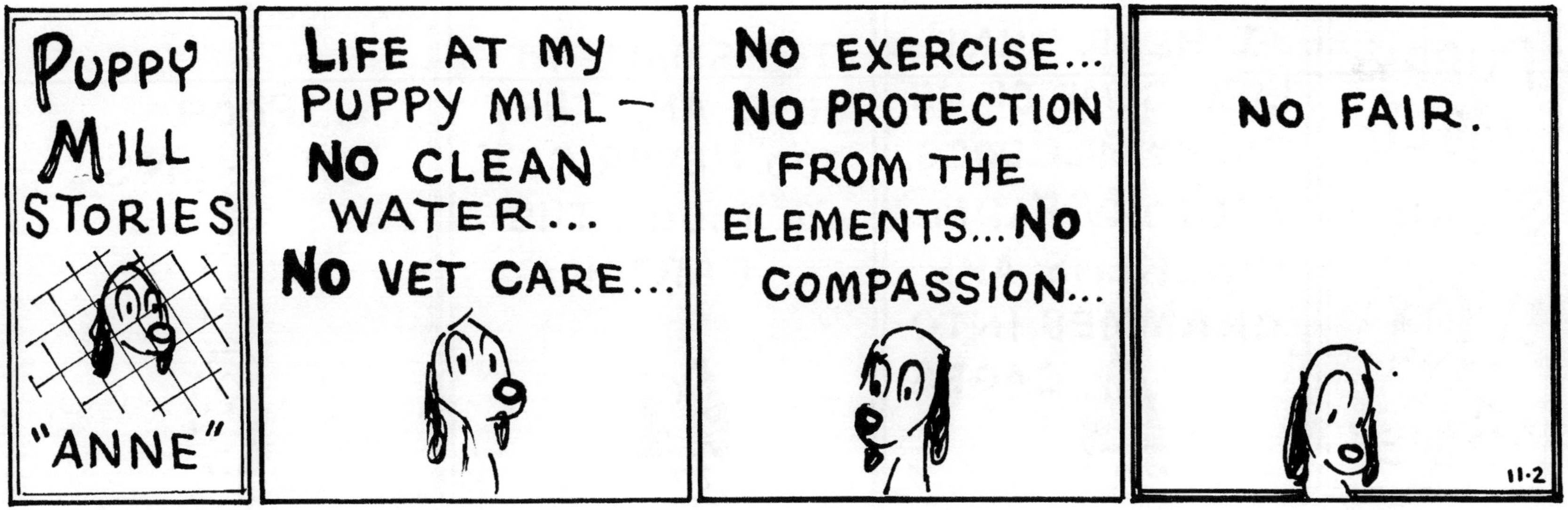
PUPPY MILL STORIES
"ANNE"
LIFE AT MY PUPPY MILL— NO CLEAN WATER... NO VET CARE...
NO EXERCISE... NO PROTECTION FROM THE ELEMENTS... NO COMPASSION...
NO FAIR.
11·2

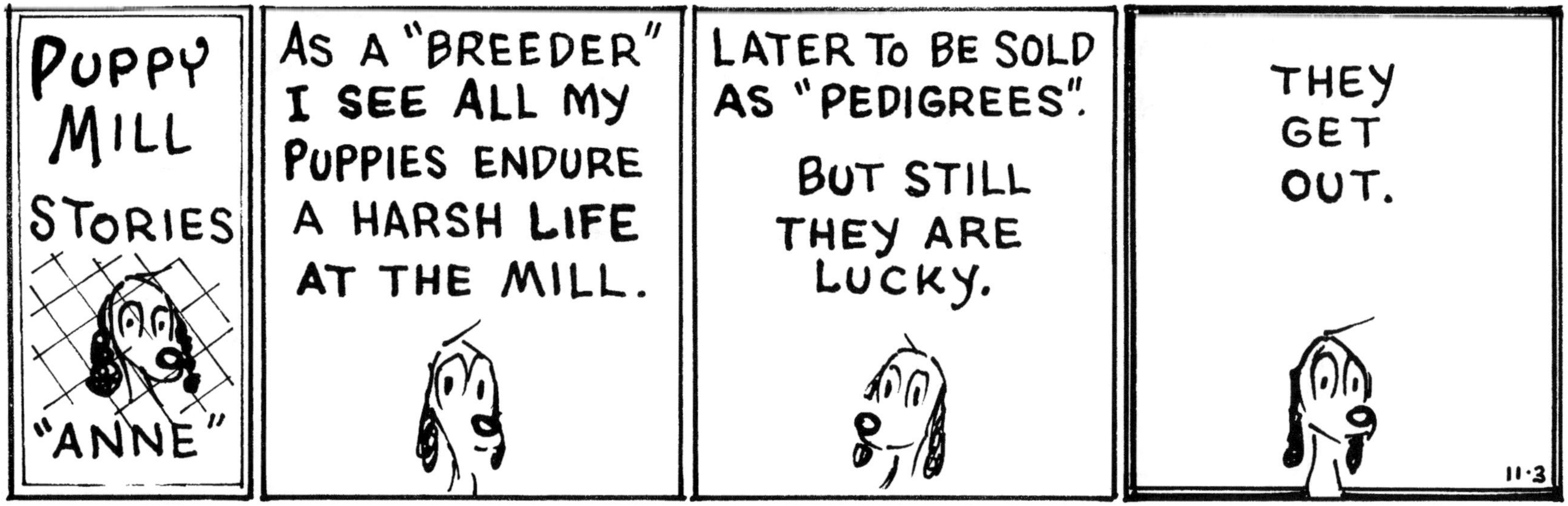
PUPPY MILL STORIES
"ANNE"
AS A "BREEDER" I SEE ALL MY PUPPIES ENDURE A HARSH LIFE AT THE MILL.
LATER TO BE SOLD AS "PEDIGREES".
BUT STILL THEY ARE LUCKY.
THEY GET OUT.
11·3

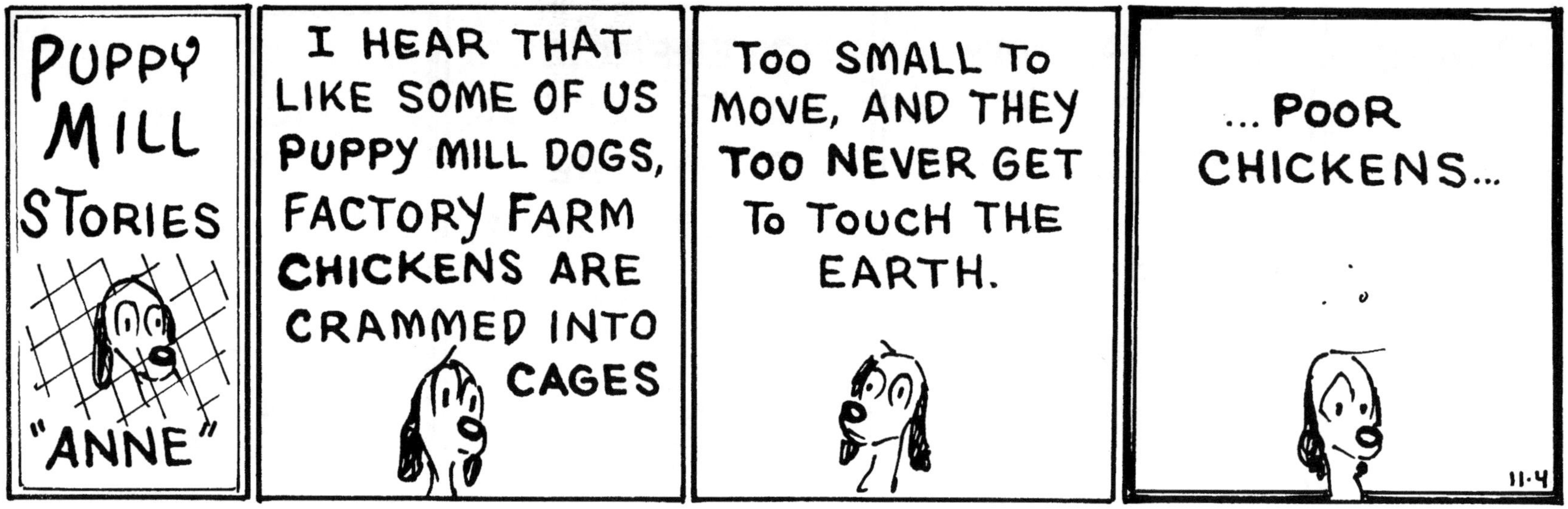
PUPPY MILL STORIES
"ANNE"
I HEAR THAT LIKE SOME OF US PUPPY MILL DOGS, FACTORY FARM CHICKENS ARE CRAMMED INTO CAGES
TOO SMALL TO MOVE, AND THEY TOO NEVER GET TO TOUCH THE EARTH.
...POOR CHICKENS...
11·4

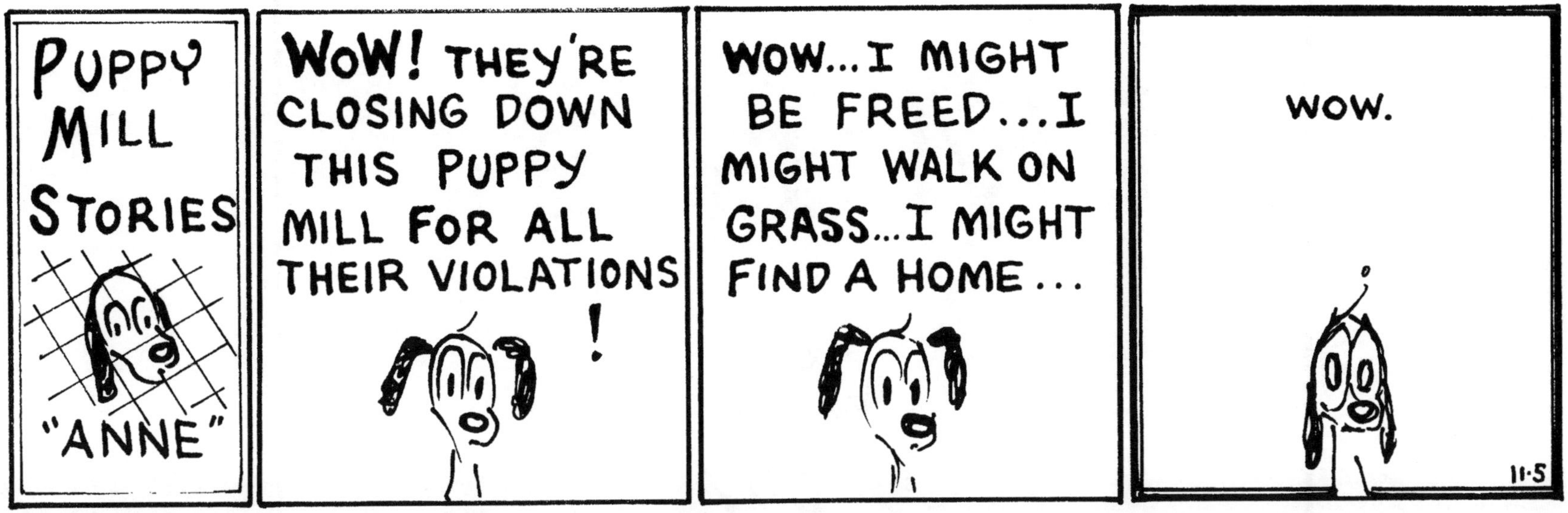
PUPPY MILL STORIES
"ANNE"
WOW! THEY'RE CLOSING DOWN THIS PUPPY MILL FOR ALL THEIR VIOLATIONS!
WOW... I MIGHT BE FREED... I MIGHT WALK ON GRASS... I MIGHT FIND A HOME...
WOW.
11·5

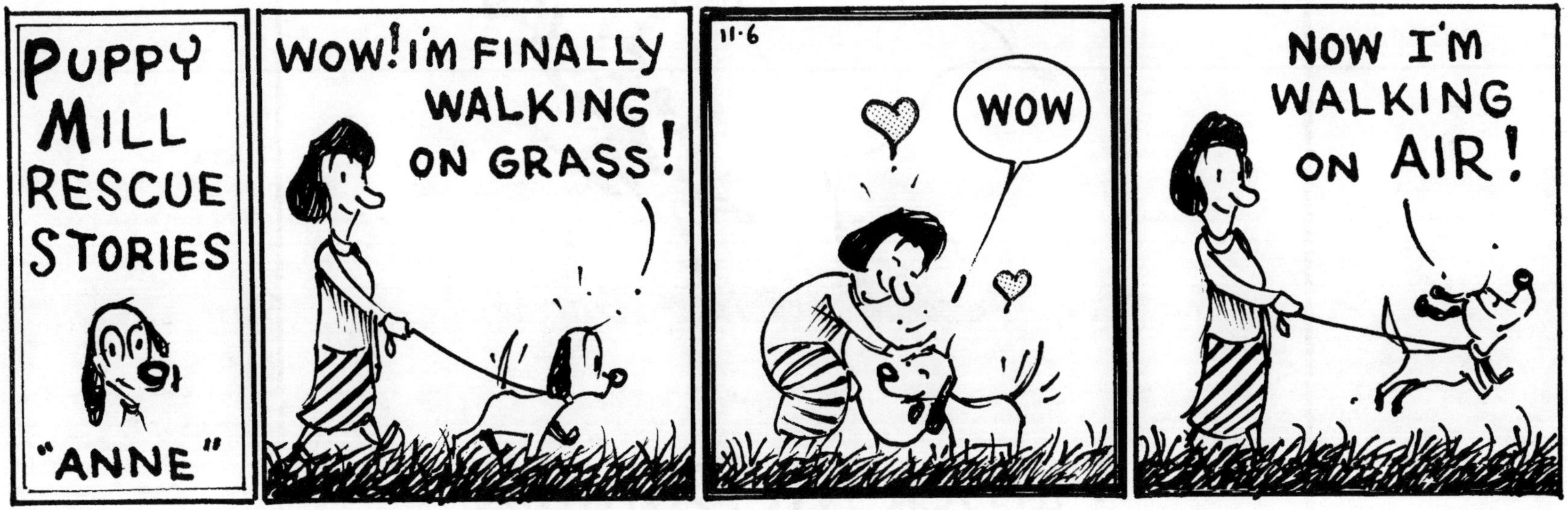
PUPPY MILL RESCUE STORIES
"ANNE"
WOW! I'M FINALLY WALKING ON GRASS!
11·6
WOW
NOW I'M WALKING ON AIR!

Mutts

Patrick McDonnell

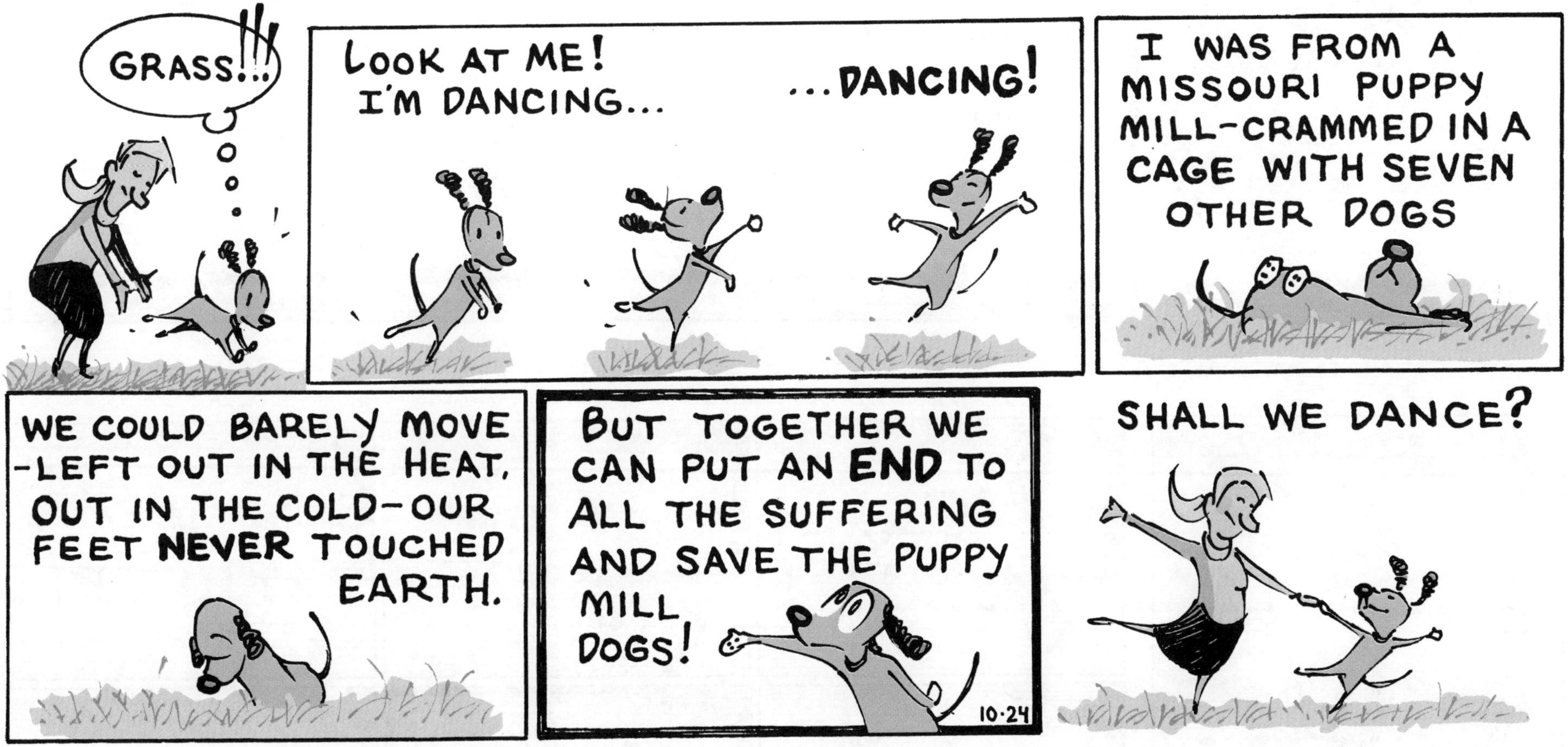

GRASS!!!
LOOK AT ME! I'M DANCING...
...DANCING!
I WAS FROM A MISSOURI PUPPY MILL–CRAMMED IN A CAGE WITH SEVEN OTHER DOGS
WE COULD BARELY MOVE –LEFT OUT IN THE HEAT, OUT IN THE COLD– OUR FEET **NEVER** TOUCHED EARTH.
BUT TOGETHER WE CAN PUT AN **END** TO ALL THE SUFFERING AND SAVE THE PUPPY MILL DOGS!
10·24
SHALL WE DANCE?

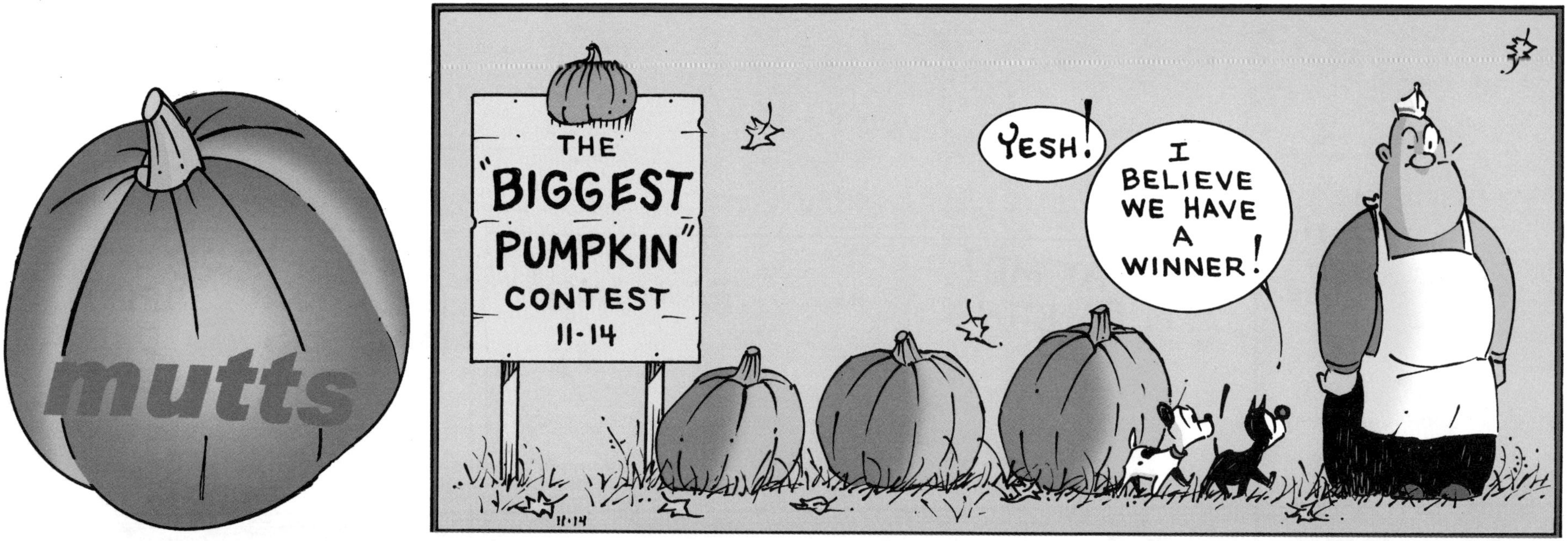
mutts
THE "BIGGEST PUMPKIN" CONTEST 11-14
YESH!
I BELIEVE WE HAVE A WINNER!
11·14

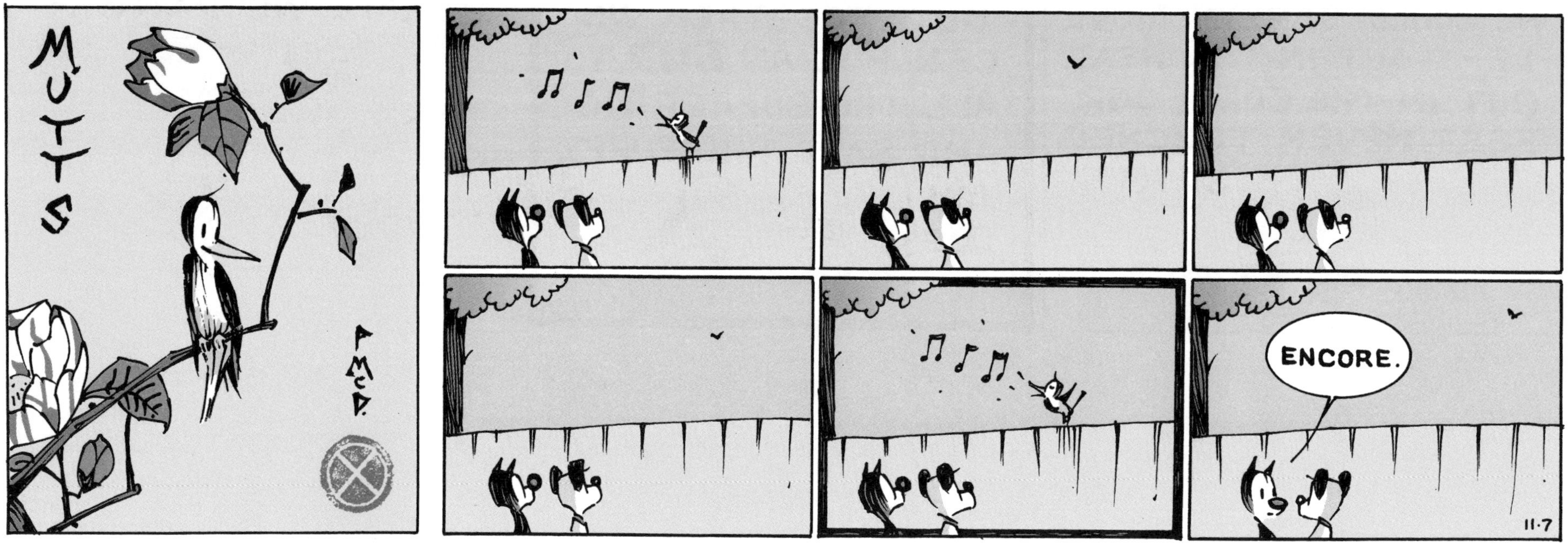
MUTTS
P. McD.
ENCORE.
11·7

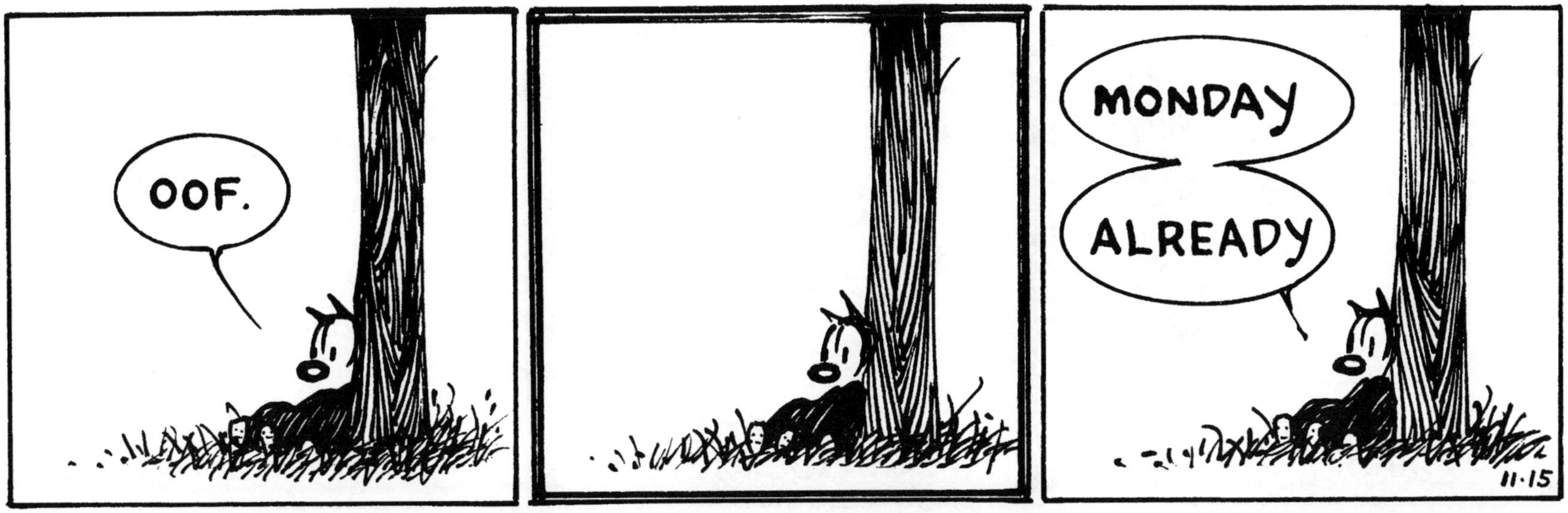
OOF.
MONDAY
ALREADY
11·15

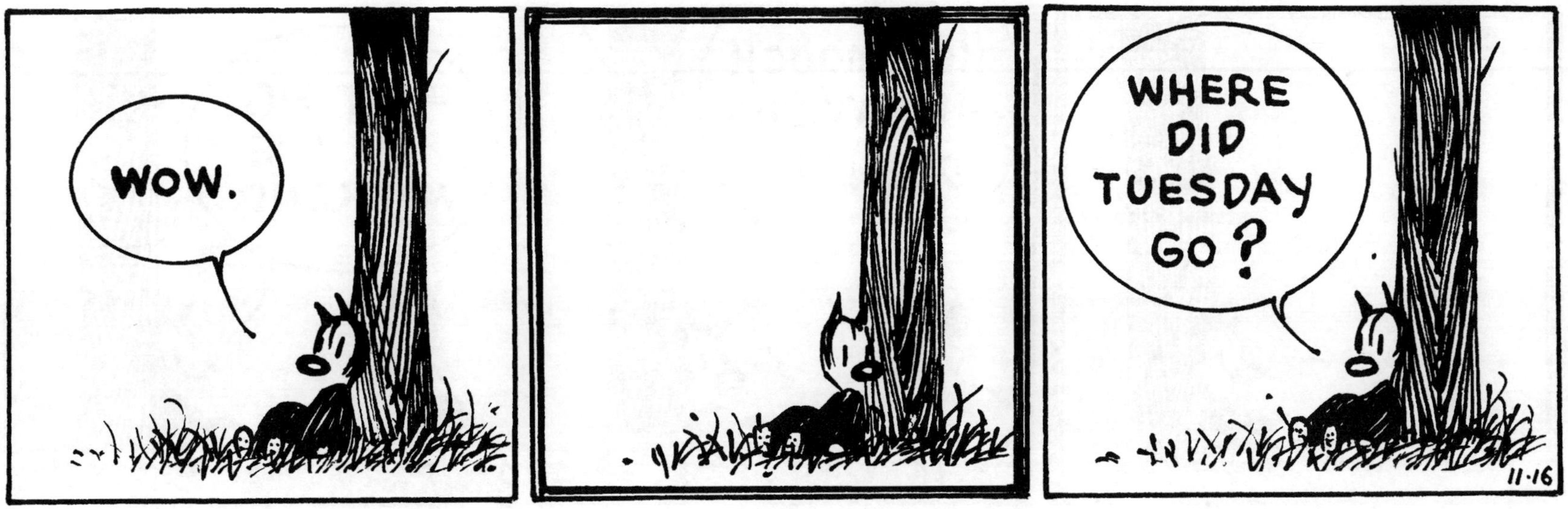
WOW.
WHERE DID TUESDAY GO?
11·16

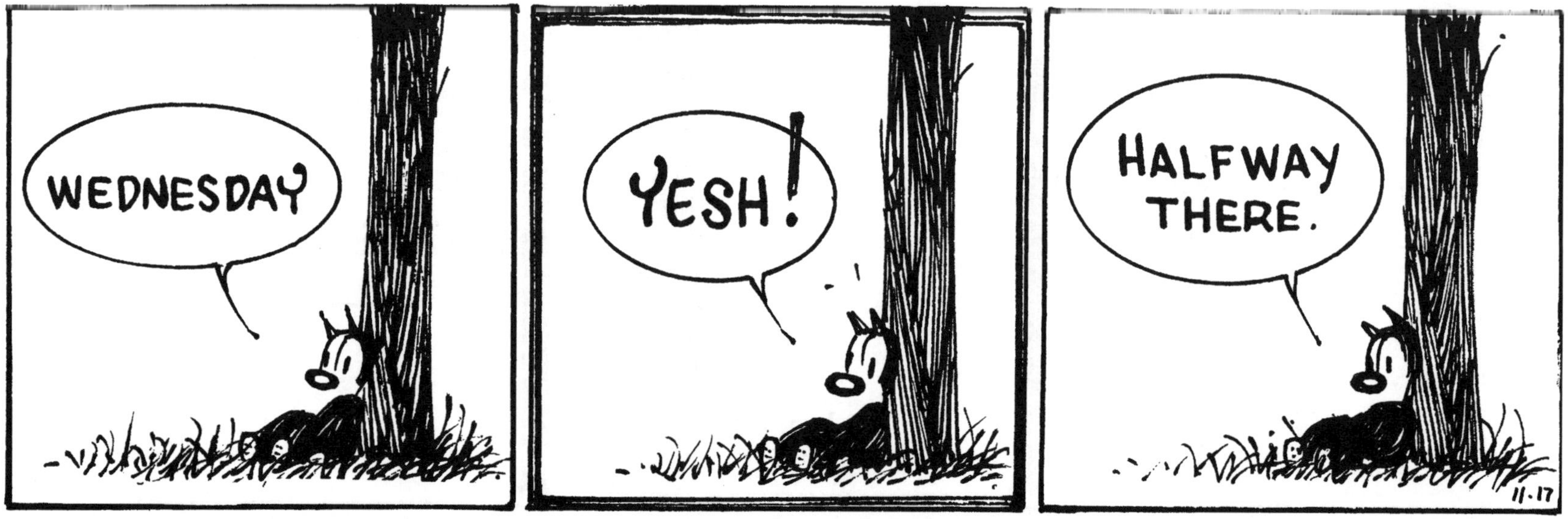
WEDNESDAY
YESH!
HALFWAY THERE.
11-17

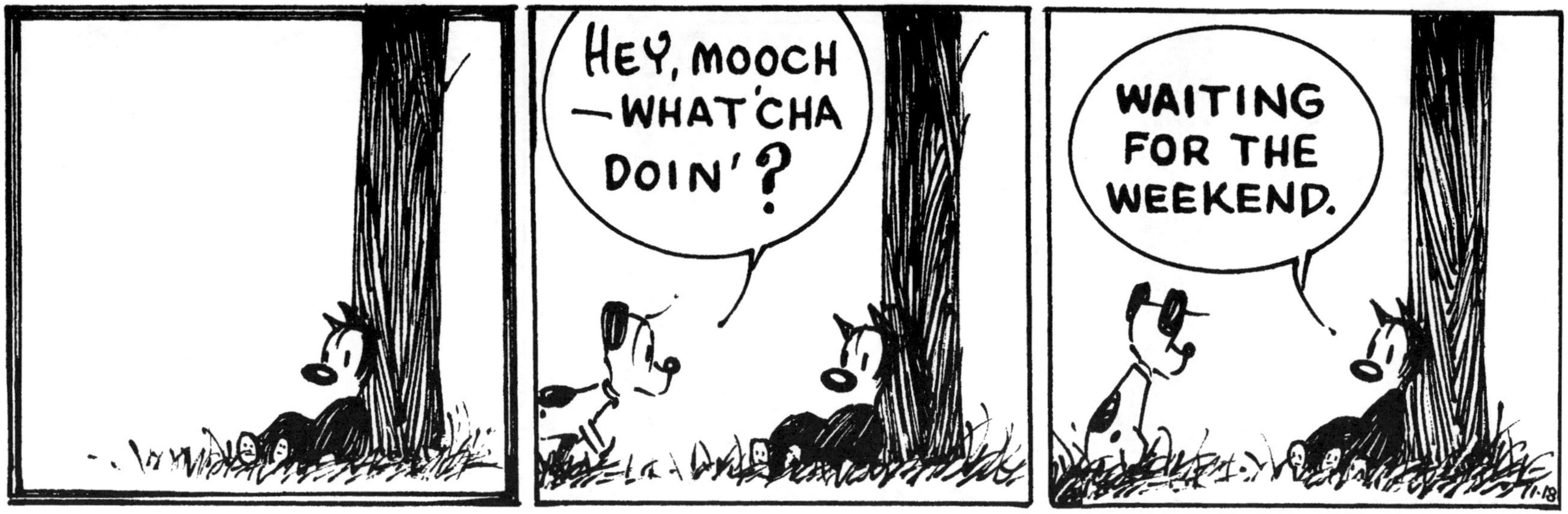
HEY, MOOCH —WHAT'CHA DOIN'?
WAITING FOR THE WEEKEND.
11-18

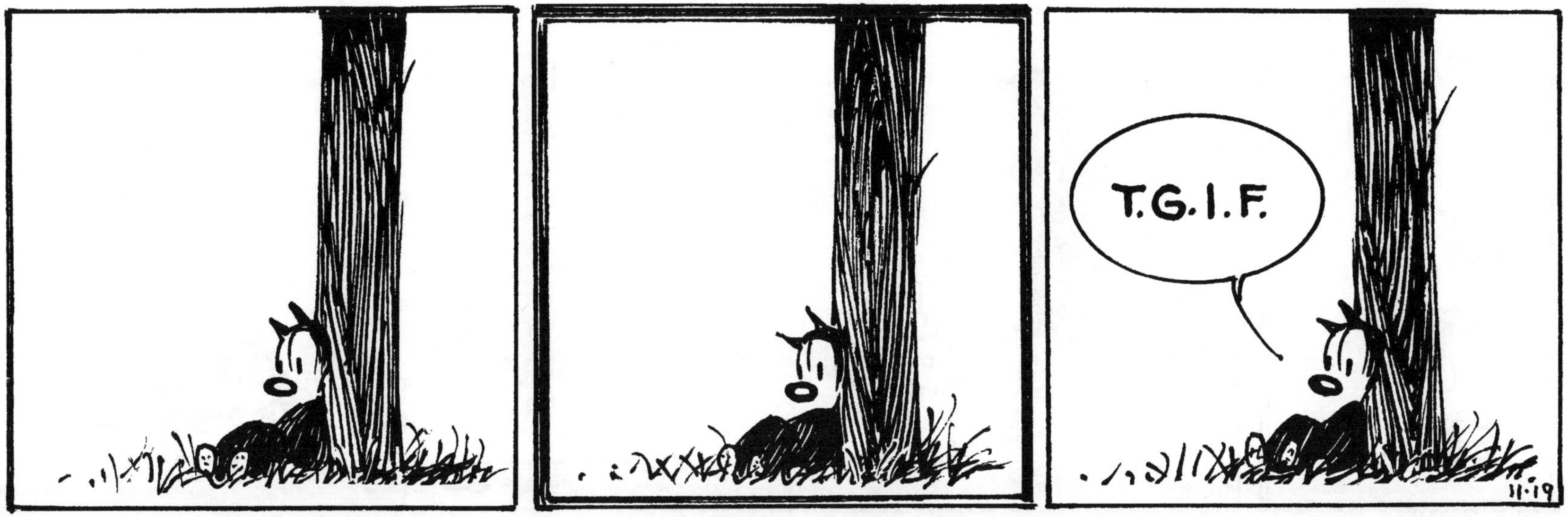
T.G.I.F.
11·19

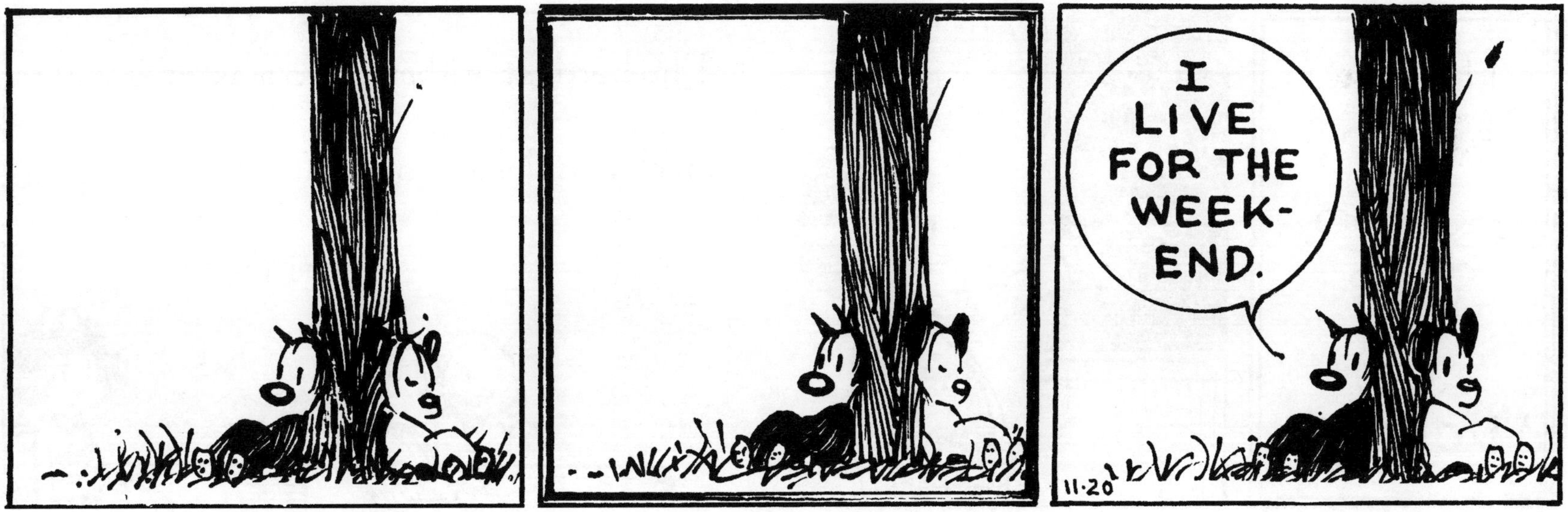
I LIVE FOR THE WEEK-END.
11·20

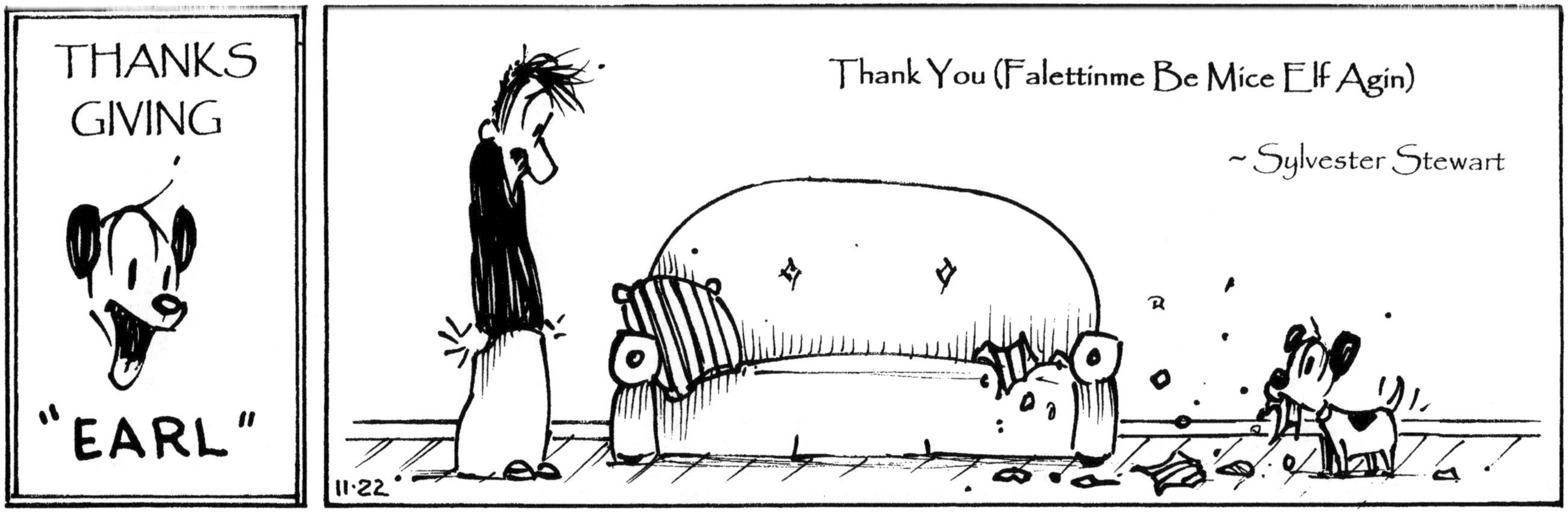
THANKS GIVING
"EARL"
Thank You (Falettinme Be Mice Elf Agin)
~ Sylvester Stewart
11·22

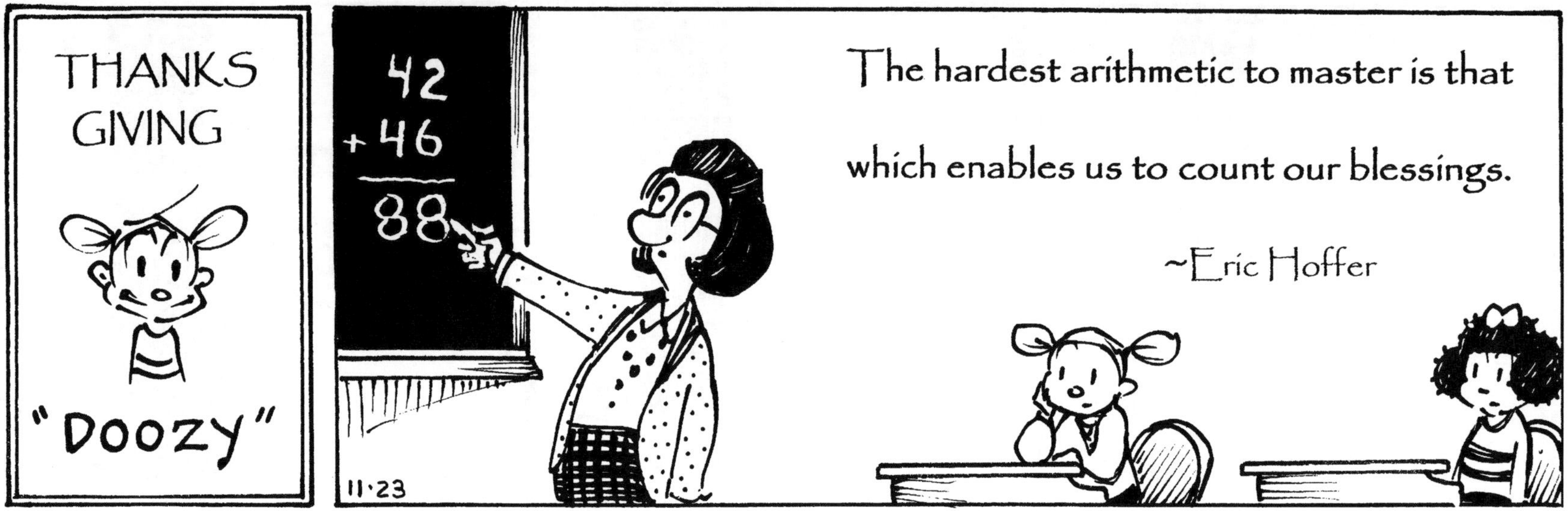
THANKS GIVING
"DOOZY"
42
+46
88
The hardest arithmetic to master is that which enables us to count our blessings.
~Eric Hoffer
11·23

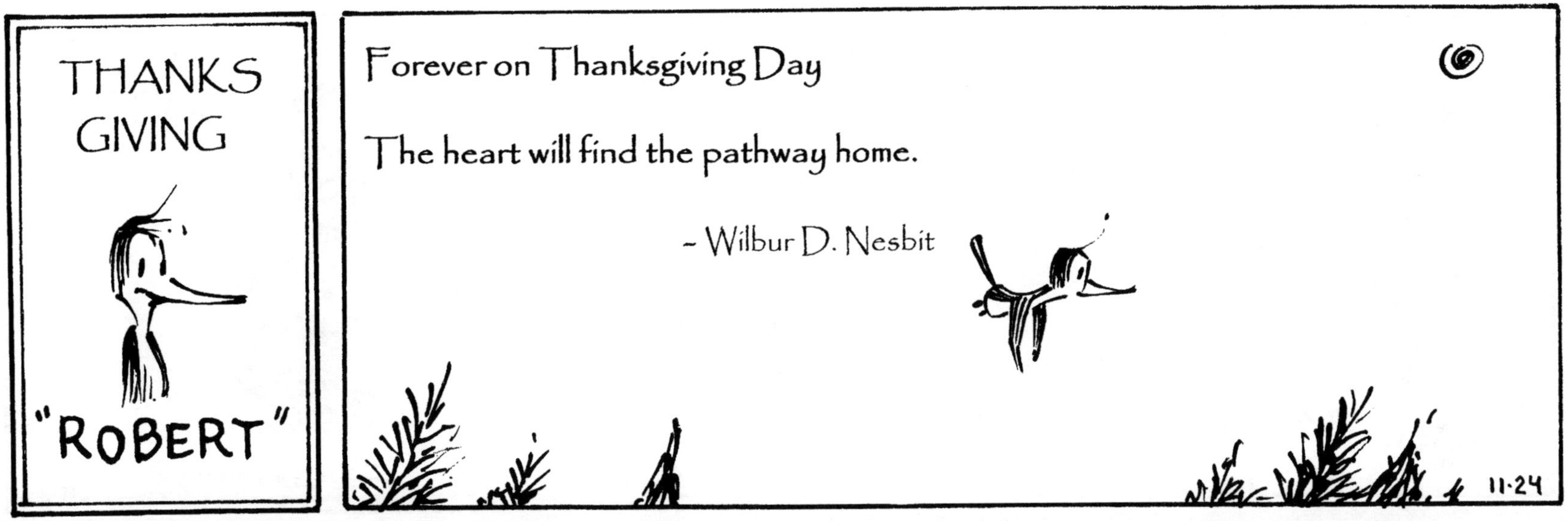
THANKS GIVING
"ROBERT"
Forever on Thanksgiving Day
The heart will find the pathway home.
~ Wilbur D. Nesbit
11·24

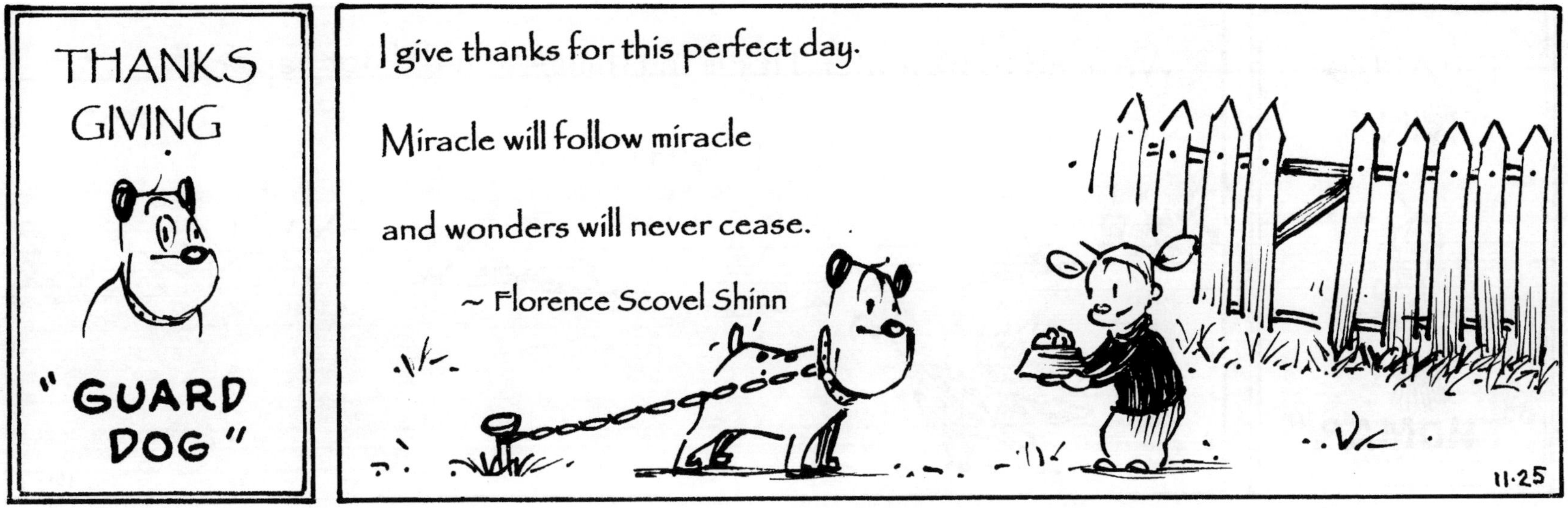
THANKS GIVING
"GUARD DOG"
I give thanks for this perfect day.
Miracle will follow miracle
and wonders will never cease.
~ Florence Scovel Shinn
11·25

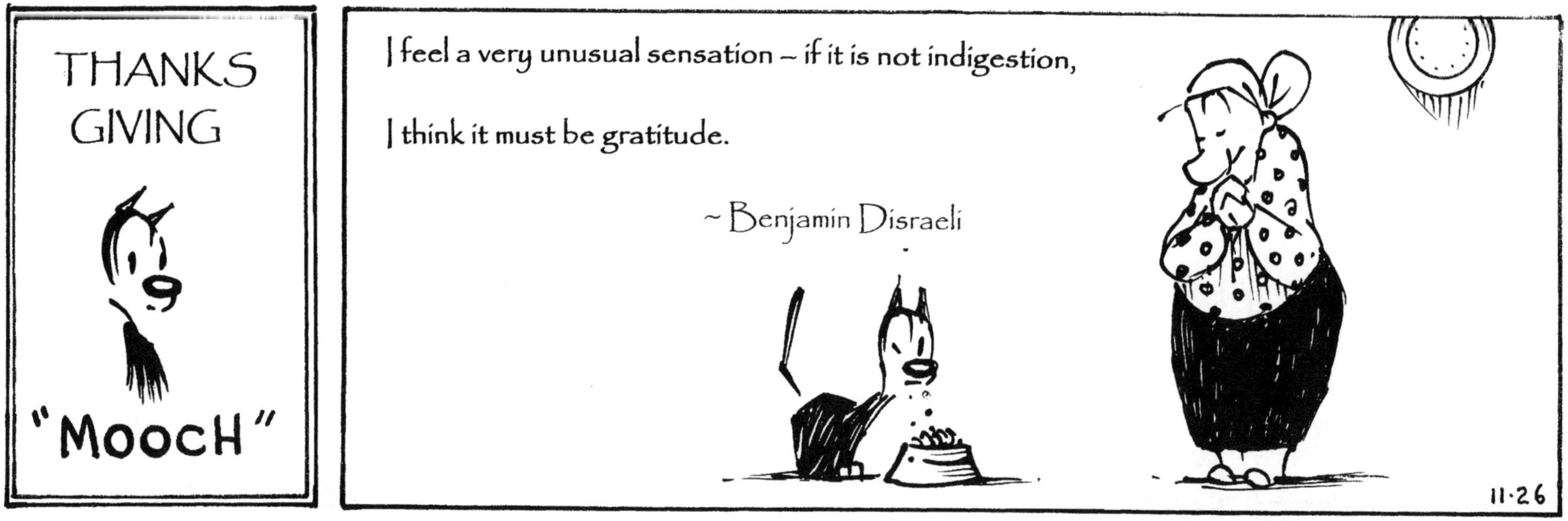
THANKS GIVING
"MOOCH"
I feel a very unusual sensation – if it is not indigestion,
I think it must be gratitude.
~ Benjamin Disraeli
11·26

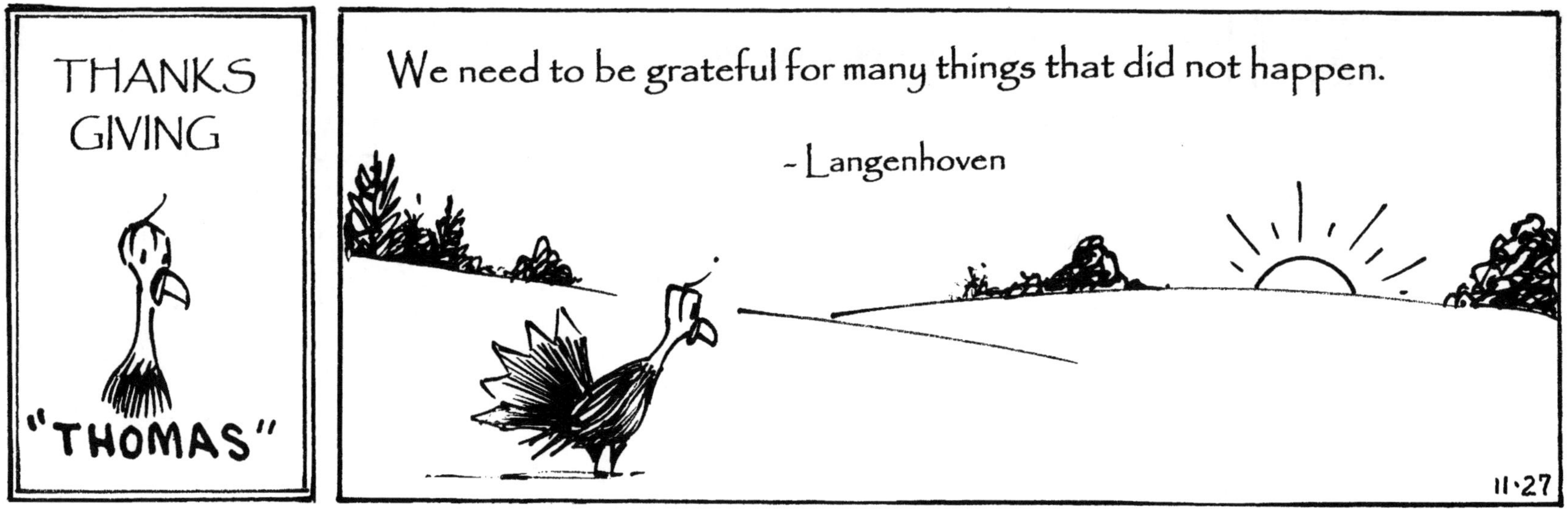
THANKS GIVING
"THOMAS"
We need to be grateful for many things that did not happen.
- Langenhoven
11·27

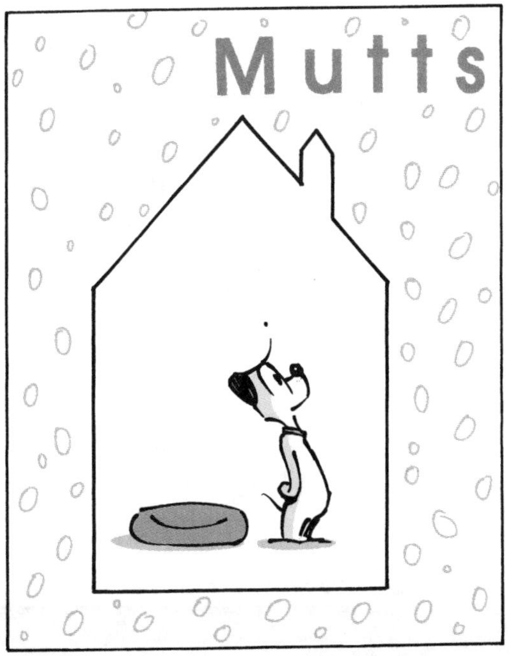
Mutts

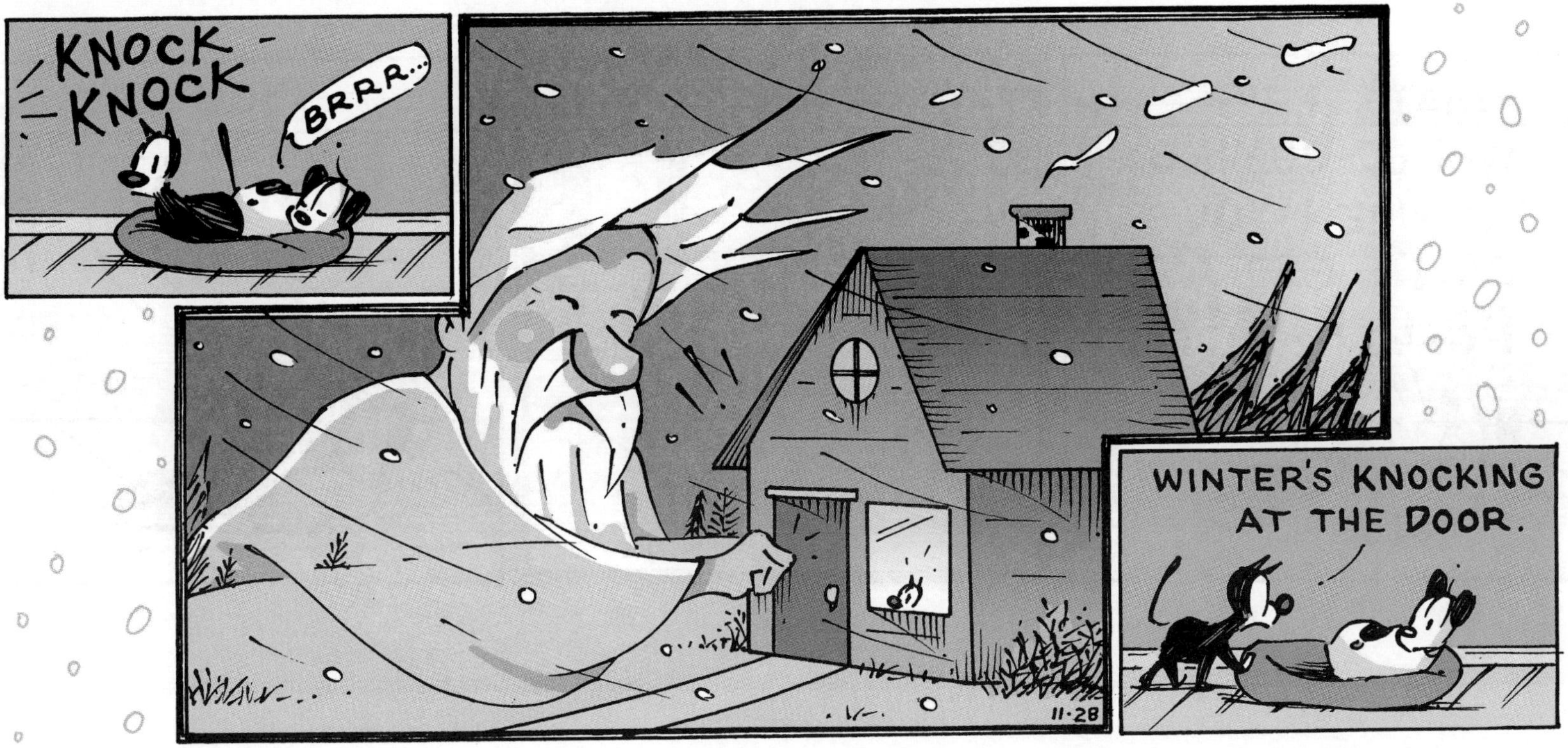
KNOCK KNOCK
BRRR...
11·28
WINTER'S KNOCKING AT THE DOOR.

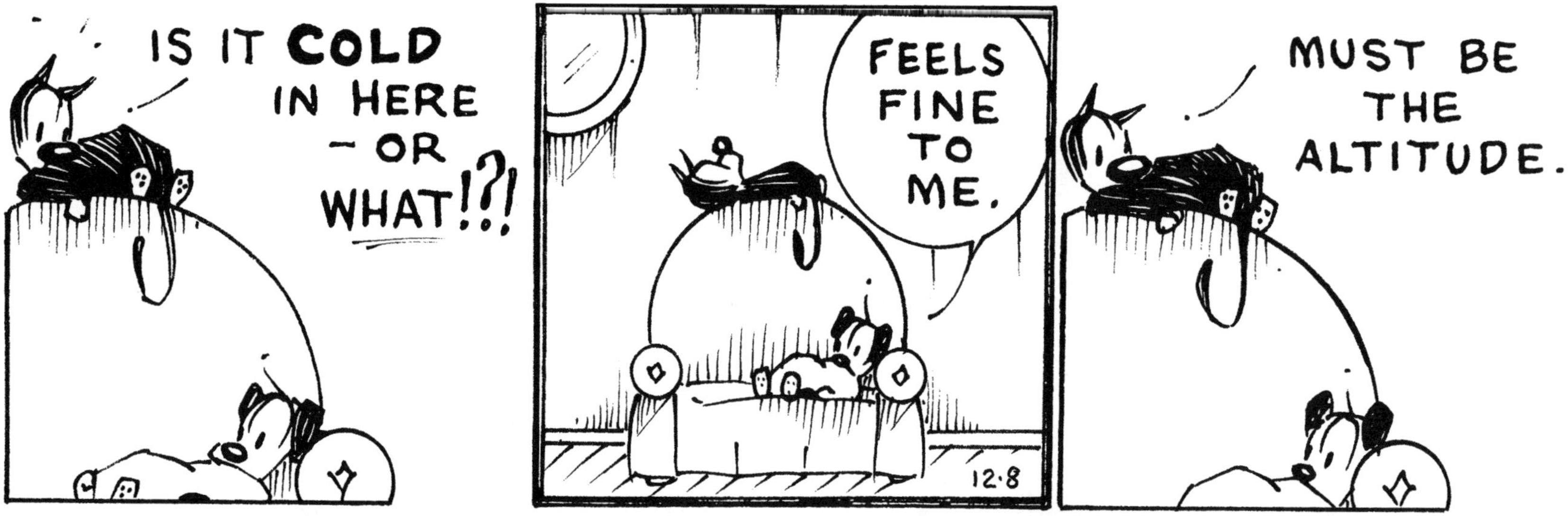
IS IT COLD IN HERE - OR WHAT!?!
FEELS FINE TO ME.
12·8
MUST BE THE ALTITUDE.

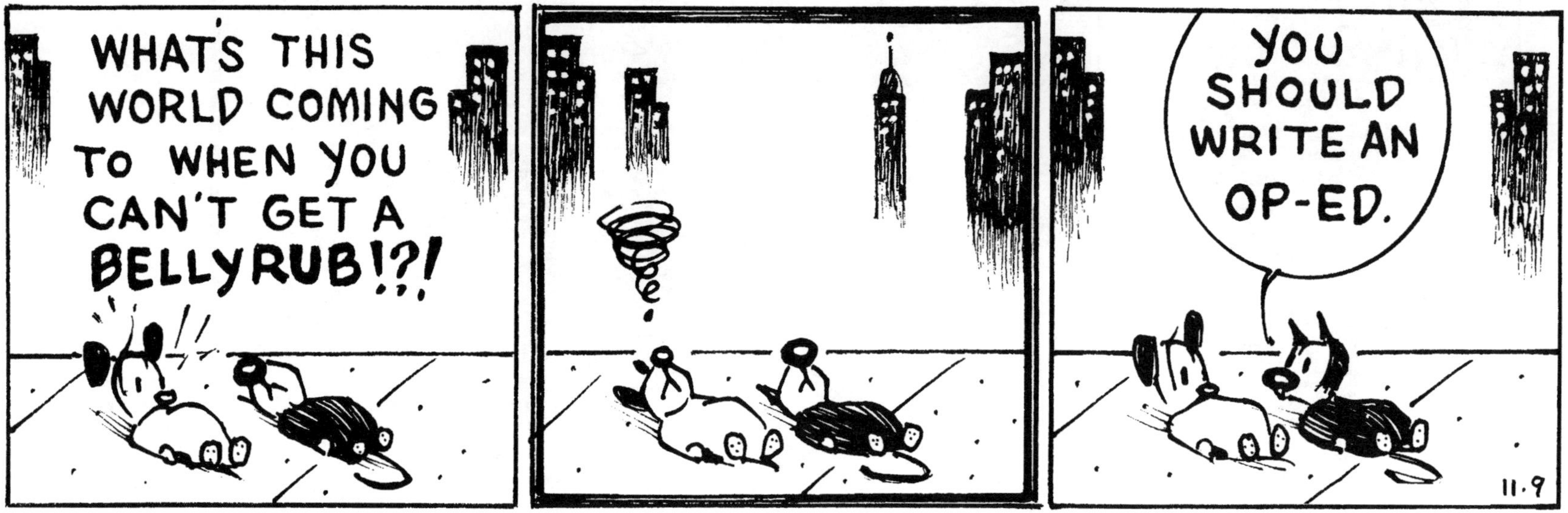
WHAT'S THIS WORLD COMING TO WHEN YOU CAN'T GET A BELLYRUB!?!
YOU SHOULD WRITE AN OP-ED.
11·9

To Do List
1. THINK OF A PUNCHLINE
OOF.
12·6

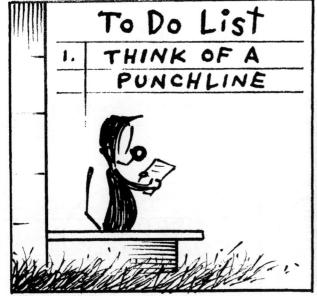

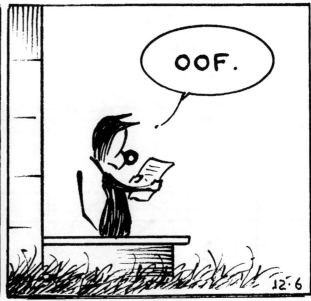

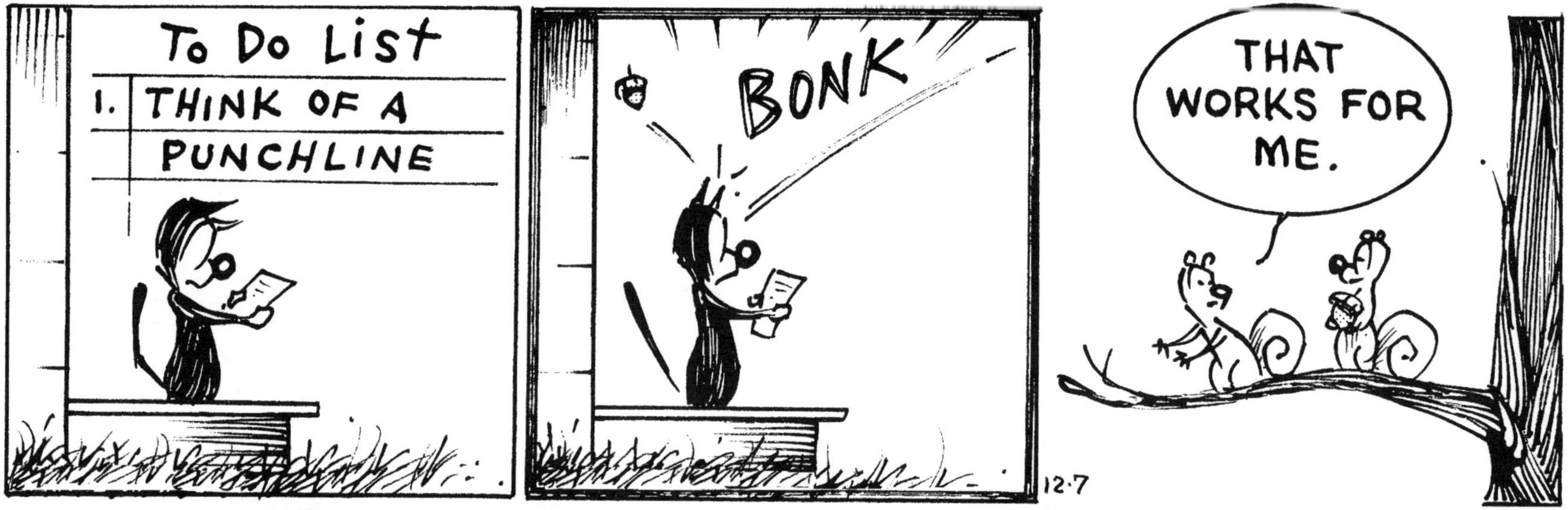
To Do List
1. THINK OF A PUNCHLINE
BONK
THAT WORKS FOR ME.
12·7

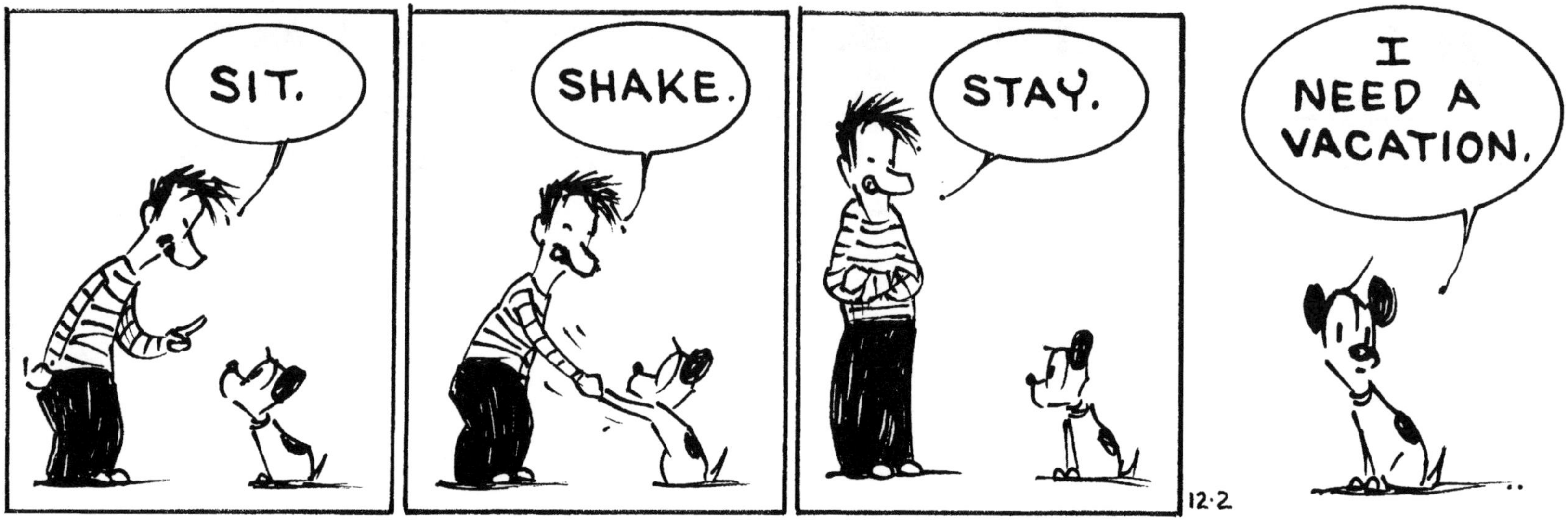
SIT.
SHAKE.
STAY.
I NEED A VACATION.
12·2

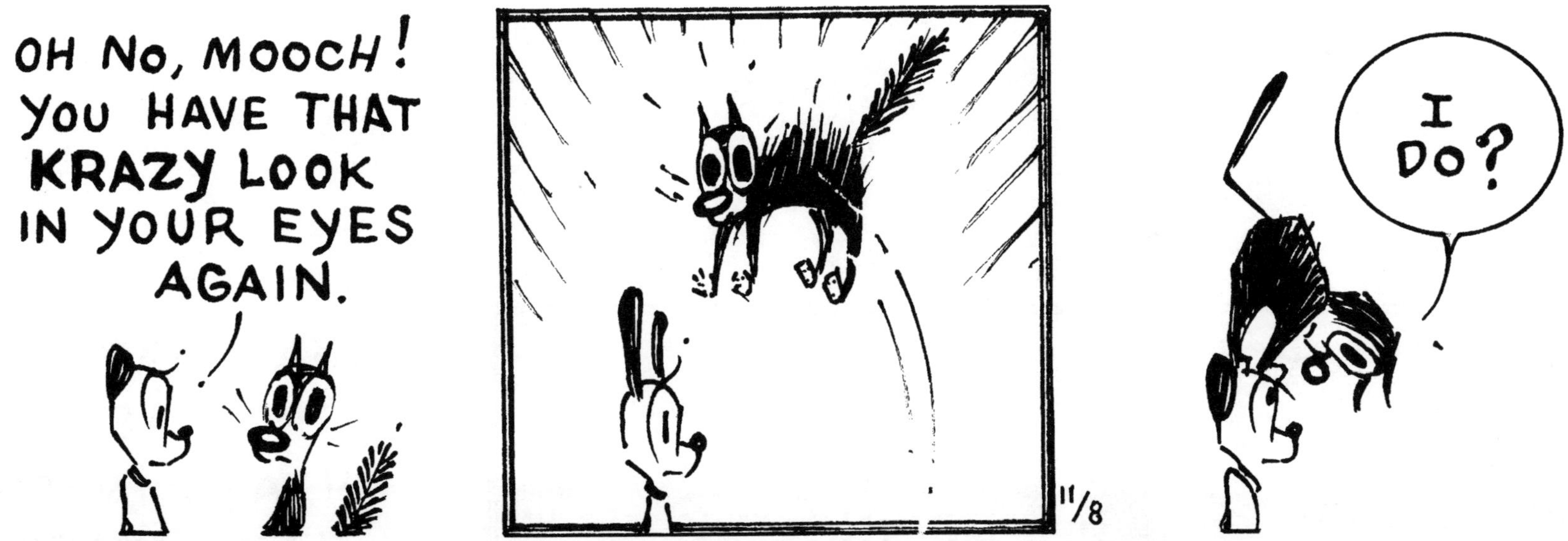
OH No, MOOCH! YOU HAVE THAT KRAZY LOOK IN YOUR EYES AGAIN.
11/8
I DO?

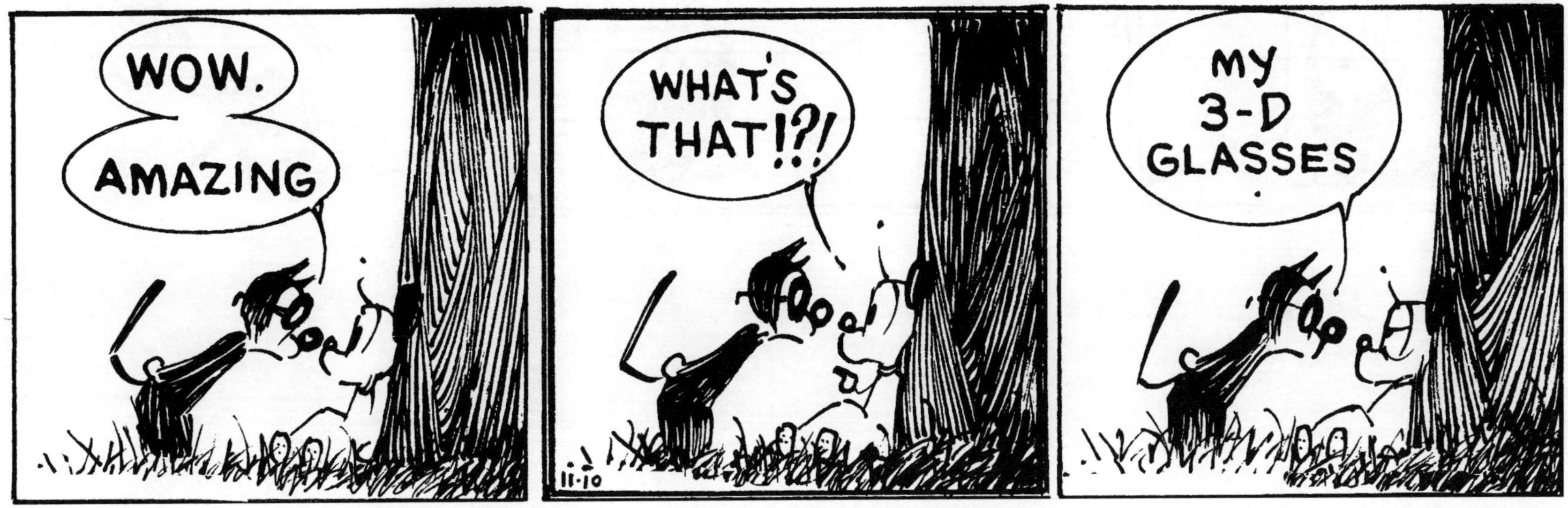
WOW.
AMAZING
WHAT'S THAT!?!
11-10
MY 3-D GLASSES

HEY, MILLIE—MOOCH WAS IN THE BASE-MENT!
I WONDER WHAT HE WAS DOING DOWN THERE!?!
12·10
WHAT HAPPENS IN THE BASEMENT SHTAYS IN THE BASEMENT.

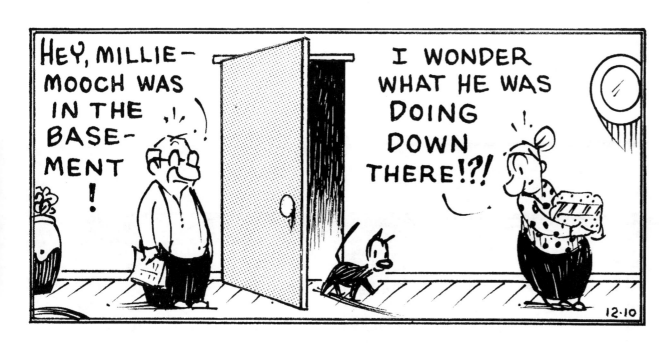

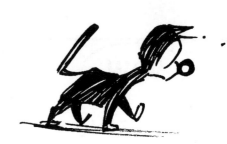

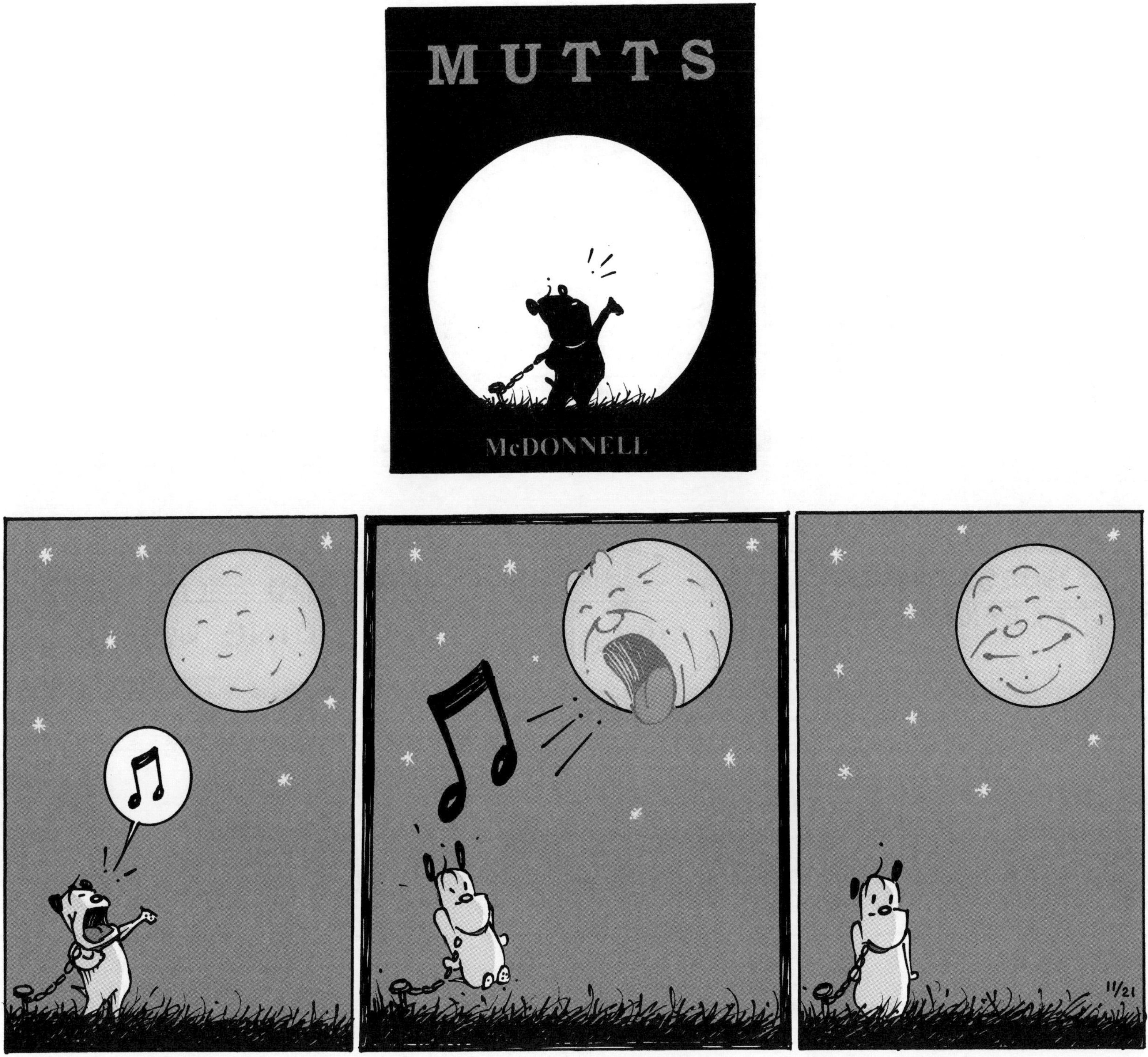
MUTTS
McDONNELL
11/21

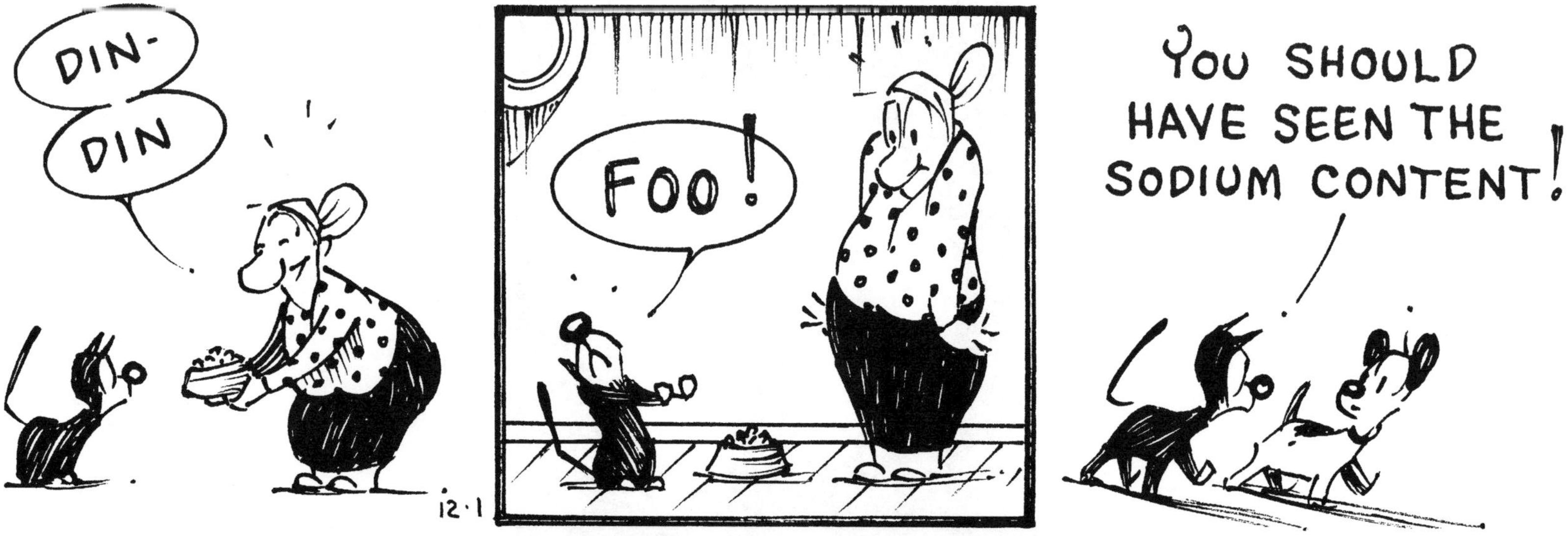
DIN-
DIN
12·1
FOO!
YOU SHOULD HAVE SEEN THE SODIUM CONTENT!

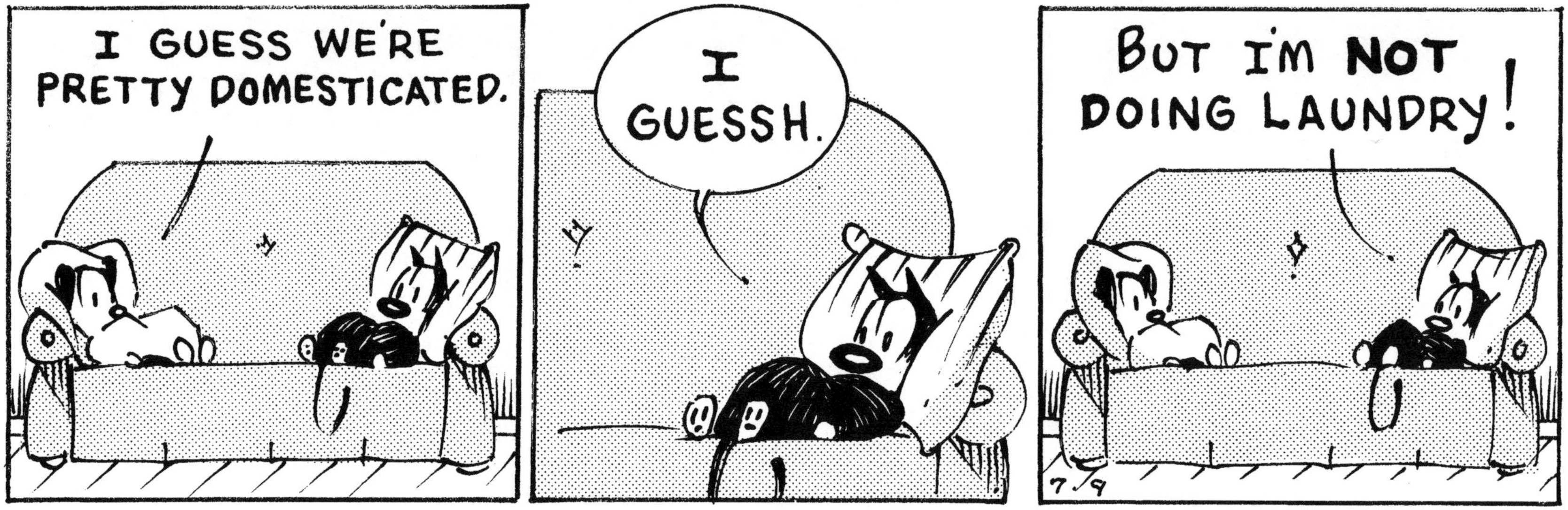
I GUESS WE'RE PRETTY DOMESTICATED.
I GUESSH.
BUT I'M **NOT** DOING LAUNDRY!
7·9

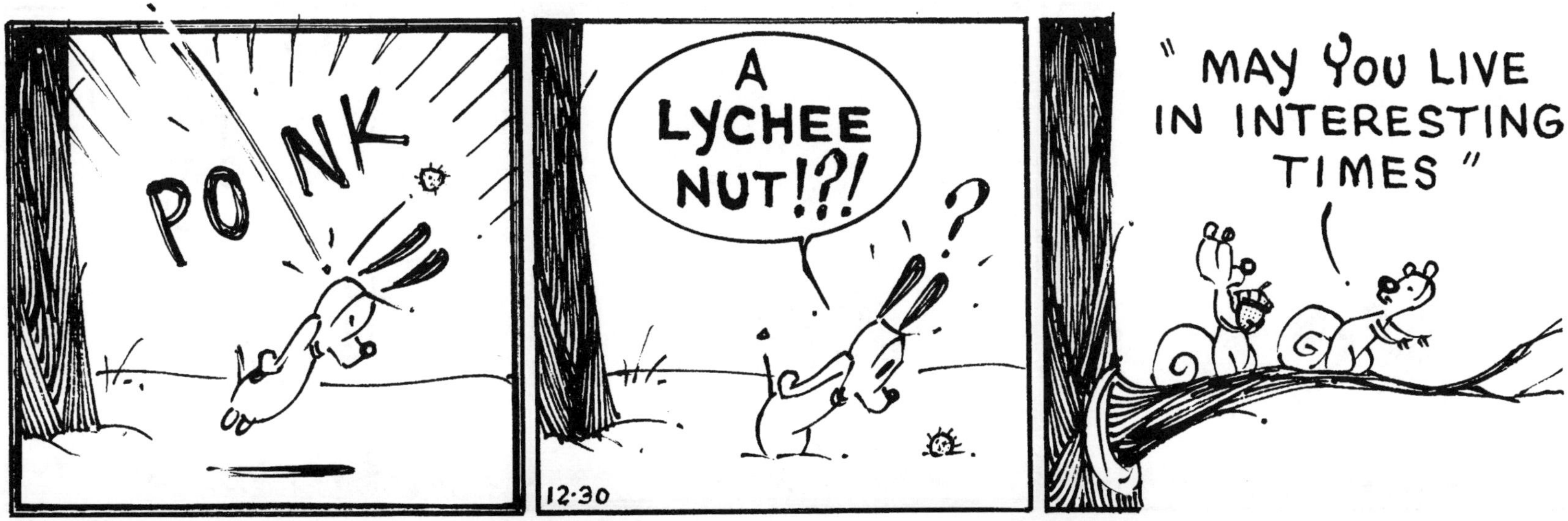
PONK
A LYCHEE NUT!?!
?
" MAY YOU LIVE IN INTERESTING TIMES "
12·30

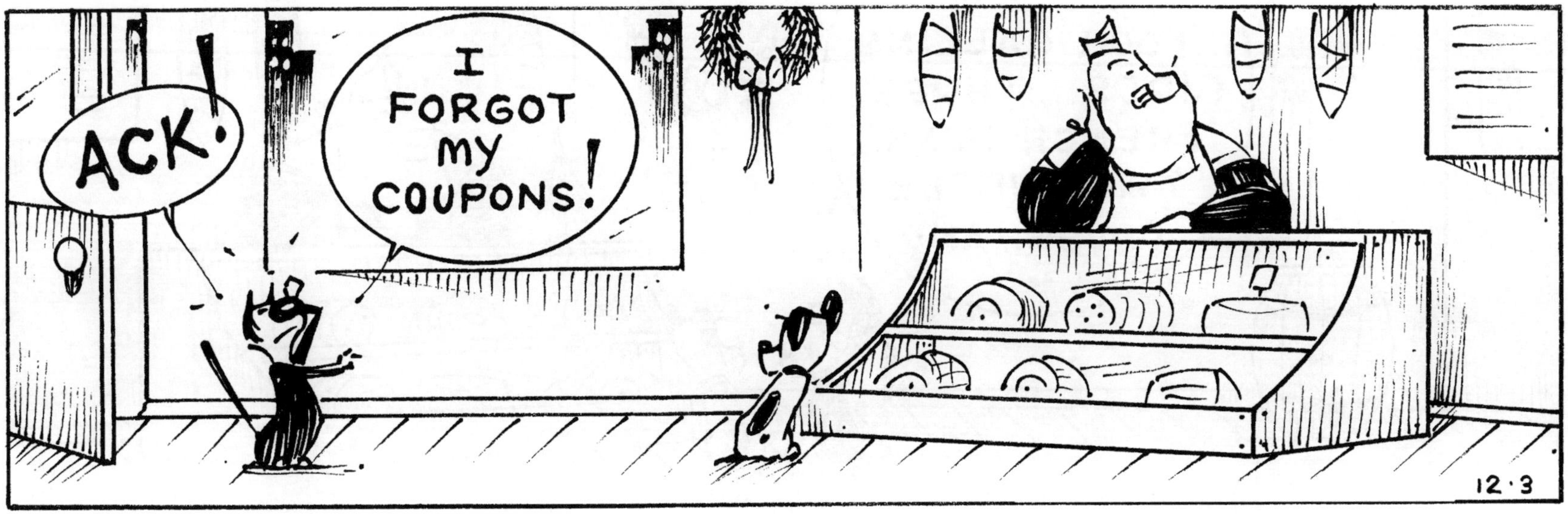
ACK!
I FORGOT MY COUPONS!
12·3

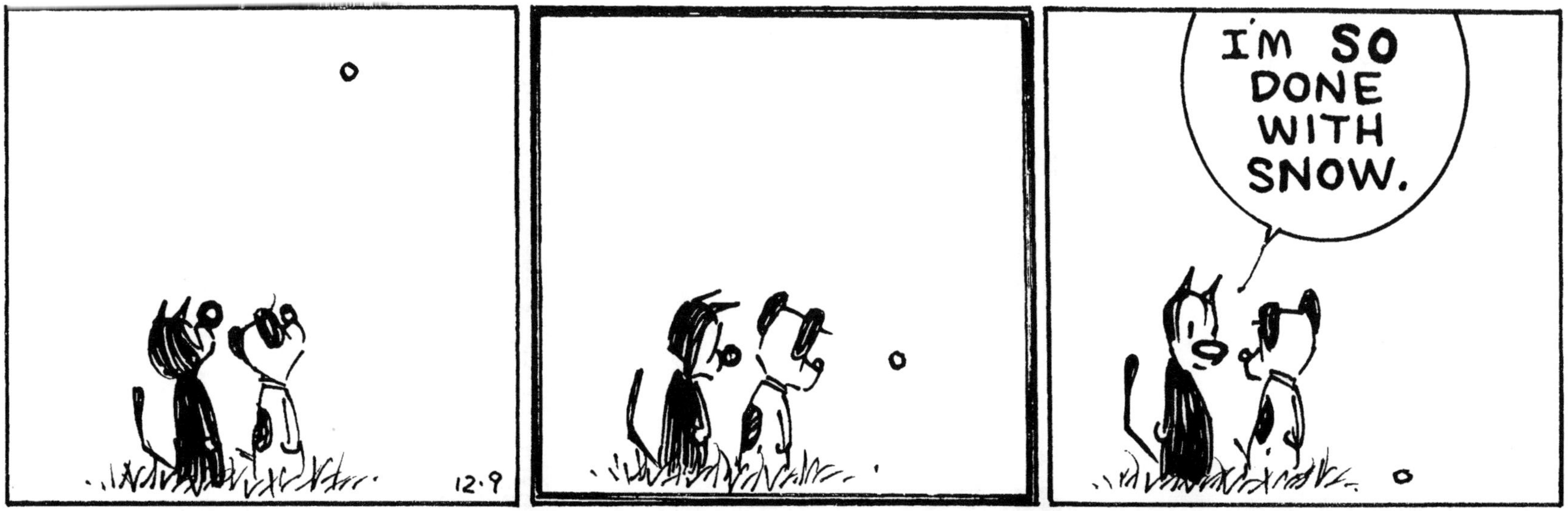
12·9
I'M SO DONE WITH SNOW.

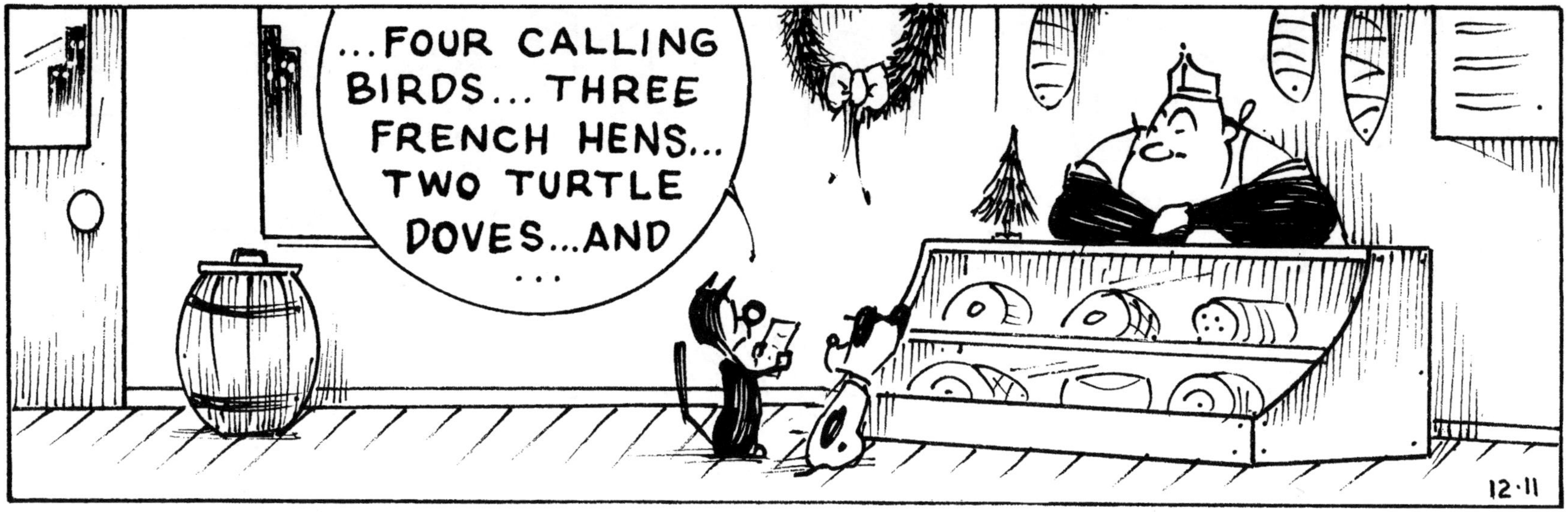
...FOUR CALLING BIRDS... THREE FRENCH HENS... TWO TURTLE DOVES...AND ...
12·11

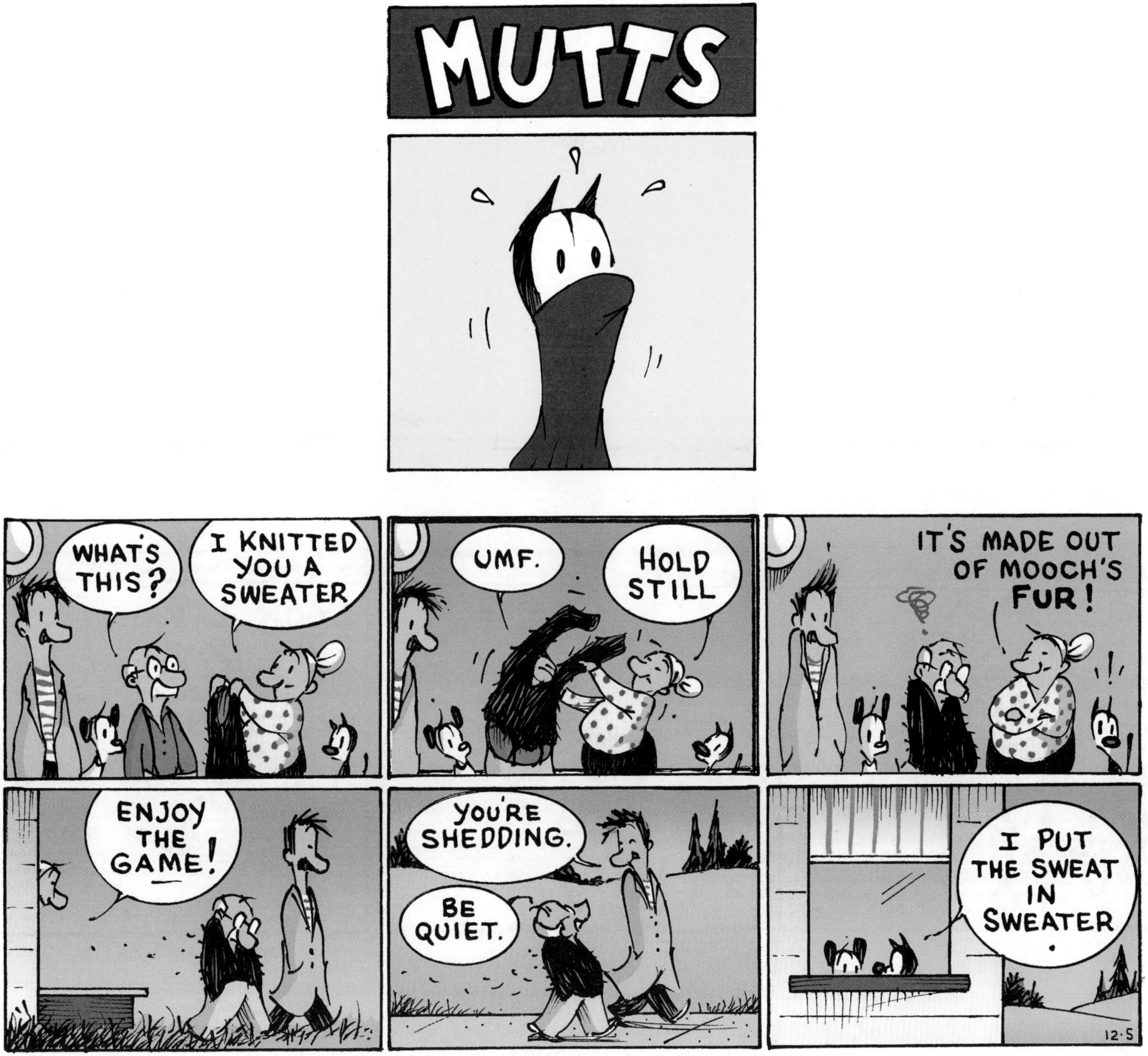
MUTTS
WHAT'S THIS?
I KNITTED YOU A SWEATER
UMF.
HOLD STILL
IT'S MADE OUT OF MOOCH'S FUR!
ENJOY THE GAME!
YOU'RE SHEDDING.
BE QUIET.
I PUT THE SWEAT IN SWEATER.
12·5

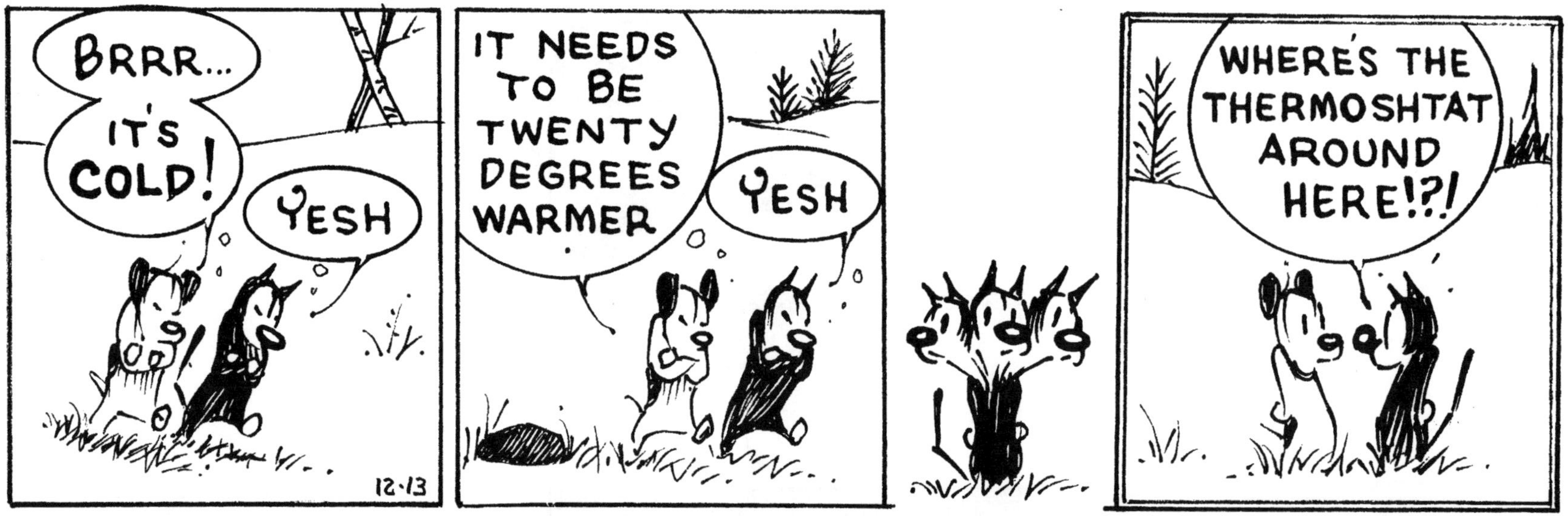
BRRR...
IT'S COLD!
YESH
12·13
IT NEEDS TO BE TWENTY DEGREES WARMER
YESH
WHERE'S THE THERMOSHTAT AROUND HERE!?!

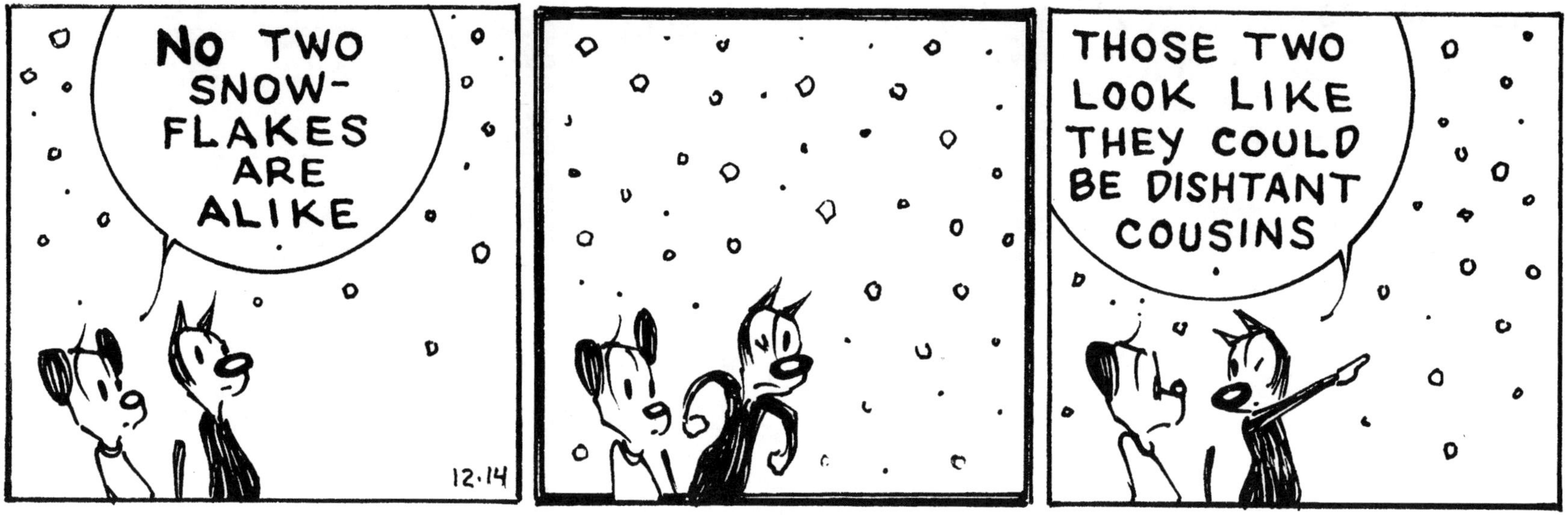
NO TWO SNOW-FLAKES ARE ALIKE
12·14
THOSE TWO LOOK LIKE THEY COULD BE DISHTANT COUSINS

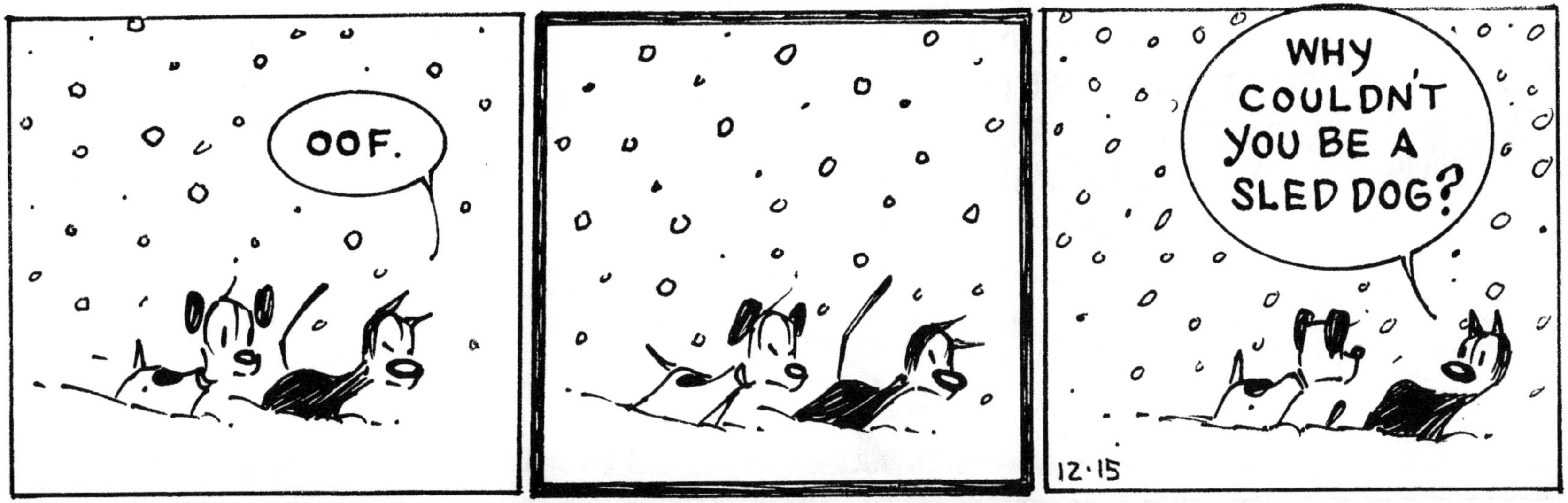
OOF.
WHY COULDN'T YOU BE A SLED DOG?
12·15

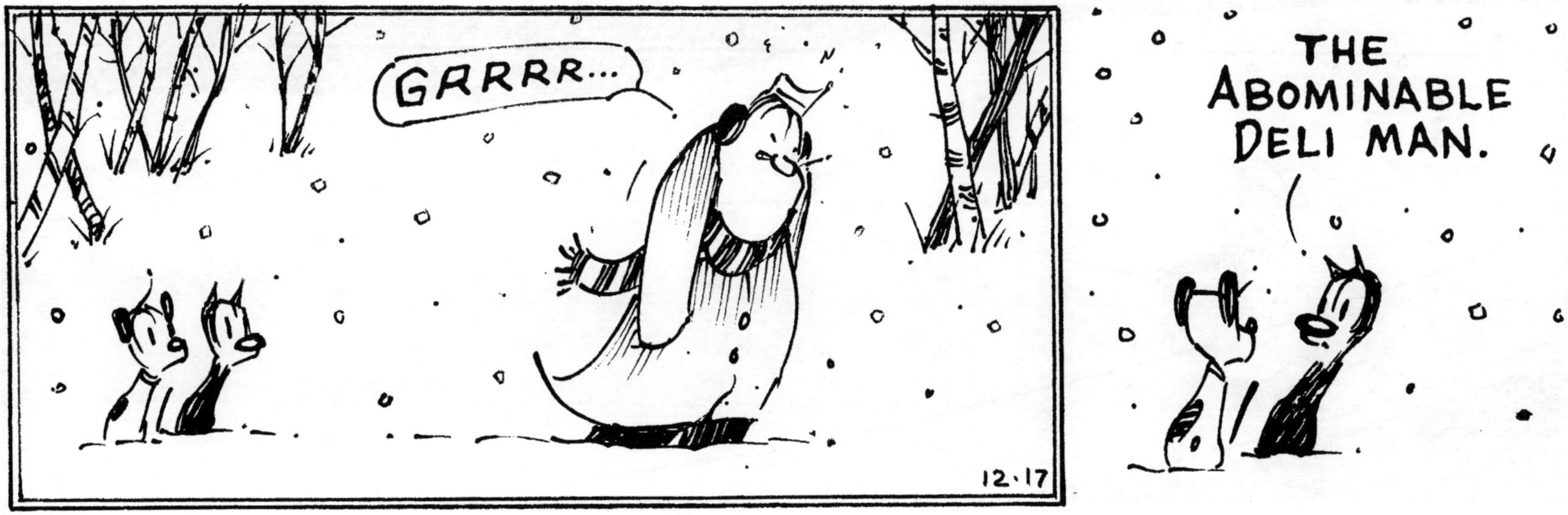
GRRRR...
THE ABOMINABLE DELI MAN.
12·17

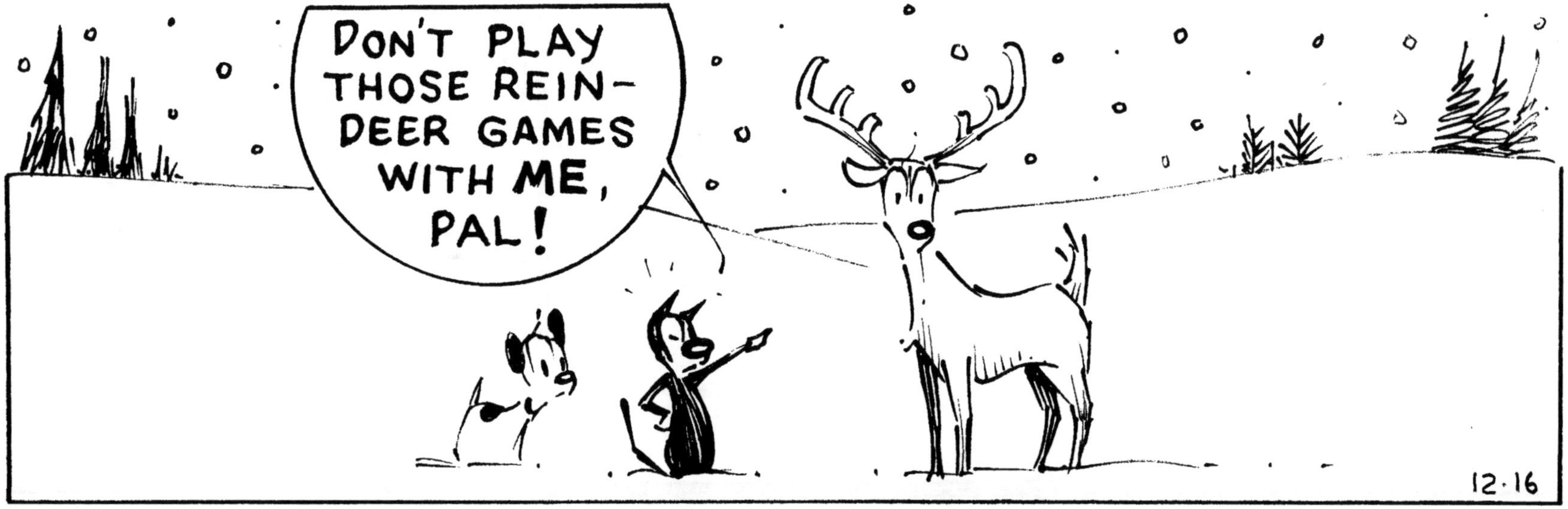
DON'T PLAY THOSE REIN-DEER GAMES WITH ME, PAL!
12·16

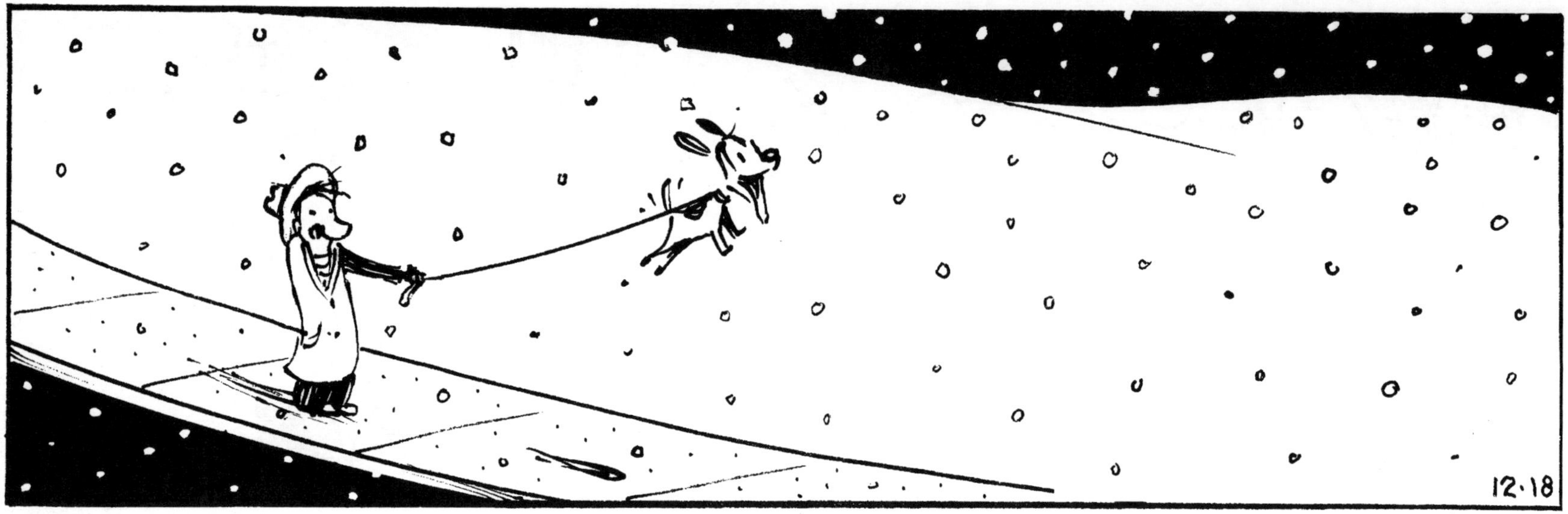
12·18

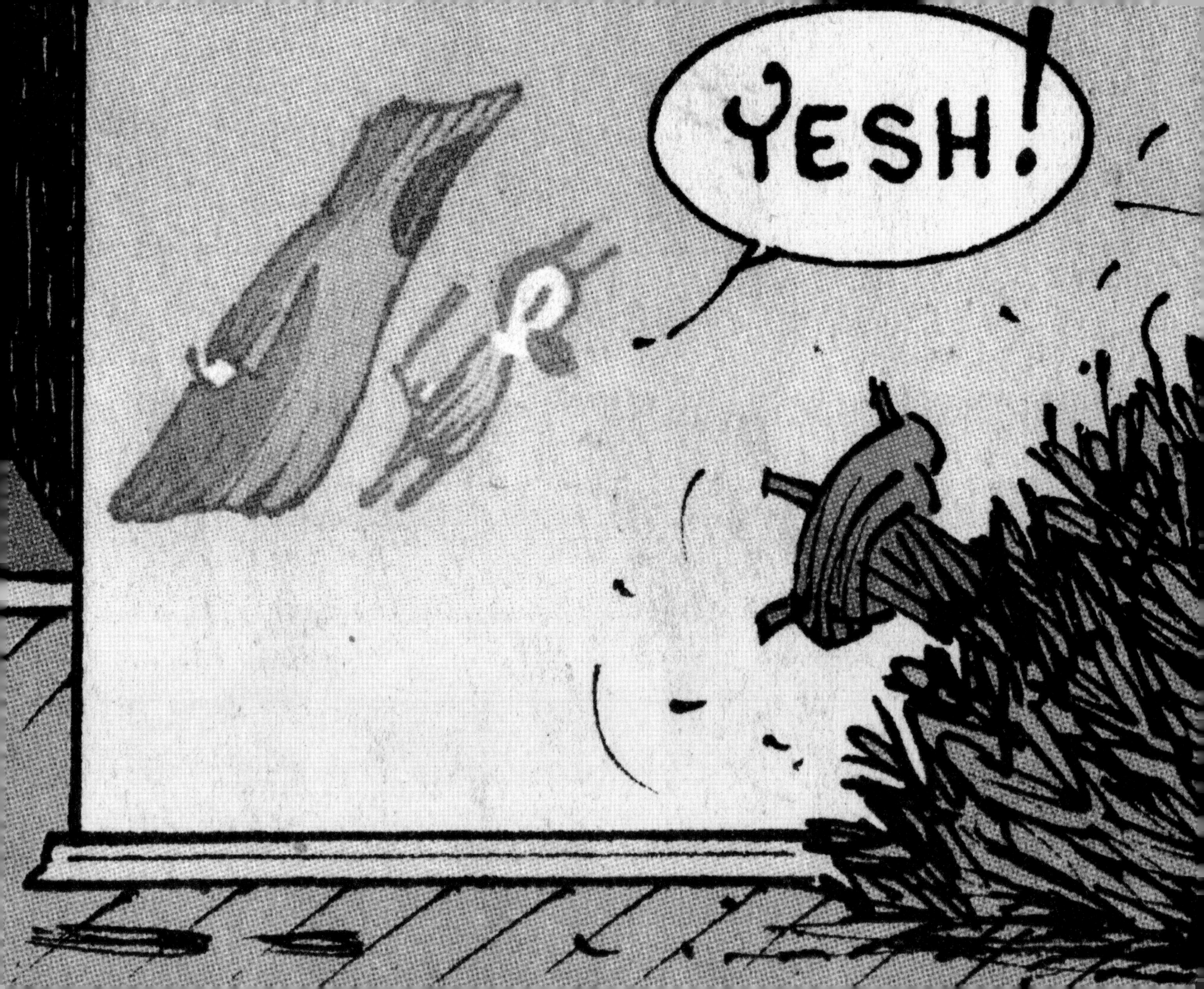
YESH!

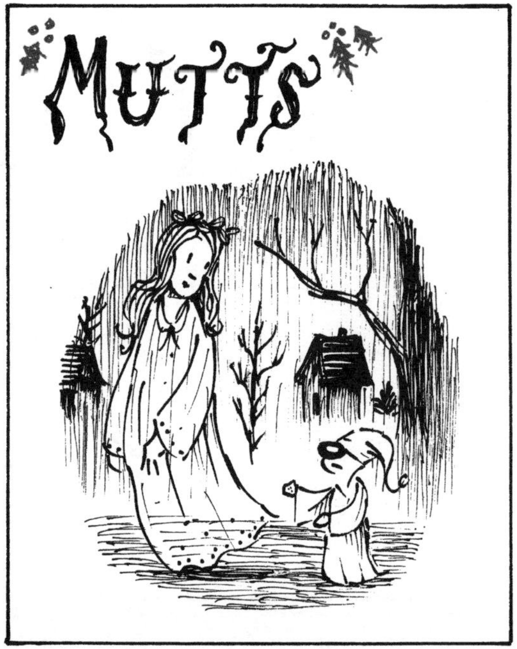
MUTTS

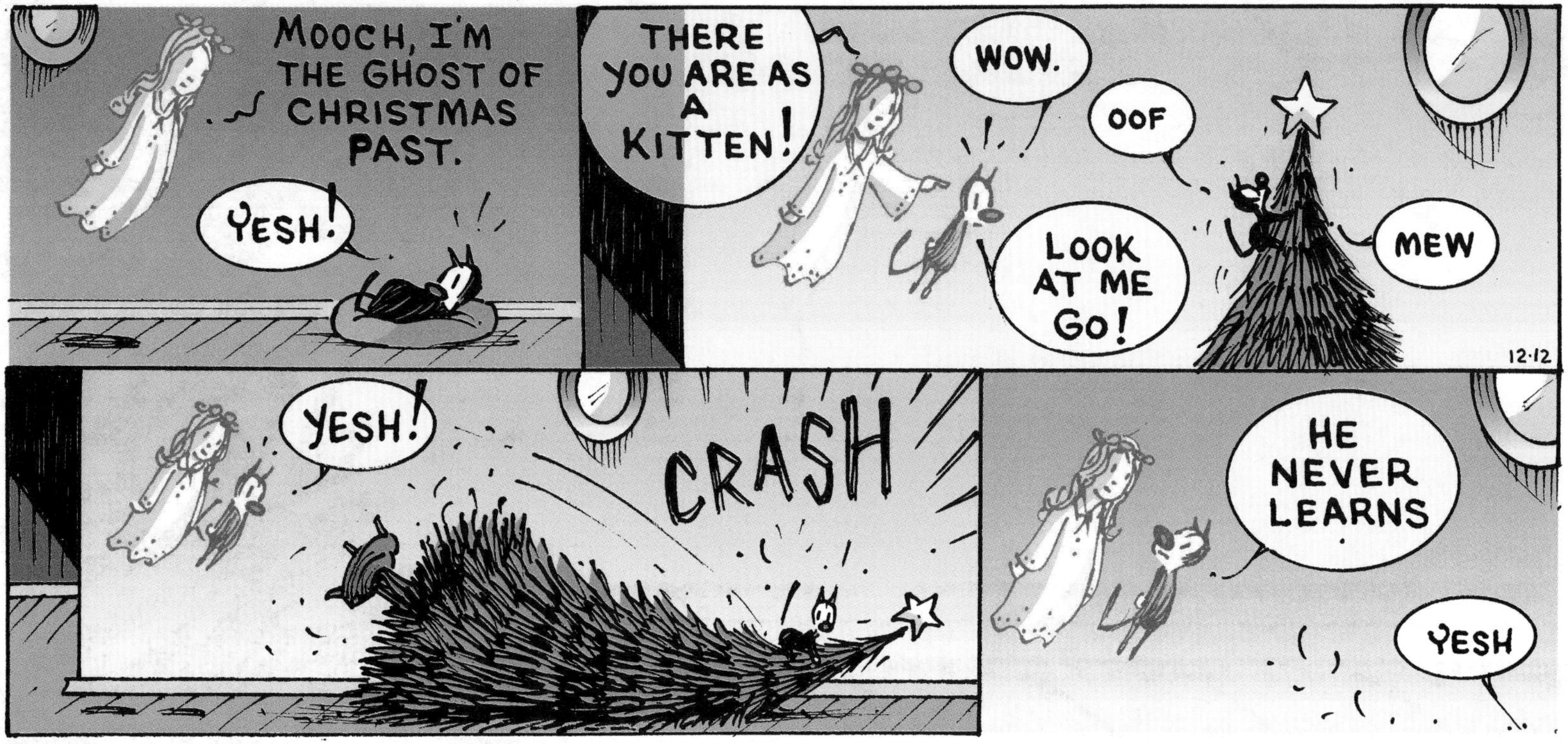
MOOCH, I'M THE GHOST OF CHRISTMAS PAST.
YESH!
THERE YOU ARE AS A KITTEN!
WOW.
OOF
LOOK AT ME GO!
MEW
12·12
YESH!
CRASH
HE NEVER LEARNS
YESH

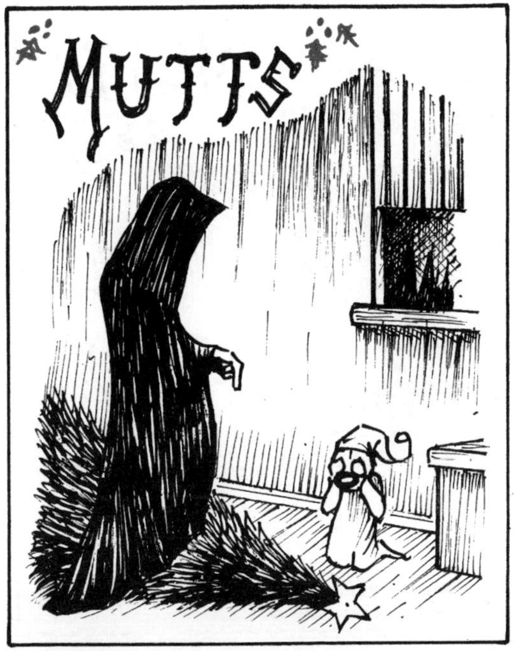
MUTTS

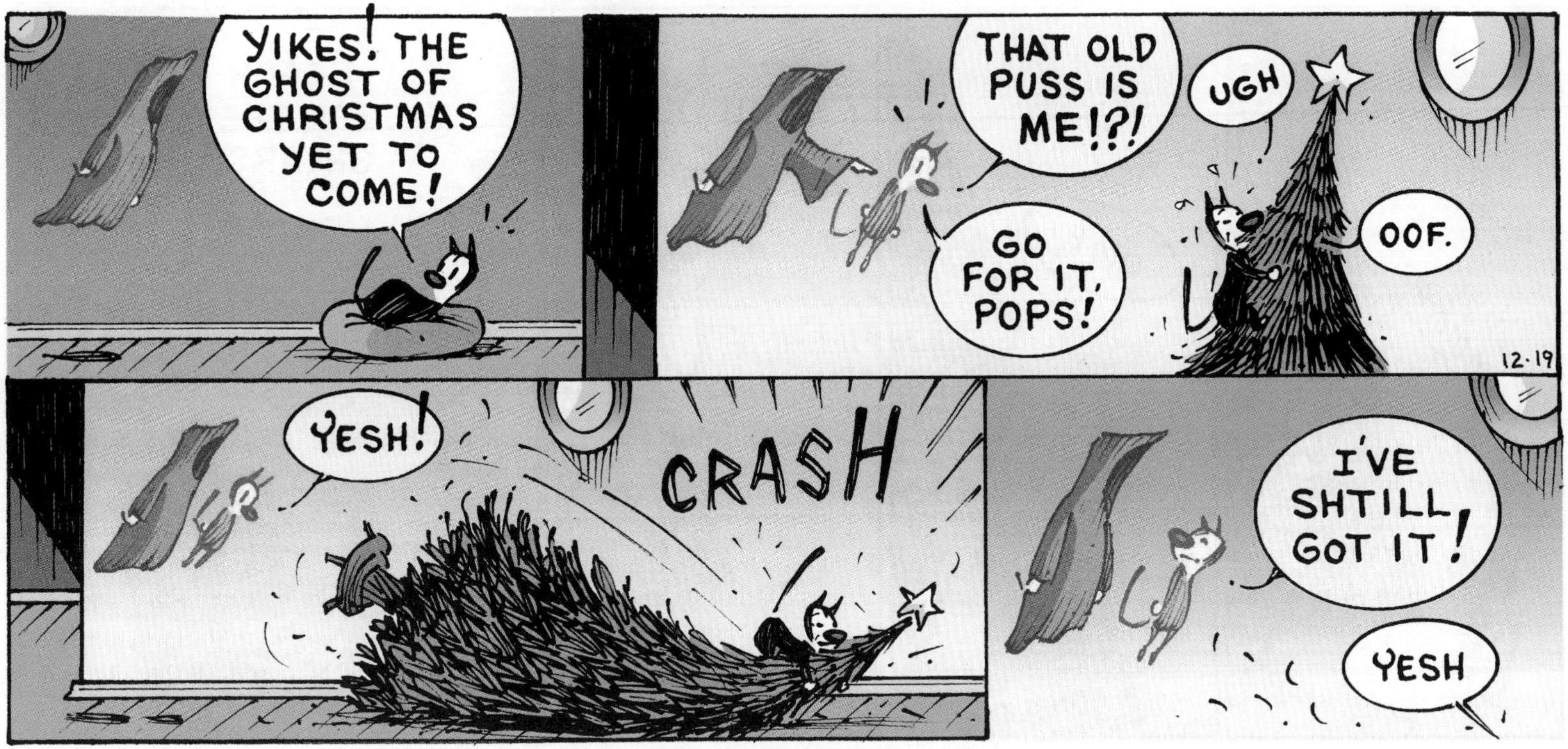
YIKES! THE GHOST OF CHRISTMAS YET TO COME!
THAT OLD PUSS IS ME!?!
GO FOR IT, POPS!
UGH
OOF.
12·19
YESH!
CRASH
I'VE SHTILL GOT IT!
YESH

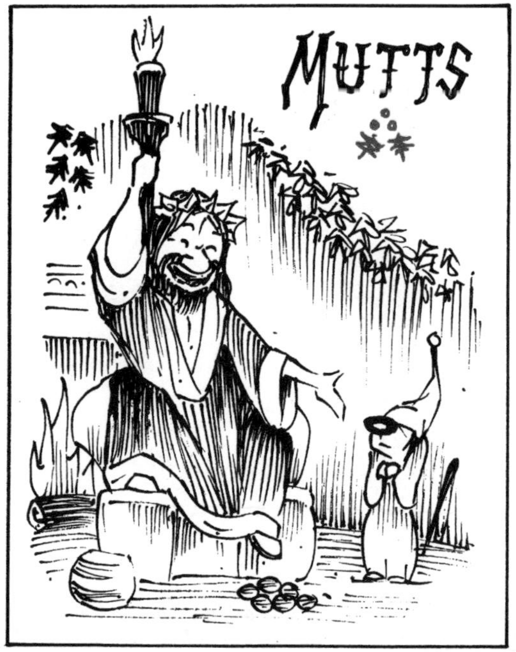
MUTTS

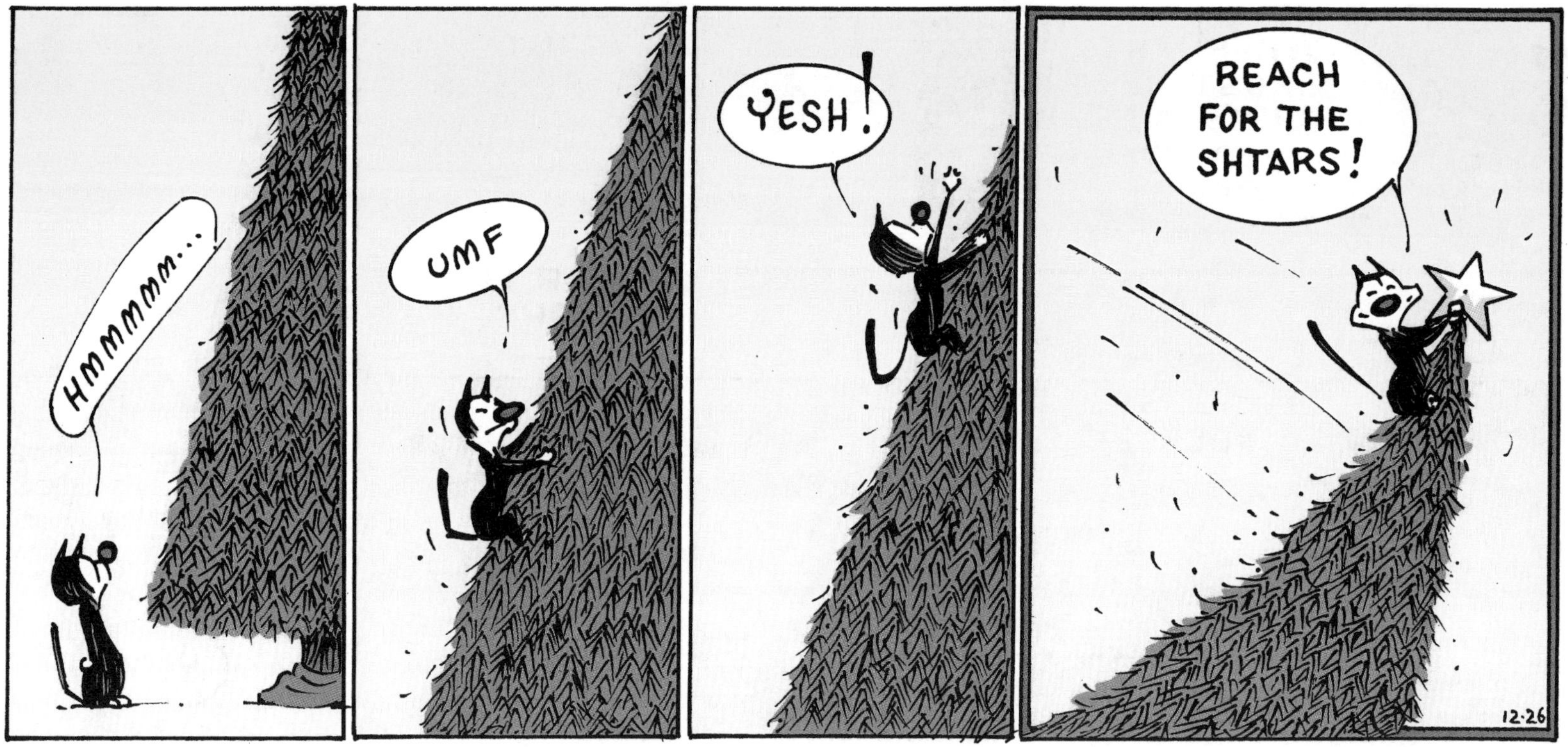
HMMMMM...
UMF
YESH!
REACH FOR THE SHTARS!
12·26

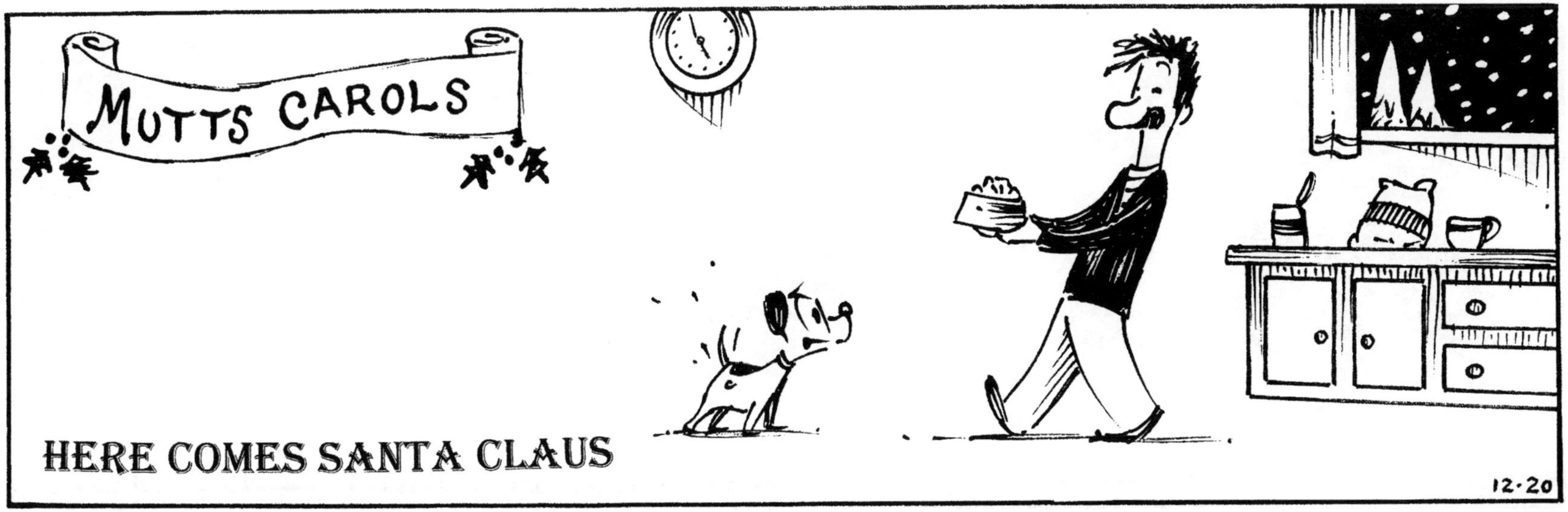
MUTTS CAROLS
HERE COMES SANTA CLAUS
12·20

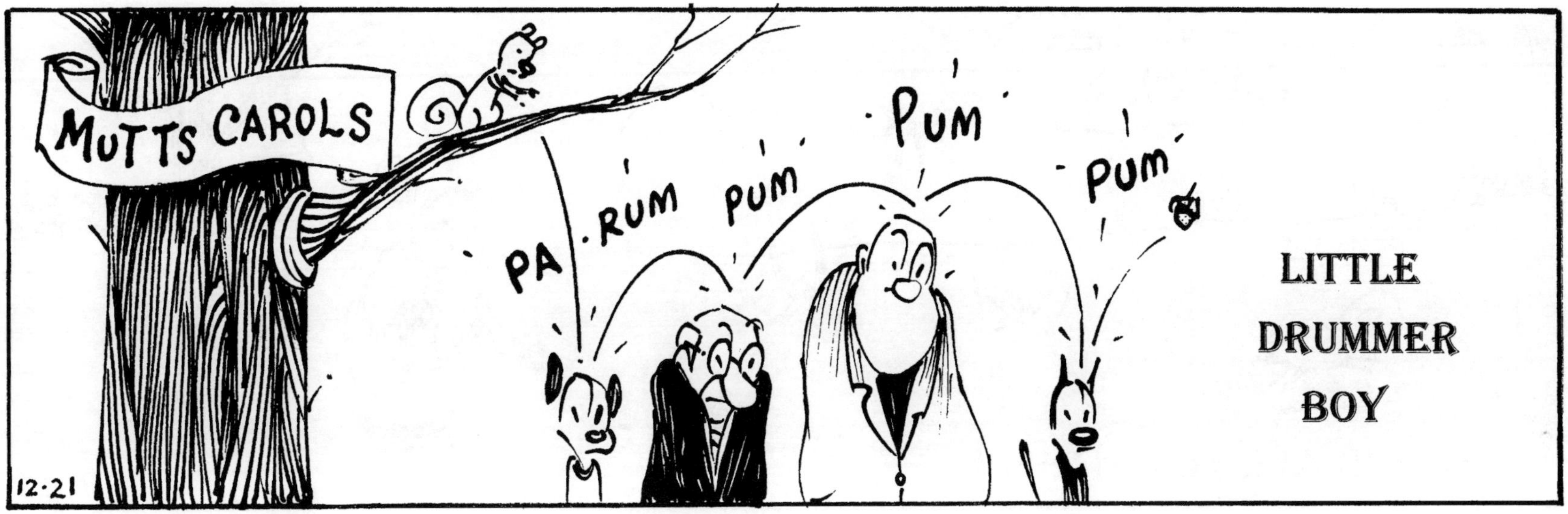
MUTTS CAROLS
PA RUM PUM PUM PUM
LITTLE DRUMMER BOY
12·21

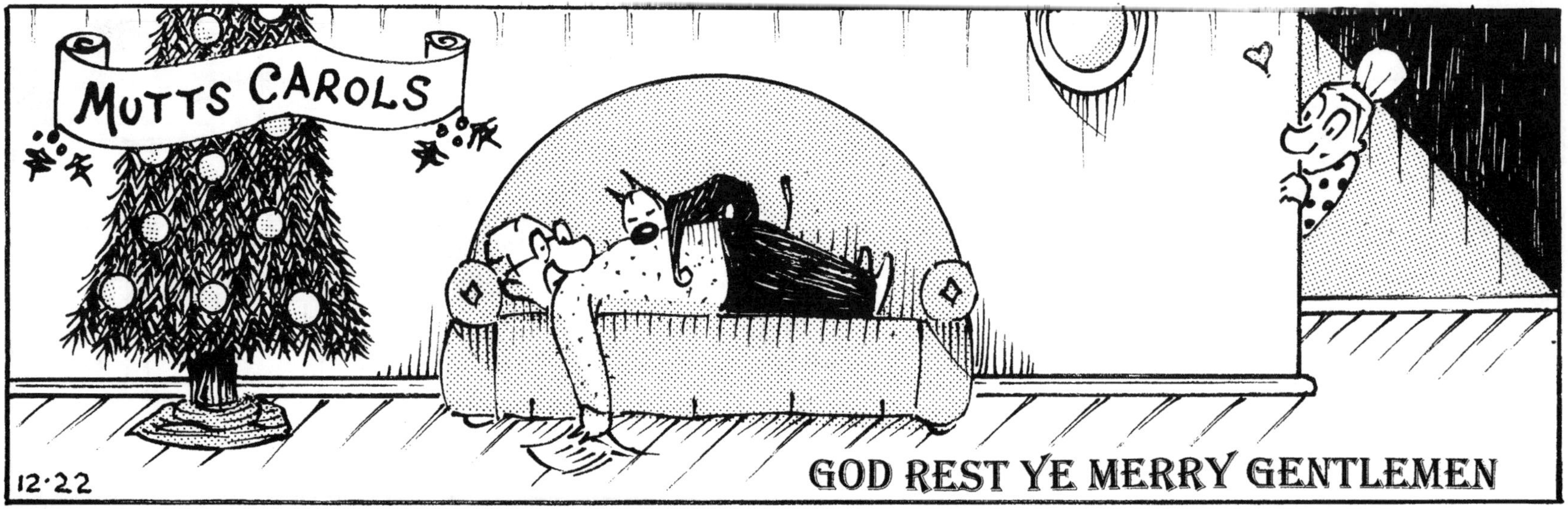
MUTTS CAROLS
12·22
GOD REST YE MERRY GENTLEMEN

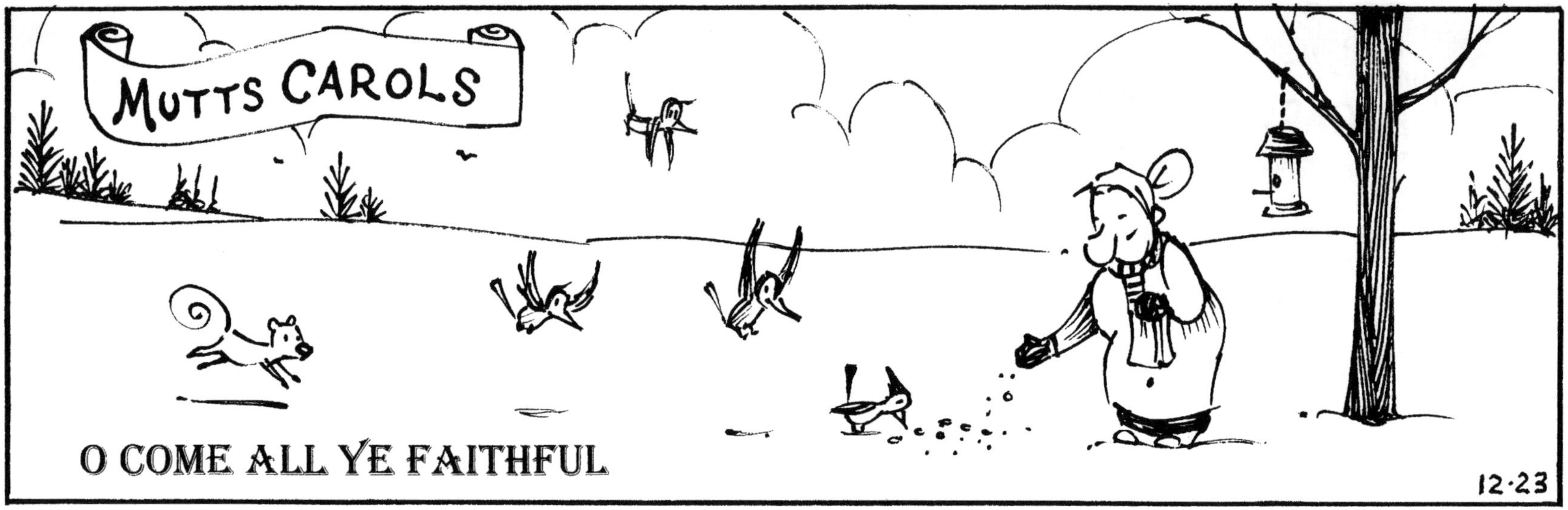
MUTTS CAROLS
O COME ALL YE FAITHFUL
12·23